Africa Yearbook

Africa Yearbook

Politics, Economy and Society South of the Sahara in 2023

VOLUME 20

Edited by

Seidu M. Alidu
Benedikt Kamski
Andreas Mehler
David Sebudubudu

BRILL

LEIDEN | BOSTON

The Library of Congress Cataloging-in-Publication Data is available online at https://catalog.loc.gov

Typeface for the Latin, Greek, and Cyrillic scripts: "Brill". See and download: brill.com/brill-typeface.

ISSN 1871-2525
ISBN 978-90-04-69696-9 (hardback)
ISBN 978-90-04-69697-6 (e-book)
DOI 10.1163/9789004696976

Copyright 2024 by Koninklijke Brill BV, Leiden, The Netherlands.
Koninklijke Brill BV incorporates the imprints Brill, Brill Nijhoff, Brill Schöningh, Brill Fink, Brill mentis, Brill Wageningen Academic, Vandenhoeck & Ruprecht, Böhlau and V&R unipress.
All rights reserved. No part of this publication may be reproduced, translated, stored in a retrieval system, or transmitted in any form or by any means, electronic, mechanical, photocopying, recording or otherwise, without prior written permission from the publisher. Requests for re-use and/or translations must be addressed to Koninklijke Brill BV via brill.com or copyright.com.

This book is printed on acid-free paper and produced in a sustainable manner.

Contents

Preface XI
Abbreviations XIII
Factual Overview (as of 31 December 2023) XVI
List of Authors XX

PART 1

Sub-Saharan Africa   3
   Seidu M. Alidu, Benedikt Kamski, Andreas Mehler, and David Sebudubudu

PART 2

African-European Relations   29
   Benedikt Erforth and Niels Keijzer

PART 3

West Africa   43
   Seidu M. Alidu

Benin   54
   Issifou Abou Moumouni

Burkina Faso   66
   Daniel Eizenga

Cabo Verde   76
   Gerhard Seibert

Côte d'Ivoire   82
   Jesper Bjarnesen

The Gambia   93
   Akpojevbe Omasanjuwa

Ghana 106
    George M. Bob-Milliar

Guinea 117
    Seidu M. Alidu

Guinea-Bissau 123
    Christoph Kohl

Liberia 130
    Aaron Weah

Mali 136
    Bruce Whitehouse

Mauritania 144
    Baba Adou

Niger 152
    Klaas van Walraven

Nigeria 161
    Heinrich Bergstresser

Senegal 178
    Mamadou Bodian

Sierra Leone 192
    Krijn Peters

Togo 200
    Hans-Joachim Preuß

PART 4

Central Africa 211
    Andreas Mehler

Cameroon 222
    Fanny Pigeaud

Central African Republic   234
    Andreas Mehler

Chad   244
    Ketil Fred Hansen

Congo   253
    Brett L. Carter

Democratic Republic of the Congo   260
    Koen Vlassenroot, Hans Hoebeke, and Josaphat Musamba

Equatorial Guinea   274
    Enrique Martino

Gabon   282
    Douglas Yates

São Tomé and Príncipe   290
    Gerhard Seibert

PART 5

Eastern Africa   299
    Benedikt Kamski

Burundi   312
    Raymond-Blaise Habonimana

Comoros   323
    Benedikt Kamski

Djibouti   329
    Nicole Hirt

Eritrea   336
    Nicole Hirt

Ethiopia   345
    Hallelujah Lulie and Jonah Wedekind

Kenya   360
    Njoki Wamai

Rwanda   372
    Erik Plänitz

Seychelles   384
    Anthoni van Nieuwkerk and Benedikt Kamski

Somalia   391
    Faduma Abukar Mursal

South Sudan   400
    Daniel Large

Sudan   410
    Antoine Galindo and Augustine Passilly

Tanzania   422
    Kurt Hirschler and Rolf Hofmeier

Uganda   438
    Moses Khisa and Sabastiano Rwengabo

PART 6

Southern Africa   453
    David Sebudubudu

Angola   459
    Jon Schubert

Botswana   472
    David Sebudubudu

Eswatini   485
    Marisha Ramdeen

Lesotho   491
    Roger Southall

Madagascar 497
Richard R. Marcus

Malawi 506
George Dzimbiri and Lewis Dzimbiri

Mauritius 514
Roukaya Kasenally

Mozambique 520
Lorraine Dongo

Namibia 536
Henning Melber

South Africa 545
Sanusha Naidu

Zambia 557
Edalina Rodrigues Sanches

Zimbabwe 565
Amin Y. Kamete

Preface

In 2003, the Africa–Europe Group for Interdisciplinary Studies (AEGIS) encouraged the creation of a comprehensive scholarly record of sub-Saharan Africa (SSA). Since then, the *Africa Yearbook* has emerged as a valuable resource for a diverse readership, providing an annual comprehensive record of the continent's dynamic landscape and promoting a deeper understanding of the region's political, economic, and social developments.

In 2024, the *Africa Yearbook* proudly marks the publication of its 20th volume. Over the years, this collaborative project has been supported by various institutions, culminating in a fruitful and lasting partnership between partners in SSA and Europe. The first volume was published by the African Studies Centre in Leiden (ASC), the Institute of African Affairs in Hamburg (IAA), and the Nordic Africa Institute in Uppsala (NAI) on the initiative of Andreas Mehler, Henning Melber, and Klaas van Walraven. In 2007, the Dag Hammarskjöld Foundation in Uppsala (DHF) joined as a fourth partner. The established international collaboration between the Arnold Bergstraesser Institute (ABI) (since 2018), the University of Botswana, and University of Ghana (both since 2020) forms the foundation of a balanced and efficient consortium of supporting institutions and editors.

The *Africa Yearbook* received the prestigious biennial Conover-Porter Award for outstanding Africa-related reference works in November 2012 from the African Studies Association and the Africana Librarians Council in the United States. This recognition signified that this annual collaborative project had become a permanent and valued feature in Africanist publishing.

For 20 years, the *Africa Yearbook* has offered annual overviews of events in Africa, grounded in scholarly research, ensuring a reliable account of domestic politics, foreign affairs, and socioeconomic progress. Developments in the four sub-regions (West, Central, Eastern, and Southern Africa) are summarised in overview articles. Additionally, each volume covers European–African relations and the continent's connections with global actors such as China, the Middle East, and the United States.

Since 2016, country-focused chronologies based on *Yearbook* chapters have been published and have gained a growing readership, testifying to their inherent value and the significance of the format. A total of 13 booklets have been published summarising the trajectories of development over 'A Decade in' Burkina Faso, Cameroon, Central African Republic, Ethiopia, Ghana, Mozambique, Madagascar, Namibia, Niger, Nigeria, Somalia, Tanzania, and Zimbabwe – and others are in the making.

Twenty years after the publication of the first volume, the continent faces novel geopolitical shifts, especially in the Horn of Africa and the Sahel region.

Additionally, complex challenges have emerged from global conflicts in the Middle East and Europe, impacting commodity prices and supply chains. Significantly, increased efforts to address colonial injustices and reparations are evident through heightened diplomatic engagements and historical acknowledgements. These developments and their potential consequences, as well as other emerging trends affecting development in SSA, are featured in this edition. To capture the evolving socioeconomic realities on the continent, the *Africa Yearbook* maintains the summary nature of its country chapters.

This project is made possible by the contributions of all country experts and the ongoing support from partner institutions within the AEGIS as well as universities on the continent. We would like to extend our gratitude to the growing number of authors who have played a part in the success of the project since 2003, especially to the 20th edition. We are grateful for the continued commitment over the years from Brill Publishers and the invaluable help provided by project managers and language editors, since 2024 Fem Eggers and Luke Finley, in the production of the *Africa Yearbook* over two decades.

The editors
Accra, Addis Ababa, Freiburg, and Gaborone, July 2024

Abbreviations

ACP	African, Caribbean, and Pacific Group of Countries (Lomé/Cotonou Agreement)
AfCFTA	African Continental Free Trade Area
AfDB	African Development Bank (Tunis)
AGOA	African Growth and Opportunity Act
AI	Amnesty International
APRM	African Peer Review Mechanism
ARVS	antiretrovirals
AU	African Union (Addis Ababa)
AUEOM	African Union Election Observer Mission
BCEAO	Banque Centrale des Etats de l'Afrique de l'Ouest (Dakar)
BEAC	Banque des Etats de l'Afrique Centrale (Yaoundé)
BRICS	Brazil, India, Russia, China, and South Africa
CAR	Central African Republic
CBLT	Commission du Bassin du Lac Tchad (N'Djaména)
CEEAC	Communauté Economique des Etats de l'Afrique Centrale
CEMAC	Communauté Economique et Monéetaire de l'Afrique Centrale
CEN-SAD	Community of Sahel-Saharan States (Tripoli)
CFAfr	Franc de la Communauté Financière Africaine (BCEAO; BEAC)
COMESA	Common Market for Eastern and Southern Africa (Lusaka)
CPI	consumer price index
CPLP	Comunidade dos Países de Língua Portuguesa
CSO	civil society organisation
DRC	Democratic Republic of the Congo
EAC	East African Community
ECA	Economic Commission for Africa (United Nations; Addis Ababa)
ECCAS	Economic Community of Central African States (Libreville)
ECF	Extended Credit Facility (IMF)
ECOWAS	Economic Community of West African States (Abuja)
EDF	European Development Fund (Brussels)
EIB	European Investment Bank (Luxemberg)
EITI	Extractive Industries Transparency Initiative
EIU	Economist Intelligence Unit
EPA	Economic Partnership Agreement
EU	European Union (Brussels)
FAO	Food and Agricultural Organization (Rome)
FDI	foreign direct investment
FOCAC	Forum on China–Africa Cooperation

FPE	Free Primary Education
FTA	free-trade area
GDP	Gross Domestic Product
GECF	Gas Exporting Countries Forum
HDI	Human Development Index (UNDP)
HIPC	Heavily Indebted Poor Countries Initiative
HRW	Human Rights Watch
ICC	International Criminal Court
ICGLR	International Conference on the Great Lakes Region
ICJ	International Court of Justice
ICT	information and communications technology
IDA	International Development Association (Washington)
IDP	internally displaced person
IED	improvised explosive device
IFAD	International Fund for Agricultural Development
IFC	International Finance Corporation (Washington)
IGAD	Intergovernmental Authority on Development (Djibouti)
ILO	International Labour Organization (Geneva)
IMF	International Monetary Fund (Washington)
IOC	Indian Ocean Commission (Quatre Bornes)
IOM	International Organization for Migration
ISGS	Islamic State in the Greater Sahara
ISIL	Islamic State in Iraq and the Levant
ISIS	Islamic State in Iraq and Syria
ISWA	Islamic State in West Africa
LNG	liquified natural gas
MoU	memorandum of understanding
MSF	Médicins Sans Frontières \
NATO	North Atlantic Treaty Organization
NEPAD	New Partnership for Africa's Development
NGO	non-governmental organisation
OAU	Organization of African Unity
OCHA	United Nations Office for the Coordination of Humanitarian Affairs
ODA	official development assistance
OECD	Organisation for Economic Co-operation and Development (Paris)
OIC	Organisation of Islamic Cooperation
OIF	L'Organisation Internationale de la Francophonie
OPEC	Organisation of Petroleum Exporting Countries (Vienna)
PIDA	Programme for Infrastructure Development in Africa
PPP	Purchasing Power Parity

ABBREVIATIONS

RCF	Rapid Credit Facility Abbreviations
REC	Regional Economic Community
RSF/RWB	Reporters Sans Frontières/Reporters Without Borders
SACU	Southern African Customs Union (Pretoria)
SADC	Southern African Development Community (Gaborone)
SAPP	Southern Africa Power Pool
SDGS	Sustainable Development Goals
SSA	sub-Saharan Africa
STP	São Tomé and Príncipe
UAE	United Arab Emirates
UEMOA	Union Économique et Monétaire Ouest-Africaine (Ouagadougou)
UHC	universal health coverage
UK	United Kingdom
UN	United Nations (New York)
UNDP	United Nations Development Programme (New York)
UNESCO	United Nations Educational, Scientific and Cultural Organisations (Paris)
UNGA	United Nations General Assembly
UNHCR	United Nations High Commissioner for Refugees (Geneva)
UNHRC	United Nations Human Rights Council
UNICEF	United Nations Children's Fund (New York)
UNOCHA	United Nations Office for the Coordination of Humanitarian Affairs
UNSC	United Nations Security Council
UNSG	United Nations secretary general
US	United States
USAID	United States Agency for International Development (Washington)
WAEMU	West African Economic and Monetary Union
WEF	World Economic Forum
WFP	World Food Programme (Rome)
WHO	World Health Organisation (Geneva)
WTO	World Trade Organisation (Geneva)

Factual Overview (as of 31 December 2023)

West Africa

Country	Area (in sq km)	Population (in m)[a]	Currency	HDI (2024)[b]	Head of State	Prime Minister
Benin	112,622	13.7	CFA Franc	0.504	Patrice Talon	
Burkina Faso	274,122	22.9	CFA Franc	0.438	Ibrahim Traoré	Apollinaire Joachim Kyélem di Tambela
Cape Verde	4,033	0.6	Cape Verdean Escudo	0.661	José Maria Pereira Neves	Ulisses Correia e Silva
Côte d'Ivoire	322,462	30.9	CFA Franc	0.534	Alassane Ouattara	Robert Beugré Mambé
Gambia	11,295	2.8	Dalasi	0.495	Adama Barrow	
Ghana	238,500	34.1	Cedi	0.602	Nana Addo Dankwa Akufo-Addo	
Guinea	245,857	14.2	Guinean Franc	0.471	Mamady Doumbouya	Bernard Goumou
Guinea-Bissau	36,125	2.2	CFA Franc	0.483	Umaro Sissoco Embaló	Rui Duarte de Barros
Liberia	111,370	5.4	Liberian Dollar	0.487	George Weah	
Mali	1,240,000	23.3	CFA Franc	0.410	Assimi Goïta	Choguel Kokalla Maïga
Mauritania	1,030,700	4.9	Ouguiya	0.540	Mohamed Ould Gazouani	Mohamed Ould Bilal
Niger	1,267,000	27.2	CFA Franc	0.394	Abdourahmane Tchiani	Ali Lamine Zeine
Nigeria	923,768	223.8	Naira	0.548	Bola Ahmed Tinubu	
Senegal	197,162	18.3	CFA Franc	0.517	Macky Sall	Amadou Ba
Sierra Leone	71,740	8.9	Leone	0.458	Julius Maada Bio	
Togo	56,785	9.1	CFA Franc	0.547	Faure Gnassingbé	Victoire Tomegah Dogbé

a (Population figures are for mid-2023 according to Population Reference Review, 2023 World Population Data Sheet: https://www.prb.org/wp-content/uploads/2023/12/2023-World-Population-Data-Sheet-Booklet.pdf)

b (Latest data from according to UNDP: https://hdr.undp.org/data-center/country-insights#/ranks)

FACTUAL OVERVIEW (AS OF 31 DECEMBER 2023)

Central Africa

Country	Area (in sq km)	Population (in m)	Currency	HDI	Head of State	Prime Minister
Cameroon	475,442	28.1	CFA Franc BEAC	0.587	Paul Biya	Joseph Dion Ngute
Central African Republic	622,984	6.2	CFA Franc BEAC	0.387	Faustin Archange Touadéra	Félix Molua
Chad	1,284,000	18.3	CFA Franc BEAC	0.394	Mahamat Déby	Saleh Kebzabo
Congo	342,000	6.1	CFA Franc BEAC	0.593	Denis Sassou-Nguesso	Anatole Collinet Makosso
DR Congo	2,344,855	102.3	Congolese Franc	0.481	Félix Tchisekedi	Jean-Michel Sama Lukonde Kyenge
Equatorial Guinea	28,051	1.7	CFA Franc BEAC	0.650	Teodoro Obiang Nguema Mbasogo	Manuela Roka Botey
Gabon	267,667	2.4	CFA Franc BEAC	0.693	Brice Oligui Nguema	Raymond Ndong Sima
São Tomé and Príncipe	1,001	0.2	Dobra	0.613	Carlos Vila Nova	Patrice Trovoada

Eastern Africa

Country	Area (in sq km)	Population (in m)	Currency	HDI	Head of State	Prime Minister
Burundi	26,338	12.2	Burundi Franc	0.420	Évariste Ndayishimiye	Gervais Ndirakobucai
Comoros	1.862	0.9	Comoran Franc	0.586	Azali Assoumani	
Djibouti	23,200	1.0	Djiboutian Franc	0.515	Ismail Omar Guelleh	Abdoulkader Kamil Mohamed
Eritrea	124,320	3.6	Nakfa	0.493	Isaias Afwerki	
Ethiopia	1,121,900	126.5	Ethiopian Birr	0.492	Sahle-Work Zewde	Abiy Ahmed Ali
Kenya	569,259	55.1	Kenya Shilling	0.601	William Ruto	
Rwanda	26,338	14.1	Rwanda Franc	0.548	Paul Kagame	Édouard Ngirente
Seychelles	455	0.1	Seychelles Rupee	0.802	Wavel Ramkalawan	
Somalia	637,600	18.1	Somali Shilling	0.380	Hassan Sheikh Mohamud	Hamza Abdi Barre
(Somaliland)	137,600	n.a.	Somaliland Shilling	n.a.	Muse Bihi Abdi	
Sudan	2,505,805	48.1	Sudanese Pound	0.516	Abdel Fattah al-Burhan Abdulrahman (Transitional Sovereignty Council); no functioning government since April 2023	Osman Hussein (acting)
South Sudan	619,745	11.1	South Sudanese Pound	0.381	Salva Kiir Mayardit	
Tanzania	945,087	67.4	Tanzania Shilling	0.532	Samia Suluhu Hassan	Kassim Majaliwa
Uganda	197,000	48.6	Uganda Shilling	0.550	Yoweri Kaguta Museveni	*Robinah Nabbanja*

FACTUAL OVERVIEW (AS OF 31 DECEMBER 2023)

Southern Africa

Country	Area (in sq km)	Population (in m)	Currency	HDI	Head of State	Prime Minister
Angola	1,246,700	36.7	Kwanza	0.591	João Manuel Gonçalves Lourenço	
Botswana	581,730	2.7	Pula	0.708	Mokgweetsi Masisi	
Lesotho	30,344	2.3	Lesotho Loti	0.521	King Letsie III	Sam Matekane
Madagascar	592,000	30.4	Malagasy Ariary	0.487	Andry Nirina Rajoelina	Christian Louis Ntsay
Malawi	118,484	19.8	Malawian Kwacha	0.508	Lazarus Chakwera	
Mauritius	2,040	1.3	Mauritian Rupee	0.796	Prithvirajsing Roopun	Pravind Kumar Jugnauth
Mozambique	799,380	33.9	Mozam-biquen Métical	0.461	Filipe Nyusi	Adriano Afonso Maleiane
Namibia	824,269	2.6	Namibian Dollar	0.610	Hage Gottfried Geingob	Saara Kuugongelwa-Amadhila
South Africa	1,219,090	60.7	Rand	0.717	Matamela Cyril Ramaphosa	
Eswatini/ Swaziland	17,364	1.2	Swazi Lilangeni	0.610	King Mswati III.	Russell Dlamini
Zambia	752,614	20.2	Zambian Kwacha	0.569	Hakainde Hichilema	
Zimbabwe	390,580	16.7	Zimbabwean Dollar	0.550	Emmerson Dambudzo Mnangagwa	

List of Authors

Issifou Abou Moumouni
PhD in Social Anthropology, Postdoctoral Fellow at the University of Bayreuth, Researcher at the Laboratoire d'Etudes et de Recherches sur les Dynamiques, Sociales et Dévélopement Local (LASDEL), Parakou, Benin, issifou.abou-moumouni@uni-bayreuth.de; issifouboro@yahoo.fr.

Faduma Abukar Mursal
PhD in Anthropology, Senior Lecturer and Researcher in the Department of Anthropology, at the University of Lucerne, Switzerland, faduma.abukar@unilu.ch.

Baba Adou
PhD student in the Department of Political Science at the University of Florida, Research Assistant at UF Sahel Research Group, adou.baba@ufl.edu.

Seidu M. Alidu
Associate Professor and Head of the Department of Political Science at the University of Ghana. His core functions as a Senior Lecturer are to conduct research, teach and provide extension services to local communities, the country and the international community at large, smalidu@ug.edu.gh.

Heinrich Bergstresser
Media Consultant, Freelance Research Associate of the Institute of African Affairs in Hamburg and Freelance Trainer of Akademie für Internationale Zusammenarbeit (AIZ) within Deutsche Gesellschaft für Internationale Zusammenarbeit GIZ, Germany, heinrich.bergstresser@web.de.

Jesper Bjarnesen
Senior Researcher, The Nordic Africa Institute, Uppsala, Sweden, jesper.bjarnesen@nai.uu.se.

George Bob-Milliar
Associate Professor at the Kwame Nkrumah University of Science and Technology (KNUST), Ghana, bobmilliar1@gmail.com.

Mamadou Bodian
PhD in Political Science, Researcher at the Institut fondamental d'Afrique noire (IFAN) of Cheikh Anta Diop University, Dakar, Senegal, papexb@gmail.com.

LIST OF AUTHORS

Brett L. Carter
Assistant Professor, Department of Political Science and International Relations, University of Southern California, and Hoover Fellow, Hoover Institution, Stanford University, blcarter@usc.edu.

Lorraine Dongo
Research Associate in the Urban Institute, University of Sheffield, l.dongo@sheffield.ac.uk.

George Lewis Dzimbiri
Lecturer in HRM & Public Administration, Malawi University of Business and Applied Sciences, gdzimbiri@poly.ac.mw.

Lewis Dzimbiri
Professor of Public Administration, Deputy Vice Chancellor at Lilongwe University of Agriculture and Natural Resources, Malawi, proflewisdzimbiri@gmail.com.

Daniel Eizenga
PhD in Political Science, Research Fellow with the Africa Center for Strategic Studies, Washington DC, daniel.j.eizenga.civ@ndu.edu.

Benedikt Erforth
PhD, Senior Researcher, German Institute of Development and Sustainability (IDOS), Bonn, Germany, benedikt.erforth@idos-research.de.

Antoine Galindo
East Africa editor for Paris based Africa Intelligence online newsletter (since 2020). Formerly freelance reporter based in Ethiopia (2013–2017) and in Ghana (2018–2019), galindo@africaintelligence.com.

Raymond-Blaise Habonimana
Studied Political Science and International Relations at Lake Tanganyika University. He holds a master's degree in Governance and Development from the University of Antwerp and an interdisciplinary and inter-university degree in transitional justice from the Université Libre de Bruxelles and the Université Catholique de Louvain, blaisepeace@gmail.com.

Ketil Fred Hansen
PhD in African History, Professor in Social Sciences, University of Stavanger, Norway, ketil.f.hansen@uis.no.

Kurt Hirschler
Freelance Political Scientist, Hamburg, Germany, kurt_hirschler@web.de.

Nicole Hirt
PhD in Political Science, Associate Fellow, Institute of African Affairs, GIGA German Institute of Global and Area Studies, Hamburg, Germany, nicolehi2001@yahoo.de.

Hans Hoebeke
Studied Political Science (International Relations) at Ghent University (1996). He is an independent consultant focused on the DRC and the African Great Lakes region. Since 2023, he has been a Regional Advisor for the European Institute of Peace (EIP). He is also an affiliate of the Egmont Institute as a Senior Associate Fellow. hans.hoebeke@gmail.com.

Rolf Hofmeier
Former Director, Institute of African Affairs, GIGA German Institute of Global and Area Studies, Hamburg, Germany, gr.hofmeier@gmx.de.

Amin Kamete
Professor of Spatial Planning, Division of Urban Studies and Social Policy, School of Social and Political Sciences, University of Glasgow, Scotland, UK, amini.kamete@glasgow.ac.uk.

Benedikt Kamksi
PhD in Political Science, Senior Researcher at the Arnold Bergstraesser Institute, Freiburg, Germany, benedikt.kamski@abi.uni-freiburg.de.

Roukaya Kasenally
Associate Professor of Media and Political Systems, Department of Social Studies, University of Mauritius and CEO of the African Media Initiative, roukaya@uom.ac.mu.

Niels Keijzer
PhD, Senior Researcher, German Institute of Development and Sustainability (IDOS), Bonn, Germany, niels.keijzer@idos-research.de.

Moses Khisa
Associate Professor of Political Science and Africana Studies, School of Public and International Affairs, North Carolina State University, USA and Research Associate at the Centre for Basic Research, Kampala. He is also a columnist for the Daily Monitor newspaper, Kampala, Uganda, mkhisa@ncsu.edu.

LIST OF AUTHORS

Christoph Kohl
Independent Researcher, Halle (Saale), Germany, christoph_a_kohl@hotmail.com.

Daniel Large
Associate Professor at the School of Public Policy, Central European University, and Fellow of the Rift Valley Institute, larged@spp.ceu.edu.

Hallelujah Lulie
PhD Candidate in Politics at the University of Oxford, hallelujahlulie@gmail.com.

Richard Marcus
Professor and Director, The Global Studies Institute and the M.A. in International Affairs, California State University, Long Beach, USA, richard.marcus@csulb.edu.

Enrique Martino
Postdoctoral Researcher at the Departamento de Historia, Teorías y Geografía Políticas, Universidad Complutense de Madrid, Spain, enrique.martino@gmail.com.

Andreas Mehler
Director of the Arnold Bergstraesser Institute and Professor of Political Science at the University of Freiburg, Germany, andreas.mehler@abi.uni-freiburg.de.

Henning Melber
Associate of The Nordic Africa Institute and Director emeritus of The Dag Hammarskjöld Foundation, both in Uppsala, Sweden, henning.melber@nai.uu.se.

Josaphat Musamba Busyy
PhD student at Ghent University in the Faculty of Political and Social Sciences, Department of Conflict and Development Studies, focusing on the socio-anthropology of security practices in areas affected by recurring conflicts in the Eastern Democratic Republic of the Congo. josaphat.musambabussy@ugent.be.

Sanusha Naidu
Senior Research Associate, Institute for Global Dialogue, sanusha.naidu@gmail.com.

Akpojevbe Omasanjuwa
Geography Lecturer, University of the Gambia, West Africa, masapele@yahoo.com.

Augustine Passilly
Freelance journalist in Sudan (2020–2023) and in Ethiopia (since 2023), writing mainly for La Croix and Le Point Afrique, passillyaugustine@gmail.com.

Krijn Peters
Professor in Post-war Reconstruction, Rural Development and Transport Services, Department of Politics, Philosophy & International Relations, Swansea University, UK, k.peters@swansea.ac.uk.

Fanny Pigeaud
Journalist, France, fanny.pigeaud@gmail.com.

Erik Plänitz
PhD in Political Science Associated Senior Researcher, Arnold Bergstraesser Institute, Freiburg, Germany, erik.plaenitz@abi.uni-freiburg.de.

Hans-Joachim Preuss
Institute for Political Science and Sociology, University of Bonn, Germany, hansjoachim.preuss@uni-bonn.de.

Marisha Ramdeen
Senior Programme Officer at the African Centre for the Constructive Resolution of Disputes (ACCORD) in Durban, South Africa, marisha@accord.org.za.

Sabastiano Rwengabo
PhD in Political Science (NUS), Independent Consultant (Fragility and Resilience Assessments, Political Economy Analyses, and Governance), Research Fellow, Centre for Basic Research, Kampala, Uganda, rwerutaoo@gmail.com.

Edalina Sanches
Research Fellow at Instituto de Ciências Sociais, Universidade de Lisboa, Portugal, ersanches@ics.ulisboa.pt.

Jon Schubert
SNF Eccellenza Professor of Urban and Political Anthropology, Division of Urban Studies, University of Basel, jon.schubert@unibas.ch.

David Sebudubudu
Professor of Political Science in the Department of Political and Administrative Studies, Faculty of Social Sciences, University of Botswana, sebudubudu@ub.ac.bw.

Gerhard Seibert
Research Associate, Center for International Studies (CEI), ISCTE-Instituto Universitário de Lisboa, Portugal, mailseibert@yahoo.com.

LIST OF AUTHORS

Roger Southall
Emeritus Professor in Sociology at the University of the Witwatersrand, Johannesburg, and Professorial Research Associate in Politics, SOAS, South Africa, roger.southall@wits.ac.za.

Anthoni Van Nieuwkerk
Professor of International and Diplomacy Studies, Thabo Mbeki African School of Public and International Affairs, University of South Africa and Visiting Research Fellow, Wits School of Governance, South Africa, anthoni.vannieuwkerk@wits.ac.za.

Klaas van Walraven
Researcher, African Studies Centre, Leiden, The Netherlands, walraven@ascleiden.nl.

Koen Vlassenroot
Director of the Conflict Research Group | Governance in Conflict Network, koen.vlassenroot@ugent.be.

Njoki Wamai
Assistant Professor of Politics and International Relations at the International Relations Department at the United States International University-Africa in Nairobi, Kenya, nwamai@usiu.ac.ke.

Aaron Weah
Director, Ducor Institute for Social and Economic Research (a Liberian-based think tank), abweah.ci@gmail.com.

Jonah Wedekind
PhD in Agrarian Studies from Humboldt-Universität zu Berlin, Germany; Political Ecologist and Economist based in Berlin and independent consultant with the Rift Valley Institute's Peace Research Facility, Ethiopia, j.wedekind@hu-berlin.de.

Bruce Whitehouse
Associate Professor of Anthropology, Lehigh University, USA, bruce.whitehouse@lehigh.edu.

Douglas Yates
Professor of Political Science at the American Graduate School in Paris, France, douglas.yates@ags.edu.

PART 1

Sub-Saharan Africa

Seidu M. Alidu, Benedikt Kamski, Andreas Mehler, and David Sebudubudu

Trends

In May, the WHO declared the official end of the Covid-19 pandemic as a global health emergency. Concurrently, the ambitious sustainable post-pandemic recovery strategies for the continent became secondary, as the ongoing war between Ukraine and Russia, along with the escalation of tensions into a bloody conflict between Israel and Hamas in the Middle East, dominated global attention. These developments also suggest that geopolitical tensions would continue to affect SSA on multiple levels, including commodity prices, financing costs, and supply chain disruptions. With 2024 being a major election year globally, the presidential polls in Russia are unlikely to bring surprises while the US presidential elections and the potential of a second term for Donald Trump could be pivotal for the continent. In this regard, another central question relates to the growing competition for economic, political, and cultural influence, especially across the Horn, between the UAE, Saudi Arabia, and Qatar, known as the 'Gulf Scramble for Africa'. How will this competition affect future cooperation with global partners such as Russia, China, the US, and the EU?

COP28 highlighted significant climate adaptation challenges for the continent, noting a fourfold increase in climate debt over the past decade due to heavy borrowing. While green hydrogen, promoted by the EU and the AU, could be crucial for fostering innovative financing and sustainable energy solutions, the road-map raises concerns about perpetuating novel forms of extractivism and increasing dependencies on the Global North.

Positions on migration from the African continent have hardened in major parts of the main destination outside the continent, i.e. Europe. With a growing number of governments and right-wing populist opposition parties openly calling for even stricter handling of what they see as illegal and unbearable migration – and European elections coming up in 2024 – more friction can be expected. At the same time, record numbers of refugees and IDPs on the continent will increase the pressure for migration – together with the long-term effects of anthropogenic climate change.

With the 140th anniversary of the Berlin Congo Conference looming in 2024, more efforts to address the atrocities of colonialism and find appropriate ways of dealing with the past will be observed. However, it was unclear whether far-reaching solutions would be found between former colonisers (still avoiding seeing the principle of reparations as justified) and African governments (still reluctant to step out of the familiar patterns of development assistance that stresses a donor–recipient relationship between North and South). Clearly, the direct successors of victims, on both community and family levels, are unhappy with the limited progress so far. The visit on 1 November of German federal president Frank-Walter Steinmeier to Songea (Tanzania), a major battle zone of the Maji Maji war with its estimated 300,000 victims, was probably only a precursor of more thorough efforts to come to terms with the repatriation of ancestral remains and cultural goods looted from Africa, including official apologies and maybe even reparations. French and Belgian colonisation have already received their share of attention, and it could be expected that injustice and violence in British colonies will also come under scrutiny again. The bicentennial of the British slave trade abolition already brought renewed attention to debates on reparations and restorative justice, with narratives increasingly influenced by the rise of right-wing populism and xenophobic, anti-immigration sentiments across Europe. Both increasing claims by 'source communities' and right-wing populism are expected to further influence public discourse on colonial reparations.

Africa in the World Economy

The debt crisis on the continent escalated to a critical level, emerging as the foremost concern in economic policies and political discussions during the year. As a result, post-pandemic recovery strategies largely took a back seat, considering also increased political instability and the re-emergence of conflicts especially across the Horn of Africa, the Great Lakes region, and the Sahel. Overall growth slowed due to external shocks, geopolitical tensions, and growing inflationary pressures.

According to AfDB data, 15 countries across all sub-regions, including North Africa, experienced increased GDP growth compared with the previous year. Notably, *GDP growth* exceeded 5% in Ethiopia and Rwanda in Eastern Africa, DRC in Central Africa, and Mauritius in Southern Africa. On average, Central Africa's GDP grew by 3.8%, Eastern Africa's by 3.5%, West Africa's by 3.2%, and Southern Africa's by 1.6% (AfDB). Eastern Africa demonstrated resilience despite ongoing conflicts in Sudan and South Sudan. In West Africa, growth was driven by strong performances from key economies such as Côte d'Ivoire, Ghana, Nigeria, and Senegal, while Southern Africa faced a mixed economic environment, with growth in Angola, Botswana, Lesotho, Zambia, and Zimbabwe, but with infrastructural challenges, particularly in power supply, hampering South Africa's performance.

The latest UNCTAD (UN Trade and Development) assessments indicate that *FDI* slightly declined in 2023. It fell by 1% in West Africa and by 17% in Central Africa. In Southern Africa, FDI inflows to South Africa decreased by a staggering 43%.

Countries experiencing coups, such as Niger, faced visible economic downturns. East Africa's FDI decreased by 3%, driven by an 11% decline in Ethiopia due to ongoing political instability and the volatile security environment.

Despite declining investor trust, the AfDB presented an overall positive *economic outlook* for 2024 but advised 'cautious optimism given the considerable global uncertainty and geopolitical tensions'. Two major factors influenced the continent's growth projection: persistent inflation and unsustainable debt servicing costs combined with rising borrowing costs. Inflation remained concerningly high compared with the global average of 6.8% based on IMF assessments. The AfDB estimated that the average inflation rate in Africa, including North Africa, was 17.8%. This trend has been evident since the outbreak of the pandemic, which nearly doubled inflation rates.

While it is widely agreed that persistent double-digit inflation necessitates more aggressive monetary policies, debt service payments have become a significant budgetary concern for almost all countries in SSA. Relying solely on increased tax collection, as a growing number of governments advocate, will not solve the issue and may reduce private sector spending and investment. Since the early 2010s, spending on *debt servicing* has increased more than fourfold, and it is projected to reach over $70 bn during 2024. The IMF estimated that in 2023, interest payments alone accounted for more than 10% of total revenues for the median country in SSA, having doubled over the course of ten years.

The year under review starkly highlighted the potential for a looming debt crisis. The challenge of maturing bilateral and syndicated loans, along with scheduled Eurobond repayments for 2024, significantly impacted budgetary planning and placed increasing pressure on governments to meet their short-term obligations. The risk of partial default due to missed debt payments became increasingly imminent, exemplified by Ethiopia's default on a Eurobond coupon payment in December, joining Zambia, which defaulted on its payments in 2020, and Ghana, which suspended payments on most of its external debt in December 2022. By year's end, the Debt Management Facility (DMF), a multi-donor trust fund, had conducted 37 technical assistance operations in 25 countries in SSA, aimed at enhancing debt management and transparency. These operations encompassed Debt Management Performance Assessment evaluations, portfolio risk analysis, and the formulation of debt strategies.

Data availability continued to pose challenges in assessing risk exposure and lending dynamics. While new initiatives such as the Africa Debt Data Base launched by the Kiel Institute for the World Economy shed some light on the lenders to the continent, a growing trend of unofficial funding commitments could be observed, particularly from the UAE and Saudi Arabia. These commitments, which do not appear on a country's balance sheet, directly affect debt transparency. *Debt negotiations* were further complicated by unclear lending volumes, interest payments, and currency denominations of loans especially from Chinese lenders, a common issue across most countries in the sub-region.

In all of this, *credit rating agencies* remained powerful actors, determining the terms under which banks and other lenders offered loans to governments. In the absence of a continental rating agency, risk assessments and, consequently, access to and conditions for financing were dominated by the three major international players that control close to 95% of credit ratings globally. Fitch, Standard & Poor's, and Moody's have been accused of biased and unfair assessments. In August, Kenyan president William Ruto openly criticised the leading credit rating agencies for hindering investment in 'junk' rated countries, which could have spurred initiatives to address fiscal vulnerabilities. Notably, by the end of the year, Fitch had not assigned ratings for DRC, Ethiopia, Ghana, Mozambique, or Zambia – all considered to have a high degree of credit risk. Countries on the continent were penalised more severely than similar economies in Latin America and Asia, resulting in a total of seven rating downgrades and six outlook downgrades for 11 African states in the first half of 2023. The AU criticised significant errors, noting that no African country received an upgrade in the first half of the year. Initiatives to counter this imbalance included proposals to establish an independent Africa-focused ratings agency and to adopt the EU regulatory model for closer supervision of international ratings agencies. Throughout the year, the AU continued its efforts to establish a private-sector-driven African credit rating agency, implement the Africa Debt Monitoring Mechanism (ADMM), and develop the Africa Financial Stability Mechanism, with concrete actions anticipated in the coming year.

Illicit financial flows (IFFs) were a key factor undermining Africa's economic stability and development, as they drained capital, reduced government revenues, and deprived public services of essential funding. IFFs were especially prevalent in extractive industries, state-owned enterprises, and the informal economy. According to Transparency International, Nigeria and DRC were particularly vulnerable to these flows, which stemmed primarily from tax evasion, corruption, theft, crime financing, and illegal markets. Little changes could be observed in *Transparency International's Corruption Perceptions Index* (CPI) 2023 rankings (based on 2022 data), with Equatorial Guinea ranking 172nd out of 180, South Sudan 177th, and Somalia 180th. As in previous years, Seychelles (20th out of 180), Cabo Verde (30th), and Botswana (39th) were the highest-ranked countries in SSA. Significantly, the rank shows a country's relative position, while the CPI score (0–100) measures the degree of public sector corruption, 0 being highly corrupt and 100 very clean. It is a direct and crucial indicator of corruption, making the score more important than the rank for assessing corruption. Regarding IFFs, Transparency International identified the DRC (score: 20/100), Côte d'Ivoire (40/100), Nigeria (25/100), and

Zambia (37/100) as being at particularly high risk of corruption. This was primarily because the informal sector was estimated to account for up to 50% of GDP in these countries. While many countries on the continent are adopting stronger legal frameworks and engaging in international cooperation to combat IFFs, enforcement remains challenging due to weak institutions and limited resources. A noteworthy development in this regard was the approval of the UN Tax Convention on 23 November, proposed by Nigeria on behalf of the UN African Group. The convention was aimed at combating corporate tax abuse and IFFs.

There was little noteworthy progress on the implementation of the AfCFTA, lending credibility to critics who argued that promoting regional trade and economic integration was a process that would likely take a decade or more. By August, 47 of the 54 signatories had deposited their instruments of AfCFTA ratification, with Comoros, Botswana, and Mozambique being the latest to do so. The states not to have done so were Benin, Eritrea (not a signatory), Liberia, Libya, Madagascar, Somalia, South Sudan, and Sudan. The three phases of AfCFTA negotiations – Phase 1 (trade in goods, services, and dispute settlement), Phase 2 (investment, competition, and intellectual property), and Phase 3 (digital trade and trade issues for women and youth) – are interconnected and require a common understanding among state parties, as well as political will at both the national and REC levels. Therefore, with negotiations on protocols of all three phases yet to be finalised, it was surprising when Kenya signed an EPA with the EU in December. The EPA established a preferential trade scheme between Kenya and EU member states, like the AGOA of the US, which could discourage regional trade integration. In October, the US government announced that CAR, Niger, Gabon, and Uganda would lose their AGOA beneficiary status from 1 January 2024, while Mauritania would have its status reinstated following its suspension in 2019.

The continent continued to navigate new geopolitical and geoeconomic dynamics, affecting sectors from fertiliser and wheat procurement to market access. In December, EU member states, the European Parliament, and the EU Commission reached a provisional agreement on the Corporate Sustainability Due Diligence Directive (CSDDD). The CSDDD was designed to enhance human rights protections, safeguard the environment, and advance international climate objectives across product value chains. However, this new supply chain legislation also highlighted significant challenges for African manufacturers, who face the risk of losing market access unless they rapidly adapt to new standards.

The conflict between Israel and Hamas highlighted growing *geopolitical fragmentation*, with some African nations showing solidarity with the Palestinians and rising anti-Zionist sentiment. The conflict also revealed internal divisions within countries such as South Africa, where domestic criticism arose when the state brought a case against Israel to the ICJ on 29 December. Meanwhile, pro-Israel nations (e.g., Kenya, Ghana, DRC, Rwanda) and neutral countries (e.g., Uganda, Nigeria) maintained their stances.

Various summits took place during the year, including the 1st Italy–Africa summit in Rome (28–29 January), the 2nd Russia–Africa summit in St Petersburg (27–28 July), and the 1st Saudi–Africa summit in Riyadh (10 November). These events reflected the continent's strategic engagement with global powers. For instance, an estimated 40 African states have signed agreements, including MoUs, on military, technical, and energy cooperation with Russia over the past two years. The declaration from the summit in St Petersburg emphasised BRICS–Africa partnership and called for actions to 'counter manifestations of neo-colonial policies that aim to undermine the sovereignty of states'. Broadly, it seemed to endorse Moscow's position in global affairs, and in doing so, it implicitly supported the annexation of Ukraine. AU representatives, including AU chair President Azali Assoumani of Comoros and AUC chair Moussa Faki Mahamat, attended the Russia summit. However, suspended AU member states such as Sudan, Gabon, and Niger were also present, illustrating that such summits extend beyond a continental approach and focus more on bilateral links. China continued its engagement with Africa during the Forum on China–Africa Cooperation (FOCAC) held in November. Shortly after his appointment, foreign minister Qin Gang travelled to Africa for high-level visits to Ethiopia, Gabon, Angola, Benin, and Egypt in January. His predecessor, Wang Yi, whom he replaced after only seven months, continued Beijing's strategic commitment, with discussions on debt restructuring and deepening trade relations. UAE also continued to expand its economic and strategic presence on the continent, committing billions in investment. Following the US–Africa leaders' summit in December 2022, the US facilitated new trade and investment deals with African countries in 2023, valued at $14.2 bn, marking a considerable increase in both the number and value of deals compared with 2022.

The theme for this year's *BRICS* summit, hosted by South Africa in August, was 'BRICS and Africa: Partnership for Mutually Accelerated Growth, Sustainable Development, and Inclusive Multilateralism'. New memberships for Egypt, Ethiopia, UAE, Saudi Arabia, Iran, and Argentina were approved, effective 1 January 2024. However, the future strategic goals of BRICS+ remained unclear. Russia, China, and Saudi Arabia have openly criticised Western dominance in multilateral bodies such as the IMF and the World Bank, suggesting that BRICS+ could emerge as a counterbalance. Contrary to the belief that China dominates the BRICS group, Russia reportedly played a crucial role in admitting Ethiopia, a nation experiencing internal instability and unsustainable debt but also record growth. With Egypt, linking Africa and the Middle East, Ethiopia, the seat of the AU, and South Africa as members, it remained to be seen whether BRICS+ will now pursue a more Africa-centred strategy.

The AU and the APRM

The year marked several firsts and milestones for the AU. Celebrating its 60th anniversary, the continental organisation became a full member of the *Group of Twenty* (G20), hence holding the same status as the EU, six decades after its predecessor, the OAU, was established in Addis Ababa, Ethiopia, in 1963. The AU's successful bid to join the G20 received international support from the EU, US, and China. This achievement can also be attributed to the institutional reforms initiated by Rwandan president Paul Kagame, which aimed to streamline the AU's foreign engagements and positions.

Comoros' President Azali Assoumani succeeded Macky Sall of Senegal as chair during the 36th AU summit in February. This marked a historic moment as Comoros became the first Small Island Developing State (SIDS) to lead the bloc. President Assoumani represented the AU for the first time at the G20 summit in Delhi and participated in an AU-led peace mission to Ukraine and Russia, both unprecedented events. Additionally, Comoros also ratified the AfCFTA just days before Assoumani assumed the *AU chairship* – notable given that the annual theme was 'Accelerating the Implementation of the African Continental Free Trade Area'. Despite the late ratification, Comoros successfully lobbied Botswana and Mozambique to ratify the agreement during the year.

Comoros' bid to head the AU was met with considerable scepticism among many member states due to the country's alleged limited diplomatic experience on the continental stage. Given the recent resurgence of unconstitutional changes of government (UCGs) in Africa, many also questioned Assoumani's credibility on the issue. This scepticism was fuelled particularly by the fact that he began his first presidential term in 1999 following a military coup, while Comoros was facing significant political challenges ahead of the 2024 presidential elections.

The *strategic agenda* of Comoros for the year closely aligned with those of the previous chair, Senegal, emphasising continental peace, multilateralism, AfCFTA acceleration, women's empowerment, climate change, food security, and digitalisation. Not surprisingly, Comoros also used the role to highlight the unique challenges of SIDS and promoted the *blue economy* agenda. On the latter, the 'Moroni Declaration for Ocean and Climate Action in Africa' signed in June was a notable achievement with the objectives of improving maritime security, increasing institutional support, and encouraging international cooperation and investment, particularly in relation to the AfCFTA. Other key topics of Comoros' chairship were the conflicts in CAR and Chad, the implementation of Ethiopia's 2022 peace agreement, and the ongoing dispute over the Blue Nile between Ethiopia, Sudan, and Egypt. As of April, the novel escalation of conflict in Sudan became a pressing issue, with the AU failing to achieve notable progress by year's end. With few exceptions, Comoros' success in driving its initiatives was limited, resulting in minimal achievements, particularly in fostering peace and structural stability on the continent.

The selection of Comoros was a race until the last minute due to competition with Kenya, as both countries had announced their candidacy for the post, which rotates among the five sub-regions of the continent. To the surprise of many, Kenya's President Ruto officially withdrew Nairobi's bid during the US–Africa summit in December 2022. This paved the way for a new *AU bureau* selected in February led by Comoros as chair, with Botswana as second vice-chair, Burundi as third vice-chair, and the outgoing chair, Senegal, as rapporteur. The position of first vice-chair, elected from North Africa and set to assume the chairship in 2024, remained vacant throughout the year. North Africa's last AU vice-chair was Egypt in 2019. Morocco and Algeria were major contenders; mainly due to the diplomatic stalemate over the status and sovereignty of Western Sahara, an AU member state, neither country withdrew its candidacy before the end of the year, and no consensus candidate was found.

The AU faced significant challenges in an increasingly complex diplomatic landscape. In addition to the escalating conflicts in the Sahel, the Greater Horn of Africa, and the Great Lakes region, the continent was impacted by international conflicts such as the Israel–Hamas war and the ongoing conflict between Russia and Ukraine. For instance, during the summit, Israeli diplomat Sharon Bar-Li was reportedly removed from the plenary hall despite having observer credentials. The AU stated that she was not the accredited ambassador to Ethiopia, while Israel blamed South Africa and Algeria, accusing them of hostility.

The AU's heavy reliance on donor *funding* remained a pressing issue. In 2015, the AU had decided that member states should self-fund 100% of operations, 75% of programmes, and 25% of the peacekeeping budget. Over 66% of the 2023 budget ($655 m) was funded by donors. Moreover, funding sources have shifted, with member states contributing less over time, from $110 m in 2019 to merely $44 m in 2023. Consequently, international partner contributions increased, from $140 m in 2019 to $195 m in 2023. Nevertheless, notable progress was made with regard to the AU Peace Fund, which was nearing its $400 m target, with a large proportion coming from member state contributions. Related to this, on 1 December, the UNSC adopted a resolution establishing a framework for UN funding of AU-led peace operations. The UN will fund up to 75% of each mission's annual budget, with the remaining 25% jointly raised by the UN and AU from other sources. This agreement was crucial for reinforcing Africa's security architecture and marked the end of more than 15 years of debate on funding African peace missions with the UN's budget. A review of the African Peace and Security Architecture (APSA) began in July, focusing on pressing topics such as the role and composition of the AU Peace and Security Council (PSC), resource adequacy to address security challenges, and enhancing preventive diplomacy on the continent.

In November, the AU requested an extension of the Transition Mission in Somalia (ATMIS) personnel drawdown, initially scheduled for September, to 31 December. The deployment schedule for uniformed personnel to carry out ATMIS's mandated tasks was extended until June 2024, highlighting ongoing issues with securing adequate funding and logistical support for the Somali National Army.

Ongoing crises and the escalation of new conflicts kept the AU PSC particularly busy. By the end of the year, six members remained suspended from AU meetings and voting, Guinea, Sudan, Burkina Faso, Mali, Niger, and Gabon, the latter two suspended since August. A total of 96 meetings were held, with 28 focusing on acute crises and countries in transition. The 15-member PSC faced challenges due to a lack of coherence between the AU and RECs, inconsistent application of 'subsidiarity', and unclear leadership roles, as seen in the response to the Niger coup and the conflict in Sudan, which was eventually delegated to IGAD. Burundi and Congo (Central Africa), Tanzania and Uganda (East Africa), Tunisia (North Africa), South Africa and Zimbabwe (Southern Africa), and The Gambia, Ghana, and Senegal (West Africa) served their second year. Tanzania, The Gambia, and Uganda are likely to seek re-election in 2024. Meanwhile, North Africa was actively campaigning for a third seat on the PSC, where West Africa currently holds four seats. The debate continued as to whether West Africa should relinquish one of its seats to North Africa or if the total membership should be expanded.

The APRM celebrated its 20th anniversary in December under the theme 'Accelerating and Deepening Governance Reform, Measures, and Intervention'. By 2023, a total of 43 states had joined the APRM, with the latest being the AU's current chair, Comoros, in February. Twenty-six countries completed initial reviews, while Kenya, Uganda, Mozambique, Nigeria, and South Africa completed second reviews. Targeted reviews were conducted in Zambia, Djibouti, Sierra Leone, Uganda, Kenya, Namibia, Senegal, Ghana, Mozambique, Chad, Lesotho, Guinea, and Comoros. A governance gap analysis was also conducted in Sudan.

The African Climate Summit, held 4–6 September in Nairobi, Kenya, focused on green growth and climate finance solutions, aligning with the APRM's goals of sustainable development. In April, the APRM signed an MoU with CARE Ratings (Africa) to enhance financial governance and transparency among member states through credit rating assessments. A sensitisation mission to Seychelles took place in August, aiming to revive the APRM process in Seychelles, which joined in 2020.

Democracy and Elections

The quality of democracy across the globe continued to be a public issue, as affirmed by indices. As in the previous year, the *EIU Democracy Index* suggested that democracy recorded 'reversals' across all the regions of the world. Using a scale of 0–10, the Index estimated that the average global democracy score declined from 5.29 in 2022 to 5.23. It rated 167 countries and grouped them into four types of regime, 'full democracy', 'flawed democracy', 'hybrid regime', and 'authoritarian regime', based on five dimensions: electoral process and pluralism, functioning of government, political participation, political culture, and civil liberties. The score for SSA decreased to 4.04, down from 4.14 in 2022. In SSA, the Index identified the tiny island of Mauritius as the only country regarded as a full democracy. The number of countries classified as flawed democracies remained at six, while 15 and 22 countries were regarded as hybrid regimes and authoritarian regimes, respectively. CAR was the worst performer in SSA, with a score of 1.18, emerging last in the region and ranked 44th. The Index suggested that SSA has a long way to go before a culture of democracy could be entrenched and consolidated, as authoritarianism reigned.

The findings of the *2024 Freedom in the World* report by Freedom House were consistent with those of the EIU Democracy Index, suggesting that democracy was in distress across the globe. Based on 2023 data, it declared that there is 'mounting damage of flawed elections and armed conflict'. This suggested that although democracy was widely embraced, it was operating under challenging circumstances and anti-democratic forces continued to oppose its being established. The distress suffered by democracy was particularly evident in developing countries such as those in SSA. Freedom House assessed 210 countries as 'free', 'partly free', or 'not free' and declared that 'the breadth and depth of the deterioration were extensive. Political rights and civil liberties were diminished in 52 countries, while only 21 countries made improvements. Flawed elections and armed conflict contributed to the decline, endangering and causing severe suffering.' The situation described by Freedom House was worrying but not surprising, because the 2023 EIU Democracy Index had shown that a substantial percentage of the world's population lived under what it described as flawed democracies, hybrid regimes, and authoritarian regimes.

The situation described above by Freedom House was more evident in Africa, as there was no noticeable change or improvement recorded. As in the previous year, out of 54 countries evaluated in Africa, 46% were regarded as 'not free', 37% as 'partly free', and only 17% as 'free'. Elections in several countries were tarnished by the prevalence of violence and allegations of fraud. In other countries, conflicts gave rise to widespread human rights violations, at times with impunity. Unsurprisingly, five countries in SSA – South Sudan, Eritrea, Equatorial Guinea, CAR, and Sudan – fell into the category of 'worst of the worst' performers in the aspect of political rights and civil liberties. Liberia offered a glimmer of hope.

The 2023 RSF *World Freedom Index* presented a concerning situation regarding the state of freedom. The World Freedom report, which considered the state of press freedom in 180 countries utilising the five dimensions 'good', 'satisfactory', 'problematic', 'difficult', and 'serious', declared that 'the situation is "very serious" in 31 countries, "difficult" in 42, "problematic" in 55, and "good" or "satisfactory" in 52 countries', noting that 'the environment for journalism is "bad" in seven out of ten countries, and "satisfactory" in only three out of ten' – suggesting a deterioration of the state of affairs. In Africa, the situation remained quite challenging, considered 'satisfactory' in 10.4% countries, 'problematic' in 45.8%, 'difficult' in 39.6%, and 'very serious' in 4.2% countries. The World Freedom Index noted that although the African continent 'has seen a few significant rises, such as that of Botswana (65th), which has risen 35 places, journalism overall has become more difficult in this continent and the situation is now classified as "bad" in nearly 40% of its countries (against 33% in 2022). They include Burkina Faso (58th), where local retransmission of international broadcasters has been banned and journalists have been deported, and the Sahel in general, which is in the process of becoming a "no-news zone". Several journalists have also been murdered in Africa, including Martinez Zogo in Cameroon (138th). In Eritrea (174th), the media remain in President Isaias Afwerki's despotic grip.' The Index suggests that journalists are operating under trying conditions, yet some of these countries present themselves as democracies. Overall, in 89.82% of countries in Africa, journalists functioned in 'problematic', 'difficult', or 'very serious' situations, clearly demonstrating that the situation was not promising.

Indisputably, democracy continued to be under attack from anti-democratic and repressive forces in SSA. Notwithstanding the challenges, elections were held in several countries. These included DRC, Djibouti, Gabon, Guinea-Bissau, Liberia, Madagascar, Mauritania, Nigeria, Sierra Leone, Eswatini, and Zimbabwe. The countries that held elections were deemed hybrid regimes or authoritarian by the EIU Democracy Index, suggesting that the conditions in most of them were not conducive to a free vote taking place. Unsurprisingly, the elections were diminished by either the prevalence of violence or accusations of fraud. However, Liberia held a promise for the region, as its elections were approved by international observers.

The Somali Federal Government announced key political reforms in May, including universal suffrage and direct elections, with the first local elections scheduled for June 2024. These reforms were met with opposition, resulting in armed clashes and declarations of autonomy by some groups.

Unconstitutional Rule: Coups or Constitutional Crisis

Since 2020, the continent has witnessed a new wave of coups d'etat and coup attempts. This trend continued in the reporting year, with two major coups occurring in Gabon and Niger. While the coup in Niger had a similar (anti-French) background as those in neighbouring Mali and Burkina Faso in preceding years, the coup in Gabon was arguably of a different kind. Preceding the coup in Gabon, incumbent Ali Bongo moved ahead in manipulating the rules for standing in elections; this was not the only effort by African elites to rule against a constitution, alter it with dubious means, or manipulate elections. The failed coup attempts in Guinea-Bissau and in Sierra Leone could equally be interpreted from this perspective.

The coup in *Gabon* on 30 August was preceded by general elections four days earlier. Incumbent president Ali Bongo Ondimba had made sure – by changing the legal provisions – that he could run for president a third time. An internet shut-down was meant to avoid the spread of critical news around election day. But when elections results were announced (giving Bongo a comfortable, while rather improbable, win of 64% of the votes), the military intervened in a clearly well-prepared scenario and against very limited resistance. Bongo and some key family members were put under house arrest. On the streets of the capital, people danced and cheered at the end of the uninterrupted dominance of the Bongo clan (with Ali's father Omar Bongo inaugurating family rule in 1967). General Brice Clotaire Oligui Nguema, commander of the Republican Guard, was sworn in as president of the transition on 4 October. While the neighbouring regimes were clearly shocked by the turn of events and at least paid lip service to loyalty to their deposed peer, there was little solidarity from other quarters, including the EU, although the AU suspended the country's membership. Oligui Nguema was not fully an outsider and was even a distant relative of the ousted president. It was fairly unclear whether the coup would in the end result in more or less acceptable governance practices in Gabon.

The coup in *Niger* on 26 July – the fifth since independence, after 1974, 1996, 1999, and 2010 – ousted President Mohamed Bazoum, seen as a close ally of France and playing the role of 'anchor of stability' in the Sahel, at least in the eyes of many decision-makers in the EU. The trigger for the coup was reportedly the decision by Bazoum two days earlier to depose Abdourahamane Tiani, the no longer trusted commander of the Presidential Guard and apparently mastermind of the later coup. However, an air force commander announced via national broadcast that the coup was 'due to the deteriorating security situation and bad governance' – a narrative that resembled justifications for successful coups in Burkina Faso and Mali in preceding years. Bazoum was detained by the Presidential Guard in the presidential palace. At first, loyalist troops and civilian demonstrators tried to reverse the situation by marching to the palace and controlling critical infrastructure. In the evening Tiani managed to present himself at state TV with representatives of all major corps of Niger's security forces and declared the take-over the act of a junta calling itself Conseil national pour la sauvegarde de la patrie (CNSP). Bazoum had over time lost the support by most of the military hierarchy, which facilitated the coup immensely. Bazoum and his wife and son remained detained, reportedly with little food, water, and electricity. Tiani declared himself president of the junta, which appointed later a civilian prime minister. ECOWAS issued a firm ultimatum on 30 July, giving the coup leaders in Niger one week to reinstate Bazoum, threatening military intervention, and imposed sanctions. This was rather a welcome development for the coup-makers, who were able to mobilise street protests against an unpopular concerted foreign intervention by both France and ECOWAS. The junta suddenly gained more popularity and declared the setting up of a militia of civilian volunteers that would fight any such military mission – and it gained open support from Russia. ECOWAS, though it prepared for some weeks for an intervention, in the end retracted its plans in the absence of a good prospect of a successful and speedy resolution of the crisis by military means. However, the CNSP was not at ease: the constitution was suspended, as were all main state institutions, with no alternative viable framework in sight. Above all, Bazoum refused to resign and kept claiming to be the legitimate president, while reports on his health condition were a source of concern; many governments showed solidarity and called for his release. On 10 December, ECOWAS promised to lift its sanctions if the junta would free Bazoum, but the junta did not give in.

A further coup attempt in *Burkina Faso* against de facto president Ibrahim Traoré was on record, though some details remained opaque. Discontent with the latest junta, which was as unable as its predecessor to reinstate security and stability in the country, had grown over months. On 27 September, a rather small protest action against Traoré broke out in Ouagadougou but was quickly quelled. Whether only taking this as a pretext or with more tangible proof, the junta now declared that it had foiled a coup attempt by high-ranking security officers. Later, the commander of the Burkinabé Special Forces and three other important officers – all under arrest – were named as the coup leaders and investigated; two further officers were in hiding. On 4 October, Traoré fired the head of the national gendarmerie.

In *Guinea-Bissau*, the bloody failed coup attempt of last year was only the precursor to a renewed attempt. On 30 November, serious fighting between two corps of the security forces broke out while President Umaro Sissoco Embaló was at the UN Climate Change Conference in Dubai. The upheaval was related to the questioning of two ministers in an anti-corruption investigation; they were placed under arrest at a police station in Bissau. Armed members of the National Guard stormed the police station and released both, though they were rearrested later. Open armed confrontations between the National Guard and special forces of the Presidential Palace Battalion followed in two neighbourhoods of the capital. On 1 December, the army captured the commander of the National Guard, who was dismissed the next day. Roadblocks were erected and ECOWAS regional stabilisation forces patrolled the streets. The fighting resulted in two people killed, six injured, and the fleeing of many National Guard officers. On 4 December, Embaló issued a decree dissolving the National People's Assembly (parliament) and ordered soldiers to be deployed at the headquarters of state media outlets to replace their directors by force. Assembly speaker Domingos Simões Pereira accused the president of carrying out a 'constitutional coup d'etat'. In fact, the constitution is explicit in stating that the legislature cannot be dissolved in the first 12 months after an election (elections were held only in June). It was obvious that the fact that the president and the majority in parliament were from opposing parties was one major driver of the crisis.

Contested election outcomes were also at the origin of a coup plot and a serious coup attempt in *Sierra Leone*. On 31 July, authorities detained at least 24 people, most of them members of the armed forces, for planning a coup, accusing them of subversion; they also issued a warrant for eight further army or police officers. A retired chief superintendent was arrested in Liberia in early August and extradited to Sierra Leone. Opponents to President Julius Maada Bio openly questioned whether there had really been a coup attempt and interpreted the arrests as an act of intimidation. But the following, more serious coup attempt on 26 November could hardly have been made up. Insurgents attacked several locations in Freetown including a military armoury geographically close to the presidential palace (which they apparently were not able to conquer) as well as a police station and the navy headquarters. A prison was stormed and nearly all inmates freed. The government placed the country under a nationwide curfew. While loyalists quickly gained the upper hand, the army attacked the residence of former president and now opposition leader Ernest Koroma, killing one of his guards. The government later accused him openly of being behind the coup attempt. Koroma was confined to his home on 9 December and later termed a suspect in the coup attempt, though he had himself strongly condemned the attack. Around a dozen military officers were immediately arrested, with further individuals apprehended in early December, most of them army or police officers. Authorities later arrested the alleged brain behind the coup, Amadu Koita, a former military officer and bodyguard of Koroma. Koita was notorious for his criticism of Bio's government on social media. By 12 December, 80 people had been arrested on suspicion of involvement in the coup while an additional 54 people were actively sought, including Koroma's daughter.

In *CAR*, President Faustin-Archange Touadéra moved ahead in his strategy to change the constitution despite quite some resistance from churches and opposition parties. Having deposed the equally resistant president of the Constitutional Court in 2022, he now pushed for a constitutional referendum, which was held on 30 July, secured and logistically supported by Russian mercenaries. The yes vote was officially given as 95%. The new text would allow Touadéra to stand in the next presidential elections.

Chad's transitional authorities remained extremely unpopular but paved the way to a legalistic end to the transition. A new constitution was prepared and received an official 86% approval rate in a referendum held on 17 December. The referendum question, to be answered by yes or no, was overly suggestive ('Do you approve the constitution submitted to you preserving the unitary state?'), and critics of Mahamat Déby disliked a good number of provisions in the text. For Déby himself, it was an important step towards the normalisation of his rule.

A second 'third term debate' (after 2010, when elderly president Abdoulaye Wade faced strong resistance when he decided to run for a third time but then lost the run-off in 2012 against current president Macky Sall) was developing in *Senegal*, where President Macky Sall was tempted to adopt a controversial interpretation of the constitution and run for a third time in presidential elections in 2024. The fact that the constitution was revised in 2016 to allow for two terms in office served as a pretext for Sall to see a third term (formally only the second under the 'new' constitution) as legally in order. However, this interpretation met with fierce resistance and even triggered violent unrest, leading to around 20 people being killed in confrontations between supporters of opposition leader Ibrahim Sonko and the security forces. Not only Sall's posture but also the thwarting of Sonko's political ambitions were contentious. On 1 June, Sonko was cleared of rape charges but was sentenced to two years' imprisonment for a minor infraction – which still would prevent him from being eligible in 2024. In this heated situation, on 3 July, Macky Sall announced that he would actually not stand, without omitting to again state that the constitution would allow him to do so. This stance was widely praised as intrinsically pro-democratic. However, the unease persisted. On 28 July, Sonko was again arrested for 'disturbing the public order'. Furthermore, different Senegalese courts saw a banning of Sonko from the electoral register as either justified or not.

Armed Conflict, Peace, and Security

Broad stretches of land and people living in those zones were exposed again to widespread violence. The topography of this insecurity did not change greatly from last year, with two major geographical belts, one from west to east and one from north to south, being quite visible. From west to east, Sahel countries Mali, Burkina Faso, and Niger, with related zones in northern parts of Benin, Togo, Nigeria, and Cameroon, plus western Chad, were exposed to jihadist insurgencies, though government armies and their supporters (ethnic militias and in some cases Russian mercenaries) did not produce more security. From north to south, a further belt from the now fully unstable Sudan, through CAR and eastern DRC, with neighbours Uganda, Rwanda, and Burundi all driving conflict dynamics but also affected by warfare themselves, could be identified. Here, rowing armed actors, at times just 'guns for hire', lived on plunder, extortion, and smuggling while claiming to protect some ethnic or religious community or other. Two further areas (Ethiopia/Somalia and western Cameroon) were not fully unrelated to these two belts but followed a somewhat different dynamic.

In terms of *fatalities* in violent conflict, the worldwide figure fell sharply from record year 2022. According to the Uppsala Conflict Data Program (UCDP), fatalities from organised violence decreased for the first time since the rapid increase observed in 2020, dropping from 310,000 in 2022 to 154,000 in 2023. In Africa, this trend was also tangible, though situations varied quite significantly. In two countries relatively prominent in recent years, a positive trend could be clearly detected: the *Ethiopian* Tigray war was ended by the Cessation of Hostilities Agreement (CoHA) signed in November 2022 in Pretoria. The conflict was considered to be the deadliest in decades, with estimates ranging between 162,000 to 378,000 civilian casualties. The Peace Research Institute Oslo (PRIO) estimated numbers of additional battle-related deaths to be as high as 100,000 in 2022 alone, but the number of fatalities went down sharply with the signing of the CoHA. This should not hide the fact that confrontations in Oromya alone produced close to 500 fatalities. Additionally, new confrontations arose when the ethnic Amhara militia group Fano felt betrayed by the government (in signing the peace agreement) and attacked security forces in the first months of the year all over the region of Amhara.

In *Mozambique*'s Cabo Delgado province, violent acts by an IS-affiliated group were brought fully under control by a SADC-mandated military peace operation. Less clear were the situations in Cameroon, CAR, Chad, Mali, and Niger, where the yearly fatalities figure fell slightly or remained constant but with little hope that a long-term positive trend would develop.

Several arenas in *Nigeria* were again hotspots, and an increase of fatalities of roughly 1,000 was recorded by the UCDP. Given that violence in the most populated country of the continent would still only affect a rather small percentage of the population, some rated the situation as not so dramatic. However, the fact that not only the north east experienced widespread violence meant that conflict was omnipresent in the minds of Nigerians.

Most concern was justified where figures either sharply rose (Somalia, Sudan, and Burkina Faso) or remained very high despite a relative decline in overall figures (DRC). The Great Lakes region was again a powder keg, with eastern DRC (North Kivu and Ituri particularly) the scene of the most horrendous acts of violence. The verbal escalation between Kigali and Kinshasa even nurtured fears that a further broad international war could unfold in which the DRC government could rely on a number of alliance partners among southern neighbours while Rwanda would trust in its superior logistical capacities. The concerted efforts between Ugandan and DRC security forces against the IS-affiliated Allied Defence Forces may have been partly successful, though the UCDP recorded the passing of a 1,000 fatalities threshold in attacks attributed to IS (in the Beni territory of Nord Kivu province and the southern parts of Ituri province). The Rwandan-backed M23 rebels clearly expanded their zones of operation, particularly in the Masisi and Rutshuru territories of North Kivu. Self-help groups, now acknowledged by the government in Kinshasa, were not always good protectors but rather an additional fighting force in conflicts between communities. In fact, in Ituri but also in an area close to the capital Kinshasa, local ethnic militias and state forces clashed and killed civilians.

In *Burkina Faso*, the level of insecurity rose sharply, and calculated fatalities increased by 135% (from 2,600 to more than 6,100). The coups in 2022 (justified by their perpetrators with reference to the incapacity of the predecessor governments) had obviously not contributed to any more peacefulness or protection of civilians. Similar developments could be seen in *Niger*, where the first half of the year was comparatively peaceful but diverse Islamist actors affiliated to either IS or al-Qaida took advantage of the coup in mid-year to step up their activities in the second half. The single most deadly attack on a military convoy occurred in early October (53 reported fatalities, both sides). In *Mali*, the post-coup regime would potentially claim a contribution to the decline in numbers of fatalities, which went down sharply (from more than 1,450 in 2022 to fewer than 500 in 2023). However, the UCDP attributed this positive development to fewer deadly attacks on civilians by IS in Sahel Province (ISSP), which in 2022 had used the security vacuum when France left Mali to kill up to 900 civilians in massacres as revenge for their support for pro-government militias. The main perpetrator of one-sided violence was now the official Malian army, which killed more than 170 civilians, 'sometimes on their own, and sometimes together with Wagner soldiers', as the UCDP noted.

Somalia was among the countries with a significant overall increase in numbers of fatalities (+4,000). Beyond the familiar confrontations between al-Shabaab and government forces plus peacekeepers, a new confrontation developed in the de facto state of Somaliland where the Dhulbahante clan organising the so-called Khatumo Administration (pledging allegiance to Somalia and calling for support from Mogadishu) clashed with forces loyal to the regime in Hargeisa in February and March.

Further declining fatality figures in *South Sudan* could be attributed to somewhat stable peace arrangements, but some speculation about under-reporting was voiced even by the UCDP. The hypothesis here was that media attention was turning to the catastrophic developments in the larger neighbouring country *Sudan*. Here, the escalation of violence was significant, 'reaching over 7,500 fatalities for the first time since the early 2000s', according to the UCDP. On 15 April, disagreement over the composition of the planned unified national army pitted the Sudanese Armed Forces (SAF) with leader Abdel Fattah al-Burhan against the Rapid Support Forces (RSF) of Mohamed Hamdan Dagalo (alias Hemedti). The confrontation was at first looked at as merely an expression of personal rivalry. However, it quickly escalated and mobilised group-based loyalties. In the capital Khartoum, urban warfare resulted in heavy casualties among civilians. The fighting spread to West Darfur, where the RSF could draw on Arab support while Masalit and other groups stood by the SAF. At the margins, intercommunity clashes also claimed many fatalities. RSF, gaining the upper hand (without decisively ending the confrontation), committed serious crimes against humanity (including rape, summary executions, torture, and forced displacement based on ethnicity). Only indirectly related, South

Kordofan developed into a separate war zone when the Sudan People's Liberation Army broke the ceasefire agreement by attacking Sudanese army units. The Abyei area remained disputed between Sudan and South Sudan (and also between two sub-groups of the Dinka ethnic group).

Among the category of Least Developed Countries (45 countries) which according to UNHCR hosted 21% of all *refugees* worldwide, African countries such as Chad, DRC, Ethiopia, Rwanda, South Sudan, Sudan, Uganda, and Tanzania stood out. At the end of the year, Sudan was the country with most *IDPs* worldwide; DRC was placed fourth, after Syria and Colombia. In Sudan, at least 5.8 m people were forced to flee their homes during the year as a result of the SAF–RSF war. Overall, 9.1 m IDPs were on record at the end of the year (including displacements from previous conflict episodes). UNHCR stated that 'Sudan constitutes the largest IDP population ever reported'. For DRC, the number of newly displaced persons in Ituri and North Kivu calculated by UNHCR was close to 2.8 m, with the number of people remaining displaced at the end of the year growing to 6.3 m.

A reconfiguration of the landscape of military peace operations, at least in West Africa, clearly started in 2023. The five largest *peace operations* worldwide continued operating on African soil, with MINUSCA in CAR, MONUSCO in Congo, ATMIS in Somalia, UNMISS in South Sudan (all with 15,000 to 18,000 troops) and MINUSMA in Mali (still numbering 13,000 troops by mid-2023). However, MINUSMA's mandate was terminated – upon a request by Bamako – by the UNSC on 30 June with a six-month drawdown period until 31 December, a landmark event. Opposition against this move was limited, as substantial frustrations (with the mission, its effects, but also the lack of gratitude locally) were widely shared by all major partners. This development was interpreted by some observers as the beginning of the end of classic blue helmet operations (not only in Africa). Indeed, MONUSCO and MINUSCA were also more or less frequently criticised by host governments, although UNMISS enjoyed rather better relationships and ATMIS, as an AU mission, at least did not receive the criticism of being 'neocolonial'. An abrupt end of those missions was not expected, however. During the year, African non-permanent members of the UNSC, above all Ghana, sought ways to shift more funding for peacekeeping from the UN to the AU. Additionally, a myriad of smaller operations were still active. A number of sub-regional organisations were also mandating missions, such as the EAC Regional Force (EACRF) operating from September 2022 to December 2023 in DRC with a troop strength of 1,500, with the SAMIDRC (the SADC Mission in DRC) set to relieve it. SAMIM (the SADC Mission in Mozambique) was officially composed of 1,900 troops and proved very effective. In West Africa, ECOWAS operated the ECOWAS Mission in The Gambia (ECOMIG) with a military strength of 1,000 and its Stabilisation Support Mission to Guinea-Bissau (with only 630). Officially, G5 Sahel still operated its Joint Force with 5,000 troops. However, the G5 Sahel, serving not least as a framework for channelling Western military aid, was on the brink, when

Mali, Niger, and Burkina Faso decided to create a new structure, the Alliance of Sahel States on 16 September. On 6 December, Chad and Mauritania, the remaining G5 Sahel countries, said that they were prepared to dissolve the G5 Sahel. The CBLT continuously offered a framework for the Multinational Joint Task Force (MNJTF) operating in the Lake Chad area against jihadist groups. Speculation about the imminent departure of Niger from this alliance was countered by an official denial on 16 November; still, it was unclear how the coup in July could not also affect this regional arrangement. The Berlin-based Centre for International Operations (ZIF) calculated a non-negligible number of 36,712 personnel in such African peace operations. The EU continued to operate advisory, capacity building, training, and military partnership missions as well as one naval operation in Africa – in Mali, Niger, CAR, Somalia, and Mozambique – mostly with limited numbers of personnel. With the departure of French troops from Burkina Faso and Niger (in October), it was unclear what would happen to the EU missions in the Sahel, which all still had valid mandates; none were immediately terminated. Most training missions had between 100 and 180 members, but the EU Naval Force in Somalia was larger, with some 330 deployed marine troops.

Epidemics and Disasters

The ongoing battles with the Covid-19 pandemic, Marburg virus disease, malaria, and Ebola further undermined the capacity of health systems in many countries across the sub-regions. In addition, the effects of anthropogenic climate change had affected the capacity of people to meet their nutritional needs due to drought and low levels of precipitation contributing to food insecurity and breakdown of their immune system, making them easily susceptible to infections and diseases. The adverse effects of climate change and disease are a lethal mix for the survival of people on the African continent.

In May, *the Covid-19 pandemic* was declared no longer a global public health emergency. This declaration was validated by the increased number of vaccinations worldwide and the reduced rate of deaths and severe illness requiring intensive emergency care. On 30 April, the WHO reported a substantial decline of 95% in reported cases and 98% in confirmed deaths compared with 2022.

Seychelles was the foremost state in the rankings in this regard, with the highest *rate of vaccination* per person of any country globally: it had reportedly administered 205 doses of Covid-19 vaccination per 100 people. Countries next in the ranking included Rwanda and Mauritius. South Africa ranked last as the most affected, with a vaccination rate of 64 doses per 100 people. Data from the WHO, as of 31 December, indicated that 368,280,983 people had been vaccinated with the complete primary series of the AstraZeneca and Pfizer vaccines.

On a more adverse note, several districts of Zambia faced *an outbreak of anthrax*. This put pressure on the public health systems and capacity in the country. The outbreak was officially confirmed on 1 November. Across the country's ten provinces, 44 out of 116 districts were affected by the epidemic. According to the WHO, on 20 November, the accumulated number of cases confirmed was 684. The Sinazongwe district was the hub of this epidemic and as a result, accounted for 42% of the confirmed cases, translating to 287 active cases and two deaths out of a total of four nationwide at the Dengeza Health Post in Sinazongwe. Other countries running the risk of acquiring anthrax included Tanzania, Mozambique, Namibia, DRC, and Uganda through regular movements of ruminants for human consumption across their borders.

In Equatorial Guinea on 13 February, the Centers for Disease Control (CDC) reported the *prevalence of the Marburg virus disease* (MVD), a rare haemorrhagic fever first reported in the Ghanaian region of Ashanti on 17 July during the previous year, claiming the lives of two people out of three cases confirmed. In Equatorial Guinea, 17 cases were confirmed with 12 deaths and, according to the WHO, the case fatality ratio reached 75%, meaning that three out of four confirmed cases resulted in fatalities. The human capital aspect of this is that health capacity tends to be overwhelmed, as five cases were confirmed among health workers, of which two died. MVD stems from the same disease family as Ebola and thus, it has significant similarities in symptoms and treatment of infected bodies. Tanzania declared an MVD outbreak on 21 March where nine cases were probable, eight cases confirmed, and six deaths recorded, with three recoveries.

Burkina Faso reported the *outbreak of dengue fever and chikungunya* during the year. According to the country's health ministry, the deadliest outbreak of dengue fever was recorded in October, killing at least 214 people. Data from the Burkina Faso health ministry revealed over 50,000 cases, mainly in the capital Ouagadougou, with the city of Bobo Dioulasso recording 20% of the cases in a single week. Mosquito-borne illness, which is prevalent among communities outside of these two urban centres, is less documented but expected to be deadlier due to lack of treatment and misdiagnosis. A chikungunya virus (CHIKV) outbreak was also confirmed in November, with at least 89 cases officially reported by Burkina Faso's Public Health Emergency Response Operations Center. CHIKV is spread through mosquito bites and can lead to death in extreme cases. Due to this outbreak, the US Centers for Disease Control and Prevention enacted a level 2 travel warning to Burkina Faso.

There were also outbreaks of yellow fever in 12 countries, including Burkina Faso, Côte d'Ivoire, Niger, Nigeria, Benin, and Togo in the West Africa; CAR, DRC, Chad, and Congo in Central Africa; and Sudan and Uganda in Eastern Africa. With a case fatality rate (CFR) of 11%, the risk assessment for the yellow fever is evaluated as moderate on the African continent and low globally. The WHO indicated that 65 m people had been vaccinated against yellow fever in Africa, with 4 m done in Sudan during a health campaign by the WHO.

Following the disruption caused by the Covid-19 pandemic, the WHO restarted the distribution of insecticide-treated mosquito nets (ITNs); the campaign began in 2022. However, as the pyrethroid-only nets proved to be ineffective, a shift towards pyrethroid-chlrofenapyr nets, deemed to be almost 50% more effective than the pyrethroid-only nets, was put into effect. October marked the distribution of Matrix-M or R21 vaccines under the auspices of the WHO and UNICEF for the prevention of plasmodium falciparum malaria in children, along with other measures and interventions such as the ITNs, RTS and S vaccines, mosquito repellent, insecticides, and artesunate-pyronaridine medications to protect the lives of African children. Around 661,714 Malawian children received at least one dose of the RTS and S vaccines in March to combat the *Anopheles stephensi* mosquitos that thrive in urban areas. All countries in the Horn of Africa were affected, in addition to Ghana, Nigeria, and Sudan.

Around mid-2023, Eastern African countries such as Somalia, Kenya, and Ethiopia experienced drought. UNOCHA noted that the prolonged droughts in countries in the Horn of Africa had left approximately 23.4 m people with nutritional uncertainties in 2023. Around, 5.1 m children in these areas were left malnourished while 2.7 m people were struggling for basic sustenance. Improved rainfall in this region over the years only slightly mitigated the adverse effects of the prolonged drought. El Niño was responsible for both the severe drought and sudden torrential rainfall experienced in this area. While the conditions resulting from the prolonged drought did not change drastically due to sudden rainfall, the rains made floods and landslides imminent. The severe impact of El Niño led to increased levels of malnutrition and displacement of people, exacerbated by climate change. The effects of climate change were felt in Africa, manifesting as disastrous climatic conditions.

The Institute of Security Studies reported that approximately 438 people died in South Kivu in DRC, with 20,000 people affected by flooding. A total of 5,000 people were reported missing, presumed dead, and properties were destroyed. In Rwanda, 30 lives were lost due to torrential rainfalls. Floods decimated communities in this region and contributed to the increased threat of infections and diseases such as malaria and cholera.

In October, the Volta River Authority (VRA) in Ghana begun a controlled release of water from the Akosombo Dam, which generates electricity for the country. This annual event happens when the volume of water in the dam and reservoir threatens the hydro plant. This time however, the water released led to flooding in low-lying communities along its course, affecting six communities: Sogakope, Mafi, Mepe, Battor, Ada, and Adidome. The National Disaster Management Organization (NADMO), responsible for dealing with disasters in the country, reported that more than 26,000 individuals were displaced by the flood, and the farms, homes, and possessions of the people living in these communities were destroyed. Education in these communities was interrupted, and the MP, together with local philanthropic organisations, had to find temporary shelters for displaced women and children since the government's response to the disaster was slow.

On 24 October, the National Assembly of South Africa received a Climate Change Bill from the executive, starting the process of a law on climate change in the country. When passed, it will usher in an era of consistent national policy approach to dealing with climate change. The bill provided a legal framework to lessen the discharge of greenhouse gases (GHGs) and heighten climate resilience. Included in the bill were national adaptation approaches to securing emission objectives and eco-friendliness with sustainable progress in development. Notwithstanding the landmark nature of the bill in South Africa's politics and law, some opposition parties objected to its conception. However, this was a solid step for South Africa and more broadly, the world, towards achieving resilience to the adverse effects of climate change.

In Sierra Leone, around $200 m is spent annually on importing rice, and the figure is likely to increase as a result of the impact of the Ebola crisis. Sierra Leone has had to continuously deal with the impact of the 2014 Ebola health crisis, which affected local rice production. A number of factors, including limited research capacity, declining soil fertility, and limited access to external agricultural inputs, including fertilisers, have worsened the plight of citizens in the West African nation. Worryingly, this situation has the potential to affect their fundamental food and nutrition needs.

Mauritania battled with an increasing wave of migration, as thousands of Mauritanians crossed the Mexican border into the US. US government data, as reported by the 'New York Times', indicates that over 15,000 individuals were apprehended at the southern border. Thousands of Mauritanians have embarked on the dangerous journey to the US, locally known as 'Jumping the Wall'. In November, the US embassy in Nouakchott announced a formal agreement between the US and the Mauritanian government to repatriate a significant number of individuals lacking the legal authorisation to stay in the US. This move sent a clear message to illegal immigrants who use Mauritania as a launch base to embark on this life-threatening journey. Mauritania has also faced, in recent times, worsening food insecurity exacerbated by the persistent arrival of refugees fleeing the ongoing conflict in Mali. In July, UNOCHA reported 91,263 Malian refugees living in and around the Mbera camp in the Hodh El Chargui region in Mauritania. Mauritania authorities noted that the refugee numbers had more than doubled within a year and now surpassed 100,000, posing a significant security threat and creating additional costs for government.

An estimated 3 m Burkinabé suffered from hunger during the lean season due to insecurity. If this situation were to continue till the end of the year, nearly

650,000 individuals would have faced extreme hunger (Integrated Acute Food Insecurity Phase Classification 5), implying that people have started dying from lack of food. Over 2 m people fled violence, increasing the growing number of IDPs. The violence that followed the political instability in the country disrupted studies in approximately one in four schools and resulted in the closure of 6,100 schools, affecting over 1 m students and 30,000 teachers. This represented a 44% increase from the previous years' figures due to insecurity. The UN reported that Burkina Faso was unable to secure up to half of the $800 m required to address this humanitarian crisis, prompting the Norwegian Refugee Council to describe the situation in the country as the 'most neglected crisis'.

PART 2

African-European Relations

Benedikt Erforth and Niels Keijzer

Amid global turbulence, key features and trends of EU–Africa relations remained largely undisturbed. Africa remained a significant trade partner for European member states, serving not only as a destination for manufactured goods and hardware but also as a vital source of raw materials crucial to European value chains. Inversely, the EU trading block (still) remained the Africa's most important trading partner and a key export destination for African agricultural and mining exports. The EU also continued to be the largest source of FDI to African states; under its Global Gateway investment – and specifically its EU–Africa Investment Package – this involvement will only increase. Another key event was the signing of an Economic Partnership Agreement between the EU and Kenya on 15 December, almost ten years after the conclusion of an agreement with the EAC that failed to materialise. Last but not least, after much self-inflicted European delay, the EU finally signed the Samoa Agreement with a selection of African, Caribbean, and Pacific states in November, replacing the Cotonou Partnership Agreement that was concluded back in 2000.

Yet while EU–African economic cooperation and trade endured, politically and diplomatically the relationship continued to experience rough waters. This year, the regular 'College-to-College' meeting between the European Commission and the AU Commission did not take place, while in November a planned AU–EU ministerial meeting was cancelled only a week in advance. While the views of the two groupings on Russia's war on Ukraine failed to converge over the year, the EU's response to and positions on the Hamas attacks on Israel of 7 October were a further and considerable source of tension in the relationship. The severity of this event was such that the EU's support for the AU's successful application for a permanent seat in the G20, provided a month earlier, was largely forgotten. Aggravating matters further, coups d'état in Niger and Gabon further reduced the European – and particularly French – role in West Africa and added to the considerable doubt around the 2022 AU–EU Summit's motto of a 'Joint Vision of a Renewed Partnership'.

Global Gateway

A year after the 2022 AU–EU Summit, it was revealed what the contents were of the hitherto elusive 'Africa–Europe Investment Package', which was valued at €150 bn and consisted of separate investment, health, and education packages. The significant delay can be attributed to two main factors. First, the reported reluctance of the AU to include the details in the Summit declaration contributed to the prolonged process. Second, Europe faced a challenging task in executing the required follow-up actions to define and implement individual investment initiatives. Achieving the mobilisation of such an amount in external investment constitutes a formidable challenge in and of itself.

The EU intended to transform the *Global Gateway initiative* into the Union's external investment and external action more broadly, and in that way to overcome a perceived lack of visibility and acknowledgement of its engagement in this area. Implicitly challenging China's Belt and Road Initiative, the Global Gateway promised large-scale infrastructure investments in five sectors: digitalisation, climate and energy, transport, health, and education and research. After being prompted by the EU foreign ministers that compose the initiative's board, the European Commission proceeded to select flagship projects featuring hard infrastructure investments where 'quick results' could be realised. Basic information on the titles and locations of projects, most in Africa, were shared in spring.

A further key moment was the convening of the *first Gateway Forum* on 26 October, which attracted heads of state and other high-level officials from the EU and its partner countries to Brussels. This forum was held a week after China convened its third Belt and Road Forum for International Cooperation, the timing once more underscoring the competition between the two policy frameworks. It was, however, fair to observe that the Global Gateway initiative and the Africa–Europe Investment Package had so far generated more momentum in Europe than in Africa.

Green and Digital Technology

The Global Gateway's list of priorities served as a clear indicator of the significance attached to the twin *green and digital transitions* within the EU's relations with the African continent. In 2023, a total of 87 projects were endorsed, with 49 dedicated to climate and energy initiatives and 11 focused on digital cooperation. By comparison, 17 projects pertained to transport, 7 to health, and 3 to education. Reflecting the strategy's emphasis on hard infrastructure, the implementation centred around this core principle.

In 2023, the Africa–EU Digital4Development (*D4D*) Hub entered its third year of action, serving as a pivotal multi-stakeholder platform aimed at bolstering the €150 bn Africa–Europe Investment Package. The Hub's primary focus was accelerating Africa's digital transformation while leveraging innovation and technology. Unsurprisingly, significant attention was directed towards data protection and digital regulation, reflecting the platform's commitment to ensuring a secure digital space. Noteworthy initiatives included collaborative efforts with the Nigerian Data Protection Commission and German development agency GIZ's Digital

Transformation Center Nigeria to organise comprehensive data protection training for processors and controllers. Additionally, the Hub facilitated knowledge exchange on data protection across East Africa, including the creation of a dedicated data protection podcast. Throughout the year, the EU maintained its dedication to enhancing trusted connectivity and expanding access to digital services, with a focus on improving affordability. In October, the EU and Finnfund joined forces to inaugurate the *Africa Connected Programme*. This initiative aims to mobilise over €1 bn in investment towards sub-Saharan African states with a focus on digital infrastructure and digital service platforms. While these commitments signified a significant step forward, it is essential to acknowledge that the infrastructure investment deficit still loomed large. Despite efforts under the Global Gateway framework, tangible progress towards bridging this gap remained elusive.

In July, the AU and the EU jointly adopted the *AU–EU Innovation Agenda*, backed by the Global Gateway infrastructure initiative. This agenda outlined a series of short-, medium-, and long-term actions aimed at fostering research and innovation cooperation between the continents, particularly in areas such as public health, green transition, innovation and technology, and science capacities, alongside addressing cross-cutting issues. Despite some positive developments, 2023 also saw challenges, notably with the introduction of the EU *Carbon Border Adjustment Mechanism* (CBAM), which sparked significant opposition, particularly in Africa and other developing regions. Although emissions reporting will become mandatory only as of 2026, the political debate on its impact was already in full swing. Studies indicated potential adverse effects, projecting a substantial annual economic cost of $25 bn for African economies combined. The CBAM was designed to prevent carbon leakage to countries with lower emissions standards, but critics raised concerns about its unilateral implementation by the EU, the lack of exceptions for low-income countries, and the absence of plans to allocate tax revenues to support the latter's transition to greener practices. The policy's short transition period and perceived shortcomings drew heavy criticism, despite its potential positive climate impacts. While governments on both sides of the Mediterranean emphasised the urgent need for a global climate transition, Africa and Europe have yet to align on a coherent vision for implementing the energy transition. Instead of leading to a unified vision, European actions in this policy area were perceived as paternalistic behaviour by African governments.

Peace and Security

While the African continent remained at the core of EU action in terms of the number of different assistance measures adopted, the volume of assistance provided to Ukraine in 2023 eclipsed the volumes allocated to the African continent.

By June, close to €6 bn of a total €12 bn for the period 2021–27 had been allocated to Ukraine. Despite the global spotlight being on the conflict in Ukraine, the EU remained actively involved on the African continent, sustaining *11 military and civilian missions* alongside a suite of assistance initiatives through the European Peace Facility (EPF). This engagement resulted in operations across various regions, including Somalia, CAR, Niger, Mali, and Libya, as well as in the Mediterranean and off the shores of the Horn of Africa.

The series of coups d'état in the Sahel coinciding with confrontations on a global level provided a hiatus in cross-continental military cooperation. In June, the Council adopted two assistance measures in support of the Nigérien Armed Forces totalling almost €5 m. An EU press release noted that this was the first time that the EU had used its Peace Facility to provide lethal equipment. The packages complemented the €65 m that the country had received earlier (in July 2022 and March) as part of the EU military partnership mission with Niger (EUMPM). It was all the more shocking for Brussels that a few months and one putsch later, the Nigérien junta terminated those defence partnerships.

At the same time, France, Germany, and other EU member states continued to wind down their military presence in the region. Following its departure from Mali in 2022 and Burkina Faso in early 2023, *France* proceeded with withdrawal from Niger in October, culminating in the departure of the last French troops from the country in December. Following the conclusion of MINUSMA, the UN Multidimensional Integrated Stabilization Mission in Mali, the last *German soldiers* departed from the country in December. Originally scheduled for 2024, the troop transfer was expedited due to the premature conclusion of MINUSMA. Additionally, logistical challenges arose following the coup in Niger, which was intended to serve as the primary exit route for the German troops. Consequently, by year's end, the US military presence constituted the last remaining significant Western troop deployment in the country.

With partnerships across the Sahel faltering, the EU was looking to foster new and reinforce other relations. To support West African partners in mitigating the violence spreading from the Sahel to the coastal region, the EU bolstered its relations with coastal countries along the Gulf of Guinea. This involved signing security and defence initiatives aimed at countering armed extremist groups that posed a threat to the northern regions of these coastal states, while also prioritising investments in trust-building within society. *Côte d'Ivoire, Benin, Togo, and Ghana* were identified as priority partners in this regard.

Ghana stood out as one of the key partners in the region – not least due to its democratic fabric. In October, High Representative Josep Borrell Fontelles visited Ghana not only to accompany the delivery of armoured vehicles to the country but also to highlight in his speeches the urgent threats that coastal states were facing and to showcase the support the EU was prepared to offer. Similarly, in July, Ghana and *Portugal* finalised a bilateral MoU aimed at enhancing maritime security in the Gulf of Guinea.

The EU continued to play an active role as a security partner in the Horn of Africa region and beyond. The anti-piracy *Operation Atalanta* marked its fifteenth year of operation. Furthermore, the EU remained committed to providing security and defence support to *Somalia* and *Mozambique*, as well as contributing to border management efforts in *Libya*. In Somalia, it remained engaged not only through its Operation Atalanta but also through its Training Mission (EUTM) and Capacity Building Mission (EUCAP), which continued to lend support to building up the Somali armed forces. The focus of the EU–Somali partnership rested on fighting the Islamist insurgent group al-Shabaab. To outline their security cooperation for the next two years, the Federal Government of Somalia and the EU finalised a Joint Operational Roadmap in May which delineates three priority areas of cooperation: supporting state-building and governance capacity, establishing a constitutional court by 2024, and fostering a more participatory democratic system.

The conflict between the Rapid Support Forces (RSF) and the Sudanese Armed Forces (SAF), which erupted in April, led to a multilateral evacuation mission. Through this operation, the EU co-facilitated the evacuation of over 1,700 European citizens on 30 flights from *Sudan*. Beyond the evacuation of EU citizens, the EU also provided humanitarian support, yet it considered the AU to be the best-suited actor to advance mediation efforts.

AU–EU Relations

On 20 November, the AU and EU were scheduled to meet for their third foreign affairs ministerial meeting. This meeting in the (in)famous building of the European Council in Brussels, informally referred to as the 'Space Egg', was postponed until further notice a week before it was due to take place. Observers speculated about reasons for this cancellation, but most probably it was linked to the differing positions on the Israel–Gaza conflict – as if the ongoing difficulties in finding common language on the war in Ukraine were not already challenging enough. Another reason may have been that the ministerial meeting was planned for soon after the signing ceremony of the Samoa Agreement on 15 November (see below), which would not have made for an easy travelling schedule.

The cancelled high-level meeting was just another indication of the somewhat paradoxical nature of AU–EU relations. Although both the basis and the case for a political partnership remained compelling, the combination of a challenging global environment and low priority and vision among EU and AU leaders meant that few concrete steps were taken to further the joint vision during the year. One indication of this was that there was no meeting between the European Commission and AU Commission in the form of their regular *'College-to-College' meeting*, last held in Brussels in November 2022.

West and Central Africa

The relationships between both West and Central Africa and the EU have been profoundly influenced by a *series of coups* that had begun in 2021 with the unconstitutional transfers of power in Mali and Chad. In 2023, the military ousted the sitting presidents of Gabon and Niger, namely Ali Bongo Ondimba and Mohamed Bazoum, respectively. Additionally, coup attempts were reported in Burkina Faso, Sierra Leone, and Guinea-Bissau. All of these events, particularly the apparent illiberal and anti-Western stance of the military leaders in Mali, Burkina Faso, and Niger, have significantly strained relations between the region and the EU. The coups underscored the failure of the lived experience of democracy to meet the demands of a majority of African citizens. Despite a prevailing belief among a majority of respondents, in repeated opinion polls, in the merits of free and fair elections, optimism regarding the potential for meaningful electoral change within their own countries was mostly low.

Consequently, trust in and cooperation with Europe, traditionally perceived not only as a staunch promoter of democracy but also as an extension of French influence in the region, have further declined. Coup leaders have capitalised on the widespread *anti-French sentiments* prevalent across the region, framing their actions as a moment of decolonisation.

In particular, the *coup in Niger* took the EU by surprise, as they had bet on Niger as a stabilising force in a highly volatile region. The country was also an essential agent in the EU's attempts to control and reduce migration via the Mediterranean to Southern European shores. After the coup in Niger, the EU swiftly condemned the military take-over and called for the restoration of constitutional order, while also endorsing the efforts of ECOWAS. In doing so, it backed the sanctions imposed on Niger by ECOWAS and acknowledged the potential for military intervention against the junta, as voiced by ECOWAS. This alignment with ECOWAS and continued support for President Bazoum led to a further deterioration of relations with the coup leaders, impacting Europe's military mandate and presence in the region.

In October, the EU adopted its own framework for restrictive measures, enabling the Union to impose *sanctions* on individuals and entities that pose a threat to peace, security, and stability, or those who violate human rights or undermine democracy. The sanctions include assets freezes and travel bans to the EU. This framework also included a humanitarian exemption, allowing for the provision of necessary aid and assistance despite the sanctions.

In response, Niger's military junta repealed a 2015 law that had criminalised human trafficking, particularly the transportation of migrants through the country towards the Libyan border. It also revoked its defence and security partnerships with the EU in early December, resulting in the termination of civilian and military missions in the country. Prior to this action, the sixth mandate of EUCAP Sahel, the regional capacity-building mission, had been extended until September 2024.

Throughout West Africa, the EU deployed three Election Observation Missions (EOM), to Nigeria, Sierra Leone, and Liberia. A follow-up mission was deployed to Ghana. None of these missions received much attention in either the local or the European media.

In *Sierra Leone*, the EU EOM confirmed 'a clear commitment among Sierra Leoneans to the democratic processes' while 'highlighting the urgent needs for reforms' especially regarding the transparent handling of election results. The same commitment to democracy was attested in *Nigeria*, where the EOM identified 'shortcomings in law and electoral administration [that] hindered the conduct of well-run and inclusive elections'. The EOM in *Liberia* came to the most positive conclusions, describing polls there as a 'remarkably close and well-administered run-off election'.

The European Union Advisory Mission (EUAM) in the *CAR* marked its third anniversary, with President Faustin-Archange Touadéra commending the substantial strides made in security sector reform, bolstered by the support of the mission. He emphasised notable achievements in enhancing interoperability among various operational units within the Central African security framework.

East Africa and the Great Lakes Region

A key event in the region concerned the long-awaited signing of the *Economic Partnership Agreement* (EPA) *between the EU and Kenya* in December. The EPA goes far beyond a 'trade in goods only' agreement, including ambitious provisions on environmental protection, gender equality, climate action, and labour rights. The bilateral agreement emerged from one originally concluded in October 2014 between the EU and the then five members of the EAC. The original agreement became stuck after Burundi, Rwanda, Tanzania, and Uganda failed to sign it, in part because as Least Developed Countries, these countries already had duty-free market access to the EU – while the EPA would also have required opening their markets to economic big brother Kenya. For Kenya, the new agreement secures continuous access to EU markets, replacing a temporary arrangement on duty-free exports granted by the EU. While the agreement brings Kenya potential benefits, critics suggested that it may distract from or even hinder ongoing economic integration efforts under the nascent African Continental Free Trade Area (AfCFTA).

In Ethiopia, the gradual normalisation of relations continued following the Cessation of Hostilities Agreement concluded in November 2022. Despite ongoing atrocities in the Tigray region and clashes that began in July in Amhara Region, in October the European Commission launched its delayed multi-annual development cooperation programme for the period 2024–27. Reflecting the real need for the EU to maintain its long-standing relations with its regional partner, the Commission reserved €650 m to continue supporting the country's development in what it called a 'transformative, inclusive and forward-looking manner'.

This year's EU–*Rwanda* political dialogue was another opportunity to showcase the advances of Global Gateway. Rwanda is a key partner of the EU especially in the digital realm. In the summer, the EU–Rwanda business forum followed suit. Organised by the Rwanda Development Board, the forum brought together policy-makers, development finance institutions, and the private sector to identify investment opportunities in high-growth sectors.

The Great Lakes region has emerged as a battleground in the global competition for resources and adjacent infrastructure investments. In October, the US and the EU jointly declared their support for the revival of the *Lobito Corridor*. This corridor aims to connect the resource-rich Congolese hinterland to the Angolan port of Lobito on the Atlantic coast. The proposed railway would follow the tracks originally laid by the Belgians and Portuguese at the turn of the century. Leading a consortium, the Swiss commodity trader Trafigura has been enlisted for this project. The primary objective is to enhance transportation efficiency and diversify supply chains in the region, which is currently dominated by China. Through the corridor, the EU aims to bolster competition in the market. Angola, Zambia, and the DRC share similar aspirations, including the desire to process ores locally instead of merely exporting them.

Southern Africa

On 9 October, agreement was reached on the conclusion of the sustainable investment facilitation agreement (SIFA) between the EU and *Angola*. The choice to negotiate the first of this kind of agreement with Angola was influenced by the abundance of raw materials within its territory. The inclusion of environmental and social dimensions of sustainable development was new in this agreement, which was primarily intended to boost investment in the country. Commitments in these areas were binding for both Angolan and European investors. The SIFA was expected to increase both the transparency and the predictability of investment-related measures, via actions such as information provision, simplified procedures, focal points, and structured consultations. Linked to the SIFA, Angola also decided to join the EPA between the EU and the SADC Group, which includes Botswana, Eswatini, Lesotho, Mozambique, Namibia, and South Africa. The further steps for the signing and entering into force of the SIFA are planned for 2024.

A perhaps less high-profile yet noteworthy event concerned the 27th EU–South Africa Inter-Parliamentary Meeting, held in Strasbourg on 18 and 19 October. Soon after the Hamas attacks on Israel, the meeting adopted a statement in which both parliaments agreed on common statements concerning Ukraine and Gaza – while in subsequent weeks this would prove not possible for their governmental counterparts. The challenging and volatile relations reached a climax during the final days of the year when, on 29 December, South Africa filed its case at the ICJ in The Hague which accused Israel of committing genocidal acts in Gaza. South Africa's initiative was inspired by a clearly anti-colonial stance and pinpointed directly the unconditional European support for Israel in the early days of the confrontation. Furthermore, not only the government but also intellectuals in South Africa compared Palestinian experiences in and with Israel with non-white experiences under Apartheid in South Africa – an analogy refuted by most European governments. This testified to the continuing challenging prospects for further foreign policy convergence between Europe and Africa after Russia's invasion of Ukraine.

Trends in EU Member State Policies

At the start of the new year, the German Ministry for Economic Cooperation and Development published a new strategy for cooperation with Africa under the title 'Shaping the Future with Africa'. Given *Germany*'s role as the second-largest provider of ODA on the continent after the US and its long-term relations with a large majority of African states, the strategy was noteworthy for setting out a distinctly value-driven approach to cooperation. It was published ahead of the adoption of a feminist development policy by the same ministry and a feminist foreign policy by the German Federal Foreign Office, both in March. It was also followed by the start of a consultation based on which the federal government as a whole will update (by summer 2024, according to the proposed schedule) its broader political guidelines regarding cooperation with African states, replacing the most recent version of 2019, which has long been overtaken by various crises, geopolitical events, and changes.

The EU's commitment to bolstering an interest-driven approach was further exemplified by a collaborative effort between Germany and *Italy*. The two governments agreed to jointly import hydrogen from North Africa, while simultaneously expanding the Southern Corridor for the transportation of both gas and hydrogen across the Alps. The plans also signified a strategic shift initiated by Prime Minister Georgia Meloni towards positioning Italy as a prominent player in foreign policy matters. Throughout her tenure, particularly in 2023, Meloni has actively forged key partnerships across North Africa. This was underscored by her inaugural bilateral visit abroad to *Algeria*, emphasising the significance she places on this partnership beyond energy security concerns alone. Meloni further demonstrated her commitment by engaging in high-level discussions in *Libya*, including a meeting with Prime Minister Abdul Hamid Al-Dbeibeh in Tripoli and hosting militia leader Khalifa Haftar. These discussions ranged from migration issues to energy and infrastructure development. Additionally, Meloni held three meetings with Tunisia's president, during one of which, alongside Ursula von der Leyen (EU Commission president) and Mark Rutte (acting prime minister of the Netherlands), she announced a €105 m assistance package to bolster the Tunisian coastguard and border police. While the focus of these discussions was controlling illegal migration from Tunisian to Italian shores, the Italian prime minister refrained from publicly criticising *Tunisia*'s democratic backsliding. Meloni's efforts heralded the announcement of the Mattei Plan, scheduled for 2024, which is expected to shape Italy's strategy for Africa in the years to come.

Towards the end of May, the government of the *Netherlands* published a new Africa strategy covering the period 2023–32, following a detailed consultation process that included a wide range of stakeholders in the Netherlands and Africa-based organisations and representatives. Similarly to many new European strategies towards Africa, it includes a prominent emphasis on shared and mutual interests as well as economic cooperation. The focus on promoting reliable partnership and ensuring credibility by strengthening policy coherence was noteworthy. Another thread in common with the German strategy was that while international and European cooperation is stressed in most sectors, in the area of migration the preference remains to keep relationships bilateral – including by signing country-to-country migration partnerships.

(Not) Signing the Samoa Agreement

After a full year of institutional limbo, with Hungary blocking the unanimous decision required by the EU's rule book to proceed with signing an international agreement with the members of the Organisation of the African, Caribbean and Pacific Group of States (OACPS), a significant part of 2023 proceeded in pretty much the same way. Successive extensions of the Cotonou Partnership Agreement, originally set to expire in February 2020, helped to avoid a so-called legal vacuum that specifically would have prevented new actions by the EIB. By April, a full two years after the agreement had originally been initialled by the chief negotiators, Hungary gave up its resistance to the signing process – without any clear returns. Yet to the dismay of those involved and invested, this resulted only in Poland taking over the role as the sole blocker of the signing process. It would take until July for the member state to be persuaded to agree to the signing. The fuzzy reasons and reasoning for the delays were in part specific to the two blocking countries concerned, but it should be observed that the (non-)cooperation between the EU and the OACPS in recent years – and a general low level of knowledge of the concluded agreement and its potential returns – did not promote a sense of urgency.

For several years, the OACPS had insisted that the location for the signing process would be the distant island of Samoa – distant from the perspective of most of the EU and OACPS representatives who would travel there. The signing process would be a key moment that would allow for most of the agreement to provisionally enter into force, while the agreement would fully enter into force once ratified by the EU member states and two-thirds of OACPS members. Following considerable preparations, large delegations travelled to Samoa and gathered in a conference centre on 15 November, with the unexpected result that only 44 of the 79 OACPS members signed the agreement. The 35 non-signing countries included Nigeria, the largest state of the group following South Africa's departure in September 2022. A few further states joined by signing bilaterally in Brussels in the remaining days of 2023, of which neither the EU nor the OACPS maintained an official count. The low level of awareness – and in some cases distorting or framing – of the agreement suggests that the subsequent ratification process will be considerably challenging, as will the translation of the new agreement into action during the coming years and decades.

PART 3

West Africa

Seidu M. Alidu

The West African sub-region was troubled with instability as a result of violence orchestrated by various insurgent and jihadist groups as well as military overthrow of constitutionally elected governments. These incidents imposed humanitarian and economic challenges on states within the region. Notwithstanding these identifiable challenges, several states in the region held presidential, parliamentary, and local-level elections to choose their political leaders, validating the strong conviction that democracy is the only game in town. Economies within the sub-region tumbled in some countries while others recorded marginal or even substantial growth, bolstered by either the increase in prices of natural resources in the global market or increased borrowing to offset balance-of-payments deficits. Both the AU and ECOWAS were busy in the year under review, addressing the military coups and instability in the Sahel region. A significant fallout from this crisis was the abandonment of France by its formal colonies and the welcoming of Russia as the new economic and security partner.

Elections and Government Reshuffles

Elections constitute the critical levers of every democracy and one of the major yardsticks for determining democratic consolidation, according to Samuel Huntington. The Varieties of Democracy report for 2023 indicated that 60 countries across the world held national elections in 2023 and out of this number, only three were improving in their democratic levels while 31 were worsening. The report further noted that elections are increasingly being undermined and the autonomy of election management bodies has been weakened in 22 out of 42 countries. This has contributed to the reversals of democracy across the world and in sub-Saharan Africa to the levels it was at in the year 2000. The democratic deficits in SSA, especially in the last five years, have been in part due to the military *coups d'état* in Gabon and Niger in 2023 and in five other countries – Burkina Faso, Guinea, Mali, Sudan, and Chad – in the region since 2020.

Notwithstanding these cases, there were several countries in the region that were still committed to democratisation through elections, no matter how flawed they might have appeared. On 20 February, the main opposition All People's Congress (APC) of *Sierra Leone* re-elected Samura Kamara as its presidential candidate in anticipation of the 24 June presidential elections. Prior to these elections, the government banned political street rallies and restricted campaign events to selected locations only as part of measures recommended by the Political Parties Regulation Commission to limit the risk of electoral violence. These measures did not achieve the intended objectives and on 25 June, a day after the election, opposition leader Kamara, accused the police of firing live bullets and tear gas at the APC headquarters which claimed a life of an APC supporter.

Eight million people participated in the 24 June elections, where the president, parliament, and municipal representatives were elected. Notwithstanding the few reported irregularities and violence, the process was declared largely peaceful, with incumbent president Julius Maada Bio beating off competition from 12 registered contestants to emerge the winner with 56% of the votes. His main contender, Samura Kamara, received 42% of the total valid votes cast. Kamara took to X to 'categorically reject' the election results, but that did not prevent the swearing in of Bio as the new president.

Mauritania held legislative, regional, and municipal elections in May – the first since President Mohamed Ould Ghazouani came to power in 2019. The elections were largely viewed as a popularity test for Ghazouani and a census on the performance of the ruling Insaf and other pro-Ghazouani political parties ahead of the 2024 presidential elections. Approximately 1.8 m voters participated in the first round of elections that took place on 13 May, to elect 176 members of the National Assembly, 13 regional council, and 238 municipal council members. Insaf won the majority of the 176-capacity National Assembly with 107 seats, won all 13 regional council seats, and secured two-thirds of the municipal council seats. The opposition party won 27 National Assembly seats, with the remaining 42 seats going to pro-Ghazouani political parties.

The electoral wave continued in *Cabo Verde*, where on 16 April, Ulisses Correia e Silva was elected leader of the MpD in internal party elections for the fourth consecutive time since 2013 with 90.1% of the votes. In preparation for the 2024 local and the 2026 legislative elections, the MpD held its 13th National Convention to elect 61 members of the party's National Directorate and 20 members of the National Political Commission; 300 delegates participated in the election, which took place between 25 and 27 May.

The internal party democratic process also proceeded in Ghana among the two dominant political parties in preparation for the December 2024 presidential and parliamentary elections. The opposition National Democratic Congress (NDC) held its primaries first, with three major contestants – former president John Mahama, former governor of the Central Bank Kwabena Duffour, and the former mayor of Kumasi, Kojo Bonsu. Dr Duffour pulled out of the contest less than 72 hours before the start of voting, citing infractions in the electoral process, and even attempted to injunct the elections. The electoral process continued, and John Mahama was overwhelming elected as the flagbearer of the party for the 2024 elections with 98.9% while Bonsu obtained 1.1% of the valid votes cast. The ruling political party, the

New Patriotic Party (NPP), held its presidential primaries on 4 November following a super-delegates congress that reduced the number of candidates from the initial ten to five on 26 August. The incumbent vice-president, Mahamudu Bawumia, was elected as the flagbearer of the NPP for the 2024 presidential elections with 60.5% of the valid votes cast.

In *Guinea-Bissau*, parliamentary elections took place on 4 June. A total of 890,000 individuals were registered by the Gabinete Técnico de Apoio ao Processo Eleitoral (GTAPE) in April to participate in an election contested by two coalitions and 20 political parties. The Partido Africano da Independência da Guiné e Cabo Verde (PAIGC) coalition won 54 out of the 102 seats, the Movimento para a Alternância Democrática (MADEM-G15, Embaló's party) won 29 seats, the Partido para a Renovação Social (PRS) secured 12 seats, the Partido dos Trabalhadores Guineenses had six seats, and the Assembleia do Povo Unido – Partido Democrático da Guiné-Bissau (APU-PDGB) managed just one seat.

The electoral wave continued in *Liberia* with the contest between the main opposition candidate, Joseph Nyuma Boakai, and the incumbent, George Weah. The challenger won with 50.64% of the valid votes cast but with a minority in the House of Representatives: the Congress for Democratic Change under the leadership of Weah won 24 seats while the United Party under the Boakai got ten. The rest of the seats were taken by independent candidates.

The electoral wave ended in Nigeria with the 25 February general – presidential and National Assembly – elections and the 11 March gubernatorial and state assembly elections. The presidential election was seen as a three-horse race between Bola Ahmed Tinubu of the ruling All Progressives Congress (APC), Atiku Abubakar of the opposition People's Democratic Party (PDP), and Peter Obi of the Labour Party (LP). The election campaign as well as the outcome had ethnic, religious, and regional undertones. Tinubu won with 8.8 m votes, representing 36.6% of the valid votes cast, while his main rival Atiku got 7 m, representing 29.1% of the votes. Peter Obi secured 6.1 m votes, representing 25.4%, with over 900,000 votes declared as invalid.

Notwithstanding the global and regional democratic backsliding, the continuous holding of elections in Africa, regardless of the flaws, gave hope that the continent was ready to provide opportunities to its citizens to determine who led them and to give them a seat in the decision-making space.

Government and Military Leadership Reshuffles

One of the key roles of political parties after elections is to form a government to execute the party's manifesto. Government formation involves making appointments, reshuffling appointees, and relieving appointees of their responsibilities. A couple of these scenarios manifested in countries in Africa after the electoral wave. In early October, the junta in *Burkina Faso* sacked the chief of staff of the National Gendarmerie, Lieutenant Colonel Evrard Somda, after he and four other military officers were accused of attempting to overthrow the government in September. The military leaders also replaced a number of officers in charge of logistics and military equipment with the intention of exerting complete control of the military equipment needed by the military to stage a coup. A partial ministerial reshuffle was also announced by President Ibrahim Traoré on 17 December in which the minister of foreign affairs, Olivia Rouamba, was relieved of his post and replaced by Jean Marie Traoré Karamoko, the minister delegate for regional cooperation. Others affected in the reshuffle included the minister of national education, mining minister, and the secretary-general.

In *Guinea-Bissau*, President Umaro Sissoco Embaló reshuffled his government in March. The minister of the interior, Sandji Fati, was appointed as Embaló's defence advisor and Soares Sambu, minister for parliamentary affairs, became the minister of interior. Malal Sané, a close confidant of Embaló, took over Sambu's position. General Celso de Carvalho, who had been the head of the secret services, was replaced by General Armando da Costa. Although no reasons were provided for the reshuffle in these sensitive positions, it was believed that the intention was to put presidential loyalists in charge in order to forestall an attempt to overthrow the government.

The reshuffles within the military establishment were not limited to military governments on the continent but were experienced by constitutional governments as well. *Nigeria*, the most populous democracy in the sub-region, had its share of shake-up in the military. After his victory on the 25 February presidential election, President Tinubu approved the retirement of all service chiefs on 19 June and immediately replaced them. Among the beneficiaries of the reshuffle were Major General Christopher Gwabin Musa, who became the new chief of defence staff; Taoreed Abiodun Lagbada, who became chief of army staff after his promotion to major general; Rear Admiral Emmanuel Ikechukwu Ogalla, who took over as chief of naval staff; and Air Vice Marshal Hassan Bala Abubakar as chief of air staff. The reshuffle continued with Major General Emmanuel Parker Akomaye Undiandeye appointed as chief of defence intelligence, Major General Valentine Uzochukwu Okoro as general officer commanding (GOC) 2 Division in Ibadan, and Hassan Taiwo Dada and Muhammed Usman assuming command of 82 Division in Enugu and 81 Division in Lagos respectively. The *redeployment* continued with Major General Adulsalami Abubakar taking command of GOC 3 Division in Jos and of the operation 'Safe Haven' while Major General Peter Paturmala Malla was moved to 7 Division as GOC and commander sector 1 of the joint task force of the North East operation 'Hadin Kai'. Major General Ibrahim Ali was redeployed as force commander to the Multinational Joint Task Force (MNJTF) in the Chadian capital N'djamena, with air force, navy, and police service witnessing similar reshuffles and redeployments.

Political Rights and Civil Liberties

Political rights and civil liberties constitute essential rights that underpin liberal democratic governments. They have to be guaranteed and enforced in any democracy to secure citizens' participation and freedom of self-determination. During the year under review there were registered episodes of human rights violations and suppression of citizens' freedom in West Africa.

In *Sierra Leone*, Amnesty International documented the killing of 27 civilians and six police officers in riots that occurred in the two northern towns of Kamakwie and Makeni in August. Similar occurrences of arbitrary arrest or detention and unlawful killings were recorded by the US State Department's country report in *Mauritania*. There were at least three cases related to police violence, including the death of human rights activist Souvi Ould Cheine while in police custody on 10 February. There were signs of torture on his body and an autopsy report revealed a fracture of the neck and possible signs of suffocation, disproving the initial police attribution of his death to natural causes.

In *Ghana*, the decision of parliament to adopt the report of the Committee on Constitutional, Legal, and Parliamentary Affairs on the Promotion of Proper Human Sexual Rights and Ghanaian Family Values Bill by parliament around July angered members of the LGBTQ+ community and their sympathisers. The private members' bill, many human rights and LGBTQ+ community campaigners believe, could endanger the lives of the thousands of lesbian, gay, bisexual, transgender, and queer people living in Ghana. Indeed, the issue of LGBTQ+ rights dominated the news for much of the year under review because of this bill.

On 16 October, a total of 12 journalists were unlawfully arrested by security forces during a demonstration against government censorship in *Guinea*. Organised by the Syndicat des Professionnels de la Presse de Guinée (SPPG), the demo called for the removal of limitations imposed on the Guinée Matin website. This incident and several others highlighted the plight of journalists in the country and also had an impact on the ranking of Guinea in the Freedom House Index. Guinea dropped from a score of 34 in 2022 to 30 in 2023, indicating challenges with civil and political rights. It was ranked 7/40 for political rights and 23/60 for civil liberties, suggesting ongoing suppression and violation of these rights.

Cases of violations of human rights and civil liberties continued in *Guinea-Bissau* when gunmen attacked the political analyst and PRS member Fransual Dias and set his car on fire on 5 May, while in September the interior minister ordered the arrest of 22 police officers for allegedly beating a teenager to death. The youth wing of the PAIGC, Juventude Africana Amílcar Cabral (JAAC), accused the government of violating the right to demonstrate when several of its members were arbitrarily arrested by the authorities. Human rights abuses also extended to the media when, on 16 April, the government ordered the closure of two private radio stations, Rádio Sol Mans and Rádio Jovem Bissau, for not paying their licence fees. The government further ordered the closure of two foreign broadcasters, Rádio e Televisão de Portugal (RTP-África) and Rádio Portugal (RDP-África), on 13 July. The violations continued throughout the year.

Finally, in *Mali*, government authorities were accused of suppressing legitimate dissent by cracking down on domestic critics. Mohamed Youssouf Bathily, a civil society activist and media commentator, was arrested and imprisoned in March after blaming the government for the death in detention of former prime minister Soumeylou Boubèye Maïga. Also, Aliou Touré, a journalist, disappeared after organising a press conference in April to demand the release of Bathily. Arbitrary arrests of citizens also affected social media influencer Rokia Doumbia, blogger and radio station owner Abdoul Niang, and Abdoul Niang, a former outspoken supporter of the military regime, for daring to demand either accountability or that the right thing be done.

Socioeconomic Developments

Democracy and democratic development ride on sustainable socioeconomic development, which provides citizens with the right frame of mind to participate in decision-making. The socioeconomic development of states in the sub-region recorded mixed growth as a result of both external and internal factors but largely due to military coups, election-induced spending, economic mismanagement, and low investor confidence because of ongoing instability. Nigeria, the economic giant in the sub-region, was not spared, making much smaller economies more vulnerable.

In *Sierra Leone*, the iron ore sector played a limited role in GDP growth as its contribution fell from 0.8% to 0.1% of the country's GDP. *Mauritania* recorded slower economic growth of 3.4% compared with 6.4% growth in 2022. This was attributed to a decrease in exports and reduced public spending. However, inflation reduced from 9.5% in 2022 to 5% in 2023. *Cabo Verde* saw an increase in tourist arrivals during the first, second, and third quarters, the UK, Portugal, Germany, and Belgium being the major countries of origin and Sal Island and Boa Vista being the major destinations. The total number of air passenger arrivals increased by 22%.

The World Bank estimated that the economy of *Burkina Faso* would grow by 3.2% compared with the recorded 1.5% in 2022. This growth was supported by an expansion of the public sector. The agricultural sector, on the other hand, continue to slump, as did gold production, in the context of the general levels of insecurity in the country. The manufacturing and construction sectors continue to be the mainstays of the secondary sector of the Burkinabé economy. In *Ghana*, an IMF debt restructuring programme affected many people in the country, especially individual bondholders. The affected bondholders blamed large-scale government expenditure as the major cause and suggested fiscal adjustments to its expenditure.

Although the government indicated that the Domestic Debt Exchange Programme was voluntary, many people lost their life savings as a result.

Guinea, according to World Bank data, experienced a decrease in inflation from 11.6% in 2022 to 9.3% in 2023. This achievement was attributed to the government's ability to control the volatility in the cost of transportation and to drastic monetary policies instituted after the military coup. Guinea also witnessed a decrease in debt-to-GDP from 36.7% in 2022 to 35.5% in 2023. In contrast, *Guinea-Bissau* recorded a huge debt-to-GDP of 83%, far above the UEMOA threshold of 70%. Similarly, the *Malian* economy fared poorly as a result of the effects of international sanctions imposed after the coup: the World Bank estimated just 1.8% growth, with 9.1% inflation. Foreign aid, which previously constituted 15% of the country's gross national income, drastically reduced during the year under review. *Liberia*'s economy also struggled, under the combined effects of Ebola and the Covid-19 pandemic, with a growth rate of 4.8%. However, there was hope that the mining, services, and agricultural sectors might expand over the coming years.

The experience in *Niger* was not different. The imposition of sanctions on the country affected the projected growth of the economy, as it was expected to fall to 2.3%. In addition to the holding up of goods at the borders with neighbouring Benin and Nigeria, prices of basic commodities and services were expected to rise. The country received less than half, i.e., $82 m in financial support compared with the $625 m expected before the military intervention. *Nigeria* witnessed relatively high prices of oil and gas due to the ongoing wars in Ukraine and Palestine and the disruptive activities of the Houthi rebels on Western vessels in the Red Sea. The total debt of Nigeria stood at $114.3 bn as of 30 September compared with $103.1 bn at the beginning of the year. Prices of goods shot up, but the country ended the year with foreign reserves of $32 bn.

Illicit Trafficking and Drugs

Cases of illicit trafficking and drugs were recorded in the sub-region. In *Mauritania*, the former president, Mohamed Ould Abdel Aziz, and ten co-defendants were charged on 25 January with illicit enrichment, money laundering, and abuse of office. Abdel Aziz was found guilty of charges of money laundering and using his office to enrich himself and sentenced to five years after a year of standing trial. He maintained his innocence while referring to the trial as a political witch hunt. In *Guinea-Bissau*, President Embaló rejected the allegation of the US that his country was a 'drug trafficking state' despite 15 years of drug finds involving high-ranking military officers.

On 11 July, a Nigerian, Ramon Abbas, also known as 'Hushpuppi', was sentenced to eight years and three months in prison by a district court in Illinois for his coordination of a multi-million-dollar fraud. He was also made to pay some $8 m to seven victims in restitution. On 29 December, another Nigerian, Olusegun Samson Adejorin, was arrested in Ghana in connection with charges related to a $7.5 m scheme to defraud two charitable organisations by impersonating their employees. A grand jury in Maryland indicted him for wire fraud, unauthorised access, and serious identity theft.

Violence, Conflict, and Wars

The year under review was marked by several incidences of violence, conflict, and wars in the West Africa sub-region. Attacks by jihadists, insurgents, and the army, against civilians and also among themselves, were fuelled by ideological, religious, political, and other grievances related to political power. Others were instigated by political instability, military coups, and counter-coups in the sub-region.

In *Sierra Leone*, several attempts, in both July and August, to overthrow the Bio government led to the arrest of 14 soldiers, three former police officers, and two civilians. The former police chief superintendent, Mohammed Turay, was also arrested, on 4 August, in connection with the coup, having fled to Liberia in March. A more serious attempt took place on 26 November in which two barracks, police stations, and prisons were attacked, leading to the escape of several prisoners. Four weeks of curfew were imposed and military checkpoints mounted to arrest the fleeing prisoners. Twenty-one people died in this incident while the former president, Ernest Koroma, was placed under house arrest and Amadu Koita, a former guard of Koroma, was arrested along with almost 80 of his colleagues.

In *Mauritania*, the volatile Sahel region continued to pose threat to the country's security. Four jihadist inmates managed to break out of the central prison at Nouakchott, killing two prison guards and injuring several others. However, their attempt to escape to neighbouring Mali was foiled by a mechanical failure in the pick-up truck they were using. An armed confrontation between the fleeing prisoners and security forces resulted in the death of one gendarme and three inmates while the remaining inmate was arrested. On 26 March, the country's security agencies reported the arrest of the alleged mastermind of the prison break.

Burkina Faso probably witnessed the most violence in the year under review, with more 1,500 attacks by jihadists, resulting in almost 8,000 fatalities. In November, dozens of soldiers, members of the VDP (Volontaires pour la Défense de la Patrie) militia, and at least 40 civilians were reportedly killed in an attack by jihadists attempting to take control of the military base in Djibo. Not only was this violence perpetrated by jihadist groups, but two media outlets – Associated Press and Liberation – reported the alleged execution of civilians by the army at a military base near Ouahigouya. Although the military denied this allegation, several other military-linked massacres, including the killings of 28 civilians in Nouna, 156 in Karma, approximately 100 in Zaongo, and 30 in Fô, gave credence to it.

Violence by jihadist groups continued in the central and northern parts of *Mali*. The Jama'a Nusrat al-Islam wa-l-Muslimin (JNIM, or Group to Support Islam and Muslims) and the Islamic State in the Greater Sahara (ISGS) were reportedly guilty of these attacks. The northern regions of Gao and Menaka were initially targeted during the first half of the year and a UN expert team in the country indicated that ISGS controlled nearly twice as much territory as it had held in mid-2022. The group attacked a large military base in the central town of Sévaré in April and briefly occupied another near Gao in September. It also attacked a large passenger vessel on the Niger River in September, killing at least 60 civilians.

The case of *Niger* was not different. The military reportedly killed 11 insurgents and captured six jihadists in the region of Tillabéri on 24 January, as well as seizing and destroying 100 motorcycles belonging to the jihadists. On 1 February, insurgents attacked the Malian refugee camp in the region of Tahoua and on 10 February, the military reported an operation against jihadists near the village of Intagamey, on the border with Mali. Seventeen soldiers died in the attack while 13 were wounded and 12 went missing. Another jihadist attack was reported at a police station in Makalondi, prompting several army operations in the border towns of Tamou and Ouanzerbé. The attacks continued unabated at Diffa, Gueskérou, and Bosso on Lake Chad, claiming the lives of five soldiers and injuring four in all.

Finally, *Nigeria* suffered attacks by suspected Fulani herders in the local government areas of Apa, Guma, and Otukpo during Easter week, killing at least 134 people. The attacks continued in the Barkin Ladi and Bokkos communities in Plateau State, with 160 people were killed. There were also reported kidnappings and killings of Christian worshippers, including Isaac Achi, a Catholic priest in the Paikoro local government area in Niger State on 15 January, and another priest, Charles Igechi, the vice-principal of St Michael College, in Benin City on 7 June. These targeted attacks continued until Christmas Eve, when worshippers were killed by armed men while attending a Catholic mass in Abakaliki local government area in Ebonyi State.

ECOWAS and Sub-regional Politics

The ECOWAS and other sub-regional bodies in the sub-region got busy in the year under review because of political instability, insurgency and jihadist activities that continued to threaten security in the region. The year begun with the opening of the 36th *AU summit* that was held in Addis Ababa, Ethiopia on 18 February & 19 February. The summit hosted numerous heads of states, dignitaries across the continent. The AU used the summit to denounce the wave of military coups that were sweeping across the continent, especially in Western Africa and maintained the suspension of Sudan, Mali, Burkina Faso and Guinea following the undemocratic changes of power in those countries.

ECOWAS, the sub-regional bloc got alarmed when on 26 July the military in Niger overthrew the constitutional government in their country and took over power. ECOWAS, under the newly inaugurated Nigerian President, Bola Tinubu, quickly responded with sanctions and threatened military action to reverse the coup and restore deposed president Mohamed Bazoum to power. Earlier in February, ECOWAS rejected the overtures of Mali, Guinea and Burkina Faso to be readmitted to the organisation. It only lifted economic sanctions against Mali and decided to impose a travel ban on top Malian officials. In a joint conference with Mali on 31 July, the two juntas declared that an ECOWAS intervention in Niger to restore deposed president Mohamed Bazoum to power would be considered a declaration of war against both countries. The joint statement followed an emergency ECOWAS summit after which ECOWAS threatened to take any measure, including military force, to reinstate democratically elected president Bazoum and restore constitutional order.

The leaders of Burkina Faso and Mali – both military regimes – declared their support for Niger against ECOWAS noting that Niger's security fundamentally affect them as well. Even though ECOWAS did not carry out its threat of military action in Niger, the three juntas on 16 September formalised their alliance with a mutual defence pact named the *Alliance des États du Sahel* (AES). The agreement allows the three countries to provide military support in the event of an attack or external aggression against any of them and proposed the creation of a political, economic, and defence alliance; a stabilisation fund, an investment bank and monetary union.

These military coups in the Sahel region incapacitated the *G5 Sahel* regional bloc, further endangering the precarious security situation in the area. Mali was the first to withdraw its membership from the bloc followed by Niger and Burkina Faso. On 6 December, Mauritania and Chad released a joint statement respecting the sovereign decisions of the departing countries. They affirmed their dedication to carrying out the necessary steps outlined in the G5 Sahel founding convention, specifically mentioning Article 20, which permits the dissolution of the alliance if requested by at least three member states.

Some leaders from West Africa, including Ghana, participated in the UNSC High-Level meeting on countering terrorism and preventing violent extremism. The meeting was aimed to strengthen cooperation between the UN and regional organisations in the fight against terrorism. Key among the issues discussed was the situation in the Sahel region, and the logistical deficits of states affected by these threats and their inability to counter it. The situation has provided justification for military interventions in Burkina Faso and Mali.

Related to this is the influence of Russia in the sub-region following the military coups that occurred in Mali, Niger and Burkina Faso. These three Sahelian countries and former French colonies have cut ties with France and increased diplomatic and security cooperation with Russia. The EU, a major funder of development and security sector assistance in Mali, imposed sanctions on the head of Wagner Group operations in Mali, as did the *UK* and *US* governments. Officials of the US expressed concern over the end of MINUSMA, and the potential implication it may have on the humanitarian situation in Mali and the region. In addition, the US Treasury Department imposed sanctions on a number of Malian army officers over their facilitation of Wagner Group operations and their alleged participation in crimes against civilians.

Also, about 30 heads of states from Africa attended the G77+China meeting in Havana, Cuba. Made up of mostly developing and emerging countries representing 80% of the world's population, the meeting discussed the Russian-Ukrainian war and its impact on their general lives and businesses, climate change and the imposition of the Western model of life on member countries.

Benin

Issifou Abou Moumouni

As an election year in Benin, 2023 was also marked by initiatives at the highest level of government to strengthen security, against a backdrop of intervention by armed groups in the north of the country. The enhancement of bilateral and multilateral cooperation enabled the acquisition of equipment and the synergy of efforts in the fight against terrorism. Despite the economic gloom decried by the population, Benin's economic situation was quite satisfactory and stable, according to the analysis of certain international institutions.

Domestic Politics

The legislative elections were among the most remarkable political events to usher in the year 2023. Held on 8 January, these elections – the ninth since the advent of the Democratic Renewal – took place in a context characterised by numerous issues and challenges.

The elections brought with them a number of innovations, issues, and challenges and learning from the last elections, which were characterised by violence and low voter turnout. This time they were both peaceful and transparent, with opposition parties able to take part. In terms of innovation, the elections were held in accordance with the provisions of Article 144 of the Electoral Code and the number of seats was increased from 83 to 109, including 24 reserved exclusively for women. The term of office for members of the National Assembly was extended from four to five years. This five-year term is renewable twice, according to Article 80 of the Electoral Code. However, with a view to the general elections to be held in 2026, the term of office of MPs elected in 2023, reduced to three years, will expire on the date on which the MPs elected in January 2026 officially take office (Article 208). Members who had already served three terms were allowed to take part in the 2023 elections. The term of office of MPs sitting in parliament from 2023 to 2026 will be counted as a full term under Article 80 of the 2019 Electoral Code.

In the end, the elections went well overall, with no major acts of violence and with an increase in voter turnout (38%). In contrast to the 2019 elections, seven parties took part, including three from the opposition: the Union Progressiste le Renouveau (UPR), the Bloc Républicain (BR), the Forces Cauris pour un Bénin Emergent (FCBE), the Union Démocratique pour un Bénin Nouveau (UDBN), the Mouvement des Elites engagées pour l'Emancipation du Bénin (MOELE-Bénin), the Mouvement Populaire de Libération (MPL), and Les Démocrates. In all, four parties failed to exceed the 10% threshold, leaving the three largest parties – UPR, BR, and Les Démocrates (the only opposition party with 28 seats) – with the majority of seats. The provisional results announced by the Autonomous National Electoral Commission were contested by the Democrats, whose president Eric Houndété denounced cases of fraud before rejecting the results. However, on 23 January, the Constitutional Court, whose decision is final, validated the results, forcing the Democrats to make do with the 28 seats allocated to them, compared with 81 seats allocated to the two parties (UP-R and BR) of the presidential camp. This configuration means that the ninth legislature can avoid the criticism of being described as a monocoloured assembly, as was the case with the previous one.

The year was marked by a government reshuffle, following which a new minister was appointed by the president to the Ministry of Foreign Affairs. After more than ten years at the head of this ministerial department, Aurélien Agbenonsi was replaced by Olushegun Adjadi Bakari, who renewed his cabinet, endorsed by the Council of Ministers on 31 October.

Another major event was the meeting initiated by the government through the minister of labour and the civil service to bring together the various players in the public services to examine draft documents drawn up with a view to improving the governance of communal public service centres (CCSPs). The meeting, which took place on 18 and 19 April, brought together, among others, those involved in the management of CCSPs and User Relations Service Offices (GSRU). The draft documents consisted of a manual of procedures for managing the CCSPs and GSRUs and a draft decree establishing a framework for consultation and management of the CCSPs and GSRUs. The aim was to provide all stakeholders with the same level of information on the management and monitoring arrangements for the operation of the CCSPs and GSRUs, and to raise awareness among the various stakeholders to improve their management.

This initiative followed the implementation of reforms in the field of public administration to modernise it through the use of digital technologies to improve the quality of public services. In line with this government policy, the Ministry of Labour and the Civil Service, with the technical and financial support of UNDP, targeted communes to set up CCSPs and user relations service counters (GSRUs). These online service centres are also part of the drive to bring public services closer to the population in general, and to government employees in particular, and to combat corruption through direct contact between employees and users. According to the monitoring report on the activities of the centres, the results already achieved were encouraging. Recent reports on the activities of the CCSPs and GSRUs have shown that an average of 600 users a month visit the 20 CCSPs and four GSRUs that have been set up, with an average satisfaction rate of over 75%. In addition, by the end of March, this system had enabled the Ministry of Labour and the Civil Service's Service Centre to record 1,081 complaints and 2,971 requests for information and queries made by users, virtually all of which were dealt with by the Ministry's relevant technical departments.

Government–union dialogue was also important in 2023. On 16 May, a negotiation meeting was held between the government and the general secretaries of the trade union centres and confederations. This first Ordinary Session of the Commission Nationale de Concertation, de Consultation et de Négociations Collectives was attended by the three orders of education, the ministers of health and justice, the minister of labour and the civil service, and the minister of state, who chaired the Commission. Discussions focused mainly on the concerns of the ministries of Nursery and Primary Education and of Secondary Education, Technical and Vocational Training.

At the start of the session, minister of state Abdoulaye Bio Tchané highlighted the achievements of the consultations and collective negotiations at the end of the Commission's sessions of 26 April, 8 September, and 6 December 2022. Over the course of 2022, the negotiations had led to an increase in the salaries of workers in the public and private sectors, and an increase in the Guaranteed Minimum Interprofessional Wage (SMIG) from CFAfr 40,000 to 52,000, with effect from 1 January. There was also the authorisation by the Council of Ministers in January 2023 of the lifting of the sanctions imposed on 305 teachers who had refused to take part in the aforementioned evaluation, and the resumption of payment of their salaries. While acknowledging the government's efforts, the unionists pointed to a number of persistent problems and made a number of demands, including the payment of 12 months' salary to AMEs (Aspirants au Métier d'Enseignement; aspirants to the teaching profession) and the improvement of working conditions for workers on certain building sites.

The desire to define a shared national vision of development has motivated Benin to carry out national long-term outlook studies. As the deadline for Vision 2025-Alafia approached, the Beninese government decided to launch the second generation of long-term outlook studies. With the launch of the Vision 2060 formulation process on 23 November, the Benin government, in agreement with all the nation's driving forces, wanted to prepare and to define Benin's radiant future by 2060. The year 2060 was chosen as the horizon, to project the desired development of Benin 100 years after its independence. The aim was to strengthen the country's capacity for anticipation and action in the face of the profound changes and transformations underway or to come, both nationally and internationally. The new vision, which will result from these studies, should make it possible to articulate a long-term national development strategy to meet the major challenges. The 2060 vision and its planning framework therefore needed to provide for everything and was to be carried out with the involvement of all the major components of the nation. It was to be based on the evaluation of the implementation of the 2025 Alafia document, capitalising on good practices from the 2016–21 Government Action Programme (PAG; Programme d'Action du Gouvernement) and the 2021–26 PAG, and was to consist of defining the major development orientations. In addition, to facilitate the involvement of all the skills required for the smooth implementation of the process, the government adopted an institutional framework responsible for coordinating and monitoring the construction of Vision 2060, validating the documents drawn up and ensuring the mobilisation of the various sections of the population. Through the launch of the process of formulating the national development vision, the government of Benin wanted to set out a clear path to the future for the benefit of present and future generations.

Following attacks by armed groups in Benin, the government redoubled its efforts to mobilise the resources needed to combat terrorism and violent extremism effectively. These efforts included the acquisition of equipment for the Benin Armed Forces. This included aircraft, drones, individual and collective protective equipment, light and armoured vehicles, and equipment for actions against the enemy which would, day by day, increase the resilience of armed forces and their ability to fight in the long term. Benin's friends did not fail to lend their support.

Foreign Affairs

On the diplomatic front, 2023 began with a working visit from 13 to 14 January by the minister of foreign affairs of the People's Republic of China. On her arrival in Cotonou, Gang Qin was welcomed by her Beninese counterpart Aurélien Agbenonci, before being received for an audience with the Beninese head of state

Patrice Talon. The various exchanges led to the signing of an MoU on the partial cancellation of Benin's debt and the renewal of Beijing's commitment to continue working together over the next three years on the various projects agreed by the two parties as part of the implementation of the nine Africa–China cooperation programmes adopted at the Forum on China–Africa Cooperation (FOCAC). These projects concerned infrastructure in the industrial and health sectors. The Chinese foreign minister's visit to Benin included a tour of the Glo-Djigbé industrial zone, to assess Benin's efforts in sectors such as textiles, renewable energies, agri-food, and pharmaceuticals. An agreement was also signed for the construction of buildings for the Confucius Institute and the Department of Sociology-Anthropology at the University of Abomey-Calavi. The protocol was signed at a ceremony held at Benin's Ministry of Foreign Affairs and Cooperation, in the presence of the respective ambassadors of the two countries. In addition, on the occasion of President Patrice Talon's state visit, and to demonstrate the excellent quality of Sino-Beninese relations, the Chinese and Beninese governments signed 13 cooperation agreements on 1 September at the Great Hall of the People in Beijing, in areas such as the economy, health, digital technology, customs, training, and communication.

Still in the context of bilateral cooperation, the year was marked by the visit of a Saudi delegation led by Abdoulaziz Abdoullah Alrgabi. During their stay in Benin from 9 to 15 February, the working visit focused on the measures to be taken to start construction work on the infrastructure that will house the Kingdom of Saudi Arabia's representation in Benin, the organisation of the Hajj, and the creation of an Islamic centre to train young Beninese Muslims.

Among the diplomatic visits Benin received was that of the Algerian minister of foreign affairs, Ahmed Attaf. On a tour of the West African sub-region, the minister paid a working visit to Benin on 25 August for talks with his Beninese counterpart, Olushegun Adjadi Bakari. Speaking to the press, President Abdelmadjid Teboune's emissary explained the reasons for his visit, which focused on political consultations on the current situation in Niger, marked by the attempted seizure of power by the military from 26 July. It emerged that Algeria remained firmly committed to rejecting unconstitutional changes in any country. Algiers' position remained in line with that of ECOWAS, which condemned the attempted putsch in Niger and imposed several sanctions on that country and the military junta. For his part, Benin's minister of foreign affairs underlined the convergence of views between Benin, Algeria, and ECOWAS on the rejection of the seizure of power by force of arms. The two countries reaffirmed their attachment to the principle of winning power through the ballot box and to the concerted search for solutions to the situation.

On 30 October, a delegation from Benin visited Germany as part of the 22nd session of Benin–Germany intergovernmental negotiations. Welcoming their relationship of cooperation and friendship, the two countries, through their representatives, expressed commitment to continuing this mutually beneficial partnership.

At the end of the discussions, the areas of intervention, the level of financial commitments, and the actions to be taken to ensure the effective implementation of the projects and programmes envisaged were defined. Thus, over the period 2023–25, an overall financial envelope of approximately €62 m, or about CFAfr 41 bn, will be devoted to implementing development projects in the areas of good governance, technical and vocational training, decentralisation, water and sanitation, biodiversity, and renewable energy. Two grant agreements were also signed on this occasion. The first, worth €20 m, will finance the construction of two technical agricultural colleges in Natitingou and Cobly. The second, worth €10 m, will benefit the Fondation des Savanes Ouest Africaines (FSOA) as part of the management of the Pendjari National Park and the W-Benin Park.

As part of bilateral cooperation, the Moroccan minister of foreign affairs, African cooperation and Moroccans resident abroad, Nasser Bourita, had a telephone conversation with his Beninese counterpart Bakari, on 12 December. The two ministers affirmed the excellent relations between the two countries. As part of the preparations for the 7th Moroccan–Beninese Joint Cooperation Commission, scheduled to take place in Cotonou in 2024, agreements and memorandums in several areas of cooperation, including the economy, were finalised. Discussions also focused on the need to maintain active solidarity and a mutually beneficial partnership as the basis for bilateral relations between the two countries. As part of the review of the diplomatic and consular map, Bakari promised to advocate the establishment by Benin of a consular presence in the Moroccan Saharan city of Laâyoune, and to carry out a mission to Dakhla to observe the region's economic and social development, with a view to forging local partnerships. For his part, Nasser Bourita decided to increase the number of training grants for Beninese executives in Morocco, and to examine the possibility of abolishing visas for Beninese nationals holding ordinary passports, in order to facilitate the free movement of people between the two countries. For the time being, Beninese citizens will benefit, from 1 January 2024, from an electronic visa facility, developed since 2023 with the Benin's brotherly and friendly countries.

In terms of multilateral cooperation, Benin took part, through the presence of Olushegun Adjadi Bakari, in the 20th Congress of Ministers of Foreign Affairs held from 16 to 17 October 2023 in Algiers. The aim of this meeting was to promote an increased and dynamic partnership between the Nordic countries of Europe and Africa. The theme of the Congress was 'Strengthening Dialogue on the Basis of Shared Values'. This annual meeting was attended by representatives of 30 states, including 20 foreign affairs ministers, and the five Nordic countries, namely Sweden, Denmark, Norway, Finland, and Iceland.

In November, Benin hosted the 44th Ordinary Session of the Council of Ministers of the African Petroleum Producers Organisation (APPO). This session, which brought together delegations from 16 countries, the secretary-general of the APPO, and the director-general of the African Energy Investment Corporation, was an opportunity for deep reflection with a view to taking courageous and responsible decisions that would be binding on all member countries. During the session, the foundations were laid for the creation of the African Energy Bank in partnership with Afreximbank. This bank would make it possible to finance energy infrastructure in the various regions of the continent to ensure energy security and sustainable development. It is envisaged that the creation of the African Energy Bank will be a reality by 30 June 2024.

Following the coup d'état that took place in Niger on 26 July, an Extraordinary Conference of Heads of State of ECOWAS member countries was held in Abuja on 30 July, in which Benin played an active part, and a series of sanctions were imposed with immediate effect. The Beninese government complied with the repressive decisions taken by ECOWAS and was one of the first countries to implement the sanctions against Niger. Public opinion was critical of the government's position. To clarify Benin's position in the crisis, the government's deputy secretary-general and spokesperson, Wilfried Léandre Houngbédji, and minister of foreign affairs Bakari held a joint press conference on 4 August. The speakers indicated that the Conference of Heads of State and Government of ECOWAS member countries was a sovereign conference and that decisions were taken behind closed doors without any external intervention. Consequently, Benin fully subscribed to the decisions of ECOWAS, as did the other countries, and would implement all of the decisions of the Conference.

Benin received material support from France in its fight against terrorism. On 20 January, a first batch of eight armoured vehicles equipped with support weapons and night vision equipment was delivered to Benin. These vehicles were supposed to provide safe transport for troops in theatres of war and protect them against the weapons used by terrorists and their homemade mines. Through this support, France once again demonstrated the quality of its relations with Benin, and further revitalised military cooperation between France and Benin, which is currently at war with terrorist groups. The fight against terrorism in the northern part of Benin had become one of the objectives of the military partnership between Benin and France. It is for this reason that France was providing support and participation in terms of equipment, training, and intelligence.

At the symbolic handover of the keys, Marc Vizy, France's ambassador to Benin, pointed out that 'The eight vehicles made available to Benin's armed forces were recently used by French units. If we have decided to part with them for the benefit of Benin, it's because we are pursuing the same objective: to provide the strongest possible resistance to the totalitarianism expressed on Benin's northern borders by jihadism. This violent extremism is hitting people hard.'

On 7 April, Benin also received a donation from France of a high-performance communications system that would be vital to the success of air and land manoeuvres. It consisted of VHF transmitters and receivers, portable radios, detection equipment, and mine-clearing equipment.

However, France was not the only country to provide material support to Benin. Benin also received support from the People's Republic of China, which provided the Benin Armed Forces with reconnaissance and combat drones to help them successfully expand and diversify their intelligence and intervention strategies in the fight against armed groups. The official handover ceremony took place on 24 March in the presence of the chief of staff of the Benin Armed Forces. These PMR-50 UAVS can be adapted to different situations. They are easy to use and equipped with grenade launchers and several other munitions. At the handover ceremony, China's ambassador to Benin, Peng Jingtao, praised the quality of relations between Benin and his country. Military cooperation played an important role in the more than 50 years of friendship between the two countries. In 2018, as part of the military cooperation between the two countries, Benin received large consignments of equipment from China, including buses, trucks (tankers, logistical trucks, and troop transporters), and weapons and ammunition. In addition, various training courses were organised for military personnel.

The US became the third country to provide support to Benin in its fight against terrorism. The donation consisted of a batch of military equipment (ballistic glasses, clothing, and communications equipment) designed to strengthen the capacity of the Benin Armed Forces in the fight against armed groups. The official reception ceremony for this donation, which formed part of the second edition of the Border Security Programme known as BORSEC 2, took place on 29 November. The donation could be seen as a demonstration of the US Department of Defence's solidarity with Benin's army, to strengthen its capacity to deal with attacks by armed groups in northern Benin. These various forms of support reflected the clear desire of these three countries to help Benin deal with the threat posed by insecurity and terrorism. Given the dynamic operating methods of armed groups, it was vital to continually strengthen the human and material capacities of the Beninese army, and this support helped to raise the operational level of personnel and the quality of equipment.

However, there was a shared awareness among Benin and its partners that training and equipment alone were not enough to fight terrorism effectively. It also required close cooperation, specialised training, and an unwavering commitment to tackling the root causes of terrorism. Against this backdrop, the Beninese government stepped up and strengthened strategic military partnerships to give its armed forces a real boost. An MoU worth an estimated CFAfr 1.3 bn was signed between the US and Benin to intensify and broaden cooperation in key areas such as intelligence, skills transfer, and specific training for FAB personnel. As part of the growing number of strategic partnerships, Benin received a 48-hour visit from the Belgian minister of defence on 1 June. Accompanied by the Belgian chief of defence, Ludivine Dedonder praised the state of military cooperation between the two countries. During their discussions with the Beninese minister of national defence and the Beninese military hierarchy, it was pointed out that in view of Benin's priorities, defence and security cooperation between Benin and the Kingdom of Belgium should be consolidated in the areas of capacity-building of human resources through the training of officer personnel, the joint organisation of military exercises, the construction of infrastructure, technical support, and mine clearance, among others. In the same context, Benin received a working visit from the chief of staff of the French Armed Forces, General Thierry Burkhard. On this occasion, he reaffirmed France's willingness and commitment to remain one of Benin's privileged partners in its drive to be a country of great resilience in the face of terrorism.

Against the backdrop of France's military disengagement from Niger, the rift between France and the Sahel countries, and the fight against armed terrorist groups in the Sahel, the chief of staff of the French Armed Forces made a point of commenting on the nagging rumour that has been spreading in public opinion for some time about the establishment of a French military base in Benin. At a press conference, he declared: 'No, there is no French military base in Benin. Nor is there a permanent military mission here. You are in Benin, and if there was a French base, you would see it.' Nevertheless, as part of the operational military partnership, there were French detachments operating with the Beninese army in response to expressed needs, and as soon as their missions are over, they leave the country.

However, the Beninese army was aware that the fight against terrorism and insecurity in general would also require sub-regional cooperation. With this in mind, Operation SAFE DOMAIN II was carried out from 11 to 15 September, to patrol and secure the maritime area of Zone E, which involves Togo, Nigeria, and Benin. Among other things, it complied with a code of conduct relating to the prevention and repression of acts of piracy, armed robbery at sea, and illegal maritime activities in economic Zone E. These manoeuvres proved to be an effective solution to the maritime difficulties and threats likely to handicap the economic development of the countries concerned. Thanks to the systematic deployment of naval resources by the various states, the operation reduced the number of incidents in the Gulf of Guinea.

On 13 December, Benin hosted the evaluation of the Yaoundé Code of Conduct adopted by the signatory states for maritime safety and security in the Gulf of Guinea. Signed in 2013, the Yaoundé Code of Conduct aims to lay the foundations for cooperation between the signatory states to suppress transnational organised crime in the maritime domain; acts of maritime terrorism; illegal, unreported, and unregulated (IUU) fishing; and other illegal activities at sea. The aim of this process was to pool the material, human, financial, and organisational resources of the states bordering the Gulf of Guinea in order to optimise the effectiveness of a concerted global fight against organised transnational crime at sea, particularly piracy and armed robbery. This multilateral cooperation aimed to prevent and repress acts of piracy, armed robbery against ships, and illegal maritime activities in West and Central Africa. The workshop in Cotonou brought together representatives of diplomatic missions, regional organisations in Benin, and the Military High Command of the Gulf of Guinea States, led by the chief of staff of the Benin Armed Forces. Ten years after its implementation, the results achieved were quite satisfactory. The various speakers praised the convincing results in terms of the proven drop in the number of acts of piracy and armed robbery in the Gulf of Guinea, particularly in Zone E. This positive assessment of the process was a sign of the strengthening of maritime cooperation and the constant support of international partners. This support has made it possible to patrol the navigable areas off the coasts of West and Central Africa, areas that have seen the highest rates of piracy of any region in the world.

As part of the drive to strengthen cross-border security, on 6 and 7 December Benin hosted the Regional Conference on the Involvement of Border Communities, with the aim of fostering regional and cross-border cooperation through the sharing of best practices, lessons learned, and challenges in order to strengthen political and institutional mechanisms for better involvement of border communities. The conference brought together representatives of national border management agencies; international, regional, and sub-regional institutions; and civil society. As a forum for sharing experiences and drawing up recommendations, this was an opportunity to renew the desire to strengthen the political framework of institutional mechanisms and technical capacities around the involvement of border communities.

Also in the area of security, 2023 saw the organisation of a day for defence attachés accredited to Benin. Organised on 26 October, this initiative, which was henceforth to be an annual event, was intended to provide a forum for direct physical exchanges between the various players involved, with a view to boosting cooperation activities. Defence Attachés Day was part of the drive to strengthen military cooperation between Benin and its various partner countries. Its aim was to provide a forum for exchanges between military attachés and Benin's senior military authorities.

Socioeconomic Developments

The year was marked by economic gloom, which can be seen as the combined effect of the Benin–Niger crisis, the ban on exports of food products to neighbouring countries, and the depreciation of the naira. The closure of the land border between Benin and Niger in application of the sanctions adopted by ECOWAS on

30 July resulted in a slowdown in economic activity. In addition, the decision taken by the Council of Ministers on 12 October 2022 to ban the export of raw cashew nuts and grain soya contributed to the deterioration in the socioeconomic situation of the population. To alleviate the situation, the Beninese government issued a press release on 16 November announcing that for the 2023/24 grain soya marketing year, trade in grain soya would be unrestricted throughout the country, and that soya exports would be unrestricted, without approval, and would take place exclusively via the port of Cotonou. The contribution to agricultural research and promotion (CRA), levied at the customs cordon and payable exclusively by exporters, was set at CFAfr 30 per kilogram of grain soya instead of CFAfr 140 for the previous season. However, these new measures were not appreciated by producers, who considered them to be of little benefit to them.

Despite this economic gloom, the indicators at national level looked rather satisfactory. On 12 September, the Beninese government announced that the international financial rating agency Fitch had awarded Benin a B+ rating with a stable outlook and estimated Benin's growth at 5.5% for 2023. Moody's also maintained its B1 rating for Benin, with a stable outlook.

A number of initiatives were undertaken to contribute to the social and economic wellbeing of the population. Some were national in scope, while others were regional. From 10 to 12 October, Benin hosted the second International Conference of the Euro-African Platform on Poverty and Migration, organised by the Euro-African Platform on Poverty and Migration (ECOPPAM), chaired by Carmen Garba, with the support of the Benin government and technical and financial partners. The conference opened on 10 October in Cotonou, chaired by minister of state Abdoulaye Bio Tchané, in the presence of the UNDP resident representative in Benin, Aouale Mohamed Abchir. The aim was to take stock of the platform's work in support of partner countries over the past two years. Participants shared information and knowledge in order to identify best practices and solutions to the problems associated with this theme.

For Abchir, this conference came at just the right time, given recent events in the Mediterranean. She pointed out that with less than seven years to go on the 2030 Agenda, any initiative to combat poverty and social inequality deserved to be supported. This was why the theme of this conference, 'Social Exclusion and Migration of Young People in Africa: Current Situation and Prospects', was of particular interest to the UNDP in Benin. Benin became aware very early on of the challenges and issues affecting its communities, and had implemented major measures (with nine projects and programmes carried out) aimed at impacting the social lives of Beninese and promoting wellbeing for all.

ECOPPAM was set up to support the international community's efforts to combat social inequality, forced migration, and poverty. It is essentially made up of NGOs. Its aim is to contribute to the consolidation of better social protection systems in

African countries, which remains the credible way of sustainably reducing poverty and combating forced migration and insecurity.

To promote local products, the fourth 'Consommons' ('Let's Consume') local month was launched, opening in Benin from 4 to 26 October. This initiative has taken on the dimension of a large UEMOA market dedicated to products from member countries. According to the UEMOA ministers responsible for trade, the aim was to enhance the value of national resources through the local processing of products and the development of consumer habits within the Union. The eight UEMOA countries – Benin, Burkina Faso, Côte d'Ivoire, Guinea-Bissau, Mali, Niger, Senegal, and Togo – took part in caravans and travelling markets in six Benin towns: Abomey-Calavi, Bohicon, Cotonou, Djougou, Parakou, and Porto-Novo. The 2023 Consommons local month marked the start of a regional rotating festival aimed at stimulating the adoption of UEMOA goods and services. In 2023, the activities on the agenda focused on two themes: first, what strategies should be used to stimulate the consumption of local goods and services in the UEMOA region; and second, at national level, the concept of ready-to-consume local products in the essential aspects of daily lives: housing, food, and clothing.

A team from the IMF, led by Constant Lonkeng, was in Cotonou from 17 to 26 October to hold discussions on the third review of Benin's programme, which the IMF supports under the ECF and the Extended Fund Facility (EFF), and on a new programme under the Resilience and Sustainability Facility (RSF). The Beninese authorities and the IMF team reached a staff-level agreement on a new programme under the RSF and on the conclusion of the third review of the EFF and the ECF. At the end of the EFF/ECF review, SDR 101.59 m, or 82% of Benin's quota (around $134 m), was to be disbursed to the state budget.

The first Artisanal Entrepreneurship and Promotion Week (SEAPA) was held from 7 to 9 December. The minister of small and medium-sized enterprises and employment promotion, Modeste Tihounté Kérékou, officially opened the event on 7 December under the theme 'Contribution of the Textile, Clothing and Agri-Food Trades to Youth Employment'. The aim was to reveal to the public, and especially to young people looking for work, the enormous opportunities offered by the craft sector in Benin. During the event, professionals from the textile and agri-food industries presented their career paths, their companies, and their products in order to arouse interest among young people. This enabled them to discover the trades in the craft sector and revealed the branches and trades likely to offer great opportunities for creating jobs and wealth for young people.

Burkina Faso

Daniel Eizenga

After seizing power in 2022, Captain Ibrahim Traoré consolidated control over his military junta by suppressing dissent and building ties with other juntas in the region. As Traoré focused on internal critics and opposition to his power grab, a growing militant Islamist insurgency besieged dozens of localities, cutting populations of displaced people off from essential humanitarian aid. Some 1 m school children had no school to attend as a quarter of the country's schools were shuttered due to rampant insecurity. A formal alliance with neighbouring juntas in Mali and Niger appeared to do little to address the worsening security situation, as millions in the region faced the highest levels of food insecurity in the last ten years.

Domestic Politics

Captain Ibrahim Traoré, an artillery officer in the Burkinabé army, held power throughout the year as the head of the country's ruling junta, the Mouvement Patriotique pour la Sauvegarde et la Restauration. Traoré came to power after ousting the junta's previous leader, Colonel Paul-Henri Sandaogo Damiba, on

30 September 2022. Despite promises to restore the country to peace after years of a worsening militant Islamist insurgency, the security situation deteriorated at an accelerated pace under Traoré. As the security situation worsened, the junta stifled dissent and criticism.

In April, Traoré declared a 'general mobilisation' initiative to provide the state with 'all necessary means' to fight jihadist attacks. The one-year conscription effort was signed by Traoré on 19 April and applied to all men over 18 years of age. Critics of the military regime found themselves forcibly conscripted by this law into the militia forces known as the Volontaires pour la Défense de la Patrie (VDP) and transported to the front lines of the conflict.

Between 4 and 5 November, Burkinabé security forces notified several journalists, civil society activists, and opposition party members that they had been enlisted to participate in security operations in various parts of the country. Human rights groups, media, and labour unions denounced the move, noting that it had been used in a targeted and punitive manner to suppress opposition to the regime. Shortly after the increased pressure from human rights groups, prominent activist Daouda Diallo was abducted in Ouagadougou by at least four unidentified men dressed in civilian clothing while getting his passport renewed. Photographs of Diallo on the frontlines surrounded by VDP militiamen circulated on social media a few weeks later.

The junta also worked to suppress the media and control information released to the public. These efforts targeted both international media and journalists and domestic media. On 2 April, two French journalists from the newspapers 'Le Monde' and 'Liberation' were expelled from the country. On 29 June, the Conseil Supérieur de la Communication (CSC), Burkina Faso's media regulatory authority, suspended the French news channel LCI and a TF1 programme following a journalist's remarks on jihadist violence in the country, which the CSC labelled false information. Then, Radio Omega, one of the most popular radio stations in Burkina Faso, was suspended by the ruling junta government for broadcasting an interview which was deemed insulting to Niger's new military leaders after that country experienced a coup in July. Radio Omega subsequently received numerous death threats from people supporting Niger's junta. In September, Burkina Faso's military junta suspended 'Jeune Afrique' for publishing two articles deemed untruthful.

On 21 November, the junta's legislative body approved a new law reorganising the CSC to increase its control of the media environment in the country. Under the new law, the junta was to have increased power to appoint key members of the CSC. It also granted the CSC authority over any content posted by bloggers, online activists, influencers, and any other individual or group with at least 5,000 online subscribers, followers, or friends.

Despite the attempts to control the information environment, reports of discontent within the armed forces did emerge during the year. On 8 September, three

Burkinabé soldiers were arrested and charged with involvement in a plot against state security. The state's prosecutor claimed that the three soldiers had confessed after investigators uncovered their plan to overthrow the junta before the promised elections. Later in September, rumours of a coup triggered calls for pro-junta demonstrations in the streets of Ouagadougou on the evening of the 26th. Hundreds of people participated in the show of support for Traoré. Four days later, in a speech on the first anniversary of Traoré's coup d'état, the army captain announced that elections were 'not a priority' and that he would undertake a 'partial modification' to the constitution. Elections had been scheduled for July 2024; however, Traoré said they should be held when it would be possible for all citizens to vote, leaving the polls indefinitely postponed.

In early October, the junta announced the sacking of Lieutenant Colonel Evrard Somda, chief of staff of the National Gendarmerie. Somda and four other military officers stood accused of staging the second attempted coup in September. Military commander Ismaël Touhogobou was killed in unclear circumstances in early October. Authorities claimed that he had attempted to resist arrest in connection with the attempted coup and that a police officer had been forced to resort to deadly force. Following these arrests, the junta replaced several officials in control of logistics and military equipment, seeking to reassert control over sensitive areas within the armed forces with junta loyalists.

Traoré also sought to reinforce his support in the civilian administration of the country. In a new presidential decree read on national television on 17 December, Traoré announced a partial reshuffle of ministerial positions. The sacking of foreign minister Olivia Rouamba surprised many observers due to Rouamba's perceived position in Traoré's inner circle. Jean Marie Traoré Karamoko, the minister delegate for regional cooperation, replaced Rouamba. Other key positions, such as the minister of national education, mining minister, and secretary-general, were reshuffled without any reason given, as were several other government officials.

On the second to last day of the year, the junta-appointed parliament authorised a revision of the constitution. The revisions include changes to juridical institutions, removing the ability of the High Court of Justice to judge in certain political circumstances, with that power relegated to the lower courts. The revisions also removed the status of French as the official language, making it a 'working language' along with English and elevating the country's national languages to official language status. The revisions passed with 64 votes in favour, five abstentions, and one against.

The aforementioned political developments, concentrated mostly in Ouagadougou, all occurred in a context of raging insecurity across the country more broadly. Attacks linked to militant Islamist groups reached all-time highs during the year with more than 1,500 attacks resulting in nearly 8,000 fatalities – more than three times the number of attacks and almost five times the number fatalities recorded in 2020.

In addition to the violence wrought by militant Islamist groups, the security forces were also credibly accused of multiple attacks on civilians. In reporting from Associated Press and 'Liberation', a video appeared to show the execution of civilians by the army at a military base near Ouahigouya. In the video, seven teenagers were shown with their hands tied behind their backs. One of the soldiers was seen hitting the head of a victim with a stone. The junta denied the validity of the incriminating video, accusing terrorists of disguising themselves as army members.

Soldiers and VDP militia were also implicated in several massacres during the year. These massacres included the killing of 28 civilians in Nouna, 156 in Karma, roughly 100 in Zaongo, 30 in Fô, and others. The authorities also cited several instances in which civilians were massacred by militant Islamist groups. In late November, for instance, dozens of soldiers, VDP, and at least 40 civilians were killed in an attack by jihadists attempting to take control of the military base in Djibo. The junta sought to use this and other attacks to further confuse the situation, urging the country's civilians not to believe media showing abuses committed by Burkinabé soldiers.

The growing insecurity across the country also hampered the ability of humanitarian organisations to respond. On 17 February, MSF announced the suspension of its humanitarian operations in Burkina Faso following the death of two of its employees in an attack in the Boucle du Mouhoun region in the north-west of the country. In July, Amnesty International issued a report detailing war crimes by armed groups, noting that at least 46 localities in the country were under siege by militant Islamist groups. The tactic, which involved blocking main roads and exit routes using checkpoints and IEDs, affected at least a million people in the country. In many of these besieged communities, civilians were prevented from farming, health centres were closed, and food and water were heavily restricted.

During the lean season, an estimated 3 m Burkinabé suffered from hunger due to the insecurity. Among those affected, nearly 650,000 individuals faced extreme hunger (Integrated Acute Food Insecurity Phase Classification 5), meaning that people were already starting to die from a lack of food. Of those able to leave their communities, over 2 m fled violence and found themselves recorded among the country's growing internally displaced population. As a further illustration of the instability, violence led to the shuttering of roughly one in four schools in the country, leaving some 6,100 schools closed. These closures affected over 1 m students and 30,000 teachers. It also represented a 44% increase since the previous year, when roughly 4,250 schools were closed due to insecurity.

According to the UN, less than half of the $800 m requested to address this humanitarian crisis had been given. Despite this, aid groups and the government scrambled to assemble funds to handle the growing needs. The lack of funds, dire circumstances, and limited media coverage and international support led the Norwegian Refugee Council (NRC) to rank Burkina Faso as the world's 'most neglected crisis' for the second year in a row.

Foreign Policy

Traoré's foreign policy looked to build stronger ties regionally with other junta-led countries and shake up ties within the broader international community by reaching out to potential new partners.

The first indications of strengthening ties between regional juntas emerged during a visit by Traoré's prime minister, Apollinaire Kyelem de Tambela, to Bamako. During the February visit, de Tambela suggested that the two countries form a federation to bolster their economic clout. The suggestion appeared to gain momentum with the announcement a week later that Burkina Faso, Guinea, and Mali (all under military rule) had agreed to form a Bamako–Conakry–Ougadougou axis to enhance cooperation and to jointly seek reintegration into the AU and ECOWAS, from which each was suspended following coups d'état.

Perhaps the strongest indication that foreign policy in Ouagadougou had shifted came in the wake of the 26 July military coup in neighbouring Niger. In a joint conference with Mali on 31 July, the two juntas declared that an ECOWAS intervention in Niger to restore deposed president Mohamed Bazoum to power would be considered a declaration of war against both countries. The joint statement followed an emergency ECOWAS summit after which ECOWAS threatened to take any measure necessary, including military force, to reinstate democratically elected president Bazoum and restore constitutional order.

Traoré's cabinet backed up their pledged support for the Niger junta by authorising military troops to deploy to Niger to help in its defence. The junta's minister of defence stated that this commitment was made in the interests of fighting terrorism and with the consideration that what affected Niger's security fundamentally affected Burkina Faso's security too. ECOWAS ultimately did not intervene in Niger and by 16 September, the juntas of Burkina Faso, Mali, and Niger had formalised their alliance with a mutual defence pact named the Alliance des États du Sahel (AES). Under the agreement, all three nations agreed to provide military support in the event of an attack or external aggression against any of them. Later in the year, at a two-day meeting in Bamako, the AES foreign ministers outlined the creation of a political, economic, and defence alliance in the form of a federation between their three countries. Their recommendations included the establishment of a stabilisation fund, an investment bank, and a monetary union. The development was seen as an attempt to legitimise the military governments and further snub ECOWAS.

Following in the footsteps of Mali, which left the G5 Sahel regional security initiative in 2022, the juntas in Burkina Faso and Niger announced that they had decided to withdraw from all organs of the G5 Sahel, including the joint force, from 29 November. The military-led governments asserted that the anti-jihadist force contradicted their aspirations for more significant independence and dignity. In a joint statement on 6 December, Chad and Mauritania, the two remaining members, expressed respect for the sovereign decisions of the departing countries and stated their commitment to implementing the necessary measures outlined in the G5 founding convention, explicitly referring to Article 20, which provided for the dissolution of the alliance upon the request of at least three member states.

As relations with neighbouring juntas developed, Burkina Faso's ties to France in particular diminished. Traoré's junta recurringly cast France as malign actors set on intervening in Burkina Faso's internal affairs. On 2 January, the military junta announced that it had expelled France's ambassador to Burkina Faso, Luc Hallade. The French foreign ministry acknowledged that it had received a letter from Burkinabé authorities in December asking the French ambassador to leave the country. This came a few days after the expulsion of two French nationals accused of espionage. The French ministry then announced France's plan to withdraw its military forces from Burkina Faso within the month, ending a French military presence in Burkina Faso since 2013.

Pro-junta demonstrators gathered in the Place de la Nation in the centre of Ouagadougou on 28 January to celebrate the removal of French troops from the country. Junta supporters carried signs reading 'Down with imperialism', and 'Down with French policy in Africa'. Additionally, there were protesters bearing Russian flags, and according to Agence France-Presse reporters, liaisons from the Russian Wagner Group had been spotted in the country. By March, the junta had officially ended an accord on technical military assistance with France which had been signed in 1961. The accord had been reviewed over the years, but with little change to its substance. Similar developments in Mali reflected something of a junta populist agenda appealing to anti-French sentiment in former French colonies in the Sahel. Tensions between France and the junta remained throughout the year and in September, the junta ordered Emmanuel Pasquier, the French embassy's defence attaché, and his personnel to leave the country within two weeks.

With France's presence diminishing, rumour and speculation soared around a possible partnership between Russia and Traoré. Since he ousted Colonel Damiba from power in 2022, observers had speculated that Traoré represented a contingent within the armed forces that wished to pursue a similar strategy as that employed in Bamako, which saw over 1,000 Russian mercenary forces contracted under the pretence of fighting terrorism. The Russian diplomatic corps quickly moved to bolster these rumours with Côte d'Ivoire-based Russian ambassador to Burkina Faso Alexei Saltykov visiting Ouagadougou for the first time in January. Among the topics discussed during the visit were increasing defence cooperation and reopening a Russian embassy in Ouagadougou.

By May, Traoré was referring to Russia a strategic ally alongside Türkiye and North Korea, each of which had provided military support for the ongoing fight against terrorism. Traoré denied that Russian mercenaries were helping Burkinabé forces in the fight against jihadists, however. He instead claimed that the 'Wagner concept' was fabricated to encourage other countries to abandon Burkina Faso. Ghanian president Nana Akufo-Addo seemed to disagree, however, when he visited on 10 May to discuss 'major issues in the region regarding the security challenge' with Burkina Faso's leaders. Ghana was increasingly concerned about Russian mercenaries working in the region, who had reportedly been spotted near the countries' shared border.

Following a July meeting between Russian president Vladimir Putin and Captain Traoré in Moscow, Traoré announced that MoUs would be signed later in the year under which the Russian federal agency for nuclear energy, Rosatom, would help to build a nuclear plant in Burkina Faso. Traoré insisted that such a facility would allow Burkina Faso to meet its energy needs. By the end of the year, after 31 years of closure, Russia announced that it had reopened its embassy in Burkina Faso. Among the stated goals was the training of specialists and national, civil, and military executives, as well as the expansion of the two countries' cooperation in the areas of trade and the economy.

Under Traoré, Burkina Faso also resumed official diplomatic exchange with North Korea and expanded its ties with Iran. The Burkinabé Council of Ministers announced the approval of an agreement for the appointment of an ambassador of the Democratic People's Republic of Korea to Burkina Faso. According to the office of the Burkinabé president, the move would facilitate bilateral cooperation in the 'security sector' and provide Burkina Faso with military materials. Following a meeting in Tehran with Burkina Faso's foreign minister, Olivia Rouamba, Iran's oil minister announced that Iran would build an oil refinery in Burkina Faso. During Rouamba's visit, Iranian president Ebrahim Raisi praised Burkina Faso for resisting 'colonialism and terrorism' and expressed Iran's willingness to share its achievements with 'friendly' African countries. Subsequently, the two countries formalised their partnership with eight new agreements within the framework of their joint cooperation commission, which held its first meeting from 2 to 5 October in Ouagadougou. The deals ranged from energy and mining to pharmaceuticals and security. The next joint cooperation commission would take place in Tehran, in 2025.

The increased ties with Russia, North Korea, and Iran alarmed Western diplomats whose governments had previously pledged significant humanitarian aid and sought to maintain defence forces in the country. US secretary of state Antony Blinken announced in March that $150 m in humanitarian aid would be given to the Sahel to support vulnerable populations and to help combat Islamist insurgencies. And despite a US policy that outlaws providing military or police aid to coup-affected regimes, the Biden administration allowed a US Green Beret unit to remain stationed in Ouagadougou in April.

However, the junta's policies made it increasingly difficult for the US to continue its support. In a December press statement, the US condemned the increasing and 'unacceptable violence' committed by extremist groups against Burkinabé civilians and institutions. The statement reaffirmed the States' commitment to helping Burkina Faso fight violent extremism but expressed concerns about the actions of authorities that have enacted programmes such as forced conscription, restrictions on political parties, and the reduction of civic space. On 18 December, ambassador Sandra Clark ended her mission to Burkina Faso. In November, US president Joe Biden nominated Joann M. Lockard to be the next US ambassador to Burkina Faso; her nomination remained pending Senate confirmation at the end of the year.

Socioeconomic Developments

According to the World Bank, the economy's GDP was estimated to have grown by 3.2% (0.5% per capita), up from 1.5% in 2022. The growth was fuelled by an expansion in the public sector, leading to the services sector accounting for nearly half of all GDP. The agriculture sector continued to slump due in insecurity and resultant inaccessibility. Manufacturing and construction kept the secondary sector growth positive, while gold production dropped further due to insecurity, despite high international gold prices. Burkina Faso's economic outlook appeared to hinge significantly on the security situation in the country, with forecasters suggesting that stabilisation in the security situation could result in consistent 4% or greater growth in coming years.

Burkina Faso ranked as Africa's fifth-largest producer of gold, with several mining operations in the country run by international companies. However, there are also many small, informal artisanal mining sites that lack regulation or oversight, contributing to frequent accidents. One such accident took place at a mine located in the western province of Tuy when at least nine people died in a collapsed shaft. Armed groups, including militant Islamist groups, targeted artisanal mining and international sites during the year. Gold production fell by more than 13% due to security concerns that caused at least five large-scale mines to close.

Junta policy also placed industrial mining operations under increased strain, with the Energy and Mining Ministry requisitioning gold on short notice from mining companies. The ministry can purchase gold in the public interest in accordance with the country's mining code, which allows for gold to be acquired directly in exceptional circumstances for reasons of public necessity. It was unclear how the junta would use the requisitioned gold. Burkina Faso's junta also revised its mining code, on 27 October, to increase the mining royalties to be collected on gold production. Specifically, the minimum royalty rate for a 'spot price' (the current market price of one ounce of gold) above $1,500 increased from 5% to 6%, with the rate further increasing to 7% for a spot price above $2,000.

Roughly a quarter of Burkina Faso's schools were shut down due to increasing jihadist violence in the region. In a press release on 21 March, the NRC announced that 6,134 schools had been closed in the country since February. UN agencies found that these closures accounted for almost half of the 13,200 schools that have closed in Central and West Africa. Only a quarter of children affected by these closures were reassigned to new schools, with the vast majority not regaining access to education. In March, the European Commission, UNICEF, and the NRC joined with the Education Cluster in Burkina Faso and other international entities to call for increased access to education for children at a conference on 'Education in Emergencies' in Brussels.

In an October joint communiqué, the EU and UNICEF announced their plan to provide emergency educational support to Burkina Faso. They pledged approximately $633,000. The funding was expected to help some 10,000 children who had been unable to attend school. Burkina Faso's education ministry also created a Radio Education Program (REP) to provide daily lessons to some 200,000–300,000 children who could not attend school due to insecurity. Funded by UNICEF, families received a radio, flash drive, and solar panel to receive broadcast REP lessons daily at 4 pm from a studio in Ouahigouya, northern Burkina Faso.

In addition to the education crisis, the Sahel faced a record number of hunger victims this year. The International Rescue Committee estimated that more than 34 m people could be impacted by food insecurity in the Sahel this year. Burkina Faso was predicted to be the most vulnerable and most severely impacted country, with approximately 16% of its population at risk of facing severe hunger. Population displacements due to conflict and climate change were responsible for the closing of health centres and restricted access to lands, limiting food production. To address the crisis, the report urged countries to focus on ensuring that affected populations could regain access to education, health, water, and food. Meanwhile, UN humanitarian agencies warned that food insecurity in West and Central Africa was at its highest level in ten years, and that the number of people without access to nutritious food could reach 48 m during the lean season of June–August 2023.

The warnings prompted concerns that catastrophic levels of hunger and food insecurity would be especially felt in conflict-afflicted areas in dire need of humanitarian aid, such as regions of Burkina Faso and Mali confronted with persisting insecurity. The UN agencies recommended that efforts should focus on boosting agricultural production to achieve greater food sovereignty and independence from imports. It also found that total acute malnutrition had increased by 83%. Burkina Faso appeared to be among the countries most severely affected, with the WFP and the FAO calling for urgent aid in response to rising food emergencies in the country.

These agencies placed Burkina Faso on high alert and prepared for 'catastrophic conditions', including mass starvation in certain locations. In December, well after the lean season, the Famine Early Warning Systems Network reported that some 300,000 people stuck in the town of Djibo continued to face the threat of famine as humanitarian access to the town remained intermittent at best.

Persistent insecurity also complicated officials' responses to health emergencies such as the outbreak of dengue fever and chikungunya during the year. According to Burkina Faso's health ministry, the country experienced its deadliest outbreak of dengue fever in recent years in October. At least 214 people died. Data revealed over 50,000 thousand cases, mainly in the capital, Ouagadougou, and the city of Bobo Dioulasso, the country's two largest population centres, with 20% of these documented cases recorded in a single week. For those outside of these two urban centres, the mosquito-borne illness was expected to be deadlier and less documented due to lack of treatment and misdiagnosis. In November, a chikungunya virus (CHIKV) outbreak was also confirmed, with at least 89 cases officially reported by Burkina Faso's Public Health Emergency Response Operations Centre. CHIKV is spread through mosquito bites and can lead to death in extreme cases. Due to this outbreak, the US Centers for Disease Control and Prevention enacted a level 2 travel warning to Burkina Faso.

The celebration of National Martyr's Day on 31 October raised questions and some debate about how the event should be commemorated in light of the current security crisis. Two different commemorations were planned concurrently. The annual holiday and celebration was established following Burkina Faso's transition to democracy in 2015. The original intent of the holiday was to pay tribute to the victims of the popular uprising at the end of October 2014 and the coup d'état of 16 September 2015. It was first declared a paid national holiday in 2016. This year, a collection of trade unions called for demonstrations to protest the security context, cost of living, and corruption, while the junta opposed these plans and pushed forward with plans for a traditional event.

Despite more than a year of junta rule and rising insecurity, Burkina Faso once again organised Africa's largest film festival in Ouagadougou. The week-long Pan-African Film and Television Festival (FESPACO) kicked off in Burkina Faso on 25 February and concluded on 4 March without major incident. Holding FESPACO in the current context was held up by many as a sign of 'resilience', continuing the event's record of never having been cancelled, despite periods of significant instability in the country and region. One hundred African films were shortlisted for the competition. Over 15,000 people attended the festival, including film celebrities hailing from Nigeria, Senegal, and Côte d'Ivoire. Tunisian film director Youssef Chebbi won the first prize for a feature-length film with his film 'Ashkal' while second place was claimed by Burkinabé director Apolline Traoré for her film 'Sira'.

Cabo Verde

Gerhard Seibert

In April, Prime Minister Ulisses Correia e Silva was for the fourth consecutive time elected leader of the Movimento para a Democracia (MpD), albeit with a slightly smaller percentage of votes and a lower turnout of voting party members than before. On several occasions, President José Maria Neves publicly disagreed with his government's decisions. The tourism sector suffered a set-back when, in October, a Chinese investor cancelled a $250 m casino project in Praia for which the concession contract had been signed in 2015. Nevertheless, the number of foreign visitors further increased, while the number of air passenger arrivals reached a new annual record.

Domestic Politics

On 16 April, Prime Minister Correia e Silva was *elected leader of the MpD* in internal party elections with 90.1% of the votes – for the fourth consecutive time since 2013. The opposing candidate, Orlando Dias, obtained only 8.9% of the ballots. Of the 32,560 registered party members, only 11,598 (35.6%) participated in the voting, held in 312 polling stations, including 29 abroad. From 25 to 27 May, the MpD held its 13th national convention, at which 300 delegates elected 61 members of the party's National Directorate and 20 members of its National Political Commission. At the gathering, Correia e Silva claimed that his party felt strengthened and ready to win the 2024 local elections and the legislative elections in 2026 alike.

On 14 July, *the National Assembly rejected a motion of no confidence against the government* with the 38 votes of the ruling MpD against the 28 votes of the Partido Africano da Independência de Cabo Verde (PAICV) and the four of the União Cabo-verdiana Independente Democrática (UCID). The PAICV had submitted the motion, alleging the continuing lack of transparency in public resource management and attempts to hide illegalities. The allegations referred to, among other things, the privatisation of the national airline, Transportes Aéreos de Cabo Verde (TACV), the management of the Tourism Fund and the Environment Fund, and the sale of the building of Cabo Verde's embassy in Washington, DC. The PAICV claimed that the government of Correia e Silva had not met its promise to increase state efficiency and transparency but instead treated the public administration as a source of political favours, while the lack of transparency in the management of public resources had become generalised. In the debate, Correia e Silva qualified the motion as completely unfounded and a result of an obsession with classifying the government's actions as not transparent by an opposition party resentful over consecutive electoral defeats.

On 30 October, the MpD majority in the *National Assembly rejected a resolution* submitted by the PAICV and supported by the UCID that advocated the official celebration of the centenary of the birth of Amílcar Cabral, the leader of the independence struggle, on 12 September 2024. Paulo Veiga, leader of the MpD parliamentary group, justified the refusal, arguing that legally, a resolution was the wrong instrument for the purpose, but his party had nothing against the memory of Cabral. He claimed that the PAICV intended more to take political advantage than to pay a sincere tribute to the historical importance of Cabral. PAICV leader Rui Semedo regretted the rejection, saying that while the historical role of Cabral was recognised worldwide, parliament, as representative of Cabo Verde's own people, had denied the commemoration of his centenary. In turn, the next day, President Neves expressed his concern about the lack of consensus in parliament on the celebration of Cabral's centenary and asked all parties involved to find a way to celebrate the anniversary fittingly.

Foreign Affairs

President Neves disagreed with several foreign policy actions of the government. On 9 May, Correia e Silva, together with a large delegation of politicians and businesspeople, left for an official three-day visit to Morrocco, where he was received by Prime Minister Aziz Akhannouch and participated in the second meeting of the Joint Commission Cabo Verde–Morrocco. In addition, Correia e Silva visited the harbour of Tanger and the Université Euro-Méditerranéenne de Fès (UEMF). Cabo Verde considered bilateral relations with Rabat as strengthened and promising, following its *formal recognition of Morrocco's territorial integrity*, i.e. its sovereignty over the disputed Western Sahara, in 2022. Both the PAICV and Neves considered the recognition of Rabat's territorial claims as a disregard for international law and the resolutions of the UN, which, since 1991, has maintained the Mission for the Referendum in Western Sahara (MINURSO) to enable the local population to choose between integration with Morocco and independence.

On 20 June in Lisbon, finance minister Olavo Correia and his Portuguese counterpart Fernando Medina, in the presence of the prime ministers Correia e Silva and António Costa, signed an MoU that provided for the *conversion of bilateral debt of €12 m* until 2025 in a Climatic and Environmental Fund to co-finance Cabo Verde's climate transition. Cabo Verde's total debt with Portugal was almost €600 m, including €140 m of bilateral debt and about €460 m of commercial debts with two Portuguese banks. At the signing ceremony, Costa declared that the remaining bilateral debt of €140 m could also be converted into the Fund if the evaluation of the operation in 2025 was positive.

On 26 July, both Correia e Silva and Neves declared that *Cabo Verde would not participate in the second Russia–Africa Summit* held on 27 and 28 July in St Petersburg in protest against Russia's invasion of Ukraine, which Cabo Verde had condemned from the very beginning at the UN and in other international forums. Correia e Silva said that before the end of the war, his government would not take any action that could be understood as support for Russia's actions.

Correia e Silva and foreign minister Rui Figueiredo Soares *participated in the CPLP's 14th Conference of the Heads of State and Government* held in São Tomé from 25 to 30 August. On 26 August, Correia e Silva inaugurated Cabo Verde's embassy in São Tomé, where hitherto it had been represented only by a consulate. He said that the opening of the embassy marked the strengthening of bilateral relations with STP and a closer relationship with the significant local community of Cabo Verdeans and their descendants. During his stay, Correia e Silva was also received by STP's Prime Minister Patrice Trovoada and President Carlos Vila Nova.

On 3 October, Germany's *federal president, Frank-Walter Steinmeier, arrived for a two-day visit to Cabo Verde*. Steinmeier addressed the National Assembly, where he expressed his admiration for Cabo Verde's democratic performance and political stability. He said that Germany and Cabo Verde were united by common values and common goals and a similar world vision concerning climate protection, the importance of international partnerships, and the defence of democracy. During his visit, the first to the country by a German head of state, Steinmeier held talks with Correia e Silva and was received by Neves, who awarded him the first degree of the Amílcar Cabral Order in recognition of his contribution to strengthening bilateral cooperation between the two countries. At the ceremony, Steinmeier claimed that Cabo Verde, committed to democracy, played a special role with a signal function within ECOWAS, where several coups d'etat had taken place.

At the invitation of the president of the European Commission, Ursula von der Leyen, *Correia e Silva participated in the Global Gateway Forum* held in Brussels on 25 and 26 October. At the invitation-only event that brought together representatives of governments from the EU and beyond with the private sector, civil society, think tanks, financing institutions, and international organisations, Von der Leyen and Correia e Silva presented a €246 m investment package to boost the green transition, sustainable transport, and digital connectivity in Cabo Verde as part of the EU's Global Gateway Strategy, launched in December 2021. While in Brussels, Correia e Silva also held talks with NATO secretary-general Jens Stoltenberg, whom he assured of Praia's commitment to international defence cooperation, and met Luxembourg's Prime Minister Xavier Bettel.

On 27 October, Cabo Verde was one of the 44 states that *abstained in the voting om the UN resolution on a humanitarian truce in Gaza*, which was adopted with 120 votes in favour. The opposition PAICV fiercely criticised the abstention as diplomatic self-isolation and a manifestation of a revolting lack of sensitivity towards the Palestinian people. In turn, Neves considered incomprehensible the government's position, since the country could not abstain when human rights and complying with the UN Charter were at stake.

On 9 December, Correia e Silva met Ukraine's President Volodymyr Zelensky during the latter's two-hour technical stop-over at the airport on Sal Island on his flight to Buenos Aires, where he was to participate in the inauguration of Argentinian president Javier Milei. *Correia e Silva reconfirmed his government's position that Ukraine was fighting for a just cause*: its sovereignty, its territorial integrity, its democracy, and its legitimate desire to join the EU. For his part, Zelensky thanked Correia e Silva for Cabo Verde's support at the UN, where Russia's military invasion was condemned by several resolutions. Two days later, Neves publicly criticised the government for a lack of the usual communication between state organs, since he had not been informed beforehand about the meeting between Correia e Silva and another head of state. The government denied the accusation by affirming that it had duly informed Neves one day before the meeting.

Socioeconomic Developments

Air and sea transport, as well as tourism, continued to dominate financial decisions and economic developments throughout the year. At the request of national airline TACV, on 2 February, the government approved a resolution authorising the General Directorate of the Treasury (DGT) to concede a *one-year extension of the term of a guarantee concerning two loans* totalling 210,265,000 Cabo Verdean escudos (CVE, €1.9 m) that the company had taken out from Caixa Económica de Cabo Verde (CECV). On 14 March, the government permitted DGT to concede another one-year extension of the payment period for a loan of CVE 441 m (€4 m) that TACV took out from Banco Cabo-verdiano de Negócios (BCN). On 15 June, the government approved one more guarantee for a loan of CVE 650 m (€6 m) that TACV took out from BCN for the acquisition by financial leasing of a second plane, a Boeing 737–8, from Boeing Capital Corporation. On 11 July, the government granted another twelve-year unconditional guarantee of almost CVE 600 m (€5.4 m) for the financial leasing of the plane, which arrived in Praia on 19 July and assumed operations on 6 August.

On 15 April, the government authorised DGT to grant the state-owned airports authority Empresa Nacional de Segurança Aérea (ASA) an eleven-year guarantee to take out a loan of $12,344,140 (€11.3 m) jointly from CECV and Banco Angolano de Investimentos Cabo Verde (BAICV) *to purchase a plane for urgent and essential public needs in the areas of maritime security and rescue operations.* Following the airports concession agreement with VINCI signed in July 2022, the ASA remained in charge of the air traffic business and maintained its 100% stake in Cabo Verde Handling. On 7 July, the ASA introduced a new air traffic control system as part of the government's technological infrastructure modernisation strategy. One year after the signing of a 40-year concession agreement, on 24 July, the French VINCI Airports effectively assumed operation of the airports through its subsidiary Cabo Verde Airports.

On 20 April, the *government signed an amendment to the existing concession agreement with Cabo Verde Interilhas (CVI) made in 2019* for the operation of seven inter-island connections. The modification allowed the government to more closely monitor the company's operations and financial management. The company, which operates three ferry boats, had needed more government subsidies than expected, while the quality of its services was considered unsatisfactory. In February, it became known that the state had paid Interilhas CVE 427,827,628 (€3.9 m) out of total debts of CVE 581,275,085 (€5.3 m) accumulated by December 2022. In addition, the government fixed a maximum amount of compensation payments of €6.6 m to cover operational deficits, whereas before the amount had been unlimited. To increase the company's revenue, the government increased ticket prices by 20% for local passengers and by 80% for foreigners – the first such price adjustment since 2013.

On 30 August, finance minister Olavo Correia inaugurated in Mindelo the 130-room Ouril Hotel, owned by the local company Grupo Mendes & Mendes. The hotel includes a 150-person conference room, two swimming pools, spa, fitness studio, three shops, and a restaurant. The new hotel in São Vicente is Grupo Mendes & Mendes' fifth Ouril hotel in Cabo Verde. Bad news arrived on 4 October, when

Li Chu Kwan, executive director of the gaming company *Macau Legend Development*, announced a decision to discontinue the project of a 15-ha casino and leisure complex on Santa Maria islet in Praia, allegedly as part of disinvestment from casinos. The construction works for the 250-room hotel, budgeted at €250 m, had been initiated in 2016 but were interrupted in 2019. In response, Correia e Silva announced the reversal of the concession for the project, creating the conditions for alternative investment on the site.

Throughout most of the year, *tourist arrivals further increased*. In the first, second, and third quarters, tourist arrivals amounted to 216,148 (+52.6%), 215,895 (+27%), and 231,532 (-3.4%) respectively. As usual, Sal Island attracted more than half of these visitors, followed by Boa Vista with more than a quarter, and Santiago with almost 10%. As in previous years, the UK was the main country of origin, representing more than a quarter of the tourists, followed by Portugal with more than 10%, and Germany and Belgium/Netherlands both with roughly 10% of the travellers. The volume of air passenger arrivals over the entire year increased by 22%, reaching the highest number ever of 927,651, including 134,485 Cabo Verdean nationals or descendants.

Côte d'Ivoire

Jesper Bjarnesen

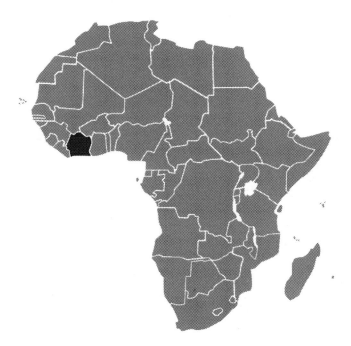

Despite an encouraging overall economic outlook and relative political stability, municipal, regional, and senatorial elections in 2023 consolidated a worrying tendency towards the entrenchment and domination of the ruling Rally of Houphouëtists for Democracy and Peace (RHDP) in Côte d'Ivoire. With a hotly contested 2025 presidential election looming on the horizon, the prospect of incumbent president Alassane Ouattara seeking a fourth consecutive term seemed to be on the cards, already stirring resistance and mobilisation among the divided and increasingly marginalised opposition. With the military take-over in Niger, the Ouattara administration also faced a shifting sub-regional political climate, in which foreign policy relations with Sahelian neighbours Mali and Burkina Faso seemed to deteriorate and little progress was made in the fight against regional jihadist extremism. At the same time, domestic security remained stable as major infrastructure investments were being finalised ahead of the African Cup of Nations football championships, hosted by Côte d'Ivoire for the first time since 1984. The Ivorian cocoa sector was the centre of international attention as unprecedented drops in production drove global selling prices to a record high.

Domestic Politics

The Ivorian political year was dominated by two electoral contests, both cementing the recent dominance of the ruling RHDP under President Alassane Ouattara. But before these important votes, one of the president's main rivals departed. On 1 August, former president and central political figure *Henri Konan Bédié died* at the age of 89 years. Bédié succeeded Côte d'Ivoire's first president, Félix Houphouët-Boigny, after his death in 1993, having served as president of the National Assembly under Houphouët for more than a decade. He was a central figure in instrumentalising identity politics in Côte d'Ivoire in the 1990s, as he sought to out-manoeuvre his closest political rival, Houphouët's prime minister Alassane Ouattara, whom he argued was ineligible because of his father's origins in present-day Burkina Faso. This strategy excluded Ouattara from the 1995 elections, won by Bédié, but also arguably laid the roots of the country's civil war, as questions about citizenship and land ownership rights rose on the political agenda and polarised Ivorian society. Bédié was ousted by a military coup in 1999 but continued to lead his party, the Democratic Party of Côte d'Ivoire – African Democratic Rally (PDCI-RDA), and remained one of three central figures in Ivorian politics until his death. In 2010, following a closely contested first round of presidential elections between these three figures – Bédié, Ouattara, and Laurent Gbagbo – Ouattara and Bédié formed an unlikely alliance, given their past rivalry, and defeated Gbagbo in the second round, with Bédié agreeing to hand the presidency to Ouattara. However, the ruling coalition was marked by the two ageing politicians' personal rivalry and eventually fell apart in the build-up to the 2020 presidential elections, which Ouattara won virtually unopposed following an opposition boycott. In his final years, Bédié became the main opposition leader challenging the Ouattara government, reaching out to his former rivals in Gbagbo's Ivorian Popular Front (FPI). He was, in this way, a political opportunist throughout his career and until the very end.

Municipal and regional elections on 2 September, broadly seen as a political testing of the waters ahead of the 2025 general elections, consolidated the ruling party's increasing dominance at all levels of government. The results were described as an 'orange wave', in reference to the party colour of Ouattara's RHDP, which swept to victory in 25 out of 30 regions, and 123 municipalities out of 201. The PDCI-RDA, under the leadership of former Credit Suisse executive Tidjane Thiam, managed to limit its losses somewhat despite internal turmoil following the death of popular strongman Bédié. The party won only two regions under its own colours: Aries and Nawa. However, an electoral alliance between the PDCI-RDA and the newly formed African People's Party-Côte d'Ivoire (PPA-CI) of former president Gbagbo signalled the latest in a long list of unlikely political partnerships between former rivals that might challenge the dominance of the RHDP in future contests. Candidates from this alliance of circumstance won two additional regions. In the municipal elections, the PDCI-RDA managed to win only one large city on its own ballot: the municipality of Yamoussoukro. Again, the PDCI-RDA's alliance with the PPA-CI ensured victory in two key municipalities within the financial capital of Abidjan: Cocody and Port-Bouët.

Shortly after the regional and municipal elections, *senatorial elections* were held in Côte d'Ivoire for the first time since the inaugural vote in 2018. Two-thirds of the 99 members of the Ivorian Senate were elected through indirect vote by an electoral college composed of local electors, while the final 33 senators were appointed directly by President Alassane Ouattara by decree on 9 October. Unsurprisingly, not least in light of the recent orange wave sweeping the regional and municipal vote, the ruling RHDP sustained its majority, extending its number of senatorial seats by eight, to a total of 58 out of the 66 elected senators. Despite the overwhelming dominance of the ruling party, the president of the Senate, Jeannot Ahoussou-Kouadio, suffered a comprehensive and unexpected defeat to no less than two PDCI-RDA candidates: Allah Kouadio Rémi and Yeboué Kouadio. The ruling party had traditionally held a majority in the Bélier region but Ahoussou-Kouadio was handed his second electoral defeat, following a similar outcome in the regional elections two weeks earlier, due primarily to his own RHDP members either abstaining or voting for the opposition candidates. During the inaugural session of the Senate on 12 September, former minister of foreign affairs Kandia Camara was unanimously elected as the new president of the Senate with 91 votes and 6 abstentions.

Although the PDCI-RDA ensured its first six senatorial seats, it was more noteworthy that the largest opposition grouping was unable to challenge the RHDP dominance in the slightest, considering that the major opposition parties had boycotted the 2018 election and therefore handed the inaugural vote to the ruling party. Gbagbo's PPA-CI failed to secure its entry into the Senate, with all candidates losing out at the polls. The independent candidates benefiting from the 2018 opposition boycott were the largest losing bloc, giving up 14 out of 16 seats in the 2023 vote.

In addition to the dire state of the joint opposition, the two rounds of elections in 2023 also gave a strong indication of the outlooks and strategies of the country's main political actors ahead of the 2025 presidential elections. On 30 September, PPA-CI spokesperson Justin Koné Katinan announced that his party rejected the results of the local and senatorial elections, accusing the Independent Electoral Commission (CEI) and the police of bias in allowing electoral irregularities and fraud. Much as in the lead-up to the 2020 presidential elections, the calls for reform of the CEI and accusations of systematic fraud were gaining force within the opposition and largely ignored by the ruling party. In a similar spirit, contestations regarding the candidacies of the main political players – including Ouattara's likely fourth-term bid, Gbagbo's claim to eligibility despite his convictions for fraud and embezzlement in the Ivorian courts, and the fates of outsiders such as former rebel leader Guillaume Soro and estranged Gbagbo loyalist Charles Blé Goudé – were shaping up to dominate the electoral campaigns ahead of the 2025 vote. These worrying signs in terms of the status of democracy in Côte d'Ivoire unfortunately represented a continuation of the overall trend following the dramatic 2020 elections – a continuity reflected in the country's Freedom House Index score of 49/100, at the low end of the mid-range of a 'hybrid regime'.

In the midst of these electoral reverberations, the political year in Côte d'Ivoire continued to deliver in melodrama, with secretary-general of the presidency Aboudramane Cisse's unexpected announcement, on 6 October, that President Ouattara had requested the *resignation of Prime Minister Patrick Achi* and dissolved his government. Although no official reason was given for this significant decision, it seemed that Achi was seen by the president as having neglected his task of overseeing the preparations for the 2024 Africa's Cup of Nations. On 16 October, the governor of Abidjan and close ally of Ouattara, Robert Beugre Mambé, was appointed as the new prime minister and tasked with proposing a new government. Although the replacement of Achi was unexpected, Mambé seemed to be an obvious choice for his replacement, as a ruling-party insider and even a possible successor as the RHDP candidate for the presidency. The replacement of a prime minister and the accompanying dissolution of the government, it should be noted, was not a new occurrence in Ivorian politics, as Mambé became the sixth holder of the office under Ouattara's presidency.

The *African Cup of Nations*, a key priority for the Ouattara government, was the focus of intense activity throughout the year, as the construction and refurbishment of venues in five Ivorian urban centres was being finalised alongside elaborate infrastructural work to facilitate the arrival of fans and journalists from across the continent. In addition to the Ivorian passion for the game of football, hosting the first African championship since 1984 was seen as a way for Côte d'Ivoire to present itself to an outside audience as a country of progress, and for Alassane Ouattara to showcase his achievements in light of the 2025 presidential race. On assuming his new role as prime minister, Mambé was seen repeatedly on construction sites around the country, inspecting the progress of roadworks and other efforts to prepare the country for an estimated 1.5 m visitors during the first two months of 2024. On 12 September, a friendly match between Côte d'Ivoire and Mali, played at the newly constructed Olympic Alassane Ouattara Stadium of Ébimpé, was cancelled mid-match due to heavy rains, raising concern that the extravagant infrastructure was not suitable for the conditions. However, the president of the African Cup of Nations Organising Committee, François Amichia, assured the sceptics that all six football stadiums would be up to the task.

Finally, the Ivorian authorities released businessman and *suspected cocaine trafficker Hussein Taan* on bail in late December. The manager of an Abidjan restaurant chain had been under arrest for more than a year following the April 2022 record seizure of two tonnes of cocaine in Abidjan and San Pedro. Hussein Taan was the fourth suspect released, after the French Dominique Amata and the Ivorian-Lebanese Richard Ghorayeb and Abbas Hamka in May, all suspected of being accomplices in an elaborate drug trafficking ring involving Côte d'Ivoire as a transit country for the cocaine trade between South America and Europe. The Ivorian Narcotics and Drugs Police Department (Direction de la police nationale chargée des stupéfiants et des drogues; DPSD) estimated that 50–60 tonnes of cocaine had passed through Côte d'Ivoire annually prior to the seizure. Trials in the case were scheduled for early 2024.

Foreign Affairs

On 6 January, Assimi Goïta – Mali's junta leader – announced the *pardoning of the 49 Ivorian soldiers* detained in Bamako on 10 July 2022. The 46 male soldiers had been sentenced to 20 years in prison for 'attack and conspiracy against the government', 'undermining the external security of the State', and other charges. Three female soldiers had been released in September 2022 and later tried *in absentia*. The soldiers were of the eighth detachment of the National Support Element (NSE), led by Lieutenant Adam Sanni Kouassi of the Ivorian Special Forces, and were deployed in support of the German contingent of the UN Mission in Mali, MINUSMA. The presidential pardon revoked the sentences of all 49 soldiers.

The 46 soldiers arrived in Abidjan the following day and were received by the president and several members of government at Félix Houphouët-Boigny International Airport. Their release marked the end of an extended diplomatic tug of war between Bamako and Abidjan, involving several regional heads of state and significant pressure from ECOWAS, reflecting the broader foreign policy landscape in a sub-region where Côte d'Ivoire had seen three of its neighbouring countries fall under military rule in recent years. The Malian junta leader stated that the pardon was an expression of the good relations between the two countries, and although Ouattara responded by welcoming the normalisation of diplomatic relations. Côte d'Ivoire continued to face a more challenging diplomatic relationship with the juntas in Mali and Burkina Faso.

The detained soldiers returned to Ivorian soil, the relationship between Abidjan and Ouagadougou became the centre of attention for the Ouattara administration's sub-regional foreign affairs. In addition to their territorial borders, Mali, Burkina Faso, and Côte d'Ivoire continued to share an interest in combating regional jihadist extremism, on the rise since 2018. The presence of jihadist groups with an allegiance to Mali-based Katiba Macina in southern Burkina Faso, in particular, had necessitated close security collaboration between the three countries.

In the eyes of Abidjan, the ousting of junta leader Lieutenant Colonel Paul-Henri Damiba by Captain Ibrahim Traoré arguably presented a further challenge in ensuring this collaboration. Upon seizing power, Traoré aligned immediately with the junta in Mali, and eventually with the coup leaders in Niger, to form an Alliance of Sahel States, opposing French interests in the sub-region and challenging broader sub-regional collaboration under the banner of the ECOWAS. Côte d'Ivoire's Ouattara, a former IMF economist, represented not only an older generation of political leaders but also a more accommodating attitude towards France and a more unequivocal commitment to ECOWAS, underlining ideological and diplomatic differences between the Sahelian juntas and the Ouattara administration.

As an apt illustration of these broader foreign policy challenges, Ouattara's estranged collaborator and former leader of the Forces Nouvelles rebel movement Guillaume Soro was received with great fanfare in both Bamako and Ouagadougou in December despite having been convicted by the Ivorian courts for an 'attempted insurrection' against Ouattara in 2019. Soro's rebel movement was instrumental in bringing Ouattara to power in the wake of the electoral crisis in 2010/11, during which more than 3,000 civilians lost their lives. Soro had gone on to serve as the speaker of the National Assembly during Ouattara's first term, before declaring his ambition to challenge his former mentor at the polls in the 2020 elections. In November, Soro announced in a brief video recording that he would be returning to Côte d'Ivoire for the first time since his conviction, despite the sentences against him, with the intention of presenting his candidacy for the 2025 elections. His visits to neighbouring Mali and Burkina Faso signalled that he was serious about these intentions and also that he could rely on the support of the juntas – a strong message to the Ouattara administration.

Notwithstanding these challenges, the release of the Ivorian soldiers seemed to signal that the Burkinabé junta and the Ivorian government would be able to continue their collaboration despite their ideological differences. In this spirit, Outtara declared in January that he had offered military equipment worth CFAfr 2.3 bn (€53.5 m) to Burkina Faso, which remains one of Côte d'Ivoire largest trading partners. However, as the year proceeded, several incidents were reported along the 600 km border between the two countries, eventually leading to the arrest of Ivorian security forces on Burkinabé territory by traditional hunters, who then handed them over to the Burkinabé military. On 16 March, three Ivorian police officers were briefly arrested in Burkina Faso. On 19 September, two Ivorian gendarmes were arrested in the village of Kwame Yar, on Burkinabé territory, and transferred to Ouagadougou, leading to intense negotiations between the two parties. In an interview on Burkinabé national television on 30 September, Ibrahim Traoré gave assurances that there was 'no problem' between 'the Burkinabé and Ivorian people' but said that the policies of the two countries 'may differ' – a thinly veiled allusion to his increasing alignment with the juntas in Mali and Niger. It was suspected that Traoré was using the detainment of the two Ivorian gendarmes as political leverage in order to push for the extradition of Burkinabé citizens detained in Côte d'Ivoire, and possibly to ensure further financial support from the wealthier neighbour to the south. The two gendarmes remained in the custody of the Burkinabé authorities at the end of the year.

The relationship between Burkina Faso and Côte d'Ivoire also increasingly involved the issue of Burkinabé citizens being displaced from borderland areas affected by the presence of jihadist groups such as Katiba Macina and Jama'a Nusrat al-Islam wa-l-Muslimin (JNIM). Urban centres across the northern Ivorian border areas saw considerable influxes in 2023. Ouattara was said to be personally involved in the matter, ordering a census of new arrivals and the implementation of a humanitarian assistance plan. Instructions were also given to the chief of staff of the armed forces, General Lassina Doumbia, to reinforce surveillance and security in the eastern and northern regions, on the border with Burkina Faso. By the end of the year, more than 50,000 people were estimated to have been displaced from Burkina Faso to Côte d'Ivoire.

Foreign preoccupation with Côte d'Ivoire's troubled regional neighbourhood was reflected in official interactions, most notably with French representatives, as Burkina Faso's military regime followed the Malian example and ordered French troops to leave the country early in the year. On 21 February, during an official visit to Abidjan, French defence minister Sébastien Lecornu announced an increase in French military support to Côte d'Ivoire in an effort to adjust the French strategy to combat the spread of regional jihadism. Later in the year, on 21 November, Alassane Ouatara was received in Paris by French president Emmanuel Macron on an official state visit, during which the Sahelian security crisis was one of the main points of conversation, with the military take-over in Niger in July adding to the list of French concerns in the sub-region.

Socioeconomic Developments

Despite continued regional and global political tensions and crises leading to harsher economic conditions, as well as more locally specific challenges to agricultural production, the Ivorian economy overall remained impressively robust in 2023, with the government signalling a strong commitment to macroeconomic stability and ongoing structural reforms in line with the National Development Plan (NDP) 2021–25. Despite higher import prices, leading to declines in domestic consumption, rising global and domestic interest rates, and falling external demand, *economic growth* remained solid, with a slight decline from 6.9% in 2022 to 6.4% in 2023. According to the World Bank, economic growth was driven mainly by continued high levels of public investment and the resilience of private investment. The key industrial and service sectors continued their growth, although at a slower pace than in recent years.

For ordinary Ivorian citizens, these conditions did not lead to dramatic improvements but did continue some generally encouraging trends. The unemployment rate registered a slight drop from 2.6% in 2022 to 2.4%, and the extreme poverty incidence (the proportion of people living on less than €2 a day) was expected to see a similar drop from 12.3% in 2022 to 12% in 2023, driven by the industry and services sectors and lower inflation, especially among food items (expected to fall from 8.9% in 2022 to 4.8%). The Ivorian HDI, however, showed a slight decline, falling from 0.550 in 2022 to 0.534, with the country dropping from a rank of 159th to 166th out of the 199 countries surveyed.

Boosting the government's plans for wider economic reforms, the IMF agreed in April to lend Côte d'Ivoire approximately $3.5 bn. The loan programme would help to preserve fiscal and debt sustainability and support reforms to promote more private-sector-led inclusive growth and a transition to middle-income country status. In addition to long-term reform initiatives, the Ivorian government was carrying the mounting costs of the preparations for hosting the African Cup of Nations in early 2024, with total costs estimated at €3.5 bn, including more than €800 m in road repairs to facilitate transportation between the six venues across five urban centres throughout the country: Abidjan (with two stadiums) and San Pedro on the coast; Yamoussoukro and Bouaké in the centre; and Korhogo in the north. Infrastructure investments were thus not limited to the construction and improvement of sports facilities but also included large-scale investment in major roads throughout the country and other amendments that would benefit the transportation of key export products such as cocoa, cashews, rubber, and gold.

At the same time, high-prestige infrastructure projects such as the construction and upscaling of football stadiums to international standards reflected the Ouattara administration's overall strategy of rebranding the country's international profile as a commercial and tourism hub in the sub-region. As a case in point, the impressive *Alassane Ouattara Bridge* across Cocody Bay in central Abidjan was inaugurated by the president on 12 August. Built by the Chinese Road and Bridge Corporation and funded with a loan of up to CFAfr 77.5 bn (approximately €118 m) from the Islamic Development Bank, the project was initially launched in 2019 by prime minister Amadou Gon Coulibaly, who passed away in July 2020. The original intention was to finalise construction in 2021, but building was delayed in part due to the Covid-19 pandemic. After the death of Gon Coulibaly, construction was overseen by minister for infrastructure and road maintenance Amédée Kouakou, who stated that the bridge was 'an emblematic work for the city'. The 634-metre bridge, which includes a 260-metre viaduct and connects the Plateau business district to Cocody, was expected to facilitate the transit of an estimated 35,000 vehicles daily across the busy city centre in the hope of easing traffic across the city. The construction was part of the broader project of infrastructural development around Cocody Bay, intended to include a water park, marina, restaurants, and high-end shopping, all expected to boost Abidjan's image as a global city attractive to foreign investors and visitors.

Although the overall economic outlook was encouraging, the Ivorian *cocoa sector* became the focus of intense scrutiny, as well as international media attention, in 2023. Throughout the year, concerns about the impact of extreme weather events on production in the world's primary exporter preoccupied actors in all parts of the global value chain. Similar concerns had been raised the previous year, particularly because of enduring problems with the so-called 'swollen shoot virus', which causes cocoa plants to rot when conditions are too humid. Early in the year, concerns about reduced outputs for the season were based on the opposite problem, namely a lack of rainfall which threatened to stifle plant growth, believed to be caused by the natural climate phenomenon known as the El Niño Southern Oscillation (ENSO), or 'El Niño' for short. With heavy rainfall mid-season, prognoses quickly shifted towards a more optimistic outlook, initially raising hopes that the mid-season harvest would recover and reach the same levels as the previous year. The outlook soon shifted again, however, as sustained rainfall led to the flooding of plantations, not only exacerbating the impact of the swollen shoot virus but also causing difficulties for producers in accessing their farms and transporting their harvest.

In response to these challenging circumstances, minister of agriculture Kobenan Kouassi Adjoumani announced in March that the fixed farmgate price paid to cocoa farmers would be raised from CFAfr 825 to 900 (approximately €1.40) per kilogram for the April-to-September mid-crop. At the end of the year, it was estimated that the total harvest had dropped by more than 30% compared with the previous season, from 2,241 metric tonnes for the 2022/23 harvest to around 1,800 metric tonnes for the 2023/24 season, contributing to a projected global deficit for the 2023/24 season of 370,000 tonnes.

This dramatic drop in supply from the Ivorian cocoa harvest, and similar conditions affecting the harvest in neighbouring Ghana, were felt internationally as well. At the end of 2023, the annual average cocoa price in London had increased by 46% compared with the previous calendar year. During the same period in New York, the average of benchmark prices rose by 35% year on year. According to the International Cocoa Organization (ICCO), in December the average daily cocoa prices reached a record-breaking €3,896 per tonne and $4,250 per tonne on the London and New York exchanges respectively. In addition to the efforts to mitigate the effect on farmers by raising farmgate prices, the Ivorian Cocoa-Coffee Council (CCC) faced the challenge of negotiating international contracts for the 2024/25 season, with multinational companies demanding that it lower prices despite a forecast of similar supply shortages. In December, CCC director-general Yves Brahima Koné announced that all sales would be halted for the 2024/25 season, 1 m tonnes in cocoa export contracts having already been sold for the 2024/25 season, including about 350,000 tonnes to multinational companies and the rest to local exporters.

Despite these overwhelming short-term challenges, plans for reforming the Ivorian cocoa sector in the long term continued, with Koné announcing in January that the share of *cocoa being processed domestically* would increase from 35–40% to around 50% as a result of the opening of two new processing plants in the south-western part of the country financed by China to enter into production in October, with a production capacity of 50,000 tonnes each. During a visit in Abu Dhabi to open a new CCC office, Koné elaborated that an agreement had been signed with the UAE for the construction of a new plant in the coastal town of San Pedro with a grinding capacity of 120,000 tonnes. The new plants would allow the Ivorian industry to process more than 1 m tonnes of cocoa annually, making it the *world's leading cocoa grinder*, surpassing the Netherlands. The opening of the CCC office in Abu Dhabi, furthermore, signalled the Ivorian intention to expand exports to global markets beyond the country's traditional reach in Europe and the US. Cocoa accounted for about 15% of national GDP and more than 40% of export earnings.

Cashew production, another agricultural sector in which Côte d'Ivoire is world-leading, posted another season with a harvest of more than a million tonnes. Concerns were raised, however, about changing global consumer attitudes and a global stock surplus leading to a shrinking demand. In response to the risk of lower selling prices on the global market, Kobenan Kouassi Adjoumani announced that the 2023 farmgate price for cashew nuts would be set at CFAfr 315 (€0.4882) per kilogram, up from CFAfr 305 in 2022. Despite government subsidies and export incentives being provided to local processors to allow them to remain competitive, cashew production was marked by the worsening export conditions, with activities in the central town of Bouaké, home of the country's largest cashew processing industry, coming to a near standstill as employers struggled to pay salaries.

There was more bad news for the country's *cotton sector*, with outputs for the 2022/23 season expected to fall by 50% to 269,000 tonnes due to infestations of 'jasside' parasites. Adjoumani announced that the government would allocate CFAfr 34.52 bn (€53.51 m) to help compensate farmers for their losses. Providing the troubled minister some relief, *natural rubber production* rose by more than 30% year on year to reach a record 1.7 m metric tonnes in 2023. Côte d'Ivoire thereby maintained its position as Africa's leading grower of natural rubber and the world's third-largest producer after Thailand and Indonesia. The rise in Ivorian rubber production was attributed to farmers shifting from cocoa and coffee production, attracted by the promise of more stable income.

Further encouraging trends were registered in the gold mining sector, with a record-breaking output of 51 tonnes, an increase of more than 6% from 48 tonnes in 2022. Mining companies operating in Côte d'Ivoire included Barrick Gold, Endeavour, and Perseus. In September, Canadian Roxgold opened its gold mine in Seguela in the north-western region, approximately 500 km north of Abidjan, aiming to produce around 130,000 ounces of gold per year. Barrick Gold said in July that its Tongon mine, the output of which was expected to rise above 200,000 ounces of gold in 2023, would continue operating until at least 2030 following a significant discovery of new deposits. The gold mining expansion, however, also posed concerns about environmental degradation and deforestation as an effect of the expansion of both industrial and artisanal mining, raising questions about how the country would comply with new EU laws preventing commodity imports linked to forest loss.

Finally, the first major discovery of *oil and natural gas* in the Ivorian sedimentary basin, the *Baleine deposit*, operated in partnership between the Italian oil giant Eni and Ivorian Petroci, entered production at the end of August, almost two years after its discovery. With production estimated at 2.5 bn barrels of crude oil and 3,300 bn cubic feet of natural gas, Baleine continued to raise hopes of a dramatic rise in revenue through exports in addition to ensuring domestic energy provision. In July, Eni's chief executive Claudio Descalzi announced the discovery of a new deposit, called 'Calao', with the potential to produce 1–1.5 bn barrels of oil, further boosting the hopes of the Ivorian energy sector.

The Gambia

Akpojevbe Omasanjuwa

The ruling party performed poorly in the April municipal elections, while imperceptible inter- and intra-party intrigues shaped a number of activities during the year. The seemingly unconstitutional appointment of executive coordinators by the president provoked the ire of his critics. Opposition parties cautiously endeavoured to remain relevant with barely three years to the next general elections, while the judiciary and National Assembly (NA) made some impression, notable among which was the passing of two contentious bills. The imprisonment of military officers conspiring to overthrow the establishment, and a permanent secretary convicted for bribery, made news. A life sentence passed on a human rights violator in Germany for crimes committed during the Jammeh administration caused elation for some. Certain ambassadors accredited to foreign countries presented letters of credence. The impact of the war between Ukraine and Russia shaped economic activities, forcing the financial authorities to adopt stringent monetary and fiscal policies to ameliorate the economic situation.

Domestic Politics

Municipal elections were conducted on 20 May, subsequent to President Adama Barrow's re-election under the banner of the new National People's Party (NPP) and the party's consequent victory in the 2022 parliamentary elections. The United Democratic Party (UDP) won all three urban municipal councils, in Banjul, Brikama, and Kanifing, where the NPP lost all except one council seat outside Brikama. The newspaper 'The Point' reported that the president's party had once again won all rural chairperson seats except in the Lower River Region (LRR), regarded as the UDP's stronghold. Barrow won massively in his native Upper River Region (URR).

Momodou Sabally, former campaign manager of the UDP, crossed the floor to the NPP in December. No reason was advanced for the defection, though it was widely believed that it was to enable the sanction imposed on him by a commission of inquiry to be overturned. The Janneh Commission, which had investigated the financial activities of former president Yahya Jammeh, indicted Sabally and consequently barred him for life from holding public office.

Also in December, the solicitor-general disclosed that the government was undertaking consultations regarding reviving the rejected 2020 draft constitution with the intention of holding a national referendum in December 2024. It was rumoured that NA members had voted against the document in 2021 because of certain clauses that could hamper the political ambitions of the incumbent president. The solicitor-general disclosed that consultations were on track to ensure consensus would be reached on the issue, while some politicians and members of the public believed that the ex post facto clauses impinging on the president's term of office would scuttle the process again. The rejected document had been meant to usher in a third republic following the end of the 22-year rule of Yahya Jammeh in 2017.

Executive coordinators for Banjul and Kanifing municipalities were appointed by the president. Although their role in governance was not clearly spelled out, Barrow had earlier, in December 2022, announced his desire to appoint governors for these municipalities to address the activities of those undermining the implementation of his programmes. Some legal practitioners were of the opinion that the appointments were unconstitutional, but a State House press release explained that by the powers granted by the constitution, the action was not ultra vires, as it was within the president's powers to establish public offices, make appointments, and terminate them, subject to constitutional provisions and acts of the NA. The release further contended that The Gambia is a unitary state, with overarching authority, and hence local councils are not separate government entities. However, nine civil society organisations signed a request to the president to rescind his decision.

Former president Yahya Jammeh reiterated that he would neither cede control of the Alliance for Patriotic Reorientation and Construction (APRC) to anyone nor tolerate any change to its structures. Speaking to his supporters in a leaked audio recording around December, Jammeh emphasised that anyone aspiring to be the party flagbearer should go elsewhere. He also warned against changing party emblems and symbols. Furthermore, he said that a council of elders and chairs who would not compromise the party's principles would be appointed to oversee its national executive committee and would be the sole conduit for communications from him on party affairs. This came at a time when several executive members of the party were reported to have been replaced. The party currently holds five HA seats.

In November, the leader of the UDP, Ousaino Darboe, admonished ambitious young politicians within its fold who were eager to succeed him, calling on them to exercise patience and focus instead on solidifying the party's support base. With barely three years until the next general election, party militants remained doubtful amid speculations of a likely split of the party when its current leader quits active politics. Darboe assured supporters not to worry over reports that people were pushing and pulling to succeed him, because any ambitious young person in the party would want to assume a leadership position. 'I just want to advise that those who want to succeed me should be patient and wait for their time', he was quoted as saying by newspaper 'The Standard'.

Another party frontrunner, Mai Fatty of the Gambia Moral Congress (GMC), had earlier, in September, suggested that the NA revoke the law outlawing female genital mutilation on the ground that despite having been proscribed since 2015, the practice continued to be practised surreptitiously. The ass conviction of three women over the issue sparked intense country-wide debate as a number of adolescent girls had been subjected to the practice. Among the driving forces behind calls for its decriminalisation were Islamic cleric Abdoulie Fatty and legislator Sulayman Saho. In an interview, the GMC leader urged parliament to amend the law and render female circumcision a choice for parents, while advocacy groups could then continue to persuade and educate parents and guardians about the practice. He said that the state should ensure that 'laws reflect the subjective moral and cultural values of societies and not foreign ideas'. A UN official called on the government, civil society, and religious and traditional leaders to dialogue on a shared vision that would prioritise the wellbeing and fundamental human rights of girls and women.

On 20 October, the administrative secretary of the ruling NPP, Seedy Ceesay, disclosed to a reporter from 'The Standard' his desire to push for a more robust relationship between his party and opposition parties, to end hostilities among their members. He said that the NPP, in its reform agenda, would prioritise engaging with opponents to foster such a relationship, based on respect and mutual understanding, in the interest of peace and stability. The paper further reported him as saying that 'we will engage our opponents to make them understand that we are not enemies but just opponents who have the same intention of building a better

Gambia. We want to start a discussion around how to foster a more cordial relationship because if you find yourself in opposition you are a government in waiting.'

Commenting on how the NPP intended to foster a cordial relationship with the media, Ceesay reiterated his party reform agenda and desire to continue improving engagement with the media. His comments followed the observation of Emmanuel Joof, chair of the National Human Rights Commission, that the growth of hate speech and derogatory remarks against political opponents, religious groups, tribes, and other minorities was threatening The Gambia's newfound freedom and democratic governance. Addressing a graduation and prize-giving ceremony at Saint Augustine's Senior Secondary in June, Joof remarked that The Gambia was a secular democracy where tolerance, co-existence, and respect for other tribes, ethnicities, religions, genders, and statuses were preserved and respected by past generations. Secularity, he further stated, does not mean that laws are anti-religion or encourage immorality, or that they do not protect the rights of people to practise their religion, as some had suggested. Secular democracy gives people the right to practice the religion of their choice but mandates that the state should not interfere in the religious and non-religious beliefs and practices of people; that one cannot declare a state religion; that one cannot establish a party based on religion or tribe; and that the state should not either give preferential treatment to or discriminate against any religion or religious group. He emphasised that although The Gambia had been spared the menace of tribal, religious, and sectarian conflict despite the 22 years of dictatorship under Yahya Jammeh, and notwithstanding the progress accomplished since 2017, the growth of hate speech and derogatory remarks against certain groups were issues that continued to threaten the country's newfound freedoms.

'The Standard' reported in May that the National Audit Office's report on the 2019 government financial statements revealed that the 22,319,958 dalasi (GMD; around $329,450) proceeds from the sale of Jammeh's assets were 'unaccounted for'. The general triplicate receipt book used for receipting monies from the sale of government assets reported by the Janneh Commission was not provided for inspection; it was claimed that the book was missing after the sale of assets. The justice minister conversely informed the NA that the narrative was misleading. However, the author of the story stood his ground, stating: 'We based our article on the latest government 2019 simplified and summarised audit report which was published in June'. The managing editor of the paper reacted to the minister's comment as to whether the newspaper paper had an agenda: 'Our agenda is to serve as a relay between the people and the government and between the peoples and engender debate on issues of national relevance so that at the end of the day the government is held accountable to an informed citizenry.'

It was reported in May that the implementation of the Truth, Reconciliation and Reparation Commission (TRRC) recommendations was progressing, under the aegis of the Ministry of Justice. As part of an ongoing effort, the ministry drafted the Special Prosecutor's Office and the Special Accountability Mechanism Bills to be presented to the NA for enactment. Through these pieces of legislation, it sought to create a mechanism that would consist of a special prosecutor's office, a hybrid tribunal, and a special criminal division of the High Court. When the Act came into effect, a victims' commission was to be established within the first quarter of 2024 to empower the commission to administer the victims' fund, admit new victims, maintain a victims' database, and also reassess and establish a fair amount of compensation for the assorted injuries suffered. The TRRC HAS investigated alleged atrocities committed during the Jammeh administration.

In the area of institutional and legislative reforms, the government, through the justice ministry, embarked on a reform agenda necessitating an unprecedented amount of draft legislation pending before the NA, with more sectoral and institutional legislation in the pipeline. Earlier in the year, the NA passed the Prevention and Prohibition of Torture Act 2023, thereby domesticating the UN Convention against Torture. The NA was expected to pass the Criminal Offences and Criminal Procedure Bills as well as the Anti-Corruption Bill. In addition to the transitional justice process, the ministry executed its mandate in the areas of criminal prosecutions, civil litigation, and the provision of quality and timely legal services to government ministries, parastatals, and The Gambia's overseas missions.

Twenty-seven new entrants to the legal profession were enrolled by the General Legal Council in December. The chief justice welcomed the new entrants and disclosed that the enrolment brought the total number of legal practitioners in the country to 554. He implored them to be honest while upholding the rule of law. During the occasion, tribute was paid to a retired justice of the Supreme Court, Gibou Janneh – one of the first six enrolled Gambian lawyers present at the ceremony. Also present were the solicitor-general and legal secretary, representing the attorney-general and minister of justice.

Meanwhile, following a Supreme Court judgment in November declaring the 1994 Bamfo Commission not properly constituted, the People's Progressive Party (PPP) issued a communiqué imploring the government to return its confiscated assets. This was after a veteran politician, M.C. Cham, challenged the composition of the Commission of Inquiry in court on the basis that its chair was not qualified as a judge or competent to practice law in The Gambia. The commission had been established following the overthrow of the PPP administration in 1994 through a military coup.

In another instance, the Westminster Foundation country representative, Madi Jobarteh, who had earlier been released on bail, was charged with seditious intention, incitement to violence, and false publication and broadcasting. He confirmed to 'The Standard' that his bail had been extended to 23 November. However, he denied the charges in his statement to the police.

In December, the family of a slain journalist, Deyda Hydara, applauded the life sentence passed down to Bai Lowe by a German court as a development representing a major step in the search for justice for those who suffered abuses during the Jammeh's 1994–2017 administration. German prosecutors accused Bai Lowe of being the car driver associated with the murders of legal practitioner Ousman Sillah, journalist Deyda Hydara, and member of the military Dawda Nyassi. Other charges included the attempted murder of Ida Jagne and Nian Sarang Jobe of the 'Independent' newspaper. Baba Hydara, son of the murdered journalist, was quoted by the 'The Standard' as describing the development as a milestone judgment on every level, and one which was only the beginning, as there were many more people to be held accountable, most importantly the main perpetrator, former president Yahya Jammeh.

The deaths of two brothers, barrister Bola Carrol and Dr Henry D.R. Carrol, within days of each other occurred in November. Bola Carrol had commenced his career as a state counsel before taking to private legal practice, while Dr Henry, who also began as a state counsel, had attained the position of solicitor-general and legal secretary at the Ministry of Justice before retiring as commissioner for law reform. The death of Reuben Phillot, an erstwhile judicial secretary, was also announced in November.

Two contentious government bills were tabled at the NA in September and November respectively. The first concerned the improvement of conditions of service for judges of the Supreme Court and judicial staff. It generated rancour, as observers were of the view that, akin to the executive and legislature, the judiciary intended to rip off Gambians by extracting their hard-earned money through taxes. The justice minister, however, retorted that the bill was in alignment with relevant sections of the constitution. Where a judge dies while holding office, the bill states: 'a lump sum equal to one-half of his or her yearly salary at the time of his or her death shall be paid to his or her surviving spouse. A judicial officer who retires at or after the age of sixty-five years, and after having served at least five years in aggregate in a judicial office, shall be paid a non-taxable lump sum gratuity in a sum equal to six months of his or her basic salary last received whilst in office.'

The other contentious bill granted lifetime benefits to ex-presidents of The Gambia and their spouses. Dubbed the Former Presidents Bill 2023, it generated fierce debate among house members and in public forums, compelling the speaker to put to the vote whether it should advance to a third reading. Of the 47 present, 30 voted yes while 17 objected. Consequently, the objectors walked out of the chambers in protest while the speaker commended those who acquiesced for defending the interest of their electorates. The bill proposed a six-month lump sum gratuity payment to an outgoing president to facilitate their transition to post-presidential life. To sustain the dignity of the first family, the bill recommended a monthly allowance equal to 25% of a deceased former president's pension, to be paid to the surviving spouse.

In another development, Corporal Sanna Fadera and seven other military officers were charged with conspiracy, in diverse places between October and

December 2022, to commit felony and treason with the intention of overthrowing the government through unlawful means. They all denied the charges. The case was presided over by Justice Basirou V.P. Mahoney in November, and upon conviction, Corporal Sanna Fadera received a 12-year prison sentence while others received various terms. Consequently, a visiting delegation of parliamentarians from the European Parliamentary Committee on Foreign Affairs urged the Gambian government to prioritise security sector reform, this being an expected landmark of democratic consolidation. The delegation also discussed other areas of mutual interest connected to current regional geopolitical challenges. It also acknowledges the ongoing work towards the setting up of a special prosecutor's office and a hybrid court in partnership with ECOWAS.

Former permanent secretary of the Ministry of Fisheries and Water Resources Bamba Banja, despite denying an allegation of bribery levelled against him, was convicted in March and sentenced to two years' imprisonment for unlawfully accepting GMD 100,000 from a foreign fishing company to facilitate the release of a vessel apprehended for engaging in illegal fishing in Gambian waters. He was also fined GMD 50,000 for the loss of income suffered by the government; in the case of default, he would serve an additional year in prison. A spokesperson for the prisons service confirmed Banja's presence in the Mile 2 prison facility. Subsequently, Banja and 36 other convicted prisoners in different correctional facilities received state pardon.

Foreign Affairs

The Ministry of Foreign Affairs, International Cooperation and Gambians Abroad stated in April that two vessels conveying 233 illegal Gambian migrants had been intercepted in Dakhla, in the disputed territory of Western Sahara. A statement issued by the ministry said that the migrant boats had been rescued by Moroccan security officers. On the basis of the cooperation between the Moroccan government and The Gambia's embassy in Rabat, the necessary arrangements were made for the repatriation of the migrants to The Gambia. The ministry also acknowledged the deaths of other Gambian migrants recorded in Senegal, Mauritania, Morocco, and the Canary Islands at different times since October. The release lamented the increase in the number of Gambians engaged in irregular migration to Europe.

'The Standard' reported in April that sustained advocacy by environmentalists had compelled the US embassy in Banjul to give up plans to erect its new embassy building at the Bijilo Monkey Park, a protected habitat for endangered fauna and flora. Clarifying its decision to search for an alternative location, the embassy said in a press release that it had 'pursued a biological assessment [of the area] which raised concerns'.

As part of an ongoing collaborative effort, the government of Nigeria in October assigned two judges to The Gambia as volunteers under the aegis of the Nigerian Directorate of Technical Aid Corps (DTAC). The director-general of the DTAC urged the judges to carry the Nigerian flag high, 'We assure you as usual, this directorate and the embassy of Nigeria in The Gambia will protect your interest and make sure you're giving the best during your service', he stated. In response, one of the judges expressed appreciation for the opportunity and promised that they would make Nigeria proud in delivering their mandate in their host community.

The ECOWAS Court of Human Rights dismissed a suit filed in July by the former prime minister of Guinea-Bissau, Aristides Gomes, in which he asked the court to suspend The Gambia, Senegal, Niger, and Nigeria from the organisation in line with Article 45 of the community's protocol and also bar them from discussions and decision-making processes relating to Guinea-Bissau for a period of not less than five years. This followed the two rounds of elections in 2019 and 2020 which had declared Umaro Embaló president, subsequently inaugurated on 27 February 2020 despite the erstwhile ruling party, the African Party for the Independence of Guinea and Cape Verde (PAIGC, Partido Africano para a Independência da Guiné e Cabo Verde), objecting to the results on grounds of electoral fraud. Holding a majority in the HA, the party had sworn in speaker Cipriano Cassamá as a rival president, but he had resigned a day later following assassination threats. In February 2020, Embaló had replaced Aristide Gomes as prime minister with Nuno Gomes Nabiam, but Aristide refused to resign. Soon afterwards, President Embaló visited The Gambia, Senegal, Niger, and Nigeria, where he was received as the president of Guinea-Bissau. Aristides, who had challenged the validity of the election of President Embaló, was angered by the actions of the four countries in welcoming and recognising Embaló as president. In a judgement delivered in May, the court upheld the submission of the plea in law and facts in support of a preliminary objection filed by The Gambia. The court cited a statement issued by ECOWAS in April 2020 that the community recognised President Umaro Embaló as the duly elected president of Guinea-Bissau.

The death of Alieu Jammeh, The Gambia's high commissioner to Sierra Leone, was announced in May. Jammeh had served as ambassador to Guinea-Bissau before taking up post in Freetown. He had been the head of the University of The Gambia's international relations office after serving as youth and sport minister for five years under President Jammeh.

In May, career diplomat Harriet King presented her letters of credence as the new British high commissioner to The Gambia. Her appointment was announced in a statement by the UK's Foreign, Commonwealth and Development Office. She took over from David Belgrove OBE, who had been accredited to The Gambia in 2020 after Sharon Wardle.

In October, the Gambian ambassador to South Africa with concurrent accreditation to other SADC countries, Fatoumata Jahumpa-Ceesay, presented her letters of credence to President Hage Geingob of Namibia in Windhoek. The occasion rekindled Jahumpa-Cessay's memory of developments that had facilitated the process of some Namibian students pursuing their education in The Gambia. She remarked that her accreditation was another milestone in 'our collective endeavours to strengthen the excellent relations between Namibia and The Gambia dating back the turbulent days of the 1980s and 90s when The Gambia resolutely supported and was in solidarity with the people of Namibia during their protracted rancorous struggle for independence'.

On an earlier occasion in March, Zambian president Hakainde Hichilema had remarked that relations between The Gambia and Zambia commenced with the similarity between the names of the two countries. He recalled how mail destined for Zambia often ended being routed in error to The Gambia and vice versa. He was speaking in Lusaka while receiving Jahumpa-Ceesay's letters of credence. During the occasion, the president emphasised the need for cordial ties between the two countries, reiterating the need for peace and security as a panacea for economic development. He enjoined Jahumpa-Ceesay to explore and enjoy Zambia's diverse and warm culture. Jahumpa-Ceesay retorted, after recalling the cordial relationship between the two countries maintained in the fields of education and the judiciary, that she would do her best to upgrade Zambian–Gambian friendship and cooperation.

Also, the Gambian ambassador to the US and Canada, Momodou Lamin Bah, in December presented his letters of credence to the governor-general of Canada, Mary Simon, who designated him as high commissioner of The Gambia to Canada. High Commissioner Bah thanked the government and people of Canada for their support for The Gambia's ongoing case over the treatment of the Rohingya in Myanmar, and for the country's development agenda. He appealed for an expansion of Canada's development assistance to The Gambia, in the areas of capacity-building for the youth and the country's diplomatic cadre, as well as the implementation of the TRRC white paper recommendations and the country's drive for food security. In response, Simon welcomed Bah to Canada and congratulated him on his new role, which she said would be to see how the two countries could better work together to make the world a better place.

In March, minister of defence Sering Modou Njie alerted law-makers to the need for government to seriously engage with the Senegalese government to respect The Gambia's sovereignty, as the country's airspace and land territory must be protected. Based on previous incidents, he made it clear that any use of the national territory should take place only with the express approval of the government of The Gambia.

In response to an interrogation raised by a member of the NA on the crisis in Foni, where several residents were traumatised from across the border by Senegalese drones, the minister commented that the matter had been addressed with the Senegalese government to enable their military planners to be extra-careful. The

Gambia Armed Forces strengthened its deployment in Foni, to support the 4 Infantry Battalion's operations as a show of force to restore the confidence of the people and protect residents in the area. The restive border area separating The Gambia and Senegal has been plagued with instability due to the activities of a separatist movement based in southern Senegal.

Commenting on the NA member's assertion that the Gambian military contingent deployed in the area to assist the camp in Kanilai had been withdrawn, Njie asserted that the Gambian deployment continued to exercise its duty around the border area to give confidence and to restore peace in the area. The minister said that the government would take steps to engage the people of Foni and the surrounding communities in the border area. 'We have engaged the border commission and they have been intensifying their efforts in the area', he said.

Following the signing of an agreement by The Gambia and Senegal enabling pursuit of criminals across the border, a Gambian security expert, Momodou Lamin Faye, decried the move as a threat to national security. Faye suggested that pursuit of suspected criminals on land across international boundaries was a grey concept which had 'no global legal basis', and that 'no global legal authority' would allow one nation to conduct incursions into another nation's territory to pursue an opposing element because the act was in breach of the sacrosanct sovereignty and territorial integrity of a nation. He aired his views in light of the fact that the agreement could escalate the crisis in the Casamance region of Senegal, which is contiguous to The Gambia. He further explained that the treaties had been signed to serve the interests of the contracting parties and not to threaten national security. Based on his analysis of the continuing rebel movement in Casamance, the agreement could escalate the decades-old unrest in the region.

Socioeconomic Developments

A news item credited to Reuters in June confirmed that government documents had revealed that it was to be made mandatory from 1 July for all pharmaceutical products from India to be inspected prior to shipment to The Gambia, following the deaths of children linked to an Indian-manufactured cough mixture. The Gambia initiated moves to address issues related to counterfeit medicines entering the country after at least 70 children, most of them under the age of five, died of acute kidney injury which medical practitioners linked to the contaminated cough mixture.

During the fiscal year, the agriculture sector grew in terms of the scale and number of projects, demonstrating the government's commitment to this sector. The finance minister disclosed, in his budget speech to the NA, that the Ministry of Agriculture (MOA) had engaged in partnerships aimed at implementing initiatives harmonising with the Recovery Focus National Development Plan. This introduced a post-Covid-19 Emergency Response Plan, focusing on bolstering the resilience of farmers through the agricultural extension policy. The policy was designed to foster sustainable production, enhance capacity, improve governance, and facilitate partnerships. The MOA prioritised the rice value chain, small ruminant improvement, and the development of a national strategy to combat and eradicate ovine rinderpest. Notably, the prevalent livestock diseases in the country, especially the contagious bovine pleurae pneumonia and new castle disease for poultry, were addressed through extensive vaccination campaigns for small ruminants and poultry. A total of 208,231 small ruminants received the required vaccinations. Also, the ROOTS project offered services such as ploughing assistance for 80 hectares of land, distributed 160 bags of urea fertiliser, and provided input materials, including 2,800 sachets of herbicide and 5,300 kilograms of seeds, through the Rural Poor Stimulus Facility programme. The small ruminant enhancement project established 20 community pasture schemes and facilitated the enlargement of 150 one-hectare farms. Food availability remained robust country-wide despite a notable increase in the prices of cereals compared with the previous year. The price increase was principally ascribed to global inflation and the ongoing war in Ukraine. Dependence on food imports exacerbated these impacts on the prices of basic commodities, further aggravated by the continuous rise in fuel prices, which led to increases in transportation costs. The National Agricultural Research Institute, in collaboration with the FAO, achieved significant progress in agricultural research. This included the final screening and availability of five groundnut varieties, five new *findi* varieties, and three cassava varieties. The institute also initiated the development of new technologies for livestock feed and soil fertility enrichment. Donor funding continued to supplement government efforts to reform the agriculture sector.

The fisheries sector faced challenges including the degradation of habitats, over-exploitation, climate change and variability, the effects of Covid-19, and the Russia–Ukraine conflict. The latter increased oil prices for seagoing fishing vessels and impacted the average cost of fish. To address the managerial gaps confronting the sector, cabinet approved the reviewed licensing fee for vessels and fish meal factories. The $25 million Climate Resilient Fishery Initiative for Livelihood Improvement Project funded by the Green Climate Fund was launched, and project implementation commenced. Two climate-friendly fish-smoking ovens, fish-drying racks, and processing equipment were installed at the Tanji and Gunjur fish-landing sites, in addition to the construction of two fish-landing platforms funded under the EU–Gambia Sustainable Fisheries Partnership Agreement. In July, The Gambia acceded to the Convention on the Protection and Use of Transboundary Watercourses and International Lakes. With support from UNESCO and the WFP, the government procured additional instruments to enhance the accuracy of weather forecasts and monitoring. In addition, the strengthening of the Climate

Change Early Warning Systems Phase II project undertook capacity-building on climate change early-warning systems for selected people in the seven local communities. The Climate Smart Rural Water Supply and Sanitation Development Project, funded by the AfDB, commenced construction of 55 solar-powered piped water supply systems to provide safe and quality drinking water to rural people. The government allocated GMD 10 m for the drilling of boreholes, reticulation systems, and solar powered systems, in addition to 110 boreholes already drilled under the supervision of the Department of Water Resources (DWR). Through an AfDB, funded project, DWR established a functional web-based monitoring and evaluation system which was launched in May.

Initiatives implemented to boost tourist arrivals included the construction of 2 km of cluster roads within the tourism development area and the construction of three new eco-lodges in the North Bank and Central River regions and URR to address the challenge of accommodation for tourists and locals in rural areas. Sotuma Samba Koi eco-lodge was completed and handed over to the tourism board, while a new craft market was also completed at Palma Rima. The Ministry of Tourism and Culture, through the National Council for Arts and Culture, completed the quadrennial periodic reporting against the UNESCO 2005 Convention on the Protection and Promotion of the Diversity of Cultural Expressions.

The finance minister disclosed that the government had provided incentives to 11 companies through the Gambia Investment and Export Promotion Agency's special investment certificate. These companies were projected to invest a total of $37.4 m, creating over 1,000 jobs. The Gambia Competition and Consumer Protection Commission handled 88 cases with a total value of GMD 1,921,250, conducted market investigations into essential commodities, and took decisive action against businesses found to be in violation of the Competition Act 2007. It also initiated bi-weekly market surveillance of essential commodities to combat anti-competitive practices, and carried out inspections of products to safeguard consumers. To enhance conditions of service and productivity, the government initiated a new employment policy for 2023–28, and in consonance with modern labour standards and practices, a revised Labour Act 2023 was enacted.

Road rehabilitation and sewage/drainage system improvement in Banjul reached its final stage of implementation. This involved the rehabilitation of the pump house at Bund Road and the installation of new pumps to evacuate storm water; 98% of the road components in the initial scope and 87% of those in the additional works were commissioned in September. As part of the OIC infrastructure development projects for hosting the heads of states summit, the upgrading of 50 km of urban roads was in progress and a new VIP Lounge and the rehabilitation of the terminal building at the airport were completed.

The energy sector was affected by the Russia–Ukraine war, leading to increases in fuel prices, devaluation of the Dalasi, and a shortfall in foreign earnings. Consequently, the prices of fuel, lubricants, and spare parts and freight and logistics challenges skyrocketed. To address the stability of fuel supplies, the National Petroleum Company constructed additional fuel stations.

With the assistance of the WFP, the US, and Caritas, the government increased the home-grown school feeding intervention in the Lower River and West Coast regions. Another plan was initiated to intervene in 186 schools, with effect from October, to the benefit of 51,000 students.

As the fiscal year drew to a close, the country grappled with an unprecedented challenging situation. Multiple developments unfolding concurrently in other parts of the world impacted the domestic economy. Increases in global food and energy prices and a high interest rate contributed to producing a grim outlook for the economy. The finance minister asserted that these concerns necessitated an inward-looking approach. Efforts were made to enhance revenue collection and prune expenditures to reinforce macro-fiscal sustainability. A draft financing approach was prepared and a domestic resource mobilisation strategy was fashioned for 2024 to fortify a resource mobilisation drive, to be supported with the resolute backing of development partners in tackling principal challenges.

Aside from high global food and energy prices, strong domestic demand reinforced inflationary pressures. Inflation reached a record high level of 18.5% (year on year) in September, although it declined to 18.05% in October. The macroeconomic environment made fiscal policy control and consolidation efforts challenging, as the central bank increased its policy rate to curb inflationary pressures.

Both fiscal and monetary policy instruments were utilised to sustain macroeconomic stability and mitigate the spill-over effects of the global economic challenges. From January to November, central bank foreign currency interventions of $59.28 m ameliorated supply-side constraints and eased the importation of essential commodities which were at critically low stock levels. Monetary policy was tightened through an increase in the policy rate by four percentage points over the course of the year to arrest rising price levels. On the fiscal front, as at October, the government subsidised fuel products by as much as GMD 479,190,238 to mitigate the effects of high global fuel prices. Other fiscal interventions included subsidies on food and agriculture inputs to the tune of GMD 664,499,675. A 30% basic salary increase for civil servants mitigated the effects of the escalating cost of living.

Approximately 67% of the population was offline by January. The internet penetration rate was at 33% in February, while internet users saw median fixed-line internet download speeds of 6.4 megabits per/second (Mbps), a 0.79 Mbps decrease from that of 2022. The Gambia ranked 170th out of 179 countries for fixed broadband internet download and upload speeds as of April 2023.

Freedom House ranked the country 56th/100 for freedom on the internet, the same position as that of 2022. The Transparency International 2023 Corruption Perceptions Index score was 37/100 while the ranking was 98th/180, a drop of 12 places from that of 2022.

Ghana

George M. Bob-Milliar

Ghana's economic decline continued in 2023. The country was officially bankrupt, but the ruling political elites were in denial. The urgent injection of funds came with conditionalities, and the country was still adjusting to the changes its return to IMF brought on. How to engage domestic and international private creditors proved challenging for the economic management team. The country's public debt ballooned to some 650 billion Ghanaian cedi (GH₵). Securing the second tranche of the $3 bn IMF bailout was partly dependent on the successful restoration of the fiscal space, debt restructuring, and the implementation of revenue mobilisation reforms, such as increases in VAT. Debt restructuring under the Domestic Debt Exchange Programme (DDEP) was controversial, with pension bondholders picketing. Inflation soared to 56.6% at the beginning of the year but ended at 26.4%. The deteriorating economic conditions triggered protests. The two major parties organised parliamentary and presidential primaries to select their parties' candidates for the December 2024 general elections. A major reshuffle of the leadership of the minority in parliament reverberated across the political landscape. The governing New Patriotic Party (NPP) was rocked by the resignation of Alan Kyerematen from and his formation of the Movement for Change. The government faced several scandals, including the national cathedral project and the discovery of several millions of dollars and cedis at the homes of a minister of state. The Akosombo Dam spillage affected over 50 communities and displaced some 30,000 people living close to the banks of Lake Volta and its estuaries. The movement towards the passage of the anti-LQBTQ+ bill gathered momentum. The fight against illegal gold mining in the country continued, but with few successes. In the domain of foreign affairs, the visit of US vice-president Kamala Harris as part of a tour of seven African countries and the president's engagements outside the country characterised the year under review.

Domestic Politics

Preparations for internal elections within Ghana's two major parties dominated local politics for much of 2023. The major parties, the governing NPP and the opposition National Democratic Congress (NDC), put their houses in order. In January, the NDC injected new blood into its leadership in parliament by reshuffling the minority front bench. Cassiel Ato Forson, a former deputy minister of finance and MP for Ajumako Enyan Essiam constituency, replaced the charismatic Haruna Iddrisu, MP for Tamale South, as the leader of the minority group. Kofi Armah Buah and Governs Kwame Agbodza were the new deputy minority leader and minority chief whip, respectively. The new appointments caused disaffection in the party. It was claimed that the communication between the old leadership and the party hierarchy was improper. While some party members and the public welcomed the leadership changes, others, including MPs, disapproved of them, arguing that they would affect the party's prospects in the general election. The party's response did not help matters. Therefore, delegations were sent to the homes of the sacked leaders to plead with them to accept the changes in the greater interest of the party.

The laying of a new constitutional instrument (CI) before parliament resulted in heated debates between the majority and minority sides. As is the norm in preparation for national elections, the Electoral Commission's (EC's) new Public Elections (Registration of Voters) Regulations Bill was laid. The minority side of the house opposed the bill. The main issues of contention centred on the requirement of proof of identification for registration. The EC proposed strictly using the Ghana Card as the sole form of identification to enrol citizens on the electoral register. Both parties agreed that registration based solely on using the Ghana Card would sanitise the register. However, they disagreed on the timing of the exercise.

A challenge mounted by Michael Ankomah Nimfah, a resident of Assin North constituency, against the eligibility of the incumbent NDC's MP for the area was adjudicated by the Supreme Court (SC). The SC's ruling was controversial in the context of Ghana's hung parliament. It portended a tilting of the balance of power and complication of the numerical strengths of the two main parties in parliament. On 17 May, in a unanimous decision, a seven-member panel of the SC directed parliament to expunge the name of the NDC incumbent MP, James Gyakye Quayson, from its roll of members. The SC came to this decision having ruled that processes leading to the election of Quayson in December 2020 had contravened Article 94(2)(a) of the 1992 Fourth Republican Constitution of Ghana, which bars a person with dual citizenship from contesting as an MP. Quayson had held dual citizenship – Ghanaian and Canadian – at the time of the filing of his nomination. He had initiated the process to renounce his Canadian citizenship beforehand, but he claimed that Covid-19 had slowed work in Canada and delayed the arrival of certification of this renunciation. The EC declared the seat vacant and rolled out a timetable for the by-election.

By-elections during the mid-term of political administrations tend to be a referendum on the performance of the incumbent regime. In that context, the 27 June by-election was an election that the ruling party wanted to win at all costs. If the seat switched to the NPP, it would have added to the slim majority the party held in parliament. The NPP, the NDC, and a third party, the Liberal Party of Ghana (LPG), all mobilised their electorates to deliver the necessary votes. However, the contest was essentially between the NPP and the NDC. The NDC maintained Quayson as its candidate. The NPP conducted parliamentary primaries and selected 40-year-old Charles Opoku as its candidate.

The government and party machinery were relocated to the constituency in the lead-up to the elections. The government engaged in project politics by hurriedly completing ongoing infrastructural projects, including new roads, bridges, and streetlights. As part of his campaigning for his party, President Nana Akufo-Addo commissioned a 70-metre steel bridge over the river Pra at Kushea. Vice-president Mahamudu Bawumia also commissioned the 31.2-km Assin Fosu main road project and an astrograph at Assin-Bereku in the constituency. The opposition NDC campaigned on its past record and appealed for sympathy votes. The party's messages targeted densely populated areas with large communities of non-indigenous migrant farmers, such as Assin Fosu, Ningo, Senchiam, Dansame, and Bongro. The economic hardships that citizens had experienced under the incumbent party could not be forgotten with the last-minute commissioning of development projects, which many considered vote buying. Quayson won the seat with 57.56%, and the NPP's candidate, Charles Opoku, obtained 42.15%.

The two major parties organised their parliamentary and presidential primaries in the year. In May, the NDC conducted primary elections to select a presidential nominee and 275 parliamentary candidates. The elections were keenly contested in some constituencies. The constituencies in Upper West Region that saw a keen contest were the Daffiama-Bussie-Issah and Wa Central constituencies. In the former,

Abu Kabiebata Kasangbata won with a slim margin. In the latter, Rashid Hassan Pelpuo, the longest-serving MP, faced three challengers but won with 871 votes to beat his closest rival, Hudu Mogtari, who obtained 708 votes. Samuel George, MP for Ningo-Prampram and a key member of the anti-LGBTQ+ group of legislators, beat off a challenge from the former constituency chair, polling 1,036 votes to defeat Michael Kwettey Nettey, who polled 626 of the total votes. Some 16 incumbent MPs lost to new entrants. A former journalist and the incumbent MP of Sagnarigu Constituency in Northern Region, Alhaji A.B.A. Fuseini, was defeated by his opponent. Some MPs in other constituencies were elected unopposed.

The NDC's presidential primary was contentious. Two Asante – Kwabena Duffour, a former governor of the Bank of Ghana and former finance minister, and the former mayor of Kumasi, Kojo Bonsu – challenged former – President John Mahama. All three candidates filed for the party's nomination, but Duffour pulled out of the contest less than 72 hours before the commencement of voting after he had tried to injunct the conduct of the elections legally. He claimed that irregularities had marred the preparations for the polls. Nevertheless, Duffour's campaign was uninspiring and lacked touch with the party's grass-roots.

On the other hand, Bonsu did not have a credible message and failed to make the case for leadership change in the NDC. Based on the certified results from the EC, John Mahama polled 297,603 votes (98.9%) of all valid ballots cast and was popularly elected. Bonsu received a paltry 3,190 votes (1.1%). This was Mahama's second win at his party's presidential primary election. Of the total 355,092 delegates certified to vote, 307,371 voted, giving the party a healthy national voter turnout of 86.56%.

In May, the NPP constituted a vetting committee to manage the party's presidential primary election. Ten men filed nominations to contest the elections. The party's constitution limits the number of presidential aspirants to five. On 26 August, the party held its super-delegates' congress, limited to 17 polling stations nationwide. The congress elected the top five from among the ten presidential aspirants for the party's 4 November National Delegates Conference. Francis Addai-Nimoh, a former MP for Mampong, and Boakye Agyarko, a former minister of energy, were tied for the fifth position and were scheduled for a second-round vote. However, Agyarko pulled out of the contest, citing a breach of party rules.

Meanwhile, Kwabena Agyepong, Joe Ghartey, and Kwadwo Poku could not achieve the required votes to proceed to the next level of the voting process. At the end of the first round of the selection process, fractures had emerged. Some candidates complained of a lack of level playing field and executive influence over the process. The president was accused of manipulating the party's electoral process to favour the vice-president. He denied this, but public statements and the behaviour of national, regional, and constituency executives appeared to suggest that the party hierarchy was firmly behind the candidature of the vice-president.

On 25 September, Alan Kyerematen, one of the presidential primary candidates, resigned from the NPP. He claimed that his supporters in and outside of government had been harassed, and that the election rules were skewed to favour the incumbent vice-president. Kyerematen had previously contested presidential primary elections in 2007, 2010, and 2014 and had served in various capacities in two governments of the NPP since 2001. He had assumed that he would be the presumptive presidential nominee after President Akufo-Addo. Members of the NPP believe in upholding the party traditions, including respecting elders, but also in rewarding loyalty and hard work. Based on this reasoning, Kyerematen believed that he had served the party well and wanted an impartial election process to enable him to contest for the presidential candidate position. He claimed that the process was biased, and as a result he broke away and launched the Movement for Change to contest the December 2024 presidential elections as an independent.

With the departure of Kyerematen from the NPP, four candidates – Owusu Afriyie Akoto, Mahamudu Bawumia, Kennedy Ohene Agyapong, and Francis Addai-Nimoh – contested the 4 November presidential primary election. Kennedy Agyapong moved up the ladder and occupied the spot that Kyerematen's departure from the contest had created, becoming the main opponent of Bawumia. His abrasive approach and unconventional campaigning resonated with the party's grassroots. He leveraged on his financial assistance to party activists and his sponsorship of party activities in the past to campaign. Distancing himself from the record of the governing party, he positioned his message well. Nevertheless, with more than 200,000 delegates voting across the 16 regions of the country, Bawumia won the NPP presidential primary with 61.43% of the total valid votes cast. His closest contender, Agyapong, came second, with 37.41%. Afriyie Akoto placed third with 0.76%, while Addai-Nimoh was at the bottom with 0.41%.

The governing NPP had won 169 seats in the 2016 presidential and parliamentary elections, making it the majority party. However, it had lost 32 seats to the opposition NDC in the 2020 elections. The party had lobbied for an independent vote to claim the majority side in parliament with 138 seats. Therefore, in preparation for the 2024 elections, the party declared all parliamentary seats open to contest. The jostling for parliamentary seats in the incumbent NPP intensified when the party opened and outlined its electoral calendar in the middle of the year. It opened nominations and vetted the candidates in December. Polls were expected to take place in 105 constituencies across the country, with some MPs going unopposed. The preparations for the primaries indicated what was to come in the new year. Battleground constituencies included Dome Kwabenya, Asante Akim Central, Adansi Asokwa, Bekwai, Bantama, Old Tafo, and Tano North. The party scheduled 27 January 2024 as the date of parliamentary primaries in constituencies with sitting MPs.

President Akufo-Addo's electoral promise in 2016 to construct a national cathedral has become a source of a major political scandal. Not only has the project become hugely controversial in Ghana in the face of an IMF bailout, but members of the secretariat have also become embroiled in the scandal at different levels. The government has spent $58 m on the project, but it is still at the foundation level. Funding for the cathedral project has been shrouded in secrecy. The North Tongu MP, Samuel Okudzeto Ablakwa, raised several issues of impropriety and infractions regarding the construction of the cathedral. He accused Reverend Victor Kusi Boateng, secretary to the Board of Trustees of the project, of engaging in a conflict of interest. In January, Ablakwa petitioned the Commission on Human Rights and Administrative Justice (CHRAJ) to investigate Boateng for conflict of interest and possession of multiple identities. Boateng filed a defamation suit against Ablakwa, and later, a contempt application was filed. The exposures presented as parliamentary oversight embarrassed the government and appeared to have forced some clergymen to resign from the board. The application to the Accra High Court sought to stop the MP from publicly commenting on the subject. In May, the court dismissed the first contempt application because it was defective.

There was an increase in public awareness of corruption in Ghana. Several ruling-party functionaries implicated in acts of corruption were investigated, helping to end political scandals. On 22 July, Cecilia Dapaah, the minister of sanitation and water resources, was forced to resign from government when news broke that her household staff had stolen $1 m in cash. This was a major political scandal, and the government moved swiftly to contain the contagion effect. The minister's resignation was followed by full investigations into the sources of the cash, and more damaging findings were made. The Office of the Special Prosecutor (OSP) searched all of the properties and bank accounts of Dapaah and discovered more foreign and local currency. The scandal significantly influenced public perception of the government's efforts at improving governance. Major improvements in relation to issues of transparency and political accountability have not been seen during the NPP administration. Ghana's overall performance in the global Corruption Perceptions Index of Transparency International was stagnant.

In July, national security was threatened when an audio recording of a private conversation between senior police officers and a politician was made public. The content of the recording involved a conspiracy to remove the incumbent inspector-general of police (IGP), George Akuffo Dampare, from office. The allegations of conspiracy to remove the IGP were captured in an audio file leaked by Daniel Bugri Naabu, a former Northern Region chair of the governing NPP. The serving police officers, commissioner of police (COP) George Alex Mensah, superintendent Emmanuel Eric Gyebi, and superintendent George Lysander Asare, and the chief conspired to remove the incumbent IGP and cause President Akufo-Addo to appoint a new IGP who would be loyal and pliant to the governing party to enable it to retain power in the December 2024 elections. A special committee of parliament was constituted to investigate the allegations in the leaked audio file. The public hearings revealed the political ambitions of some of the officers at the top echelons of the police service. Underlying this was the overt politicisation of the police service and how partisan considerations influenced Ghana's security management.

In December, former president John Mahama delivered a speech at the ninth Ghana CEO Network Business Cocktail, outlining his vision for a major economic policy – the 'Mahama 24-Hour Economy'. Mahama's speech to the captains of industry laid out a transformative blueprint for Ghana's development. The initiative was to address unemployment, maximising the available resources and putting the nation to work through a three-shift work schedule. It would include legislative support, tax incentives for private sector operators, and regulations to facilitate businesses operating 24/7 within the economy. The state would create an enabling environment for companies participating in the initiative by offering reduced power tariff costs during off-peak hours and funds to support strategic industries.

Foreign Affairs

The president and senior government officials engaged in important diplomatic missions during the year. In February, the president received the letters of credence of new envoys from the Guinea, Mauritius, Bangladesh, New Zealand, and Canada. All five nations have maintained diplomatic relations with Ghana since independence.

In June, the Ghanaian president hosted other African and Caribbean politicians at the 30th Annual Meeting of the African Export-Import Bank (Afreximbank) in Accra. President Akufo-Addo and Prime Minister Mia Mottley of Barbados, among other leaders, addressed participants at the four-day meeting, held under the theme, 'Delivering the Vision: Building Prosperity for Africans', which featured keynotes, panel discussions, and plenaries focusing on African trade, trade finance, and development issues. The implementation of the AfCFTA was a key theme for discussion.

In March 2023, US vice-president Kamala Harris made Ghana her gateway to a seven-day African tour. The tour was considered part of Washington's charm offensive to counterbalance the growing Chinese and Russian influence on the continent. In Accra, Harris met President Akufo-Addo and Ghanaian feminists, and delivered a speech on women's empowerment to young Ghanaians. Her comments at a press conference on supporting freedoms and building an inclusive society were interpreted by some as US promotion of gay rights in Africa, a subject that has divided the country. The controversial 'Promotion of Proper Human Sexual Rights and Ghanaian Family Value' was debated in Ghana's parliament during Harris's visit. Even though Harris did not directly comment on the LGBTQ+ issue, the speaker of Ghana's parliament interpreted her call for 'equality and freedoms of all people' as an intrusion into a sovereign nation's domestic affairs. Speaker Alban Bagbin described the comments by Harris as 'undemocratic'. Harris also visited the slave castle in Cape Coast.

The president participated in the UNSC high-level debate on countering terrorism and preventing violent extremism. It aimed to strengthen cooperation between the UN and regional organisations in the fight against terrorism. Terrorism in the Sahel has threatened the stability of several countries. The issue of terrorism and how poorly equipped national armies have become was used as the justification for the military coups in Burkina Faso and Mali.

Ghana's promotion of diaspora affairs was acknowledged in October. President Akufo-Addo was awarded the Star Prize for the Black History Makers Award in New York, in recognition of his promotion of diaspora engagement, investment, and cultural exchanges. Relatedly, in December, the president launched the Diaspora Engagement Policy. This provides the framework for active engagement with the African diaspora for collaborative socioeconomic transformation. It aims to strengthen ties with the global Ghanaian community.

The G77+China convened a meeting in Havana, Cuba during the year. The group comprises developing and emerging countries representing 80% of the world's population. President Akufo-Addo joined some 30 heads of state and governments from Africa at the meeting. The imposition of the Western model, the Russia–Ukraine conflict, and climate change were some of the pressing issues delegates discussed at the conference.

Ghana played a diplomatic role when the military seized power in Niger in July. The response from ECOWAS that saw the suspension of Niger from the regional body had repercussions for Ghanaian traders. The closure of Niger's international borders denied Ghana a vital source of food commodities. Ghana imports onions, shallots, garlic, leeks, and certain roots and tubers from Niger.

In November, Swiss federal councillor Ignazio Cassis visited Ghana to deepen bilateral and multilateral cooperation. The Swiss delegation met the president and senior government ministers. The meeting focused on economic relations between the two countries.

Socioeconomic Developments

The Covid-19 pandemic and the Russia–Ukraine war lenses have explained Ghana's economic difficulties, but Ghana's economic decline has not surprised many. The country had long been the standard for economic growth and political stability on the continent. Yet underneath the successes were deep cracks centring on the structure of the economy. Ghana's economy has not seen any major transformation since the 1920s. The Guggisberg economic model bequeathed by the departing

British colonialist to the new leaders was maintained with little change. There is little value addition to exportable commodities from Ghana. In addition, the liberation of the economy has thrown open the country's borders for the dumping of manufactured goods from China and the industrialised world. As a result, any small external shocks throw the economy off gear. Western-style liberal democracy has complicated socioeconomic development in Ghana. In seeking votes from citizens, governing parties have spent lavishly and increased the public debt over the years. Elections are expensive in Ghana, and election-year budget overruns are now institutionalised.

The debt restructuring directed by the IMF programme affected several vulnerable groups. The government DDEP engaged financial sector operators and representative groups of individual bondholders. The individual bondholders formed an association known as the Individual Bond Holders Association of Ghana (IBHAG) to safeguard their interest in the debt exchange programme, and the leadership of the IBHAG held meetings with the Ministry of Finance to discuss the modalities for the exchange. Another group, the Ghana Individual Bondholder Forum, convened by Senyo Hosi, demanded to be excluded from the programme. The group offered suggestions for fiscal adjustments to government expenditures, arguing that haircuts would be unnecessary if the government cut its expenditure. The government indicated that the DDEP was voluntary. The IMF programme brought some discipline into the fiscal policy space. Yet like most IMF-inspired austerity programmes, debt restructuring denied many people their life savings. The 2023 budget incorporated several revenue measures, including VAT increases and removing benchmark values on imports. Ghana received the first tranche of support under the IMF programme, signalling progress.

The widespread hardships introduced by the austerity measures appeared to compound the corruption issue. Transparency International's Corruption Perceptions Index showed that corruption remained a major development issue in Ghana. The maintenance of its position at 43 showed that Ghana had not done much to improve perceptions of corruption in governmental circles.

The issue of LGBTQ+ rights dominated the news for much of 2023 as parliament considered the private Promotion of Proper Human Sexual Rights and Ghanaian Family Values members bill. Activists and moderate advocates for LGBTQ+ rights were harassed, compelling many to go underground. On 5 July, Ghana's parliament voted to adopt the report of the Committee on Constitutional, Legal, and Parliamentary Affairs on the bill. The action of parliament put in jeopardy the lives of hundreds of thousands of lesbian, gay, bisexual, transgender, and queer Ghanaians. Like elsewhere in Africa, debates on homosexuality were narrowly focused and played on the emotions of Ghanaians.

The year became one of protests as the economic crisis deepened. A section of the population took to the streets to express discontent, and there were several waves of demonstrations against the government on one issue or the other. Social problems including high inflation, high levels of debt, high costs of living, corruption, unemployment, and poor working conditions triggered protests in Accra and other urban centres. Four protests were particularly significant. The three-day #OccupyJulorBiHouse protests were staged from 21 to 23 September. The start date of the demonstration was historically significant, as it was the birthday of one of Africa's greatest pan-Africanists, Kwame Nkrumah. The protest was organised by Democracy Hub and was aimed at forcing President Akufo-Addo and his government to urgently address the worsening economic conditions and corruption issues in the country. The demonstrators marched to Jubilee House, the seat of government, to present a petition to the president but were prevented from doing so. Police officers mounted a roadblock near the 37 Military Hospital and blocked the protesters from getting close to the president's office. Protesters carried placards and Ghanaian flags and lamented the high cost of living. On the first day of the protest, 49 protesters were arrested and detained at various police stations in the city.

The #OccupyBoG Protest was organised in October. The organisers included the minority caucus in parliament, the pressure group Arise Ghana, and Justice for Ghana. The protesters demanded the resignation of the governor of the Bank of Ghana, Ernest Addison, and his deputies. The bank had reported a loss of GH¢ 60.8 bn in its financial statement, which many Ghanaians found unacceptable. Some of the bank's actions were said to have contributed to the worsening economic situation in the country. The central bank printed about GH¢ 77 bn to support government expenditure. The protesters alleged that the governor and his officials were incompetent, and this collective incompetence, they claimed, contributed to the financial difficulties of the bank.

The IMF-inspired debt restructuring affected many government bondholders. The government's decision to include pensioner bondholders in the DDEP triggered the formation of an association. In February, the Pensioner Bondholders Forum began picketing at the premises of the Ministry of Finance. The senior citizens' picket gained momentum when retired former chief justice Sophia Akuffo joined the protest. Gold Coast Fund customers also picketed at the same venue. On 28 November, dissatisfied customers of the defunct Gold Coast Fund Management staged a 32-hour protest outside the Ministry of Finance headquarters building, demanding the release of their locked-up investments. To hammer home their frustrations, the customers slept in the open overnight at the ministry building.

The government's financial sector clean-up exercise and the prosecution of offenders were still ongoing. Ato Essien, the former chief executive officer of the collapsed Capital Bank, entered a plea bargain with the state but could not meet the terms the court imposed on him. Consequently, he was sentenced to 15 years' imprisonment for his inability to pay the full amount of GH¢ 90 m to the state.

Ghana's Forestry Commission warned that widespread illegal mining activities were destroying the country's forests. Since assuming office in 2017, President Akufo-Addo had promised to eliminate unlawful mining, known locally as 'galamsey'. The environmental damage that illegal mining has caused Ghana was debated across the country. Despite the state's intervention, with many policies to discourage the youth, many new areas, including forest reserves, were infringed upon. Foreigners' involvement in illegal mining attracted the attention of the law enforcement agencies. Aisha Huang, a notorious Chinese national engaged in the galamsey business, was lucky once when the state failed to prosecute her and instead deported her back to China. Her return to Ghana was secret, but her re-engagement in the mining industry attracted the attention of security agencies. She was arrested on a mining-related offence and tried and jailed in 2023. She was jailed for four and a half years after she was found guilty of mining without a licence. Relatedly, the Asantehene, Otumfuo Osei Tutu II, added his voice to complaints over the lack of progress in the fight against galamsey. As the overlord of the Asante kingdom, Otumfuo warmed chiefs leasing lands for unauthorised mining activities to stop the practice or risk destoolment.

In October, the Volta River Authority (VRA) started a controlled release of water from the Akosombo Dam. The authority releases water when the volume in the dam and reservoir threatens the hydro plant. This is usually an annual affair; however, the speed and timing of increased water volumes concerned the manager of the plant. The water release led to flooding in low-lying communities along its course, as Sogakope, Mafi, Mepe, Battor, Ada, and Adidome. The National Disaster Management Organization (NADMO) reported that the floods displaced more than 26,000 individuals. They also destroyed farms, homes, and other possessions. Education was interrupted, and local authorities had to find temporary shelters for the displaced women and children. The government's response to the disaster was slow.

Guinea

Seidu M. Alidu

Guinea confronted significant political and economic developments in 2023. Under the provisional government helmed by General Mamady Doumbouya, following the 2021 military coup that deposed President Alpha Condé, efforts to stabilise governance and lay the groundwork for forthcoming elections were foremost. This era was marked by ambitious political reforms and anti-corruption measures. Despite its abundant bauxite reserves, which underpin the national economy, Guinea continued to struggle with inescapable poverty and a high rate of joblessness, impeding broader economic advancement. There was excessive upheaval in the socio-political atmosphere, as widespread protests demanded better living conditions and an expedited handover to civilian rule. In response, the government initiated several projects aimed at enhancing infrastructure and public services, thereby fostering economic growth and restoring public confidence. To improve its economic prospects, Guinea actively sought to fortify its diplomatic ties with international and regional partners. Thus, 2023 was a year of measured headway as Guinea endeavoured to achieve political stability and economic rejuvenation.

Domestic Politics

General Mamady Doumbouya still retained executive and military control of the administration of Guinea as the sole leader of the military junta and interim president under the umbrella of the Comité national du rassemblement et du développement (CNRD). General Doumbouya's style of leadership has played an effective role as part of his maintaining power, control, and order during this transitional period. This style has been one of a strict military discipline and tact. His priority as acting president has been to eradicate the existence of corruption among government officials and the reconstruction of a new democratic government and civilian rule.

The opposition postponed a 9 March rally to allow for peace discussions, which were mediated by the minister of religious affairs and the imam of Conakry's Grand Mosque. Despite this, demonstrators and security police clashed in Conakry on 14 March, killing one person. The Forces Vives de Guinée (FVG) made a series of demands, including an end to harassment of activists and political leaders, the repeal of the protest prohibition, and restitution for those jailed during pro-democracy marches. Website Guineenews reported on 14 March that some protesters had battled with police personnel in Conakry between the Hamdallaye and Bambeto districts, blocking traffic for nearly an hour. One person was killed during fresh skirmishes and gunfire around midnight.

To recoup stolen assets, the Guinean government initiated several anti-corruption activities in 2023, including inquiries into the financial transactions of former officials. The trial of Ibrahima Kassory Fofana, Mohammed Diane, and Oye Guilavogui, three ministers accused of corruption and misusing public funds, was adjourned by a Guinean court on 14 March due to their non-appearance. The accused believed that because the military had established a partial judiciary, it was not independent and that their arrests were planned, and their absence was intentional. The FVG called off the protests the day before they were scheduled to begin again on 20 March. It presented the government with a list of demands, which included compensating those detained during pro-democracy movements, ending the persecution of activists and political figures, and lifting the prohibition on protests.

The FVG then staged a two-day demonstration on 10 and 11 May, calling for the release of their leaders who were in custody as well as the return of constitutional government. Seven demonstrators lost their lives because of security forces' harsh response to these protests. The FVG demanded that harassment of activists and political leaders stop, that the protest prohibition be lifted, and that those jailed during pro-democracy demonstrations receive compensation. They also accused the government of using excessive force.

The US State Department reported significant cases of human rights violations under General Doumbouya's regime, including but not limited to arbitrary or unlawful arrest and killings, torture, cruel, inhuman, and degrading treatment of civilians by the government, unlawful interference with privacy, and the punishment of family members for alleged offences committed by a relative. There were also reports of gender-based violence, including female genital mutilation, people trafficking, and restriction of freedom of movement and residence. Additionally, reports indicated that overcrowding in prisons across the country was one of the major causes of the deaths of prisoners, besides malnutrition.

On 11 October, Lamine Waraba Sacko, a Rassemblement du Peuple Guinéen (RPG Arc-en Ciel) supporter, was arbitrarily detained by BAC8 Anti-Crime Brigade operatives, according to the US State Department's report. A covert audio recording of Sacko led to charges that he had incited violence. Citing infractions of Criminal Process Code 358, his attorney, Salifou Beavogui, denounced the arrest as illegal. The randomness of Guinea's law enforcement methods was brought to light by this episode.

A total of 12 journalists were arrested by security personnel on 16 October during a demonstration against government censorship organised by the Syndicat des Professionnels de la Presse de Guinée (SPPG), which called on the government to remove limitations on the Guinée Matin news website. This incident brought to light the ongoing difficulties that the media in Guinea faced, including government harassment and censorship, which in turn cause a great deal of self-censorship among journalists. Guinea's journalists had a difficult summer because of intimidation and censorship by the government.

The administration began a few dialogues to promote communication and reconciliation. To address the future of the nation, a platform for national discourse was created that brought together different actors from the political, social, and civil society spheres. Nonetheless, some opposition parties continued to harbour doubts regarding the sincerity of the junta's commitment to inclusive dialogue and a true democratic transition.

There were substantial obstacles and little progress during General Mamady Doumbouya's military-led administration. The country's score in the Freedom House index fell from 34 to 30 out of 100, indicating that problems with civil freedoms and political rights still existed. With scores of 7/40 for political rights and 23/60 for civil freedoms, this decrease was indicative of persistent suppression of the opposition, violent dispersal of demonstrations, and severe media restrictions. Guinea climbed somewhat from 147th to 141st place out of 180 nations on Transparency International's Corruption Perceptions Index despite these set-backs. Attempts to combat systemic corruption targeting former officials were responsible for this slight improvement, although it remained a big problem overall. While the efforts of the transitional government were commendable, they were seen as inadequate and insufficient for a thorough transformation. In general, the political climate was marked by tight military control, limited democratic progress, and ongoing struggles with corruption.

Foreign Affairs

On the diplomatic front, on 11 and 13 September, the Guinean government, in collaboration with the IOM, organised a forum to strengthen strategic collaboration with the Guinean diaspora. The event, chaired by Kabele Soumah, secretary-general of the Ministry of Foreign Affairs, African Integration, and Guineans Living Abroad, brought together 53 presidents of councils representing Guineans living abroad. This collaboration between the Guinean government, IOM, and the EU aimed to pave the way for a sustainable partnership between Guinea and its diaspora, and to mobilise the diaspora for Guinea's socioeconomic development. Discussions focused on the strategic role of the diaspora, opportunities for cultural and technological exchanges, and mechanisms to ensure the protection of the diaspora, and of their investment in Guinea. The collaboration also facilitated the return of Guineans abroad and assisted in setting their lives back on track by creating employment opportunities, small businesses, and career workshops. A few thousand migrants have returned home since being displaced by the coup, through an IOM voluntary return programme.

The 36th AU Summit was held in Addis Ababa, Ethiopia, on 18–19 February, attended by numerous dignitaries, including heads of state such as South African president Cyril Ramaphosa, Kenyan president William Ruto, and Rwandan president Paul Kagame. The AU reiterated its 'zero tolerance' for undemocratic changes of power and maintained the suspension of four countries – Sudan, Mali, Burkina Faso, and Guinea – ruled by military leaders following coups. ECOWAS also decided to maintain sanctions on Mali, Guinea, and Burkina Faso, imposing travel bans on government officials and senior leaders from these countries. The position adopted by the AU to maintain the sanctions on these countries was justified on the basis that the political volatility caused by military coups stood opposed to what AU represents, as it seeks to pressure military-led governments to restore their administrations to civilian rule and thus promote respect for democratic principles on the African continent.

At midday on 21 September, President Mamady Doumbouya addressed the UNGA, highlighting the epidemic of military coups in Africa, particularly in French-speaking countries south of the Sahara. He emphasised that the real putschists were those who manipulated constitutional texts to stay in power indefinitely. Doumbouya justified the September 2021 coup in Guinea as a necessary response aimed at preventing the country from descending into chaos. He criticised the imposed Western democratic models and called for a focus on African solutions, stressing that Africa should not be categorised by foreign powers but should be seen with new eyes. In an indication of the bold assertion of Guinea's position in local governance and foreign affairs, General Doumbouya said that his administration would charter a course of governance based firmly on African agency.

On 19 December, Rwandan minister of state Kabarebe James hosted Soumaila Savané, Guinea's ambassador to Rwanda, in Kigali. Their meeting focused on enhancing bilateral ties and expanding cooperation between Rwanda and Guinea. The two countries have maintained resident missions since their bilateral relations gained momentum in March 2016, marked by President Paul Kagame's official visit to Guinea, where he held discussions with his counterpart. During this visit, significant agreements were signed including the Framework Cooperation Agreement; agreements on diplomatic consultation; visa waivers for certain passport holders; cooperation in health, development planning, and environmental management; and the Bilateral Air Service Agreement (BASA). These agreements underscored the commitment of both nations to deepening collaboration across various sectors, to mutual benefit.

Socioeconomic Developments

Inflation was volatile in Guinea during the year under review, denoting the economic pressures faced in all sectors since the coup and ominously affecting consumer prices and costs of living. The World Bank noted that Guinea had experienced progress in inflation in 2023, as it decreased to 9.3% from the previous year's 11.6%. The decrease can be attributed to the controlling of the volatility in transportation costs and monetary policies instituted after the coup. Albeit that there was some progress in inflationary terms, the budget deficit grew to 1.6% of GDP compared with the previous year's 0.9%. GDP growth was attributable to the implementation of infrastructural projects which increased the gross domestic product by 1.41%. Due to repayment of secured domestic debt, the debt-to-GDP ratio dwindled from 36.7% in 2022 to 35.5% in 2023.

Agriculture remained the driving sector of Guinea's economy, as it was in the previous year. The sector employed more than half of the rural working population of the country, contributing immensely to the income of rural households, which constitute most of the Guinean populace. The Guineans agricultural specialties of rice, maize and cassava yields increased by 5–10% after government and international support programmes were instituted and more modern farming techniques were implemented. In securing a boost to the economy via the agricultural sector, the government made a significant investment in rural infrastructural development such as the construction and maintenance of roads and road networks to improve access to farms and markets.

In farming communities, the Guinean government executed projects to construct facilities for the bulk storage of farm produce and irrigation networks for continuous and reliable supply of water. This push by the state contributed to an increase in infrastructural development, tightening the infrastructural gap. The World Bank

'Macro Poverty Outlook' estimated that the fiscal contribution of agriculture to the Guinean economy would decrease in the next year, from 5% to 3% of GDP, to be replaced by the mining sector.

On 11 July, the Guinean government, represented by the minister of environment and sustainable development, in collaboration with UNDP launched an environmentally sustainable initiative named Guinée forestière. Eight municipalities in Guinea stand to benefit from the project. Koulé, Kokota, Niosomoridou, Diécké, Bignamou, Wassérédou, Gouécké, and Mousadou will all take advantage of the smart integration of climate information and farming practices to achieve yield increases as a result of 97% of all farmlands being irrigated naturally. The project was contracted for five years' duration with a $8.85 m financial package, and was projected to support 651,800 people, cutting the unemployment rate, according to the 2023 UNDP report on Guinea.

Due to agricultural expansion, deforestation has been a major ecological setback for Guinea. This has contributed to intensified land degradation and loss of vegetation. Improper mining practices such as sand winning and improper quarrying have additionally strained the natural resources of Guinea, reducing the capacity of these natural resources to support communities. The launch of Guinée forestière will help to address these ecological predicaments and to strengthen climate resilience, as well as promoting agricultural and mining practices and providing financial aid to empower local communities to protect their environment, according to the IOM.

The HDI evaluated Guinea in 2023 with an overall score of 0.472 compared with its previous year's overall score of 0.468. This minimal increase of 0.004 indicated a negligible improvement in the overall human development metrics. Notwithstanding the progress, the overall score for both years is low, reflecting ongoing challenges in improving the quality of development in Guinea.

Guinea-Bissau

Christoph Kohl

Like previous years, 2023 was characterised by pressure on government critics and media professionals, for which state president Umaro Sissoco Embaló and his entourage were held partly responsible. The authoritarian Embaló continued to interpret the constitution unilaterally in his favour by appointing governments that did not enjoy the support of parliament. The long-awaited parliamentary elections were held in June, more than a year after the dissolution of the legislature, and resulted in a clear victory for the opposition. Once again, Embaló delayed the formation of a government and refused to appoint the leader of the opposition coalition. The president used an alleged coup attempt as a pretext to dissolve parliament once again and install a government that suited him. Guinea-Bissau was able to recover slightly in economic terms, although structural deficits persisted.

Domestic Politics

At the beginning of March, Embaló *reshuffled the government*. He appointed the previous minister of the interior, Sandji Fati, as his defence advisor. Fati was succeeded by Soares Sambu, who had previously been minister for parliamentary affairs. Sambu was in turn succeeded by Malal Sané, a confidant of Embaló. General Armando da Costa became the new head of the secret services, replacing General Celso de Carvalho. On 1 April, education minister Martina Moniz announced her resignation in light of conflicts with school headteachers. Parliamentary elections took place on 4 June. In the run-up to the elections, diasporan Bissau-Guineans complained that the census to update the electoral register was being carried out in only a few places. At the end of April, the Gabinete Técnico de Apoio ao Processo Eleitoral (GTAPE) announced that more than 890,000 citizens had registered for the elections. The UNDP pledged to cover 30% of the election costs; for the first time, Guinea-Bissau would have to bear 70% of the costs – around $10 m – and it was announced at the end of May that the government would have to take out a loan of $2.7 m for this purpose. For the first time, several parties – the União para a Mudança (UM), the Partido da Convergência Democrática (PCD), the Movimento Democrático Guineense (MDG), and the Partido Social-Democrata da Guiné-Bissau (PSD) – formed an electoral alliance under the leadership of the Partido Africano da Independência da Guiné e Cabo Verde (PAIGC). However, in mid-April, at the request of a pro-government party, the Supreme Court prohibited the PAIGC from using the party flag – which historically formed the basis for the national flag – for election campaign purposes. The Supreme Court also objected to the name of the alliance and its symbol; the name ended up being Plataforma Alliança Inclusiva (PAI) – Terra Ranka. The election campaign began on 13 May, with two coalitions and 20 parties competing. In mid-May, human rights activist Fodé Mané spoke of a climate of fear and suspicion. The election result was a slap in the face for President Embaló: the PAIGC coalition won 54 out of 102 seats, the Movimento para a Alternância Democrática (MADEM-G15, Embaló's party) achieved 29 seats, the Partido para a Renovação Social (PRS) ended up with 12 seats, the Partido dos Trabalhadores Guineenses six and the Assembleia do Povo Unido – Partido Democrático da Guiné-Bissau (APU-PDGB), which provided prime minister, Nuno Nabiam, only one seat.

The *convening of the newly elected parliament* was delayed until 27 July. In addition, Embaló repeatedly declared that, as president ('boss'), he alone would head the government. After Embaló rejected the appointment of PAIGC leader Domingos Simões Pereira as prime minister, the latter was elected parliamentary leader. Embaló had already declared on 19 May that he would not appoint either Pereira or Geraldo Martins (also PAIGC) in the event of an election victory. The PAIGC coalition formed a *government* with the PRS and PTG, and only on 8 August did Embaló appoint the former finance minister and confidant of Pereira, Geraldo Martins (PAIGC), as prime minister. On 13 August, Martins presented his government of 19 ministers and 15 state secretaries. Meanwhile, critics once again accused

Embaló of establishing a kind of 'shadow government' by appointing a further six advisors, which Embaló denied.

On 27 September, Embaló announced his intention to run again in the *presidential elections* scheduled for 25 November 2025.

On 19 October, the president of the *Supreme Court*, José Pedro Sambú, was relieved of his duties by the judicial council, the Conselho Superior da Magistratura Judicial, on suspicion of interfering in court proceedings. A few days later, Sambú dismissed the four judges who had obtained his suspension, accusing them of exceeding their competence. On 6 November, however, Sambú announced his resignation from office, citing the presence of armed men outside his home who were preventing him from leaving the building. Pereira in turn accused Embaló of having placed the armed uniformed men outside Sambú's house.

On 1 December, two men in uniform were killed in gunfire between the National Guard and the Presidential Guard. Shortly afterwards, the armed forces declared that they had the situation under control, and Victor Tchongo, head of the National Guard was arrested. According to reports, members of the National Guard had removed two members of the government – finance minister Souleiman Seidi and finance secretary António Monteiro – from a police building on 30 November and taken them to an unknown location. Both were there for questioning by the attorney-general, who is close to Embaló. As in previous years, the finance minister had paid money to companies to settle state debts – around $10 m in 2023 – and this was blown up into a scandal by circles close to Embaló. Both Embaló and his MADEM-G15 party subsequently spoke of a *'coup'*. On 4 December, Embaló dissolved parliament again. Although Prime Minister Martins initially remained in office from 12 December, Embaló took over the interior and defence portfolios. On 13 December, police forces used tear gas to prevent members of parliament from the previous governing coalition from entering the parliament building. On 20 December, Embaló dismissed Martins and appointed Rui Duarte Barros (PAIGC) as his successor, without the consent of the dissolved parliament. The government consisting of 24 ministers and 9 state secretaries on 'presidential initiative' was made up of all parties, but MADEM-G15, APU-PDGB, and PRS were dominant.

Human rights remained under pressure: at the beginning of January, the Liga Guineense dos Direitos Humanos (LGDH) denounced a physical attack on a trader on 30 December 2022 and the inaction of the authorities. Domingos Simões Pereira was again prevented from leaving the country at the beginning of February; in mid-May, he criticised an 'environment of intimidation' on his return from a trip abroad after the roads to the city centre and the PAIGC headquarters were blocked by representatives of the authorities. At the end of February, the media reported that the UNHRC had publicised the questions it had raised in the case of the lawyer and political radio commentator Marcelino Intupé, who had been beaten by gunmen in November 2022, after the Bissau-Guinean government failed to respond. At the beginning of March, the LGDH warned of 'growing signs' of political extremism, particularly in predominantly Muslim eastern Guinea-Bissau, where differences over the interpretation of 'religious commandments' were becoming increasingly frequent. On 3 May, authorities locked down the headquarters of the umbrella union União Nacional dos Trabalhadores da Guiné (UNTG). On 5 May, gunmen attacked political analyst and PRS member Fransual Dias and set his car on fire; Dias accused Embaló of being behind the attack. In an open letter addressed to the interior ministry in October, the LGDH criticised an increase in police violence and accused the government of complicity in atrocities. A short time later, interior minister Adiato Nandigna ordered the immediate arrest of 22 police officers, including a head of department, for allegedly beating a teenager to death in September. In mid-November, PRS member of parliament Farid Fadul accused the Presidential Guard of attacking him for allegedly filming the presidential palace. The PAIGC youth organisation Juventude Africana Amílcar Cabral (JAAC) accused the authorities of arbitrarily arresting several young demonstrators and thus violating their fundamental rights. However, in March, President Embaló announced his intention to punish adults who send children to beg on the streets; this practice, which is promoted by Islamic marabouts, is a problem in many West African countries. Embaló also declared war on the forced marriage of girls – another practice that is widespread primarily among Muslims in the east.

Freedom of the press was also under threat: on 16 April, as it did in 2021, the government ordered the closure of the private radio stations Rádio Sol Mans and Rádio Jovem Bissau, allegedly because they had not paid their licence fees. According to reports, the terrestrial broadcasting of the Portuguese public foreign broadcasters Rádio e Televisão de Portugal (RTP-África) and Rádio Portugal (RDP-África) was suspended from 13 July. The government had ordered the closure of RTP-África after criticising the political reporting of RTP and RDP; government spokesperson Fernando Vaz rejected the accusations and referred to technical problems. In mid-August, 18 months after its closure due to unpaid licence fees, the new government ordered the reopening of the private Rádio Capital, which was known to be critical and had already been raided by gunmen in 2020 and 2022. A media union accused the new government of intimidation on 8 December, and three days later of organising 'censorship' when a new director of the state radio company entered the facility with uniformed personnel at the behest of the state president.

Regarding *security*, in March, Embaló announced that he would 'soon' be stationing a second criminal investigation department (Polícia Judiciária) in the centre of the country; adding to the one in the capital. On 22 July, he inaugurated the country's first military training school in Cumeré, 35 km from Bissau.

Long-standing PRS chair Alberto Nambeia died in Portugal on 25 January. On 24 September, the country celebrated the fiftieth anniversary of its independence;

Embaló pushed ahead with 'militarisation' by introducing 16 November as Armed Forces Day.

Foreign Affairs

Foreign policy highlights included Embaló's *state visits* to France and Portugal: on 26 January, he was received by his French counterpart Emmanuel Macron in Paris. Embaló's visit on 24 October to his Portuguese counterpart Marcelo Rebelo de Sousa, the first since Guinea-Bissau's independence, was met with criticism: the diaspora association Firkidja di Púbis called Embaló an 'authoritarian leader, dictator' who was responsible for human rights violations. At the end of January, an organisation representing the interests of former Bissau-Guinean colonial soldiers had already called on Portugal to keep the promises it made in 1974 (on pensions and Portuguese citizenship).

South–South cooperation also remained important: Guinea-Bissau granted asylum to the former CAR head of state and rebel leader François Bozizé in March. On 17 April, Paul Kagame was the first Rwandan president to visit Guinea-Bissau. In mid-April, nine Bissau-Guinean students were surprised by the outbreak of civil war in Sudan; they managed to return home via Egypt and with the help of Senegal on 3 May. In the run-up to the BRICS summit in South Africa in August, it became known that Guinea-Bissau had expressed an interest in membership.

On 9 July, Guinea-Bissau's chairship of ECOWAS came to an end and was taken over by Nigeria. The ECOWAS summit on 10 December approved the extension of the ECOMIB (ECOWAS Mission in Guinea-Bissau) stabilisation mission; however, the mandate of the mission, which has been (re)deployed since 2022, was supposed to be reviewed.

On 27 August, it was announced that Guinea-Bissau would take over the chairship of the lusophone community of states, the CPLP, for 2025–27.

Socioeconomic Developments

On 29 November, following several reviews, the IMF executive board certified the country's progress under the 26-month ECF worth $38.4 m, agreed on 30 January: the new government was implementing structural reforms to mitigate risks in the energy and financial sectors, maintaining macroeconomic stability, and pursuing fiscal consolidation (salaries, tax revenues, debt management, etc.). The IMF projected economic growth of 4.2% for 2023 (as in 2022) and inflation of 8% (similar to 2022), due to rising international food and fuel prices. The overall fiscal deficit was expected to amount to 5.6% of GDP in 2023, while public debt was expected to decline to 76.5% of GDP. By November, the IMF had released a total of $17.7 m in funds. In mid-September, the government had reported that public debt was at 83% of GDP, breaking the threshold of 70% set by UEMOA. After the cashew crop – cashews are the main export product – was weak in 2022, a strong season was expected for 2023.

Rising costs of living also affected Guinea-Bissau: on 22 August, the government decreed that a (50 kg) bag of rice should be reduced to CFAfr 17,500 (previously around CFAfr 23,000). Intermediaries complained that the reduction came at the expense of their profits. On 4 December, the government decreed a further reduction in the price of rice, while on 28 December the successor government expressed concern about the renewed rise in rice prices (now CFAfr 20,000). On 12 September, the government decreed a reduction in the price of bread from CFAfr 200 to CFAfr 150 from 24 September. However, some bakeries announced a boycott and temporarily stopped bread production. The government ordered the closure of bakeries that opposed the price reduction.

Guinea-Bissau remained dependent on international *development cooperation*, debt relief, and projects. In January, Spain announced the resumption of development cooperation. At the same time, Russia announced that it would be cancelling all of Guinea-Bissau's debts. In April, it was announced that the Global Agriculture and Food Security Programme (GAFSP) launched by the G20 countries would also support vulnerable communities in Guinea-Bissau to improve food resilience. According to reports from August, Guinea-Bissau was to benefit from an ECOWAS programme aimed at reducing youth unemployment through capacity building in the agricultural sector. On 3 December, the World Bank announced that it had provided $266.5 m to improve internet connectivity, including in Guinea-Bissau. At the end of November, the government announced that it had joined the African Export-Import Bank (Afreximbank), a pan-African financial institution under the auspices of the AfDB which provides governments and trade in Africa with loans.

The *exploitation of nature* remained a problem: in January, the destruction of the Mbatonha Park in Bissau, which had been upgraded with EU funds only in 2018, was enforced by police violence. President Embaló defended the replacement construction of a mosque, a hospital, and a school with Turkish support, declaring that the 'national interest' outweighed environmental concerns. In January, Senegalese officials accused the rebels of the Mouvement des Forces Démocratiques de la Casamance (MFDC), which also used Guinea-Bissau as a retreat, of smuggling cannabis and wood. At the beginning of February, a new building for the Instituto Nacional das Actividades de Pesca, which combats illegal fishing, was inaugurated with funding from the EU. According to estimates, West African coastal states, including Guinea-Bissau, lose $2.3 bn in revenue every year due to illegal fishing. Illegal fishing also threatened biodiversity, as the Instituto da Biodiversidade e Áreas Protegidas (IBAP) warned in October. 'Anarchic' logging caused 'extremely worrying' conditions in the forests after the export of logs was banned but logging was permitted again in 2020. There had been no forest inventory since 1983.

Despite 15 years of drug finds in Guinea-Bissau, in which high-ranking military officers have also been involved, Embaló claimed at the end of October that Guinea-Bissau was not a '*drug trafficking* state' and rejected the corresponding accusations of the US.

A case of *state piracy* occurred on 28 August when a fishing boat was seized in Bissau-Guinean waters by the navy of neighbouring Guinea and released only in exchange for the transfer of $25,000 to a Senegalese account, according to the Associação dos Armadores e Industriais de Pesca da Guiné-Bissau (ANAPI).

The supply of *water and electricity* remained precarious: at the beginning of April, reports emerged that around 80% of water wells in the south of the country were not working due to a lack of maintenance; nationally, access to drinking water met only 67% of demand. Bissau was without electricity from 17 October onwards after the Turkish company Karpowership, which operated a power plant ship in the port, stopped supplying electricity. The energy ministry then pledged to immediately settle $6.6 m of the $10 m debt. Karpowership was supplying 30 MW of electricity per month in 2023 at a cost of $3 m. At a financing summit in Dakar in February, the member states of the Organisation pour la Mise en Valeur du Fleuve Gambie (OMVG), including Guinea-Bissau, were granted further financing for hydropower generation.

On 12 April, the government announced the creation of its own *airline*, Guiné-Bissau Airlines, in cooperation with the Canadian company Ajitaa-Aeronautics; the last state-owned airline had gone bankrupt in 1998. In October, the Togolese Asky Airlines announced that it also wanted to fly to Bissau.

Various areas of the public sector went on *strike* over outstanding salaries or additional lines, such as the largest hospital in the country, Simão Mendes Hospital, in March and December and the education sector in March.

Liberia

Aaron Weah

Since the signing of the Accra Comprehensive Peace Agreement, Liberia has had four democratic elections. These elections have transitioned the country away from war to peace, reinstated a constitutional order, and consolidated political parties' structures. They have also enhanced the notion of 'one person, one vote' and emboldened citizens to vote for a candidate of their choosing. Though much has been achieved, embedding an open, transparent, and accountable domestic political system remained a challenge in 2023. There was little public trust in the impartiality of the judiciary, with suspicion of political interference rife. Practices of systematic corruption across the three branches of government were reminiscent of the impunity of the civil war years. The legislature adopted a resolution to investigate war and economic crimes. Public expectations were high that it would explore the correlation between wartime impunity and post-war corruption. Human right challenges also abounded. Prolonged pretrial detention, mysterious deaths, and everyday challenges for people living with disability persisted. At the same time, social economic conditions revealed that the cost of living was surging due to inflation and unstable market conditions. Among the basic commodities affected by price increases were petrol, diesel, and rice (Liberia's staple food). The rising cost of living was exacerbated by a recent wave of fire disasters across Monrovia. The source of these tragic fire incidents is still being investigated, but some have attributed to the power grid and the poor regulation of power supply. More than 34 years since the civil war, the minister of foreign affairs led a new diplomatic intervention to have Liberians living as refugees repatriated.

Domestic Politics

In a context in which more than 20 political parties are registered to contest elections, no single political party in Liberia has been able to win without the strategy of a grand coalition. In 2023, the political opposition's chances of defeating George Weah's Congress for Democratic Party (CDP), a grass-roots political institution with one of the largest populist appeals across the country, at the polls appeared grim following the collapse of the CPP (Collaborating Political Parties). Originally, the CPP coalition had comprised the All Liberia Party (ALP), the Alternative National Congress (ANC), the Liberty Party (LP), and the Unity Party (UP). To make up for this and increase the chances of winning, 2023 started with opposition parties seeking to forge a new alliance.

Alongside this were questions involving the constitutionality of voter registration and challenges to voters' registration. Liberia issued its first biometric voter registration (BVR) during the year. The process was rolled out in two phases. Phase one started with six counties: Bomi, Grand Bassa, Grand Cape Mount, Gbarpolu, Margibi, and Monsterrado. Phase two was used to complete the remaining nine counties. The final register showed 2,498,904 registered electors. Out of this number, 2,471,183 were determined to be active while 27,192 were flagged as duplicates and 529 tagged as suspected underage. Though the BVR was meant to improve effectiveness and accuracy, the process was fraught was controversy. For example, the National Election Commission's (NEC's) voter registration officers denied some potential voters the right to register. These denials were fuelled by the perception that young voters are often trucked from one district to another. Others were denied on the basis of the perception that they were under the voting age. Some were denied due to the perception that they were Sierra Leonean nationals, Guineans, Ivoirians, or Burkinabés who had crossed over the border to enhance the chances of one of the candidates.

The phenomenon of voter trucking, whereby affluent political aspirants provide logistical support and financial reward to eligible voters (mostly young people) to travel from one electoral district to another in order to register and vote, was on the rise, and it lay at the heart of the cost of politics in Liberia. Some candidates have viewed this as provocative and unfair to others who have sought to be transparent, fair, and patriotic in the exercise of their civil and political rights. This led to violent clashes during the period of voter registration.

Some of the major political parties organised youth militants into brigade-like formations. Young Liberians, some of them first-time voters and most of them born after the Accra Comprehensive Peace Agreement, have been mobilized around ideas of militancy by party leaderships, the latter belonging to the pre-war generation of Liberian society. The primary role of these so-called militants is to instil fear in the hearts and minds of their respective political opponents. News reports suggested that vandalism of campaign materials, political rallies, and scuffles over the double scheduling of presidential rallies were often led or instigated by these militants. Some conflicts turned violent and led to the destruction of property, injuries, and deaths. Four people were confirmed dead in a violent dispute involving the Congress for Democratic Change (CDC) and the UP in Foya and Konia, Lofa County. Violence and disputes flared up in other counties, including Nimba, Grand Gedeh, and Grand Cape Mount. These disputes led to an increase in court cases. This was Liberia's first election since the departure of the UN Mission in Liberia, ECOWAS, and the AU Elections Observation Mission. To ameliorate tensions, Goodluck Jonathan held closed-door meetings with the NEC and political parties as well as the leading contenders, Joseph Nyuma Boakai and George Weah. These diplomatic interventions ultimately helped Weah concede defeat to the UP, setting in motion a seamless transition from one government to another with Boakai's inauguration at the start of 2024.

In a tightly contested poll, Boakai defeated Weah with 50.64% of the valid votes cast. The marginal difference exposed not just the fractures in Liberia's post-war politics but the challenges in governing a society divided straight down the middle. The divisions portrayed during the elections were reproduced in the legislature. In the House of Representatives (HoR), the CDC, formerly the ruling party, won 24 seats while the Unity Party (UP), though now the ruling party, won ten. Somewhere in the middle was the independent bloc, with the rise of independent representatives revealing a certain level of distrust between the electorate and political parties. Survey research measuring trust has shown that CSOs and religious institutions have the highest levels of trust in the country, while key organs of the state, including the legislature, are trusted by less than 50% of people (SCORE Index Liberia). The 2023 Afrobarometer survey revealed that the majority of the electorate (61%) claim that representatives and senators are not accountable to their constituents after election, while 55% maintain that elections provide an adequate opportunity to remove those who are less accountable. As a consequence of the electorate's decision to vote in greater numbers for independent candidates, no political party could gain an absolute majority to influence policy change without consensus building.

The rule of law was central on the agenda of judicial reform, picking up from where former president Ellen Johnson Sirleaf left off. The implementation of rule of law was envisioned as a means of reinstituting a culture of accountability, to dismantle the culture of impunity left in the wake of the civil war. Reform of the judiciary was expected to tackle the growing trend of human rights violation. The Independent National Commission of Human Rights of Liberia (INCHRL) uncovered patterns of systematic human rights abuses, with violations such as prolonged pretrial detention, poor-quality and unsafe detention facilities, rape and other sexual violence, and occurrences of mysterious deaths. Investigation revealed that mysterious deaths in the western and south-eastern parts of the country were linked to a pattern of enforced disappearances. In a few incidents, victims who had disappeared were found with body parts removed. The INCHRL determined that some of the mysterious deaths were ritualistically motivated. One of these incidents involved the Liberia National Police (LNP). The victim was arrested and held in police custody for investigation; he was later discharged but never made it home, and was then found dead with body parts extracted. The INCHRL filed a petition before the LNP's Professional Standards Division (PSD) asking for a statement on the matter. The failure by the state to apprehend perpetrators and bring them to justice further revealed some of the challenges in the executive and judiciary branches of government. The INCHRL report also highlighted the level of neglect and social stigmatisation of people living with disability (PwD) and those affected by mental illness. PwD and mental health issues remained among the most intractable human rights issues in Liberia. Liberians in these categories suffered from discrimination, social stigmatisation, and cruel, degrading, and inhumane treatment. These human rights problems persisted without any meaningful remedy in sight, according to the INCHRL. In a related development, the government filed a case of aggravated assault and attempted murder against a US missionary, Lucas Richards. Richards, involved in an extra-marital affair with Jessica Lloyd, the alleged victim, was accused of her attempted murder in September 2023. The case garnered significant public interest. The judge of Criminal Court B ruled that the prosecutor had insufficient evidence to find the defendant guilty. However, 'Frontpage Africa' reported a leaked audio recording in which settlement was discussed, in collusion between the prosecution and defence lawyers. In response to this development, Moima Briggs Mensah, representative of District 6 in Bong County, declared the verdict disturbing. She called for a joint committee on the judiciary and gender to review the matter.

Foreign Affairs

In 2023, Liberia appeared in the international press for two reasons in particular. One involved the Israeli–Palestinian conflict in Gaza while the other related to diplomats' involvement in sex abuse scandals.

On 12 December, Liberia, along with ten other countries including the US, voted against the ceasefire in the Gaza. Sarah Safyn Fyneah, ambassador and permanent representative of Liberia to the UN, explained that the decision was based on the directives of Dee-Maxwell Saah Kemayah, the Liberian foreign minister. In a latter communication, Ambassador Fyneah clarified that Kemayah's position contradicted that of President George Weah. She made this clarification in a press statement exonerating herself of what appeared to have been a diplomatic blunder. In a context where South Africa filed a case against Israel in the ICJ on 29 December, the support for Israel military aggression against Palestine shown by Liberia – the only African country to take this stance – was unpopular.

In another development, President George Weah dismissed deputy minister Henry Fahnbulleh. Fahbulleh's dismissal was linked to his intervention in addressing a rape allegation against foreign minister Kemayah, who had previously served as ambassador as part of Liberia's permanent mission at the UN. Wynee Cummings, a female member of staff in the permanent mission, accused Kemayah of having committed sexual assault while he served as ambassador.

Meanwhile, Moses Browne, Liberia's permanent representative to the Maritime Office of the IOM, and Daniel Tarr, an official of the IOM, were accused of sexual assault against two young Korean girls. The two officials had made contact with the girls during a trip to Seoul, South Korea, for official government business, and were accused of behaviours that were determined to be inappropriate and in contravention of Korean laws. On 5 April, a court in Busan, Korea, found both Browne and Tarr guilty of sexual assault and sentenced them each to nine years. Families of the convicted officials pleaded with President Weah to intervene in the scandal to have the two officials brought back home. In particular, the mother of Browne pleaded with Weah to have her son released. The government of Liberia engaged with the Republic of Korea through official diplomatic channels to explore other options pertaining Browne and Tarr, but all efforts proved futile.

In other developments, Liberia issued a new regulation on diplomatic passports. This regulation sort to modify an earlier regulation initiated in 2016. The earlier regulation set the expiry date of a diplomatic passport at two years, while the new regulation, under the leadership of minister Kemayah, extended it to six years. The criteria stipulating who is entitled to carry a diplomatic passport were also changed. The original criteria had stipulated that diplomats' children were entitled to carry diplomatic passports as long as the children were below the age of 18. Children over 18 were not eligible. Minister Kemayah's modification of this rule allowed the children of diplomats to carry diplomatic passports even once aged 18 years and above.

Socioeconomic Developments

Liberia's economy was still reeling from the effects of Ebola and Covid-19 – themselves only the latest events in ten years during which the country has been in a state of flux, influenced by a convergence of geopolitical crises, regional developments, and domestic challenges. These circumstances have had an adverse impact on social wellbeing and economic growth. In particular, they have impacted the cost of living in the form of commodity prices.

However, in 2023, the 4.8% growth rate, as well as a projection of 5.6% for 2024, revealed an economy on the rebound. Economic analysis determined that the macroeconomic conditions were expected to become more favourable. The mining sector was expected to expand, likewise services and the agriculture sub-sector. Coming out of an election year, inflation was expected to ease in 2024 due to a stable exchange rate and the calm of non-electoral activities.

Yet prices of basic commodities increased, and Liberia's Central Bank estimated that GDP growth would have declined from 4.8% in 2022 to 4.5% in 2023. Worse still, inflation rose sharply from 7.6% in 2022 to 10.5% in 2023. The rise in inflation was attributed to the rise in domestic food prices in the global market on fuel prices. In July, the price of imported rice increased: this raising of the cost of the national staple food was attributed to an increase in global rice prices, leading to a certain level of scarcity and food security concerns. The devaluation of the Liberian currency further exacerbated economic conditions, $1 now being equivalent to 195.39 Liberian dollars. The devaluation placed pressure on communities. At the same time, reports showed that the deplorable state of the roads in rural Liberia remained a constant factor in the rising cost of vehicle maintenance, repair, and rental.

Fire disasters were on the rise in Liberia, imposing further hardship on families and communities. In late 2023 and continuing into 2024, churches, homes, and businesses were razed to the ground. Communities impacted by this growing trend included West Point Township, Central Monrovia, Old Road, Paynesville, Garnerville, and Bushrod Island. Fire disasters in these communities rendered families homeless and lacking in personal effects. Effective corrective action will entail significant reform: essentially, it would have deal with some of the dysfunctions left in the wake of the civil war. The response times of the fire department are revealing of the fact that Liberia's post-war reform prioritised some institutions believed to be more important than others. The National Fire Service was not among the key agencies that benefited from the security sector reform programme, and beyond one central office and location, the fire department has not evolved logistically. The service was largely centralised in downtown Monrovia, without the operational ability to operate effectively throughout Monrovia and across the country. Monrovia, originally designed and built to accommodate 350,000 people, is now host to one-third of the country's 5.3 m population, following a surge in rural to urban migration after the war. This has led to systematic overpopulation in almost every neighbourhood. Failure to implement zoning laws has led to squatters erecting structures haphazardly, including makeshift structures placed in alleyways, some of which are meant to be used as routes in the case of emergencies. Systematic reform will be necessary to render the fire department efficient and make neighbourhoods safe again.

Mali

Bruce Whitehouse

The Malian government strengthened its position both domestically and internationally in 2023, cementing its authority and muzzling dissent at home while rebuffing pressure from abroad to accelerate the country's transition to democratic rule. Violence by armed jihadi groups persisted, however, and conflict resurged between government security forces and ethnic Tuareg rebels in the country's northern regions. The Malian government stepped up its criticism of UN peacekeeping operations in the country and demanded the departure of UN troops. The mission's withdrawal during the final months of the year removed many constraints on the government's ability to set its own security agenda. The government pursued new international partnerships and sought to further remove the country from the influence of France, its former colonial ruler. Yet Mali's priority of asserting its sovereignty, while popular domestically, came with economic costs, and the national economy remained fragile and the country's people insecure.

Domestic Politics

Mali's *military government worked to consolidate its power* in defiance of international criticism and pressure to cede power to a democratically elected regime. Led by president Assimi Goïta and his civilian prime minister Choguel Kokalla Maïga, the government sought to establish a new constitution that further centralised power in the hands of an already powerful presidency. After the new draft constitution was presented to the public in February, a coalition of Muslim civil society leaders opposed it because it maintained postcolonial Mali's status as a secular republic. A referendum on the draft, originally scheduled for March, was finally held in June. The government claimed that 97% of voters had approved the document and that 38% of voters had participated in the referendum, but independent observers estimated turnout to be much lower. The new constitution, according the head of state the authority to dictate policy and dissolve parliament, was officially adopted in July. In addition to buttressing presidential power, it established a new senate and downgraded the status of French from 'official language' to 'working language'. Although the government reported that the June referendum had been run smoothly, in September a regime spokesperson announced that presidential elections which had been scheduled for February 2024 would be indefinitely postponed for 'technical reasons'. The government remained popular at home, but this postponement stoked concerns among pro-democracy activists and foreign governments about the prospects for the country's return to civilian rule.

Violence by armed jihadi groups, against both government and civilian targets, caused significant disruption and destruction throughout the year, mainly in central and northern regions of the country. Most of this violence was attributed to Jama'a Nusrat al-Islam wa-l-Muslimin (JNIM, or Group to Support Islam and Muslims) and ISGS. A report by HRW alleged that hundreds of civilians had been killed and tens of thousands displaced in ISGS attacks taking place in the northern regions of Gao and Menaka during the first half of the year. In August, a report by UN experts said that the area of Malian territory under ISGS control had nearly doubled between mid-2022 and mid-2023. JNIM forces also constituted a severe danger throughout central and northern Mali. They assaulted a large military base in the central town of Sévaré in April, briefly occupied another near Gao in September, and attacked a large passenger vessel on the Niger River in September, killing at least 60 civilians. JNIM also blockaded the northern town of Timbuktu from August to December, preventing goods from reaching inhabitants and repeatedly shelling the city's airport. In November, suspected jihadi fighters kidnapped about 40 civilians from a bus near the central town of Bankass. Analysis by ACLED (the Armed Conflict Location & Event Data Project) estimated that the level of violence against Malian civilians between January and August was 38% higher than during the same period of the previous year.

Amid diminishing UN presence in Mali (see next section), long-stalled peace talks between ethnic Tuareg rebels and the government finally collapsed and *violence between Tuareg rebels and the Malian army intensified*. The Coalition des Mouvements de l'Azawad (CMA, or Coalition of Azawad Movements), the umbrella organisation representing Tuareg-dominated separatists who had fought in 2011–12 for an independent state in northern Mali named 'Azawad', withdrew from constitutional talks with the government in January. The following month, three of the CMA's largest component groups merged to form a new alliance, the Cadre stratégique permanent or CSP. Government security forces arrested 12 CMA members in north-eastern Mali in April, accusing them of terrorism, while Malian air force jets (recently acquired from Russia) flew low over the northern town of Kidal and other Tuareg strongholds, a bold show of force in regions from which the Malian military had been absent for several years. In August, amid escalating tensions, the CMA withdrew its representatives from Bamako and fighting was reported between government and CMA forces in a few locations in the north. CSP forces began attacking government military bases and patrols throughout northern Mali in September. In early October, a large convoy including Malian army and Russian troops (believed to be working for the semi-private Wagner Group) departed the northern city of Gao bound for rebel-held Kidal. Fighting and airstrikes began in Kidal in early November, and by 14 November, Malian and Russian forces had occupied the town. The government celebrated the taking of Kidal as a major victory, and President Goïta promised to continue the military offensive until the government had control over all Malian territory. Later in November, a court in Bamako opened an investigation into alleged money laundering by CMA and JNIM leaders. In December, CSP-affiliated fighters blocked the major roads linking northern Mali with Algeria, Mauritania, and Niger. By late December, all armed groups that had signed the Algiers peace accord with the Malian government in 2015 had withdrawn from it and called for international mediation. In Bamako, however, President Goïta announced a new peace process without foreign involvement – one that would guarantee the country's territorial integrity, national unity, and state secularism. The CMA refused to participate in this process.

As the tempo of Malian military operations increased, *losses of government aircraft* mounted only months after Mali's air force had acquired several new planes and helicopters from Russia. An army helicopter crashed in Bamako in April, killing its three crew members and injuring at least nine civilians on the ground. In September, Tuareg rebels released photographs of two air force jets that they claimed to have shot down over northern Mali, and a large Russian-built cargo plane registered to the Malian air force crashed upon landing at the Gao military airport, killing all aboard. Despite the existence of photos and video footage of these crashes, the government neither acknowledged the losses nor announced casualty figures.

While the government's military offensive was broadly supported by members of the Malian public, especially in Bamako and other major cities, *government authorities cracked down on domestic critics.* A prominent civil society activist and media commentator, Mohamed Youssouf Bathily, was arrested and imprisoned in March after blaming the government for the death in detention of former prime minister Soumeylou Boubèye Maïga. In April, journalist Aliou Touré disappeared shortly after holding a press conference calling for Bathily's release. August saw a Malian social media influencer, Rokia Doumbia, fined and imprisoned for criticising the military's failure to quell insecurity and high inflation. That same month, a blogger and radio station owner named Abdoul Niang was arrested in Bamako and later charged with defamation and making false statements about the justice system. He was freed on bail to await trial. Days later, a political activist named Adama Diarra, formerly an outspoken supporter of the military regime, was arrested after expressing his disagreement with its decision to postpone elections. Diarra was sentenced to prison in September for impugning the credibility of the government. In December, police arrested a Muslim cleric, Chouala Bayaya Haïdara, after he characterised the detention of government critics as unjustified. At year's end, Bathily, Doumbia, Diarra, and Haïdara remained imprisoned; the whereabouts of Touré was unknown.

Foreign Affairs

Mali's military regime pursued its strategy, initiated in 2021, of distancing the country from many of the states and multilateral organisations upon which it had formerly relied for economic and security assistance. Tensions persisted or mounted between Mali and foreign governments and regional bodies that criticised the Malian military's human rights record and reluctance to organise elections. This dynamic was especially acute regarding *the UN Multidimensional Integrated Stabilisation Mission in Mali* (MINUSMA), the multinational peacekeeping force mandated in 2013 to enhance security and protect civilians in the country. In February, the Malian government expelled MINUSMA's human rights director from the country after his division had released reports and organised testimony at a January hearing of the UNSC that were critical of the Malian military's human rights record. Subsequent UN reports called attention to increasing levels of violence in Mali during the previous year and accused Malian and Russian combatants of killing over 500 civilians in the central town of Moura in 2022. Anti-MINUSMA demonstrations were held in Bamako and other cities in the first half of the year, fuelled by popular discontent with the UN mission. On 16 June, citing a lack of trust between its officials and the mission, the Malian government demanded that MINUSMA be withdrawn from Mali 'without delay'. On 30 June, the UNSC unanimously voted to terminate the mission's mandate, announcing that its withdrawal would be completed by the end of the year. UN peacekeepers began evacuating their bases in central and northern Mali in August, turning them over to government security forces. Approximately 1,000 UN personnel left Kidal hurriedly in October as the government's military offensive closed in on the town. At least 39 peacekeepers were injured by roadside bombs during their ground evacuation after the Malian government barred the UN from flying out its personnel or receiving air support. MINUSMA completed its pull-out from the country by late December.

Malian relations with other regional bodies and Western donor governments were similarly strained. In February, ECOWAS rejected overtures from Mali, *Guinea*, and *Burkina Faso* (all three of which the organisation had earlier suspended following military coups) to be readmitted to the organisation. While the regional body lifted economic sanctions against Mali, it chose to impose a travel ban on top Malian officials. The *AU* similarly refused to reinstate Mali to the organisation in February. The *EU*, formerly a major funder of development and security sector assistance in Mali, levied sanctions on the head of Wagner Group operations in Mali, as did the *UK* and *US* governments. The US Treasury Department also sanctioned a number of Malian army officers over their facilitation of Wagner Group operations and their alleged participation in crimes against civilians. US officials expressed concern over the end of MINUSMA, citing potentially adverse humanitarian consequences for the Malian people. Mali's relations with *France* remained marked by mutual antagonism. Malian officials asked the UNSC not to use France as the sponsor of Mali-related resolutions in March. In August, the French government stopped issuing visas at its consulate in Mali, a move which the Malian government quickly reciprocated. In September, France suspended the issuance of student visas for applicants in Mali, Burkina Faso, and *Niger*, and French foreign ministry officials asked concert venues in France not to host artists from the three countries. In December, Mali withdrew from a long-standing double taxation treaty with France, as did Niger.

In contrast, the Malian government continued its campaign to build stronger ties with several non-Western partners, especially *Russia*. Russian foreign minister Sergey Lavrov visited Bamako in February and December, while President Goïta attended the Russia–Africa summit in St Petersburg in July. Russia delivered significant military aid to Mali and arranged to send supplies of fertiliser and wheat. Russian officials announced the creation of nearly 300 university scholarships for Malian students at Russian universities, planned a new high-capacity gold refinery, and expressed interest in the construction of a power-generating nuclear reactor in Mali. Russia also provided diplomatic support to Mali in the UNSC, most prominently by vetoing a French resolution to renew UN sanctions against Mali in August. *China* sold military equipment, including dozens of armoured vehicles, to Mali in March, and in December, following a visit to Beijing by Malian foreign minister

Abdoulaye Diop, it promised to eliminate most of its import duties on Malian goods. Mali took delivery of military drones from *Türkiye* in February. Malian officials also discussed enhanced economic cooperation with *Iran*: Colonel Sadio Camara, Mali's minister of defence, travelled to Tehran in June to discuss bilateral relations and arms purchases.

The country also established closer diplomatic and military cooperation with neighbouring *Burkina Faso*, and in January the two countries discussed prospects for political federation. After a military coup toppled the civilian president of *Niger* in July, the governments of Mali and Burkina Faso expressed solidarity with the Nigérien coup leaders. With all three countries now under military rule and facing similar threats from armed jihadi groups, especially in their shared border region, they moved to form a security alliance. In August, the Malian military sent combat aircraft to Niger, ostensibly to help defend the new Nigérien regime against threatened military intervention by ECOWAS. Speaking at the UNGA the following month, foreign minister Diop warned against any ECOWAS attack on Niger. The presidents of Mali, Burkina Faso, and Niger announced the establishment of the *Alliance des États du Sahel* (Alliance of Sahelian States, AES) in September, with the goal of facilitating military cooperation and coordination as well as closer diplomatic and commercial ties among the three countries. They framed the alliance as a step towards greater sovereignty and opposing neocolonial (i.e., French) influence. The three presidents met in November to discuss the possibility of creating a new regional bank and airline and establishing a monetary union. In December, their prime ministers attended a rally in Niger to encourage public support for the tripartite alliance. The foreign ministers of Mali, Burkina Faso, and Niger met in Marrakesh later that month to discuss an economic and political alliance linking their three countries more closely with *Morocco*.

Malian relations with its southern neighbour, *Côte d'Ivoire*, remained under strain following Mali's detention of 49 members of the Ivoirian military in 2022 for allegedly seeking to overthrow the Malian government. The Ivoirians were pardoned by President Goïta and returned home in January following mediation by ECOWAS and the president of *Togo*. Ties with Mali's northern neighbour, *Algeria*, grew increasingly tense as Algerian leaders, hoping to forestall renewed fighting on their southern border, sought to reinvigorate Mali's peace process formalised under the 2015 Algiers accord. Algeria's foreign minister travelled to Bamako in April to discuss the future of the peace process with President Goïta, and both governments signalled their commitment to relaunching the process. After Algeria received a delegation representing various Tuareg rebel groups in December, however, the Malian government summoned the Algerian ambassador in Bamako to protest what it characterised as Algeria's interference in Mali's internal affairs. Both countries subsequently recalled their ambassadors.

Socioeconomic Developments

Mali's economy remained frail, partly due to the lingering effects of international sanctions implemented the previous year, many of which were not eased until several months into 2023. A report by the World Bank estimated Mali's annual economic growth at only 1.8%, with inflation at 9.1%. Foreign aid, which had previously constituted up to 15% of Mali's gross national income, became scarce as many donor governments reduced or ended their aid programmes in the country, and Mali's new foreign partners were unable to reverse this trend. Nonetheless, some significant inflows of aid remained. In June, the World Bank inaugurated new aid programmes worth CFAfr 131 bn ($217 m) for projects pertaining to land reclamation and the improved collection of economic statistics.

In *infrastructure development*, the AfDB allocated $33 m for the construction of power lines connecting Mali to planned solar energy projects in Mauritania. Consumer electricity delivery grew increasingly erratic throughout the year as Energie du Mali (EDM), the state-owned power utility company, was beset by financial woes stemming from rising fuel costs and heavy demand. In the transport sector, the Malian government relaunched passenger rail traffic between Bamako and the western city of Kayes following a five-year suspension of service. However, this traffic was interrupted again after only five months by a train derailment and had not been resumed by year's end.

In the *industrial sector*, in February the Malian government announced plans to relaunch COMATEX, a parastatal textile company which had ceased production at least five years earlier. In the *mining sector*, foreign investors expressed concern after the government drew up a new mining code that proposed to raise Mali's required national stake in mining interests from 20% to 35%. Existing gold and lithium mines were to be exempted from the change. In March, the government began reviewing industrial mining contracts already in effect, with the aim of renegotiating their terms. Gold production for the year was estimated at 72.5 tonnes, up 0.3 tonnes from 2022. Development continued of new lithium mines in Bougouni and Goulamina. The mine at Goulamina, operated by the Australian company Leo Lithium, inaugurated production in June, but the government halted raw lithium exports in September pending a new round of negotiations with the company.

In *agriculture*, national cotton production reached an estimated 690,000 tonnes in 2023, down from 760,000 in 2022 but still securing first place for Mali among West African cotton-producing countries. The Malian grain harvest was estimated at 10.9 m tonnes, up 6% from 2022.

In *social affairs*, food insecurity increased due to violence and inflation. A report by the WFP and FAO listed Mali among several countries at rising risk of food emergency, and UNICEF estimated that 1 m children in the country faced acute malnutrition and 200,000 faced death by starvation. As unprecedented electricity outages caused rising frustration across the country, the path towards greater security and social harmony remained highly uncertain. Many schools closed due to political violence and insecurity, especially in central and northern regions of the country; by year's end, these closures affected nearly 500,000 Malian children.

Mauritania

Baba Adou

Legislative, regional, and municipal elections were held in May. The ruling party and its allies secured a landslide victory, positioning President Mohamed Ould Cheikh El Ghazouani for a potential second term. The year-long trial of former president Mohamed Ould Abdel Aziz concluded with a five-year sentence for corruption-related charges. Ten co-defendants also received varying sentences. Meanwhile, more than 15,000 Mauritania immigrants made their way to the US through its southern border, and a violent prison break by four jihadist inmates almost disrupted the country's successful record of countering terrorism. On the foreign affairs level, Mauritania continued to maintain regular relations with its neighbours despite changing regional alliances following a wave of military coups in the Sahel and West Africa. The G5 Sahel, the regional bloc that Mauritania helped to found, was crippled due to the withdrawal of four members, three of them having taken the coordinated decision to leave in 2023. Despite promising energy prospects and declining inflation, Mauritania witnessed slow economic growth in 2023. Food insecurity impacted 16% of the population in the year.

Domestic Politics

On 25 January, former president (2008–19) Mohamed Ould Abdel Aziz and ten co-defendants, including former ministers, businesspeople, and family members, went on trial. Abdel Aziz faced charges of abusing his office, illicit enrichment, money laundering, and nepotism during his time in office. On 4 December, the trial culminated in a five-year sentence for Abdel Aziz, who was found guilty of charges of money laundering and using his office to unlawfully enrich himself but was cleared of other allegations. The prosecutor had asked for a 20-year sentence. Throughout the trial, the ex-president consistently asserted his innocence, emphasising that he was being targeted for his attempts to re-enter the political sphere. A few weeks before he went on trial, Abdel Aziz had lashed out against the current president, Mohamed Ould Cheikh El Ghazouani. In a 90-minute-long Facebook Live address, he criticised the current president, expressing regret for supporting him in the 2019 elections and describing it as a significant mistake.

Mauritania had maintained its status as a security exception in the volatile Sahel region: since 2011, the country had not reported any terrorist attacks. However, this streak of successful anti-terrorism efforts was abruptly halted in March. Four jihadist inmates managed to escape from the central prison in the capital Nouakchott, during which they killed two prison guards and injured two others. Their attempt to flee to neighbouring Mali was thwarted when their pick-up truck broke down in the desert, drawing the attention of local nomads. A confrontation between the army and the fugitives ensued in the desert, hundreds of kilometres from Nouakchott, resulting in the death of one gendarme and three of the escapees. The fourth fugitive was captured with minor injuries. This week-long crisis laid bare the vulnerability of Mauritania's security image. Adding to the complexity, a pick-up truck laden with explosives, believed to be from northern Mali and connected to the prison escape, was discovered parked in a neighbourhood in Nouakchott. On 26 March, the police said that they had arrested the man they believed to be the mastermind behind the prison escape attempt. Other than this incident, the country generally remained relatively stable and secure within the volatile Sahel region.

In May, Mauritania held its first legislative, regional, and municipal elections since President Ghazouani came to power in 2019. The elections were viewed as a test for Ghazouani ahead of the 2024 presidential elections and resulted in a landslide victory for the ruling party Insaf and other pro-Ghazouani parties. The first round took place on 13 May, with approximately 1.8 m voters participating to select candidates for the 176 seats in the National Assembly, 13 regional councils, and 238 municipal councils. The results of both rounds gave Insaf a sweeping majority, securing 107 out of 176 seats in the National Assembly as well as control of all 13 regional councils and two-thirds of the municipalities. Ten other parties allied with the presidential majority secured 42 seats, while the remaining 27 went to opposition parties. Despite allegations of fraud and irregularities, the opposition participated in the second round and continued to engage in parliamentary activities. In July, the new deputies elected retired general Mohamed Ould Meguett, former chief of staff of the armies, as the new head of the National Assembly with an overwhelming majority. This reflected a trend of significant military influence in Mauritanian politics, with key positions held by military personnel since at least 2018, including the presidency, the head of the National Assembly, and the minister of national defence. Following the elections, President Ghazouani appointed a new government, the fourth since he came to power in 2019. Prime Minister Mohamed Ould Bilal retained his position, which he has held since August 2020, while nine new ministers joined the cabinet. The remaining ministers either retained their positions or were reassigned. Similarly to Ghazouani's previous cabinet reshuffles, these changes did not indicate a significant shift in policy or personnel.

In 2023, thousands of Mauritanians crossed the Mexican border into the US, with US government data, as reported by the 'New York Times', indicating that over 15,000 individuals were apprehended at the southern border. This surge made Mauritania the leading African country in terms of the total number of migrants to the US, a notable figure considering that the country's population is less than 5 m. Despite the surge of immigrants making headlines, the Mauritanian government was mostly silent on the issue. In November, however, the US embassy in Nouakchott announced on its website that it had worked with the Mauritanian government to repatriate a significant number of individuals lacking legal authorisation to stay in the US. The embassy highlighted that in recent years, thousands of Mauritanians had undertaken the dangerous journey to the US, locally known as 'jumping the wall'. The repatriation flights, according to the embassy, were aimed at sending a clear message to those involved in illegal immigration that they would face life-threatening risks and would be promptly returned. The embassy commended the active cooperation of the Mauritanian government, indicating its commitment to international obligations.

The US's 2023 'Country Reports on Human Rights Practices' noted no significant change in the human rights situation in Mauritania, highlighting persistent issues such as arbitrary or unlawful killings, harsh prison conditions, and arbitrary arrest and detention. At least three cases related to police violence dominated the news in 2023. On 10 February, the death of human rights activist Souvi Ould Cheine while in police custody sparked outrage. While the death was initially attributed by the police to natural causes, his family confirmed signs of torture on his body. An autopsy revealed a neck fracture and signs of possible suffocation as potential causes of death, leading to the arrest of police officers and agents involved. On 14 September, 11 defendants were referred for trial before the Criminal Court for the murder of the activist. In May, protests erupted following the death of Oumar

Diop after police arrested him. The Public Prosecutor's Office in the region of Nouakchott-Ouest concluded that the final forensic report, conducted in Morocco, indicated that the death had been caused by cardiac arrest resulting from excessive consumption of cocaine mixed with alcohol. Following the release of this report, the family decided to proceed with the burial but continued to reject the results. In a press conference held in Nouakchott on 12 June, the family and their lawyers stated that Diop had been tortured and had died before being taken to the hospital. Police also killed another young man in Boghé in eastern Mauritania during a protest that occurred following the death of Diop. The family and their lawyers held a press conference on 13 May in which they vowed to pursue justice despite government pressure to close the case. The family accused Mauritanian authorities of sending deputies and tribal chiefs to pressure them instead of investigating the death, claiming that the victim had been buried without their consent. The minister of the interior and decentralisation announced an investigation into the murder.

On 2 October, imams and religious leaders protested in front of the parliament in Nouakchott against a draft bill addressing violence against women, claiming that it contradicted Islamic principles, despite the government's assurances that it did not. The bill, named 'Karama' ('dignity' in Arabic), was a revised version of a gender law that MPs had previously rejected twice before being put up for a vote. The government claimed that the new law adhered to Sharia and had been submitted to the National Fatwa Council for review.

Foreign Affairs

The year was marked by regional instability, significantly influencing Mauritania's foreign relations both regionally and globally. The wave of military coups that swept the Sahel region led to the incapacitation of the G5 Sahel regional bloc, headquartered in Nouakchott. Following the withdrawal of Mali from the G5 Sahel in May 2022, Mauritania and other member states continued their efforts to keep the organisation functioning and to bring Mali back into the fold. During a speech in Nouakchott on 10 July, President Ghazouani called on Malian authorities to rejoin the G5 Sahel and its joint force. Ghazouani expressed regret over Mali's withdrawal, noting that it disrupted the geographical continuity and deprived the G5 Sahel of Mali's valuable contributions. He expressed hope that the withdrawal would be only temporary.

However, the withdrawal was not temporary. In fact, two other member states, Niger and Burkina Faso, followed in the footsteps of Mali, leaving Mauritania and Chad alone in the regional organisation. On 6 December, the two remaining member states released a joint statement respecting the sovereign decisions of the departing countries. They affirmed their dedication to carrying out the necessary steps outlined in the G5 Sahel founding convention, specifically mentioning Article 20, which permits the dissolution of the alliance if requested by at least three member states.

The year also witnessed the increasing influence of Russian presence in the Sahel, with three Sahelian countries, Mali, Niger, and Burkina Faso, cutting ties with France and strengthening diplomatic and military cooperation with Russia. While maintaining relations with Russia, Mauritania aligned with the West and officially criticised the prevalent anti-French sentiments in the Sahel. Russian minister of foreign affairs Sergey Lavrov visited Nouakchott on 8 February and met with President Ghazouani. During a press conference with his Mauritanian counterpart, Lavrov expressed Russia's support for Mauritania in its fight against jihadists. This was despite the fact that in March 2022, Mauritania had supported a UN resolution calling for Russia to immediately halt its military operations in Ukraine, in contrast to many African nations that either abstained or chose not to participate in the vote. Additionally, Lavrov announced plans to diversify trade and economic ties between the two countries and confirmed that President Ghazouani would participate in the Russia–Africa summit in St Petersburg in July, although in the event, prime minister Mohamed Ould Bilal participated in the summit instead of Ghazouani.

Meanwhile, Mauritania continued to strengthen its relations with the EU, France, and the US. In an interview with the French newspaper 'Le Figaro' on 29 September, Ghazouani remarked that Africa's expectations from France were excessive, potentially contributing to rising anti-French sentiments in some Francophone countries. He emphasised that this sentiment was exacerbated by 'virulent populism', particularly through social media.

Relations between Mauritania and the EU were dominated by immigration, the economy, and aid cooperation. European Commission president Ursula von der Leyen and President Ghazouani launched a new Team Europe Initiative on the eve of the Global Gateway Forum in Brussels on 25 and 26 October. This initiative, part of the EU's broader Global Gateway offer, aims to support investment in Mauritania's energy transition and the decarbonisation of its economy. Specifically, it focuses on developing the country's green hydrogen industries. In 2023, the EU allocated €8.5 m in humanitarian aid to Mauritania. It also provided an additional €3.1 m to address the urgent needs created by the increased influx of refugees from Mali.

On 17 October, Spain's interior minister, Fernando Grande-Marlaska, announced increased coastal surveillance in Mauritania and Senegal to deter migrants from reaching Spain. This reflected an improvement in anti-migration cooperation among Mauritania, Senegal, and Spain. The minister stated that the Guardia Civil would use CN-235 aircraft in these operations to prevent migrant boats from departing for the Canary Islands.

In October, the US reinstated Mauritania to the African Growth and Opportunity Act (AGOA), from which it had been suspended in 2019. The decision came, as explained by the Office of the US Trade Representative, after Mauritania had demonstrated significant advancements in labour rights and the eradication of forced labour. Effective 1 January 2024, this reinstatement closely followed US president Joe Biden's decision to terminate AGOA benefits for Gabon and Niger due to unconstitutional post-coup government changes, along with Uganda and CAR, which lost their benefits due to human rights violations.

Mauritania strengthened its relations with China. In August, President Ghazouani undertook a five-day state visit to China, during which the two countries signed an agreement to boost collaboration in various areas as part of the Belt and Road Initiative, which Mauritania joined in 2018. During the visit, the two countries also signed an MoU under which China agreed to cancel 760 m Mauritanian ouguiya (MRU; equivalent to $21 m) of Mauritania's debt. However, the specifics of how much this relief package constituted in relation to Mauritania's total debt to China were not disclosed.

Mauritania also notably enhanced its relations with Algeria during 2023. The two countries signed seven partnership agreements across various sectors in January during a business forum at the Algerian Manufacturing Fair held in Nouakchott, with the participation of 166 Algerian companies from both the public and private sector. This event reflected the commitment of Mauritania and Algeria to bolstering their economic cooperation, highlighted by their joint initiative to construct a 772 km road connecting Tindouf in south-western Algeria to Zouerate in northern Mauritania. In April, Ahmed Attaf, Algeria's new minister of foreign affairs, made his inaugural foreign visit to Mauritania. Additionally, in September, the Algerian Union Bank, Algeria's first bank to operate abroad, opened a branch in Nouakchott.

Socioeconomic Development

Mauritania's socioeconomic landscape in 2023 was characterised by both hopes and challenges. According to World Bank figures, the Mauritanian economy grew at a slower pace, with a growth rate of 3.4% compared with 6.4% in 2022. This slowdown was attributed to a notable reduction in public spending and a decrease in exports caused by weaker industrial activity. However, inflation fell significantly, from a high of 9.5% in 2022 to 5% in 2023. Based on the IMF's preliminary data, the current account deficit also decreased, to 9.8% of GDP in 2023 compared with 16.7% at the end of 2022.

Mauritania's gas prospects faced challenges in 2023. On 1 August, BP, working on the Grande Tortue Ahmeyim offshore gas project between Mauritania and Senegal, announced a slight delay in natural gas production. The company stated that the timing of the expected first gas, initially planned for November 2023, would be moved to the first quarter of 2024 due to a delay in completing sub-sea work. Despite this set-back, several major oil and gas companies expressed interest in investing in Mauritania's energy sector. In February, Mauritania and Shell signed a production-sharing agreement for section C2 of the coastal basin within Mauritanian territorial waters. In April, Qatar Energy secured a deal with Shell to obtain a 40% stake in Shell's C10 block, situated in offshore Mauritania. In October, Mauritania received observer member status in the Gas Exporting Countries Forum (GECF), a coalition that holds 70% of the world's natural gas reserves and constitutes 42% of the global natural gas market.

Mauritania also embarked on initiatives to develop green hydrogen projects. On 8 March, the country signed an MoU with German project developer Conjuncta, Egypt's energy provider Infinity, and the UAE's Masdar for a $34 bn green hydrogen project. The project aimed to produce up to 8 m tons of green hydrogen or other hydrogen-based end products annually, with an electrolyser capacity of up to 10 gigawatts, according to a joint statement from Conjuncta, the involved companies, and the Mauritanian government.

In March, Mauritania launched the Multidimensional Poverty Index (IPM-M) to monitor poverty eradication efforts. The index goes beyond income to measure poverty, considering health, education, employment, and living standards. According to the IPM-M, 2.3 m Mauritanians (56.9% of the population) lived in multidimensional poverty, lacking in education, health, living standards, and employment. Children aged 0 to 17, accounting for over half of the population, were the poorest group, with 61.9% living in multidimensional poverty.

Mauritania faced a heightened risk of a food crisis due to Russia's exit from the Black Sea grain deal. Unlike its Sahelian neighbours, Mauritania heavily relies on wheat imports, with nearly a fifth sourced from Ukraine. The disruption in this key supply chain could destabilise prices of staple foods such as bread, as noted by some experts. Russian president Vladimir Putin announced at the Russia–Africa summit that Russia would provide free grain shipments to six African nations, but Mauritania was not among the recipients.

Relief Web's projections for the 2023 lean season (June–August) estimated that five regions in Mauritania were expected to be in the 'Pressure' phase (IPC 2) while the remaining eight regions were projected to be in the 'Crisis' phase (IPC 3). During this period, an estimated 694,612 people, 16% of Mauritania's population, were expected to be food insecure. Of these, 17% were expected to be in the 'Emergency' phase (IPC 4) while 83% would be in the 'Crisis' phase (IPC 3). In the previous year, Relief Web had estimated that the food-insecure population was 440,765 people, or 10% of Mauritania's population. Among them, 12% were in the 'Emergency' phase (IPC 4) and 88% were in the 'Crisis' phase (IPC 3).

The worsening food insecurity in Mauritania was exacerbated by the persistent arrival of refugees fleeing the ongoing conflict in Mali. As of July, OCHA reported that the number of Malian refugees living in and around the Mbera camp in Hodh Ech Chargui Region exceeded 91,263. In an interview with 'Le Figaro', the Mauritanian president noted that the refugee population had more than doubled in a year, surpassing 100,000 people. He highlighted that apart from Nouakchott, no Mauritanian city was home to such a large population. As he explained it, the presence of these migrants had led to significant costs, particularly in terms of security.

Niger

Klaas van Walraven

On 26 July, more than a decade of rule by the Parti Nigérien pour la Démocratie et le Socialisme (PNDS) came to an end as putschists toppled President Mohamed Bazoum. Led by the presidential guards, officers of the armed forces joined what was a corporate putsch fuelled by discontent over a range of issues, including dismissals, military cooperation with France, the fallout of the arms procurement scandal, and jockeying for the largesse expected from petroleum exports. In search of legitimacy, the junta, led by General Abdourahamane Tiani, tapped into anti-French sentiments, whipping up nationalist passions. As Bazoum's principal backer, France refused to recognise the military regime. ECOWAS countries, led by Nigeria, also declined to accept what was presented as one coup too many in the sub-region and imposed sanctions while threatening military intervention. Tiani refused to budge and confronted France in a weeks-long stand-off culminating in the severance of ties. Relations with ECOWAS deteriorated, and towards years' end, the regime contemplated withdrawal from the organisation. As sanctions led to the closure of borders, growth fell. The budget was slashed and prices and shortages increased, as did concerns over the humanitarian consequences of the sanctions.

Rains were abundant but too brief to allow all cereal crops to mature. Harvests were disappointing.

Domestic Politics

On 1 April, the army chief of staff Salifou Modi was dismissed and replaced by Major General Abdou Sidikou. Some military personnel believed that Bazoum was using Modi as a scapegoat for the security crisis, while there were speculations about a possible coup. But the key move against Bazoum came from the presidential guards, the elite force usually loyal to Niger's heads of state. On 26 July, guards were ordered by their leader General Abdourahamane Tiani to detain the president in his residence. A spokesperson for the self-styled Conseil national pour la sauvegarde de la patrie (CNSP) announced that the *government had been overthrown*. The following day, key figures of the armed forces expressed support for the putsch. Chief of staff Abdou Sidikou backed the coup to avoid bloodshed but was sidelined by his predecessor Salifou Modi, US-trained Brigadier General Moussa Barmou, and General Tiani, who declared himself head of state.

Tiani claimed that Niger's security situation was deteriorating and questioned the lack of security cooperation with Mali and Burkina Faso. He was an appointee of Bazoum's predecessor Mahamadou Issoufou and linked to him by his wife's family. His *relations with Bazoum* had deteriorated, and the president was reportedly considering his removal, likely to consolidate his position vis-à-vis Issoufou loyalists within the PNDS. Investigations into the arms procurement scandal were also said to have unnerved officers. Bazoum's attempts to gain control of structures concerned with oil production, which sidelined Issoufou's son Mahamane Sani Mahamadou, also known as 'Abba', and were opposed by PNDS chief Foumakoye Gado, may also have played a role.

On 7 August, the CNSP appointed a *new prime minister*, Ali Mahamane Zeine, member of the Mouvement National pour la Société de Développement, one-time ruling party with ties to the military. Zeine formed a government on 9 August which included Salifou Modi as minister of defence. Brigadier General Mohamed Toumba took the interior ministry, Bakary Yaou Sangaré became foreign minister, and the oil ministry went to Mahaman Barké, to the detriment of Issoufou's son Abba.

Bazoum refused to step down. Although detained, he was able to communicate, including with US officials and France's president Emmanuel Macron, and he even published an article in the 'Washington Post' stating that he was a hostage. Western countries called for his reinstatement. Tiani threatened that Bazoum would be executed in the case of military intervention, and the conditions of the *president's detention* deteriorated. In mid-August, the new regime said that it would prosecute

Bazoum for high treason and undermining security. On 16 September, Bazoum retaliated by filing a lawsuit with the ECOWAS Court of Justice. The government announced that it had foiled an attempt, on the night of 18–19 October, to liberate the deposed president, claiming that it involved the use of helicopters belonging to a foreign power. In mid-December, the ECOWAS Court of Justice ruled that Bazoum had to be reinstated. The ruling was ignored.

The new regime made arrests among members of the PNDS, including several ministers. On 31 July, Abba was put in detention in a government villa, together with the PNDS chair Foumakoye Gado. *Former president Issoufou*, who had continued to exercise influence under his successor, negotiated with the military for Bazoum to be reinstated but declined to condemn the coup, giving rise to speculations about collusion with Tiani. Issoufou's disagreements with Bazoum had become more frequent. However, his influence under Tiani was in decline; his reputation was stained by the opaqueness of his role.

In search of legitimacy, the *military played the nationalist card*. Free rein was given to simmering anti-French (and anti-Western) sentiments as well as hostility to the PNDS in Niamey – an opposition stronghold. The day after the putsch, people pillaged its headquarters and burned vehicles. Pro-coup rallies at the National Assembly and in the city of Dosso drew at least 1,000 and several hundred participants respectively. On 31 July, thousands reportedly took part in a rally in Zinder. Whipped up by social media networks, in which some key figures were said to have Russian connections, demonstrators denounced the French military presence. M62, a coalition of civil society groups, played a role in Niamey on 30 July when a rally was held at a football stadium. According to the military, some 30,000 people attended (this was disputed by the French ambassador). Brigadier General Mohamed Toumba gave a fiery speech. Thousands of demonstrators turned up at the French embassy. People tried to storm the complex before being dispersed by tear gas grenades fired from the grounds. The consulate was badly damaged.

Social-media-driven rumours fed excitement (essentially limited to the urban environment), while on the cultural scene musicians contributed patriotic songs and videos. Amid the *stand-off with France and ECOWAS*, rallies were staged in the month after the coup. Demonstrators were on the streets of Niamey on 3 August (independence day) waving Russian flags. On 6 August, another rally took place, also attended by members of the military, and on 9 August, M62 called for Westerners to be taken hostage to force out French and other Western troops. Other rallies followed on 20 and 27 August, on the latter date at France's military base near Niamey. Rumours suggested that some demonstrators were being paid. Nigeria cut electricity supplies, plunging numerous cities into darkness. On the day of the attack on France's embassy, Paris decided to evacuate French and other Western nationals. The operation concerned some 1,000 people, half of whom were French. As relations with France deteriorated, further rallies were held on 1–3 September to protest its military presence.

On 19 August, General Tiani said that civilian rule would be restored after a *transition of three years*. A one-month 'inclusive national dialogue' would be held to prepare the ground. The Maison de la presse du Niger expressed concern about threats against journalists, and a civil society representative complained that anti-coup sentiments could not be aired. Reports spoke of demonstrations in support of Bazoum in Niamey and Tahoua, a PNDS stronghold where Tuaregs and Arabic speakers were rumoured to have come under attack. Former minister Rhissa Ag Boula, a Tuareg dignitary and Bazoum confidant, announced on 8–9 August the formation of a Conseil de la resistance pour la république in support of the deposed president. The *military cracked down* on dissent. On 30 September, Samira Sabou, a journalist and human rights campaigner, was detained on an accusation of disturbing public order; she was released on 1 October, charged with treason.

On 24 January, the military reportedly killed 11 *insurgents* and captured six in Tillabéri Region; arms were seized and more than 100 motorcycles were destroyed. The *anti-jihadist operation* Niya suffered two injuries. On 21 January, the army engaged insurgents claiming allegiance to Islamic State West Africa Province; one militant was reported killed. On 1 February, insurgents on motorbikes attacked a camp of Malian refugees in Tahoua Region; on 10 February, the army announced an ambush by jihadists near the village of Intagamey on the border with Mali. Seventeen soldiers died in the attack, 13 were wounded, and 12 went missing. Land and air forces responded in March with operations in which 79 insurgents were allegedly killed and troops pursued militants deep into Malian territory (Niger's armed forces were now allowed to cross the border). On 4 March, a police station was attacked in Makalondi on the border with Burkina. On 30 March, the army reported having killed insurgents near Tamou, while others were pushed across the Burkinabé border at Ouanzerbé. M62 had before the coup accused the military of a massacre in Tamou in October 2022, leading to the arrest of its leader on 23 January.

In mid-March, Nigérien troops who were part of the Force Multinationale Mixte (FMM) active in the *border region with Nigeria* 'neutralised' 20 Boko Haram fighters and arrested 83 others. Earlier on, 30 Boko Haram fighters, fleeing their rivals of Islamic State (IS), had been captured along with hundreds of women and children, who were brought to the city of Diffa. On 8 April, IS insurgents staged an attack near Diffa while on 13 April, others attacked a military patrol in Gueskérou; three soldiers were allegedly killed, four injured. The following day, two soldiers were killed near Bosso on Lake Chad.

There was a *downturn in attacks* compared with the previous year. The reasons remained unclear, and improvements were more pronounced in the south-east. Civilians continued to suffer from 'taxes' levied by insurgents, many of whom in the west were marginalised Peuls (besides Tuaregs). The Bazoum administration made attempts via intercommunal forums to improve interethnic relations; some led to community agreements and the return of quiet. The overall picture was varied, and hundreds of schools in Tillabéri Region remained closed. In early May, there was an attack on islands in the Niger River at Dessa in which four were killed; thousands of inhabitants fled to nearby Ayorou. On 7 May, seven national guards died near the Samira gold mine on the border with Burkina. Two insurgent leaders were arrested in a joint Nigérien–French operation on the same border in July. More than 10,000 civilians fled in the wake of killings on 3 July after jihadists had issued an ultimatum. On 15 July, one police officer and four civilians were killed in Tillabéri; five days later, insurgents attacked Anzourou, north of Tillabéri.

A *new surge of attacks* in the west came in the wake of the coup, the causes of which remained unclear although seasoned army contingents were withdrawn to Niamey in defence against intervention by ECOWAS. Around 10 August, three soldiers were allegedly killed in a clash; six had been reported killed in western Niger the previous day. Four perished at a locality in Tillabéri Region, and six national guards and ten militants died in a clash at Sanam, north-east of Filingué, on 13 August. Two days later, 17 soldiers died in an ambush near Torodi at the border with Burkina; the army claimed that more than 100 insurgents had been 'neutralised', but more than 30 civilians died in raids on villages along the Niger River. On 20 August, 12 national guards died in an ambush at Ansougou; two days later, the army claimed to have killed an unknown number of assailants. Kandadji, the location of the hydroelectric dam under construction, was attacked on 28 August; 12 soldiers and 7 militants died when hundreds of insurgents stormed the town with motorbikes. The town was attacked a second time on 28 September, when several soldiers were killed. The fighting erupted during a counter-insurgency operation in which 100 militants were allegedly killed and stolen cattle seized. In early October, the media reported dozens of casualties among the military in unspecified attacks. Salifou Modi, as the new defence minister, attended the burial of 60 military at Tilia.

In a *change of strategy*, Nigérien forces began operating with troops from Mali. They claimed to have killed at least 30 insurgents in air strikes, while seizing weapons and drugs (4–8 December). Another 40 insurgents were reportedly killed, also in air strikes, in Tillabéri Region between 17 and 19 December. On 20 December, a market in Tillabéri was hit by a government drone, according to militants. Two days earlier, a report by insurgents had claimed that Samira had been the scene of another insurgent attack. At the end of the month, 11 people died in attacks on villages on the border with Burkina; in another incident, south of Niamey, one soldier was killed and five wounded.

Relative calm in the south-east was maintained after operations in March. On 10 May, 1,400 followers of Boko Haram, fleeing IS rivals and on their way to islets in Lake Chad, were intercepted on the border with Nigeria. Three days later, FMM troops killed 20 insurgents and captured 83 others. This was followed, at the end of the month, by operations with Nigeria in which 55 jihadists were reported killed, as well as two soldiers. On 16 June, seven soldiers were killed in a landmine explosion at Chétimari, west of Diffa. In the same region, the media reported on 10 December that the army had killed at least 11 insurgents.

Foreign Affairs

ECOWAS, the AU, the UNSC, and the EU, as well as France, the US, and other European countries, *condemned the unconstitutional take-over of the country*. Bazoum's incarceration drew special criticism. With some 1,500 troops in the country, and its military presence controversial at best, France calculated that its security interests were at stake. It rejected the fait accompli and refused to recognise the new regime. Development aid and budget support were cut and military accords suspended. Diplomatically, France followed the stance taken by ECOWAS, which did not rule out intervention if the armed forces did not return to barracks. Tiani's regime vowed that it would defend itself against 'aggression' by sub-regional powers and France.

Against this background, the stand-off at the embassy took shape. During confrontations with demonstrators, the ambassador called former president Issoufou for help, which led to intervention by General Modi, the new defence minister. President Macron warned that France would react 'immediately and without compromise' if its nationals or interests were attacked. On independence day, while French news channels were blocked, Tiani's regime renounced military accords with France. This was rejected by Paris, which said that the decisions came from an illegitimate government. On 25 August, Niger's regime *declared the ambassador persona non grata*, giving him 48 hours to leave. The ambassador refused to comply, and President Macron publicly applauded him, unhelpfully adding on 28 August that without the French presence, Niger would no longer exist. On 29 August, the ambassador was stripped of his immunity and security forces were ordered to expel him. Thousands of demonstrators gathered at France's military base in Niamey to increase pressure; doubtless there was an element of coordination with the regime.

Against the backdrop of inaction by ECOWAS, the French blinked first. On 24 September, Macron announced that *France would withdraw* its troops and ambassador. The withdrawals were completed by 22 December. At the end of the month, the French embassy was closed and local staff dismissed. On 23 November, Niger announced that it was ending all cultural cooperation, forcing the closure of French cultural centres. It suspended cooperation with the OIF due to its ties with France. The rupturing of ties was unprecedented even compared with the 1974 Kountché coup. It was accompanied on 4 December by the severance of accords with the EU.

On 30 July, ECOWAS *heads of state* convened in the Nigerian capital Abuja under Nigeria's fresh president, Bola Tinubu. It was decided to *suspend ties* and block land borders (the trade embargo included humanitarian aid), while keeping the threat of military intervention in reserve. The putschists were given a week to return to barracks. While the chiefs of staff of ECOWAS states convened in Abuja on 2 August, an ECOWAS delegation travelled to Niamey. Led by former Nigerian leader Abdulasalami Abubakar, it included the sultan of Sokoto, the traditional leader with influence in parts of Niger. It could not reach agreement, and the regime refused to allow another delegation of ECOWAS, the UN, and AU to come to Niamey on 8 August, citing concerns about public anger over sanctions. The previous day, Tiani and Brigadier General Moussa Barmou met the former emir of Kano and the ex-governor of Nigeria's central bank for talks. With Tiani's refusal to budge, ECOWAS reconvened on 10 August and mandated the deployment of a 'standby force'; France applauded the decision. Côte d'Ivoire, which received support from Senegal, announced that it would provide a battalion of 850–1,100 troops. On 16 August, it was announced that Niger had recalled its ambassador from Abidjan. An ECOWAS meeting in Ghana's capital Accra on 17–18 August reiterated the organisation's *readiness to use force*.

On 19 August, a delegation made up of the sultan of Sokoto, the ECOWAS Commission president, and Abdulasalami Abubakar arrived in Niamey and met with Tiani and Prime Minister Zeine, while also being allowed to see the incarcerated Bazoum. Tiani came with a three-year timetable for the restoration of civilian rule, but this was rejected by ECOWAS. Victoria Nuland, the US acting deputy secretary of state who met with Moussa Barmou on 7 August, was told that Bazoum would be killed in the case of intervention. In reality, there was considerable *opposition in the sub-region* to such plans, notably in Northern Nigeria, culturally close to Niger. Senators from Northern Nigeria as well as religious leaders, youth activists, and opposition politicians voiced concerns. On 12 August, a delegation of Muslim clerics visited Niamey in an attempt to mediate an end to the crisis. They met General Tiani, who claimed he was open to a diplomatic breakthrough. Ghana's opposition politicians also protested against the ECOWAS plan. Togo received a visit by defence minister Modi on 7 August and made it clear that it was willing to help Niger circumvent sanctions. Later, on 6 November, Niger called on Togo's President Faure Gnassingbé to mediate while on 8 December, Tiani flew to Lomé to reinforce bilateral ties (Togo's foreign minister repaid the visit on 14 December). Idriss Déby, the president of non-ECOWAS member Chad, who participated in the first ECOWAS summit in Abuja, flew to Niamey afterwards to mediate; he met separately with Tiani and defence minister Modi, as well as seeing Bazoum. Chad made it clear that it would not take part in any intervention; on 15 August, Prime Minister Zeine flew to Ndjamena for talks, eulogising neighbourly ties. Algeria agitated against intervention in the AU Peace and Security Council. It proposed a six-month transition period, but Tiani retorted that this would be decided by the 'national dialogue'. On 9 October, Algeria announced that it had discontinued mediation.

Burkina Faso and *Mali* fiercely opposed intervention. While pre-coup ties with Mali had been poor, the fellow putschist powers threatened to leave ECOWAS and come to Niger's defence. On 24 August, the three countries agreed to boost cooperation in the struggle against insurgents and deploy troops to help fight an ECOWAS force. On 16 September, the three signed a security pact. The 'Liptako-Gourma' charter established an Alliance des États du Sahel (AES) whose members vowed to come to each other's aid in the case of security threats or aggression. On his first trip abroad, on 23 November, General Tiani flew to Bamako to meet the leaders of Mali and Burkina. On 2 December, Niger and Burkina Faso announced that they would leave the French-backed G5 Sahel alliance, following the example of Mali. Their decision took effect on 29 November. On 12 August, Moussa Barmou also met the military leaders of *Guinea*, who expressed their support for the new regime.

On 10 December, ECOWAS decided to *maintain sanctions*. Its summit in Abuja was attended by Ouhoumoudou Mahamadou and Hassoumi Massaoudou, respectively prime minister and foreign minister under Bazoum, which Tiani saw as a provocation. On 3 December, Nigeria's foreign minister reiterated the demand for Bazoum's release; this was rejected by Tiani. Niger's foreign minister said that his country was considering leaving ECOWAS altogether; he also referred, in the same vein, to leaving WAEMU (this would prove more difficult in view of the monetary cooperation involved).

The *US managed to continue ties*, for the time being. With two air bases and 600 to 1,100 troops in Niger, and also against the backdrop of Russia's mercenary intrusions in neighbouring countries, it feared jeopardising its security investment. Rather than the robust (French-backed) ECOWAS approach, it preferred a diplomatic way out, alternating strong statements with conciliatory ones. For some time, the US declined to call the take-over a coup (as this would trigger a legally required suspension of aid). On 5 August, Washington announced that it would pause certain aid programmes. On 19 August, the new US ambassador, Kathleen Fitzgibbon, took up her post in Niamey. Meanwhile, US secretary of state Antony Blinken welcomed the ECOWAS stand, and acting deputy secretary of state Nuland called her talks with Niger's military on 7 August frank and difficult. She was refused a meeting with Tiani and defence minister Modi and denied access to Bazoum.

On 14 September, the US announced that it had resumed reconnaissance flights. Barely a month later, on 10 October, it formally declared the take-over to be a coup d'état. This was justified with a reference to insufficient diplomatic progress. However, it was understood that the US would maintain its troops, to monitor the jihadist threat. On 12–13 December, the assistant secretary for African affairs, Molly Phee, after attending the 10 December ECOWAS summit, met Prime Minister Zeine in Niamey. She announced that aid cooperation would resume in phases, on condition of a rapid transition to civilian rule. *Rumours of Russian intrusion* strengthened Tiani's position. On 4 December, a Russian delegation visited Niamey. It was received by Tiani, and the two sides signed documents on military cooperation. Prime Minister Zeine visited Moscow on 29 December.

A testimony to its blunt and callous approach, on 11 October, the regime announced that it would expel the UN humanitarian coordinator, blaming the world body for obstructing its international recognition. Niger's new foreign minister Sangaré had not been allowed to address the UNGA in September.

Having reservations about military intervention, the AU called for a study on the economic, social, and security implications involved. In a statement on 22 August, the continental body 'took note' of ECOWAS's intervention plan.

Socioeconomic Developments

With the imposition of sanctions, the *growth forecast* was predicted to fall to 2.3%. *Prices* went up as lorries were held up on the borders with Benin and Nigeria, while freight was blocked in Benin's port of Cotonou. By mid-September, medicine stocks had fallen by between 33% and 55%. On 15 November, the UN resumed humanitarian flights.

A World Bank study estimated that Niger received just $82 m in *development aid* (out of $625 m) and only $254 m in financial support, compared with $1.66 bn before the putsch. Normally, 55% of the budget stemmed from aid. The government managed to pay the July–August salaries of state employees and security forces. On 6 October, it cut the *budget* back to $3.2 bn (a reduction of around 40%).

With more than 70% of electricity normally coming from Nigeria, the country suffered *severe power shortages*. Work on the Kandadji hydroelectric dam was discontinued; employees were dismissed. By December, the Tiani regime claimed that construction of the oil pipeline to Benin was finally completed, with the first oil said to be exported the following January. There was no ban on uranium exports. French company Orano continued to operate its only mine at Arlit, with Niger's military providing security. Canadian firms were still active in exploration and on 10 August signed a convention for a subterranean mine between Arlit and Agadez.

Problems for *IDPs and refugees* continued unabated. According to the UN, the entire western region counted some 150,000 IDPs, with 700,000 refugees in the country as a whole, half of whom were IDPs. By August–September, only 39% of funding had been raised in an appeal by UNHCR. The new regime repealed the law banning human trafficking, enacted on request of the EU, an important source of income in Agadez Region.

Torrential *rains* caused *floods* affecting well over 150,000 people. While rains were abundant, they were too brief to ensure the maturation of crops everywhere. *Harvests* fell short.

Nigeria

Heinrich Bergstresser

The political scene of 2023 was dominated by the elections in February and March at both federal and state levels. Against the backdrop of the statutory end of President Muhammadu Buhari's two terms in office, the electorate witnessed a three-way battle which might have changed the political landscape. With a historically low turnout, Bola Tinubu won with the support of just 10% of eligible voters; he was thus given a rather weak political mandate in a time of multiple domestic crises. Once again, and contrary to justified expectations, the electoral commission failed in its pledge to guarantee the transparency of the elections and missed the opportunity to retain a minimum of trust in the electoral process. In the end, however, President Tinubu using the powers vested in his office without any hesitation, and, with the support of the hegemonic part of the dominant faction of the power elite, postured as willing to confront head on some of the economic issues undermining the country, despite the numerous security challenges.

Domestic Politics

The most prominent issues were the *general elections*, scheduled for 25 February (presidential and National Assembly) and 11 March (gubernatorial and state assemblies), and the ongoing precarious security in most parts of the country. At the beginning of the year, all eyes were on the elections at which, constitutionally, the presidency of Muhammadu Buhari would end. After months of heated campaigning characterised to a certain extent by an ethnic-religious undercurrent, the presidential election culminated in a three-way battle which, over the course of the year, was filled with drama. However, none of the other 15 candidates and their respective running mates were thought to have any chance of winning.

The candidate of the ruling All Progressives Congress (APC), 71-year-old Bola Ahmed Tinubu, an ethnic Yoruba of Muslim faith who had twice been governor of Lagos State, had named Kashim Shettima, an ethnic Kanuri of Muslim faith and former governor of Borno State, as his running mate. This position, however, has marginal executive powers. Only under exceptional circumstances such as the critical illness or untimely death of the incumbent would the vice-president temporarily or fully take over the leadership. The even older candidate of the opposition People's Democratic Party (PDP), Atiku Abubakar, an ethnic Fulani of Muslim faith from Adamawa State and former vice-president under Olusegun Obasanjo's eight-year presidency, ran for the country's highest office for the sixth time. Atiku had chosen a hardly known adherent of the Christian faith of Igbo extraction, Ifeanyi Okowa, governor of Delta State, as running mate, a choice which did not go down well with the more-favoured Nyesom Wike, then governor of Rivers State. This ill-advised decision was the final strategic blunder in a chain that had begun with the appointment of Iyorchia Ayu, a northerner from Benue State, as party chair two years earlier and further reduced Atiku's chances of winning. The third in the group, Peter Obi, a 62-year-old ethnic Igbo of Christian faith and former two-time governor of Anambra State, was the Labour Party's (LP's) presidential candidate. He announced Yusuf Datti Baba-Ahmed, of Muslim faith and a well-known and rather young politician and academic in Kaduna State, as his running mate. In a sense, Obi's candidacy electrified young people predominantly on *social media* both in Nigeria and within the vast Nigerian diaspora, thereby creating an image of a 'star' who would immediately move into the presidential villa and change the future of Nigeria. In reality, however, the campaign was superficial, and it was Obi who was blamed for having played the ethnic-religious card too much, thereby discouraging many sympathisers from voting in his favour or encouraging them to abstain. Furthermore, he lacked the necessary party machinery at state and local government levels, particularly in the Muslim-dominated North.

As previously, in the run-up to elections, widespread election-related violence and serious crime prevailed, as well as logistical and technical problems within the *Independent National Electoral Commission* (INEC). One of the worst of several appalling incidents happened in Ihiala local government area in Anambra State on 10 February, when gunmen ambushed the advance security team of the PDP vice-presidential candidate, Okowa, killing three police officers. INEC, for its part, was struggling to finalise the release of 'Permanent Voters' Cards' (PVCs) at both ward and local government level. On 28 January, days after the official deadline, INEC once again extended the deadline for the collection of PVCs by a further week. In addition, digital technology such as the Bimodal Voter Accreditation System (BVAS) and the INEC Result Viewing Portal (IReV) raised expectations of transparency, trust, and accountability in the elections – expectations that INEC was only partially able to fulfil on election day, despite unprecedented financial resources and support from the various state security services. Nevertheless, and notwithstanding sharp criticism from both civil society and international observers, it was widely accepted that the elections were not to be regarded as totally flawed.

INEC registered 93.5 m voters – an all-time high – among them more than 7 m first-time voters and some 40% in the 18–34 age group. In the end, 87.2 m eligible voters collected their PVCs. However, on 25 February only some 25 m (28.5%, a historic low) cast their votes in the *presidential and National Assembly elections* at the 176,846 polling stations.

Tinubu polled 8.8 m (36.6%) and won by a clear margin, with his main rival, Atiku, taking just 7 m (29.1%) votes. The other main contender and supposed icon of the youth, Peter Obi, trailed well behind with 6.1 m (25.4%) votes. However, many votes – more than 900,000 – were declared invalid. To put the result in perspective, only 10% of those holding a PVC delivered victory. Tinubu was the only candidate who fulfilled the two conditions required for victory: polling the majority of votes and passing the threshold of at least 25% of votes cast in at least 24 states plus the Federal Territory of Abuja (FCT). In fact, he fulfilled the second condition in 29 states. As expected, Tinubu performed badly in the Igbo heartland of the South East, in the states of Delta and Edo, and in Abuja. Atiku suffered bitter defeats in the two most populous states: Lagos in the South West and – even more painfully – Kano in the North; he also trailed far behind in the South East. Obi, on the other hand, made a poor showing in the South West, except for Lagos State, performed very poorly in the states of the North, and had mixed results in North-Central, but was victorious in the FCT. In a nutshell, the elections, especially the presidential election, demonstrated a *slightly changed political landscape* which partially called certainties into question and, to some extent – at least for the foreseeable future – triggered a three-way political split.

On 1 March, INEC declared Tinubu the duly elected fifth president of the Fourth Republic. Atiku, Obi, and the Allied Peoples Movement (APM) rejected the decision and challenged it at the *presidential election petition tribunal*. Shortly before the inauguration on 29 May, the Supreme Court, on 26 May, dismissed the PDP's petition to stop Tinubu and his running mate, Shettima, being sworn in. The PDP maintained that Shettima's nomination was not valid. Three days earlier, the election tribunal had ordered the merging of the petitions filed by Atiku, Obi, and the APM. Towards the end of the drama, the APM withdrew its suit.

On 6 September, the tribunal confirmed Tinubu's presidency and, in a 12-hour ruling, also addressed some fundamental issues. The two most important of these related, first, to the status of the FCT, which in the context of a presidential election was to be treated as the 37th state and, second, to the electronic transmission of results by the BVAS, which should be at the discretion of INEC. As expected, the plaintiffs disputed the verdict and filed an appeal at the Supreme Court.

In the run-up to the court's final verdict, the *legal wrangling* shifted to tertiary institutions and courts in the US. Atiku, in an unprecedented move, sought to prove that Tinubu's Chicago State University (CSU) certificate, received in the late 1970s, was forged and that consequently, he should be ineligible. CSU, however, was loath to hand over the documents, a decision that triggered a court case in Illinois. On 20 September, the Magistrate's Court ordered the university to release Tinubu's academic records, a ruling that the defendant disputed at a further court. However, on 2 October, the court affirmed the judgment of the lower court, insisting that Atiku had the right to have access to the records and ordering their release within 48 hours. In the end, the records, in particular copies of certificates, were – at least to some extent – patchy and revealed some inconsistencies.

The drama ended when, on 26 October, the Supreme Court, in a *unanimous verdict*, dismissed the petitions of both Atiku and Obi. As far as the former's case was concerned, the court maintained that it lacked the jurisdiction to assess evidence which had not been tendered before the lower court and pointed out that the grounds for the appeal had nothing to do with forgery, nor did they directly concern the president. The court also held that Atiku had neither proven his allegation of widespread rigging during the election nor won the election. In Obi's case, the only issue was the alleged inappropriate nomination of the vice-presidential candidate, which, according to the court, had been resolved earlier and would not be retried. The court's verdict maintained its rather cautious criticism of INEC's failure to upload the results in real time, and argued that public confidence in the electoral process was thereby diminished.

The *results of the National Assembly elections resembled those of the presidential elections*. The AFC secured a majority in both the 109-member Senate and the 360-member House of Representatives, although compared with the election of 2019 it lost several seats. The PDP trailed far behind, but eventually the two parties managed to gain some 75% to 80% of the seats in the National Assembly. The LP won just under 10% of the seats in the Senate and almost three dozen in the lower house, a respectable result. Apart from the New Nigeria People's Party (NNPP), which secured a landslide victory in its stronghold of Kano State, some of the smaller parties snatched one or two of the seats in the upper or lower house. The NNPP's ingrained local success even paid off in the National Assembly, where the party became the fourth-strongest force. Attempts by quite a few political heavyweights in both leading parties to be elected or re-elected into parliament were unsuccessful. One such heavyweight was the former governor of Kebbi State, Abubakar Atiku Bagudu (APC). Several disputed results were challenged at election tribunals and generally ended up at the Court of Appeal.

Against the backdrop of INEC's poor logistical and technical record, *gubernatorial and state assembly elections* were shifted back by a week to 18 March; the aim was to gain time and readjust or reconfigure the BVAS and IReV. As on previous occasions, state assembly elections were held in all 36 states with 990 seats, but only 28 gubernatorial mandates were contested because the tenure of eight sitting governors had not yet expired. Seventeen APC front-runners triumphed, while the PDP won nine states – all but three of them (Adamawa, Bauchi, and Zamfara) in the South. NNPP candidate Abba Kabir Yusuf was victorious in Kano State, LP candidate Alex Otti in Abia State. Several months later, on 11 November, three gubernatorial elections took place outside the statutory election cycle in the states of Bayelsa, Imo, and Kogi; all but one (Bayelsa) were won by the APC candidate. The previous year's out-of-cycle gubernatorial election in Osun State had been won by the PDP candidate, Ademola Adeleke; this was the starting point of legal wrangling at the tribunals, at the Court of Appeal, and subsequently at the Supreme Court. On 9 May, the Supreme Court upheld the decision of the lower court which had declared Adeleke the rightful governor even though the election petition tribunal had voided his victory on 27 January.

The *turmoil* continued when the election tribunal sacked Abba Kabir Yusuf of the NNPP (20 September) and Abdullahi Sule of the APC (2 October) in the states of Kano and Nasarawa while declaring their respective runners-up duly elected. While the Court of Appeal affirmed the ruling against Yusuf (17 November), it reversed the judgment in favour of Abdullahi Sule (23 November). In Zamfara State, Dauda Lawal (PDP) won the gubernatorial election against the incumbent Bello Matawalle, whose petition was dismissed by the tribunal. On 16 November, however, the Court of Appeal declared the gubernatorial election inconclusive and ordered INEC to conduct fresh elections in some local government areas. Plateau State, confronted with a similar development, became a focal point of the judiciary's many inconsistencies when, on 19 November, the election of Caleb Mutfwang (PDP) as governor, confirmed by the tribunal, was nullified by the Court of Appeal and the APC candidate installed in his place. The reasoning of this court was extremely contradictory, maintaining that Mutfwang was not validly sponsored by the PDP, a party which allegedly had no structure in the state.

Nevertheless, the tribunal's verdict had a telling impact on all elected PDP state assembly and National Assembly members who lost their seats in favour of the APC.

Mutfwang, as expected, gave notice of appeal to the Supreme Court. In contrast, the legal options of parliamentary candidates were exhausted at the Court of Appeal.

In January of the following year, the Court of Appeal's verdicts on the gubernatorial elections in the states of Kano, Plateau, and Zamfara were overturned by the Supreme Court, which once again raised questions about the competence of and confidence in the *judiciary* as a whole. This notwithstanding, the other judgments were in line with those of the Court of Appeal, which had affirmed INEC's certificates of return.

The *seventh legislative period* was inaugurated on 13 June. Following the inauguration, the House of Representatives elected APC members Abbas Tajudeen from Kaduna State and Benjamin Kalu from Abia State as speaker and deputy speaker. APC senator Godswill Akpabio from Akwa Ibom State emerged as Senate president, while Ibrahim Barau Jibrin from Kano State was elected as his deputy. On 3 October, the Senate passed an amendment to its standing orders to the effect that future Senate presidents or their deputy presidents must have served at least one term as senator.

As in previous elections, however, *women were significantly under-represented*. Only some 10% of more than 15,000 candidates were women, of whom just 4% – 72 women – were elected. Slightly more than a dozen made it to the National Assembly; some, in the single-digit range, were elected as deputy governor, and almost 50 made it to the various state assemblies.

Soon after the swearing-in ceremony, President Tinubu dissolved the *governing boards* of all federal parastatals, agencies, institutions, and government-owned companies. In successive steps, the entire state apparatus at federal level – except for the national judicial council – was restructured and, on an unprecedented scale in Nigeria's history under civilian rule, new personnel were appointed. On 2 June, Tinubu made first appointments to *key positions* within the presidency, such as Femi Gbajabiamila, the then speaker of the House of Representatives, as the president's chief of staff, and George Akume, former governor of Benue State and minister under Buhari, as secretary to the federal government.

Soon afterwards, on 9 June, Godwin Emefiele, governor of the Central Bank, along with his four deputies, was suspended and later arrested and charged with corruption and treason. He was succeeded by Olayemi Cardoso, whose nomination, along with that of his new deputies, was confirmed by the Senate on 26 September. On 19 June, Nuhu Ribadu, former chair of the Economic and Financial Crime Commission (EFCC) was named the new national security advisor and head of the national counter-terrorism centre. Ajuri Ngelale, one of the spokespersons in Tinubu's campaign council, was appointed as special advisor on media and publicity (31 July). Further important appointments were made, such as that of Kayode Egbetokun as substantive inspector-general of police (19 June).

In mid-August, the president presented his *cabinet*. Key positions were handed to Lateef Fagbemi (minister of justice and attorney-general of the federation), Wale Edun (minister of finance and coordinating minister of the economy), and Abubakar Atiku Bagudu (budget and economic planning). Another former governor, Muhammad Baduru, was – surprisingly – given the defence portfolio, while career diplomat and then serving ambassador in Germany Yusuf Maitama Tugger emerged as minister of foreign affairs. In a deft move, Nyesom Wike, the PDP heavyweight in Rivers State and the main opponent of Atiku, was appointed minister of the FCT. As expected, Tinubu – like all incoming presidents of the Fourth Republic – retained the decisive petroleum ministry. By year's end, half a dozen appointees who had been elected to the National Assembly triggered compulsory by-elections in February of the following year.

These appointments notwithstanding, the most far-reaching decisions concerned the *military*. On 19 June, the president approved the immediate retirement of all service chiefs and appointed replacements, triggering a massive shake-up and redeployment. While Major General Christopher Gwabin Musa took over as the new chief of defence staff, Taoreed Abiodun Lagbada, of the same rank, became chief of army staff and was promoted to the next rank; Rear Admiral Emmanuel Ikechukwu Ogalla emerged as chief of naval staff and Air Vice Marshal Hassan Bala Abubakar as chief of air staff. Major General Emmanuel Parker Akomaye Undiandeye was named chief of defence intelligence. Major General Valentine Uzochukwu Okoro assumed duty as general officer commanding (GOC) 2 Division in Ibadan, Hassan Taiwo Dada and Muhammed Usman of the same rank took command of 82 Division in Enugu and 81 Division in Lagos respectively, and Major General Adulsalami Abubakar was named GOC 3 Division in Jos and commander of the operation 'Safe Haven'. Another major general, Peter Paturmala Malla, moved to 7 Division as GOC and commander Sector 1 Joint Task Force of the North East operation 'Hadin Kai' while Ibrahim Ali, of the same rank, was redeployed as force commander to the Multinational Joint Task Force (MNJTF) in the Chadian capital N'djamena. The navy, the air force, and the police force underwent similar restructuring.

Soon afterwards, on 30 June, and in line with a long-standing military tradition, all *officers of the upper echelons* who were senior to the newly appointed service chiefs had to offer their retirement. On 19 December, however, the army hosted a lavish farewell party for all 113 generals who had left the service in the last 12 months or who were to retire before year's end. Shortly afterwards, 47 brigadier generals and 75 colonels were promoted by the Nigerian army council to the next rank.

More was to come when dozens of judges were recommended by the national *judicial council* to President Tinubu to serve at the Supreme Court, the Court of Appeal (20 divisions with not less than 49 judges), and the Federal High Court (37 divisions with a targeted number of 100 judges). When, on 21 December, the

Senate confirmed 11 new appointments, the Supreme Court was fully represented by 21 justices for the very first time. Earlier, in July and September, the Court of Appeal and the Federal High Court had seen a remarkable increase of 23 new judges.

Towards the end of Buhari's term in office, on 17 March, the then president assented to only 16 of 35 *amendments to the constitution* – to the disappointment of most legislators. These amendments were part of a package, the fifth such package proposed during the Fourth Republic. Among the amendments that Buhari approved were the provision for the financial independence of state assemblies and the judiciary at state level, as well as changes to the inaugural sittings of all legislative houses where a quorum of at least two-thirds was required.

President Tinubu and his government inherited multifarious security problems even though several *notorious gangs* had previously been smashed and hundreds of perpetrators arrested or killed. Some of the worst incidents happened in the states of Benue and Plateau in central Nigeria. During Easter week (3–7 April) for example, gunmen, suspected to be Fulani herders, raided communities in the three local government areas of Apa, Guma, and Otukpo, killing at least 134 people. Later, on 20 October, four commercial banks in Otukpo were robbed by armed men and several customers, operatives, and passers-by were killed while others were injured. During the Christmas period, well-coordinated armed groups, also believed to be herders, attacked several communities in Barkin Ladi and Bokkos local government areas in Plateau State, leaving some 160 people dead.

In addition to the *kidnapping and killing* of innocent citizens, Christian clerics and worshippers, particularly Catholics, were systematically targeted by kidnap gangs or hired assassins. On 15 January for example, Isaac Achi, a Catholic priest was killed in his rectory in Paikoro local government area in Niger State by alleged Islamists who gained entry and set the house ablaze. His colleague Collins Omeh escaped with gunshot wounds. On 7 June, another Catholic priest, Charles Igechi, vice-principal of St Michael College in Benin City, was shot dead in Okha local government area while on his way back to the college. In the late evening on Christmas Eve, three worshippers were killed by armed men while attending mass in a Catholic church in Abakaliki local government area in Ebonyi State. Even nuns were not immune to being targeted, as was demonstrated on 21 August (Imo State) and 5 October (Ebonyi State), when four Catholic nuns and three nuns along with a seminarian and their driver, respectively, were abducted and held hostage. While the former were set free three days later, the latter spent 11 days in captivity until, as in most cases, an undisclosed ransom was paid.

Over the course of the year – except perhaps on polling days – terror attacks, organised killings, kidnappings, and extortion by *Islamic State West Africa Province* (ISWAP) and various bandits were everyday events in the Muslim-dominated North East and North West. The military – some 50,000 of whom were deployed in internal operations – responded to such attacks with their own strikes, many of which led to the deaths of their adversaries. Although, according to the defence headquarters, close to 7,000 Islamists, bandits, and other criminals and quite a few of their commanders – such as Abu Iliya and Abu Zahra – were neutralised or arrested – such as Abdulmumin Otaru – and although some 4,500 hostages were rescued, the crime rate remained high in most parts of the country. According to two think tanks – National Security Trackers (NST) and the Armed Conflict Location & Event Data Project (ACLED) – over the course of the year, 3,841 people were killed and 4,243 abducted by non-state actors.

The *death toll among the military* was also quite high. One of the worst incidents took place in Niger State on 13 August, where 36 military personnel lost their lives in an encounter with cattle rustlers allegedly loyal to Abubakar Abdallah, better known as the notorious Dogo Gide. Many bandits were killed, but 12 soldiers suffered the same fate and several others sustained serious injuries. The situation worsened considerably when a helicopter that had made several trips to evacuate the wounded and recover corpses was shot down and burned by the bandits the following day.

Despite the heavy death toll of the security services, they were accused of widespread culpable negligence and of holding the public in contempt. In Nasarawa State, on 24 January, an *airstrike* killed at least 40 people, allegedly terrorists but in fact cattle herders. Initially, the air force tried to conceal the deadly incident, but months later, on 17 May, they had to acknowledge their responsibility for the operation. Against the background of a new initiative against terrorists, bandits, and other criminals, initiated by the army on 6 October, a similar incident occurred in Kaduna State on 3 December when the air force accidentally bombed a religious celebration observing Maulud; 120 civilians were killed. At first, the military again denied any responsibility, but under the pressure of civil rights activists, eventually admitted its offence.

As in previous years, the government's *anti-corruption campaign* yielded mixed results, with numerous convictions but quite a few set-backs. According to EFCC it secured close to 1,700 convictions from January to September although in a few cases the *judiciary was quite lenient* towards some defendants who were sentenced to several years' imprisonment but then given the option of paying a fine. One lawyer, Umar Hussaini, for example, was convicted of a 1 bn naira (NGN) fraud and sentenced to seven years' imprisonment on 29 March, but given the option of paying a NGN 100 m fine. On 23 June, Scales Olatunji, a member of a syndicate of internet fraudsters, was not so lucky when the Court of Appeal in Cross River State upheld the long prison sentence handed down by a Federal High Court the previous year for defrauding the Norwegian government and its citizens to the tune of NGN 525 m.

Although the EFCC's record had slightly improved, several charges against prominent people were struck out by the courts. The Federal High Court in Abuja acquitted Stephen Oronsaye, former head of service of the federation, on a charge of a NGN 190 m pension fraud indictment on 5 June. Shortly afterwards, on 14 July, the same court freed former Imo State governor Rochas Okorocha for the third time in relation to alleged fraud and corruption while in office. The most bizarre case, however, occurred when the Supreme Court overturned the conviction of former senator Peter Nwaoboshi, who was serving a seven-year prison sentence for corruption, and ordered his release on 7 July. In December, and to the delight of the government and business circles, the Financial Action Task Force (FATF) praised Nigeria's efforts to have itself removed from the *'grey list'*, on which the country was placed in February, in the foreseeable future

The precarious security situation in most parts of the country, as well as the government's wilful abuse of press freedom, had various consequences for *human and civil rights*. The media, particularly during the elections, was the main target of the security forces, with fifth columns of political pressure groups and paid claqueurs. According to the International Centre for Investigative Reporting (ICIR), at least 39 journalists and other media professionals were harassed, molested, and even detained over the course of the year. About half of the incidents happened during the general elections in February and March. The Cybercrimes Act – which served as a useful tool in deterring election-related violence – was also increasingly used by the state to deter its critics.

The case against those accused of the gruesome murder of young Christian student Deborah Samuel Yakubu the previous year was dismissed. She had been stoned to death for alleged blasphemy against the prophet and then burned by the mob. On 30 January, a magistrate's court in Sokoto, capital of the state of the same name, struck out the case and released the suspects from custody. The judge justified his verdict on the grounds of lack of evidence and of diligent prosecution. However, various courts passed death sentences for serious crimes. The one that made headlines was the *death sentence* passed by the High Court in Osun State on billionaire Abdulrahman Adedoyin, the owner of Hilton Honours Hotel in Ile-Ife and Oduduwa University. On 30 May, along with two other defendants, he was found guilty of the murder of one Timothy Adegoke, a postgraduate student of Obafemi Awolowo University back in 2021 who had lodged in the hotel. The circumstances, however, remained dubious, since the defendant refused to enter the witness box.

On 18 April, some good news was reported when the Abuja Federal High Court nullified several sections of the Companies and Allied Matters Act 2020 (CAMA). The court maintained that these sections were not consistent with the provisions of the constitution. At the time, it was widely believed that the Act would enable authorities to *clamp down on NGOs and the media* whenever they saw fit.

Against the backdrop of the *precarious security situation in the Igbo heartland*, the Nnamdi Kanu saga continued and took a new twist. On 15 December, the Supreme Court criticised the government's forcible repatriation of Kanu – the leader of the proscribed Indigenous People of Biafra (IPOB) movement – from Kenya but refused to accept the illegal action as a justification for dropping the charges of terrorism and treasonable felony against him. The Supreme Court overturned the verdict of the Court of Appeal (which had claimed that the Federal High Court could no longer try Kanu) and ordered the continuation of the trial at the very court where the proceedings began back in 2015. In addition, the court maintained that any case arguing violation of Kanu's rights should have been tried as a civil suit.

Finally, three years after the violent suppression of the nationwide #EndSARS protests against *police brutality* in 2020, at least 15 protesters were still detained – most without trial – in Kirikiri Medium Correctional Centre and Ikoyi Medium Security Correctional Centre in Lagos.

Foreign Affairs

Nigeria's *foreign policy* was – to a degree – reshaped by the new leadership. Immediately after INEC declared Tinubu as duly elected president on 1 March, both the US and the UK congratulated the president elect, while acknowledging shortcomings which should be addressed about the way the elections were conducted. Although relations have improved in recent years, the US delegation that attended Tinubu's inauguration was led by Marcia Fudge, secretary of state in charge of housing and urban development. This rather modest representation also applied to the UK government, which sent Andrew Mitchell, minister of state for development and Africa at the Foreign, Commonwealth and Development Office, to head the delegation.

Over the course of the year, however, relations with the US and UK, which are home to the largest *Nigerian diasporas*, were once again mainly dominated by legal and crime issues. On 11 July, Jacob Olalekan Ponle, better known as Woodberry, an associate of another Nigerian *international fraudster*, Ramon Abbas, alias 'Hushpuppi', was sentenced to eight years and three months in prison by a district court in Illinois for his coordination of a multi-million-dollar fraud. In addition, he was made to pay some $8 m to seven victims in restitution. Both had been arrested in Dubai in 2020. Soon thereafter, on 20 July, the Federal High Court in Abuja ruled that two Nigerian brothers, Samuel and Samson Ogoshi, were to be extradited to the US charged with sexual extortion involving numerous young men and teenage boys via social media. The defendants, who were arraigned in a court in Michigan on 14 August, were charged with having caused the death of at least one youth, Jordan DeMay, the previous year. On 29 December, one Olusegun Samson Adejorin was arrested in Ghana. He was indicted by a federal grand jury in Maryland for wire fraud, serious identity theft, and unauthorised access to a protected computer; these charges related to a $7.5 m scheme to defraud two charitable organisations by impersonating employees and gaining access to their email accounts.

Earlier, on 16 February, the US signed an agreement with the Nigerian government under the Kleptocracy Asset Recovery Programme for the return of some $1 m stolen by Deprieye Alamieyeseigha, the late governor of Bayelsa State. The Diezani Alison-Madueke saga continued against this background. In March, Alison-Madueke, the former Nigerian minister for petroleum resources, along with Nigerian businessmen Olajide Omokore and Kolawole Akanni, were investigated and indicted for *money laundering* in the US. This involved the proceeds of corruption offences under the Kleptocracy Asset Recovery Programme. By year's end, the programme had lapsed with no decision reported.

Nigeria's *precarious security situation* had a direct impact on the US mission. In an unprecedented incident, a convoy of nine – five US embassy staff and four mobile police escorts – was ambushed in Ogbaru local government area in Anambra State on 16 May. Seven people were killed and two abducted. The group was travelling in advance of a planned visit by mission personnel to a US-funded flood response project in the state. Some days later, on 19 May, the two hostages were rescued by security forces and five suspects were arrested shortly after.

This gruesome incident notwithstanding, efforts to strengthen the US – Nigerian partnership were underlined by the joint celebration of the upgrade to Kainji air force base in Niger State on 27 April; this was attended by high-ranking officers from both the US and Nigeria. The $38 m base improvements were undertaken against the backdrop of a larger $500 m US foreign *military deal*, which includes the delivery of a fleet of 12 A-29 Super Tucano aircraft as well as precision munition and training; the aircraft will be stationed in Kainji. This is the biggest US armed export deal in sub-Saharan Africa to date. In addition to improved military partnership, the US focused on expanding economic cooperation, an emphasis which was reflected in a visit by assistant secretary for energy resources Geoffrey Pyatt, who attended an energy security dialogue (18–20 June). On 17–19 September, Nigerian-born deputy treasury secretary Wally Adeyamo visited Nigeria, looking to strengthen economic ties and to *counter China's growing influence* on the continent – highlighted by a rare visit of Chinese warships to Africa's Atlantic coast on 2–6 July at Lagos harbour and the commissioning of nearby Chinese-built Lekki deep seaport back in January. Earlier, on 21 June, Bill Gates attended the Pan-African Youth Innovation Forum in Lagos, where he criticised poor investment in the nation's health sector. On 28 July, Richard Gingras, Google global vice-president, met President Tinubu in Abuja; Tinubu underscored his government's desire to create 1 m digital jobs.

As in previous years, Nigeria's *relations with the UK* were shaped by various legal issues and by frequent official visits by Nigeria's top politicians. In January, two presidential candidates, Atiku and Obi, were in the UK explaining their objectives should they win the forthcoming elections; Tinubu had made a similar presentation in December of the previous year. Later, on 6 May, then President Buhari attended the coronation of King Charles III and extended his stay by a week for dental treatment. On 24 June, President Tinubu made a short private trip to London after attending the New Global Financing Pact summit in Paris (22–23 June); this was his first visit abroad as president.

One of the most bizarre cases in Nigeria–UK relations came to an end in a UK court when, in March, former deputy president of the Nigerian Senate Ike Ekweremadu, his wife Beatrice, and a Nigerian physician practising in the UK, Obinna Obeta, were convicted of *organ trafficking*. This was the first conviction based on a contravention of the Modern Slavery Act 2015. The couple had been arrested at Heathrow Airport in June of the previous year and charged with conspiracy to facilitate the travel of one David Nwamini Ukpo to Britain; Ukpo was a Nigerian street trader and was paid a large sum of money to donate his kidney to their sick daughter, Sonia. On 5 May, the court imposed heavy sentences: Ekweremadu was to spend nine years and eight months in prison, his wife was given a jail sentence of four years and six months and the physician a ten-year sentence.

On 2 October, Diezani Alison-Madueke, who had left Nigeria in 2015, appeared before a London court accused of a £100,000 bribe paid in the UK in return for awarding multi-million-pound oil and gas contracts. She was granted bail of £70,000, to be paid before leaving the court, and was ordered to wear an electronic tag. The Nigerian government made a fresh request on 29 October for her *extradition to Nigeria* in relation to a $2.5 bn fraud in which the former minister was allegedly involved. She was facing several charges which might have fallen under the jurisdiction of the UK, the US, the UAE, or Nigeria. On 22 December, a master's student, Somtochukwu Okwuoha, was found guilty of making terror threats against Dundee University. He was sentenced to a 40-month jail term and subsequent deportation.

The UK, along with the US, remained the *preferred destination* of Nigerians. In the first half of the year 132,000 visas were issued to Nigerians. In the previous year, the number was 324,000, about 10% of all visas issued. The British High Commission opened a visa application centre in Port Harcourt in August and a temporary one in Enugu in September, in addition to the centres in Abuja and Lagos. Previously, on 23 May, the UK government had announced that, at the beginning of the following year, foreign graduate and postgraduate students on non-research courses would not be allowed to bring family members into the country.

There was good news for Nigeria, however, when on 23 October, the saga involving Nigeria and the British Virgin Islands-based company Process and Industrial Development Limited (P&ID) was settled in Nigeria's favour after 13 years of legal wrangling. The company had been accused of breach of contract, dishonest, bribery, and fraud. Against all the odds and despite many obstacles, Nigeria won its bid to overturn a $10 bn *arbitration award* in favour of P&ID. A UK court finally upheld Nigeria's petition on the grounds that the process by which P&ID had secured a long-term contract to construct and operate a gas processing plant was fraudulent.

Over the course of the year, *relationships with the EU* and its member countries, particularly Germany, were intensified. Special vocational training programmes designed for young people were sponsored by the German government in collaboration with the Nigerian Ministry of Labour and Employment; otherwise, cooperation focused on the energy sector. President Tinubu attended the fourth G20 summit on investment which took place in Berlin on 20–21 November and tried to attract more foreign investment to his country. Germany and Nigeria also signed two agreements, the first on the supply of 850,000 tonnes of Nigerian gas per year to Germany with the prospect of expanding this to 1.2 m tonnes, the second covering renewable energy projects worth $500 m. Against the backdrop of the COP28 in Dubai (30 November to 13 December), attended by both German chancellor Olof Scholz and President Tinubu, Siemens Energy signed an agreement with the FGN Power Company (Nigeria) to expedite the implementation of the Presidential Power Initiative. Scholz had visited Nigeria on 29–30 October and met President Tinubu and the ECOWAS Commission president, Omar Alieu Touray. This visit was aimed at strengthening bilateral relations and Scholz was accompanied by high-ranking German businesspeople, together with a delegation concerned with cultural programmes.

On 21 March, after the hectic election campaign, president elect Tinubu left for France on a month-long vacation amid speculations that he was travelling to attend to his health. Much later, on 3 November, the president expressed his appreciation to France for the return of *$150 m in loot* stolen by former military dictator Sani Abacha. In addition, the two governments signed a $100 m agreement to promote investment in the ICT and creative arts industries.

Against the backdrop of the Russian invasion of Ukraine, the Russia–Africa Economic and Humanitarian Forum took place in St Petersburg on 27–28 July, attended by Nigeria's vice-president Kashim Shettima.

President Tinubu emerged as ECOWAS's new chair at the 63rd Ordinary Session of the Heads of State and Government in Bissau, the capital of Guinea-Bissau, on 9 July. On 26 July, he was confronted with his first foreign affairs challenge when the president of Niger, Mohamed Bazoum, was ousted in a *military coup*, an action which was condemned by Tinubu and which led to hectic diplomatic activity within ECOWAS. At short notice, a special ECOWAS meeting was held in Abuja on 30 July under Nigeria's leadership; sanctions were imposed on Niger (Nigeria's direct neighbour) and the junta was given one week to leave the stage and allow Bazoum to return to power; otherwise, the regional organisation threatened to use force to reinstate the ousted president. Shortly thereafter, on 3 August, Nigeria's chief of defence staff hosted a meeting which saw nine colleagues from the region attending.

President Tinubu soon had to accept *ECOWAS's limited powers* in handling such a complex issue. On 4 August, the Nigerian Senate passed a resolution rejecting the president's request to deploy Nigerian troops in an attempt to restore democratic rule in Niger and suggested that political solutions could resolve the crisis. On the same day (4 August), the junta refused to receive an ECOWAS delegation led by Abdulsalami Abubakar, Nigeria's last junta leader. However, on 9 August, Lamido Sanusi, former governor of the Central Bank of Nigeria and deposed emir of Kano, together with two emirs from Niger, met the junta leader Abdourahmane Tchiani; on 13 August, a team of Nigerian Islamic scholars met Tchiani, who refused to capitulate.

Nigerians were particularly affected by the crisis in Sudan; some 2,600 were evacuated in June and July, of whom a good number had been studying there. A further 1,200 had to leave other crisis-ridden African countries.

President Tinubu had a busy travel schedule. Although Nigeria's relations with China had to some extent cooled off, Nigeria remained committed to *expanding its presence in Asia*. Thus, at the sidelines of the G20 summit in New Delhi in India (9–10 September), Tinubu, along with top Nigerian businesspeople such as Aliko Dangote, Tony Elumelu, Allen Onyema, and Femi Otedola, attended a Nigeria–India roundtable. In addition, on 20 October, the first batch of 1,001 beneficiaries of Kano State foreign postgraduate scholarships, numbering 150, left for India.

On 11 September, Tinubu made a stop-over in the UAE, where his meeting with President Mohamed bin Zayed resulted in the UAE *lifting the visa ban imposed on Nigerians*. Furthermore, Emirates resumed flights to Nigeria ten months after suspending its operations over its inability to repatriate $85 m of revenue from Nigeria. On 20 April, the Nigerian private airline Air Peace started direct flights from Abuja and Lagos to Israel. Later (on 10 November), the Nigerian president attended the first Saudi Arabia–Africa summit in Riyadh.

Prior to that, on 19 September, Tinubu addressed the 78th UNGA in person and, on 27 October, Nigeria along with 119 other member countries, voted in favour of a *humanitarian ceasefire* in the ongoing conflict between Israel and Hamas. On 24 February, Nigeria had backed the resolution calling for an end to the war and demanding that Russia leave Ukrainian territory. Finally, on 10 October, having received only three votes, Nigeria failed to join the UNHCR for the 2024–26 term.

Socioeconomic Development

During the period under review, *oil and gas prices were relatively high*, a situation largely triggered by the Russian invasion of Ukraine, the Israel – Hamas encounter in Gaza, and the attacks of Houthi rebels on western vessels in the Red Sea on their way to the Suez Canal. Over the course of the year, prices for Nigeria's high-quality crude oil averaged at $83 per barrel, but at no point did the production level reach the OPEC quota of some 1.7 m barrels per day (b/d). Apart from the months of March and October, when production reached some 1.5 m b/d, the level did not pass the 1.3 m b/d mark. This was due to widespread mismanagement, pipeline sabotage, and highly organised oil theft. On 8 February at a hearing in a Senate committee,

Mele Kyari, CEO of the Nigerian National Petroleum Company (NNPC) disclosed that about 4,800 *illegal pipelines* were in operation, causing a loss of more than 400,000 b/d, which translated into an annual financial loss of more than $8 bn. Another $10 bn at least, but probably much more, was being lost annually to petrol subsidies and non-transparent purchases. To partially compensate the loss, the NNPC began drilling a first oil well in Nasarawa State in the North in March; this followed two other northern states which had begun drilling the previous year.

The *first private oil refinery*, the Dangote refinery, located in the Lekki free zone with a capacity of 650,000 b/d and 3 bn cubic feet of gas per day, is financed and run by Nigerian business tycoon Alike Dangote. However, already in 2021, NNPC had received government approval to buy a 20% stake valued at some $2.7 bn in the refinery. This refinery was commissioned by then President Buhari on 22 May, although operations began only in October, with some 350,000 b/d. Apart from the NNPC, multinational oil companies such as Shell and ExxonMobil began to supply additional charges of crude oil.

As of 30 September, the *total public debt portfolio* of the federal government, the 36 federal states, and the FTC stood at $114.3 bn, compared with $103.1 bn at the beginning of the year. To a large extent, the seemingly manageable amount of $41.6 bn in external debt encouraged President Tinubu to copy his predecessor's economic policy of brinkmanship, borrowing large sums on the international and domestic money markets. In April, for example, Nigeria received a so-called 'palliative' $800 m loan from the World Bank to pay cash transfers of NGN 25,000 each to 15 m vulnerable households suffering as a result of overdue reforms and a rampant inflation rate of close to 30%. The increase in the price of foodstuffs was even greater. The domestic debt portfolio, however, amounted to $72.7 bn, of which the states' share, including Abuja, came to $7.5 bn. At year's end. Foreign reserves stood at $32 bn.

On 3 January, then President Buhari eventually signed the *2023 federal budget* into law. The budget totalled NGN 21.8 trillion ($49 bn) and was based on a benchmark of $75 per barrel of crude oil and a production estimate of 1.7 m b/d, as well as on an exchange rate of NGN 446 to $1. As in previous years, the National Assembly increased the president's proposal to its own advantage by 6.4% and the oil benchmark by $5. In addition, the implementation of the 2022 supplementary appropriation bill of $2 bn was extended to 31 March and later to 30 June. On 30 October, however, the federal executive council approved another supplementary budget of NGN 2.1 trillion ($2.8 bn) for 2023 which the law-makers passed within days and the new incumbent, Tinubu, approved on 8 November. With an allocation of NGN 604 bn, national security and defence were the main beneficiaries. The budget deficit was NGN 13.7 trillion, about 6.1% of GDP; the threshold set by the Fiscal Responsibility Act 2007 stipulates 3%. Once again, this deficit came as no surprise given that the annual petrol subsidy of at least $10 bn was still in place at year's end, and it remained unclear whether the end of this subsidy would become a reality by mid-2024 as claimed.

The many inconsistencies of *economic and fiscal policy* were particularly visible when the redesigned naira 200, 500, and 1,000 banknotes were supposed to replace the old ones at 31 January. The aim was to curb cash in circulation and, *inter alia*, allegedly to hinder large-scale vote buying at the forthcoming elections. This decision, however, had at best a marginal impact on the outcome of the elections. Nonetheless, the whole process eventually got stuck in a quagmire when, on 8 February, the Supreme Court temporarily halted the phasing out of the old bank notes until further notice. Later, on 29 November, in another far-reaching decision, the court ruled that both old and new bank notes remained legal tender, and the whole process ended as a pricey storm in a teapot.

At the 2024 budget presentation on 29 November, the president introduced his apparently over-ambitious federal budget of NGN 27.5 trillion ($34.8 bn), based on an exchange rate of NGN 750 to $1 and an oil price benchmark of $77 per barrel. In fact, at year's end, the exchange rate on the *parallel market* was about NGN 1,200 to $1, and it was widely expected that the gap between the official exchange rate and the parallel market would continue to grow. Nevertheless, the economy was expected to grow at a rate of 3.7%, with an inflation rate of about 21%, a budget deficit of close to 4% of GDP, and an annual debt service making about 45% of the expected total revenue of NGN 18.3 trillion.

Finally, Akintola Williams, a founding member and the first president of the Association of Chartered Accountants of Nigeria, passed away on 11 September at the age of 104. Onaolapo Soleye, finance minister under the Buhari-led military junta, died days after his 90th birthday. On 26 March, retired lieutenant general Oladipo Diya, former chief of general staff and temporary deputy and later a political prisoner of military dictator Sani Abacha, passed away at the age of 78; Frank Kokori, former general secretary of the National Union of Petroleum and Natural Gas Workers, who was one of the major opponents of the dictator, died on 7 December. Earlier, on 9 April, Bola Ajibola, a controversial lawyer and judge at the ICJ, had passed away. Last but not least, the *first female major general* and first commander of the Nigerian army medical corps, Aderonke Kale, died on 8 November at the age of 84.

Senegal

Mamadou Bodian

Domestic politics in Senegal were dominated by significant events leading up to the 2024 presidential election. The spotlight was on the opposition leader, Ousmane Sonko, who faced multiple legal challenges, imprisonment, and potential disqualification from the race. In a politically tumultuous environment, migration became a crucial public debate issue, with many Senegalese, especially the youth, undertaking perilous journeys to the Spanish Canary Islands despite government efforts to curb illegal immigration. In terms of foreign policy, despite its tarnished image due to domestic unrest and human rights abuses, Senegal attempted to strengthen its ties with traditional partners while maintaining its diplomatic leadership by actively participating in international organisations and playing a vital role in UN peacekeeping missions. Senegal also hosted international forums on food security, climate change, and human rights, promoting sustainable growth and global cooperation. Economically, Senegal experienced 4.3% growth, up from 4.0% in 2022, driven by solid secondary sector performance and improvements in agriculture, despite high inflation and political unrest. The country continued to address governance challenges, attract foreign investments, and focus on energy sovereignty and development initiatives.

Domestic Politics

A series of *high-profile trials ongoing from the previous year* marked the political landscape. On 2 January 2024, two members of the opposition PUR (Parti de l'Unité et du Rassemblement, or Party for Unity and Rally), Amadou Niang and Massata Samb, were sentenced to six months in jail for assaulting fellow MP Amy Ndiaye Gniby from the ruling BBY (Benno Bokk Yakaar; United in Hope) coalition during a parliamentary session in December 2023. The court also ordered the men to pay CFAfr 5 m francs ($8,200) in compensation to Gniby, who was pregnant at the time of the assault, which occurred during a budget debate.

The case that drew the most attention was that of opposition leader Ousmane Sonko, who went through a series of politically charged trials. On 31 January, he was summoned to court over a defamation complaint by tourism minister Mame Mbaye Niang, whom Sonko accused of embezzling CFAfr 29 bn. His trial on 2 February sparked calls for protests, raising concerns of unrest, as his March 2021 arrest on rape allegations had led to riots and 14 deaths. Sonko missed the court date, with his lawyers claiming that he had not received a summons. The trial was postponed to 16 February, when hundreds protested in Dakar as Sonko left the courthouse. Police later smashed Sonko's car windows, forcibly removed him, and escorted him home, citing disruption. Postponed to 16 March, the trial culminated in unrest when Sonko's convoy was blocked, prompting police to extract and escort him to court while blocking his estimated 5,000 supporters, who continued protests from the previous day. On 30 March, the court sentenced Sonko to a two-month suspended term for libel, ordering him to pay CFAfr 200 m to Mame Mbaye Niang, keeping him eligible for the 2024 elections. Prosecutors appealed, and on 8 May, the court increased his sentence to six months suspended and upheld the damages. Sonko, claiming government injustice, did not attend the appeal, rendering him ineligible to vote or run in 2024.

In addition to his defamation case, Sonko faced rape charges dating back to 2021, following allegations by a female massage parlour employee. After delays, the trial ended on 23 May, with the prosecutor seeking a ten-year sentence for Sonko, who did not attend. While the verdict was scheduled for 1 June, Sonko began a 'freedom caravan' on 26 May from Ziguinchor, where he is mayor, to Dakar. This was intercepted by security forces after protests led to a death in Kolda. On 1 June, the court acquitted Sonko of rape but sentenced him to two years for 'corrupting the youth', again affecting his eligibility for the 2024 presidential election. This led to severe unrest, with 16 to 30 deaths reported. Authorities announced an investigation into the alleged use of vigilantes by the government to suppress protests. The arrest of Sonko, who had been barricaded in his home in Dakar by security forces, was expected at any moment following his 1 June conviction. Finally, on 28 July – just a few days after the barricades at his home were lifted – he was arrested. He was placed in pretrial detention on 30 July on eight new charges, including 'incitement to insurrection' and 'endangering state security'. Sonko described an incident on his Facebook page just before his arrest where he had attempted to forcibly retrieve a security agent's phone to demand the deletion of images taken of him returning from Friday prayers. The opposition YAW (Yewwi Askan Wi; Liberate the People) coalition condemned his arrest and the dissolution of his party, PASTEF (African Patriots of Senegal for Work, Ethics and Fraternity), on 31 July. On 16 August, Sonko was admitted to intensive care after a 19-day hunger strike. He ended the strike on 2 September due to health concerns.

Meanwhile, political and *legal battles* over Sonko's eligibility for the 2024 election continued. On 30 August, the minister of justice declared Sonko ineligible due to his conviction. On 14 September, Sonko's lawyers filed petitions with the ECOWAS Court of Justice to suspend PASTEF's dissolution and restore political rights for Sonko and his party. On 29 September, the DGE (Direction Générale des Elections) refused to issue sponsorship forms to the 'Sonko Président 2024' coalition, arguing that Sonko was no longer on the electoral roll. Throughout October, Sonko's lawyers appealed to Senegal's Supreme Court, contesting the refusal to provide sponsorship forms and the dissolution of PASTEF. An appeal was also filed with the Tribunal d'Instance de Ziguinchor to protest Sonko's removal from the electoral roll. The Supreme Court rejected Sonko's request for the right to collect sponsorship forms due to his removal from the electoral rolls. However, a lower court judge in Ziguinchor reinstated Sonko's eligibility and ordered that he be allowed to obtain sponsorship forms. The state announced plans to appeal this decision. Senegal's electoral commission urged the DGE to reinstate Sonko and provide the sponsorship forms, but the DGE refused. On 17 October, Sonko resumed his hunger strike, awaiting a ruling on his eligibility for the 2024 elections. By 23 October, he had reportedly slipped into a coma. Despite his condition stabilising by 15 November, Sonko was sent back to prison based on his physician's recommendation, just days before the Supreme Court decided on his electoral status. On 17 November, the Supreme Court overturned the ruling that had allowed Sonko to run, closing the case.

In response, PASTEF announced on 19 November that it would sponsor Bassirou Diomaye Faye as a new candidate while maintaining Sonko's candidacy. On 12 December, a Dakar court reconsidered Sonko's electoral reinstatement, and it ruled in his favour on 14 December, which was met with public support. However, by 20 December, authorities were still refusing to provide the necessary documents for Sonko's candidacy. With a pressing deadline of 26 December, Sonko could not obtain the sponsorship forms required for the February election.

Amid political tensions and trials, Senegal's electoral process has seen significant developments. On 24 April, the presidency removed Idrissa Seck, a former prime minister and runner-up in the 2019 election, from his position as head of the Economic, Social, and Environmental Council after he declared his candidacy for the 2024 presidential election and refused to support Macky Sall. This led to Seck's Rewmi (Nation) party withdrawing from the ruling BBY coalition, potentially endangering its parliamentary majority. On 10 September, President Sall nominated Prime Minister Amadou Ba as the BBY candidate for the upcoming presidential elections, avoiding protracted primaries after announcing he would not seek a third term. On 22 September, former prime minister Mahammed Boun Abdallah Dionne resigned from the ruling party and declared his candidacy, reflecting internal contestation within the party. These developments prompted Sall to announce a new government of 39 ministers on 11 October, focusing on smooth election organisation, addressing economic and social challenges, optimising public services, and advancing the Emerging Senegal Plan. Six new ministers were appointed and two departed, with Amadou Ba designated the presidential candidate.

The *electoral reform* adopted at the national dialogue in June reduced the number of citizen sponsors required, initially set at 1% and 0.8% of the general electoral roll. It introduced an optional sponsorship system, combining citizen sponsorship, limited to between 0.6% and 0.8% of the general electoral roll, with the sponsorship of elected representatives, requiring support from either 4% of deputies to the National Assembly or 20% of heads of territorial executive bodies (mayors or departmental council presidents). This reform aimed to avoid duplication between competing candidacies, with each voter authorised to sponsor only one candidate. The start date for collecting sponsorship for the 2024 presidential election, initially set for 28 August, was postponed to 27 September, when each candidate had to appoint an agent at the Ministry of the Interior to collect citizens' sponsorship forms. To ensure the transparency of the electoral process, a new opposition coalition named the Front for Inclusiveness and Transparency of Elections (FITE) was formed on 11 November, calling for free and transparent elections and denouncing the 'erosion of democracy' under President Sall's government. All of its 35 members were to be candidates for the upcoming presidential election, including former prime minister Aminata 'Mimi' Touré and Ousmane Sonko, who continued to demand his reinstatement on the electoral roll. Seventy-nine people submitted their candidacies to the Senegalese Constitutional Council for the February 2024 presidential election before the 26 December deadline. The examination of candidacy files by the Constitutional Council began on 26 December and was to continue until 12 January 2024, with the official list of approved candidates to be announced on 20 January 2024. Among the candidates were Amadou Ba, supported by President Sall; Idrissa Seck, who came second in the 2019 election; and the imprisoned Sonko, whose eligibility remained uncertain.

The year was tumultuous for *civil liberties*, marked by arrests and significant downgrades in international rankings, indicating increased government repression. Amnesty International reported increasing repression of civil liberties ahead of the 2024 election. On 10 January, journalist Pape Ali Niang was released after more than two months in detention for sharing government secrets and reporting on Sonko's alleged rape case. Niang had been on a hunger strike since 24 December 2022. His release was conditional on refraining from travel and from commenting on the case. On 9 March, former prime minister Cheikh Haguibou Soumaré was detained for allegedly defaming President Sall in an open letter claiming that he had given €12 m to French far-right politician Marine Le Pen. Soumaré was released the next day under judicial supervision. On 10 May, a teenager was killed and 30 others were injured during a protest in Dakar's Ngor neighbourhood. Protesters, demanding the construction of a high school instead of a police station, were fuelled by Sonko's call for civil disobedience. On 6 December, Senegal's civil liberties ranking was downgraded to 'repressed' by CIVICUS, citing the jailing of Sonko and violent protests. The downgrade was so severe that Senegal was ranked alongside countries governed by military juntas. On 13 December, Senegal launched a pilot scheme to reduce prison overcrowding by releasing prisoners with ankle monitors. Critics argued that it did not address deeper justice system issues.

Despite political turmoil, the Senegalese government made notable changes in its *armed forces*. On 4 April, Senegal celebrated its 63rd Independence Day Parade under the theme 'Armed Forces and Preservation of Natural Resources' in Dakar, marking the first parade since the pandemic. Thousands joined, and President Sall praised the armed forces' efforts in preserving territorial integrity amid widespread dissatisfaction with alleged corruption and high living costs. On 6 April, President Sall dismissed General Cheikh Wade, the Chief of General Staff of the Armed Forces (CEMGA), and appointed General Mbaye Cissé as his successor on 10 April. General Cissé, a US Army Command and General Staff College graduate, had previously served as Sall's chief of staff and director of CHEDS (Centre des Hautes Études de Défense et de Sécurité). The reshuffle occurred in a tense political climate ahead of crucial elections. On 25 April, President Sall appointed Senegal's first female army general, Fatou Fall. A medical colonel and expert in hepatology and gastroenterology, Fall enlisted in the army in 1985 and became a professor at Université Cheikh Anta Diop. She now heads hepatology and gastroenterology at the Hôpital Principal de Dakar.

Senegal faced numerous *security challenges* this year, marked by fatal road accidents, clashes among fishermen over illegal practices, and significant drug seizures by the navy, all highlighting the pressing need for improved safety and enforcement measures. The issue of road safety came to the fore on 8 January when a bus crash in Gnivy village, Kaffrine region, resulted in at least 40 fatalities and 100 injuries. The accident was caused by a tyre puncture that led the bus to collide with another. President Sall declared three days of mourning in response. Just a week later, on 16 January, another tragic accident in Sakal, Louga region, claimed 19 lives and injured 25 more when a bus swerved to avoid a donkey. These incidents underscored the urgent need for traffic safety reforms, prompting the government to ban night buses and the importation of used tyres.

Environmental protection emerged as another critical challenge on 8 April when artisanal fishermen clashed over using banned monofilament fishing nets. These nets, though prohibited since 1987, had continue to be used due to poor regulation within the fishing sector, threatening the critically endangered humpback dolphin in the Sine Saloum Delta. This incident highlighted the ongoing struggle to enforce sustainable fishing practices and protect marine life. Cybersecurity became a significant concern on 26 May when Senegal's government websites were paralysed by a cyber-attack by the hacker group 'Mysterious Team'. The group, implementing a denial-of-service attack, claimed solidarity with Senegalese citizens and disrupted government operations, revealing vulnerabilities in the nation's cyber-defences. The fight against drug trafficking took centre stage with two major cocaine seizures by the Navy. On 28 November, nearly three tonnes of cocaine were intercepted off the coast of Senegal, followed by another seizure of three tonnes on 16 December. These operations, among the largest in Senegal's history, underscored the country's role as a transit point for South American cartels trafficking drugs to Europe and other regions. The increasing frequency of such seizures pointed to the growing challenge of combating drug trafficking and its associated crimes.

The *migration crisis* in Senegal escalated, with thousands attempting perilous journeys to the Canary Islands, leading to tragic incidents and significant interceptions by the Senegalese navy, alongside international support from Spain to curb illegal migration. Between 1 January and 31 August, nearly 11,500 migrants arrived in the Canary Islands. The Senegalese navy intercepted over a thousand would-be migrants throughout the year. On 10 July, a boat with 101 passengers left Fass Boye, aiming for the Canary Islands. By 16 August, a Spanish fishing vessel rescued 37 survivors in weakened conditions after days without food. On 24 July, at least 15 Senegalese migrants died when their wooden pirogue capsized off Dakar's coast. Despite the Senegalese navy's rescue efforts, many continued to die attempting the journey. In August, several boats carrying at least 300 people went missing. On 14 August, approximately 60 Senegalese were presumed dead after their canoe was found off Cape Verde. A week later, 37 migrants were rescued off Cape Verde, but 64 others were unaccounted for. On 6 September, the Senegalese navy intercepted 118 migrants off the coast of Saint-Louis. The tragic death of young Senegalese filmmaker Doudou Diop in July highlighted the perilous journey. He was documenting the journey when the Moroccan navy intercepted his boat; 71 people were rescued but 14, including Diop, died. In late September, the Senegalese navy intercepted four boats carrying 605 migrants attempting to reach the Canary Islands. On 30 October, Spain provided six drones and additional resources to help Senegal tackle the migration crisis. By 5 November, over 32,000 migrants had reached the

Canary Islands, exceeding the 2006 crisis numbers. Contributing factors included a lack of jobs, high living costs, depleted fish stocks, poor healthcare, and political unrest. President Sall ordered emergency measures to curb illegal migration, including actions by multiple ministries to address the crisis. In late December, reports emerged of 'pseudo-legitimate' travel agencies in Dakar offering migrants packages to the US–Mexico border, exacerbating the crisis.

Foreign Politics

Growing political tensions and internal challenges related to numerous politically charged trials drew global attention, highlighting the complexity of the political situation in Senegal ahead of the February 2024 presidential election. Following the cabinet reshuffle on 11 October, Ismaïla Madior Fall left his position as minister of justice to become minister of foreign affairs and Senegalese abroad, replacing lawyer Aïssata Tall Sall, who now heads the Ministry of Justice.

In *African relations*, Senegal prioritises diplomatic and cooperative approaches to regional crises, emphasising its active participation in ECOWAS meetings to address political and security challenges in West Africa. On 21 September, President Sall, during an interview with France 24 and RFI at the 78th session of the UNGA in New York, discussed the coup d'état in Niger on 26 July. He emphasised that while diplomatic solutions were preferred for resolving the crisis, military intervention remained on the table. Furthering this diplomatic engagement, on 6 December, Madior Fall attended the 51st session of the ECOWAS Mediation and Security Council in Abuja. The Council focused on the political and security situation in the region, particularly the political transitions in Burkina Faso, Mali, and Guinea. It also addressed recent political and security developments in Sierra Leone and Guinea-Bissau and the electoral processes in Ghana and Senegal. Notably, this session extended a diplomatic hand to the military juntas, underscoring Senegal's commitment to seeking collaborative and peaceful resolutions to regional conflicts.

Senegal's engagements with the *Arab and Muslim world* include high-level discussions on bilateral and regional issues, support missions for citizens abroad, and showcasing national achievements in economic and social forums. On 23 January, President Sall met with Egyptian president Abdel Fattah al-Sisi to discuss bilateral, African, and international topics. On 25 and 26 July, Annette Seck, the minister delegate to the minister of foreign affairs and Senegalese abroad, travelled to Dakhla, Morocco, following instructions from President Sall. This mission aimed to support Senegalese citizens awaiting repatriation after failed emigration attempts. Seck met with local authorities, visited Senegalese citizens in various centres, and arranged for over 50 injured compatriots to be flown back on an air force flight while preparing to repatriate over 400 others by land starting from 27 July.

On 10 November, following trips to London and Yaoundé, the foreign minister visited Riyadh, Saudi Arabia, for the fourth Senegal–Saudi Arabia Joint Commission session. This high-level meeting allowed the Senegalese private sector to explore partnerships with Saudi investors and was marked by several cooperation agreements between Senegalese ministries and Saudi authorities. On 10 December, at the 21st Doha Forum, themed 'Inclusive Economic Systems for Sustainable Growth', President Sall highlighted Senegal's growth and social inclusion. On the sidelines, he met with His Highness Sheikh Tamim bin Hamad Al Thani, the emir of Qatar, strengthening friendship and cooperation between the countries and addressing significant political, economic, and developmental issues. In his address, President Sall emphasised public policies promoting growth and social inclusion, mainly through the Emerging Senegal Plan (PSE), which aimed to transform the economy through massive investments.

Senegal strengthened its partnerships with *Western democracies* through strategic dialogues and agreements, hosting visits from high-level officials, and securing cooperation agreements in various sectors. On 24 January, President Sall received British minister for international development Andrew Mitchell to discuss the fruitful Senegalese–British partnership and shared interests. President Sall thanked the UK for supporting the AU's bid to join the G20. Shortly before, on 20 January, US treasury secretary Janet Yellen met with President Sall and finance minister Mamadou Moustapha Bâ to discuss promoting economic growth together. Yellen indicated that the US planned to expand trade relations with Senegal while ensuring fairness in multilateral organisations such as the World Bank and the IMF. She also engaged with businesswomen at a US-funded incubator in Dakar and visited Gorée Island during her ten-day Africa tour.

On 24 January, President Sall thanked Senator James Risch for a phone call on which they discussed mutual interests and the excellent US–Africa partnership. Continuing the strategic dialogue, on 20 June, during a state visit to Lisbon President Sall was received by Portuguese President Marcelo Rebelo de Sousa. They held a tête-à-tête and signed partnership agreements to strengthen economic and commercial cooperation between the two countries. On 23 August, during a working visit to Berlin, Aïssata Tall Sall held discussions with her German counterpart, Annalena Baerbock. They explored the historical relations between Senegal and Germany and exchanged views on international issues and African concerns, leading to an agreement on regular political consultations. On 15 December, Senegal's new foreign minister, Ismaïla Madior Fall, and his Spanish counterpart, José Manuel Albares Bueno, held a working session and signed a memorandum on sports, along with agreements to enhance cooperation in air transport, tourism, education, culture, maritime transport, fishing, economy, finance, trade, security, migration, politics, diplomacy, and the military. During their discussions, they addressed irregular migration, agreeing to create job opportunities for young people in their homeland to combat the phenomenon. This included implementing measures to prevent irregular migration and initiatives for youth employment and employability.

Senegal's interactions with *BRICS countries* focused on expanding practical cooperation, participating in summits to enhance strategic partnerships, and supporting initiatives. During his address at the extended session of the 15th BRICS summit on 24 August, themed 'BRICS and Africa: Partnership for Mutually Accelerated Growth, Sustainable Development, and Inclusive Multilateralism', President Sall praised the BRICS' openness in accepting six new member countries and advocated for the reform of global governance in a peaceful environment.

On 14 May, Zhao Leji, chair of the standing committee of China's National People's Congress, arrived in Dakar for an official three-day visit. The visit aimed to expand practical cooperation between Senegal and China. Both parties described the talks as friendly and productive, highlighting their co-chairing of the Forum on China–Africa Cooperation. The Chinese official pledged continued support for the PSE, the government's flagship programme, and advocated for further collaboration on China's Belt and Road Initiative. On 25 July, President Sall departed Dakar for St Petersburg to attend the second Russia–Africa summit on 27 and 28 July, attended by about 20 African heads of state and government. Sall reiterated his stance on restoring free trade in cereals. Before this, he officially visited the Russian Republic of Tatarstan on 25 and 26 July, where Tatarstan president Rustam Minnikhanov received him. The two leaders reaffirmed their commitment to strengthening friendship and cooperation, particularly in the petrochemical, automotive, agricultural, and sports industries. President Sall also welcomed the interest of the KAMAZ group in establishing a truck assembly plant in Senegal to serve the West African market. Sall participated in the 15th BRICS summit in Johannesburg from 22 to 24 August. He met with Chinese president Xi Jinping to review Sino-Senegalese cooperation and expressed his desire to strengthen their dynamic and mutually beneficial relations. On the sidelines of the summit, Sall also met with Indian prime minister Narendra Modi. They discussed energy, infrastructure, and defence, expressing satisfaction with the unique and historic partnership between India and Senegal, which has become increasingly economic. Modi emphasised that India considered Senegal a valued development partner.

Senegal's commitment to *regional and international leadership* was evident in its contributions to peacekeeping missions and active participation in UN initiatives. The country played a crucial role in UN peacekeeping, with over 2,000 soldiers in CAR, Guinea, and Gambia. On 1 March, the country paid tribute to three MINUSMA peacekeeping mission soldiers killed by an IED in Mali, reaffirming its commitment to Mali's stability amid rising jihadist violence. On 23 November, President Sall inaugurated the UN House in Diamniadio, attended by Romanian president Klaus Werner Iohannis and deputy UNSG Amina Mohammed. This eco-friendly building will house the 34 UN agencies in Senegal, enhancing synergy among UN entities and reinforcing Senegal's global diplomatic position.

Senegal also advocated for Africa's inclusion in global economic decisions and hosted significant events. On 21 July, President Sall participated in a virtual Global Crisis Response Group meeting to address the impact of the Covid-19 crisis impact and identify urgent solutions. On 18 September, President Sall arrived in New York for the 78th UNGA. He met with partners to strengthen bilateral relations, participated in a session reviewing the SDGs, and launched the campaign 'Bridging the Gap: Investing in Water' to improve African drinking water access. On 9 March, Aïssata Tall Sall received UNHCR Filippo Grandi in Dakar, expressing gratitude for his commitment to refugee issues, followed by a refugee naturalisation ceremony. President Sall played a central role in advocating for Africa's global inclusion. He urged G20 members to give Africa a voice in global economic decisions, highlighting the continent's investment opportunities. On 9 September, Sall celebrated the unanimous G20 decision to admit the AU as a full member, a significant milestone for Africa's international role.

Senegal actively engaged in *international forums* to address critical issues such as food security, climate change, human rights, and security challenges. These platforms allowed the country to advocate for regional development, sustainable growth, and enhanced global cooperation. On 25 January, President Sall participated in a three-day food security summit in Dakar, emphasising land reform and Africa's need for self-sufficiency to reduce dependency on imports and aid. The Russia–Ukraine conflict was noted to have worsened food security in Sahel. Akinwumi Adesina, president of the AfDB, announced a $10 bn commitment over five years for food and agriculture development. On 26 January, President Sall met with leaders from Kenya, Burundi, Zimbabwe, Namibia, and IFAD. From 28 February to 2 March, the UN Office for West Africa and the Sahel (UNOWAS), Switzerland's Federal Department of Foreign Affairs, and Senegal's CHEDS organised a conference in Dakar on preventing violent extremism in West and Central Africa. Experts discussed policies, structures, and inclusive political dialogue to combat extremism, emphasising multi-level cooperation. On 1–2 December, President Sall participated in COP28 in Dubai, stressing the importance of reducing greenhouse gas emissions, managing losses and damages, mobilising resources, and ensuring a fair energy transition. He highlighted the need for Africa to receive accessible funding through transparent procedures. On 12 December, he attended the 75th anniversary of the Universal Declaration of Human Rights in Geneva, reaffirming Senegal's commitment to social progress, peace, security, and the rule of law.

On 25 October, Senegal and the EU launched five critical projects under the Global Gateway initiative to address the food and economic crisis. President Sall and EU president Ursula von der Leyen signed agreements covering food security, vocational training, urban transport, environment, and digitalisation. These projects include training and employment provisions, restructuring public transport in Dakar, support for governance, clean-up of Hann Bay, and initiatives to promote inclusion and innovation. On 26 October, at the Global Gateway Forum in Brussels,

President Sall highlighted the need for public and private investment in Africa's health sector, calling for a regional hub near Blaise Diagne International Airport to improve health emergency responses. Sall attended the African Food Systems Summit on 6 September, after the first African Climate Summit in Dar es Salaam, Tanzania. This event aimed to position Africa as a hub for innovation, investment, and resilient food systems. On 30 November, Sall opened the Dakar International Forum on Peace and Security, themed 'Africa of Potentials and Solutions in the Face of Security Challenges and Institutional Instability'. He emphasised the need for peace to realise Africa's potential and called for dialogue to resolve disputes, stressing the importance of overcoming partisan divisions to build coalitions for national stability.

Socioeconomic Development

Senegal's economic growth rebounded to 4.3% from 4.0% in 2022, demonstrating resilience amid global economic challenges. This recovery was driven by solid performance in the secondary sector and a moderate improvement in the primary sector, bolstered by better agricultural conditions and the easing of ECOWAS sanctions against Mali, one of Senegal's key export partners. However, private consumption growth slowed, reflecting a decline in purchasing power due to high inflation, and investment was affected by uncertainties linked to the socio-political climate. On the supply side, activity in the tertiary sector was hampered by social unrest and political tensions. Inflation remained elevated at 5.9%, down slightly from a record 9.7% in 2022, primarily due to continued pressures on commodity prices. The government maintained high energy subsidies at 4% of GDP but moderated its approach to public investment reductions, focusing on strategic sectors to boost long-term growth.

Public revenues increased by 24%, helping to narrow the budget deficit to 5.8% of GDP from 6.1% in 2022. Public debt rose to 78% of GDP, reflecting ongoing deficits and increased borrowing for infrastructure projects. The current account deficit widened slightly to 18.0% of GDP due to high import costs, although improved export performance provided some offset. The banking sector remained stable, with loans to the economy growing by 21.0% and delinquency rates decreasing to 11.0%. According to the World Bank, the poverty rate remained at around 36%, with economic growth continuing to be concentrated in urban areas while rural populations dependent on agriculture saw slower progression.

Despite efforts to improve governance, Senegal needed help with corruption and misuse of funds, though it continued to attract significant foreign investment and support for its development initiatives. Transparency International's Corruption

Perceptions Index score of 43/100 indicated that Senegal (ranking 70th/180) remained in the red zone, where it was last year. On 7 February, Senegalese prosecutors ordered preliminary investigations into the suspected abuse of funds designated to combat Covid-19. This probe followed a December 2022 report on the Covid-19 Impact Fund by the Court of Auditors, which exposed billions of CFAfr in expenditures unrelated to addressing the pandemic. The report prompted civil society to mobilise and file an official complaint demanding an investigation into the potential embezzlement of Covid-19 funds.

Despite this set-back, the business environment remained favourable. Senegal was capitalising on its significant gas reserves to emerge as a notable gas producer in West Africa, attracting interest from foreign partners and investors. The International Islamic Trade Finance Corporation (ITFC) and Senegal signed a €400 m agreement on 30 January to support the 2023 annual plan of a five-year framework agreement signed in 2021. Under this agreement, Senegal committed to continuing the Emerging Senegal Plan and the ITFC pledged continued support to help Senegal develop critical sectors such as agriculture, energy, health, and the private sector. The parties also signed an Arab–African Trade Bridges agreement to facilitate agricultural, pharmaceutical, and e-commerce trade, complementing the AfCFTA agreement. The ITFC has supported trade and development financing in Senegal since its inception in 2008.

Senegal benefited from substantial investments and financial support from international institutions, aiming to boost economic growth, address climate challenges, and support entrepreneurship. On 28 February, the IFC, a World Bank subsidiary, announced a €242 m investment in Sococim Industries, Senegal's largest cement manufacturer, to increase low-carbon production. This investment will help to decarbonise the industrial production sector in Senegal, provide jobs, boost the economy, and address housing inequities. It is IFC's first 'green loan' for African material-based manufacturing. Senegal aims to replace old clinker lines with more fuel-efficient ones, potentially reducing carbon emissions by 312,000 tonnes annually.

On 12 May, the IMF and Senegal agreed on a $1.9 bn package to finance various facilities in the country. The deal, subject to IMF executive board approval in mid-June, required Senegal to prioritise debt reduction policies, combat money laundering and terrorism financing, and adapt to climate change. This package included $1.5 bn under the Extended Fund Facility and ECF and $327 m for the Resilience and Sustainability Facility to support Senegal's climate efforts. On 30 August, the AfDB's Project to Support and Enhance the Entrepreneurial Initiatives of Women and Young People (PAVIE) was extended for another year. This project has helped young fishers triple their income and aims to decrease illegal immigration. In three years, 3,200 young adults and women obtained training in specific trades and 3,176 informal businesses were formalised, with 6,441 businesses financed for CFAfr 38 bn ($63 m). Launched in 2020, PAVIE focuses on training, business formalisation, funding, and post-funding follow-up to ensure sustainability.

On 24 October, the IMF reached a staff-level agreement to disburse CFAfr 126 bn ($203 m) to Senegal, completing the first reviews of the Extended Fund Facility, ECF, and the Resilience and Sustainability Facility. If approved by the IMF board, Senegal will receive an additional CFAfr 40 bn ($65 m) for a climate facility. This move reflects confidence in the Senegalese economy despite political disturbances over the past year.

Senegal advanced its energy sovereignty with new power plants and renewable energy projects while enhancing cooperation in the oil and gas sector to ensure equitable economic benefits. On 13 February, President Sall inaugurated a new power plant in Senegal, expected to produce 120 megawatts of energy to power over 500,000 households around Thiès. The plant in Malicounda in the Mbour region represented an investment of approximately CFAfr 101 bn ($165 m) and aimed to increase Senegal's energy sovereignty. A second power plant, previously built in Malicounda, was to have an output of 20 megawatts. Senegal aims for universal access to electricity by 2025, supported by the PADAES Energy Access Scale-Up Project launched in June 2022.

On 22 September, the West African Development Bank (BOAD) agreed to finance a CFAfr 15 bn ($24 m) 30 MWp (Megawatt peak) photovoltaic power plant with an electric storage system in Niakhar, Fatick region. This initiative will increase electricity supply and stability, reduce production costs, and decrease dependence on fossil fuels. As part of Energy Resources Senegal's plan to deploy 500 MW of solar capacity in West Africa by 2025, the plant will help achieve these goals. On 22 February, Senegal and Nigeria signed a MoU to enhance cooperation between their oil and gas industries. The agreement included guidance on implementing energy laws, boosting workforce skills development, and addressing critical infrastructure issues. Hydrocarbon production, postponed due to the Covid-19 crisis, was scheduled to begin mid-2024, offering an opportunity to accelerate equitable investment in human capital and the energy transition, though revenues and exports are not expected until 2035.

Socioeconomic challenges persisted in Senegal, particularly in traditional sectors such as fishing, and recent political unrest disrupted key markets, highlighting the need for ongoing support and development efforts. When authorities in Saint-Louis announced a new offshore gas project in 2015, it raised hopes in the fishing community. However, residents reported in April that the project instead caused despair and hardship. Climate change, foreign competition, and the impacts of the Covid-19 pandemic have disrupted fishing revenues, and 90% of Saint-Louis's 250,000 residents depend on fishing. The gas project restricted fishing access, leading to economic distress and forcing some women into prostitution to support their families. Violent demonstrations significantly disrupted the sheep market during Eid-al-Adha (Tabaski) in June. Herders faced challenges selling their animals due to fears over theft and disruption. Authorities estimate billions of CFAfr were lost, as only 42,000 sheep reached the capital before the holiday. Political unrest over the conviction of opposition figure Ousmane Sonko contributed to the market disruption.

Sierra Leone

Krijn Peters

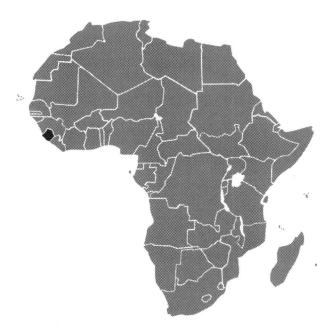

The year proved to be a highly eventful one, posing several challenges to Sierra Leone as a democratic state. In June, presidential, parliamentary, and municipal elections took place which saw incumbent president Julius Maada Bio of the Sierra Leone People's Party (SLPP) beating his main opponent, Samura Kamara of the All People's Congress (APC). However, there were reports by national and international monitoring bodies of irregularities and violent incidents during the elections. Violence erupted in July in the capital that the government considered to be part of a failed coup attempt. Unrest spread again in November, and on a more serious scale, with an armoury, barracks, and police stations attacked. Prisons were also over-run, resulting in hundreds of prisoners escaping. This second coup attempt was thwarted too and Sierra Leone returned to stability, although under heightened security, by the end of the year.

Domestic Politics

On 20 February, in preparation for the *24 June presidential elections*, the main opposition party – the APC – re-elected Samura Kamara as its presidential candidate. Kamara was a foreign minister under the APC government and ran for the presidency in 2018, narrowly losing out to the then opposition candidate Julius Maada Bio.

In December 2021, Kamara, with other former APC ministers, had been accused of embezzling more than $2.5 m in public funds, earmarked for the refurbishment of the country's consulate in New York. On 23 February this year, following an unsuccessful appeal by Kamara to the High Court to dismiss the case, the court began the trial. This was subsequently adjourned to the middle of March, and later to 14 July. Crucially, this latter date was after the presidential elections, allowing Kamara to participate as a candidate. Indeed, on 3 May, the Electoral Commission stated that Kamara had filed his application two days earlier. The incumbent President Bio filed his application with the Electoral Commission one day later, on 2 May.

A report released by Amnesty International on 20 March looked into the August 2022 riots in the northern towns of Kamakwie and Makeni, to which the Sierra Leone Police (SLP) had reacted harshly and in which 27 civilians and six police officers had been killed. The SLP stated that the use of violence had been 'proportional, reasonable and necessary', and argued that Amnesty International had not taken into account the violence and savagery that led to the killing of police officers.

In the run-up to the elections on 3 April, the government banned political street rallies, restricting campaign events to one specific location. While the government stated that it had taken this decision to limit the risk of violence, following suggestions by the independent state body the Political Parties Regulation Commission, its opponents considered the banning of this tradition yet another restriction of civil and political rights. One person died on 21 June following APC-organised protests over alleged incorrect voter registration data. The day after the election, on 25 June, Kamara accused the police of having fired live bullets and tear gas at the APC headquarters where party members had gathered to await the results, claiming another life.

The 24 June elections for the country of 8 m people saw it voting for a new president, a new parliament, and new municipal representatives. At least a third of the candidates for the parliamentary and municipal elections were required to be women, following the recent passing of legislation on gender equality and women's empowerment. The voting was for the most part peaceful, although irregularities and some violent incidents were recorded. These included the delayed opening of polling stations, particularly in the capital Freetown. Mohamed Konneh, the chief electoral commissioner, stated that the Electoral Commission's staff had been attacked by civilians in several polling stations. Bio beat the other 12 registered contestants, including his main rival Kamara. Of the 3.4 m people who had registered to vote, more than half were below the age of 35, reflecting the country's youthful population. At the time of the elections, President Bio was 59 and Kamara was 72.

The night after the election, the EU Election Observation Mission expressed concerns about the 'ongoing vote tabulation process'. Chief observer Evin Incir pleaded for 'full transparency' from the Electoral Commission. These concerns were echoed by the Carter Center, which had also sent a delegation. The following day, 26 June, the EU mission provided further details of acts of violence at ten polling stations and stated that it had received reports of the use of live bullets in three districts, while again criticising the lack of transparency in the vote tabulation process.

A day later on 27 June, the Electoral Commission announced the results, which showed that *President Bio had received 56% of the votes*, passing the 55% threshold required to be reached in order to make a run-off redundant. Kamara received 42% of the votes. On social media site X, Kamara immediately posted: 'I categorically reject the outcome so announced by the electoral commission'. Nevertheless, Bio was sworn in as the new president on the same day as the announcement of the results. On 1 July, Kamara doubled down on his accusations and asked for an investigation into the elections.

The president's party, the SLPP, also achieved a majority in the parliamentary elections, capturing 81 seats. The APC secured 54 seats, with the remaining 14 seats of the 149-seat parliament allocated to paramount chiefs. None of the other political parties managed to secure any seats. In the end, nearly 2.8 m votes were cast, representing a turnout of 82.9%.

Further concerns were raised by the EU's Election Observation Mission and the US Department of State on 14 July, both of which questioned the integrity of the official results and called for an independent investigation into the elections. Eventually, at the end of August, the US imposed visa restrictions for certain Sierra Leonean officials for their involvement in alleged vote rigging. Nevertheless, President Bio pushed ahead and announced his new cabinet on 15 July. One of his first actions as re-elected president was to appoint key members of his *26-member cabinet*, including Manty Tarawalie, who was appointed as minister of state in the Office of Vice-President; Henry Kpaka, who was appointed to lead the Ministry of Agriculture and Food Security; and Mohamed Tarawally, who was appointed as attorney-general and minister for justice. The minister appointed for foreign affairs and international cooperation was Timothy Kabba, while Isata Mahoi was appointed to the Ministry of Gender and Children's Affairs. Julius Matta was appointed as minister of mines and mineral resources. Additionally, five resident ministers were appointed covering the various regions of the country.

Violence erupted in the capital in July, caused, according to the government, by an attempt to overthrow the government of President Bio. Subsequently, the police arrested fourteen soldiers, three former police officers, and two civilians. On 4 August, the Liberian authorities arrested Mohammed Turay, a former chief superintendent of the SLP, who had fled to the neighbouring country in March 2022. This was on the request of the Sierra Leonean authorities in relation to Turay's alleged involvement in the failed coup attempt.

On 19 October, following negotiations between the SLPP and the APC, and under the mediation of ECOWAS, the AU, and the Commonwealth, the APC promised to end its refusal to take part in any level of government, which it had imposed following the controversial June elections. In exchange for the APC's participation, the government promised to end the bringing of legal cases driven by political motives and to release political detainees. Kamara hoped that his case concerning accusations of graft would also be dropped, as it was considered by the APC to be politically motivated. However, on 13 December, the Sierra Leone Court of Appeal ordered the arrest of Kamara for his alleged involvement in the sale of government-held shares in a mining company. This illegal transaction supposedly occurred in 2012, when Kamara was the finance minister under the APC government of President Ernest Bai Koroma. At the same time, Koroma was ordered by the appeal court to pay more than $15 m within 30 days in relation to a suspected corruption case.

On 26 November, a second, and arguably more serious, *coup attempt* took place. Attacks took place on the military armoury, two barracks, including the main Wilberforce barracks in Freetown, and two police stations. Shots were exchanged. Two prisons, including the main Freetown Central Prison at Pademba Road, were over-run, with hundreds of prisoners escaping, evoking memories of the 1997 coup and prison outbreak which had started the ten-month rule of the rebel Revolutionary United Front (RUF) and renegade military Armed Forces Revolutionary Council (AFRC) during Sierra Leone's decade-long civil war.

A curfew was announced which remained in place for four weeks, and checkpoints were set up by the security forces. It soon became clear that the armoury break had been unsuccessful and that those involved in the attempted coup had been driven to the outskirts of the capital. ECOWAS, the US embassy, and the EU were quick to condemn the coup and the violence, calling for respect for the constitutional order. The following day, an army spokesperson stated that 13 soldiers had died in the previous day's event. In the end, the death toll rose to 21 people.

On 9 December, Koroma was put under house arrest. On 12 December, the police announced that he was suspected of having taken part in the organisation of the coup. A number of former guards of the former president, including Amadu Koita, were also considered suspects. In total, 80 people were arrested. By this point, security forces had recovered five of the seven rocket launchers and 29 of the 47 assault weapons that had been taken during the attacks on the armoury.

Foreign Affairs

On 4 March, President Bio attended the Fifth UN Conference on Least Developed Countries in Doha, Qatar. During his speech he affirmed his country's commitment to advancing the SDGs. Also in Doha, on 8 May, he participated in a high-level session discussing global challenges to food security and indigenous knowledge systems.

In the middle of March, Sierra Leone's minister of foreign affairs and international cooperation, Professor David Francis, visited the People's Republic of China, leading a high-level delegation including minister of finance Sheku Fantamadi Bangura and ambassador Ernest M. Ndomahina. They met with the Chinese minister of foreign affairs Qin Gang to discuss opportunities for further collaboration to enhance socioeconomic growth. Among these were the financing and construction of the Lungi Bridge. Sierra Leone's international airport in Lungi is separated from Freetown by an estuary approximately 6 km wide. Other points of discussion focused on much-needed investments in the agricultural sector.

On 2 April, Guinea reported that it had seized more than 1,500 kilos of cocaine stashed on a ship flying the Sierra Leonean flag. Among the ten-person crew, all of whom were arrested, four were from Sierra Leone.

President Bio attended the inauguration ceremony of Asiwaju Tinubu, president of the Nigeria, on 29 May. Bio represented both Sierra Leone and the African Peer Review Forum of Heads of State and Governments, for which he acts as the chair. Nigeria, the regional power, contributed the majority of the Economic Community of West African States Monitoring and Observation Group (ECOMOG) troops that were active during Sierra Leone's civil war in the 1990s and early 2000s.

On 9 July, President Bio attended the 63rd Ordinary Session of the Authority of Heads of State and Government of ECOWAS in Guinea-Bissau. An important agenda item was the sub-regional instability and threats to peace plaguing the West African region.

On 6 September, President Bio attended the three-day *Africa Climate Summit* in Nairobi. He was one of the many African leaders who reminded the global community to abide by the commitments made at the Paris Summit for a New Global Financing Pact, which stated that no country would have to choose between climate action and development aspirations. A week later, the president flew to New York to attend the 78th Session of the UNGA. There he made preparations for Sierra Leone to serve its 2024/2025 term as a non-permanent member of the UNSC.

In November, Bio, among many other African heads of states, attended the Africa Investment Forum's 2023 Market Days in Marrakech, Morocco. The Forum was focused on promoting and facilitating project deals. Among its stakeholders were investors, project sponsors, and policy-makers.

Representatives from West Africa, led by President Nana Akufo-Addo of Ghana and President Macky Sall of Senegal, arrived in Sierra Leone on 23 December for the preparation of a *'security mission'* following the recent failed coup attempt. A force was expected to be established to help to stabilise the country, similar to the ECOWAS forces deployed in Guinea-Bissau and The Gambia. The Ghanian and Senegalese presidents met with President Bio to discuss the security situation.

Socioeconomic Developments

In a context in which Sierra Leone ranked 182nd out of 189 countries on the UN's 2020 Gender Development Index, a *pivotal gender equality law* was passed on 19 January. Women in private and public entities would now be entitled by law to equal pay and training opportunities and to have at least three months of maternity leave, to prevent the all-too-common practice of women being fired when they become pregnant. Furthermore, and perhaps most importantly, private and public entities would now be required to reserve at least 30% of their jobs for women. To prevent entities from fulfilling their quota by hiring women only for low-pay menial jobs, the 30% rule was also to apply to senior and managerial jobs. Non-compliance would result in financial penalties for every violation.

Sierra Leone holds huge deposits of iron ore, with most of it transported by rail to the country's dedicated deep-sea harbour and then shipped. While in 2022, 0.8% of the country's GDP increase was attributed to iron ore, this fell to just 0.1% in 2023. With little value added, iron ore export will remain limited in its GDP contribution. However, on 30 March, construction of an *iron ore processing plant* capable of processing 12 m tonnes per year began in Ferengbeya in the district of Tonkolili. Once finished, the plant will be the largest in West Africa. It is operated by the Kingho Mining Company, a subsidiary of the Leone Rock Metal Group. The cornerstone-laying ceremony for the $230 m plant was attended by President Bio, the Chinese ambassador, and the president of Leone Rock Metal Group/Kingho Energy Group.

Between 17 and 28 August, an IMF team visited the country in relation to the sixth and seventh reviews of the country's economic and financial programme. This programme was supported by the IMF's ECF, which began in 2018 and which has already disbursed more than $125 m to the country. The IMF team leader, Christian Saborowski, commented on the country's economy, flagging up inflation – which had reached 50% by August – and the depreciation of the national currency, the leone, as key concerns putting Sierra Leone at risk of not being able to service its debts.

At the same time, the cost-of-living crisis made it challenging for ordinary civilians to get by. Containing expenditure by the state was an agreed action, although the IMF and the government agreed that social spending should be protected. Additionally, they agreed that extra attention should be paid to domestic revenue collection. GDP growth of 2.7% was forecast for the year, but expectations were expressed that this should increase in the following year. On 5 June, the IMF executive board signed off on the sixth and seventh reviews, releasing nearly $21 m to Sierra Leone, while simultaneously extending the ECF by five months. Following the eighth and final review, the release of $20.7 m was approved by the IMF executive board in November. A total of $166.6 m has been disbursed, aimed at strengthening and stabilising the country's macroeconomic situation.

Previously, Sierra Leonean banks have not allowed interoperability among different banks, requiring their customers to hold multiple bank cards, which can be very expensive. But in May, the National Payment Switch was officially launched by President Bio, interconnecting the six main commercial banks. This allowed for financial transactions among the banks, mobile money operators, and microfinance institutions, providing much more convenience for customers who, irrespective of their payment service provider, could now receive and send money through different means, including ATMs, mobile money, dedicated agents, and the internet. This interoperability was also helpful for people in rural areas where banking services are scarce but mobile data coverage is common. A next step, already announced, will be the added service of enabling time-sensitive payments, allowing for 24/7 transactions and fostering further financial inclusion in a country where many adults still have no formal transaction account.

US ambassador David Reimer stated in mid-August that due to the irregularities in the June election, the Millennium Challenge Corporation (MCC) compact, a substantial five-year government-to-government support package worth $450 m, would be put on hold and reviewed. On 13 December, the MCC board of directors met in Washington, DC. While the country passed its scorecard, ambassador Bryan David Hunt, who replaced Reimer on 23 August, stated that the decision depended on more than just the scorecard result. The following day, it was announced that Sierra Leone would be reselected as eligible to continue developing a compact agreement.

In July, VPN service providers Surfshark and internet watchdog NetBlocks presented their 2022 global internet censorship report. It noted that in 2022, the Sierra Leonean government had disrupted internet services on two occasions, due to protests and political turmoil. This put the country in the top-five African countries in terms of occasions of internet censorship.

On 24 October, the World Bank released a report entitled 'Sierra Leone Economic Update 2023: Enhancing Value Chains to Boost Food Security'. The report argued that a stable macroeconomic environment was beneficial to the agricultural sector, but that the government should also focus on increasing agricultural productivity and stimulating cash-crop production for export while simultaneously achieving rice self-sufficiency. Around $200 m a year is spent on importing rice, and this figure was still increasing. Ever since the 2014 Ebola health crisis, local rice production has been falling, due to a number of factors including limited research capacities, declining soil fertility, and limited access to external inputs such as fertilisers. Worryingly, the report noted that in mid-2022, more than 80% of all households in Sierra Leone were unable to meet their fundamental food and nutrition needs.

On 14 December, a $65 m grant was approved under the World Bank's Inclusive and Sustainable Growth Development Policy Financing. This was the third and final grant under this initiative, aimed at supporting the government in addressing and improving the accountability of the public sector, gender equality, land management practices, governance of the mining sector, and macroeconomic stability.

Togo

Hans-Joachim Preuß

The postponement of the parliamentary elections scheduled for December led to conflicts between the newly formed opposition and the government, although these were resolved without violence. The north of the country was once again subjected to attacks by jihadist groups, which led to changes in the military leadership right up to national level. With international support, both military and development policy initiatives were stepped up in the affected regions. The government continued to take vigorous action against media professionals and civil society organisations if it or its representatives felt attacked. In terms of foreign policy, Togo continued to distinguish itself as a mediator in intra-African conflicts, and it also played an active role on the international stage as a self-confident advocate of African political and economic interests. The results of the census corrected the population figure downwards. Economically, Togo was able to consolidate its growth, even if the growing debt limited the fiscal room for manoeuvre for government spending in the future.

Domestic Politics

Two topics were at the centre of public interest under this section. On the one hand, it was eagerly awaited how the opposition would organise itself in view of the parliamentary and local elections announced for the end of the year. Second, increased attacks by jihadist groups in the north of the country led to calls for improved security for the local population, which resulted in increased military, economic, and social measures.

The last election to fill the National Assembly in 2018 was boycotted by the largest opposition parties, which had joined forces in the so-called C14 coalition. Most of these parties came together for the 2020 presidential elections in the Dynamique Monseigneur Kpodzro (DMK) movement initiated by the long-serving archbishop of Lomé and supported the candidacy of former prime minister Agbéyomé Kodjo. After Kodjo was defeated in the elections but still claimed victory, the DMK refused to engage in any dialogue with the government and practised fundamental opposition. In the elections scheduled for December of this year, the majority of the groups united in the DMK and other opposition parties voted in favour of participation. As Kpodzro and Kodjo refused to toe this line, the other members formed a new alliance, the Dynamique pour la Majorité du Peuple du Togo (DMP), left the DMK, and prepared for the election campaign.

After a long wait and complaints about the delay in setting the final date for the elections, it was only announced in November that they would be postponed to the first quarter of 2024, which was not in line with the constitution and led to angry protests from the opposition. The DMP had already successfully called for broad voter registration in early summer and demanded an increase in the number of seats from 91 to 117 so that all constituencies could be included. However, it criticised the way the constituencies were drawn up, which did not take sufficient account of the respective number of voters. The background to this displeasure was that the populous electoral districts in the south of the country, which are closer to the opposition, were not given more weight. For example, the Maritime region, with just under 17% of the population, was allocated only 17 seats and the Grand Lomé region, with 27% of the population, only 11 seats in parliament, whereas the central region of Kara, stronghold of the president's family, received over 19 seats. It remains to be seen whether the government will honour the date next year, which has already been postponed twice, or set a new one. These uncertainties led to the opposition parties falling behind the ruling party in the planning of their respective campaigns.

Villages and security force bases in the northern regions were once again affected to a considerable extent by armed attacks by the Groupe de Soutien à l'Islam et aux Musulmans, which is part of the Al-Qaida network. The government rarely commented on the number of victims of the attacks; enquiries by national and international media mostly went unanswered. In one of the rare official announcements, figures were given at the end of November: a total of 31 people were said to have been killed, 29 wounded, and 3 disappeared in a total of 11 attacks, not including the most recent attack at the beginning of December. Even though Togo itself has not yet been a staging area for Islamist terrorists, the partially forest-covered areas of the country provided them with temporary shelter. In addition, the flourishing smuggling trade in the border region allowed them to obtain food, fuel, and motorcycles. As a result of the insecurity, in addition to around 20,000 refugees from Burkina Faso, who fled to Togo due to the insecure situation and insufficient food in their country, over 30,000 Togolese had to leave their villages; more than a thousand citizens fled to Matéri in neighbouring Benin. Food aid was provided by the WFP to support the refugees; further humanitarian aid came from other international actors such as USAID and the EU.

The security emergency in the region was extended for a further year in April. The unsatisfactory management of the terrorist threat by the security forces once again led to the replacement of military leadership positions. The previous commander of the Togolese paratroopers, Lieutenant Colonel Lantiembé Kombate, was appointed head of the Koundjoaré military operation. For the next three years, this operation will have a budget at its disposal to combat terrorism of over €650 m, which is high by Togolese standards.

During a round of talks with representatives of the World Bank, Prime Minister Victoire Tomégah-Dogbé explained the president's new strategy. According to him, military measures were not enough, as terrorism had its roots in poverty. Togo was therefore addressing three dimensions in its fight against terrorism: the defence of the territory with armed force through Operation Koundjoaré, the eradication of violent extremism through increased cooperation with religious and traditional local leaders, and the improvement of the population's access to basic social services through the programme to strengthen resilience in the region of Savanes. International donors such as the USA, China, Germany, the World Bank, and BOAD (Banque Ouest-Africaine de Développement) agreed to finance large parts of this regional programme.

It was not only in the north of Togo that the armed forces made a name for themselves. In October, representatives of the newly introduced military jurisdiction were presented to the public. Just one month later, the high-ranking officers accused of the murder of Bitala Madjoulba, commander of the elite unit the Bataillon d'Intervention Rapide, including the former commander-in-chief of the army, General Félix Kadangha, were sentenced to long prison terms. Parallel to the start of the trial, the president filled or refilled important military positions, such as the leadership of the Presidential Guard. Observers saw this change – surprising in view of the insecurity in the north of the country – as an attempt by the president to surround himself with soldiers loyal to him and nip any conspiracy in the bud in view of the military coups that are becoming more frequent throughout West Africa.

With 234 newspapers and magazines, 94 radio stations, and a dozen television stations, Togo has a rich media landscape. Despite severe restrictions on the exercise of press freedom, the general climate in Togo has improved – after a marked slump in 2022. Reporters Without Borders ranked the country 70th out of 180 for press freedom, 30 places higher than in the previous year. However, some incidents of intimidation of media professionals contributed to widespread self-censorship. For example, the critical newspaper 'L'Alternative' was banned in March after its editor Ferdinand Ayité fled the country shortly before his conviction for 'defamation'. However, the Committee to Protect Journalists awarded him its 2023 Press Freedom Prize in November. At almost the same time, the publication of the most widely read newspaper 'Liberté' was banned for a month. In November, two journalists, Loïc Lawson and Anani Sossou, were imprisoned for three weeks after reporting on the burglary of a minister's home, during which large sums of cash were stolen. They were released three weeks later.

Civil society organisations mainly worked in charitable, humanitarian, and developmental areas; only a few were involved in the defence of human and civil rights. Due to the legal situation, the government was able to administratively hinder the activities of these groups, for example by delaying registrations, without which neither the recruitment of staff nor the implementation of measures is possible – obstacles that were criticised by the UN rapporteurs. In an open letter to the president, human and civil rights organisations also complained about restrictions on freedom of assembly and freedom of expression. In March, for example, a meeting of civil society organisations that wanted to discuss the findings of the Court of Auditors' report on discrepancies in the use of Covid-19 funds was banned by the prefect of the coastal region. Freedom House continued to rate Togo as 'partly free', with an unchanged score of 42 out of 100 points. The minister responsible for human rights, Christian Trimua, who had held the position since 2020, moved to the President's Office in September. A successor had not been appointed by the end of the year.

Foreign Affairs

Against the backdrop of the military coups in the Sahel and other West African countries, Togo has established itself as a skillful mediator for African conflicts. In March, l'Alliance Politique Africaine (APA) was founded at Togo's instigation.

Its purpose is to provide an informal platform for consultation, political dialogue, multidimensional cooperation, and collective action. It currently has ten members: Angola, Burkina Faso, CAR, Gabon, Guinea, Libya, Mali, Namibia, Tanzania, and Togo.

Both the president and his foreign minister Robert Dussey worked hard to reach an understanding between ECOWAS and the coup plotters, especially Niger. In doing so, they clearly distanced themselves from the hard line taken by the new ECOWAS chair, Nigerian president Bola Tinubu, and Patrice Talon, president of neighbouring Benin, who have threatened military intervention by the alliance. In the general debate at the UN, Dussey declared that Togo had never gone to war with its neighbours and had no intention of doing so. Togo additionally offered the military government the opportunity to open an embassy in Niamey and agreed to mediate between Niger and ECOWAS on the lifting of sanctions after a Nigérien ministerial delegation in Togo asked the president to act as a facilitator. Togo had already organised the so-called 'Forum de Lomé pour la Paix et la Sécurité' in October, which was attended not only by the foreign ministers of the Sahel states but also by the AU and the UN. The current topic was the question 'How to strengthen political transitions towards a democratic governance in Africa?' Togo granted asylum to Burkina Faso's head of state Paul-Henri Damiba, who came to power in a military coup, after he himself was deposed in the subsequent coup. The foreign minister maintained close relations with the new interim president Ibrahim Traoré.

Representatives of the Sudanese civil war parties met in Lomé in July to discuss a possible settlement and agree on a corridor for humanitarian aid deliveries. This presidential initiative was intended not to replace the peace efforts initiated by Ethiopia, Egypt, and Chad but to support them. One success of another mediation effort by Togo that was widely recognised in West Africa was the release of the 46 Ivorian members of the UN peacekeeping mission in Mali, MINUSMA, who were imprisoned in that country, accused by the junta in Bamako of attempting to overthrow the government and sentenced to 20 years in prison each.

Following Togo's admission to the Commonwealth of Nations last year, the foreign minister took part in the Commonwealth Days, which were organised in Rwanda, for the first time. For Togo, the new community also offers access to a market of 2.5 bn consumers in Africa and on other continents. Trade with its Anglophone West African neighbours Ghana and Nigeria, as well as with Rwanda, is to be intensified. Singapore and India are already among the investors in the Togolese economy. The UK alone provided the new member with around €75 m for the expansion of the overland road from Sokodé to the Beninese border and announced further funding for infrastructure measures.

However, establishing and intensifying new relationships did not mean turning away from old partners. The EU – above all, France and Germany – continued to enjoy privileged access to the head of state. Germany and France were the largest bilateral donors; on the multilateral side, donors were the EU, the World Bank, and the IMF. Relations with China have intensified over the past 50 years; Togo is part of the Chinese Belt and Road Initiative and thus a priority beneficiary in the construction of roads, bridges, and transport facilities. At the same time, deliveries of goods from Taiwan rose sharply. The partnership with Russia remained important due to its military support. The partnership with Türkiye was also emphasised for the same reasons. The exchange of goods with India has increased continuously; imports of Indian goods accounted for the highest share of Togo's import volume, at over $6 m. Togo has a long-standing partnership with Israel; it is assumed that the government also has access to the spyware 'Pegasus', developed in Israel to spy on opposition members. At international level, Togo was an advocate of a new composition of the UNSC with much greater participation from the African continent. The country's voting behaviour in the plenary of the UNGA can be seen as an attempt not to offend any of the various partners and not to submit to any bloc logic. In the votes on the Ukraine war, Togo abstained or did not take part; in the case of the Palestine resolutions calling for a ceasefire, Togo was one of the few African countries to abstain.

In November, Togo signed the Post-Cotonou (Samoa) Agreement between the EU and the Organisation of African, Caribbean and Pacific States (OACPS). Foreign minister Dussey has been the chief negotiator of the OACPS for the past five years and expressed the clear wish after the ceremony that this would lead to a paradigm shift in cooperation between the two groups of countries, in line with the expectations of the South for independence, respect, dignity, justice, and equality.

In terms of military cooperation, Togo benefited from good relationships with diverse partners. Israel provided intelligence support and trained individual battalions for rapid interventions. France and the USA provided structural cooperation in Lomé, including the training of general staff officers. Since mid-2022, Türkiye has delivered six Bayraktar TB2 drones, which can be armed and have been involved in operations in the north. Russia, for its part, delivered nearly a dozen Mi-35 and Mi-17 helicopters (with crews) by 2023 and sent some military advisors. The commander-in-chief of the Germany-based Africom, Michael Langley, visited Togo in July and discussed current security issues in the north and the Gulf of Guinea with the country's leadership.

Socioeconomic Developments

The official results of the 2022 census were released in spring. The most surprising outcome was that national and international statistics had previously estimated the population at around 9 m people, around 1 m higher than the figure now calculated. The population grew by 2.3% annually. Even though only 43% of Togolese people live in cities currently – in Africa as a whole the figure is more than half – the urban centres have experienced rapid and large growth. At the time of the survey, a quarter of the population was already living in the Grand Lomé region; in the rural regions, the population grew at a much slower rate due to increased emigration. Togo's citizens living abroad were also recorded statistically for the first time; their number totalled just under 1 m. Fewer than 100,000 of these live outside the African continent, including just under 60,000 in European countries. This could have an impact on election results in the future, as the diaspora has so far been only incompletely involved in national elections.

Growth remained robust in 2023 with an estimated rate of 5.2%, but slowed compared with the 5.8% of 2022 as the government shifted from an expansionary to a more restrictive fiscal policy. The inflation rate fell back from 7.6% to 5% following the rise in prices induced by the Ukraine war last year, especially for cereals and energy. Average per capita income at current prices rose again following the slump in the previous year; nevertheless, income distribution remained extremely unequal. At 58.5%, the poverty rate in rural regions was more than twice as high as in the cities (26.5%). Added to this was the lack of educational and healthcare facilities in these areas, as well as a deficient infrastructure for transport, communication, electricity, and water. The Assurance Maladie Universelle health insurance scheme for all citizens, which has been announced for years, was further prepared. After the president's flagship project was incorporated into the Institut National d'Assurance Maladie (IMAM) in the previous year, the government decided to split the management of the insurance between IMAM (for state employees and civil servants) and the Caisse Nationale de Sécurité Sociale. A new target date of 1 January 2024 was set for the introduction of the system.

Foreign trade grew compared with the previous year. At 6.4%, the growth in exports of goods exceeded that in imports at 5.3%. Nevertheless, the trade balance remained chronically in deficit; export revenues covered only around half the value of imports. Around half of Togo's exports were destined for other ECOWAS members. This meant that unlike its neighbours, the country was less affected by global economic upheavals.

At the end of the year, Togo reached an agreement with the IMF on an ECF totalling $390 m for three and a half years, which still has to be submitted to the IMF board for a decision. Ambitious targets were agreed for this. The most important agreements with the IMF were aimed at reducing the budget deficit to 3% of GDP by 2025 and at the same time consolidating expenditure that could support growth and promote economic inclusion of vulnerable groups. A low execution rate of public investment planned for 2023 and spending cuts already reduced the budget deficit in 2022 from 8.3% of GDP to 5.8%. The fiscal strategy was also based partly on measures to increase domestic resource mobilisation by an ambitious 0.5% of

GDP per year. It was planned to utilise public spending more efficiently; however, nothing was announced about how this would be achieved. In addition, the government intended to strengthen social security despite fiscal constraints, including by expanding cash transfers based on the creation of a standardised social register and a platform for biometric identification. The promised structural reforms included broadening the tax base and improving the efficiency of tax collection.

Nevertheless, a record budget was set at the end of December, which for the first time exceeded the equivalent of €3 bn and was therefore more than 10% higher than the previous year's budget. The fact that the budget deficit is still expected to be lower was justified by higher planned government revenue, including a 14% increase in tax revenue. The deep-water port of Lomé also played a significant role in the improvement in the revenue position: almost 9 m tonnes of imports were handled, 10% more than in the previous year. Exports rose by 38% to 2.3 m tonnes in the same period. With a 50% share of GDP and 75% of customs revenue, it was an important pillar of the economy and the state. Transit between Togo on the one hand and Burkina Faso, Mali, and Niger on the other played an important role: 92% of goods transhipped came from or went to Sahel countries. As a result of the ECOWAS sanctions against the coup plotters in Niger, transit from Lomé via Burkina Faso to Niger also increased, as goods destined for this country could no longer be transhipped via the Beninese port of Cotonou.

A large part of the budget deficit was covered by concessionary loans or private bonds raised on regional and international financial markets. Togo's debt increased in the current year. Public debt was expected to account for 67.2% of GDP in 2023, compared with 66.3% in the previous year. Two-thirds of this was attributable to foreign debt.

The government continued to endeavour to make Togo attractive to foreign investors. According to internal data, FDI in the current year up to and including the third quarter reached a value of €33 m, which would mean a significant decline by the end of the year if extrapolated. The Heritage Foundation, which compiles an annual global ranking of the investment climate, downgraded Togo's 'Economic Freedom Score' from 55.3 to 50.9 – the third time that Togo's position has deteriorated in comparison with its neighbouring countries. The parameters 'government integrity', 'property rights', and 'judicial effectiveness' were seen as particularly critical. In addition, bribery of public officials continued to play an important role, with a low score of 31 on a scale of 0 to 100 – only a slight improvement on the previous year – and Togo was ranked 126th out of 180 countries in Transparency International's Corruption Perceptions Index 2023, placing it in the midfield of African countries. The recent contract with the Moroccan Office Chérifien de Phosphates, which intends to use local phosphate deposits to produce fertilisers for Togo and its neighbouring countries, was therefore very much welcomed. Togo's intention was to become independent of fertiliser imports and to promote domestic agriculture, the productivity of which in the country is among the lowest in West Africa.

As a result, local production was not sufficient to guarantee the population's food supply. Despite sufficient rainfall and a 5% increase in cereal production, 6% of the population was affected by food insecurity. Especially in the Savanes region, which borders Burkina Faso, the number of people in need of food increased, partly because around 20,000 people from Burkina Faso had fled there. In July, the government presented an action plan aimed at eradicating hunger in Togo within seven years.

PART 4

Central Africa

Andreas Mehler

The year 2023 was another one of continued armed violence in half of the countries of the sub-region, with all of the consequences of this in terms of internal displacement and flight to neighbouring countries. Family rule was the established pattern of domestic politics in Equatorial Guinea, Chad, Congo, Cameroon, and Gabon – in this last case at least until the military coup in August. The impact of this event on at least one sub-regional organisation was evident as Ali Bongo Odimba had been the current chair of CEEAC. The regional integration process did not progress substantially, and last year's announcements that a merger of CEMAC and CEEAC would be accelerated were not followed by concrete action. Economically, the effects of the Covid-19 pandemic were (at last) largely under control, but the countries of the sub-region fared quite differently in terms of growth and inflation rates.

Democracy and Elections

The rather unexpected and popular *coup in Gabon* on 30 August, doing away with dynastic rule by the Bongo family, sent a clear message to the entire region: the legitimacy of experiments to operate father-to-son transitions appeared quite limited, and only repression could uphold such political systems. In this sense, Gabon's comparatively mild autocracy under the Bongos was also an outlier – with the regimes in Cameroon, Chad, Congo, and Equatorial Guinea ready to use all means to stay in power. However, there were indications that the politically informed parts of the population in all of those countries were carefully watching events in Gabon and drawing lessons from them. Inevitably, the military hierarchy became ever more an actor to watch in all countries of the sub-region.

Only two countries held *national elections*: Gabon – leading to the aforementioned coup – and DRC, where President Félix Tshisekedi was able to secure a second term in office after controversial elections. However, in CAR an equally important and controversial referendum was held on the adoption of a new constitution. CAR's president, Faustin-Archange Touadéra, had worked for the envisioned outcome using dubious means, including getting rid of the president of the Constitutional Court in 2022 in order to allow himself to stand for a third term in presidential elections scheduled for 2025. Opponents had appealed for a boycott of the referendum and civil society groups and the episcopal conference questioned the need for a new constitution, but to no avail. Russian mercenaries provided both security and logistical help for the referendum, held on 30 July, which produced an overwhelming official 95% approval (with a hardly credible participation rate of over 57%). CAR's descent into a personal dictatorship continued. As a reminder: in the mid-1990s it was still one of the greater hopes for democracy in the sub-region.

Elections in *DRC* were – as always – an enormous organisational challenge in a large and highly fragmented country which, above all, was partly in an undeclared state of war. Pre-electoral violence overshadowed the polls (presidential, legislative, and municipal elections), with the spokesperson for the main challenging party murdered in July. Rather expectedly, many polling stations could not open on election day, but some managed in the following days. The result was favourable to the ruling party. A game of alliances and exclusions provided Tshisekedi with enough clout to claim a landslide victory (over 73% of the votes in the presidential elections), though parts of the elite understandably cried foul. Despite all manoeuvres, main opponent Moïse Katumbi was able to win in the south-eastern part of the country, allowing him to remain a considerable challenger to the president. In the parallel parliamentary election, not all seats could be attributed due to persisting situations of war, mostly in the east. Tshisekedi's party alone could not claim a majority in the National Assembly, but it was set to dominate parliament by counting on the support of a long list of alliance partners winning enough seats.

The general elections in *Gabon* held on 26 August were preceded by changes in the legal provisions and were held in a nervous climate, with internet shut-downs and the banning of international broadcasters. On 30 August, the military seized power after the announcement of results attesting victory – with 64% of the votes – for the incumbent president, Ali Bongo Ondimba. While the coup was greeted with jubilation on the streets of the capital for doing away with Bongo family rule, the military junta propelled General Brice Clotaire Oligui Nguema to the top position: it was noteworthy that he was a distant relative of the deposed president. By putting Bongo and close relatives under house arrest, the junta tried to distance itself from the clan. Oligui Nguema was sworn in as transitional president on 4 October. The full implications of the coup were not yet palpable by the end of the year.

Overall, democracy was not 'the main game in town': the fact that Bongo's efforts to bend the constitution for a third term in Gabon had not in the end produced the calculated result was only one side of the coin. The other side was that this strategy still produced an unconstitutional change of government. With Mahamat Déby (Chad) holding on at the top of an unconstitutional government and Touadéra (CAR) in a position to change the constitution as he wished, this year made clear once again the thin surface of legality of ruling in Central Africa.

The well-known Freedom House Index did not record major changes in any countries in the sub-region. *São Tomé e Príncipe* (STP) remained the clear outlier ('free', with its score for combined political rights and civil liberties remaining constant at 84 out of 100), outscoring all other countries, which were firmly positioned in the 'unfree' category (while in all other African sub-regions 'partly free', i.e. somewhat hybrid, non-authoritarian, and non-democratic, countries could be found). While the scores of DRC (19), Congo (17), Chad (15), and Equatorial Guinea (5) were unchanged, CAR declined further to the same extremely low rating as Equatorial Guinea (i.e., 5) and Cameroon also slightly worsened (from 16 to 15). The Varieties of Democracy project, providing scores for five different dimensions of democracy, positioned the countries of the sub-region similarly, though here Chad had the worst score in the 'liberal', 'electoral', and 'egalitarian' dimensions while in the 'deliberative' and 'participatory' dimensions of democracy Equatorial Guinea remained in last place. One may have doubts as to the precision of such indexes, but the broad picture was both plausible and familiar: an overall depressing absence of democracy in the sub-region (ignoring the tiny island republic of STP), with Chad and CAR slowly approaching the level of the most hardcore tyranny of the sub-region, i.e. Equatorial Guinea – while the authorities' capacity to impose oppression still varied (with CAR having less means than Chad and Equatorial Guinea).

Instability, War, and Peace

Also depressing was the continued state of armed conflict in the sub-region. Four countries – Cameroon, CAR, Chad, and DRC – already used to repeatedly witnessing armed encounters with significant consequences for civilians again all had quite troublesome times.

No end was in sight to *Cameroon*'s secessionist conflict in the Anglophone part of the country: security forces, a myriad of armed secessionist movements, and pro-government militias all used violence for short-term military gains – with more damage done to the civilian population than the respective immediate opponents. The peace process was apparently at a dead end, with no international facilitation showing any progress and no decisive military success that could be expected. International attention declined further, though the consequences of 'low-intensity warfare' were growing with every year during which market relations were interrupted, school teaching was not continuously provided, and overall trust in state institutions was reduced to a minimum.

In *CAR*, the military balance swung somewhat in the government's direction, with its Russian allies at times showing superior capacities to armed opponents. However, the UN peace mission MINUSCA remained more important in defending civilians, protecting refugees, and enabling much-needed humanitarian assistance to be delivered to an exhausted population in about half of the territory. Armed opponents were still either in control of large territories in the centre and the east, or at least capable of fighting back government forces in the west. With the transfer of former president and warlord François Bozizé from neighbouring Chad to Guinea-Bissau in early March, one important player was now effectively sidelined.

Chad's illegal government under Mahamat Déby Itno faced some security challenges in more or less all of its border zones (West/Lake Chad, north/Tibesti, south/CAR border, and east/bordering Sudan's unsafe Darfur region), but arguably to a lesser degree than in preceding years. The main destabilising factor originated in the abused population, mostly in the capital N'Djamena, tired of decades of warlord politics at the helm of the state and of ever more degrading living conditions. A somewhat diffuse fear of a more or less discreet Russian-backed intervention to topple the last pro-French government in the Sahel was also recorded. The regime was anxious to uphold Western, mostly French support; it could also be that such supposed threats from Russia were instrumental in maintaining this support. The mixture of brutal repression and Chad's rather effective sub-regional and international diplomacy permitted a continuation of a cynical political style with little regard for ordinary people.

The DRC saw a new experiment with regional peacekeeping, separate from (and somewhat instead of) the MONUSCO mission, which at best had stabilised some war zones but had not decisively turned the country into a functioning entity. The eastern parts of the country, particularly the provinces of North Kivu and Ituri, were as unstable as ever. Arguably, both domestic and international actors had also contributed to this interim balance sheet: it was easy for government officials and opponents to blame all failures on the UN mission without promoting peace themselves. But also, aggressive or unstable neighbours (Rwanda and Uganda as well as Burundi and CAR respectively) exported some of their problems, including armed actors, to DRC. The new force #mandated by the EAC Regional Force (EACRF) quickly showed its limitations too. The government in Kinshasa finally opted not to prolong its mandate, and the withdrawal of EACRF troops was accomplished in December. The mission was replaced by one that had the blessings of the SADC (the SADC military force to the DRC; SAMIDRC); this move made Kigali even more nervous. The danger of a full war between tiny but well-armed Rwanda and large but disorganised DRC loomed large – with some further actors becoming involved as they had in preceding episodes of international warfare in the area. The big game of international alliances was complemented by local reconfigurations: so-called 'wazalendo', self-acclaimed patriotic local vigilantes, now clearly had the blessing of the government and mostly targeted 'foreigners', not least Tutsi, which again was seen as a provocation in Kigali.

As in previous years, populations were subject to *mass displacement* as a result of conflict events. The DRC counted 6.5 m IDPs and about 960,000 refugees abroad at year's end, while also hosting refugees itself, mostly from CAR (about 212,000) and Rwanda (207,000), according to UNHCR statistics. Sparsely populated CAR alone was the origin of a still-growing number of 765,000 refugees, but the number of IDPs had gone down by over 20% to 535,000 by year's end. Cameroon hosted the largest number of refugees from CAR, i.e. about 354,000. Also still growing was the number of registered refugees originating from Cameroon, now standing at 163,000 (mostly sheltered by Nigeria), while the number of IDPs skyrocketed to close to 1.1 m. Chad now hosted about the same number of refugees, with a spectacular increase of refugees coming from Sudan, standing at 572,000 at year's end.

A number of armed actors could clearly be termed 'transnational'. In the Central Africa region, all border zones of Chad and CAR harboured fighters who would fight on both sides of the border. This applied most clearly to the *Boko Haram* insurgency in the Lake Chad area (with Nigeria, Niger, Chad, and Cameroon affected), but also to other groupings. The Multinational Joint Task Force recorded some progress when it was able to hand over 46 repentant Boko Haram members to Chadian authorities in late August. Splits between ISWA factions also became obvious. However, the expanding Jama'tu Ahlis Sunna Lidda'awati wal-Jihad (JAS), one of the factions, increasingly preying on civilians in Chad's Lake Region, was a major source of concern. Uganda and DRC cooperated in containing the Allied Democratic Forces (ADF) rebellion that originated in Uganda but operated mostly in DRC, and that had paid allegiance to ISIS since 2019. Arguably best equipped among these transnational fighting forces, the M23 in eastern DRC clearly had Rwandan support. Armed opponents of the regime in Bangui now felt attracted to fight as 'guns for hire' in Sudan's expanding civil war, at least temporarily. Some progress could be noted, however, namely in the containing and disarming of the legendary Lord's Resistance Army (LRA): in two rows, LRA fighters laid down their weapons and surrendered in July and August to authorities of CAR and Uganda, in a move expected to make the rather inaccessible zone stretching from CAR, DRC, and South Sudan, to Uganda at least somewhat safer.

Human Rights and Transitional Justice

In these circumstances, it was not surprising that human rights were grossly harmed throughout the region. A number of special reports by human rights NGOs stood out.

Regarding *Cameroon*, in July Amnesty International documented a whole list of atrocities committed since 2020 in a thoroughly researched report titled 'With or Against Us', focusing on Northwest Region in particular. Special attention was given to armed conflicts between Mbororo Fulani herders and sedentary farmers; here, the report claimed that Mbororo militias were being 'supported or tolerated by the authorities'. That may have been the case, but the Mbororo themselves were equally targeted by armed separatists and suffered from increasing discrimination as 'foreigners' even though they had been living in the area for decades, if not centuries. The report also raised doubts as to whether crimes committed by the security forces were being properly prosecuted (confirming the widespread impression of one-sided impunity). An interesting detail of the report was the verified equipping of armed separatists with weapons originating from, *inter alia*, Russia, Israel, and Belgium, though many were also taken from the Cameroonian army. Seventeen international and national CSOs used the opportunity of the regular Universal Periodic Review (UPR) for Cameroon by the UN in November to issue strong recommendations focusing on the two Anglophone regions, where civilians have been the victims of unlawful killing, murder, sexual violence, destruction of homes, and abduction, attributing the responsibility in equal shares to Cameroon defence and security forces, pro-government militias, and armed separatist groups'. The most specific recommendation was to 'ensure that people arrested in the context of the Anglophone crisis are promptly brought before an ordinary court that upholds international fair trial standards, and not before military courts'. Obviously, the government was not capable of or interested in upholding minimal legal standards.

In April, HRW issued a report on the increasing repression of civil society, opposition, and media in the *CAR*. The report, 'Closing Civic Space', pinpointed in particular the actions of two pro-government organisations, one officially banned but tolerated (Galaxie Nationale) and the other increasingly violent (les Requins; literally: the Sharks) intimidating any opponent to the constitutional referendum permitting President Touadéra to stand in a further election. For *Chad*, early in the year HRW published a report on the 20 October 2022 crackdown on protesters in N'Djamena. The numbers of casualties during 'Black Friday' was highly disputed, ranging from the official 73 to estimates by local human rights organisations of over 300. Torture and intimidation were common throughout the year.

Reporting about human rights violations in *DRC* usually centres on the eastern provinces, but this time other places were also in focus. Intercommunal violence in the Kwamouth territory (in the west) from June 2022 to March 2023 was addressed in a HRW report issued on 30 March which claimed that at least 300 people had been killed in armed encounters between Téké and Yaka communities over disputed customary taxes and access to land. In addition, houses, schools, and health centres had been destroyed. The deployed security forces had allegedly added to the plight of civilians by committing extrajudicial executions, looting, and sexual violence. More than 50,000 people had been displaced by the violence.

Together with the local Initiative pour la Bonne Gouvernance et les Droits Humains, AI published a substantial report in September on the collateral damage for the local population of cobalt and copper mining in and around the city of Kolwezi in DRC's southern province, Lualaba. Four case studies were investigated in which commercial mining had resulted in forced evictions from land and the burning of houses. The increased scramble for the two minerals had to be put in the context of the global search for clean energy technologies (in which copper is needed) and lithium batteries (for which cobalt is needed).

At least one series of events in the east was also documented by NGO reports: on 6 February, HRW accused the Rwanda-backed M23 of having committed summary executions and forced recruitment of civilians in DRC since late 2022, while the army was also criticised for collaborating with 'ethnic militias with abusive records'. HRW called on Rwanda to end its military support for the M23. Four months later, on 13 June, HRW was able to publish further evidence on documented grave human rights violations by the M23. Based on interviews conducted under difficult circumstances eight unlawful killings and 14 cases of rape by M23 fighters were considered undisputable. Further credible reports on over a dozen other summary killings by M23 forces were received but could not be independently verified. The indiscriminate shelling of three heavily populated areas by M23 had reportedly killed seven and injured three. This was most probably only the tip of the iceberg, as reporting was so difficult in this war zone. Finally, on 16 December, HRW warned of the risks of more election-related violence in the context of the upcoming ballot. In the preceding weeks, a number of violent encounters between different political camps had occurred, as documented by the human rights watchdog.

Though international NGOs were mostly silent on human rights violations in *Congo*, the local Centre d'Action pour le Développement (CAD) reported on a close-to-fourfold increase of incidents from 2022 to 2023. Organisations and media were courageous enough to draw attention to a number of problematic events and situations, including the ongoing detention of two rivals to President Sassou Nguesso in the 2016 elections.

Transitional justice cases produced fewer headlines than in previous years, though a potentially intricate case was building up on the horizon: DRC's minister of justice personally handed over an official letter (dated 18 May) to the ICC asking the court's prosecutor to initiate an investigation into war crimes and crimes against humanity committed by both the Rwandan Defence Forces and M23 since January 2022 in North Kivu. The case was transferred to ICC Pre-Trial Chamber II on 15 June. By contrast, the most prominent case of the ICC with a Central Africa focus was more or less terminated when the judges announced, on 17 October, the release of Anti-balaka leader Maxime Mokom, after the Office of the Prosecutor had dropped the charges against him – justifying the decision by lack of evidence and the unavailability of witnesses against the accused. This was not well received by victims. Mokom was among a number of prominent armed regime opponents sentenced by the appeals court in Bangui in September – *in absentia* – to life imprisonment. According to Mokom's lawyers at the ICC, a key defence witness was arrested in CAR in October; earlier property from Mokom's house in Bangui would have been seized. The ICC sent an undisclosed message to CAR authorities towards the end of the year, potentially in protest. Both international and national courts seemed unable to deliver undisputable justice, in this case at least. Two other Anti-balaka leaders

(Alfred Yekatom and Patrice-Edouard Ngaissona) remained in custody in The Hague and their trial continued at the end of the year. Ex-Séléka leader Mahamat Said Abdel Kani's trial also continued after he had pleaded not guilty in April. The arrest warrant by the ICC against CAR warlord Mahamat Noureddine Adam remained active, but the suspect remained at large. The same can be said of the commander of the Forces Démocratiques pour la Libération du Rwanda Sylvestre Mudacumura, accused of crimes against humanity committed in eastern DRC, whose arrest warrant even dates back to 2012. The work of the Special Criminal Court in Bangui went more or less unnoticed. On 20 July, the appeals chamber revised a decision by the trial chamber in the proceedings against commanders of the armed 3R movement; otherwise, little transpired from this hybrid court created back in 2015.

Socioeconomic Developments

In December, the IMF issued its usual report on the CEMAC area, claiming that overall economic recovery would have gained momentum in 2022, supported by higher hydrocarbon prices. This was relevant only for the petroleum and gas producers within CEMAC – so not for CAR. Despite a number of positive trends, the IMF claimed that reforms would be needed to address recent fiscal slippages.

The IMF's World Economic Outlook, published in April 2024, provides data on individual economies. Projected *GDP growth* rates in the reporting year were solidly on the increase in Cameroon (+4.0%, from +3.6%) and Chad (+4.4, from +3.1%) and most strongly in Congo (+ 4.0%, from +1.7%), while Gabon's growth rates went down (+2.3%, from +3.8%) and STP's economic growth decreased from +0.1% to −0.3%. More dramatic were recorded changes in Equatorial Guinea, where the IMF calculated −5.9% (from +3.2% in 2022, the only positive year in the last period). On a low level, the GDP of CAR grew from 0.5% to 0.7% – not enough to bring a much-needed boost to the economy. Though it still had the highest projected GDP increase, DRC's growth rate fell (from +8.8% to +6.1%). Inflation hit the population very strongly in both DRC and STP, with consumer prices rising by around 20%. In Cameroon, prices were also quite strongly on the rise (by 7.3%). The ratio of government debt to GDP varied very strongly, with DRC the least indebted (14.3%) and Congo the highest (100.8%), and all others having debt ratios between 35 and 57%.

The World Bank, in its 'Africa Pulse' publication in October, compared estimated annual average per capita growth rates for 2022–25 with those in 2001–19, which give an overview of relative performance in recent years. Only DRC was in the group of 'improved performers' while CAR, Congo, and Gabon were listed as 'falling behind performers' (i.e., with weak performance in both observation periods), and Chad, Equatorial Guinea, and STP as 'slipping' (i.e., with a clearly worse performance in recent years). Cameroon was the only country where the performance remained roughly as it was (classified as 'stuck in the middle'). The overall positive development of GDP in DRC over many years had to be put in context of the very high inflation, which strongly reduced private consumption. The five 'resource-rich countries' of the sub-region (Chad, Congo, DRC, Equatorial Guinea, and Gabon; in the World Bank's classification these are those with more than 10% of GDP generated in the mining sector) had profited from higher prices for oil (or metals in the case of DRC) on the world market in 2022 and early 2023; in the case of Congo, production of oil products was also significantly increased, an expected positive effect on growth.

Levels of corruption remained apparently without any major changes, though some countries changed their rank within the Transparency International's Corruption Perceptions Index. The scores remained fully stable (i.e. low) since last year in Cameroon, CAR, Chad, and Equatorial Guinea. DRC was the one country that improved its score for the second year in a row (+1, but still ranked rather low at 162nd). Gabon was still the second best-ranked country, at 136th/180 (losing one rank), though far behind the only well-rated country, i.e., STP at rank 67.

Sub-regional Organisations

CEEAC held two ordinary and two extraordinary summits. The 22nd Ordinary Session was held in Kinshasa on 25 February, with a number of political crises on the agenda, including those in Chad and Burundi. Four countries were not represented by their heads of state (Angola, Cameroon, Equatorial Guinea, and Rwanda). The absence of Rwanda's Paul Kagame may have facilitated a final statement that unequivocally condemned the M23 rebellion in eastern DRC, which clearly had Rwandan backing. Félix Tshisekedi (DRC) handed over the chairing role to his Gabonese counterpart Ali Bongo Ondimba, who convened the 23rd Ordinary Session of the Conference of Heads of State and Government on 1 July in Libreville, roughly two months before he was ousted by the coup in Gabon's capital. The focus of this second high-level gathering was firmly on the funding requirements of the sub-regional integration process. While last year saw some movement in the direction of a (fully indicated) merger of the main sub-regional organisations (i.e. CEEAC and CEMAC), this dynamic did not produce new tangible results. Instead, the final statement of the summit simply displayed general satisfaction with permanent contacts between the two, and also concerted action in the process of rationalisation of the two RECs in Central Africa. Gilberto da Piedade Verissimo (Angola), the president of the CEEAC Commission, participated at the Russia–Africa Summit from 26 to 29 July in St Petersburg, and both sides praised this intensification of contact. The coup in Gabon subsequently altered the picture of 'business as usual': after a videoconference organised on 31 August, an extraordinary CEEAC summit was convened in Djibloho (Equatorial Guinea) on 4 September by Teodoro Obiang Nguema, the vice-president of the organisation acting on behalf of the impeded president (i.e., Bongo); four member countries were not present (Burundi, Cameroon, DRC, and Rwanda). The summit suspended the membership of Gabon and ordered a provisional relocation of the organisation's headquarters to Malabo. A further extraordinary summit was held at the same location on 15 December at which Gabon's coup leader and transitional president Oligui Nguema reaffirmed his intention that the transition would last for only 24 months. *Inter alia*, the heads of state expressed concern with regard to the health of their deposed peer Ali Bongo Ondimba and upheld Gabon's suspension of membership. The official facilitator in Gabon's transition process, CAR president Faustin-Archange Touadéra, saw his mandate confirmed. It is notable that a similar suspension was not decided with the unconstitutional take-over by the junta in Chad two years earlier (though Tshisekedi had been designated facilitator, similarly to Touadéra now).

Earlier, an ordinary *CEMAC* summit was held on 17 March in Yaoundé. The heads of state and government were invited to evaluate the effectiveness of the CEMAC Economic and Financial Reform Programme, but the result of this check was not published. The final communiqué was full of praise for the resilience of the sub-region after its having faced economic challenges in the preceding years. The summit endorsed the appointment of new officials to head the community's institutions, most particularly the Commission. As the terms of office of the president, the controversial Daniel Ona Ondo (Gabon), but also of his vice-president and four commissioners, had expired, new office holders were nominated: Baltasar Engonga Edjo'o (Equatorial Guinea) took the helm of the Commission assisted by Charles Assamba Ondogo (Cameroon); the further commissioners were Fulgence Likassi-Bokamba (Congo), Nicolas Beyeme-Nguema (Gabon), Ngabo Seli (Chad), and Francial Giscard Baudin Libengue Dobele-Kpoka (CAR). The presidency of CEMAC passed from Paul Biya (Cameroon) to Faustin-Archange Touadéra. Remarkably, all other heads of state of member states (i.e. Mahamat Idriss Déby Itno, Denis Sassou Nguesso, Ali Bongo Ondimba, and Teodoro Obiang Nguema Mbasogo) also attended. Despite the usual self-congratulatory style of allocutions, one could detect some level of criticism of the outgoing Commission team when Edjo'o called for 'the restoration of the Commission's credibility', but also collegial governance, promotion of transparency, and strict respect for the regulations of the Community during the handing-over ceremony on 6 June. Reading between the lines, this alluded to severe problems within the Commission. In fact, the new Commission ordered an audit of the preceding management, and in November, the Paris-based 'Jeune Afrique' quoted from a leaked report on Ondo's mismanagement, speculating about the necessity of taking judicial action. A donor roundtable in Paris on 28–29 November organised to seek funding for a number of integrative infrastructure projects was particularly successful; CEMAC was able to mobilise around €9.2 bn, with the UAE providing the lion's share.

Ghana's president Nana Akuffo-Addo invited his peers to the Third Extraordinary Session of the Assembly of Heads of State and Government of the *Gulf of Guinea Commission* in Accra on 25 April. The clear focus of the gathering was on maritime security. Obiang Nguema was the only Central African head of state present, while Congo, DRC, Gabon, and STP were represented on a ministerial level. Not fully exceptionally, Cameroon was absent from yet another important summit. Akuffo-Addo invited further West African countries to join the organisation (so as to permit the full coverage of the Gulf of Guinea from Cabo Verde to Angola).

The CBLT did not formally hold a summit, but a number of important events were organised, including a high-level conference in Niamey (Niger) on 23 January, sponsored by Germany, Norway, UNDP, and OCHA. The conference's official aim was to find mechanisms (1) for a faster return to peace and (2) to strengthen the resilience of people living in the Lake Chad basin, hard hit by the Boko Haram crisis and the devastating impacts of climate change. The 4th Lake Chad Basin Governors' Forum for Regional Cooperation on Stabilisation, Peace Consolidation, and Sustainable Development was held in N'Djamena on 7 July and, as could be expected, focused on security issues.

Cameroon

Fanny Pigeaud

Political tensions appeared to be on the rise following the sordid murder of the director of a private radio station, in which agents and officials of a counter-espionage service were implicated. Given President Paul Biya's age (90 years), the presidential election scheduled for 2025 fuelled political ambitions and rivalries within the ruling party, but also within the opposition, which lost one of its veterans, Ni John Fru Ndi, who succumbed to illness. Under pressure from the IMF, the government was compelled to reduce fuel price subsidies; this had a negative impact on inflation and put considerable strain on private households. While President Biya appeared eager to strengthen ties with Russia, his administration became embroiled in a diplomatic row with the Canadian government over the negotiations to end the war in the country's two Anglophone regions, where armed groups and the regular army continued to clash with each other and commit atrocities against the civilian population.

Domestic Politics

The political and social climate was poisoned by the *murder of Martinez Zogo*, director of the private radio station Amplitude FM in Yaoundé, whose horribly mutilated body was discovered in a vacant lot on 22 January. His assassination sent shockwaves throughout the country, bringing out into full daylight the multifaceted decay that is eating away at the heart of the state. Very quickly, it became clear that this was not the work of ordinary individuals: one senior executive, Lieutenant Colonel Justin Danwe, and some 20 agents, most of them gendarmes, of the Direction Générale de la Recherche Extérieure (DGRE), a counter-espionage service, were arrested a few days later on charges of having participated in the abduction of Zogo, aged 51, as he was driving his vehicle on the evening of 17 January, and of having subsequently tortured and killed him. The DGRE director-general himself, divisional commissioner Léopold Maxime Eko Eko, appointed by decree of President Paul Biya, was placed in pretrial detention in connection with the investigation into this sordid crime, jointly conducted by the police and the gendarmerie. His exact responsibility in this affair remained to be determined. According to the details that surfaced in the weeks following the discovery of the body, the members of the murder squad, some of whom later admitted their involvement, had acted on orders of a certain Jean-Pierre Amougou Belinga, an archetypal figure of the Biya era. Formerly the manager of a small newspaper and a master in the art of blackmail, Amougou Belinga had, in just a few years and in obscure ways, become the prosperous and arrogant owner of L'Anecdote, a media group that owns several newspapers and television channels. A few years earlier, Martinez Zogo, whose real name was Arsène Salomon Mbani Zogo, had himself patronised this mysterious businessman who maintained a large clientele thanks to his fortune. In the weeks that preceded his assassination, Zogo had devoted several editions of the very popular radio show 'Embouteillage', which he moderated himself on his radio station, to the affairs of Amougou Belinga. He accused him of having become rich and influential thanks to wrongfully appropriated public funds. He also implicated finance minister Louis-Paul Motazé, describing him as the one who had made Amougou Belinga a billionaire. Zogo had also spoken of the close ties that existed between the boss of L'Anecdote and the powerful minister of justice, Laurent Esso. During the first weeks of the investigation, the names of these two ministers were mentioned several times. The NGO Reporters Without Borders even claimed, though without providing any proof, that Laurent Esso was suspected of having been involved in the murder. Over the course of the year, the case gave rise to several judicial entanglements. In early December, the examining magistrate of the Yaoundé military court in charge of the investigation, Sikati II Kamwo, ordered the provisional release of Amougou Belinga and Eko Eko, but he rescinded this decision almost immediately without explanation. A few days later, on instruction from Paul Biya, he was replaced by Lieutenant Colonel Pierrot Narcisse Nzié, who held this new office concurrently with that of vice-president of the military tribunal.

According to some analysts, Zogo had found himself at the centre of a clan war that was playing out between the various factions of the Rassemblement Démocratique du Peuple Camerounais (RDPC) in view of Paul Biya's succession, and had been used by some to bring down others, only to become a victim himself in the end. Whether or not this was the case, his murder heightened the existing tensions within the circles of power. The rapidly approaching *presidential election of 2025* was taking up increasing room in the political calculus of the party barons. The rivalries seemed particularly strong between the clan to which the two ministers Esso and Motazé visibly belonged and that of Ferdinand Ngoh Ngoh, secretary-general of the presidency. Various rumours, both relayed and fuelled by social media, suggested that the latter was determined to steer the course of the investigation into the assassination of Zogo in order to eliminate competitors, including Eko Eko. Meanwhile, Paul Biya, who celebrated his 90th birthday a few days after Zogo's murder, remained as silent as always but continued to issue instructions to his aides.

In spite of its internal divisions, the RDPC, the senior functionaries and ministers of which repeatedly advocated Paul Biya's candidacy for the 2025 presidential election throughout the year, stood united for the *senatorial elections* of 12 March, which enabled it to consolidate its electoral supremacy: it won all 70 seats at stake in this indirect election (the electoral college is made up of regional and municipal councillors), in which ten parties took part. In accordance with the electoral code, the president of the republic subsequently appointed 30 other senators, 24 of whom were also members of the RDPC. The remaining six came from six other parties: the Mouvement pour la Défense de la République (MDR); the Alliance Nationale pour la Démocratie et le Progrès (ANDP); the Front pour le Salut National du Cameroun (FSNC); the Union Nationale pour la Démocratie et le Progrès (UNDP); the Union des Populations du Cameroun (UPC); and the Social Democratic Front (SDF), which had previously held seven seats. Marcel Niat Njifenji, aged 88, was confirmed as president of the Senate, a position he had already held ever since its creation in 2013. The opposition claimed that the election had been marred by irregularities, accusing the RDPC of having engaged in organised fraud. Three political parties filed complaints and called for new or partial elections. The Constitutional Council dismissed these appeals. At the same time, Cavayé Yeguié Djibril, aged 83 and also a member of the RDPC, was reappointed as president of the National Assembly, a position he had held for 31 consecutive years. However, the end of the year brought complications for him: an internal audit report uncovered malpractice in the management of the National Assembly's financial accounts that had led to the disappearance of CFAfr 2.7 bn (more than €4 m) in the space of a few months. The report showed that two-thirds of the institution's budget – set at CFAfr 23 bn (€35 m) – had been spent in only six months. Djibril was forced to solicit additional funds from the president of the republic in order to complete the year.

On the opposition side, an era came to an end with the *death of Ni John Fru Ndi*, the president and founder (in 1990) of the SDF, which had been the main opposition party for two decades before withering away. 'The Chairman', as he was popularly known, died on 12 June, aged 81, after a long illness. He received a state funeral and was buried on 29 July in Baba, his native village in the vicinity of Bamenda, in Northwest Region. His funeral took place under heavy military guard due to the security crisis in the region. In October, his right-hand man and vice-president, MP and businessman Joshua Osih, aged 54, was elected leader of the party for a five-year term. A few months earlier, the SDF had been in the throes of party in-fighting: nearly 30 of its officials, including MP Jean-Michel Nitcheu, were expelled in February for having criticised Ni John Fru Ndi's leadership. The SDF was not the only opposition party to experience dissent, exacerbated by the prospect of the upcoming presidential election of 2025. Maurice Kamto's *Mouvement pour la renaissance du Cameroun* (MRC) also witnessed several resignations and exclusions. The authority of Kamto, who had come in second in the last presidential election, was increasingly disputed. A number of MRC officials were of the opinion that the former minister delegate to the minister of justice and barrister, now aged 69, was too old to run for president in the next election. Some of them coveted his seat, such as for instance the lawyer Michèle Ndoki. On 7 May, Kamto held a meeting in Yaoundé, his first in the capital since the presidential election of 2018. Addressing an audience of 2,000, he mentioned cases of corruption, called for the liberation of activists from his party who were still in prison, describing them as hostages of the government, and accused President Biya of being responsible for the current situation in Cameroon, which he deemed catastrophic.

Alongside these various tensions, a political event of a special kind drew considerable attention in the latter part of the year: Franck Emmanuel Biya, aged 52 and *eldest son of the president*, made his first public appearance. On 9 October, this businessman, who has become increasingly present at his father's side without ever having held an official position, was joined by the prefect of Mfoundi while on his way to Mbankolo, a neighbourhood of the municipality of Yaoundé II, where a landslide had claimed the lives of some 30 people the day before. After spending nearly an hour at the scene of the tragedy, he went on to visit the coordinator of the 'Franckist' movement, an organisation that was actively campaigning for his candidacy in the presidential election of 2025. One month later, Biya's son was back in the news when he spoke at a political meeting of an RDPC section in France, an event that was filmed and broadcast on social media. On this occasion, Franck Biya stated that his father remained the leader of the party – a view to which he himself seemed to have subscribed – and that it was necessary to follow in his footsteps and accompany him. Earlier in the year, photographs circulating on social media showed Biya's son by the side of various celebrities: the former world-class tennis player Yannick Noah, who has settled in Yaoundé; the French football hero Kylian Mbappé, on his first visit to Cameroon, from where his father originated; and the boxer Francis Ngannou.

Still under-reported in the media, the *war in the Anglophone regions* of the Southwest and Northwest regions retained the same configuration as in previous years, with the regular army fighting various armed groups. However, the latter appeared to be partly weakened, some having lost their foreign funding as a result of the arrest of their leaders in the US. In early July, Amnesty International nonetheless denounced atrocities (extrajudicial executions, homicides, torture, rape) that were still being perpetrated against civilians by both members of the security forces and armed separatists. The armed groups also continued to carry out abductions for ransom and to impose a boycott on education, attacking schools, students, and teachers. They caused disruptions at the start of the 2023/24 school year: on 7 September, a few days after the reopening of schools, at least three civilians were killed in Southwest Region by presumed separatists who shot at car passengers and set fire to vehicles. According to the UN, at least 2,245 schools were prevented from operating all year round, thereby impacting the lives of hundreds of thousands of children.

Several other bloody incidents involving armed groups attracted the attention of the media. The first took place on 7 May when the self-styled Ambazonia Defence Forces (ADF) assassinated journalist Anye Ndé Nsoh in Bamenda, only to express their regrets afterwards, claiming that he had been targeted by mistake – at least according to a video posted online by Capo Daniel, one of the group's exiled leaders. Only a few days later, some 30 women were kidnapped in the same region by the group known as the Amba Fighters. The women were abducted in the village of Kedjom Keku after having taken part in a demonstration to protest against monthly taxes imposed by the Amba Fighters, namely CFAfr 10,000 (€15) for men and CFAfr 5,000 (€7.50) for women. According to certain media outlets, some of the women had been tortured. They were released after a week. On 4 October, in Guzang (Northwest Region), armed members of a further group, known as the Ambazonia Governing Council, forced dozens of local inhabitants to attend the execution of two civilians whom they accused of treason. According to the group's spokesperson Lucas Asu, who lives in exile in Canada, the two victims had collaborated with the Bataillon d'Intervention Rapide (BIR), an elite unit that reports directly to the president of the republic. On 6 November, some 20 people, including women and children, were killed in a nighttime attack on the village of Egbekaw, in the Southwest. Gunmen shot inhabitants in their sleep and set fire to houses. Another attack, carried out on a bar by men who arrived on motorcycles, took place on 25 November in

Bamenda, claiming the lives of at least five people and wounding nine others. The government stuck to its story that it was ready to engage in dialogue with the armed groups but that their leaders were unwilling to do so.

By the middle of the year, it was estimated that over 638,000 people had been *displaced* from the Anglophone regions and at least 1.7 m people required humanitarian aid. In April, UNHCR announced the closure of its field office in Buea (Southwest Region) due to lack of funding, even though it was responsible for caring for precisely those who have been displaced from the Anglophone regions. UNHCR also closed its office in Touboro (North Region), a focal point for 42,000 refugees from CAR. Prior to these closures, UNHCR had kept track of 480,000 refugees, including 320,000 from CAR in the Adamawa and North regions and 126,000 Nigerians in Far North and North.

In Far North Region, the terrorist group *Boko Haram* was still active, engaging in murder, kidnapping, and looting. According to HRW's World Report 2024, 246 attacks were recorded between January and July, causing the death of 169 civilians. On 3 August, for instance, a series of attacks left a trail of blood in the town of Darak, in the department of Logone-et-Chari, claiming the lives of five civilians. No one claimed responsibility for the attacks, but according to some observers, they had been carried out by members of Boko Haram, which is well known in the same area for extorting money from the population and kidnapping people. In early July, Far North Region also experienced torrential rains that destroyed the crops.

As for the *fight against corruption*, there was only one event of note: Edgar Alain Mébé Ngo'o, the once powerful and controversial ex-minister of defence and former chief of police, incarcerated since 2019, saw his pretrial detention converted into permanent detention when he was sentenced to 30 years of prison in late January. He was found guilty of embezzlement of CFAfr 23 bn (€35 m), aggravated money laundering, favouritism, and corruption. His wife was found guilty of embezzlement of CFAfr 5 bn and favouritism, and sentenced to ten years in prison. An inspector of the treasury and former technical advisor to the ministry of defence and a colonel who had once been a close collaborator of Mébé Ngo'o were also found guilty of having embezzled public funds and were each sentenced to 25 years in prison. The ex-minister insisted that his trial was politically motivated, claiming that one year before his arrest, the secretary-general of the presidency, Ferdinand Ngoh Ngoh, had threatened to send him to prison. One month after his conviction, an IMF mission undertook a 'governance and corruption diagnostic assessment' at the request of the Cameroonian authorities. The IMF report concluded, among other things, that the judicial sector had a very poor reputation in terms of governance and that the mechanisms for the recruitment, promotion, and disciplining of judges and judicial personnel lacked transparency. The IMF report also concluded that a significant part the country's economic activity and public administration takes place outside of formal rules and legal frameworks, with very little transparency, control, or risk of anyone being held accountable for corrupt behaviour. According to the report, the government's actions revealed complex relationships between politicians, senior civil servants, and the business community, and the decision-making process was highly centralised.

Foreign Affairs

For the first time in 41 years, President Biya flew to *Russia* to attend the Russia–Africa Summit held in late July. Prohibited, like some of his African counterparts, from flying over European airspace, Biya was forced to travel by way of Türkiye. Eight government ministers, his wife, and his son Franck accompanied him on this trip. He met with Vladimir Putin on 28 July, one day after signing an agreement on the mutual exemption from visas for holders of diplomatic and service passports. President Biya took the opportunity to introduce his son to his Russian counterpart, as well as to other officials, on the sidelines of a dinner hosted by the Kremlin on the same day.

Prior to this visit to Russia, Biya had already undertaken another official trip: in June, he attended the Summit for a New Global Financial Pact in Paris, to which his son Franck also accompanied him. At the same time, *tensions erupted between Cameroonian and French diplomats*: in June, Lejeune Mbella Mbella, Cameroonian minister of foreign affairs, refused to allow Jean-Marc Berthon, French ambassador for LGBTQ+ rights, to enter the country to attend an event on gender and sexuality hosted by the Institut Français du Cameroun in Yaoundé. The minister invoked the Cameroonian penal code, which punishes anyone who has sexual relations with a person of the same sex with up to five years in prison. Subsequently, the French diplomatic corps in Cameroon was struck by a tragedy: on 18 August, the lifeless body of Christian Hué, head of chancery at the French consulate in Douala, was found at his home. Initial findings pointed to suicide, but an investigation was opened under the direction of the regional division of the judicial police and of the gendarmerie legion of Littoral Region, joined by members of the French embassy's security service. The investigators did not rule out the possibility of a link between this death and the previous opening of an inquiry into a suspected trafficking of entry visas to France. Later in the year, on 4 November, President Biya received the French minister of foreign affairs, Catherine Colonna, and the secretary-general of the *OIF*, Louise Mushikiwabo, in Yaoundé, both of whom had come to Cameroon to attend an OIF conference.

The war in the Anglophone regions gave rise to tensions between *Canada* and Cameroon. On 20 January, the Canadian minister of foreign affairs, Mélanie Joly, announced that her country had accepted a mandate to facilitate the peace process between the Cameroonian government and relevant armed groups. The leaders of some of the most powerful groups, all living abroad, including Lucas Ayaba Cho of the Ambazonia Governing Council and Ebenezer Akwanga of the African People's Liberation Movement, confirmed that negotiations had been conducted in the greatest secrecy for several weeks. But on 24 January, the Cameroonian authorities denied ever having entrusted any foreign country or external organisation with the role of mediator. According to the Paris-based news magazine 'Jeune Afrique', President Biya, finally yielding to US and French pressure after two failed attempts at negotiation, had indeed consented to talks in May 2022, to be held under the guidance of Prime Minister Joseph Dion Ngute, with Canada as facilitator – which in turn solicited the expertise of the Swiss NGO Centre for Humanitarian Dialogue (HD). Discreet meetings took place in Canada from December 2022 onward, bringing together leaders of armed groups and emissaries of the Cameroonian state. The reason that Yaoundé subsequently chose to deny any negotiations of this kind was probably linked to the rivalries and ambitions among the aides of the head of state: some of them sought to thwart the initiative while it was supported by others, a process that has become typical of Paul Biya's entourage. In March, just as the associate deputy minister of foreign affairs was due to travel to Cameroon in an attempt to relaunch the mediation, the Cameroonian minister Lejeune Mbella Mbella cancelled his visit.

There was also friction between N'Djamena and Yaoundé regarding the shareholder structure of the Cameroon Oil Transportation Company (Cotco), which operates the Cameroonian section of the *Chad–Cameroon pipeline*. On 20 April, N'Djamena recalled its ambassador in Yaoundé for consultations to protest against Cameroon's support for the purchase of Cotco shares by the British company Savannah Energy. The managing director of the Société Nationale des Hydrocarbures (SNH), Adolphe Moudiki, aged 84, had planned to increase the SNH's stake in Cotco by means of a partnership with Savannah Energy in order to counter Chad's hegemonic claims over this strategic enterprise. In this way, he hoped to acquire 10% of Savannah Energy's assets in Cotco. Totalling CFAfr 26.7 bn (nearly €41 m), this transaction would have allowed the SNH to increase its share in Cotco's capital from 5% to 15.2%. However, the Chadian state considered itself the rightful owner of the shares purchased by Savannah Energy since the nationalisation of the assets held by Esso's Chadian subsidiary. On 27 April, Chad's interim president Mahamat Idriss Déby received Ferdinand Ngoh Ngoh, who had been sent by Biya to attempt to settle this dispute. At this meeting, Déby allegedly secured Chad's right to buy back the shares of another shareholder in Cotco: Petronas, a Malaysian oil company that owned 30% of Cotco at the time. But the affair did not end there. After initially approving the acquisition of Esso's shares by the SNH, Biya eventually disavowed Moudiki, thereby forcing the SNH to abandon his plan.

In the middle of the year, a business conflict put a damper on relations between Cameroon and *South Africa*, in June prompting the South African minister of international relations and cooperation, Naledi Pandor, to express concern regarding the treatment of South African companies in Cameroon. The situation began when the Cameroonian billionaire and businessman Baba Ahmadou Danpullo obtained a court order freezing the accounts of the Cameroonian subsidiary of the South African company Mobile Telephone Network (MTN) in Cameroon. Danpullo believed that he had been wrongfully dispossessed of properties he owned in Johannesburg by South Africa's First National Bank, which had indeed seized and liquidated them in 2020 following Danpullo's failure to meet several payment deadlines. The latter estimated his losses, resulting from what he qualified as acts of 'spoliation', at CFAfr 256 bn (€390 m). One of his South African partners, with whom was by this time in conflict, the Public Investment Corporation, was one of the main shareholders of MTN Cameroon. After several rulings in his favour by the Cameroonian courts, the billionaire suffered a set-back towards the end of the year: the Littoral Region Court of Appeal suspended a decision of the lower court in Douala-Bonanjo which had ordered the Cameroonian bank Société commerciale de banque (SCB) to transfer CFAfr 270 m (€410,000) belonging to the MTN to Danpullo.

Socioeconomic Developments

The balanced *budget* adopted in late 2022 was set at CFAfr 6,345.1 bn (€9.6 bn), up by 4.4% from that of the previous year. It counted on CFAfr 807 bn in oil and gas revenues, CFAfr 3,528.1 bn in tax and customs revenues, and CFAfr 250.4 bn in non-tax revenues. In order to achieve these revenues, the government resorted to substantial tax hikes for businesses as well as small taxpayers and also increased the fees for certain public services. On the expenditures side, the government allocated CFAfr 15 bn to help the regions affected by the security crisis. Above all, however, it lowered fuel subsidies under insistent pressure from the IMF. Subsidies on oil products, which had amounted to CFAfr 1,000 bn in 2022, were reduced to around CFAfr 640 bn in 2023, resulting in higher prices at the pump. In combination with climatic disruptions and the adverse effects of the war in the Northwest and Southwest regions, this increase in fuel prices had an impact on the standard of living of Cameroonian households. It contributed to a *general rise in prices*, with the average annual inflation rate reaching 7.4%, according to the National Institute of Statistics (INS). Food and transportation were hit by inflation rates of 12.8% and 11.5%, respectively. Inflation was higher for local products (+8.1%) than for imported products (+5.6%). The INS pointed out that this was only the third time in 29 years that Cameroon had experienced such a high inflation rate, after 32.5% and 9%, respectively, in 1994 and 1995, following the 50% devaluation of the CFAfr in January 1994.

In order to lessen the shock, the government raised the *guaranteed minimum wage* (Salaire Minimum Interprofessionnel Garanti, SMIG) in March. It was raised from CFAfr 36,270 to CFAfr 41,875 (€63.8) for public servants. For employees of the agricultural sector and related occupational fields, representing the country's largest workforce, the raise was from CFAfr 36,270 to CFAfr 45,000 (€68.6). In other sectors, it was fixed at CFAfr 60,000 (€91.47). Pleased with these increases, the labour unions nevertheless pointed out that the government, by assigning different values to the SMIG according to categories of workers, was violating the labour code, which allows only one universal increase. In June, the president of the republic had to sign an ordinance increasing the state budget to CFAfr 6,726.9 bn (€10.2 bn). This revised budget provided for a reduction in current and capital expenditures of nearly CFAfr 100 bn and for additional expenditures towards the repayment of debts, or an increase by CFAfr 308.2 bn to CFAfr 1962 bn. The proportion of expenditures for debt repayment thus reached 30% of the total revised budget. This budgetary revision also increased the amount of emergency aid to support vulnerable households in certain regions. As a whole, however, these social expenditures remained at a modest level, namely CFAfr 180.3 bn.

By late October, the state had earned CFAfr 559,402 bn in *oil and gas revenues*. These earnings were 11.5% lower than in the same period of the preceding year, when they had amounted to CFAfr 632,703 bn. The SNH had sold 19.9 m oil barrels, compared with 20.8 m in the same period of 2022. The sale of LNG, on the other hand, rose by over 8.7% to reach a total of 2,181 m cubic metres.

At year's end, the growth of real GDP was estimated at around 4%. The budget deficit was expected to drop, from 1.1% of GDP in 2022 to 0.7% in 2023. On 30 September, the outstanding debt of the public sector amounted to CFAfr 12,510 bn, according to the Caisse autonome d'amortissement, the state agency responsible for the management of public debt. This outstanding debt represented 43.9% of GDP at the time.

Relations between the Cameroonian authorities and the *IMF* were relatively good. Late in the year, the IMF concluded the fifth reviews of the economic and financial reform programme funded by the ECF and the Extended Credit Mechanism (ECM). It immediately disbursed CFAfr 45 bn to Cameroon, bringing the total amount disbursed under the terms of these two agreements, concluded in July 2021, to roughly CFAfr 345 bn. The IMF also extended the programme, which had been scheduled to end in July 2024, by one year, which was to result in additional funding of CFAfr 87 bn. In exchange, the country was expected to generate more domestic revenues that are not linked to oil. In particular, the IMF recommended that it should improve the efficiency and procurement of public expenditures, limit recourse to exceptional procedures for expenditures, and strengthen the management of public enterprises. The AfDB, for its part, approved a loan of CFAfr 49 bn (€74.25 m) for the implementation of the first phase of a support programme for the recovery of the electricity sector.

For several days in December, the country experienced a *fuel shortage* that mostly impacted the large cities, including Yaoundé and Douala. According to the government, this disruption was due to adverse weather conditions that delayed the arrival of three oil tankers coming from the port of Lomé. SONARA, Cameroon's only oil refinery, which has been inoperative since a fire devastated it in 2019 and owes CFAfr 374 bn (€570 m) in debts to oil traders, appeared to be seeing the beginning of a solution to its many problems: the government signed contracts to restructure its debts with several of its creditors, including Trafigura and Vitol. Cameroonians had to endure *power grid disruptions* throughout the year. The company Energy of Cameroon (Eneo), a 51%-owned subsidiary of the British investment firm Actis that manages the sale and distribution of electricity, was on the verge of bankruptcy, largely due to unpaid bills owed by the state and its dependent entities, including the decentralised territorial authorities but also public enterprises such as the Compagnie camerounaise d'aluminium (Alucam) and Camwater, the public company responsible for public water services and water purification. Due to its financial difficulties, Eneo did not pay its suppliers, including the Electricity Development Corporation (EDC) and SONATREL, the public company managing the power distribution network, and the Globeleq subsidiaries, namely the power stations operated by the Kribi Power Development Corporation (KPDC, 216 MW) and the Dibamba Power Development Corporation (DPDC, 88 MW), which alone supply about 20% of the country's available megawatts. Demanding the payment of CFAfr 107 bn from Eneo, Globeleq shut down these two power stations towards the end of the year, thereby forcing Eneo to ration electricity on its Southern Interconnected Network, which covers several large cities including Yaoundé and Douala. To prevent these disruptions from spoiling the holiday season, the government agreed to pay part of Eneo's debt to Globeleq. The state also created a new company, the Kikot Hydro Power Company (KHPC), which it owns in equal shares with the French company EDF. Launched in September, this business entity had plans to build a new hydroelectric dam by 2030.

The *mining sector* witnessed a significant change on the legal front: a new mining code was adopted by the National Assembly and the Senate in late 2023. A previous code had been passed in 2016, but its application decree was never promulgated. The new code provided the legal basis for Sonamines, created in 2020, to become the sole entity responsible for the buying and marketing of gold and diamonds. The SDF deplored the fact that this text did not put an end to the logic of centralisation and did not encourage local economic transformation or the development of an industry. The Ministry of Forestry and Wildlife also took decisions that sparked controversies. In July, it was criticised by environmental NGOs, including Greenpeace Africa, for having allowed a company, Sextransbois, to exploit part of the Ebo Forest in the Littoral Region, within the framework of a forest management unit. According to the NGOs, the ministry had not respected the law before granting this permit. Since 2020, Ebo Forest has been the object of a conflict between the government and various organisations that seek to protect the environment and local inhabitants. According to NGOs and scientists, the decision to create a forest management unit in this forest posed a serious threat to its biodiversity. The Ebo forest is reputed to be one of the last remaining intact forest tracts in the Gulf of Guinea and is home to an exceptional level of biodiversity, including several animal species at risk of extinction, such as chimpanzees that are not found anywhere else.

While the country remains the world's fourth-largest producer of *cocoa*, its exports dropped significantly during the 2022/23 season due to illegal exports to Nigeria, which were partly organised by armed groups. According to the Ministry of Trade, these illegal exports reached unprecedented levels: between 10% and 20% of production, or 30,000 to 60,000 tons, evaded control of the state during the 2022/23 season, leading to losses of CFAfr 70 bn. To curb this phenomenon, the authorities imposed armed escorts on the convoys transporting the cocoa beans produced in Southwest Region, the main production area along with Center Region.

In the educational sector, the movement called 'On a trop supporté' ('We have endured too much'), which emerged in February 2022, resumed its protests in September 2023: public school teachers from nursery school all the way up to high school went to their workplaces but did not teach classes to protest against their salary conditions. This *strike* forced the government to hold talks with the teachers' unions. In late November, they were received by a technical advisor of the general secretariat of the presidency. In his end-of-year speech, President Biya asserted that the government had made significant efforts with regard to teachers, speaking of more than CFAfr 72 bn (€109 m) disbursed in 2023 and announcing an additional CFAfr 102 bn for 2024. Under these conditions, he added that the teachers must end their strike, promising that the dialogue would continue with the 'recognised unions'.

As in the preceding year, the overall *health situation* was marked by a cholera epidemic, which broke out in October 2021 and resurged again in 2023. In May, five regions were affected: Center, Littoral, West, South, and East. Center Region, where the capital Yaoundé is located, was considered the epicentre of this outbreak, with 760 registered cases, of which at least 27 proved fatal. According to the Ministry of Health, the epidemic claimed a total of 374 lives, with a fatality rate of 2.24%. The Littoral, Southwest, and Center regions had reported the highest number of cases since October 2021, namely 7,606, 6,027, and 2,050, respectively.

In July, the country witnessed one of the worst urban catastrophes of its history: the collapse of a four-story apartment building onto another residential building in Douala claimed the lives of at least 40 people. Célestine Ketcha-Courtès, Cameroon's minister of urban development, declared that the collapsed building had had no construction permit and admitted that building regulations are rarely respected.

Central African Republic

Andreas Mehler

President Faustin-Archange Touadéra managed to get a firm long-term grip on power by pushing for a new constitution revoking presidential term limits, which was adopted by referendum. The opaque and executive-heavy process was contested by the opposition, but to no avail. The peace process saw some superficial progress, not least because a number of rebel movements split, with some factions accepting dissolution. However, the ever more widespread use of explosive devices meant that civilian populations, particularly in the north-west, could not live in peace. The economic situation remained dire, with the IMF intervening to help a government that did little by itself. Turmoil in neighbouring countries (Chad and Sudan) somewhat altered the familiar regional picture, making CAR look less vulnerable in comparison and even allowing Touadéra to be designated facilitator in Gabon's post-coup crisis, though he could not point to a major improvement in his own country.

Domestic Politics

Originally, the main item on the electoral calendar was the annual ritual of announcing the technically difficult and financially expensive *local elections* – initially this time for September 2023 – only to then postpone them to the next year, as has happened repeatedly since 2016. Political parties variously published conditions for their participation in the polls. However, these elections were obviously not the main priority of the government. On 7 September, the first round of local elections was finally rescheduled for 13 October 2024, with a second round not planned until for 26 January 2025.

Instead, President Touadéra announced on 30 May that a *referendum* on a new constitution would be held as soon as 30 July, and the state office Autorité Nationale des Elections (ANE) started to prepare for the event, which would be fully state-funded (in contrast to local elections, where UNDP tried to collect donor contributions). A campaign directorate was installed, headed by the first deputy speaker of the National Assembly, Evariste Ngamana, one of Touadéra's favourite fixers. On 25 June, the episcopal conference questioned the relevance of the referendum in the face of 'the socio-political and economic situation prevailing in our country'. The presidency nevertheless published the draft constitution on 10 July, allowing only for a short public debate; however, the main and expected elements had already been hotly debated since mid-2022. The draft contained an extension of the terms of the president (Article 67) and members of the National Assembly (Article 98) from five to seven years, also removing term limits (the key element of debate). By allowing the president to appoint a vice-president (a new position; Article 65), it bolstered the power of the president further. By declaring a 'CAR citizen of origin' to be only someone whose two parents were both equally CAR citizens of origin (Article 10) – and one condition of being elected as president was to fulfil this condition – an ultra-nationalist and exclusive definition was chosen. Furthermore, individuals who have created or have been affiliated with armed groups would be ineligible to contest legislative elections. Important, but less controversial, was the abolishment of the Senate, created *de jure* in 2015 but never established as a second chamber. Some checks on executive power by parliament were abolished and the requirements for amending the constitution lowered. The opposition platform Bloc Républicain pour la Défense de la Constitution (BRDC), created the previous year, questioned not only the content of the draft but also the legitimacy of the drafting and referendum processes. The rebel alliance Coalition des Patriotes pour le Changement (CPC) called for a boycott, as did main political parties including Kwa Na Kwa (KNK; former president François Bozizé's party), the Mouvement de Libération du Peuple Centrafricain (MLPC), the vocal Parti Africain pour une Transformation Radicale et l'Intégration des États (Patrie), and the Union pour le Renouveau Centrafricain (URCA), all of which called on the population to stay at home. On 14 July, the BRDC organised a public march; only a few hundred people attended but most heavyweights of the opposition showed up, demonstrating a high level of solidarity among them. Former prime ministers Anicet-Georges Dologuélé (URCA) and Martin Ziguélé (MLPC), as well as the outspoken Crépin Mboli-Goumba (Patrie), marched together on the streets of Bangui in protest against the referendum. This did not have a strong effect, though: the referendum was held as scheduled. The Constitutional Court, purged last year of those opposed to Touadéra's plans, announced the results of the referendum on 21 August (95% yes votes with a rather improbable 57.2% participation rate, immediately denounced by the BRDC and civil society groups). With the promulgation of the new constitution on 30 August, the CAR entered its 'Seventh Republic'.

President Touadéra addressed the nation one day later on the premises of the National Assembly, promising to remain committed to the peace process but also to end the era of impunity. However, the government's attitude towards its civilian democratic opposition remained openly hostile. On 11 December, the bureau of the National Assembly, headed by its president Simplice Sarandji, a very close collaborator of Touadéra already when they had leading positions within the University of Bangui, decided to reduce the remuneration of the most prominent opposition MPs, invoking their extended absence from the country. The decision targeted Dologuélé, Ziguélé, and Ephrem Dominique Yandocka, the leader of a smaller party (Initiative pour une Transformation par l'Action, ITA). When Yandocka returned, he was arrested in the early hours of 15 December by heavily armed gendarmes and detained for alleged involvement in a coup plot. These were all clear signs of further backsliding towards full *authoritarian rule.*

The *security situation* improved in parts of the country, particularly in the capital, Bangui. On 3 March, leader of the rebel alliance CPC and former head of state François Bozizé was forced by the Chadian government to leave the country for Guinea-Bissau. On his arrival, he reaffirmed his grip on the CPC in a declaration, as well as his continued opposition to Touadéra. The CPC (or its affiliates) appeared weakened by this relocation, losing territorial control but not all of its military capacities. Trade routes and mining sites remained the focus of rebel attacks.

In March and April, Anti-balaka elements and rebels of Retour, Réclamation et Réhabilitation (3R), all members of the CPC, repeatedly attacked positions of the security forces (Forces Armées Centrafricaines, FACA) and their Russian allies in the *West* with the latter's bases assaulted in Bossemptele (Ouham-Pendé Prefecture), in Niem (Nana-Mambéré), and in Kadjama (Ouham). One incident was also recorded near the Cameroonian border when suspected Anti-balaka combatants set the gendarmerie post of Besson ablaze on 24 January. The increasing use of landmines and other explosive devices threatened the life of civilians as well. Frequent abductions for ransom on both sides of the Cameroon – CAR border were blamed on rebels by both governments. A major clash occurred on 15 May near Benzambé (Ouham) when rebels attacked a protected convoy of traders and four soldiers were killed. On 3 July, a vehicle of a foreign company was ambushed near mining sites in Gobolo (Nana-Mambéré), and four FACA soldiers and two civilians were killed in the event (and an international mine worker wounded). FACA and Russian 'instructors' launched series of air attacks on mining sites in Ouham in the second half of October, resulting in casualties. A local commander of the Mouvement Patriotique pour la Centrafrique (MPC) was killed in one such event. 3R combatants tried to regain control of mining sites with indiscriminate use of violence, as well as kidnappings. As an example, on 18 November, five international mine workers were abducted from the Zoungo mines; they were released only on 14 December for ransom. As in past years, the start of the transhumance period triggered further attacks, but also cattle theft and reprisals. On 21 December, 3R combatants, allied with Fulani herders, attacked a FACA position in Nzakoundou (Lim-Pendé) in an act of retaliation. According to UN sources, 22 civilians and one soldier were killed and some 3,500 civilians displaced. Paoua, the capital of the same prefecture, witnessed serious intercommunal confrontations in November after a Christian was allegedly killed by a Muslim. When the gendarmerie refused to hand over the arrested suspect, a mob destroyed houses and properties of Muslims.

Mining sites were clearly mostly targeted by the contending parties in the *Centre*, particularly its Northern part. Unité pour la Paix en Centrafrique (UPC) contingents attacked positions of security forces in Wawa (Ouaka Prefecture, with the highest concentration of Wagner troops) on two occasions (15 March, 15 April), resulting in nine deaths. The Chimbolo mining site (also in Ouaka) was the scene of the killing of nine Chinese mine workers on 19 March, but it was impossible to establish responsibility. With frequent incursions by the CPC occurring in the area, UN peacekeeping mission MINUSCA attempted to keep the Mbrès–Bamingui axis open, enabling FACA to pursue its operations against rebel forces. In one operation on 31 July, CPC combatants killed 13 civilians in Diki (Bamingui-Bangoran). At least twice (2 and 24 November), the UPC attacked positions held by the security forces and its Russian allies between Kabo and Moyenne-Sido, but the latter were able to repel the militia. However, thousands of civilians were forced to flee to Chad. In a new phenomenon, drones attacked two camps of security forces and Russian instructors on 10 December in Kaga Bandoro (Nana-Grébizi Prefecture), killing three. The government had restricted the use of drones to its own already in February (*inter alia*, prohibiting peacekeepers from using them). MINUSCA also reported that drones had flown over its bases in several locations.

The security situation was particularly volatile in the *East*, especially in the prefectures of Haut-Mbomou and Vakaga. Several clashes between Russian instructors using helicopters – apparently not always operating jointly with official security forces – and CPC elements occurred at the end of January when four Russians were reportedly killed. CPC forces attacked army positions on 14 February in Sikikédé (Vakaga), a key town for the illegal arms trade with Chad and Sudan and the scene of many confrontations in 2022. Civilians were displaced and 20 soldiers abducted (released on 4 April in the presence of MINUSCA). The nearby gold mining sites around Gordil were apparently also a motivation for all conflict parties to remain engaged with the two opposed factions of the Front Populaire pour la Renaissance de la Centrafrique (FPRC), one led by Nourredine Adam (feeding the trade route to Sudan) and the other by Hissène Abdoulaye (to Bangui). On 5 May, the CPC briefly reconquered Tiringoulou, causing massive displacement of the population, but it had to track back when MINUSCA intervened. A new, clearly ethnically identified self-defence group, Azande Ani Kpi Gbe ('Too Many Azandes Have Died') emerged in March, alleging that the prefect of Haut-Mbomou was colluding with the UPC. Fighters of the group clashed with the UPC on 15 March and had to retreat to Mboki. As a result, 600 civilians had to take refuge in neighbouring South Sudan. From 21 to 23 April, Azande Ani Kpi Gbe fighters and unidentified South Sudanese clashed in Obo, the prefecture's capital. MINUSCA concentrated on keeping the Zemio–Mboki–Obo–Bambouti axis open but met with resistance from the new group, which mostly targeted Fulani and other Muslim civilians (suspected of being allies of UPC). The local military balance was still in favour of the UPC. In a further major clash on 20 June in Mboki, Azande Ani Kpi Gbe lost 48 and the UPC only four fighters; five civilians were also killed. In the absence of any state authority, MINUSCA deployed more peacekeepers to Obo and Mboki in September to stop the attacks on humanitarian organisations and the mass displacement of civilians. In summer, tensions were also high in Haute-Kotto Prefecture, mostly around Sam Ouandja, when Russian elements tried to dislodge CPC forces from the area. An attack on a gendarmerie post by fighters of the CPC-aligned (but not officially a member) Parti pour le Rassemblement de la Nation Centrafricaine (PRNC) on 4 July resulted in the death of three gendarmes and two civilians. CPC combatants also attacked a MINUSCA patrol, killing one peacekeeper. But MINUSCA also killed three combatants, including one close associate of UPC leader and CPC chief of staff Ali Darassa. With the conflict in Sudan intensifying, more incidents occurred in the north-east. UPC reportedly recruited additional combatants, mostly in Vakaga Prefecture. On 28 December, a MINUSCA patrol apprehended three Sudanese combatants, confiscated their weapons and ammunition, and handed them over to national authorities. Unidentified Sudanese combatants were responsible for several armed confrontations, killing at least four civilians and destroying property.

On 28 April, President Touadéra chaired a ceremony to mark the *dissolution of two armed groups* who had signed the Political Agreement in 2019 (Révolution et Justice-Belanga Branch and Séléka rénovée). Potentially more important was the dissolution of Abdoulaye Hissène's FPRC wing, though it had cooperated with the government already for quite some time, plus factions of the MPC and the Front

Démocratique du Peuple Centrafricain (FDPC). MPC leader Mahamat Al-Khatim announced the MPC's departure from the CPC coalition in October. At the end of November, the minister of state in charge of disarmament, demobilisation, reintegration, and repatriation, Jean Willybiro Sako, travelled to Chad and met with Al-Khatim. In a press statement, the return of the MPC to the Political Agreement was announced and the Chadian minister for public security and immigration, Mahamat Charfadine Margui, was designated as facilitator. However, on 24 December, 16 MPC members publicly dissociated themselves from the initiative and instead committed themselves to the CPC alliance. More irritating was the massive recruitment of former Anti-balaka (and other) fighters into FACA without due vetting processes or human rights training. In November, over 500 new recruits were enrolled who had received five months' training by Rwandan instructors. According to estimates by the UN panel of experts, FACA now stood at 14,000–15,000 elements (9,700 was the original target). In this context, it was hardly surprising that the *demobilisation* process advanced only slowly, with the UN mission regularly announcing the processing of rather limited numbers of former rebels. However, one faction of the Lord's Resistance Army (LRA) participated in a MINUSCA-led programme of demobilisation and repatriation (to Uganda); 127 ex-combatants and their associates left the South-East in July, and in August a further 16 individuals were repatriated by authorities of both countries.

The country's justice system, the hybrid *Cour Pénale Spéciale* (CPS), and the International Criminal Court (ICC) were all variously in the headlines. On 20 July, the Appeals Chamber of the CPS confirmed the decisions taken by its Trial Chamber in 2022 which had convicted three 3R members for crimes against humanity and war crimes committed in 2019. Warlord Abdoulaye Hissène, despite the dissolution of his FPRC wing, was arrested on 5 September in Bangui, where he lived as a free man after participating in last year's political dialogue. The once powerful and dreaded warlord had erroneously believed that he had found a stable arrangement with the government. Hissène had been a minister in the short-lived Séléka-dominated government in 2013–14 but was also on the list of individuals sanctioned by the UN, the EU, and individual countries. The CPS charged him with crimes against humanity and war crimes committed in 2017 in Mbomou Prefecture, while the Bangui Court of First Instance charged him separately with conspiracy and undermining state security. On 16 September, Anti-balaka leader Edmond Patrick Abrou was arrested by the CPS and charged with crimes against humanity and war crimes committed in the village of Boyo (Ouaka), in 2021. On 5 December, the CPS opened the trial against ten individuals accused of the same crimes committed in Ndélé (Vakaga) in 2020 during clashes between the two main FPRC factions; this was adjourned three days later. Among others, the *Bangui Court of Appeal* convicted *in absentia* former president François Bozizé, UPC leader Ali Darassa, MPC leader Mahamat Al-Khatim, FPRC leader Nourredine Adam, and Anti-balaka leader Maxime Mokom on 21 September for undermining the internal security of the state through the creation of the CPC, as well as for a number of other issues including murder, rebellion, destruction of public property, and crimes committed against peacekeepers in late 2020 and in 2021. They were sentenced to lifelong forced labour. Mokom, the confirmation of whose charges had only begun on 22 August, was for his part released by the ICC in The Hague on 17 October after the court's prosecutor withdrew charges, citing a lack of evidence and witnesses. Two other Anti-balaka leaders' trials were ongoing at the ICC.

Foreign Affairs

In his address to the nation on 31 August, President Touadéra also had a message to the outside world: 'Our country, endowed with immense natural resources, is still prey to the permanent covetousness and hegemonic ambitions of certain Western powers, which result in illegitimate embargoes and economic sanctions.' However, the government was rather less verbally aggressive towards the UN and the EU compared with earlier years. In fact, the UNSC, through its Resolution 2693, had only four days earlier lifted some of its sanctions on supply, sale, or transfer of arms and related material as well as the provision of assistance, advice, and training to the CAR security forces – while still maintaining a sanctions regime and renewing the mandate of its Group of Experts. This expert panel had detected a good number of infractions against the existing sanctions regime, not least in conjunction with Russian aircraft, in its most recent report – at least, the necessary exemption notifications were rarely provided.

In the region, neighbours *Chad* and Sudan posed new challenges. A substantial group – estimated at several thousand in number – of Chadian opponents to the regime in N'Djamena had found a rear-base in the notoriously unstable north-west of CAR (Lim-Pendé Prefecture) since late 2022. A different group of Chadians asked for permission to settle further east in Vakaga in April. Border security was therefore an important diplomatic issue. On 9 February, Angola's president João Lourenço convened a meeting in Luanda with Touadéra and Mahamat Idriss Déby Itno, the transitional president of Chad. Apparently other issues were discussed in this context, not least with regard to exiled leaders of rebel movements who had discretely been lodged in Chad. On 3 March, N'Djamena stated that François Bozizé, leader of the rebel coalition CPC and former CAR president, had left for a new exile in Guinea-Bissau – i.e. thousands of miles away instead of on Touadéra's doorstep. A joint military operation by the two countries' armies attacked the camp of Déby's opponents, not all of them armed, north of Paoua on 15 May, killing dozens and at least provisionally dispersing the rest. Only on 8 June did Prime Minister Félix Moloua and the special representative of the secretary-general for CAR (and head of MINUSCA) Valentine Rugwabiza go to Lim-Pendé Prefecture to get first-hand impressions of the humanitarian needs after the arrival of tens of thousands of displaced people fleeing violence in Chad. Turmoil in the region on both sides of the border persisted, leading to further displacements.

Following the onset of fighting in the *Sudan* on 15 April, at least 600 Sudanese soldiers reportedly fled into Chad's border zone with CAR, where they were disarmed. Sudanese elements including disgruntled Janjaweed fighters also ended up in CAR. Discussions regarding the deployment of a tripartite joint force (CAR, Chad, Sudan) at the border triangle around Tissi went back and forth, but not a lot of progress was made in such circumstances. On 6 September, Moloua and Rugwabiza went to Birao to listen to the challenges and concerns of the local population provoked by the influx of more than 20,000 refugees from Sudan. In his speech, Moloua encouraged local communities to welcome Sudanese refugees. President Touadéra travelled to Juba, capital of *South Sudan*, on the invitation of his counterpart Salva Kiir Mayardit. On 1 September, they signed agreements to enhance security, defence, and economic cooperation.

Surprisingly, given the notorious instability of CAR, the government was able to generate some level of international respectability. On 17 March, President Touadéra took over the rotating presidency of CEMAC from Paul Biya (Cameroon) at the regular summit in Yaoundé. He also assumed the rotating presidency of CEEAC on 6 July. Additionally, his peers at CEEAC chose him on 31 August to be the facilitator in *Gabon*'s crisis after the coup in that country – while in the past Omar Bongo (president of Gabon 1967–2009) or Denis Sassou Nguesso (Congo) had consistently assumed such roles in the region, not least when CAR's own developments had worried neighbours. Touadéra travelled to Libreville on 6 September, where he met, among others, coup leader General Brice Oligui Nguema and toppled president Ali Bongo Ondimba, son of Omar. These first talks began a discussion on a road-map for dialogue and the return of constitutional order in Gabon, further refined on 4 October when a delegation from Gabon led by Oligui Nguema was received by Touadéra in Bangui.

A delegation of the AU's Panel of the Wise led by former Burundian president Domitien Ndayizeye visited CAR from 5 to 11 March and confirmed its support for the full implementation of the Political Agreement (of 2019) through the Luanda road-map. On 15 November, through Resolution 2709, the UNSC decided to extend the mandate of MINUSCA until 15 November 2024 with a substantial troop size of 14,400 uniformed elements. The influence of *Rwanda* was steadily growing within the mission (not least via Rugwabiza), but also within other UN agencies, through military and police cooperation as well as private investment.

Russia remained the most important partner of the regime. Dozens of Wagner militiamen were flown in specifically to guarantee security around the 31 July referendum, but they even more actively took part in distributing voting and campaign material. Only a few days earlier (27–28 July), Touadéra participated as one of 15 African heads of state at the Russia–Africa summit held in St Petersburg, where he was warmly welcomed by Vladimir Putin. Putin promised grain shipments to several embattled African nations, including CAR, but these did not materialise quickly. The death of Wagner head Yevgeny Prigozhin on 23 August in a dubious plane accident stoked public confusion as to Russia's role in CAR at first but did not lastingly affect bilateral relations. The possibility of establishing a Russian military base was mentioned by CAR's ambassador to Russia in May. In this context, it was perhaps less surprising that major Western powers did not voice criticism of the referendum process, potentially because both France and the US feared an even closer relationship between Moscow and CAR.

Socioeconomic Developments

On 3 January, the government decreed a significant increase in the price of petrol amid widespread fuel shortages. Prices of diesel were increased by 70%, gasoline by 50%, and kerosene by 78%, with the consequence that most customers tried to procure fuel illegally – meaning that the increases did not have the calculated positive effect on state revenues. The shortages, directly related to the crises in Sudan and Chad (and temporary border closures), also hampered the delivery of humanitarian aid and the conduct of military operations by FACA. Households were hit hard by the price hikes, if only indirectly. Their purchasing power had decreased for years already as a cumulative effect of the Covid-19 crisis in 2020, conflict intensification in 2021, and Russia's war in Ukraine in 2022. Several parts of the public sector, including health and education, were severely affected. Trade unions in these two sectors called for nationwide strikes beginning in February, calling for salary increases and better working conditions. Touadéra engaged directly with the trade unions on 14 and 15 March and was able to achieve a temporary suspension of the strikes

The IMF sent a mission to Bangui which confirmed the urgent need for not only further humanitarian assistance but also concessional budgetary support. The suspension of budgetary aid by all major donors in 2021 had hit the government's capacities severely. Also, a majority of the population were living on the edge, with a projected 49% experiencing high levels of acute food insecurity. The latest figures released by the World Bank covered 2022 but were also highly instructive: nearly two-thirds of the population (65.5%) lived below the poverty line. On 27 April, the IMF's executive board of directors therefore approved an ECF worth $191.4 m and immediately disbursed $15.2 m. On 29 April, President Touadéra, in a direct response to the IMF's expectations, instructed his ministers to promptly implement required measures, including electronic tax reporting and petroleum sector reform.

Still, by the end of the year, the IMF had revised real GDP growth downwards to 1% while it revised inflation slightly upwards to 6.5%. Budget support increased by 22% to $59.3 m with the support of the World Bank and the AfDB.

The regime did not backtrack on its *cryptocurrency* dreams but adjusted its policy. On 20 January, the government instituted a task force to elaborate a more complete legal framework for the utilisation of crypto assets. On 23 March, the National Assembly accepted an amendment that harmonised the country's law (adopted in 2022) with regional and international financial standards. The obligation for economic agents to accept cryptocurrency as payment was revoked. However, in May, the parliament adopted a bill that made the sale and purchase of land and natural resources via cryptocurrency possible. Observers did not expect a quick change of financial transaction practices. Nevertheless, the risk that the country would dip into a yet greater crisis was enumerated by the World Bank in its CEMAC Barometer released on 30 November, which listed, above all, a failure to repeal or amend the recently adopted tokenisation law – likely to pose several systemic risks to macroeconomic and financial stability, including money laundering, and to derail prospects for FDI. In this risk assessment, further aspects included the potential failure to implement policies addressing fuel supply shortages, the inability to mobilise concessional donor support, a reversal of still-shaky security gains, and the tightening of regional and global financial conditions, which would necessarily increase debt service costs.

Though the estimated number of *IDP*s had gone down in December 2022, during the year it was rather stable at around 512,000 (as of 31 December) – a mere 4,000 less than a year before. The number of CAR citizens taking *refuge* in neighbouring countries stood at nearly 670,000 by year's end (with Cameroon hosting the largest number, close to 350,000); the overall figure dropped by roughly 50,000 compared with the previous year. But in parallel, a sharp increase (by 82%) to 65,440 refugees and asylum seekers from neighbouring countries was observed, owing mainly to the outbreak of conflict in Sudan and Chad. These refugees were stranded in areas already unstable and prone to violent incursions by all sorts of armed actors, with little local capacity for the provision of help.

Chad

Ketil Fred Hansen

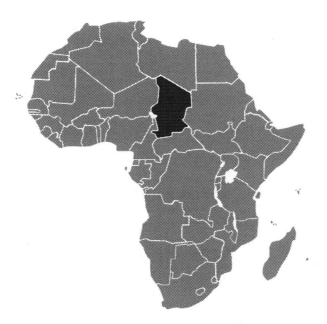

Very few political demonstrations took place in Chad compared with the average year. Fearing for their lives after experiencing the deadly 'Black Thursday' (20 October 2022), potential protesters preferred to remain calm. An accord negotiated and signed in Kinshasa (DRC) accorded amnesty to both perpetrators and victims of the Black Thursday massacres. As a result, Succès Masra, the leader of the opposition political party Les Transformateurs, was able to return home after more than a year exiled in the USA. In December, a new constitution was adopted by referendum. Cordial relations with numerous countries in the Middle East were further developed and new business deals, often including military equipment and natural resource extraction, were signed. The regime continued to nurture close relations with France, despite anti-French sentiment among most civil society groups.

Domestic Politics

Translating resolutions from last year's 'inclusive and sovereign national dialogue' into practice, and managing the aftermath of Black Thursday, absorbed much time and energy throughout the year.

On 23 February, the regime-appointed *Commission Nationale des Droits de l'Homme* (CNDH) published its report on the protest action and repression of 20 October 2022, concluding that responsibility was shared between the government and the organisers of the demonstrations for the violent results. Acknowledging that the regime's bloody repression of the protesters could not be justified, the CNDH made it clear, however, that the demonstrators 'were not peaceful', that they had 'vandalised public and private property', and that the 'physical integrity of certain citizens' was attacked. On the other hand, former presidential counsellor turned 'politico-militaire' and leader of the Parti Socialiste sans Frontières (PSF) Yaya Dillo, a cousin of President Mahamat Déby, called the regime's reactions on Black Thursday a planned genocide of certain populations from southern Chad. Until the report, the regime's official death toll had been 73 while other human rights NGOs had proclaimed some 300 killed. The CNDH, however, determined that 128 had been killed, 518 injured, and 943 arrested.

On 27 March, an act of *presidential grace* liberated 259 of the jailed and collectively and randomly sentenced demonstrators. On 13 May, however, the High Court, for this special case transferred from N'Djamena to the desert prison Koro Toro, sentenced 36 of the remaining demonstrators to five years behind bars and fines of CFAfr 200,000 (some €300) each, and CFAfr 10 m (€1,500) collectively in reparations. Another 74 were condemned with lesser penalties but pardoned by President Déby ten days later. By the end of May, 507 were still imprisoned for taking part in the Black Thursday demonstrations. Both international and national human rights NGOs accused the regime of torturing hundreds and killing dozens of the jailed demonstrators – accusations that the authorities denied.

The president pardoned other prisoners as well. On 21 March, 454 fighters from the Front pour l'Alternance et la Concorde au Tchad (FACT) were condemned, most of them to life imprisonment, for having taken part in the attempted coup and killing of Déby two years earlier; 380 of them were given reprieve by the president on 5 April. The amnesty did not include any of the 55 FACT fighters sentenced *in absentia*, including FACT's leader, Mahamat Mahdi Ali. In May, ten military officers and one NGO activist, Baradine Berdei Targuio, accused of an attempted coup in January, were amnestied and liberated.

The most remarkable presidential pardon was the one signed on 31 October, in Kinshasa. The head of the opposition party *Les Transformateurs*, *Succès Masra*, had on numerous occasions publicly proclaimed President Déby's full responsibility for the violent crackdown on demonstrators on 20 October 2022. Exiled in the US,

Masra had regular contact with American NGOs such as the National Endowment for Democracy and the National Democratic Institute and informed the US Senate Committee on Foreign Affairs on the importance of organising transparent presidential elections in Chad in line with the AU's Charter on Democracy, without allowing the head of the Conseil Militaire de Transition (CMT), the provisional junta government, Mahamat Déby, to participate.

On 8 June, the regime issued an international warrant of arrest for Masra, accusing him of undermining the constitutional order and challenging state institutions. On 5 October, when Masra informed the public about his intention to return to Chad, the arrest warrant was widely circulated in social media. Three days later, police arrested 72 supporters of Les Transformateurs as they prepared for their leader's return. The announced return was delayed while a presidential pardon and *amnesty* was negotiated by the transitional minister of national reconciliation, Abderaman Koulamallah, and facilitated by DRC president Félix Tshisekedi in Kinshasa. Signed on 31 October, the accord was never made public but included amnesty for all of those responsible for the Black Thursday violence, i.e. both those responsible for killing the 128 demonstrators and those among the protesters accused of looting, disturbance of public order, and other minor offences. Succès Masra arrived in N'Djamena on 3 November, calling on his supporters to adopt peaceful behaviour and attitudes.

Following up on the decision made during the inclusive national dialogue (October 2022) to establish a *new constitution*, the Déby-appointed drafting committee presented this constitution to the Conseil National de Transition (CNT) on 27 June. Some formally important changes included the re-establishment of a prime minister as the head of government, the High Court of Justice, the Supreme Court, and the Senate. The age of eligibility for becoming president was lowered from 40 to 35. However, candidates had to have been born in Chad to two Chadian parents. Presidential terms were limited to two terms of five years each, down from six.

Although the president still retains control over important nominations and decisions, Chad's fifth constitution is probably the most democratic ever. Of the Déby-appointed 197 representatives in the CNT, which replaced the elected members of the repealed National Assembly, 174 voted in favour of the constitution. The *referendum* on 17 December, planned since the beginning of the year, also gave some sort of popular legitimacy to the new constitution, though the populace could only vote yes or no to the question 'Do you approve the constitution submitted to you preserving the unitary state?' Though this was criticised as a biased question, explaining the content of the 232-paragraph-long new constitution would have been impossible in a country where still half of all men and two out of three women are not literate.

The organisation established to prepare for the referendum, the Commission nationale chargée de l'organisation du référendum constitutionnel (*Conarec*), was criticised for being partial. All representatives were appointed by President Déby. Furthermore, members and sympathisers of the Mouvement Patriotique du Salut (MPS) mobilised massively for a yes vote, campaigning all over the country. While members of the organising committee received high salaries and per diems, several hundred lower-stratum members of the MPS also received material benefits as helpers and service providers in the organisation of the referendum. In addition, huge sums were distributed to motivate people to vote – and specifically to vote yes. As this was widely known, many political opposition parties called for the referendum to be boycotted. Among the harshest opponents were Albert Pahimi Padacké, former prime minister and head of opposition party Rassemblement National des Democrates Tchadien (RNDT-Le Réveil), and Yaya Dillo. Succès Masra had also called for a boycott of the referendum until October. However, after his return to Chad on 3 November he first argued that people were free to vote as they wanted and then, when the referendum approached, argued for 'oui'.

Many within the political opposition characterised the referendum as having been manipulated and the outcome fabricated. Observers from the CEEAC and the Community of Sahel–Saharan States (CEN-SAD), on the other hand, declared the referendum inclusive, transparent, and credible. On 29 December, the Supreme Court officially declared the results: more than 4 m (85.9%) had voted yes while only 695,461 had voted no, with 285,384 ballots invalidated. The turnout was given as 63%, judged satisfactory by the regime in terms of confirming that the new constitution had popular legitimacy.

In a *restructuring reform of the national army* and the national intelligence agency, many people were dismissed while others were hired. Reportedly, some 4,000 intelligence agents without a clear job description were fired during the year. On 13 June, 40 generals were suddenly retired, while 43 new generals were nominated by decree a week later. Among them was Daoussa Idriss Déby, uncle of the president, an educated engineer without any formal military proficiency. By the end of the year, Chad had some 600 generals – about twice as many as the US.

Delayed by months due to lack of funding, the DDR process was formally launched on 16 October with an extraordinary $5 m fund made available by the UN to cover the costs. Some 20,000 men were to be (re)integrated into the army, others into the police, customs, or civil administration. Budgeted for at $32.5 m, the DDR process was still in vain by the end of the year.

Foreign Affairs

Leaked US intelligence revealed that in January–February the paramilitary group *Wagner* formed a military training site in the CAR near the Chadian border, with the aim of recruiting some 300 Chadian rebels and toppling President Déby. The information was denied both by *Russia* and Wagner. On 23 February, Chad voted in favour of the UNGA resolution that demanded Russia 'immediately, completely and unconditionally withdraw all of its military forces from the territory of Ukraine'. Despite this, the Russian ambassador in N'Djamena held numerous meetings with high-level administrative officers and business leaders in Chad, discussing possible aid and collaborations. In a move interpreted as a sign of dissent over Russia's war in Ukraine, Chad was represented by its minister of foreign affairs, not the head of state, in the second Russia–Africa summit, organised in St Petersburg on 27–28 July.

Chad, surrounded by countries with cordial relations with Wagner, reapproached Russia politically after the death of Yevgeny Prigozhin, the head of Wagner, in August. By the end of the year, President Mahamat Déby had started planning an official visit to Moscow (to take place early 2024).

The *German ambassador* to Chad was expelled on 8 April, after criticising President Déby for the very violent repression at Black Thursday demonstrations and for not confirming that he would not take part in the next presidential elections – delayed since October 2022 and yet to be scheduled. As a reaction, Germany likewise expelled Chad's ambassador from Berlin. Despite this obvious escalation, diplomatic relations were not discontinued between the two countries.

Other Western diplomats in N'Djamena had on various occasions noted that according to Article 25 in AU's Charter on Democracy, ratified by Chad, '[t]he perpetrators of unconstitutional change of government shall not be allowed to participate in elections held to restore the democratic order or hold any position of responsibility in political institutions of their State'. After the expulsion of the German ambassador, diplomatic critics were silent. However, the *EU* decided to freeze its military assistance as a result of the incident, only to resume it in November, officially in light of political opening and liberalisation within the CTM. The EU then delivered military aid worth €12 m to strengthen the national army operating on the frontier with the CAR. Humanitarian aid was not put on halt. In fact, the EU mobilised €25 m more than originally budgeted for in the context of the heavy influx of refugees from Sudan since 15 April, which reached some €57 m in total.

French president Emmanuel Macron and President Déby retained cordial relations, neither of them criticising the other's regime publicly. Déby was received twice in Paris by Macron, on 6 February and 18 October, to discuss bilateral relations, especially security, trade, and humanitarian aid. In between, the two presidents also met on other occasions, for example in June during the summit for a 'new global financial pact' in Paris and during the COP28 meeting in Dubai in December.

France retained around 1,000 troops in Chad. While most of them were stationed in the air base in N'Djamena, some 40 troops were located in Faya-Largeau in the northern Borkou-Ennedi-Tibesti (BET) prefecture and a small number in Abéché, 150 km from the Sudanese border.

On 5 September, a French military nurse shot and killed a Chadian soldier in the French infirmary in Faya-Largeau. Described as self-defence by the French authorities, the incident ignited a mass demonstration in the town. Later, in a press release dated 28 September, 21 civil society and political opposition leaders in N'Djamena urged the immediate departure of all French military forces based in Chad. On 1 December, the opposition further called for the 1,500 French troops ordered to leave *Niger*, some of whom had arrived in Chad from 19 October onwards, to leave the country immediately.

Immediately after war-like violence erupted on 15 April between the *Sudanese National Army* and the paramilitary *Rapid Support Forces* (RSF), formerly known as the Janjaweed, inhabitants of Darfur began to flee to Chad. Within the first 48 hours, some 20,000 Sudanese arrived. Despite the formal closure of the Chad–Sudan border on 19 April, some 40,000 new refugees arrived during the following three weeks. Towards the end of the year, OCHA had registered close to 530,000 new refugees from Sudan to Chad, adding to the 430,000 Sudanese refugees already living in one of the 13 refugee camps in the eastern part of the country. Close to 90% of the new refugees from Sudan were women and children. As the conflict in Sudan intensified, Chad was accused publicly by the Sudanese government of supplying military equipment to the RSF lead by Mohamed Dagalo, better known under his nickname Hemedti (29 November). Chad denied this and recalled its ambassador from Khartoum pending an official apology. Hemedti is an Arab Rizeigat and has family connections within the CMT in Chad.

Not convinced by the CNDH report on Black Thursday published in February, the *US* renewed the 'call for full investigations of these events and accountability for anyone responsible for human rights violations and abuses'. Like many others, the US considered the CNDH too closely linked with the regime to be objective. Washington did not officially comment on the Kinshasa accord signed with Masra, or on the constitutional referendum making it possible for members of the CMT to stand for president. Officially, the US policy towards Chad continued to prioritise building democratic institutions and secure peace.

President-in-office for the *G5 Sahel*, Mohamat Déby transferred powers to Niger's President Mohamed Bazoum during the annual G5 Sahel meeting, organised in N'Djamena on 20 February. Diplomatically and financially backed by the EU and the World Bank, the alliance, initiated mainly by the Chadian and French governments in 2014, had not managed to meet its objectives of fighting rebellions and creating peace in the Sahel. As Niger and Burkina Faso left the G5 Sahel on 3 December in a clearly anti-French show of power, remaining members Chad and Mauritania (Mali had already left in May 2022) were forced to issue a common statement on 6 December to dissolve the G5 Sahel.

Chad maintained multiple partnerships in the Middle East. In the presence of President Déby and Israeli prime minister Benjamin Netanyahu, Chad inaugurated its embassy in Tel Aviv, *Israel*, on 2 February. Full diplomatic relations had been re-established in 2022 after being interrupted since 1973. Military collaboration and security, including weapons and intelligence, were the main points discussed between Déby and Netanyahu. Nevertheless, since Israel's disproportionate retaliation against Palestine after 7 October, Chad, a country with a Muslim majority, has supported all of the UNGA resolutions on the Gaza crisis with the aim of bringing about a cessation of hostilities. On 4 November, Chad's *chargé d'affaires* in Israel was recalled 'for consultations'.

In March, President Déby met in Doha with Qatari minister of foreign affairs Sheikh Mohammed bin Abdulrahman bin Jassim Al Thani, who reassured him that Qatar would continue to support Chad financially in following up the Doha peace accord (signed with more than 40 rebel groups in August 2022), including the DDR process. Qatar opened a charity office in N'Djamena to facilitate various aid and humanitarian activities, contributing, among other things, to the Islamic World Educational, Scientific and Cultural Organisation's regional educational centre in N'Djamena, opened on 27 November.

In April, Déby undertook a pilgrimage to Mecca and met with Saudi representatives. In November, the *Saudi–Arab–African Economic Conference* was organised for the first time. The Saudi Private Investment Fund, a global fund of more than $700 bn chaired by Prince Mohammed bin Salman attracted numerous heads of states in Africa to the three-day event, which in Chad's case especially promoted mining, energy, and tourism.

The *United Arab Emirates* (UAE) considered Chad one of its most important strategic partners in Africa. President Déby made an official visit to Dubai in June during which important military cooperation agreements were signed, in addition to one on energy and another on mining. On that occasion, the UAE also accorded a loan worth $1.5 bn to support the transition to civilian rule in Chad. In August, six Nimr MCAV-20 Calidius armoured vehicles and various security equipment arrived in Chad from the UAE. This has to be seen in the light of regional developments: Western media claimed that the UAE had provided military support to the paramilitary Rapid Support Forces in Sudan through the international airport in Amdjarasse, home town of the Déby family in north-eastern Chad some 60 km from Sudan. Both the UAE and Chad maintained, however, that the UAE had delivered only food aid and medical equipment, including a mobile field hospital, to support Sudanese refugees in Chad. On 3 August, the UAE opened an aid coordination office in Amdjarasse to support humanitarian aid to the Sudanese refugees.

Regimes in south-eastern Europe continued to court the Chadian government. Relations between *Türkiye* and Chad remained friendly, and Chad continued to purchase military equipment from Türkiye. Most importantly, in July Chad's air force received two ANKA-S drones and three HÜRKUŞ-C attack close-up bomber aircraft.

Hungary repeatedly sent high-level official delegations to N'Djamena (on 5 July, 6 November, and 7 December). Major issues reportedly discussed were bilateral trade, migration, and security. At the request of President Déby in September, Hungary agreed to send 400 troops to Chad to help combat terror and contain migration. By the end of the year, the troops had not yet arrived.

Socioeconomic Developments

Close to half of the population lived in poverty, one-third in *extreme poverty*. Poverty slightly decreased while extreme poverty increased, indicating the increasing economic disparity within the country. Increased inequality was also indicated in the nutritional data. According to UNICEF, acute malnutrition among children under five had decreased by 5% since the previous year, affecting some 1.8 m children. However, severe malnutrition had increased by 15% from 2022 to 2023, affecting 480,000 children. Thus, close to 8% of children under five years suffer from severe malnutrition in Chad. Severe malnutrition was spread throughout the country, but north-eastern parts, the region bordering Sudan, and the area around Lake Chad were particularly hard hit.

With 865 deaths for every 100,000 live births, Chad had among the highest maternal mortality in the world. A very high 16.4% of all mothers were younger than 19 years old when giving birth for the first time. On the World Bank's Human Capital Index, Chad scored 0.30, the second lowest in the world. This indicates that a child born in Chad in 2023 will, on average, be 70% less productive when grown up compared with a child receiving adequate-quality education and health services.

As always, it was very difficult to confirm key economic figures as official statistics varied considerably from one office to another. For example, the inflation rate ranged from 3.7% to 13.2% according to different sources while economic growth varied from −0.2% to +3.5%. The oil sector represented some 85% of all exports and contributed more than half of the official tax revenues.

Transparency International's Corruption Perceptions Index ranked Chad as a highly corrupt country, although slightly less so than last year. It was placed on 162nd/180 on the index, with only three African countries perceived as more corrupt.

By the end of the year, 1.1 m people lived as refugees in Chad, up by some 500,000 from 2022. This near doubling was due to the conflict in Sudan from April onwards. In addition to the 900,000 refugees from Sudan, the number of refugees from the CAR, Cameroon, and Nigeria – some 180,000 – remained steady. Adding to this, due to violent conflicts and harsher climatic conditions, Chad had close to 400,000 IDPs. With the country very vulnerable and not prepared for climate change, the

'G5 Sahel Region Country Climate and Development Report' estimated that Chad's annual GDP would decline in the near future by 4–10%, due to climate change. On April 6, the World Bank granted Chad 150 m in aid to make N'Djamena more resilient to the impacts of climate change, especially floods.

Deliveries of oil and gas were short for a month from mid-April. According to the authorities, this was due to lack of maintenance of Exxon's extraction equipment. On 31 March, almost all members of the CNT voted in favour of nationalising Exxon's assets in Chad, recently sold, unlawfully according to the Chadian regime, to London-based Savannah Energy. Savannah Energy launched a court case against the expropriation and nationalisation, which was not yet concluded by the end of the year.

On 17 April, prices of diesel increased by more than 20% to CFAfr 700 per litre, while petrol remained the same (CFAfr 518/litre). By the end of the month, most motorcycles, cars, buses, and lorries, as well as generators and machinery, had stopped all over the country. One of several short *strikes* erupted, organised by the teachers' union on 8 May, to protest the lack of petrol and poor availability of electricity. Only some 12% of households have access to electricity – in principle. As power outages are extremely frequent, even this figure does not reflect reality.

Between mid-April and the end of May, numerous deadly encounters took place in various villages in the region of Logone Oriental, near the CAR border. In the department of Mont de Lam, 22 people lost their life on 18 April. Some organisations claimed that the clashes were between local peasants and unknown herders, while others, including the government, insisted that the upheaval was caused by Chadian rebels hiding in the CAR. To gain control, the CMT deployed additional troops from the national army along the Chad – CAR border.

An official statement declared 'a dozen' bandits killed in a joint military mission between the CAR and Chad on 16 May. As revenge, on 17–19 May, three villages were put on fire by armed men in the canton of Andoum. Churches and houses were plundered, hundreds of cows and multiple motorbikes stolen, and some 25–40 people killed and hundreds wounded.

Clashes due to conflict over gold mining between autochthonous and foreign fortune hunters also occurred in the area around Miski. Although a peace agreement, facilitated by the powerful director of the presidential cabinet Idriss Youssouf Boy, was signed on 8 January, conflict erupted again on numerous occasions. During the first week of June, 25–40 men were killed in the Tibesti region during fighting between two rebel groups – the Conseil de commandement militaire pour le salut de la République (CCMSR, a breakaway faction of FACT) and the Front de la Nation pour la Justice et la Démocratie au Tchad (fndjt) – and government soldiers.

Congo

Brett L. Carter

With the next presidential elections scheduled for 2026 and legislative elections for 2027, the year represented a relative pause in the electoral calendar, which opposition leaders used to organise. In April, three opposition parties formed a new coalition, which quickly demanded that the government of President Denis Sassou Nguesso release its political prisoners. Civil society organisations, meanwhile, sought to draw attention to the government's record of corruption and human rights abuses, with one consortium alleging the theft, between 2003 and 2014, of $25 bn of state funds and another documenting a nearly fourfold increase in human rights abuses relative to 2022. The ruling Parti Congolais du Travail (PCT) and its allies claimed 71 of the Senate's 72 seats in indirect elections, while the coup in neighbouring Gabon sparked rumours of an imminent coup against Sassou Nguesso and sustained calls for his resignation. The coup animated the government's foreign policy, as Sassou

Nguesso lead regional efforts to punish Gabon's new military regime, primarily to deter senior military officers in Congo from following suit. Although the government was poised to emerge as one of the world's leading exporters of LNG, living standards stagnated for most citizens, who confronted a chronically high unemployment rate, persistent inflation, and reductions in public services.

Domestic Politics

The year began with *fresh reports of massive corruption*. In January, France's 'Libération' newspaper published a series of articles that documented how Lucien Ebata, the chief executive officer of commodities trading firm Orion Oil, had emerged as one of Sassou Nguesso's chief money launderers, in part by using shell companies registered in Monaco and Switzerland. According to French investigators, 'Libération' reported, Orion Oil routinely overcharged Congo's state oil company the Société nationale des pétroles du Congo (SNPC) for refined products, with margins reaching 61%. After these transactions, Orion Oil's accounts were subjected to large cash withdrawals. 'Libération' also reported that Lucien Ebata, apparently on Sassou Nguesso's behalf, had made financial transfers to Liberian president George Weah, former IMF president Dominique Strauss-Kahn, former European Commission president José Manuel Barroso, Nobel Laureate and 'New York Times' columnist Paul Krugman, Belgian magistrate Jean-Paul Moerman, former Italian prime minister Mario Monti, and former French prime minister Manuel Valls. The payment to Valls allegedly occurred in 2016, when Valls was contemplating a run for the French presidency. In response, Sassou Nguesso's spokesperson, Thierry Moungalla, accused 'Libération' of defamation.

Fresh reports of widespread *human rights abuses* quickly followed. On 22 February, Congo's leading human rights organisation, the Centre d'Action pour le Développement (CAD), released its human rights report for 2022. Led by Tresor Nzila, who in 2021 was forced out of the Observatoire Congolais des Droits de l'Homme (OCDH) by the Sassou Nguesso government, CAD documented 572 human rights violations during the preceding year, including arbitrary detentions, torture, extrajudicial executions, and forced disappearances. The government appeared to ignore CAD's calls for it 'to clean up the security apparatus'. Weeks later, on 26 March, the government blocked an opposition rally to commemorate the deaths of former president Marien Ngouabi and Cardinal Emile Biayenda, in which Sassou Nguesso is widely believed to have been implicated.

Elections to the Senate were held on 20 August. As in years past, the elections were indirect, with the six regional senators elected by Congo's regional councils. Of the Senate's 72 seats, the ruling PCT won 52, allied parties and pro-Sassou Nguesso independents another 19, and the opposition just one. This result was lopsided even by Sassou Nguesso's standards. Pierre Ngolo was re-elected to the Senate presidency on 13 September, his second term atop the upper chamber. A longtime Sassou Nguesso ally, Ngolo had served as secretary-general of the PCT since 2011. In his valedictory address, Ngolo called for the 'progressive improvement of the electoral system', which, given the regime's long record of electoral fraud, many observers noted was deeply ironic. One of Sassou Nguesso's daughters, Andréa Carole, was elected the Senate's first quaestor, charged with managing Senate finances.

On 30 August, a group of senior military officers, led by General Brice Oligui, deposed Gabonese president Ali Bongo, ending nearly 50 years of Bongo family rule. The *coup in neighbouring Gabon* sent shockwaves through Brazzaville. Days later, news of an ongoing coup against Sassou Nguesso spread widely on Twitter, forcing Thierry Moungalla to forcefully deny them. On 16 September, opposition leaders called for a two-year 'democratic transition' to avoid the 'extreme solutions' that had occurred in Gabon. Sassou Nguesso, opposition leaders argued, should be forbidden from participating in the 2026 elections. On 3 October, four NGOs called for a 'political transition' before the 2026 presidential elections, again, they said, to avoid a military coup. As evidence of dissent within the military, the NGOs cited the 2018 conviction of General Norbert Dabira for plotting to assassinate Sassou Nguesso.

With presidential elections scheduled for 2026 and legislative elections for 2027, the opposition used the pause in the electoral calendar to organise. On 13 April, three parties, including the Rassemblement pout la Démocratie et le Développement (RDD), founded by former president Jaques-Joachim Yhombi-Opango, formed a *new umbrella coalition*, the Alliance poul l'Alternance Démocratique en in 2026 (2AD2026). Destin Gavet, its first president, called on the government to release General Jean-Marie Michel Mokoko and André Okombi Salissa, whom he dared to call 'political prisoners' despite the sensitivity of this term in Congolese public discourse. Sassou Nguesso's chief rivals in the 2016 presidential election, Mokoko and Okombi Salissa remained in prison, currently serving 20-year jail sentences for 'undermining state security'. On 10 July, the Union des Démocrates Humanistes-Yuki (UDH-Yuki) opened its extraordinary congress. Without a president since the death of Guy Brice Parfait Kolélas on 22 March 2021, its efforts to elect a new president faltered when delegates were unable to agree on a successor. On 27 November, UDH-Yuki announced that it would reconvene on 22 December, but the meeting was postponed until January, reportedly due to difficulty raising the funds required to stage the congress. On 25 November, Jean-Félix Demba Ntelo was elected president of the Fédération de l'Opposition Congolaise (FOC), the umbrella group formed in the run-up to the 2015 constitutional referendum. Demba Ntelo replaced Clement Mierassa, head of the Parti Social-démocrate Congolais (PSDC) since 1990. As director of the Composante Jean-Marie Michel Mokoko collective, Demba Ntelo had been an outspoken critic of Sassou Nguesso's human rights record, leading, in particular, the efforts to secure General Mokoko's release from prison. One of Congo's three opposition platforms (the other being the Union Panafricaine pour la Démocratie Sociale (UPADS), party of Pascal Lissouba, the only democratically elected president in Congo's history), the FOC currently has no seats in the National Assembly or Senate.

As the opposition sought to organise, several *human rights NGOs* expanded their activities. On 31 July, several NGOs, including OCDH, filed a civil lawsuit in Brazzaville courts against 'X', alleging the theft, between 2003 and 2014, of $25 bn of state funds. Observers widely interpreted the X as a reference to the Sassou Nguesso family. The state prosecutor apparently refused to initiate an investigation. On 11 August, 15 NGOs called on the government to help defray the rising costs of food and gas amid rapid inflation. On 21 August, the OCDH released a report alleging that Chinese and West African mining firms in the Sangha region were paying no taxes and disregarding environmental regulations, apparently with the acquiescence of key government officials. On 21 October, the Association pour le Respect du Droit des Populations Autochtones, du Développement Durable et du Droit de l'Homme (ARPA2DH) accused Chinese firms of using mercury and other illicit products in gold mining operations in Kouilou. On 8 December, CAD released its 2023 annual human rights report, which documented nearly 2,100 human rights violations, up from 572 in 2022. Again, the violations included extrajudicial executions, forced expulsions, and a range of attacks on individual and collective liberties. Independent media declined as well, as several independent newspapers shuttered due to financial difficulties. Meanwhile, the government rebuffed calls to provide the same subsidies to independent media outlets that it does to state-owned outlets.

The year ended on two sombre notes. *Henri Lopes* died on 2 November. A giant of African literature, Lopes had served as Sassou Nguesso's ambassador to Paris since 1997, just after he emerged victorious from the civil war and reclaimed the presidency. Lopes's support for Sassou Nguesso appeared never to waiver, yet his novels – especially 'The Laughing Cry', published in 1982 – routinely criticised corruption and human rights abuses by African presidents. After his death, his widow, from Haiti, acknowledged that discussion of his public support for Sassou Nguesso was off limits even in his personal life. Less than three weeks later, on 20 November, at least 32 young people died in a *stampede at Brazzaville's Michel d'Ornano Stadium*, where the government was staging an open recruitment drive for the army. At least 145 were injured. The stampede occurred at night, when applicants forced open a gate to enter the recruitment area. The week before, the army had announced its intention to hire some 1,500 new young people. The stampede was widely viewed as an indicator of chronic, widespread unemployment among young people. The government declared a national day of mourning and promised to indemnify families with payments of just over €7,000, in part to avoid a public funeral. Although CAD called for the resignations of the ministers of interior and defence, by the end of the year it was unclear whether anyone had been formally sanctioned for the stampede.

Foreign Affairs

The *coup in Gabon* oriented Sassou Nguesso's foreign policy. CEMAC is dominated by several of the world's longest-tenured dictators, including Sassou Nguesso, Equatorial Guinea's Teodoro Obiang, and Cameroon's Paul Biya. To discourage their senior military officers from following suit, they had to punish Oligui. Immediately after the coup, they suspended Gabon from CEMAC and imposed financial sanctions. The AU, chaired by Chad's longtime foreign minister under the late Idriss Déby Itno, also suspended Gabon. In response, Oligui mounted a diplomatic charm offensive. After visiting Obiang in Malabo on 19 September, he travelled to Oyo, Sassou Nguesso's native village, on 1 October. The sanctions remained in place at year's end, however. The disinformation campaign that suggested Sassou Nguesso was facing a similar coup had *Russia*'s fingerprints, which was striking given the series of military cooperation agreements that Brazzaville and Moscow had recently signed. Observers wondered whether it was an attempt by Russia's Wagner Group to generate new business in Congo.

Sassou Nguesso's *relationship with Paris* continued to deteriorate. On 26 June, while attending the Summit for a New Global Financing Pact in Paris, Sassou Nguesso addressed the ongoing 'biens mal acquis' investigation in French courts, which had confiscated several Sassou Nguesso family properties and increasingly appeared to be targeting the president's son, Denis Christel. In an interview on France 24, after denying that Congolese prisons held any political prisoners, Sassou Nguesso declared that 'everything is permitted in France when it comes to smearing African authorities'. Relations with Paris deteriorated further on 3 October, when his personal jet, a Falcon 7X built in 2014, was auctioned in Bordeaux. Seized by French authorities in June 2020 as part of the Commisimpex affair, it fetched just €7.1 m, far less than the estimated market price of €25 m. After the sale, Thierry Moungalla attacked the French authorities, suggesting that the jet should have been protected by diplomatic immunity. Even after the sale, the Sassou Nguesso government still owed Commisimpex, owned by Mohsen Hojeij, a Lebanese businessman, nearly €2 bn. These financial improprieties provided the backdrop for a September exhibition at Paris's Quai Branly Museum that debuted new portraits of African presidents by Kehinde Wiley, the New York-based portrait artist who famously depicted former US president Barack Obama for the Smithsonian's National Portrait Gallery. The exhibition was widely criticised, including by 'Le Monde' newspaper, for depicting dictators such as Sassou Nguesso and Rwanda's Paul Kagame alongside such democratically elected presidents as Ghana's Nana Akufo-Addo and Nigeria's Olusegun Obasanjo.

As in years past, Sassou Nguesso fashioned himself Central Africa's *elder statesman*, in part by hosting several high-level delegations from Africa and Europe and mediating several regional conflicts. After hosting a UN meeting on rebel activity in eastern DRC on 16 January, over the subsequent five weeks Sassou Nguesso held bilateral discussions in Brazzaville with Rwandan foreign affairs minister Vincent Biruta, DRC president Félix Tshisekedi, and Burundian president Évariste Ndayishimiye. In late February, he turned to the crisis in Libya and the Sahel broadly, welcoming Nigérien president Mohamed Bazoum, who was deposed in a palace coup on 26 July. French president Emmanuel Macron spent five hours in Brazzaville on 3 March, between visits to Gabon, DRC, and Angola, marking the first visit by a sitting French president since Nicolas Sarkozy in 2009. With Paris reconsidering its military footprint in Africa, the two discussed the crises in Libya and eastern DRC, and Macron reportedly pressed Sassou Nguesso to adopt a more pro-Ukraine stance on the war in Europe. On 16 May, South African president Cyril Ramaphosa announced that several African presidents, including Sassou Nguesso, would attempt to negotiate an end to the Russian–Ukraine war in June; longtime Sassou Nguesso confidant and weapons supplier Jean-Yves Ollivier was reportedly coordinating the effort. On 7 July, Sassou Nguesso hosted newly elected Kenyan president William Ruto for a state visit, during which the latter addressed the Congolese parliament.

Sassou Nguesso also sought to buttress his international reputation by casting himself as an *environmental steward*. On 26 October, he opened the Summit of the Three Tropical Forest Basins, encompassing the Congo, Amazon, and Borneo Mekong river basins. The three-day event hosted some 3,000 participants, including the presidents of DRC, Kenya, Rwanda, Togo, Guinea-Bissau, Comoros, and Gabon, but, notably, none from South America or Asia. It was unclear what the summit achieved. On 9 December, during the COP28 summit in Dubai, the Congolese government signed a partnership agreement with France and the EU that was to provide $50 m – and potentially more in the future – for forest conservation. These efforts were overseen by the minister of forests, Henri Djombo, who has held this position since Sassou Nguesso's 1997 return and is widely regarded as among the government's most corrupt figures.

Socioeconomic Developments

The economy grew by roughly 4.4%, the first time the real *GDP growth* rate had exceeded 2% since 2014. This increase was almost entirely driven by an increase in oil production after three years of contractions. This production increase appeared poised to continue. On 28 December, Italian oil major Eni announced the introduction of gas into its Tango Floating Liquefied Natural Gas (FLNG) facility, off the coast of Pointe-Noire. Tango was scheduled to produce Congo's first LNG cargo, from the Marine XII concession, in early 2024. Construction continued on a second FLNG facility, which was scheduled to come online in 2025. When it does, Congo could emerge as one of the world's *top five LNG exporters* and a key supplier to Europe, which is seeking to diversify its sources away from Russia. Eni held a 65% interest in Marine XII as part of a production-sharing agreement that runs until 2039. Russia's Lukoil held a 25% interest and the SNPC held 10%.

Despite the increase in oil production, living standards remained low for the vast majority of citizens. The total *unemployment* rate was 20%, though for young people – who comprise more than half of the population – it reached 42%. Meanwhile, the cost of living increased. The consumer inflation rate reached 3.2%, the highest since 2016. With an official debt-to-GDP ratio exceeding 90%, the government relied on its ECF agreement with the IMF, approved on 21 January 2021, to manage its fiscal position. As part of the agreement, the IMF required the Sassou Nguesso government to restrict spending, in part by cutting fuel subsidies. The first reduction, which went into effect on 31 January, lead to a 5% increase in the price of fuel. The second, on 15 July, generated a 25% increase. Notwithstanding these price increases, citizens experienced widespread fuel shortages in February and again in September, causing a further increase in the black market price. The shortages were caused, in part, by the SNPC's monopoly on fuel imports and its inability, given its chronic indebtedness, to purchase sufficient supplies on the global market to satisfy domestic demand. Citizens also reported *widespread power outages* in November and December, as Congo's primary power plant, responsible for some 70% of the country's electricity, underwent maintenance.

Despite its financial position, the government witnessed the launch or completion of several *high-profile construction projects*. On 3 May, Sassou Nguesso launched the construction of a new headquarters for the SNPC in Pointe-Noire, part of its 25th anniversary celebration. The new 16-storey headquarters will be finished in 2025. On 20 May, Sassou Nguesso launched the construction of a road connecting the northern regions of Sangha and Likouala, which will ultimately link northern Congo with the CAR and Chad. The project is financed by the BDEAC (Banque de développement des États de l'Afrique centrale; Development Bank of the Central African States), will cost nearly $2 bn, is being constructed by a Chinese firm, and will take roughly three years. The road was the last of 11 projects approved in 2020 to further integrate the sub-region. On 22 June, the government signed a 30-year concession agreement that will let Abu Dhabi's AD Ports develop and operate the New East Mole Port in Pointe-Noire. AD Ports planned to invest more than $500 m during the life of the concession, including roughly $220 m during the initial 30-month construction period. On 23 October, Sassou Nguesso inaugurated a two-tower complex in Brazzaville, the city's highest, which cost nearly €300 m and was financed by the Chinese government. One tower will host a five-star hotel, the other an office building. The project was widely criticised given the lack of affordable housing in Brazzaville. The offices were located in the neighbourhood of Mpila, near Sassou Nguesso's private residence but relatively far from Brazzaville's central commercial district.

Democratic Republic of the Congo

Koen Vlassenroot, Hans Hoebeke, and Josaphat Musamba

Two dynamics dominated the political and social context in the Democratic Republic of the Congo. One was the electoral process, which was concluded with presidential, parliamentary, provincial, and local elections held on 20 December. As expected, incumbent Félix Tshisekedi won the presidential elections and succeeded in gaining a large majority in the national parliament. The overall participation rate was the lowest since the first post-war elections and multiple irregularities affected the credibility of the electoral process. The second dynamic was the further intensification of the conflict with the Rwandan-backed M23 in North Kivu Province. Tensions between the DRC and Rwanda built up further, creating growing fear of a direct military confrontation. Regional efforts to reduce tension had limited success. Growing distrust between the DRC and Kenya led to an end of the EAC military intervention in North Kivu. This was replaced by a SADC-led military initiative. Both the Nairobi peace process focusing on internal dynamics within the DRC and the Luanda peace process targeting regional actors involved in the current conflict had little impact. In other parts of eastern DRC, security conditions also worsened due to intensified military activity of Congolese and foreign non-state armed actors. At the end of 2023, a record 6.9 m IDPs were recorded in the DRC.

Domestic Politics

Public debate centred mainly around the *presidential, parliamentary, provincial, and local elections*, which were held on 20 December. Voter registration for these elections started in December 2022 and was originally scheduled to end on 17 March. From the start, opposition leaders, including Martin Fayulu and Moïse Katumbi, raised concerns about the registration process favouring the presidential majority, denouncing an imbalance in registration sites to the benefit of the Kasaï provinces, which are considered strongholds of the Union pour la Démocratie et le Progrès Social (UDPS), Logistical constraints, technical challenges, and security conditions also caused delays in the registration of voters in Rutshuru and Masisi (North Kivu) and in the Kwamouth territory of Mai-Ndombe Province, where intercommunal violence persisted. On 13 March, the Commission électorale nationale et indépendante (CENI) declared that 70% of expected voters were already registered and on 25 April, the registration process was officially closed. According to the CENI, 95% of an expected 50 m potential voters were registered at that point, almost half of whom were women. In the Kivu provinces and Ituri, armed groups contributed to this registration in areas under their control. The external audit of the voter register, which was conducted by a team of international and national experts, was validated by the CENI on 22 May. The validation was criticised by observers and the political opposition for its apparent lack of transparency and credibility. Similarly, the vote on the draft law on the distribution of seats for the national and provincial legislatures and municipal and local elections met with a boycott by the political opposition. It also triggered allegations from within the presidential majority of discrepancies between the number of voters and the number of allocated seats. This did not stop the National Assembly and the Senate from voting in favour of the law on 5 and 15 June, respectively. The next step was the publication of the provisional lists of candidates and political groupings on 11 August. Over 25,000 candidates were eventually validated for the national legislative elections, more than 44,000 candidates for the provincial legislative elections, and 31,000 candidates for the communal elections. Most of these candidates were men. At 43%, female candidates represented a considerable share only in the case of the municipal elections. Former president Joseph Kabila and former presidential candidate Martin Fayulu wanted a revision of the existing legal and institutional framework for the electoral process before confirming their participation. On 30 October, the Constitutional Court validated 26 candidates for the presidential election, adding two more to the 24 who had been declared admissible by the CENI on 8 October. Technical and capacity issues continued to impact the preparations of the elections and triggered fierce reactions by the political opposition and civil society actors, who denounced the lack of transparency and inclusiveness in the electoral process. The electoral campaign was officially launched on 19 November.

The elections prompted a repositioning of political parties and a *reshuffling of alliances*. One of the main opposition forces, the Front Commun pour le Congo (FCC), also known as the Kabila Coalition, announced soon after its formation that it would boycott the electoral process because of the lack of a consensual legal and institutional framework to guide the process and prevailing insufficient security conditions in some parts of the country. Several of its members left this alliance to start their own political parties and join the Tshisekedi alliance. In contrast, Moïse Katumbi, who leads the party Ensemble pour la République, had already announced his candidacy for the presidential elections in December 2022. He was followed by opposition leaders Martin Fayulu (whose coalition Lamuku did not participate in the parliamentary, provincial, or local elections), Augustin Matata Ponyo, and Delly Sesanga. In May, these opposition leaders organised demonstrations in Kinshasa against the electoral process, describing it as 'chaotic', and to denounce increasing insecurity and the high costs of living for ordinary Congolese citizens. The demonstrations met with a fierce reaction by the Congolese National Police. Other *acts of intimidation* against the political opposition were reported during the electoral process. In July, Ensemble pour la République spokesperson and member of the National Assembly Chérubin Okende was found dead in Kinshasa, leading to allegations of a politically motivated crime and triggering fear among political actors about their own security. Also in the former province of Katanga, tensions mounted between the youth wings of different political factions, stirring up ethnic antagonism between Kasaïens and Katangese communities. To avoid further division among the opposition and to have a stronger common voice, presidential candidates Matata Ponyo, Seth Kikundi, and Frank Diongo announced in November, at the start of the electoral campaign, their withdrawal from the elections and their support for Moïse Katumbi.

The Tshisekedi regime developed several strategies to reinforce its hold on the electoral process and secure a political victory. One way of doing this was to *bring political heavyweights on board in the government*. On 23 March, a new 59-member government was announced. The government was again led by Prime Minister Jean-Michel Sama Lukonda, who had announced his first cabinet on 12 April 2021. Two new members of government were former leaders of rebel movements in the 1998–2003 war. Jean-Pierre Bemba, leader of the Mouvement pour la Libération du Congo (MLC), became deputy prime minister and minister of defence, while Antipas Mbusa Nyamwisi, the leader of the Rassemblement Congolais pour la Démocratie – Mouvement de Libération (RCD-KML), became minister of state and minister for regional integration. Both had a solid base in regional geopolitics, as both were allies of Uganda during the Congo war. Mbusa in particular remained controversial due to persistent rumours about the role of his network, i.e. former RCD-KML commanders, in the prevailing insecurity in the Grand Nord, the area of operations of the Allied Democratic Forces (ADF). Their appointment also was meant to secure their support for Tshisekedi's electoral campaign, as both were considered key political leaders in their home regions. Significantly, the former chief of staff of President Tshisekedi, leader of the Union pour la nation congolaise (UNC), and one of the main political protagonists of South Kivu Province, Vital Kamerhe, was appointed vice-prime minister for economy. Kamerhe had been sentenced to 20 years in prison for embezzlement in 2020 before being acquitted on appeal in 2022. Another pre-electoral strategy was the creation of the so-called Union sacrée de la nation, a majority coalition of several hundred political parties and movements that served as an electoral platform in support of the re-election of President Tshisekedi. The same platform had to secure a parliamentary majority following the elections. Influential members of this union included, besides Kamerhe and Jean-Pierre Bemba, Senate president Modeste Bahati Lukwebo (of the Alliance des forces démocratiques du Congo; AFDC) and Christophe Mboso (of the Alliance des Bâtisseurs pour un Congo Emergent; ABCE), as well as Augustin Kabuya of Tshisekedi's UDPS. In September, François Muamba was appointed head of Tshisekedi's electoral campaign team . Muamba led the Conseil présidentiel de veille stratégique, a specialised service of the Presidency set up in March 2020. He had served as a minister during the Mobutu and Joseph Kabila regimes and was the MLC secretary-general between 2005 and 2011.

As with previous elections, the December vote suffered from several challenges and irregularities. First, with a 43% participation rate – or just 18 m people voting – the turnout remained very low. Second, irregularities tainted the elections, partly as a result of the CENI's obstinacy in maintaining the election date, despite the logistical difficulties encountered in deploying electoral material to all polling stations. This positioning of the CENI could be explained by pressure from both the government and the opposition to organise the elections as scheduled and not try to postpone them. In some cases, the poll was eventually extended for up to six days – in clear violation of the electoral law. Despite this extension, over 11,000 out of 75,500 polling stations failed to operate, mainly because of a lack of electoral kits, voter lists, ballot papers, etc. According to the 60,000-strong observer mission organised by the Conférence épiscopale nationale du Congo (CENCO) and the Eglise du Christ au Congo (ECC), 27% of polling stations did not open at all. Widespread and flagrant irregularities were observed, e.g. CENCO observers documented over 5,000 incidents, affecting the integrity of the results. In 60% of cases, such incidents interrupted the voting, Other observers mentioned voting machines being found in the hands of and manipulated by specific candidates. And in still other cases, voters were reported to have been either bribed or intimidated outside polling stations. These irregularities led CENCO to conclude that the polls constituted organised disorder on a grand scale. In parts of eastern DRC, security forces or armed groups were actively involved in the organisation of the elections, supported specific candidates, and committed acts of intimidation or issued threats of violence against voters.

On 31 December, the CENI published its collected results. As expected, the presidential elections gave Tshisekedi 73.3% of the valid votes cast. His main opponent, Moïse Katumbi, secured only 18% of the vote, and Martin Fayulu 5%. Tshisekedi also gained a large majority in parliament. In total, 500 members of parliament had to be elected. More than 40 political parties gained seats. The Union sacrée secured over 390 seats, with the UDPS winning 69, Kamerhe's UNC and Lukbwebo's AFDC 35 each, and Bemba's MLC 17. The main opposition force, Katumbi's Ensemble pour la République, won 18 seats. While the opposition took a fierce stance against these results, describing the elections as fraudulent and calling for a rerun, domestic and international observation missions acknowledged the many irregularities yet largely accepted the outcomes. In the territories of Masisi and Rutshuru (North Kivu), which are partially controlled by the M23 rebel group, no elections were held. As a consequence, Congolese Hutu and Tutsi communities saw their political representation in the national and provincial assemblies significantly reduced. As a compromise, it was concluded that both territories would remain represented by candidates elected during the 2018 election.

In several parts of the country, *security further deteriorated*. The main hotspot of insecurity continued to be North Kivu, yet high levels of insecurity also remained persistent in a number of specific areas in Ituri and South Kivu. In *North Kivu*, despite the building up of the Congolese army's capacity through the rallying of non-state armed groups and inviting of regional military forces, M23 was able to advance considerably. Increased evidence of extensive Rwandan military support for the rebel group gave nationalistic and populist rhetoric new impetus as a mobilising force. On 4 May, the Senate passed a law allowing the establishment of a military reserve force. According to the law, civilian volunteers could be included in a reserve force in case of a need to defend the country's territorial integrity following an external threat or aggression. While the law did not directly apply to existing armed groups, it did not fail to achieve the intended catalyst effect. Such a call to defend Congo's territorial integrity fed into armed groups' raison d'être. Following the announcement of the reserve force, many of these armed actors transformed themselves into *'wazalendo'* ('patriotic' in Swahili) reservists, thus granting themselves formal status. In order to gain some form of official credibility, they formed themselves into the Volontaires pour la Défense de la Patrie (VDP), a loose coalition of multiple wazalendo groups. The strategy of the Congolese army units to mobilise these wazalendo groups in the fight against M23 further contributed to the ambivalent relationship between armed groups and the regime: while still considered non-state armed actors, they became integrated into formal security policies and strategies. This approach strengthened the position of armed groups in their zones of operation but further complicated the restoration of state authority in such areas. At the same time, the proliferation of wazalendo groups raised further security concerns and contributed to high levels of violence, including arbitrary arrests, targeted killings, the strengthening of parallel forms of justice and taxation, and intercommunity tensions. Not all armed groups joined this new coalition of wazalendo groups, leading to regular clashes and divisions between and within different often ill-disciplined armed groups.

Other groups in Congolese society also started to use the term 'wazalendo' to mobilise against the presence of international and regional forces. One such group was the Agano la Uwezo – Wazalendo, a politico-religious movement operating in Goma. In the early hours of 30 August, members of the Republican Guard entered the premises of a radio station in Goma belonging to this group, after it had called on its members to demonstrate later that day against the presence of the UN stabilisation mission MONUSCO, the EAC Regional Force (EACRF), international NGOs, and Westerners in general in the region. During the first moments of the intervention of the security services, several people were killed, including a police officer who was lynched by church members in an act of revenge. Following the first attack, the military operation spread to the sect's church, where many of its members had gathered in preparation for the demonstration. What followed was an extremely brutal and deadly raid by the Republican Guard, leaving at least 56 people dead and many more injured. For Goma's population, the attack was bitter proof of the official security services' lack of commitment to protecting them, despite the state of siege which had been put in place since May 2021. During a roundtable hosted by President Tshisekedi in August to discuss the impact of the state of siege in the provinces of Ituri and North Kivu it was concluded that it would gradually be eased.

At the start of 2023, *M23* continued to advance and expand its territory following new offensives, leading to the control of urban centres such as Nyamilima in the Rutshuru territory and Rwindi in Virunga National Park. At the end of January, M23 occupied the village of Mushaki and briefly took over control of the mining centre of Rubaya, before withdrawing. Tensions further escalated between DRC and Rwanda, leading to several cross-border incidents and growing fear of a direct military confrontation between the two countries and further regional escalation. On 24 January, a Congolese fighter plane was targeted by fire from the Rwandan Defence Forces (RDF) before landing in Goma. As the Sukhoi (SU-25) left the airspace of the Masisi territory bound for the town of Goma, according to the Rwandan government it left Congolese airspace and entered into Rwandan airspace. A few days later, Congolese and Rwandan naval forces clashed on Lake Kivu. The next month, the Congolese army was accused by Rwanda of having fired at a Rwandan border post near Bukavu, and in early March, the Rwandan army reported that a Congolese soldier had crossed into Rwanda and opened fire on Rwandan soldiers, killing one of them. In the midst of armed clashes between loyalist Congolese forces and Rwandan-backed M23 rebels, stabilisation initiatives were put in place at the regional level. Kinshasa demanded the withdrawal of M23, leading to a partial and temporary retreat in January. This was also in line with the conclusions of the Luanda declaration of 23 November 2022, which stipulated the full withdrawal of M23. The vacation of occupied territory was monitored by the EACRF, which was supposed to take over military control. Over the following months, M23 again expanded its area of control, amid regular clashes with the Congolese army and despite its stated commitment to a negotiated ceasefire. In March, it briefly took control of part of the city of Sake, located 25 kilometres from Goma and the only part of the axis of Goma that remained under Kinshasa's control, before being repulsed by the Congolese army. The next months saw a friable cessation of hostilities between M23 and the Congolese army yet also an intensification of violent clashes between M23 and wazalendo groups and the Forces démocratiques de libération du Rwanda (FDLR). Regular attacks against civilians and arbitrary arrests by M23 units were also reported in their zones of operation. From October, military confrontations between M23 and the Congolese army again intensified.

Ituri also saw a dramatic increase of violence against civilians, reaching the highest levels since 2017. The alliance of the Coopérative pour le développement du Congo/Union des révolutionnaires pour la défense du peuple Congolais (CODECO/URDPC) was clearly the dominant armed actor and was involved in fatal attacks against civilians and camps for internally displaced Hema people in Mongbwalu, Djugu, and Tchomia, as well as attacks on military targets and acts of ammunition seizure. Retaliatory attacks by Zaire, an armed group claiming to defend the Hema, also caused considerable numbers of casualties. Much of the fighting was centred around gold mining sites yet was also connected to long-standing conflict between Hema and Lendu communities over land and power. Other ethnic communities also became increasingly militarised, with armed groups defending the interests of their respective communities. Two major coalitions were noteworthy: the G5, comprising armed groups representing CODECO/URDPC-targeted communities; and the G3, including CODECO/URPDC, the Front patriotique et intégrationniste du Congo (FPIC), and the Force de résistance patriotique de l'Ituri (FRPI). In January, the G5 approached the Nairobi peace process facilitator and former Kenyan president Uhuru Kenyatta to ask for the exclusion of CODECO/UFDRC from the process. On 2 June, an agreement was signed between the leaders of CODECO, Mouvement d'autodéfense populaire de l'Ituri (MAPI), the FRPI, and the FPIC to cease hostilities, but violence resumed soon after the signing. CODECO/URPDC also expanded its operations to Mahagi and Aru, causing additional civilian casualties and displacement. In Irumu, rival factions of the FPIC clashed as part of an internal power struggle and a fight over the control of mining sites. Land-related disputes between Nande and Lese communities also further escalated with the involvement of armed groups, despite the signing of an agreement between community leaders.

The geographic expansion of ADF activities into Mambasa and Irumu further complicated the security context in Ituri and intensified existing tensions between local communities. The continued Shujaa joint military operation of the official Congolese and Ugandan armies, i.e. the Forces armées de la République Démocratique du Congo (FARDC) and the Uganda People's Defence Force (UPDF), in the territories of Beni (North Kivu) and Mambasa (Ituri) had the effect of destabilising and dispersing the ADF into smaller units, leading to a slight reduction in the number of violent events. It also forced the group to constantly change its headquarters and positions and adapt its operational mode. Its search for new operational bases was considered the main motive for the further expanding of its area of operations into Ituri. As part of a strategy to counter the military pressure of the Shujaa operation, it targeted and killed hundreds of civilians and committed several cross-border attacks into Uganda. Improvised and homemade explosive devices were used to kill civilians in the urban centres of Beni and Kasindi. The ADF strengthened its regional ties with Da'esh and was by some observers considered to have become a local branch of this network. Some armed actors operating in Ituri were also believed to have built collaboration with the group. In April, the Congolese and Ugandan army chiefs of staff met in Beni to evaluate the Shujaa operation and prepare its next phase. It was acknowledged that the successful dismantling of ADF bases and the neutralisation of several commanders had triggered retaliatory violence against civilians. The spread of ADF attacks in Ituri also inspired a popular protest in Bunia in April.

On 19 December, the UNSC voted to extend its mission *MONUSCO* for one more year, until 20 December 2024. A comprehensive three-phase disengagement plan agreed between MONUSCO and the government in November was meant to facilitate a gradual, responsible, and sustainable handover of responsibility. This withdrawal would come a year earlier than originally scheduled and followed a request from the government for its acceleration. By June 2024, the mission was to be closed down completely in South Kivu and its activities limited to Ituri and North Kivu. The mission had been deployed since 1999 but had seen a shift over time in its mandate, moving the protection of civilians to supporting the stabilisation and strengthening of state institutions and key governance and security reforms, the facilitation of humanitarian access, and the demobilisation and civil reintegration of former combatants. In March 2013, a specialised intervention brigade was created as part of the mission intended to strengthen peacekeeping operations by directly targeting non-state armed groups. Over the last years, the mission had become increasingly unpopular among Congolese citizens and demonstrations had been held regularly in Goma, Beni, Bukavu, and Kinshasa against its presence and lack of impact on the security context, despite its 13,000-plus military personnel and 2,000 police. The UNSC decision also followed a general trend among UN peacekeeping missions elsewhere in Africa, such as UNITAMS (the Integrated Transition Assistance Mission in Sudan) and MINUSMA (the Multidimensional Integrated Stabilization Mission in Mali), where state authorities have asked for their fast and full withdrawal. However, in light of FARDC's concentration on fighting M23, some observers feared that the end of the MONUSCO mandate might create a security vacuum in other conflict-affected regions.

Foreign Affairs

The DRC's regional and international diplomacy was predominantly influenced by the deepening conflict with Rwanda and with M23, as well as by the impact of the December elections. Where 2022 had been mostly oriented towards the deployment of the EACRF to deal with M23, disillusion with the force and growing frustration with the perceived lack of support from the EAC at large led to an increasingly fraught situation. From early 2023, Kinshasa sought backing from its partners within the SADC, while also intensifying its bilateral partnership with *Burundi*. The AU also stepped in, in an effort to improve the coordination and coherence of regional peace efforts. Beyond peace and security, Kinshasa pursued increasingly active climate diplomacy and developed economic partnerships on mineral resources with key investors (the US, the EU, and China). Also in 2023, the DRC ended its chairing of the SADC and the CEEAC.

Relations with Uganda, Rwanda, and Burundi remained complex and intricately linked. The DRC was suspicious about the role of *Uganda* in the M23 crisis. M23 maintained considerable backing in Uganda; the Ugandan government did not act against the group's control of the Bunagana border post, a major artery for M23's logistics and economic networks. UPDF troops deployed in the EACRF did not engage in any operations against M23. Kinshasa, however, maintained the joint Ugandan – DRC Shujaa military operation against the ADF. Uganda also kept its road-building project in the Grand Nord territory of Nord Kivu. In March and August, the DRC and *Burundi* further deepened their military cooperation with the signing of a defence and security agreement. Burundian troops (Force de Défense Nationale du Burundi; FDNB) had been operating in South Kivu to counter Burundian armed opponents active in the province (such as the Résistance pour un état de droit au Burundi/RED-Tabara and les Forces nationales de liberation/FNL) since 2021. In addition to these troops, in March, Burundi deployed a contingent to North Kivu as part of the EACRF. From September onwards, Burundi also deployed Burundian troops – operating in FARDC uniform – in North Kivu. These troops were fully embedded within the Congolese armed forces. This increased collaboration between the two countries contributed to existing tensions between Burundi and Rwanda.

The conflict between *Rwanda* and the DRC reached its most critical point in the course of 2023, and fears appeared of a direct military confrontation. Conflict narratives led to a build-up of military forces. Kinshasa invested in the acquisition of armed drones and relied heavily on its small air force and long-range artillery systems to counter and neutralise concentrated RDF-M23 forces. On the ground, it also depended on a number of non-state armed actors, including Rwandan FDLR elements. In 2023, Rwanda and M23 further intensified their operations. At the end of the year, this included, among other things, the deployment of more advanced mobile air defence systems. In response to this escalation, the US intensified its diplomacy with both countries with a visit by the director of national intelligence Avril Haines in November. The US called on both countries to end their collaboration and support to the FDLR and M23 respectively. In response, the DRC government ordered the army to stop such collaboration and a few military commanders were subsequently arrested.

The regional crisis also saw a further political escalation, due to the launch, in December, of the Alliance Fleuve Congo (AFC), a coalition of politicians built around M23 that also included the Twirwaneho, a Banyamulenge armed group from South Kivu. The AFC was led by Corneille Nangaa, the former head of the CENI (2015–21). At the time of its launch, the AFC seemed mainly to be offering a home to frustrated politicians. It also provided a structure, resources, and a political narrative to attract disgruntled leaders of armed groups and political opposition forces. The aim of the organisation went beyond those set by M23, as the group set its sights on taking power in Kinshasa. The AFC's public launch in Nairobi, during the last stretch of the run-up to the Congolese elections and at a time of considerable frustration between Kenya and the DRC, was taken badly in Kinshasa. In an immediate response, Kinshasa recalled its ambassadors from Nairobi and Arusha (i.e. the EAC headquarters) for consultations.

Regional initiatives continued their efforts to deal with the security crisis in eastern DRC, but with limited success. The *Nairobi peace process* focused directly on internal dynamics in the DRC while the *Luanda peace process* targeted regional actors involved in these dynamics. The main effort was the planned cantonment of M23 forces, which required the EACRF as a confidence-building force and buffer between the FARDC (supported by local wazalendo armed groups) and the M23 (supported by the RDF). To support its efforts, the EAC also established its own Monitoring and Verification Mechanism (EAC-MVM). With the deployment of the EACRF, M23 transferred some areas to the regional forces. These steps were deemed unsatisfactory by Kinshasa, which considered the regional force too sympathetic to the Rwanda-backed rebel group. The EACRF deployed its forces to North Kivu, and M23 and FARDC observed a fragile ceasefire that lasted until October, when several wazalendo groups, with support from Kinshasa, waged an offensive against M23. While this was initially seemingly successful, the fortunes on the ground changed and M23 eventually managed to expand the area under its control. On 8 December, the mandate of the EACRF expired, after having been extended for three months at the 8 August EAC summit in Nairobi.

Angola, the coordinator of the Luanda peace process, aimed to act in support of the cantonment process. On the ground, Angola's mediation was supported by an Angolan Ad-Hoc Verification Mechanism. On 17 March, the Angolan parliament endorsed the deployment of a maximum 500-strong military contingent to protect the cantonment site for M23. The deployment would depend on the existing conditions in cantonment areas. Kinshasa and M23, however, could not reach consensus on the location of the cantonment. So far, Angola has refrained from directly deploying its troops to the eastern DRC.

On 27 June, the *AU* organised the 1st Quadripartite Summit of the EAC, CEEAC, ICGLR, and SADC. The meeting adopted a 'Joint Framework on Coordination of Peace Initiatives in Eastern DRC' agreed by the different RECs, as well as a coordination group. Tshisekedi participated in the meeting while Rwanda was represented by its foreign minister. A follow-up meeting of the chiefs of defence of the key signatories was organised in Addis Ababa on 6 October.

Kinshasa increasingly looked for support from *SADC* forces which had already intervened twice in recent years: in 1998, when the rebel movement *Rassemblement Congolais pour la Démocratie* (supported by Rwandan troops) was at the doorstep of Kinshasa; and in 2013, when the organisation deployed the Force Intervention Brigade (FIB) to operate in support of MONUSCO to track down non-state armed groups. The FIB, composed primarily of SADC forces from South Africa, Tanzania, and Malawi, remained deployed in North Kivu. However, to the frustration of the SADC, over time it had lost much of its operational capacity. In February, the DRC sent a military delegation to several SADC countries, followed by a (previously planned but delayed) SADC inspection mission to eastern DRC in late February and early March. At the subsequent SADC summit in May, the organisation agreed in principle to the deployment in North Kivu of a SADC military force to the DRC (SAMIDRC). The force's mandate was based on the organisation's principle of 'collective self-defence and collective action', outlined in its 2003 Mutual Defence Pact. Upon the deployment, SADC communicated that the pact also applied to 'any armed attack perpetrated against one of the state parties'. SAMIDRC sent its first elements to North Kivu in December, at around the same time that the EAC completed the withdrawal of its forces from the DRC. Since its presence on the ground commenced, the SADC has been decried by M23, Rwanda, and the AFC as part of a coalition including the FARDC, THE FDLR, non-state armed groups operating under the wazalendo banner, Burundi, foreign mercenaries, and MONUSCO. Rwanda also attempted to stop any AU and UN support to SAMIDRC. The first commander was a South African, and the composition reflected that of the FIB (i.e., with South Africa, Tanzania, and Malawi providing the core troops).

On the diplomatic front, the revitalisation of the Peace, Security and Cooperation Framework Agreement (PSCF), originally concluded in 2013 by 11 African countries with the UN, the SADC, the AU, and the ICGLR as guarantors, became a Congolese foreign policy goal in the course of 2023. In May, President Tshisekedi appointed veteran of regional politics Professor Alphonse Daniel Ntumba Luaba to head the DRC's National Follow-up Mechanism (or MNS – *Méchanisme National de Suivi*) under the PSCF. Ntumba Luaba re-dynamised the MNS and embarked on a mission to rebalance national and regional commitments among PSCF signatories. The DRC government was unhappy about a considerable imbalance in its national commitments compared with other signatories. This issue was discussed among the signatory states at a meeting in Durban, South Africa, in October and November. While Kinshasa seemed to have accepted that some of the national commitments, such as security sector reform, were in line with the aim of the agreement, it considered others, such as decentralisation and economic development, to be within the realm of national sovereignty. It also wanted other national commitments, such as democratisation and reconciliation, to be extended to the other signatories and not be limited to the DRC only.

At a meeting of the UNHRC in Geneva on 27 February, President Tshisekedi called for the reactivation of the tripartite talks with Rwanda on the return of Congolese refugees to the DRC and Rwandan refugees to Rwanda. A first round of talks was held in Geneva in May, followed by two further rounds in Nairobi in June and November. Talks including local and traditional authorities were supposed to be held in Goma, but these were cancelled due to security concerns for the Rwandan delegates.

From October 2022, Félix Tshisekedi was also the CEEAC mediator for the political crisis in Chad. Under DRC facilitation, on 31 October, part of the Chadian opposition signed an agreement with the government in N'djamena.

In recent years, the DRC has placed increased importance on its climate diplomacy. In 2022, this led to a partnership agreement between *Brazil*, the DRC, and *Indonesia*. In August 2023 at the 'Amazon Summit', the DRC co-signed the 'United for Our Forests' statement with Indonesia, the *Republic of Congo*, Brazil, and several other Amazon basin states. Also, a $40 m deal with tech company Okala was signed in December to finance the measurement, valuation, and protection of Congolese biodiversity and carbon natural assets. Okala committed itself to supporting the management of national parks and key landmarks.

The government's relations with Western actors (mostly the EU and US) remained strong, despite these actors' concerns about the electoral process. On 20 July, the EU decided to provide support to the 31st Brigade of the Congolese armed forces, a programme executed by the Belgian Ministry of Defence. A total budget of €20 m under the European Peace Facility was aimed at countering Congolese criticism over similar EU support to Rwanda for its military operation in Mozambique.

One element of controversy was the cancellation by the EU of its electoral observation mission to the DRC on 29 November. Brussels considered it impossible to deploy its observers throughout the country given that the government had raised security objections about the use of communications equipment as well as other technical conditions that would have prohibited the observers from working independently.

Socioeconomic Developments

Economic *growth* maintained strong momentum. According to the World Bank, real GDP growth in the DRC was expected to reach 6.8%, after peaking at 8.9% in 2022 and 6.2% in 2021. This was mainly attributable to the mining sector, despite the expected slowing down of its output growth from 22.6% in 2022 to 11.7% in the reporting year. According to the IMF, by the end of September, cumulative copper exports had increased by 13% year to year, and cobalt saw a decline of 4% because of a sharp slowdown in prices. Non-mining sectors (particularly services) were expected to show a modest increase in growth, from 2.7% in 2022 to 4.2%. On the demand side, according to the AfDB, economic growth was driven by robust exports and investment. Inflation was expected to go up from 9.2% in 2022 to an estimated 20.7%, particularly due to higher food and energy prices and a sharply depreciating currency (28.4% in October year to year against the US dollar). Similarly, according to the World Bank, the account deficit was expected to further increase, from 2.9% of GDP in 2022 to 4.7%. Higher import prices and volumes and persistent deterioration in terms of trade were presented as the main causes of this increase. On the other hand, it was expected that inflows from external financing would lead to the accumulation of international reserves, estimated to go up from 7.9 weeks in 2022 to 10 weeks (close to $7 bn) on average in 2023 and 2024. The fiscal deficit was projected at –1.3% of GDP, only 0.3% lower than in 2022, despite a prudent fiscal policy and increase in revenue and aid. Continued exceptional spending for security and election purposes did not permit a further reduction of the deficit.

The DRC remained among the five poorest nations in the world; with a value of 0.481, it ranked 180th in the HDI, and more than 60% of the population lived on less than $2.15 a day. The intensification of armed conflict and violent clashes further affected the *precarious socioeconomic and health conditions* of ordinary civilians in several parts of the country, producing one of the worst current global humanitarian crises. According to OCHA, out of a population of 113 m, more than 27 m people were in direct need of assistance. Despite being one of the highest priorities in government social spending (30% of the budget was reserved for the ministries of education, health, social, and humanitarian affairs), little was achieved in practice. In February, a Humanitarian Response Plan was launched by the government and humanitarian donors with the aim of raising $2.25 bn in support of the needs of 10 m vulnerable people. In October, a record 6.9 m people were internally displaced, the majority living in the conflict-affected provinces of South Kivu, North Kivu, Tanganyika, and Ituri. Particularly in North Kivu, humanitarian conditions became critical, with more than 600,000 IDPs living around Goma in makeshift shelters without access to food, drinking water, or health services. More than 85% of displacement was caused by armed violence. The nutrition situation also remained critical, particularly in conflict-affected regions, where 34% of the population were at emergency levels of food insecurity.

DRC's endowment with strategic minerals (copper and cobalt) is key for the global energy transition. Because of its abundance in hydroenergy potential, the DRC presented itself as a country that could provide the necessary support to this transition. Both the EU and the US expanded engagement with the DRC on natural resources. The DRC, *Zambia*, and the *US* signed an MoU on the electric vehicle battery industry in December 2022. In October 2023, the EU signed a strategic partnership with the DRC on value chains for critical raw materials. In collaboration with the EU and the US, the DRC also partnered with Zambia and Angola for the further development and extension of the Lobito Corridor, a transnational railway of 1,300 km connecting the Katangese and Zambian mineral-producing regions to the Atlantic Ocean. The formal objectives of the Lobito Corridor are to maximise and promote trade, investment, and economic integration among and between the DRC, Angola, and Zambia. Investors include the EU, the AfDB, and the Africa Finance Corporation. The railway services and logistics of the project will be managed by a consortium including the Portuguese Mota-Engil Group and Belgian private railway operator Vecturis SA.

As well as Western investors returning to the DRC, the country was also renegotiating the terms of the controversial minerals-for-infrastructure Sicomines agreement of 2008 with China.

Equatorial Guinea

Enrique Martino

Instead of the familiar mix of oil and corruption, the year's main stories were propelled by a new combination of gas and anti-corruption campaigns. After the cabinet reshuffle following the elections held late in 2022, the vice-president, Teodoro Nguema Obiang Mangue, widely known as Teodorín and for being found guilty of embezzlement in various courts abroad in the past, led the charge against the 'corrupt' local elites. In Malabo, Moscow, and Minsk in the second half of the year, five meetings took place between the country's leadership – either President Teodoro Obiang Nguema Mbasogo or Teodorín – and Russia's President Putin or Belarussia's President Lukashenko. This helped to drown out the attention being given (by the European Parliament and UN bodies) to the persecution and kidnapping of prominent political exiles, including those with Spanish citizenship. In major oil news, ExxonMobil finally revealed its exit plans in October and began to transfer its full stake and assets in the famed Zafiro site to state-owned GEPetrol. The scrapping of the Zafiro floating production storage and offloading (FPSO) unit after an explosion on the offloading vessel late last year had disconnected dozens of wells for months and directly resulted in the second-worst plunge of GDP in decades. Teodorín's firm grip on power bolstered expectations of authoritarian stability and apparently convinced Marathon Oil and Chevron to expand investment in and production of LNG, the new hydrocarbon backbone of the country.

Domestic Politics

President Obiang remained active despite his age, hosting international summits in his newly built 'legacy' towns Sipopo and Ciudad de la Paz – in reality not much more than shiny conference centres – and attending events such as the Saudi–Africa summit in Riyadh on 10 November. However, Obiang appeared most content when signing copies of his latest memoir 'El sueño de una Guinea mejor' ('The dream of a better Guinea') at a book launch in the Gran Hotel Djibloho of Ciudad de la Paz. In contrast, local news often featured his son Teodorín inaugurating or pushing for the completion of *public works* (schools, hospitals, university campuses, and the like) and leading legal initiatives focused on the protection of minors. Teodorín's *anti-corruption campaign* ironically became the centrepiece of domestic politics. His commanding leadership was apparent in new, partially televised cabinet meetings and special anti-corruption 'investigation' sessions, which he presided over from his ornate seat at the head of a gilded table. The more formal elements of the new anti-corruption commission received increased funding, to the fanfare of the IMF, and were led by the *new prime minister*, Manuela Roka Botey, the first woman but not the first minority-ethnic Bubi to hold the position. She was formerly the minister for education but was not on record for any newsworthy appearances or statements in the past years, and therefore, Teodorín ran no risk of being overshadowed by this appointment. Instead, he announced her promotion personally, stressing his country's 'commitment to gender equality' on his active X (formerly Twitter) account.

Teodorín's own 'investigation' initially focused on his half-brother Ruslan Obiang Nsue, who was accused of selling an aeroplane belonging to the national airline in the Canary Islands and pocketing the proceeds. The interrogations led to the quick surfacing of new evidence that implicated other former high-ranking officials in *corruption*, most clearly those linked to Gabriel Mbaga Obiang Lima, Teodorín's half-brother and rival, who was once considered a presidential succession favourite by US oil companies. In spring, accused of forging Obiang's signature for various fraudulent projects, Lima's father-in-law and deposed finance minister Valentin Ela Maye was placed under house arrest. In the *cabinet reshuffle* on 2 February, Teodorín's ally Fortunato Ofa Mbo Nchama, a former IMF trainee, banker at the BEAC, and chair of the BDEAC, assumed control of the crucial Ministry of Finance. Intriguingly, Antonio 'Tony' Oburu Ondo became the new hydrocarbons minister. He was known as Obiang's 'economics guru' and a very reliable backer of Teodorín, as he is married to Teodorín's cousin (his mother's brother's daughter).

In a humiliating turn, Gabriel Obiang Lima, who had been in charge of the Ministry of Mines and Hydrocarbons (but could also be blamed for more than a decade of economic downturn), was relegated to the newly created minor Ministry of Planning and Economic Diversification, dedicated to national accounting statistics.

Last year's deadly pre-election crackdown on the *banned party* Ciudadanos por la Innovación (CI) ended in June with its leader Gabriel Nsé Obiang receiving a 29-year sentence from a Malabo military court for charges including insults to security forces. This followed the September 2022 violent raid on his home and party headquarters. The public broadcaster TVGE aired the mass trial, showing Nsé and 50 co-defendants in ochre prison uniforms loosely seated in what appeared to be a high-end conference venue. The EU's chief diplomat, Josep Borrell, called the sentences 'harsh'. In Juan Carlos Ondo Angue, a new *opposition figure* emerged beyond the established range of political parties. Ondo Angue, a former judge, announced the creation of his new platform, Nexos-GE, on the anniversary of Obiang's 1979 coup, 3 August, and claimed to be dedicated to exposing human rights violations and highlighting that the regime's 'growing ties to China and Russia [are] regional and global security threats'. In August, Teodorín's anti-corruption campaign used X to display documents meant to show Ondo Angue's abuse of power and engagement in extortion during his time as the president of Malabo's Supreme Court. It was also widely known that he is the son of Purificación Angue Ondo, a retired ruling-party big-wig from Mongomo, from the Esangui clan, and the former ambassador to the US and Spain, popular for being an anti-colonial militant in the 1960s and a champion of women's rights in the country.

The main protagonist of the exiled opposition groups this year was certainty the *MLGE3R*, (Movimiento para la Liberación de Guinea Ecuatorial Tercera Republica), founded in Spain in 2018 by Martin Obiang Ondo Mbasogo, the son of the founder of the FDR (Fuerza Demócrata Republicana), which had tried to halt Teodorín's rise to power since the late 1990s. The leader of the MLGE3R is a distant relative (a kind of grandson-in-law) of President Obiang. Notoriously, the movement comprised exiled military personnel from Mongomo who were sentenced *in absentia* by the government for their alleged participation in the 2017 Christmas coup attempt. In 2019, several MLGE3R leaders and members had been lured away and then kidnapped from Spain, via South Sudan, and 'disappeared', most likely into the new Oveng Azem prison near Mongomo.

The year opened with a bombshell news item on 4 January that spread across the Spanish press. It was revealed that an ongoing investigation was being carried out by a judge from the Spanish High Court (Audience Nacional) into the *kidnapping* of two Spanish citizens, and the prime suspect was Carmelo Ovono Obiang, another son of President Obiang and his chief of foreign security. A resolution by the European Parliament on 16 February titled 'Violence against opposition activists in Equatorial Guinea, notably the case of Julio Obama Mefuman' referred to this case. Obama Mefuman was a former Spanish legionary and MLGE3R member. He had been kidnapped in South Sudan in 2019 and tortured on the same presidential plane as the other MLGE3R members. He mysteriously died in mid-January in the Mongomo prison. Spanish newspapers then also revealed that it was Obama Mefuman's recorded testimony, smuggled out from his jail cell, which had been originally submitted to a Spanish judge in September 2022 that had kick-started the investigation. His death was attributed by the government to 'illness', possibly 'diabetes'.

Foreign Affairs

In April, MLGE3R members met with Spanish politicians, advocating for an *international arrest warrant* against Carmelo Ovono Obiang. Subsequently, the Spanish state attorney requested the judge to issue such a warrant, citing Ovono Obiang's failure to appear in court in March. In May, the case was also discussed in the Spanish Congress, where almost all parties pressed the Spanish government to condemn Equatorial Guinea and to prosecute the regime's criminal ongoing surveillance of exiled opponents. By the early summer, the Spanish High Court had removed the international arrest warrant and passed the investigation into kidnapping and torture into the hands of Equatorial Guinea's own courts. Amnesty International then pursued Spain in a special report submitted to the UN Committee Against Torture in July for its 'failure to comply with its international human rights obligations' resulting from the High Court's effective *discontinuation of the investigation*. The UN Working Group on Arbitrary Detention decided to open its own investigation, which it analysed in a closed session in September, with the widespread hope that its findings might lead to UNHRC-recommended sanctions. The EU Diplomatic Service's confidential recommendations were submitted to Josep Borrell, who was formerly the Spanish foreign minister in 2018 and last met Obiang a few weeks before refusing the latter's invitation to attend the celebration of the 50th anniversary of independence from Spain on 12 October 1968. Borrell has also been embroiled in the rescue of opposition figures in the country with Spanish citizenship in the past.

Teodorín came out in full public support of Albert Ondo Ossa, who claimed to have been the real winner of the *Gabonese elections* in August and who was sidelined by Ali Bongo being declared the election winner and then shortly after again by General Brice Oligui Nguema's post-election coup. Teodorín's assertions of democratic violation and Western interference were notable and well received in Gabon among Ondo Ossa's supporters. A CEEAC summit followed the coup, announcing a temporary shift of the organisation's headquarters from Libreville to Malabo, and the rotating presidency passed from Ali Bongo to Obiang. Obiang presided over the 5th Extraordinary Summit of CEEAC in Ciudad de la Paz (Djibolo) as the new chair, but the coup general's lobbying in Malabo managed to achieve the postponement of the CEEAC headquarters' relocation.

The political dynamics in the region after the coup in Gabon appeared to play in Obiang's favour, following his last-minute exclusion from President Emmanuel Macron's Summit for a New Global Financing Pact in Paris in June – a meeting attended by nearly all other CEEAC presidents. Initially it seemed that *French–Equatorial Guinean relations* were improving, with Macron's 'Africa' envoy, Christophe Bigot, visiting Malabo in January and proposing a presidential meeting and Macron engaging Obiang at a climate summit in Libreville shortly thereafter. But the relationship was still determined by the ongoing 'ill-gotten gains' saga targeting Teodorín. French legislators announced the earmarking of a €6.1 m fund for restitution initiatives, gained through the auctioning off of Teodorín's luxury cars and other ornamental items that filled the mansion at 42 Avenue Foch in Paris, worth at least €150 m. The mansion, still occupied by members of the Equatorial Guinean diplomatic corps, remained stacked in an escalating case of legal claims and counterclaims at the ICJ. In June, Teodorín was ordered to pay additional property taxes by the Paris Court of Appeal. The NGO Redress, in a special briefing by Tutu Alicante of EG Justice, suggested utilising *confiscated funds* to offer compensation to corruption victims through scholarships, journalism training programmes, and investment in cultural and artistic projects that would foster a 'culture of free expression'. At the UNGA in September, Teodorín focused on extending an investment invitation to the business community of all 'friendly countries'. Antonio 'Tony' Oburu, assumed the presidencies of both OPEC and the GECF, committing to 'eradicating energy poverty' at the GECF ministerial meeting in Sipopo on 10 October.

Russia rekindled its past interest in Equatorial Guinea – the island of Bioko once hosted a Soviet fleet of fishing vessels and submarines for much of the 1970s. At the Russia–Africa summit in July, Teodorín advocated for the re-establishment of the Russian embassy in Malabo – a proposal that was accepted and announced in December. The Russian ambassador was to join the dwindling ranks of resident European ambassadors from Spain and France. On 2 November, Obiang led a significant delegation to Moscow for a 'working breakfast' tête-à-tête with Putin, signalling a desire to align with or join BRICS, and Putin noted that he was pleased that relations were being restored and developed. On 9 December, Belarusian president Aleksandr Lukashenko, who had probably facilitated the meeting with Putin, arrived in Malabo, receiving a warm welcome from Teodorín at the airport, complete with a display by traditional dance troupes. Obiang had already first travelled to Minsk on 6–8 September and issued a statement that harked back to the days before US oil totally monopolised the country's hydrocarbon economy and denounced the 'diktat of Western multinationals'. The Belarusian industry minister proposed transforming the port of Bata into a hub for distributing *Belarusian engineering products* such as tractors across the region. Teodorín returned to Moscow in mid-December, to secure technico-military deals with senior Ministry of Defence officials, including on security, maritime navigation, and aviation. He also met with the director of the Russian Space Agency (Roscosmos) to discuss launching a communication and tracking satellite, a step towards what Teodorín termed 'space sovereignty'.

Socioeconomic Developments

The major outlets of the international press focused mainly on the March outbreak of the contagious *Marburg virus*, which subsided after quarantine measures and about a dozen deaths. The WHO declared the outbreak over in June. The difficulty of gathering social and economic data was admitted by the Independent Evaluation Office of the UNDP, which regretted the 'scarcity' of up-to-date data from government and non-government sources. The IMF put the *decline of GDP* at −6.2% in its 2023 outlook for Equatorial Guinea, marking the second-sharpest drop since its records began almost half a century ago but close to the −5% average in the past decade. The almost $300 m loan or bailout from the IMF had expired in 2022, though its 'recommendations' were still being implemented, including the gradual reduction of fuel subsidies, which accounted for 1.3% of GDP in 2022. The social consequences of the economic decline and privatisation were muted because of the relatively high baseline of the ongoing decline: the country's GNP remained higher than Bermuda's and its GDP per capita was comparable to that of South Africa. Nevertheless, HDI figures showed a gradual decline since 2015, ranking Equatorial Guinea 145th out of 191 countries, with *social spending* remaining at an extremely low 1.6% of GDP (in 2022).

The country maintained a large fiscal surplus of 13.5% of GDP in 2022, marking the first time in years that it had accumulated net foreign assets at the BEAC. The IMF's 2023 Staff Report (Article IV Consultation) noted that hydrocarbon production constituted a little less than 50% of GDP, but the *construction industry*, the most significant non-hydrocarbon sector, remained heavily dependent on hydrocarbon revenues. The government cleared nearly €100 m in overdue payments to Chinese and Belgian construction companies during 2022, a part of which was deposited in local banks, which helped to address the IMF's main concern about the need to 'recapitalise' the larger '*ailing banks*' in the country. Nevertheless, outstanding arrears, principally to construction firms, stood at almost €900 m as of August. Equatorial Guinea's banking sector faced challenges, with the world's highest rate of non-performing loans according to the World Bank (57.9% of total loans in the first quarter of the year). A new agreement with Ivorian credit risk-rating agency firm Bloomfield Investment Corporation was aimed at helping to deal with international interest rate variability and imported inflation. Meanwhile, over the summer, Société Générale withdrew from the country, selling its subsidiary (SGBGE) to the Vista Group headquartered in Conakry. Emirati group Terminals Holding LLC took control of the new Malabo airport, and an agreement with Turkish Albayrak Holding was signed for port operations.

A focus on developments in the oil and gas sector is crucial because the politics of the country is highly dependent on it. The steeper-than-usual GDP drop can be attributed to the explosion at Zafiro. After almost three decades of pumping out over 1 bn barrels of oil from Zafiro, the Exxon era drew to a close. The Zafiro blend of crude, still drawing a high premium in global markets, continued to be taken out through the floating Serpentina unit on site. All of Exxon's remaining assets were scheduled to be passed on to the management of the new minister 'Tony' Oburu and Teresa Isabel Nnang Avomo, a 36-year-old Spanish-Guinean geologist and former reservoir engineer at Repsol who replaced Oburu as director of the GEPetrol in February.

While underwater oil reservoirs and state revenues seem to be slowly disappearing, there was great dynamism in *gas*, exports of which have held at stable level over the past decade and which in the last year or two has become the country's primary hydrocarbon as well as the focus of intense speculation and investment. According to GECF data for 2022, the country produced almost 3% of the world's internationally marketed production of LNG and ranked fourth in Africa for LNG exports (at 5.74 bn cubic metres, after Egypt, Nigeria, and Algeria). All gas was piped in from Marathon Oil's Alba field and Chevron's Alen field and later liquified at the LNG plant at Punta Europa near the international airport of Malabo. In all of these ventures, GEPetrol held a minority but important share. In a February press release, Marathon Oil's chief executive officer (CEO) emphasised the company's commitment to extending the life of the country's 'gas monetisation infrastructure' facilities, through the ongoing phases of the so-called *gas mega hub*, which aims to extend pipelines and wells connected to this onshore liquefaction train on a secured oceanic enclave. Marathon and Chevron bucked the trend of withdrawal by US firms from the wider region. The end of the year, 31 December, marked the long-awaited end of the contract for *gas pricing* with Shell. Under this agreement, Shell and other British intermediaries had for almost two decades purchased LNG from the plant at a low fixed price linked to the American Henry Hub price. Marathon Oil's CEO highlighted the potential for an imminent doubling of profits due to its finally being able to sell directly at the more lucrative European and Asian rates for gas.

Cameroonian president Paul Biya endorsed the 'gas mega hub' project in the Douala basin. In March, during the 15th CEMAC conference of heads of state, a joint development agreement was signed between Biya and Obiang encompassing the new fields Yoyo and Yolanda, adjacent to Alen but extending into Cameroonian waters and also under *Chevron's ownership*. In December, Chevron also announced its intention to buy from Exxon its exploration blocks adjacent to Zafiro, where gas discoveries have been made. GEPetrol continued its focus on the unexploited Fortuna field, with an estimated 3.8 trillion cubic feet of gas in deeper but untapped waters south-west of Zafiro. New developments were here linked to Golar LNG, led by Tor Olav Trøim, a protégé of an eccentric Norwegian tanker magnate, who met with Teodorín in Malabo in August. Olav Trøim commended Teodorín for creating a favourable 'business climate', promised to put 'our cash in the national banks', and talked up the plan to develop the Fortuna field by connecting it to a new *deep-water floating LNG unit* that was still under construction.

Shortly after becoming Teodorín's new hydrocarbon pointman at the ministry, Oburu signed new production-sharing contracts near Chevron's still-maturing Alen field, with Africa Oil Corp, a modest-sized firm with many ties to former Marathon Oil employees. By November, the company had sold its blocks as there was a '*staggering industry interest*' in their 'exploration block', so 'close' to a 'high-end LNG plant'. Oburu had previously lived in London for 15 years as director of sales for GEPetrol. Several smaller – in some cases only one-person – London-based firms, including Antler Global Ltd and Europa Oil & Gas, acquired an exploration block near Alen in October. They confidently announced a '90% chance of finding a commercial discovery' estimated at 1.3 trillion cubic feet, branding it a 'high quality, low risk, and high reward asset in shallow water'. An influx of speculators usually signals the kick-starting of a boom. Even Lars Windhorst, the German investor famous for his 'billionaire lifestyle', paid a familiar visit to Teodorín in November to discuss 'gas'.

Despite the *managed decline* of the Ceiba and Okume oil-only fields off Rio Muni, co-owned by Houston's Kosmos and London's Panoro and Trident, the appointment of Oburu as minister also spurred a wave of new licences and blocks being awarded around this complex. Norwegian drill operators, specialised in 'redeveloping mid-life oil assets' by extending undersea taps to new wells, were engaged. Previously, Teodorín had hindered Trident's attempts at making inroads, including the thwarting of its 2019 bid for Zafiro, likely due to its CEO's French nationality. The patience of the founder and CEO of Trident, Jean-Michel Jacoulot, paid off. In April, he was welcomed at Teodorín's palace, with the vice-president promising him his 'full support' after pledging $400 m in new investment in *exploration and extraction*. Trident is an unlisted company, backed by New York's private equity firm Warburg Pincus, which also funds the Kosmos ventures.

In November, the Turbogas power generation facility at Punta Europa, which provides much of Bioko's energy, transitioned from a 21-year Marathon Oil maintenance contract to a new arrangement with China Machinery Engineering Corporation (CMEC). This shift occurred after Teodorín had directed the treasury to settle payments of several million euros overdue to CMEC. The firm, which engages in water treatment, supply, and various building and construction projects, also received a significant advance payment as part of this deal. In June, Oburu met with Sinopec Group's Qu Bin, who signalled an entirely new interest in oil and gas exploration, suggesting that last year's public tension between the US and China around the alleged plan to build a naval base in Bata's deep port has been muted but is trickling down into the energy sector.

Gabon

Douglas Yates

On 30 August, the military seized power in Gabon after the announcement of the results of the presidential election had proclaimed victory for the incumbent president, Ali Bongo. An outpouring of unbridled joy on the streets of Libreville erupted when news of the coup broke, and it was even celebrated in other African countries with long-standing autocrats. After the coup, the new transitional government headed by General Brice Clotaire Oligui Nguema tried to get to grips with the tangle of assets held in Libreville, Paris, Dubai, and London by former heir apparent Noureddin Bongo, favourite son of the ousted president, and his associates.

Domestic Politics

On 12 January, President Ali Bongo replaced his *prime minister* Rose Christiane Ossouka Raponda with Alain-Claude Bilie By Nze, who established himself as one of the new strongmen of the Bongo system. With the departure of Ossouka Raponda, to whom she was close, first lady Sylvia Bongo lost some influence within Gabon's government; he also supported Ali Bongo in the highly contested presidential elections of 2016. Sylvia Bongo's influence in the presidential palace had been dynastic ever since her husband's 2018 stroke. She had been jockeying for her eldest son Noureddin Bongo to replace him once Ali Bongo's re-election was assured.

On 2 April, on the 55th anniversary of the creation of the ruling Parti Démocratique Gabonais (PDG) by his father Omar Bongo, Ali Bongo spoke for the first time of his stay in Morocco from 2018 to 2019 after he'd suffered a stroke in Saudi Arabia. The purpose of his speech was to assure his PDG supporters, and through the filter of the mass media his voters, that he had completely recovered from his stroke and was ready to assume another five-year term. Bongo spoke in front of more than 5,000 PDG activists in the capital city Libreville. 'We had arrived in Morocco, and I spent a few days there first, trying to find myself. The king, my brother, our brother, our brother', Bongo cried, displaying a weakness that belied his desire to appear strong. 'The king did everything for me!'

Behind the scenes, everybody knew that Bongo could no longer recover all of his abilities. Ali's (jailed) former cabinet advisor Brice Laccruche Alihanga had told Sylvia Bongo that it was necessary to think about Ali Bongo stepping down. After the coup, Ian Ghislain Ngoulou, Noureddin's cabinet director, confessed that he and other clanspeople of the Valentin-Bongo branch of the ruling family had been asked to silence Alihanga: 'We had to keep power by all means'. This information was confirmed by Alihanga on his release from prison on 20 October. He summed up the reason that he had been held incommunicado for four years in three points: the first was that he had opposed the galloping mismanagement of the former first lady and her son; the second was that in view of the physical condition of the president, he had suggested on several occasions that Ali Bongo should withdraw from political life to rest; and the third was that he 'strongly opposed the stated will of former first lady Sylvia Bongo Ondimba and her son Noureddin Bongo Valentin to take power in Gabon, by any means possible'.

Democratic opponents of the 'Bongo clan' spent the year trying to organise fair elections. But the president had used the super-majority of his ruling party in both chambers to revise the electoral code so that all elections – presidential, legislative, regional, and local – would be held at the same time. This would ensure a complete PDG sweep of all government institutions in one single fraudulent ballot. On 6 April, the National Assembly and the Senate convened in a bicameral 'Congress' to adopt the proposed *constitutional revisions* with 86% of the votes. These revisions harmonised the election dates and duration of all political mandates (president of the republic, senators, deputies, and local elected officials) to five years, removed term limits for all political offices, and adopted a single-round voting procedure for all political elections. Aligning legislative elections with the presidential election would strengthen the president's influence over the political system and restrict the scope of the parliamentary majority, confining it largely to rubber-stamping executive directives.

On 17 July, a new force, the opposition platform Alternance 2023 and COTED-Gabon (Consortium de la Société civile pour la transparence électorale et la démocratie au Gabon) filed a *petition for the annulment of the revision of the electoral code* within less than 45 days of the general elections. The opposition considered this new electoral law a democratic step backwards, favourable only to the incumbent Ali Bongo and his ruling PDG. The appeal was nevertheless rejected by the Constitutional Court, presided over by PDG loyalist Marie Madeleine Mborantsuo, a former mistress of the late Omar Bongo, the president's father.

General elections were scheduled for 26 August. A field of 19 candidates was approved by the electoral commission to challenge Bongo, including Alexandre Barro Chambrier, a former PDG minister of mines who tried to rally other candidates around him without success, and Albert Ondo Ossa, a former education minister under Omar Bongo, who had challenged Ali Bongo back in 2009. On 18 August, less than two weeks before the election, six opposition parties joined together under the Alternance 2023 banner and chose Ondo Ossa as the unified opposition candidate. Chambrier threw his support behind Ondo Ossa.

Electioneering by the Bongos followed. In order to disable the opposition from verifying any ballot-counting procedures, the PDG announced indefinite restriction of internet access and a nightly curfew on the evening of the election. The same day, the PDG government suspended broadcasts by all three French media channels, France 24, RFI, and TV5Monde. Silence reigned until 30 August, when the Gabonese Elections Centre announced on STE television that Bongo had won with 293,919 votes (64.3%), defeating Ondo Ossa's 140,690 votes (30.8%) and the 12 other candidates, who split the remainder.

On 30 August, the military seized power. There was immediate popular support in the streets when news of the coup broke, and it was soon being celebrated in other African countries with long-running leaders. Ali Bongo went on social media pathetically asking his 'friends' in the international community to intervene. (African social media turned his video plea for help into a TikTok meme called 'Make Noise'.) The military, represented by the Republican Guard, temporarily dissolved all institutions of government and forced the retirement of the president, who was placed under house arrest. All this was greeted with popular jubilation as a *'coup de libération'*.

On the same day army colonels and elite soldiers of the Republican Guard formed a junta: the Committee for the Transition and Restoration of Institutions (CTRI). General Brice Clotaire Oligui Nguema was sworn in as transitional president on 4 October. Son of a Téké mother and a Fang military officer, born in the province of Haut-Ogooué (the clan fief of the Bongos), Oligui Nguema was a cousin of Ali Bongo and thus a blood member of the Bongo dynasty. Aide-de-camp under the late Omar Bongo, Oligui Nguema found himself, after the 2009 election of Ali Bongo, exiled as a military attaché at embassies in Morocco and then Senegal. Belonging to Omar Bongo's family had contributed to his promotions up the ranks of Republican

Guard, but it took a while for the second generation of Bongos to trust him. After her husband's stroke, first lady Sylvia Bongo called him back to Gabon when she suspected that her husband's half-brother Frédéric Bongo was possibly fomenting a coup. Oligui Nguema subsequently became commander-in-chief of the Republican Guard, replacing Grégoire Kouna, Omar Bongo's nephew from the paternal branch, who had reached retirement age.

On 23 October, Frédéric Bongo was dismissed from the army by Oligui Nguema. Frédéric flew to Paris, where he procured legal representation for forthcoming battles over his family's vast offshore wealth. Already on 12 October, Sylvia Bongo, suspected of embezzling public funds, had been jailed. Charged on 28 September with money laundering, forgery, and falsification of records, she remained under house arrest in Libreville after the coup brought down the curtain on decades of dynastic pilfering.

On 7 September, President Oligui Nguema appointed Raymond Ndong Sima as *new prime minister of the transitional government*. Sima was an outspoken Fang critic of Ali Bongo. Originally a PDG baron, he had served as Ali Bongo's prime minister from 2012 to 2014, then resigned to run against him for president in 2016, and again ran against him as part of an opposition coalition in 2023. On 8 September, General Oligui Nguema decided to call in political heavyweights to serve in Sima's first government – figures who were close to his predecessors, Omar and Ali Bongo. He reappointed former 'barons' to head the institutions they had managed previously (the National Assembly, Senate, Cabinet of Ministers, and Constitutional Court, and the Economic and Social Council) thereby asserting his seizure of power with the 'selectorate' (elites whose support is necessary for the survival of any authoritarian regime) by ensuring continuity with the past. These reappointments led to satirical weekly 'The Nganga' calling the August coup 'a rupture without a real rupture'.

But on 6 October, General Oligui, realising the danger he had created, put some of his own loyal men in key positions, and in late September he made sweeping appointments, surrounding himself with military personnel, figures from the provinces of Haut-Ogooué and Woleu-Ntem and a handful of Bongo clanspeople who had been unhappy with the Valentin-Bongo branch's efforts to transfer power to Noureddin. Changes came to both the *visible and the invisible power structures* of Gabon. On 20 October, the Freemasons chose Jacques Denis Tsanga to replace Ali Bongo as Grand Master of the Grande Loge du Gabon.

Foreign Affairs

On 19 January, Noureddin Bongo (acting in his capacity as a private businessman) set up a new London investment firm. It was an open secret that *the Bongo dynasty had embezzled billions of dollars* into 'offshore' trusts over 66 years in power, so this so-called 'business' news was not very surprising. But efforts to prosecute it in

France had nevertheless failed. French justice suspected several members of the family of having 'knowingly' benefited from a significant real estate asset 'fraudulently' acquired in France by their patriarch, president of Gabon from 1967 to his death in 2009. But on 15 March, the Paris Court of Appeal changed the course of French justice, reversed the roles of accuser and accused, and granted 'plaintiff' status to the government of Gabon, making it the first country involved in the long-running anti-corruption case to obtain that status, and providing the Bongos with access to the investigation file. In contrast, on 29 July 2022, five other children of Omar Bongo had been indicted in France, accused of having profited from their late father's ill-gotten real estate. Among them were Pascaline Bongo, eldest daughter and former chief of staff for her father; Omar Denis 'Junior' Bongo, grandson of Congolese president Denis Sassou Nguesso; Jeanne Matoua; and Joseph Matoua. These dynastic rivals were indicted for 'concealment of embezzlement of public funds', 'active and passive corruption', 'money laundering', and 'misuse of corporate assets'.

On 24 February, Ali Bongo and *Congolese president Denis Sassou Nguesso* appeared ready to bury the hatchet. These two neighbouring presidents, who had been on frosty terms for years, hoped to use the One Forest Summit in Libreville to set aside their grievances. One bone of contention had been the attitude of Sassou's grandson, Omar Denis 'Junior' Bongo, whom Ali Bongo believed was financing the political opposition from Brazzaville. On 21 July, the Brazzaville dowry of Omar Denis 'Junior' sparked hopes for a détente with Gabon when President Sassou gave his fiancée's family a dowry at a ceremony in Brazzaville in the presence of Omar Bongo's eldest daughter (i.e. Ali Bongo's sister) Pascaline Bongo. This *trans-dynastic diplomacy* heralded a further thaw in relations between the two clans, and thus, the two countries. After the August coup, General Oligui came to Congo on 11 October to ensure that his new regime would have support from President Sassou. Oligui's plane landed late in the morning at Ollombo airport, in the centre of the country, near Oyo, where a face-to-face meeting was held between the two men followed by lunch. Notable among the members of the welcoming committee was Omar Denis 'Junior' Bongo, whose mother, the late Edith Lucie Bongo Ondimba, had been Sassou's eldest daughter.

During the first half of the year, before the August coup, relations with *France* resembled the normal pattern of secret intrigue, public diplomacy, and scandalous judicial investigation. On 18 May, Juan Rémy Quignolot, a former French Foreign Legion soldier accused of espionage by the CAR who had been arrested by CAR authorities in 2021, was evacuated to Libreville and arrived in France three days later. His release had been the subject of intense, secret negotiations between Paris and Bangui since March, with help from the Gabonese intelligence services. On 27 June, Paris presented a military restructuring plan to Bongo and other African presidencies. The Elysée and the defence ministry held discreet consultations with a handful of African 'partners' to present the reorganisation of France's military presence on the continent.

To escape judicial investigations into his family's ill-gotten goods, President Bongo had moved offshore assets to London, sent his eldest son Noureddin to English private schools, and joined Gabon to the British Commonwealth in 2022. But the August coup reversed this trend, allowing France to bolster its long-standing position and safeguard its interests. Officially, on 30 August, France condemned the coup and called for respect for democratic institutions and processes. But shortly after taking office, on 1 September, General Oligui held talks with the French ambassador to Gabon, Alexis Lamek, as well as that embassy's head of the French external intelligence service (DGSE). Oligui was quick to convey his strategy to French authorities, emphasising his intent to strengthen ties with Paris. According to reports, he also engaged in discussions with the French government in Paris to underscore Gabon's commitment to the French presence and the continuity of the DGSE in Gabon. He made it clear to his French counterparts that the current situation in Gabon was *unrelated to the recent coups in Guinea, Burkina Faso, and Niger*, which all adopted vehemently anti-French policies.

On 12 December, General Oligui appointed a new ambassador to Paris, wanting to keep civil servants too closely linked to the former regime and former first lady Sylvia Bongo at a distance, including, therefore, the country's ambassador to France, Liliane Massala, who had headed the Gabonese embassy in Paris since September 2020 and was particularly influential under Bongo's presidency thanks to her close relationship with the former first lady. Noureddin Bongo and Massala's son Antony were close friends. Massala was replaced by Gabon's Ethiopia envoy, Marie-Edith Tassyla-Ye-Doumbeneny.

Gabon's relations with *China* were revealing of the change of direction in foreign policy since the August coup. On 4 April, then president Ali Bongo had gone to Beijing for a state visit, including a meeting with President Xi Jinping. During another April visit by Bongo, Beijing had upgraded its relations to a 'comprehensive strategic cooperative partnership', which is considered by China the highest level of bilateral relations. On the afternoon of 19 April, President Xi held talks at the Great Hall of the People with Ali Bongo. In dynastic republican style, Peng Liyuan, wife of President Xi, and Sylvia Bongo, were also present at the welcoming ceremony, which included the signing of the strategic cooperation agreement. Bongo had been openly changing sides in the global East–West conflict. But after the August coup, on 7 September, General Oligui Nguema's decisive first foreign policy step at the helm of Gabon's transitional government was to freeze Beijing's recent hard-won deal with Bongo to create a naval base in the country. Beijing had been searching for a location to build a military base along Africa's Guinea Coast. That is no longer expected to happen.

Socioeconomic Developments

Crude *oil production* in Gabon averaged 233 barrels per day (bbl/d) from 1973 to 2024. By the end of this year, production was reported at 226 bbl/d in December, an increase from 218 bbl/d in November. The traditional French oil major that had historically produced most of Gabon's oil, TotalEnergies EP Gabon, reportedly produced 158 bbl/d, which was stable compared with the previous year. Much of this oil was produced through improved operational efficiency and the first positive results from the well intervention campaign having offset the natural decline of the fields. French family firm Maurel & Prom produced 15.4 bbl/d in 2023 from its share of the Ezanga permit, an increase of 5% compared with 2022. On 17 April, British firm Tullow Oil announced that it would be getting back to its roots in oil exploration. Having reduced its debt, the British firm wanted to invest in an offshore block in Gabon.

The big *oil business news* during the year was the announced withdrawal of Assala Energy's sole shareholder, investment fund Carlyle, a move closely followed by Bongo a few months before the presidential election. Carlyle Energy specialises in private equity, real assets, and private credit and is one of the largest mega-funds in the world. On 25 January, Indonesian national energy company Pertamina had moved to take over Carlyle's Assala Energy in Gabon. The presidential palace went into discussions with Pertamina. On 20 April, the Franco-British oil junior Perenco hurried to sell its share in the Atora field before Carlyle sealed its sale of its shares. Perenco wanted to quickly sell its share for $50 m, indicating that it no longer wanted to work with the future owner of Assala Energy's majority share. The negotiations were delayed by the August coup.

Noureddin Bongo's 30 August arrest also left a whole raft of UK, US, and French consultants out of work and at a loose end. Some had been working on Ali Bongo's re-election campaign while others had already been preparing for the first months of a new term. On 7 November, it was reported that the junta was tracking down Noureddin's dubious London assets. Since the August coup, the new government had been trying to get to grips with a tangle of offshore assets held in Dubai and London by Noureddin and his associates. On 6 November, it prepared to pre-empt the sale of Carlyle's oil assets. Until the August coup, Maurel & Prom had been the best-placed bidder for US investment group Carlyle's Gabonese oil interests. But the new junta in Libreville arranged an alternative all-Gabonese take-over plan. On 20 December, it was reported that General Oligui had instructed oil minister Marcel Abéké to do all he could to bring in fresh funds and take back control of certain fields. Carlyle's oil assets appeared to be the key target of this decree.

On 30 September, involved in tricky negotiations because of his long-standing business relations with the Bongo clan, Indian tycoon Gagan Gupta also tried to save his investments in Arise Integrated Industrial Platform. General Oligui met with Gupta, who was close to Noureddin Bongo. But Gupta spent several days of enforced waiting before being allowed to meet with the new transitional ruler. On 19 May, an independent assessment commissioned by the Forest Stewardship Council concluded that Olam Palm Gabon had cleared over 24,000 hectares of forest, as well as between 900 and 1,823 hectares of non-forest areas with high conservation value. This was the basis of the complaint that Mighty Earth filed with the Forest Stewardship Council (FSC) in 2016. In May 2019, Mighty Earth and Olam entered into an alternative dispute resolution process. 'Olam and Arise are shell companies all belonging to Bongo and their associates', was the comment on social media sites, in an accusation widely shared by Gabonese observers. 'Gagan Gupta had never invested in Gabon; he had only participated in embezzlement.'

On 11 September, oil companies with business interests in Gabon were being called to account. On 19 September, despite officially denying that it was carrying out an audit, Gabon's Ministry of Hydrocarbons had asked the oil companies operating there to provide a list of all payments made to the state from 2020 to 2023. Perenco, Maurel & Prom, and Assala remained calm after the coup. Oil operators in the country continued to produce oil and worked to build good relations with the new power, whose choices of oil and gas officials were reassuringly well-known figures.

On 18 October, the new oil minister Marcel Abéké faced a challenge from foreign investors, having announced new measures aimed at improving the country's drawing power with foreign operators. Yet his efforts had little impact on his intended audience, whose interest had already waned before the coup. On 19 October, rivals Maurel & Prom hoped for the post-coup reallocation of Carlyle's assets. The new regime in Libreville needed to give its verdict on the planned sale of Carlyle's oil assets in Gabon to Maurel & Prom. Ali Bongo's government did not formally approve the deal, and some disappointed parties believed they had an opportunity to get back into the running with the new transitional government. But the affair had still not been closed by year's end. On 20 November, Perenco was in the junta's crosshairs, as General Oligui Nguema's administration investigated the alleged links between the country's leading oil operator and two members of the Bongo family.

São Tomé and Príncipe

Gerhard Seibert

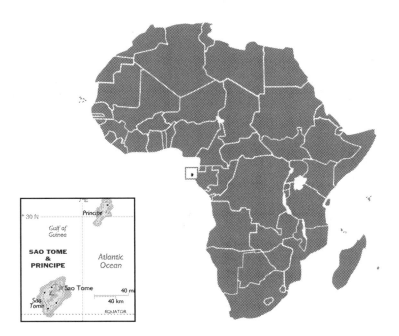

Altogether, 30 members of the miliary and one civilian were charged with crimes committed on 25 November 2022 in the context of an armed attack on army barracks that had been thwarted. Pressured by the IMF, the government introduced a 15% VAT to increase revenue. Prime minister Patrice Trovoada spent most of his time on official travelling abroad. An investment by a Turkish company in the energy sector was expected to end recurrent power cuts.

Domestic Politics

The shocking details of the violent repression of an armed attack in the previous year continued to provide major headlines. Following the detention of six military personnel in December 2022, on 10 February another *five members of the military were put in pretrial detention* for their involvement in the death of four detainees on 25 November 2022. According to the criminal investigation report released by the public prosecutor on 23 February, 14 men had been actively involved in the assault on the barracks, including two former Buffalo soldiers (Santomeans who served in Apartheid South Africa's 32 'Buffalo' Battalion), Arlécio Costa and Gonçalo Evaristo Bonfim, who were both killed in detention, together with two others. The public prosecutor charged eight suspects, all young soldiers except for one civilian called Bruno Lima Afonso, with the violent change of the rule of law, attempted homicide, mayhem, and possession and use of prohibited arms. The proceedings against Delfim Neves and six other suspects were filed due to a lack of evidence.

On 16 March, *the public prosecutor charged 23 military personnel*, including former chief of general staff of the armed forces Olinto Paquete, vice-chief of general staff Armindo Rodrigues, and Colonel José Maria Menezes, for their involvement in the atrocities committed in the aftermath of the failed assault on 25 November. Twenty soldiers were charged for their active participation in 14 cases of torture and four cases of homicide. The three high-ranking miliary officers were additionally charged with omission, since they had failed to prevent the crimes. In June, the proceedings against Paquete for torture and homicide were halted due to a lack of evidence, but the accusation of crimes of omission was maintained.

On 31 August, eight detainees accused of participation in the assault on the barracks who had been detained since 28 November 2022 were released, since the nine months' maximum for preventive detention had expired. On 25 September, the court postponed the trial of Afonso and ruled that the seven soldiers had to be judged by a military court. Consequently, on 23 November, *a 15-member military tribunal was established*. Only one of its members had graduated in law, while the other judges from the security forces lacked legal training. Finally, on 20 December, a court sentenced Afonso to 17 years of imprisonment, including two on probation, and payment to the state of a fine of $9,000. His defence lawyers announced that they would appeal the verdict at the Supreme Court.

As demanded by the IMF, on 19 May, the *National Assembly adopted a law on the introduction of VAT* from 1 June. The general VAT rate was to be 15%, while a reduced 7.5% rate was applied to several essential goods. In addition, special regimes of 7% and 2% VAT were to be charged for businesses with reduced turnover. VAT was expected to increase the state's tax revenue and broaden the tax base. On 13 December, Mário Sousa, the director of taxes, revealed that since its introduction the Ministry of Finance had collected VAT of 240 m São Toméan dobra (STN; €9.7 m), significantly more than the STN 183 m (€7.4 m) originally expected.

On 1 June, the ruling Acção Democrática Independente (ADI) and Movimento de Cidadãos Independentes – Partido de União Nacional (MCI-PUN) in the National Assembly adopted a *law on the compulsory retirement for judges older than 62 years*. Consequently, four judges of the Constitutional Court, all considered government opponents, were forced to retire, leaving the court with only one judge. The law was widely considered as retaliation since in 2019 the four removed judges had cancelled a decision in favour of returning the disputed Rosema brewery to its former owners António and Domingos Monteiro, the MCI leaders. On 15 June, the National Assembly, with the votes of the ADI and the MCI-PUN, appointed four new judges to the Constitutional Court. On 11 July, they announced their first decision: the return of the Rosema brewery to the Monteiro brothers. Angolan businessman Mello Xavier, who in 2018 had regained control of the brewery thanks to a Supreme Court verdict, fiercely protested, but in vain.

On 28 July, *foreign minister Alberto Pereira resigned* following controversial declarations that Portugal and Angola had not sufficiently promoted the teaching of Portuguese in Equatorial Guinea, a former Spanish colony and since 2014 the ninth CPLP member state. On 9 August, Trovoada entrusted Gareth Guadalupe, the minister of the presidency of the council of ministers and parliamentary affairs, to additionally assume Pereira's portfolio until the formal appointment of a new foreign minister.

Foreign Relations

In contrast to his predecessor Jorge Bom Jesus, Prime Minister Patrice Trovoada continuously travelled abroad on official missions. June was a particularly busy travel month.

On 18 February, minister of finance Genésio da Mata and Angola's minister of state for economic coordination, Manuel Nunes Junior, signed a bilateral agreement of economic cooperation. Mata declared that the agreement would open new business opportunities and *reschedule São Tomé's huge debts with Angola*, including the $252 m debts of fuel company ENCO with Sonangol and $68 m of bilateral debts.

From 5–9 March, Trovoada headed a government delegation at the 5th UN Conference on the Least Developed Countries (LDC) in Doha, Qatar. STP was included in a list of LDCs expected to *be graduated into the category of middle-income country (MIC)* in 2024, a promotion achieved by only six countries since 1994. The country had met two of the three criteria (income and human assets) for the first time in 2015 and for the second time in 2018. In his address, Trovoada said that the international community had to support his country's fight against poverty and for greater economic growth to enable it to successfully make the transition to MIC.

From 19–20 March, National Assembly president Celmira Sacramento (ADI) participated in the *Second International Parliamentary Russia–Africa Conference* held in the State Duma in Moscow. In her address, Sacramento stressed her country's historical relations with Russia, which had always supported the independence struggle and university education. Nevertheless, on 23 February, STP had been one of the 141 countries which voted in favour of the UN resolution to end Russia's war against Ukraine.

On 27 April, Trovoada headed a government delegation on a 24-hour visit to Malabo, where he was received by Equatorial Guinea's president, Teodoro Obiang Nguema, and his son and designated successor, vice-president Teodoro Nguema Obiang Mangue (Teodorín). The talks on bilateral cooperation included funding part of the costs for the CPLP summit in STP in August.

Although STP was not invited, on 6 May, *Trovoada participated in the coronation of King Charles III* and Queen Camilla in London. Upon his return, he justified the trip by claiming that what was most important was his presence and the opportunity he had to meet with several delegations, including the presidents of Brazil and Angola, with whom he had also spoken about the financing of the CPLP summit in STP.

On 5 and 6 June, Trovoada participated in Abidjan (*Côte d'Ivoire*) in the Africa CEO Forum, co-hosted by Jeune Afrique Media Group and the IFC. On the sidelines of the Forum, Trovoada was received by Ivorian president Alassane Ouattara and met other participants. On 8 June, in Washington DC, Trovoada met Anna Bjerde, the World Bank's managing director for operations, with whom he discussed his government's inclusive growth agenda and options for energy transition and expanding electricity access. On 11 June, in Brasília, Trovoada was consecutively received by *Brazil*'s finance minister, Fernando Haddad, Admiral Jose Augusto Vieira da Cunha de Menezes, Chief of Staff of the Navy, and foreign minister Mauro Vieira. Vieira declared that Trovoada's visit marked the resumption of the priority given to African countries as part of President Lula da Silva's foreign policy. From 18–21 June, Trovoada attended the 30th annual meeting of Afreximbank held in Accra, *Ghana*. In his address, he complained about the migration of young educated African professionals to Europe. He appealed to African leaders to give hope to their youth and managers so that they would remain in their home countries.

On 14 July, Trovoada, accompanied by his wife Nana and the ministers Mata and Guadalupe, paid an *official one-day visit to Kigali*, where they were received by president Paul Kagame and first lady Jeannette Kagame. Trovoada declared that the visit's objective was to resume economic and technological cooperation with Rwanda, established in 2017 during his previous government. On 19 and 20 July, Trovoada visited *Chad* and *Congo* (Brazzaville) where he was received by transitional president Mahamat Idriss Déby and president Dennis Sassou Nguesso respectively. With both heads of state, Trovoada discussed bilateral cooperation and issues related to the CEEAC, including regional cooperation, climate change, terrorism, and poverty.

On 27 August, *STP hosted the CPLP's 14th biannual Summit of Heads of State and Government*, at which the theme was 'Youth and Sustainability'. The summit adopted economic cooperation between the members as the organisation's new general objective. At the meeting, STP's president Carlos Vila Nova took over the CPLP's two-year rotating chairship from Angola's João Lourenço.

On 20 September, Trovoada addressed the 78th annual UNGA in New York. He claimed that his country was one of the main victims of climate change, the degradation of ecosystems, and economic dependence. He argued that the leaders of the G20 were responsible for the climate crisis and that international financial institutions continued to ignore his government's social and environmental objectives, denying access to necessary financial resources. He condemned both the Russian invasion of Ukraine and the increasing number of coups in Africa. On the sidelines of the UNGA, Trovoada participated together with his wife Nana in a reception offered by US president Joe Biden and first lady Jill Biden.

From 10–11 October, in Bali, Trovoada participated in the First High-Level Meeting of the *Archipelagic and Island States Forum* (AIS Forum). The meeting was attended by 32 of the 51 AIS countries, including Japan and the UK. On the sidelines of the forum, Trovoada was received by *Indonesia*'s president Joko Widodo and met *East Timor*'s prime minister Xanana Gusmao.

On 13 October, *Trovoada chaired a donor roundtable* organised by the IMF Africa Department in Marrakech (*Morocco*). He claimed that foreign donors had pledged a total of $160 m in assistance for the period 2024–26. On 17 October, in London, Trovoada was one of the invited speakers at the Tenth Africa Summit of the 'Financial Times'. On the 25th, Trovoada left on his own initiative for a one-day trip to Kinshasa, where he met DRC president Félix Tshisekedi to mediate in the tensions between the DRC and Rwanda.

Socioeconomic Developments

On 14 January, the government suspended the agreement on the management of the *port authority* Empresa Nacional de Administração dos Portos (ENAPORT), signed by the former executive in 2022 with the Ghanaian Safebond Consortium, arguing that it was prejudicial to national interests. On 20 December, minister of infrastructure Adelino Cardoso signed instead a five-year management contract for STP's port with Africa Global Logistics (AGL), a subsidiary of the Geneva-based Mediterranean Shipping Company (MSC). Seven days later, the ENAPORT workers' union threatened to go on strike if the agreement was not cancelled, since it would violate workers' rights.

On 8 March, the *inter-island ship service was resumed* when the Greek-built passenger and cargo ship 'Olivia C', owned by a local Portuguese businessman, made its first voyage from São Tomé to Príncipe island. The regular inter-island sea connection had been interrupted following the shipwreck of the 'Anfitrit' in April 2019, when 17 passengers drowned. Filipe Nascimento, president of Príncipe's regional government, declared that he hoped the new vessel would ease Príncipe's double insularity. Return passage from São Tomé on the new ship cost $130, while a return flight between the islands was $270.

On 29 April, the Angolan-owned UNITEL, the country's second-largest telecommunications provider with a 17% market share, was the first in STP *to introduce 4G mobile service*. Inoweze Ferreira, UNITEL's general manager in São Tomé, declared that the introduction was the first step in speeding up the process of transforming the country's digital economy. On 8 August, the Companhia Santomense de Telecomunicações (CST) followed, launching its own 4G service. At the ceremony, Jorge Frazão, the Portuguese CEO of CST, said that the new service, with an investment of €2.3 m, would cover 90% of the national territory and would practice lower tariffs than previous ones.

On 23 October, Trovoada announced an agreement with the Turkish company EB Group on the supply and operation of five new diesel generators worth €11 m in the thermoelectric power station of the public energy utility Empresa de Água e Electricidade (EMAE) in the capital. These would increase *electricity production* from 12 mw to 22 mw, above national demand – estimated at 19 mw. Under the agreement, the state supplied EB Group with all necessary fuel free of charge. For the duration of the agreement, the company was exempted from all tax payments. Following the installation of the new generators, on 26 December, EMAE announced the resumption of regular electricity supply after months of constant power cuts.

On 27 December, *Brazil's oil company Petrobras* signed a farm-in deal with Shell with stakes of 45% in EEZ (exclusive economic zone) blocks 10 and 13 and 25% in block 11. Shell remained the operator in the three blocks, where it kept a 40% interest in each. The National Oil Agency (ANP) held the usual 15% stake in each of the three blocks, while Portuguese Galp Energia's 20% participation in block 11 remained unchanged. Petrobras' decision marked both its first engagement in the archipelago and its return to the African continent, from which it had completely withdrawn in 2018 following several corruption investigations as part of Brazil's Lava Jato operation (2014–21).

PART 5

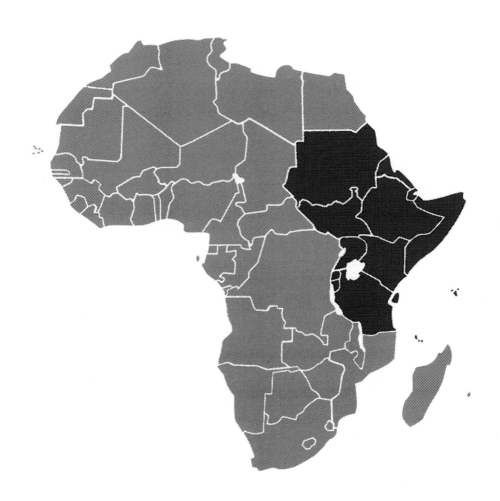

Eastern Africa

Benedikt Kamski

Despite earlier hopes, the Greater Horn of Africa again faced major challenges in 2023, raising doubts about its trajectory towards lasting peace and stability. Eastern Africa grappled with several new issues, including the delayed implementation of the peace agreement in Ethiopia and the outbreak of a deadly new conflict in Sudan in April. Additionally, concerns arose over Ethiopia's claims to Red Sea access, which were voiced multiple times by government officials throughout the year, indirectly alienating the country's neighbours. The ongoing crisis caused by the M23 insurgency in eastern DRC triggered multi-layered bilateral tensions across the Great Lakes region. Amid these challenges, Kenya attempted to position itself as a diplomatic and economic pillar under President William Ruto's leadership. Eastern Africa also held the AU chair, with Comoros actively putting the issues faced by Small Island Developing States on the continental agenda. Maritime trade flows through the Gulf of Aden and the Bab al-Mandeb Strait saw major disruptions towards the end of the year due to an increase in attacks on commercial ships by Houthi rebels from Yemen, affecting global trade flows through the Suez Canal and directly impacting supply chains in Eastern Africa by year's end.

IGAD's efforts to mediate in the Sudan conflict and support peace agreement implementation in Ethiopia had limited success, once more highlighting the organisation's challenges in fulfilling its mandate. Conversely, Somalia was admitted to the EAC, expanding the bloc to eight member states and increasing the potential for regional trade. However, Somalia's admission, coupled with the ongoing security and governance challenges in the DRC and South Sudan, could eventually have the opposite effect and weaken the EAC as an REC. Despite these concerns, the upgrade of the Addis Ababa–Djibouti transport corridor, financed by the World Bank, marked another important step towards regional economic integration.

Both conflict and climate change affected regional dynamics during the year. Prolonged floods and droughts, along with people fleeing war zones, significantly increased the number of IDPs and regional refugees, particularly impacting Burundi, Ethiopia, Somalia, South Sudan, and Sudan. The aggregated number of food-insecure people across the region surpassed 60 m by the end of the year.

Despite these growing crises, Eastern Africa showed economic resilience. The region had the highest number of countries with growth rates exceeding 5%. Especially high inflation rates could impact the outlook for achieving the SDGs in the medium term, reflecting a broader continental trend. The debt crisis, which influenced economic trajectories across the continent and will continue to do so, took its toll also on the sub-region, as seen in the overall contraction of growth.

Further challenges loom, with scheduled debt repayments for 2024 for several states, stalled negotiations with creditors, and the announcement of austerity programmes. The outlook for 2024 was therefore mixed.

Political Developments

Eastern Africa was not spared the significant repercussions of multiple global crises and novel geopolitical divides. Instability increased especially across the Greater Horn of Africa and the Great Lakes region. The region felt the direct impact of global developments, which triggered the further escalation and prolongation of conflict in Sudan and exacerbating existing bilateral tensions. Renewed agitation for political change was evident across several countries, especially in Kenya, where sporadic demonstrations against President Ruto during his first year in office foreshadowed growing discontent over debt- and inflation-related austerity measures and the government's failure at economic inclusion.

There were early indications that the region could see *political shifts* in the years to come. In Rwanda, the ruling Rwandan Patriotic Front (RPF) changed its leadership structure, which could be interpreted as a generational shift. Yet President Paul Kagame, who took office in 2000, also announced his candidacy for the 2024 presidential elections. Similar dynamics were observed in Burundi, where President Évariste Ndayishimiye dismissed a number of senior party members and recruited young technocrats, despite challenges from the ruling party.

Long-serving leaders such as Uganda's Yoweri Museveni, Eritrea's Isaias Afwerki, and Djibouti's Ismaïl Omar Guelleh were confronted with growing demand for political change. President Guelleh has officially announced that he will not run in 2026, but it remained unclear who would succeed him within the ruling-party coalition. All indications were that for a planned transition, a handpicked successor would be chosen in the foreseeable future. Meanwhile, more speculations emerged that Muhoozi Kainerugaba, the son of President Museveni, might be preparing for a presidential bid in Uganda. Additionally, concerns about political stability in Eritrea were growing. However, despite the increasingly ageing leadership of the ruling People's Front for Democracy and Justice (PFDJ) and the lack of scheduled elections, the prospects for political change remained difficult to determine. President Isaias rose again above the country's status as sub-regional pariah and repositioned Eritrea as a major military player in the region following the war in Tigray and ongoing fighting in the region of Amhara in Ethiopia. In South Sudan, President Salva Kiir announced his candidacy for the long-awaited December 2024 elections, yet by the end of the year it was still unclear whether elections would take place, despite the passing of an amended National Election Act. In Comoros, the unofficial phase of the presidential election campaign began during the second half of the year amid a fragmented political landscape. President Azali Assoumani, also the current AU chair, was running for a fourth term in the January 2024 election. The opposition called for a boycott, citing fear of irregularities and interference by the security forces.

More promising developments could be observed early in the year in Tanzania, where President Samia Suluhu Hassan lifted the ban on political rallies as part of the '4Rs' strategy (Reconciliation, Resilience, Reform, and Rebuild). The lifting of the ban also prompted the return of exiled politicians and fuelled hope for increased political inclusivity ahead of the 2025 elections.

Djibouti held parliamentary *elections* in February, which went largely unnoticed and produced no surprises, with the ruling party securing 58 out of 65 seats. Conversely, Seychelles witnessed the establishment of new political parties, signalling a promising path towards more secure political pluralism. Overall, political dynamics in Eastern Africa were characterised by a mix of enduring leadership, growing public discontent, and evolving electoral landscapes.

The year 2022 had ended on an overall *promising note in Sudan and Ethiopia*. The signing of a framework agreement in Khartoum indicated a return to the democratic transition process that had stalled with the military coups of 2021. Similarly, the *Cessation of Hostilities Agreement (CoHA)* of November 2022 marked the official end of combat operations in Ethiopia and set out conditions for peaceful dialogue between the Tigray region and the federal government. However, in Sudan, the failure to integrate the paramilitary Rapid Support Forces (RSF) into the national forces, as defined in the framework agreement, led to a full-out war in April with no viable solution in sight by year's end. Efforts to mediate the conflict, including international interventions by various stakeholders, failed completely, resulting in severe economic decline and a humanitarian crisis. In Ethiopia, the delayed implementation of the CoHA led to increased fragmentation among political and armed groups. The rise of the armed Fano movement led to a worsening of the already fragile security environment in Amhara and armed confrontations continued throughout the year, forcing the government to declare a state of emergency in August. As in Sudan, this was triggered largely by an attempt to integrate regional forces and rebel movements, such as the Fano, into the national forces. In the Oromia region, the armed insurgency led by the Oromo Liberation Army (OLA) persisted. Peace talks between the OLA military leadership and the federal government in May failed to reach an agreement and large parts of Oromia remained in a state of lawlessness and lack of state control.

Following long negotiations, the Somali federal government and regional leaders agreed on major reforms to introduce universal suffrage and direct elections for the office of the president, national representatives, and local and regional councils, with local elections set for June 2024. However, these reforms encountered opposition, resulting in armed clashes and some regions declaring autonomy. Overall,

Somalia remained in a state of insecurity amid these growing political tensions. Despite the government's renewed and coordinated efforts to combat terrorism, al-Shabaab (Harakat al-Shabaab al-Mujahideen) was the most significant threat to stability, having developed enhanced operational skills and persistent attacks throughout the country. ISIL-Somalia's growing presence in Puntland added another destabilising element to the security landscape.

Growing instability in the Great Lakes region, fuelled by complex alliances involving several militias backed by Rwanda, the Congolese army, and Burundi, exacerbated regional instability and triggered a new humanitarian crisis. In eastern DRC, the year was marked by intensified clashes between M23 rebels and government forces. Kinshasa refused to negotiate with the well-equipped M23, which was allegedly receiving support from Rwanda.

Much related to the novel escalation of conflicts as well as growing political fragmentation in already weak states of the region, Eastern Africa faced significant *human rights challenges*. Yet there were also positive efforts and steps taken towards improvement. For example, the peace agreement in Ethiopia and the announcement of a domestic-led transitional justice mechanism fuelled renewed hope for an inclusive national dialogue process. Nevertheless, ongoing conflicts in the Amhara region and a prolonged state of emergency highlighted the need for continued focus on accountability and stability after the end of the civil war. Similarly, South Sudan's legislative developments, including ratifying the AU Protocol on the Rights of Women in Africa, were promising, even though systematic repression of media and civil society remained of high concern. Meanwhile, in Burundi, the expansion of the Truth and Reconciliation Commission to include the diaspora indicated a renewed commitment to addressing past injustices in a more inclusive manner. However, justice reforms still needed fulfilment, and reports of human rights violations persisted.

Under particular threat was the *LGBTQ+ community*. The escalation of legal restrictions and violence, with governments enacting stricter laws and increasing persecution despite international condemnation, was a concerning and dangerous trend. Uganda enacted a new Anti-Homosexuality Act in May that criminalised same-sex acts with severe penalties, including the death penalty for 'aggravated homosexuality'. In Tanzania, the LGBTQ+ community also faced increasing restrictions and arrests, with social media accounts closed and advocacy organisations deregistered. Similarly, Ethiopia's LGBTQ+ community reported a surge in online and physical attacks in August 2023, primarily due to incitement on TikTok. Following Uganda's anti-homosexuality legislation, Kenyan MP George Peter Kaluma proposed a bill to criminalise LGBTQ+ activities, which naturally heightened fears among LGBTQ+ individuals and human rights advocates.

The region, as in previous years, showed mixed progress and little notable improvement on *press freedom*. In its 2024 World Press Freedom report (based on

2023 data), RSF ranked Eritrea unchanged at 180th out of 180 states, with Djibouti (161st), Sudan (149th), Somalia (145th), Rwanda (144th), and Ethiopia (141st) again among the worst performers in the region. Seychelles, the best performer for more than a decade, dropped three ranks to 37th.

Corruption challenges remained prevalent across Eastern Africa, with varying degrees of efforts to combat the misappropriation of funds. Somalia, despite ranking last (180th out of 180 states) in Transparency International's 2023 Corruption Perceptions Index, made some progress with new anti-corruption legislation and high-profile trials, though significant governance challenges remained. Somalia scored 11 on a scale of 0 to 100, marking it as highly corrupt. Seychelles again stood out positively, ranking 20th out of 180 and first in SSA. However, the country faced high-profile corruption cases, including money laundering still linked to the Pandora Papers leak. Ethiopia dropped again in its ranking, falling from 94th in 2022 to 98th in 2023. Eritrea (score: 21) was grappling with military corruption, with bribery among army officials, including cases of human trafficking and smuggling, reportedly rampant. In Djibouti (score: 30), a political system deeply intertwined with corruption and patronage particularly affected the transportation and logistics sectors, hindering development. In contrast, Rwanda (score: 53) presented a more positive picture, with a zero-tolerance strategy towards corruption. Overall, despite established anti-corruption institutions and novel legislation, impunity and collusion persisted with few notable exceptions. Moreover, anti-corruption initiatives carried the risk of political abuse to eliminate political rivals, as it happened in Comoros with the case of former president Ahmed Abdallah Sambi, as well as other instances across the region.

Transnational Relations and Regional Conflict Configurations

The *geopolitical and geoeconomic landscape* of Eastern Africa became more complex in 2023, with the emergence of new and shifting alliances. This complexity can be linked to global conflicts such as those in the Middle East and the war between Russia and Ukraine. Additionally, the so-called 'Gulf Scramble for Africa', involving the UAE, Saudi Arabia, and Qatar actively competing to expand their political and economic as well as cultural-religious influence in the region, was creating new geoeconomic and geopolitical dynamics. These dynamics are complex to understand and analyse due to the intricate interplay of regional and international interests, shifting alliances, and the varying economic and political strategies of the Gulf states. They also affect future cooperation with other global partners such as Russia, China, the US, and the EU.

While the involvement of *Gulf states* promised substantial economic benefits for individual countries, it also risked exacerbating existing conflicts, as evidenced very clearly in Sudan. The Emirati role in the region was pivotal, crystallising a number of alliances. The UAE, openly aligned with Ethiopia, supported the RSF in Sudan, and positioned itself in contrast to Saudi interests especially in Sudan. Türkiye's involvement was also notable, as it supplied drones to Ethiopia for the Tigray conflict and the Turkish Armed Forces remained a central partner in Somalia's maritime security. Overall, the multitude of foreign players increased the pressure on all countries in the region to either choose sides or remain neutral, forced to navigate a delicate balance of power.

The US seemingly focused on countering the UAE's influence in the Horn of Africa. This involved a multifaceted strategy of increasing support for Somali governance, enhancing military presence in Djibouti, and mediating regional disputes. Additionally, the growing bilateral ties of Eritrea with China, Russia, and Saudi Arabia – significantly, the president, who usually shies away from travel, visited all of these countries during the year under review – raised alarm bells for the US administration. Eritrea's strategic location at the Red Sea makes it a potentially valuable partner for both China and Russia, who are seeking to expand their influence across the region, including the Red Sea. In February, Russian foreign minister Sergey Lavrov announced that Russia was awaiting legislative approval from Sudan for a long-planned naval base on the Red Sea. Given the de facto absence of a functioning government, a final decision was not made. Russia's quest for a naval base on the Red Sea could further complicate the strategic balance in the region, adding another layer of complexity to the already intricate geopolitical landscape.

Similar to *US initiatives*, *the EU* showed renewed commitment to aligning international efforts for stability in the Horn of Africa. The visit of the EU special envoy to the Horn, Annette Weber, to the UAE underscored the EU's interest in supporting negotiations for a ceasefire and political resolution in Sudan. Also, the foreign ministers of Germany and France jointly travelled to Ethiopia, and the growing list of 'special envoys' for the Horn and Red Sea from China, the US, and Europe, continued their engagement.

Security in the Red Sea remained a significant concern due to ongoing conflicts and attacks on commercial shipping. The Israel–Hamas conflict in Gaza and related Houthi maritime attacks disrupted shipping routes, leading major carriers to suspend Red Sea transits. These disruptions had economic implications for regional ports, affecting their revenue and operations, as well as disrupting wider supply chains in the sub-region. This was an additional strain following the repercussions for global logistics of the Covid-19 pandemic and delays to shipments of goods especially following the Russian invasion of Ukraine. Operation Prosperity Guardian, a US-led military initiative launched in December, aimed to protect commercial shipping in the Red Sea from Iran-backed Houthi rebels in Yemen. Piracy incidents off the coast of Eastern Africa had declined considerably during 2022. However, in reaction to these novel maritime security challenges, the EU announced in January the extension of the mandate of the Naval Force Operation Atalanta until the end of 2024.

Commercial seaport access was a critical issue in this context. The Suez Canal, a vital source of income for Egypt's economy as well as transhipment hubs such as Djibouti, reached record revenue of $9.4 bn in 2023, according to estimates of the EIU. However, at the same time, the ports in Sudan, Eritrea, Djibouti, and Somaliland faced reduced vessel availability and increased costs. By contrast, ports such as Mombasa, Dar es Salaam, and Beira saw increased traffic from the Persian Gulf but still relied on the Suez Canal, leading to higher costs and delays.

Meanwhile, France and Djibouti launched a review of their defence agreement, significant since Paris maintained its largest overseas military base in Djibouti. This review reflected broader security concerns and the shifting strategic priorities in the region.

In August, Ethiopia's acceptance into BRICS+, along with Egypt, represented a major diplomatic achievement for the Horn of Africa. With the country set to officially join the group on 1 January 2024, Ethiopia's inclusion is hailed as a regional triumph, even though the economic advantages have yet to be fully determined. With Addis Ababa and Cairo continued to be entangled in bilateral disputes over the use of the waters of the Blue Nile, both countries joining the group of states of BRICS+ came as a surprise. In July, Ethiopian prime minister Abiy Ahmed visited Cairo to revive talks regarding the Grand Ethiopia Renaissance Dam (GERD), which Ethiopia had announced as 90% complete in April and for which the fourth filling was finalised in September. A joint statement with Egyptian president Abdel Fattah al-Sisi aimed to finalise an agreement over the use of the Blue Nile within four months. By the end of the year, no binding agreement had been reached. Ethiopia also criticised a League of Arab States resolution in May, arguing that the issue should not be politicised and should involve only Nile riparian countries, accusing Egypt of adhering to colonial-era water allocation stances.

In 2023, the *nature of warfare in Eastern Africa* underwent a significant shift as paramilitary forces increasingly challenged national armies and state structures. This trend was particularly evident in the civil war in Sudan, where by October, territorial control was unclear between the RSF and SAF, including in the capital Khartoum. Throughout the year, the fighting intensified in brutality, with freelance militias and regional powers further complicating the situation. A similar pattern was also observed in DRC and in Ethiopia. In Ethiopia, militias in the Amhara and Oromia regions fought against federal and regional government forces, forming unclear alliances and disrupting national army command structures. In eastern DRC, the government continued to refuse negotiations with the *M23 rebel movement* about its future, including political integration and entry into the army. M23, drawing from the Congolese Tutsi community, was well equipped and organised, resembling a national army. Meanwhile, the Congolese army remained weak and disorganised, relying on weapons from China and Russia. By December, the East African Force of troops from Burundi, Kenya, South Sudan, and Uganda, had withdrawn from eastern Congo as Kinshasa still refused to negotiate under the current conditions. As a result, DRC – Kenya relations were tense, and DRC – Burundi relations were also strained due to Burundi's unilateral military actions against M23. Uganda had troops in eastern DRC and potentially supported M23, hence also complicating relations with Rwanda. Rwanda was accused of supporting M23, providing weapons, recruits, and intelligence, which it denied. Diplomatic relations between DRC and Rwanda were severed, with both countries accusing each other of misconduct.

Another area of growing strategic significance was the *Western Indian Ocean*, with African coastal countries relying on ports dominated by trade with Indian Ocean nations and China. These nations are expected to see significant population and economic growth over the next 25 years. China has strengthened ties with Comoros and other African Indian Ocean island states, highlighted by its ongoing observer status in regional organisations, reflecting the importance of strategic and cooperative climate action in the region.

In September, Kenya hosted the first African Climate Summit (ACS) in Nairobi, focusing on climate justice, green growth, and finance solutions for Africa and emphasising increased investment in the continent. President Wavel Ramkalawan of Seychelles also used his speech during the UNGA in September to call for global cooperation on *climate change*, ocean conservation, sustainable development, and maritime security. COP28 was another venue for countries of the region to emphasise the growing threats of climate change and its economic implications. The growing recognising of the 'blue economy' at continental, regional, and national levels could further booster novel funding mechanisms and cooperation agreements.

Socioeconomic Developments

Eastern African countries showed varied *economic performance* in terms of GDP growth, inflation, and debt. The region's growth averaged 3.5% according to AfDB estimates. Notably, Eastern Africa had the most countries of any SSA region with GDP growth exceeding 5%, including Rwanda (7.6%), Ethiopia (6.1%), Tanzania (5.2%), and Uganda (5.3%). Kenya also performed well, with 5.6% growth, driven by agriculture, services, and household consumption.

Inflation trends remained concerning yet showed a declining tendency. Djibouti's inflation reduced from 11% to 1.2%, Uganda's inflation dropped to 2.7% while Tanzania was equally able to control inflation at 3.8%. In Comoros, inflation fell from 12.4% to 9.1%, and Rwanda's dropped from 21.7% to 11.2%. By contrast, Ethiopia's official inflation remained high, at 34.2%, in March but had dropped to 30% by December, according to government estimates. Burundi also grappled with high inflation, at 30%. High inflation in Africa is problematic because it erodes purchasing power and increases the cost of living, making essentials such as food and healthcare less affordable and pushing more people into poverty. It also deters investment by creating economic instability. Both Ethiopia and Burundi are cases in point.

Eritrea presented a unique case regarding loan financing and its *debt situation*. During a visit by AfDB president Akin Adesina in September, President Afwerki described the bank as a 'partner of choice' in advancing sustainable economic development. However, Eritrea operates without a national budget. If the AfDB extends loans to Eritrea, the funds are directed to the ruling PFDJ or the government-controlled Red Sea Corporation, both of which have been targeted by sanctions for international criminal activities. In this regard, it is also noteworthy that the AfDB largely relies on payments from Western countries and the creditworthiness of its Western shareholders. According to AfDB estimates, Eritrea had the highest debt-to-GDP ratio in the region, at 164.7%. Kenya's public debt was 69.1% of GDP, Burundi's was 72.7%, and Ethiopia's stood at 46.37%. Uganda's public debt reached 52% and South Sudan's was 54%, compounded by political instability. Comoros' debt rose to 38.2% of GDP, while Somalia significantly reduced its external debt to 6% through the HIPC initiative. Seychelles improved its debt-to-GDP ratio to 56.7%, and Djibouti continued to face debt concerns despite some restructuring progress. Rwanda effectively managed its debt under IMF agreements. Overall, China remained the largest creditor of the region, with a growing number of bilateral funding and financing agreements from the UAE.

In December, Fitch downgraded Ethiopia's credit rating from CC to C due to a missed $33 m payment, further reducing it to RD (restricted default). Meanwhile, in February, JP Morgan, the fifth-largest investment bank and financial services company globally, established a regional office in Nairobi, underscoring Kenya's growing prominence in the global marketplace and as a financial hub in Eastern Africa.

In July, Tanzania took significant steps to address its US dollar shortage by restoring the inter-bank forex market and ending dollar rationing, thereby boosting its official reserves to cover four months of imports. In September, the Addis–Djibouti corridor received a $730 m upgrade from the IDA, aimed at enhancing regional connectivity and logistics across the Horn of Africa.

On *regional economic integration*, a World Bank study published in September highlighted that money transfer fees within the EAC were among the highest in the world. Transaction costs reached as high as 35% for transfers from Tanzania to Kenya, 30% to Uganda, and 20% to Rwanda. Even the least expensive route, from Kenya to Rwanda, cost around 7.5% – almost double the cost of sending money from the US to South Sudan. The IMF pointed out that these elevated transaction costs were significant obstacles to the EAC's common market and suggested a currency union as a solution to reduce and streamline costs. However, it seems unlikely that EAC member states will form a currency union due to the associated loss of monetary policy independence. This concern is particularly significant given the region's diverse economic structures and the consequent need for individual fiscal policies.

Overall, the *economic outlook* remained cautiously positive. Ethiopia, Kenya, Rwanda, Tanzania, and Uganda were expected to be among the world's fastest-growing economies in 2024, highlighting the potential for continued economic progress in Eastern Africa.

More concerning were the *growing challenges related to food security*, human wellbeing, and climate change. Historic droughts and flash floods induced by El Niño have significantly worsened food insecurity, compounded by recent years of crises. Climate shocks, along with economic downturns and conflicts, have deepened the already looming humanitarian crises across large parts of Eastern Africa.

Sudan's escalating conflict led to more internal displacements and increased humanitarian needs. Heavy rains and flooding as a result of El Niño hit parts of Eastern Africa, including Burundi, Ethiopia, Kenya, Rwanda, Somalia, South Sudan, Sudan, Tanzania, and Uganda. Between September and mid-December 2023, 479 people died and over 5.2 m were affected, according to OCHA. Nearly 2 m were displaced in Kenya, Somalia, Uganda, Burundi, and Ethiopia. The most affected countries were Somalia (2.5 m), Ethiopia (1.5 m), South Sudan (451,000), Kenya (546,000), and Sudan (89,200).

After a multi-year drought, the Horn of Africa faced further impacts from the El Niño phenomenon. From September, heavy rains affected 5.2 m people in Burundi, Ethiopia, Kenya, Somalia, South Sudan, and Sudan, causing floods and landslides. Over 4.5 m people were displaced by these climate-related disasters, with 68,000 cases of cholera reported. Forecasts for 2024 predicted unusually wet conditions, likely leading to more displacement, disease outbreaks, and food insecurity (UNHCR).

The Horn of Africa and the Great Lakes region remained a critical area for *humanitarian support* due to the complex interplay of climate change, armed conflicts, and economic challenges. According to UNHCR figures, the region hosted 5 m refugees and asylum seekers, accounting for one in six refugees globally. Additionally, by the end of December there were 19.4 m *IDPs* due to conflict and natural disasters, with over 578,000 refugees returning to their countries of origin in 2023.

Conflicts caused extensive displacement. Sudan saw 6.1 m newly displaced people and over 1.5 m refugees fleeing to neighbouring countries, with 962,000 refugees remaining by year's end, according to UNHCR. South Sudan hosted 386,000 refugees and had 2 m IDPs, with about 2.3 m South Sudanese refugees in neighbouring countries. Burundi hosted 87,513 refugees and had seen over 234,000 returnees since 2017. Rwanda hosted 135,000 refugees, including nearly 14,000 Congolese fleeing ongoing conflict in 2023. Tanzania hosted 229,000 refugees and had assisted nearly 165,000 Burundians in voluntary returns since 2017. Uganda hosted 1.6 m refugees, with over 99,000 new arrivals in 2023 and Kampala alone hosting nearly 137,000. In February, Kenya introduced a significant policy shift by granting city status to the Dadaab and Kakuma refugee camps, thereby permitting refugees to work within these areas. Uganda continued to be a key host for refugees, accommodating the largest refugee population in Africa and the third-largest worldwide, as reported by EU Civil Protection and Humanitarian Aid.

Humanitarian needs in Eastern Africa surged due to conflict and climate disasters, doubling the number of food-insecure people to 63 m and increasing the number of displaced people by 44% to 23 m by the end of 2023, according to WFP. The Regional Bureau for Eastern Africa received $1.7 bn, with the US contributing $974 m. South Sudan, Somalia, Sudan, and Ethiopia received $1.3 bn, 79% of regional funding and 16% of global WFP funding. During the year, the WFP assisted over 32 m people, mainly in Ethiopia, Somalia, South Sudan, and Sudan. In a significant move to counter corruption in the aid system, the EU suspended WFP funding in Somalia in September due to aid theft and misuse. This followed similar actions by the WFP and USAID in Ethiopia in April. While these measures were an understandable reaction to systemic corruption, they were unlikely to bring significant improvements and could, in fact, worsen the situation for the affected populations. The aid freeze endangered the livelihoods of many, potentially leading to more severe systemic issues. Notably, US officials estimated that the incidents uncovered could represent 'the largest theft of foreign food aid ever'.

Sub-regional Cooperation and Organisation

Regional and continental organisations were actively managing conflicts in Sudan and the Great Lakes region. Notably, the expansion of the EAC, with Somalia set to join the regional bloc, represented a significant step towards the objectives of the AU Agenda 2063. Contrary to earlier speculations, Eritrea did not rejoin IGAD. President Afwerki, who had a history of undermining multilateral institutions, continued to favour Gulf partnerships over African multilateralism.

During the year, IGAD faced numerous challenges amid ongoing regional crises. On 13 June, Djibouti was appointed as the new chair, replacing Sudan, which remained as vice-chair despite the de facto state collapse since April. A significant development was the formation of a 'Quartet' on Sudan, chaired by Kenya and including South Sudan, Ethiopia, and Djibouti, to address the conflict between the RSF led by Mohamed Hamdan Dagalo and the army led by Abdel Fattah al-Burhan. In July, three months after the outbreak of hostilities in Sudan, IGAD convened a meeting in Addis Ababa to discuss the crisis. However, the Sudanese army chief al-Burhan declined the invitation, citing Kenya's involvement due to perceived bias. Despite a lack of tangible achievements as a mediator in the conflict, the IGAD Quartet Group received appreciation for its detailed report on the situation in Sudan. Its efforts in addressing the crisis were recognised during the 41st Extraordinary Session of the IGAD Assembly of Heads of State and Government in December.

The EAC experienced notable economic and political developments during the year. In November, during the 23rd Ordinary Summit of EAC Heads of State, a communiqué directed the council to develop a road-map for Somalia's integration into the EAC and report on progress at the next summit. South Sudan's president assumed the role of EAC chairperson, marking a shift in regional leadership. The EAC officially announced on 1 May that troop-contributing partner states, including Burundi, Kenya, South Sudan, and Uganda, had deployed contingents to eastern DRC. During the 22nd Extraordinary Summit of EAC Heads of State in Nairobi on 5 September, the mandate of the EAC Regional Force (EACRF) in Eastern DRC was extended until the end of the year, ensuring continued support for peace and security in the region. The EACRF played a noteworthy role in stabilising Eastern DRC throughout 2023, successfully restoring peace and security in various regions and enabling residents to return to their homes. However, ultimate stability and resolution of the situation were not achieved, and it remained unclear how security dynamics with M23 would evolve. On 3 December, the EACRF began withdrawing its troops from Eastern DRC, with the first group of Kenyan troops departing from Goma airport after completing a year-long deployment.

On 13 June, the *East Africa Legislative Assembly* passed a resolution allowing EAC partner states to halt the use of US dollars in both local and international transactions, promoting the use of regional currencies. In June, Kenya signed an Economic Partnership Agreement (EPA) with the EU, ending a ten-year block and causing bemusement among EAC member states during the Eastern African chairship of the AU, themed around accelerating the implementation of the AfCFTA. The EPA was initially blocked by Tanzania, Uganda, and Rwanda due to concerns about opening their economies to European firms. Ruto positioned himself as a de facto leader within the EAC despite not being its chair, hence overshadowing Burundi as the current chair. He actively invited Ethiopia to join the EAC and supported Somalia's verification process for membership, reflecting his ambition to strengthen regional integration.

The *AU Peace and Security Council* (PSC) concentrated much of its efforts on the East and the Horn of Africa during the year. There were 13 sessions in total, the highest number for any region. Unlike in 2022, when discussions were centred mainly on Somalia and the African Transition Mission (ATMIS), the agenda in 2023 shifted significantly due to the outbreak of conflict in Sudan in April. The PSC held seven meetings to address the situation in Sudan, six dedicated solely to the conflict and one that included discussions on Sudan as part of broader regional issues in the Horn of Africa.

Significant developments occurred regarding the status and planned withdrawal of ATMIS. The PSC extended the deadline for the drawdown of 2,000 troops to 30 June and prepared for a further reduction of 3,000 troops by 30 September, while emphasising the need for stabilisation in liberated areas. However, in September, the decisions on troop withdrawal were reversed following Somalia's request for a 90-day technical pause, highlighting especially the need for additional funding.

Surprisingly, Ethiopia was less of a topic during the year, When it was, the primary focus was on the AU Monitoring Verification Mechanism (MVM). A planned field mission in February was not executed, meaning that a chance was missed to assess conditions and support peace efforts. On 15 March, the AU MVM mandate was extended until December 2024. Approximately $1 m from the AU Peace Fund was allocated on 10 April to support the national Disarmament, Demobilization, and Reintegration (DDR) process.

South Sudan's transition process received renewed attention. The council urged the Revitalised Transitional Government of National Unity (R-TGoNU) to complete all transitional tasks by the extended deadline of December 2024, emphasising that it was unlikely that a further extension would be granted. The year ended with unclear prospects for these conflicts.

Burundi

Raymond-Blaise Habonimana

Burundi experienced significant socio-political events in 2023, both domestically and regionally, marking a dynamic year for the country. The Burundian courts sentenced General Alain Guillaume Bunyoni, former prime minister and strongman of the presidential party, to life imprisonment. His trial marked a clear split between the pro-Nkurunziza and pro-Ndayishimiye factions. The activities of the Congrès National pour la Liberté (CNL), the main opposition party, were suspended by the authorities, making it increasingly difficult for its members to express their opinions and organise freely. The year also coincided with Burundi's presidency of the EAC, which enabled President Évariste Ndayishimiye to position himself at the regional level, cutting short the option of diplomatic isolation that his predecessor had opted for. Despite this glimmer of diplomatic hope, the economic situation was alarming due to the opaque ways in which public affairs were managed, the trial-and-error approach, and the global economic situation. Several cases of fuel shortages and basic needs affected daily life. The human rights situation did not improve, and human rights defenders were not spared.

Domestic Politics

On the political front, the president of Burundi, General Évariste Ndayishimiye, tried to channel his efforts into a developmentalist discourse. Without naming individuals, he openly criticised those in power monopolising the country's wealth and misappropriating public assets. In many speeches, the president criticised justice sector officials, economic operators, and lazy citizens. However, analysts wondered whether the president really held power, or whether there were other command centres parallel to the central command. President Ndayishimiye dismissed several senior members of his party. What emerged from the new appointments was a desire to recruit young technocrats to serve the country. However, young people came up against a system in which the ruling party controlled the state, making it difficult to carry out reforms.

On 2 October, for the second time since assuming office in 2020, the president *reshuffled* his government. Four ministers were dismissed. Of the 15 ministers who made up the government, four – Sanctus Niragira, minister of agriculture and livestock; Sylvie Nzeyimana, minister of public health; Ezéchiel Nibigira, minister of youth and sport and the East African Community; and Déo Rusengwamihigo, minister of the civil service – were dismissed to make way for Prosper Dodiko, Lyduine Baradahana, Gervais Abayeho, and Venuste Muyabaga respectively. The ministerial reshuffle was the subject of debate among observers of Burundi, who wondered whether it was a technical or a political move. The new ministers all came from the ruling Conseil National Pour la Défense de la Démocratie – Forces pour la Défense de la Démocratie (CNDD-FDD). No member of the opposition parties held a ministerial post.

In the run-up to the 2025 elections, Burundi's minister of the interior, Martin Ninteretse, *suspended the activities of the main opposition party*, the CNL, throughout the country. In his decision, taken on 2 June and made public on 6 June, the minister explained that the political party was going through an internal crisis. However, CNL president Agathon Rwasa spoke of interference in his party's affairs by his opponents. According to him, these were just ten people, compared with the thousands of CNL militants who supported Rwasa.

President Ndayishimiye sought to (re)position himself as the strongman, by distancing himself from the generals who inherited the CNDD-FDD system and who held commanding positions. In this context, the Burundian courts requested a *life sentence* for the former prime minister, General Guillaume Bunyoni. In December, according to the court, 'The former Prime Minister was sentenced to life imprisonment for the seven crimes of which he was accused, including plotting against the Head of State to overthrow the constitutional regime, an attempted assassination of the Head of State using fetishes, insulting the Head of State and the Prime Minister and undermining the internal security of the State'. Bunyoni was also convicted of illegal enrichment and destabilising the economy. The court ordered the confiscation of four houses and buildings belonging to him, as well as a plot of land and 14 vehicles. The co-accused, including Désiré Uwamahoro, the Burundian officer at the head of the riot squad, were sentenced to 30 years.

On the security front, in December, the RED-Tabara rebel group attacked Gatumba, a border area with the DRC. According to a statement by the Burundian authorities, *20 people were killed*, many of them civilians. Established in the early 2010s, the group challenges the legitimacy of the current government in Burundi but had been forgotten for several years. According to Thierry Virculoun, Crisis Group's senior Central Africa consultant, RED-Tabara is a Burundian armed opposition group that emerged after the 2015 crisis and moved to South Kivu in the DRC, on the border with Burundi. The group carried out attacks against Burundian forces for several years after 2015, but it had not carried out any significant action against the Burundian army since 2021. In the wake of this attack, President Ndayishimiye said during a public broadcast in Cankuzo province on 29 December that Rwanda was supporting the rebels of the RED-Tabara movement. According to him, 'these groups are housed, supplied and financed by Rwanda'. Further, 'Rwanda needs to know that continuing to support those who kill children means creating hatred between the populations of these two countries. It is not normal to supply those who kill children'. Ndayishimiye's accusations against Rwanda were seen as a step backwards in the gradual warming of diplomatic relations with its northern neighbour, which had been severed since the 2015 socio-political crisis in Burundi. This came at a time when the position of the two countries on the crisis in the east of the DRC was also increasing tensions.

Burundi will hold legislative elections in 2025. This is a crucial period for the country. In December 2023, a new team for the Independent National Electoral Commission (CENI) was put in place by the National Assembly. SOS Torture stressed that the current chair of the CENI, Prosper Ntahorwamiye, was well known for having been its spokesperson from 2012 to 2020, a period during which Burundi organised at least three elections (2010, 2015, and 2020) marred by irregularities that led to a serious socio-political crisis in 2015 against the backdrop of the controversial candidacy of the late president Pierre Nkurunziza. The new CENI team therefore did not seem to meet the criteria of independence in the eyes of public opinion, because of partisan affiliations or social proximity to the ruling CNDD-FDD. There was clear partiality and lack of professionalism in the preparation of the elections.

In March, the president decreed Organic Law No. 1/05 on the determination and delimitation of the provinces, communes, zones, hills, and quarters of Burundi. The number of provinces fell from 18 to 5 and the number of communes from 119 to 42. The number of zones and hills/quarters increased significantly, from 339 to 447 for zones and from 2,910 to 3,036 for hills/quarters. The new division had implications for the 2025 and 2025 elections, as a new electoral code must comply with it. The Ministry of the Interior presented draft laws revising Organic Law No. 1/14 of 2020 on the organisation of local government and Organic Law No. 01/11 of 2019 on the electoral code. According to the Minister of the Interior, there were three main reasons for this amendment: to bring the electoral code into line with law no. 1/05 of 2023 on the determination and delimitation of the provinces, communes, zones, collines, and quarters of the country; to resolve the difficulties encountered by the CENI in implementing certain provisions of the law in force; and to take account of the recommendations arising from the evaluation of the 2020 electoral process. Two main changes proposed for the new electoral code provoked political debate: the issue of the nomination deposit and the members of polling stations. On one hand, the deposit was increased for candidates at the various levels: to 100 m Burundian francs (BIF) for the presidential post, BIF 2m for parliamentary candidates, and BIF 200,000 to be elected to a communal council. On the other hand, article 38(3) of the draft electoral code stipulates that provincial and communal electoral commissions, as well as polling stations, are to be set up with a view to ensuring political neutrality. For opposition political parties, this concealed the intent to exclude political parties from these compositions. Kefa Nibizi, chair of the political party Codebu, commented 'We are going to put what we call representatives of religious denominations, civil societies, but who, in reality, are militants of the party in power'.

Timid progress was made in the fight against corruption. Public authorities made anti-corruption speeches. In July, at the opening of the government retreat in Ngozi, President Ndayishimiye declared that the fight against corruption and injustice was on the agenda. Again, in September, at the opening of the 2023/24 judicial year at the Ingoma stadium in Gitega, Ndayishimiye called on 'corrupt judges to wake up before it's too late'. However, corruption still existed in Burundi, despite the rhetoric. The country was ranked 162nd out of 180 countries in the 2023 Transparency International Corruption Perceptions Index, based on 2022 data, compared with 171st the previous year. Abriel Rufyiri, president of OLUCOME, the Anti-Corruption and Economic Malpractice Observatory, deplored the fact that public procurement accounted for 70% of the state budget, and that it was one of the most corrupt areas in the country. He called for the AU Convention on Preventing and Combating Corruption to be implemented. The governor of the central bank, the BRB (Bank of the Republic of Burundi), was sacked and taken by the military to the dungeons of the National Intelligence Service, where he spent months in Mpimba central prison. He was released three months later without trial. He was accused of passive corruption, undermining the functioning of the national economy, money laundering, and misappropriation of public property. However, according to the CSO 'Parole et actions pour le réveil des consciences et l'évolution' des mentalités (PARCEM), the BRB's dependence on the Presidency of the Republic limited its capacity for action and its efficiency. The BRB had become a department of the presidency, which explained why any disagreement between the presidency and the governor of the BRB triggered dismissals. PARCEM condemned this interference by the president in the operation of the BRB and suggested that the BRB should report to the Ministry of Finance.

The Truth and Reconciliation Commission (TRC) continued its work. It also went beyond the borders to expand its contacts. From 28 June to 1 July, members of the TRC travelled to Brussels to meet the Burundian diaspora. Despite the Commission's determination to reach out to all stakeholders, the meeting was faced with challenges that undermined the search for truth and reconciliation in Burundi. The diaspora is divided along partisan and historical lines, the TRC is perceived by some victims as an instrument of the ruling party, and it is accused of exploiting the memory of Burundians.

The National Commission on Land and Other Assets (CNTB) completed its mandate in March 2022, with some of its powers transferred to the TRC. The TRC thus now had a dual role: overseeing finding the truth and making reparations. This is an enormous task given the length of the period covered (1884 to 2008). Land disputes were increasingly a source of tension between communities, hence the need to effectively resolve ongoing disputes in a spirit of reconciliation.

The human rights situation continued to give cause for concern. The Burundi Human Rights Initiative (BHRI) pointed out that President Ndayishimiye's unkept promises to reform the justice system cast a shadow over his reputation. The BHRI described how judicial officials and prison directors frequently violate the law or obey instructions from intelligence agents or prosecutors not to release certain prisoners – particularly those accused of political or security-related offences. The Iteka League reported that at least 495 people were killed in various parts of the country in 2023, alongside 795 cases of arbitrary arrest. Freedom House qualified Burundi as 'not free', as in 2022.

Nor were human rights defenders spared this year. On 14 February, five human rights defenders were arrested by national intelligence agents and accused of rebellion and undermining internal state security and the functioning of public finances. The charges appeared to relate only to their relationship with an international organisation abroad and the funding they received from this organisation. Two of the defenders worked for the Association of Women Lawyers in Burundi (Association des femmes juristes du Burundi, AFJB) and three for the Association for Peace and the Promotion of Human Rights (Association pour la paix et la promotion des droits de l'Homme, APDH). All five were initially charged with rebellion, but this charge was only maintained for three of them during the trial. The charge of undermining the functioning of public finances was eventually dropped for all five. All were released on 28 April; five were acquitted of undermining internal state security; three were acquitted and two were convicted of rebellion, fined BIF 50,000 ($25), and handed a two-year suspended sentence.

In addition, Burundian authorities restricted the freedoms of people from LGBTQ+ groups. In March, police arrested 24 delegates at a seminar in Gitega on entrepreneurship and charged them with 'homosexuality and incitement to debauchery and prostitution'. The President raised his voice against the practice of homosexuality, calling for the liquidation of gay people: 'Personally, I think that if we see this type of individual in Burundi, we should put them in a stadium and stone them to death. And it wouldn't be a sin for those who do it'. Earlier in the year he had already called for homosexuality to be 'banned' and gay people 'treated as pariahs'.

In July, Fortuné Gaetan Zongo, the special rapporteur, in his oral update to the UNHRC, expressed concern over systematic self-censorship in the country, arbitrary arrests, reprisals, and the use of trumped-up charges against human rights defenders and journalists. He raised the alarm about Burundi 'becoming a forgotten crisis' and called on Burundi's friends not to forget Burundians, 'who are thirsty for justice and dignity'.

Journalist Floriane Irangabiye was arbitrarily arrested on 30 August 2022 and is currently serving a ten-year prison sentence for criticising the government, Amnesty International, the Burundi Human Rights Initiative, the Committee to Protect Journalists, and Human Rights Watch said. 'Floriane Irangabiye was convicted simply for doing her job as a radio journalist', said Tigere Chagutah, Amnesty International's regional director for East and Southern Africa. 'Her conviction and imprisonment are a travesty and flagrant violation of her rights to freedom of expression and to a fair trial.'

Public space continued to be dominated by the CNDD-FDD. Paramilitary training run by the Imbonerakure youth league was stepped up nationwide under the guise of transmitting patriotism and entrepreneurship spirits. The Imbonerakure held several meetings ranging from ordinary meetings to *Imbonerakure Day*, as if to demonstrate its strength. These practices alarmed the opposition, which denounced the militarisation of young people. In October, Martin Zongo, the Burundi UN expert, called for the protection of civic space.

Foreign Affairs

Burundian diplomacy was very active in 2023, ranging from the pursuit of dialogue with its bilateral and multilateral partners to other potential partners. The presidency of the EAC enabled President Ndayishimiye to take part in several summits of the sub-region's heads of state.

In terms of political and diplomatic gains, Burundi occupied several diplomatic posts that raised its profile, as minister Albert Shingiro stated in July while presenting cooperation and foreign affairs achievements. These included the post of chief of staff of the Central African Multinational Force (FOMAC). The heads of state of ECCAS took note of Burundi's offer to host the new Court of Auditors of ECCAS, provided for in the Community's revised treaty. The heads of state also approved the appointment of Burundian politician the Honourable Léonce Ngendakumana as a member of the Council of Elders of ECCAS.

On 4 February, Burundi hosted the 20th Summit of EAC Heads of State. Rwandan president Paul Kagame also attended the summit. His visit to Burundi made headlines in the local media: the Rwandan president had not set foot on Burundian soil for more than 11 years. His last visit was in July 2012, when Burundi celebrated 50 years of independence. On the sidelines of the summit, the Burundian and Rwandan presidents held talks behind closed doors.

In relations with the AU, Moussa Faki Mahamat, chair of the AU Commission, visited Burundi in March, invited by President Ndayishimiye. This visit happened a few days after Ndayishimiye's election to the AU during the 36th Ordinary Session of the AU.

In May, UNSC António Guterres visited Burundi. The UNSC praised Burundi's role in regional peace initiatives in the east of the DRC. 'I would also like to pay tribute to Burundi's positive role in the region, and above all to the efforts undertaken by the Burundian president in his capacity as chairman-in-office of the East African Community', Guterres said during his visit to Bujumbura.

Again in May, the minister of foreign affairs of the Russian Federation, Sergey Lavrov, paid a working visit to Burundi – the first time in the 60-year history of relations that a Russian foreign minister had visited the country. Lavrov said that Russia would continue to cooperate in the fields of health, particularly in the fight against infectious diseases, and peaceful nuclear energy. In relation to education, he announced that Russia had increased the quota of scholarships for Burundian students in Russia for 2023/24.

In June 2023, Gervais Ndirakobuca, prime minister of Burundi, took part in a summit for an international financial pact in Paris. His participation was criticised by human rights organisations. The Initiative for Human Rights in Burundi (IDHB) called it a 'disgrace' for France to host a man cited for serious crimes in Burundi. In 2022, Ndirakobuca was under EU sanctions for his role in the violent crackdown on demonstrators against the last term of President Pierre Nkurunziza.

Burundi was actively involved in restoring peace, security, and stability in several African countries, including Somalia, CAR, and DRC, where it had troops on the ground as part of UN, AU, and EAC-led peace missions. The president was also involved in restoring peace in DRC through the Nairobi peace process. Burundi was elected vice-president of the 77th session of the UNGA and won the support of the ECCAS for the presidency of the UNGA in 2029.

In accordance with bilateral military agreements signed between DRC's Félix Tshisekedi and Évariste Ndayishimiye at the end of August, Burundi had four battalions (around 3,200 soldiers) in this part of the DRC as part of the EAC force, plus another battalion sent to North Kivu at Kinshasa's request. The involvement of Burundian troops in the DRC remained a topical issue in Burundi. The troops were less motivated and the losses on the ground were enormous.

In July, Burundi's first lady, Angeline Ndayishimiye Ndayubaha, was nominated for the UN Population Award for her efforts in raising awareness and ensuring the full development of all sections of the population. However, the first lady's travels outside the country began to attract criticism because of their cost, against the backdrop of the precarious economic conditions that Burundi was experiencing.

The Burundian presidency of the EAC enabled the country to forge stronger diplomatic relations and break with its isolation from the world. Ndayishimiye has held the baton of command of the EAC since July 2022. At the 23rd Ordinary Summit of Heads of State of the EAC, held in Arusha on 24 November, he handed over command to Salva Kiir, president of South Sudan.

In Bujumbura, on 21 November, the government of Burundi and the AfDB signed two grant agreements totalling $13.15 m to implement Phase 1 of the Water Sector and Climate Resilience Building Support Programme (PASEREC-Phase1).

In November, Burundi signed the Samoa Agreement. This cooperation agreement between the Organisation of African, Caribbean and Pacific States (OACPS) and the EU was the successor to the Cotonou Agreement, which had entered into force in 2003 – a new legal framework for relations between the two bodies. The agreement covered priority areas such as human rights, democracy and governance, peace and security, human and social development, inclusive and sustainable economic growth and development, environmental sustainability and climate change, and migration and mobility.

Although relations between the EU and Burundi appeared to be evolving, the European Council renewed the restrictive measures it adopted on account of the situation in Burundi for a further year, until 31 October 2024. The restrictive measures in force applied to one person, Mathias/Joseph Niyonzima, alias Kazungu, an officer of the National Intelligence Service. This person was subject to an asset freeze, and EU citizens and companies were prohibited from making funds available to him. He was also subject to a travel ban preventing him from entering or transiting through EU member states.

To diversify its partners, Burundi strengthened relations with Russia and China. In July, the president of Burundi attended the second Russia–Africa summit and held talks with his counterpart Vladimir Putin. Among the areas of cooperation identified were military cooperation and the use of uranium for civilian purposes. After Russia, the head of state travelled to China, where he took part in the opening ceremony of the World University Games in Chengdu. He met his counterpart Xi Jinping and visited various companies, in particular those manufacturing agricultural machinery, cooking oil, and cereal seeds. In August, President Ndayishimiye took part in the 15th BRICS summit in South Africa. In September, accompanied by the first lady, he took part in the Summit of Heads of State and Government of the Group of 77 and China, held in Cuba. During his stay, he met his Cuban counterpart Miguel Díaz-Canel. In an interview with the newspaper 'Iwacu' in September, Claude Bochu, the EU ambassador to Burundi, criticised the cooperation between Burundi and Russia, asking 'What does Russia bring to Burundi in terms of development, apart from vague promises?'

Socioeconomic Developments

The economy was disrupted by domestic factors, as well as by the global economic situation, including the war in Ukraine. The trade balance remained in deficit, aggravated by the difficulty of accessing foreign currency for imports. Prices of basic products such as sugar, fertilisers, petroleum products, and beverages rose significantly. The government increased the price of petroleum products four times, making the Burundian economy increasingly fragile. The repercussions on the lives of the Burundian people were enormous. According to USAID, by mid-September, fuel prices had risen sharply by around 35%, representing an increase of almost 40% on July and 65% on the previous year's prices. The inflation rate remained high from the start of the year, reaching around 30% in August. Prices of basic foodstuffs remained considerably high, ranging from 30% to 75% above the previous year's prices and from 80% to 120% above the five-year average.

For the 2023/24 financial year, the general budget amounted to BIF 3,923 bn, or $1,387 m, compared with BIF 2,392.3 bn in 2022/23 ($1,176.4 m), an increase of 63.9% that can be explained by the government's major ambitions, particularly in the infrastructure sector, including the railway project, and production. Consequently, state expenditure increased by 65.23% compared with the budget for 2022/23. Significantly, a large proportion of the state's revenue came from domestic tax collection. The increased taxes covered wine, cigarettes, flight tickets, telephony. The tax burden was not the reason for the rise in prices, but depreciation of the BIF or devaluation had something to do with it. Economic growth accelerated to 2.7%, compared with 1.8% in 2022, according to the World Bank. Agricultural production was expected to recover, assuming favourable rainfall and good distribution of fertiliser, albeit chemical fertilisers increased in price by 10% in September.

In March, the WFP highlighted the prevalence of food insecurity. Overall food insecurity was 42%, with 36% of households moderately food insecure and

6% suffering from severe food insecurity. Compared with the same period in 2022, this was a sharp deterioration, with the proportion of food-insecure households having more than doubled from 20% (including 1% in severe food insecurity) in March 2022.

Headline inflation accelerated to 26% in July, driven by increases in food and fuel prices. The price of basic foodstuffs increased, bringing food inflation to 35.8% in July compared with 24.5% in July 2022. Fuel shortages worsened in June due to supply disruptions caused by the war in Ukraine. The fiscal deficit was projected to decline to 6.7% of GDP, from 12.1% in 2022, due to cuts in current expenditure and small increases in revenues. Public debt was expected to reach 72.7% of GDP, from 68.4% in 2022, driven by disbursements under the IMF's ECF programme.

In 2023, total public debt continued to rise; it had increased by 26.1% by the end of June 2023, reaching BIF 6,027.6 bn compared with BIF 4,779.3 bn at the end of June 2022, according to the Monetary Policy Committee report for the second quarter of 2023. Data from the BRB showed that total public debt represented 59.8% of GDP and remained below the standard of 50% of GDP, agreed in the macroeconomic convergence criteria of the EAC.

Therefore, on 17 July, the executive board of the IMF approved a 38-month arrangement under the ECF with access to $200.2 m (or about $261.7 m, representing 130% of quota). This agreement was a sign of hope for the Burundian economy, which was facing several challenges, including a shortage of foreign currency and a trade deficit. The agreement aimed to help the country cope with the difficult macroeconomic situation it was experiencing, and to support the authorities' reform programme, aimed in turn at reducing vulnerabilities linked to public debt, recalibrating monetary and exchange rate policies to restore external viability, and promoting inclusive economic growth and good governance. An IMF team led by Mame Astou Diouf, mission chief for Burundi, visited Bujumbura in September and held follow-up discussions during October with Burundian authorities on recent developments and progress towards the objectives of the new arrangement under the ECF.

The education sector did not improve during the year, and faced several challenges including lack of infrastructure, high drop-out rates, low quality of education, and the living conditions of students' families, which also affected the education system. The school province of Cankuzo recorded more than 9,000 drop-outs during the 2022/23 school year. To counter this phenomenon, the Burundian government set up a system of school canteens. The budget allocated to this programme was increased to BIF 12.5 bn for the 2023/24 budget year. However, there was still a long way to go to reach the target: the programme reached 670,000 schoolchildren out of a target of more than 2 m. In November, China pledged $1.5 m to support the school canteens programme through the Action Bonne Foundation, for which the first lady was responsible.

Repatriation operations for Burundian refugees continued. The UNHCR counted a total of 17,780 returnees at the end of September, returning from Tanzania (12,121), Kenya (89), Rwanda (325), DRC (4,504), Uganda (570), Mozambique (48), and other countries (123).

The country had a low unemployment rate (17.2% in urban areas; 1.1% in rural areas), according to the ILO. Under-employment affected 53.4% of the working population, particularly those aged 15–35 and women (57.9%) more than men (47.87%).

Living conditions for women did not improve. Amnesty International called on Burundi to introduce a decisive law on gender-based violence to bring it into line with regional and international standards. The organisation stressed the importance of improving the 2016 law, the provisions of which violate human rights such as the right to privacy and the principle of non-discrimination. AI recommended that the National Assembly take a survivor-centred approach, revising Article 21 of the GBV law on the obligation of direct neighbours to intervene to ensure that actions, in particular the reporting of a crime, are not taken against the wishes of the victim.

Access to drinking water remained a concern for many localities, including the municipality of Bujumbura. In Burundi, the Régie de production et de distribution d'eau et d'électricité du Burundi (REGIDESO) is responsible for the water supply. Supply has remained virtually unchanged in Bujumbura and the provinces for the past 20 years, while the population has grown steadily. As a result, drinking water is becoming a rare commodity, forcing Burundians to drink water from the river. Burundi's health ministry declared an outbreak of cholera on 6 September, with 15 cases reported in the western part of the country, which is prone to water shortages.

On the health front, tangible results were achieved. UNICEF supported the Burundian government's polio immunisation campaign. More than 2.8 m children aged 0–7 years were vaccinated by the end of August. Again, there was hope with the progress made in the fight against malaria. Burundi will benefit from the 18 m doses of the very first anti-malaria vaccine allocated to 12 African countries for 2023–25.

In April, the flooding of the Ruzizi River again affected the population of Gatumba. Climatic disasters were responsible for 89% of displacements in Burundi, according to the latest figures from the Displacement Monitoring Matrix (DTM). An estimated 10,000 people were affected, displaced by the floods at the beginning of May in the Gatumba area. A $350,000 project to build protective dikes on the river was designed to strengthen the resilience of inhabitants of the area, who are often victims of the effects of climate change. However, environmentalists did not see the value of these dikes, arguing that as the land in the Gatumba area is arable, it would be difficult to control the waters of the Rusizi and Lake Tanganyika. They instead proposed the relocation of populations in the area at high risk of flooding.

Comoros

Benedikt Kamski

Comoros entered the continental stage on taking over the chairing of the AU, which shaped both domestic and foreign politics during the year. Despite initial widespread doubts due to the alleged diplomatic and financial shortcomings of the small nation, President Azali Assoumani's chairship received favourable assessments as leader of the first Small Island Developing State (SIDS) to hold this position. The early phase of the 2024 presidential election campaign kicked off at the end of the year, highlighting a trend of growing authoritarian tendencies in the country. Relations with France remained cordial and stable, not least as a result of France's support for Comoros during its AU tenure. Migration and maritime security were key issues throughout the year, both in bilateral relations with France and within the broader context of the Western Indian Ocean, involving other international powers. The country's economic growth was marginal but positive, with increased government expenditures. Assoumani actively promoted the 'blue economy', successfully positioning SIDS as key stakeholders in global climate change and trade policy on the continent.

Domestic Politics

Politics in Comoros were defined by the country's AU chairship, while the presidential election campaign for the January 2024 polls took centre stage domestically during the second half of the year, with early campaigning. The political party landscape in the country remained divided. The *Inter-Comorian National Dialogue* of 2022 did not achieve its goals: no political rapprochement between the ruling Convention for the Renewal of the Comoros (CRC) and opposition forces was achieved.

President Azali Assoumani was elected *AU chairperson* during the 36th AU Assembly of Heads of State and Government in February. A core team of technical and political advisors was appointed to support Comoros' first chairship in Addis Ababa, Ethiopia. Mohamed Issimaila, an academic and former education minister, was appointed by decree as the task force coordinator. Imam Abdillah, a specialist in multilateral African organisations and head of cooperation at the Ministry of Foreign Affairs, and Fatima Alfeine, a diplomatic advisor with the rank of ambassador who brought experience in the Sahel region and the UN, assisted the president throughout the year with his AU-related tasks. Other task force members were Colonel Soilih Abdallah Rafik, head of the General Directorate of Civilian Security (DGSC) with extensive experience in multilateral diplomacy and the Comorian armed forces; and Youssoufa Mohamed Ali (Belou), appointed defence delegate in September 2021. Assoumani's eldest son, Nour El Fath Azali, has been his private advisor since 2019. Former prime minister Hamada Madi (known as Bolero) was another key advisor who brought a strong network across the continent, reportedly supporting Assoumani's visits as AU chair to Guinea, Burkina Faso, and Mali.

Presidential elections were scheduled for the last weeks of the AU chairship in early 2024. Assoumani had never allowed any doubts to arise about his intention to stand for a fourth consecutive term. This had been made possible by a controversial referendum in 2018 that voided the 2001 constitution and the so-called 'Fomboni Agreement', which had ensured a rotational presidency among the three main islands – Grand Comore, Anjouan, and Mohéli. Comoros had experienced a total of 20 coups since independence in 1975, one of which brought Assoumani to power in 1999. The constitutional change also removed the three vice-presidential offices meant to ensure the equal representation of the three islands in the executive branch. Significantly, it also ended the presidential term limits, paving the way for Assoumani's latest bid for the presidency.

Since his highly contested 2019 election victory, Assoumani had faced growing *criticism for authoritarianism, nepotism, and restricting democratic space*. The president wields significant influence over the judiciary, with the ability to appoint and dismiss Supreme Court judges. In a notable instance of this power, he removed

Harimia Ahmed, the chief magistrate in charge of election oversight, in December, just one month before the presidential elections. Moreover, his primary rival, former president Ahmed Abdallah Sambi, had been out of the political scene since his arrest in 2018 on charges of embezzlement, for which he received a life sentence in 2022. In this high-profile case, Sambi and Mohamed Ali Soilihi, former vice-president, were charged with high treason and corruption in November 2022. Comoros scored 20 out of 100 and ranked 162nd on Transparency International's *Corruption Perceptions Index* for 2023 (based on 2022 data).

The *election campaign* was marred by a de facto ban on public political gatherings since 2019. Reports of arbitrary detentions and restrictions on opposition campaigning increased towards the end of the year, heightening political tensions. Assoumani campaigned under the slogan 'Gwa Ndzima' ('All at Once' in Shikomori). Despite highlighting infrastructure achievements during his campaign, he faced criticism for the persistent poverty affecting 45% of the population, along with frequent power and water issues. Opposition parties repeatedly called for a boycott of the January 2024 poll, claiming that it would not be free or fair. They also demanded the release of political prisoners, the replacement of the Independent National Electoral Commission (CENI) with an independent body, and the guarantee of the exclusion of the military from interference in the electoral process. At the end of the year, five candidates besides the incumbent had announced that they would stand in the elections – Salim Issa Abdallah, Daoudou Abdallah Mohamed, Bourhane Hamidou, Mouigni Baraka Said Soilihi, and Aboudou Soefo.

Press freedom in Comoros faced significant challenges. While the constitution guarantees the freedom of the press, stringent defamation laws resulted in widespread self-censorship by the media. Journalists regularly faced intimidation, attacks, arrests, threats, and censorship. In February, four journalists were interrogated for defamation in relation to allegations against an executive of the Office de Radio et Télévision des Comores (ORTC), each receiving a nine-month suspended sentence and a €300 fine in August. The National Union of Journalists condemned the increasing trend of summoning journalists, calling it the 'systematisation of the night at the brigade'. The RSF World Press Freedom Index ranked Comoros 75th in 2023 (based on data from 2022) with a score of 62.25, improving to 71st in the 2024 ranking with a score of 61.47 (based on data from 2023). The 2024 Freedom in the World report (based on 2023 data) rated Comoros 'partly free' with a score of 42/100, unchanged from 2023.

In August, Assoumani made *antisemitic remarks* during the inauguration of a mosque in Maraharé (Anjouan Island). The official webpage of the Anjouan governorate published a video of his speech in which he referred to the 'damned Jews' (French: 'les maudits juifs'). Controversially, Assoumani was still AU chair when he made these remarks, which received little public attention.

Foreign Affairs

The *AU chairship* of Comoros marked the first time that a SIDS has headed the continental organisation. Assoumani successfully raised the country's international profile through what observers described as especially personal determination. AU officials and diplomats noted his active involvement during his tenure, which saw him represent the continental bloc at several international summits, including the G20, as well as during an AU-led peace mission to Russia and Ukraine in June. President Assoumani made sustainable maritime resource management a core topic of his agenda, highlighted by the 'Blue Future Ministerial Conference on Blue Economy and Climate Action in Africa: Island and Coastal States at the Forefront', held in the federal capital Moroni in June. Despite overall benevolent assessments, Comoros achieved few meaningful results in addressing continental issues related to security and structural stability such as in the Great Lakes, across the Horn of Africa, or in the Sahel.

Securing funding for the AU chairship was a big challenge for the small island nation, leading the Comorian government to seek support from several international partners, including the UAE, Saudi Arabia, China, the UNDP, and the Bill & Melinda Gates Foundation. The UAE reportedly provided an aeroplane and covered travel costs during the chairship, while *France*, approached by Assoumani prior to his appointment, financed additional staffing at the Addis Ababa embassy through Expertise France. Naturally, speculation arose about the conditions tied to France's support due to the contested status of *Mayotte*, the fourth island of the archipelago and an overseas department of France. Significantly, Assoumani had again declared Mayotte's sovereignty at the UNGA in September 2022, but he avoided the topic during his AU tenure. Despite strong political and socio-cultural ties, relations between France and Comoros were contentious, especially in and over the status of Mayotte. Comoros relies heavily on its diaspora in France, numbering around 300,000 people, whose remittances are crucial, amounting to approximately three times the country's domestic revenues. In April, Paris launched the 'Wuambushu Operation' in Mayotte aimed at relocating 20,000 illegal migrants from Mayotte back to Comoros, and security forces dismantled shanty towns on the island. Migration to Mayotte continued to be a pressing issue. Approximately half of Mayotte's population (around 175,000 people) are non-French citizens, most of them Comorians. The forced repatriation of Comorians from Mayotte was met with harsh criticism from the government in Moroni. The operation was eventually scaled down by France but clearly highlighted the complexities in Franco-Comorian relations.

The *United States* and Comoros signed a Joint Statement of Cooperation in February, strengthening their partnership across several areas. For instance, the US provided Covid-19 vaccine doses through the COVAX facility and pledged $5 m via USAID and the Department of State to support food security, energy, and workforce development. The US government also announced a maritime security assistance package for Comoros, including unmanned aerial vehicles (UAVs) and training, to improve the archipelago's maritime capacities.

Comoros ratified the *AfCFTA* agreement on 19 February, only days prior to Assoumani assuming the AU chair under the annual theme 'Acceleration of the AfCFTA implementation'. Following more than 17 years of negotiations and the establishment of a working party as long ago as October 2007, Comoros came a step closer to joining the WTO. By the end of the year, negotiations were close to conclusion and Comoros was expected to join in early 2024.

Key bilateral partners and donors, including France, China, Saudi Arabia, and Japan, remained unchanged from previous years. Notably, the US government's increasing involvement in the region should be interpreted as a strategic response to China's growing influence. China has strengthened its diplomatic and economic ties with *African Indian Ocean Island states* such as Comoros and Seychelles, as evidenced by the observer status of Beijing in the Indian Ocean Commission, the Indian Ocean Tuna Commission, and the Indian Ocean Rim Association. The geostrategic importance of the Western Indian Ocean is significant for both China and the US, highlighting the region's critical role in their broader geopolitical strategies.

Socioeconomic Developments

Economic performance was affected by slow progress in modernising infrastructure and improving the business environment. Critical needs included enhancing development management capacities such as better partner coordination, effective resource mobilisation, and strengthening the statistical system; and improving waste management and the social protection system.

GDP growth was 3.1%, up from 2.6% in 2022, driven mainly by the services and agriculture sectors, according to the AfDB Africa Economic Outlook for 2024. Growth was projected at 4% in 2024 and 4.6% in 2025, supported by government initiatives, the IMF, and the expected positive effects of AfCFTA and WTO membership. With increased household consumption due to strong remittance flows, inflation decreased from 12.4% to 9.1%, aided by stable global prices and a reduction in the central bank's reserve requirement rate from 15% to 12.5% (AfDB). *Inflation* was expected to decline further, though the budget deficit would remain high, with the current account deficit projected at 5.8% of GDP in 2024, according to AfDB estimates. To address the high cost of living, the government adjusted civil servants' salaries, increasing the state payroll by 3% to approximately $68.4 m out of a $237.1 m budget. This triggered a teachers' strike from mid-November 2023 until the end of the reporting period.

By the end of 2023, the public debt stock had risen to 38.2% of GDP, up from 34.0% at the end of 2022, according to World Bank data. AfDB assessed the overall fiscal risks as remaining high due to a fragile domestic context and global uncertainty, with heavy reliance on imports, remittances, and foreign aid.

As part of the 2023 *IMF Article IV Consultation* and the ECF arrangement, the IMF completed its review, allowing for an immediate disbursement of Special Drawing Rights (SDR) of 3.56 m (approximately $4.77 m). The four-year ECF arrangement, approved on 1 June, giving access to SDR 32.04 m (approximately $43 m), helped to support economic recovery, evidenced by a rebound in tourism figures and public investment projects.

In June, the World Bank announced an additional $15 m grant, which increased the total aid package to $85 m, with support from Agence Française de Développement. The funds are earmarked to revamp the three main ports in the three Comoros islands, including the $60 m renovation of the port of Boingoma on Mohéli Island, which sustained major damage as a result of Cyclone Kenneth in 2019 and other less severe tropical storms after that. Despite its critical vulnerability to natural disasters, Comoros did not face major flood hazards.

Comoros presented its *second Voluntary National Review* in July. The country achieved the SDG target for maternal mortality, with a ratio of 53 deaths per 100,000 live births, and made significant strides in reducing child mortality, to 36 deaths per 1,000 live births. Education saw improvements, with the number of public primary schools offering preschool classes rising from 233 in 2022 to 257 in 2023 (UNICEF). Infrastructure projects, such as the construction of the El Maarouf Hospital and Galawa Hotel, along with the new energy law promoting renewable electricity production, were expected to support economic recovery. According to UNICEF, Comoros had a population of approximately 870,000, with 44% living in poverty and 67% residing in rural areas. The nation faced significant challenges, including frequent disruptions in electricity and water supply and the absence of a garbage collection system. Socially, the situation remained fragile, with a poverty rate of 38.4%, a slight improvement from 39%, and stable unemployment at 6.5%, despite high levels of under-employment.

The EU supported Comoros' growth strategy under the Emerging Comoros Plan (ECP) 2030. The Public Health Emergency Preparedness and Response Plan (2022–26) identified 4,000 households at risk from volcanic eruptions and ranked disease probability at the highest level.

Djibouti

Nicole Hirt

President Ismaïl Omar Guelleh remained in power and his ruling party *Rassemblement Populaire pour le Progres* (RPP) unsurprisingly won a landslide victory in the parliamentary elections, which took place in February and were boycotted by most opposition parties. The economy recovered and trade activities resumed after relative peace had been restored in Ethiopia following the November 2022 peace deal. Poverty and food insecurity remained endemic. The country made progress in strengthening its renewable energy sector, and a new wind farm was inaugurated in September near Lake Ghoubbet. In addition, Djibouti continued its ambitious space programme and launched its first satellite in November with the purpose of collecting environmental data. The government signed an MoU with a Chinese company to construct an international space port with a rocket and satellite launching site.

Domestic Politics

President *Ismaïl Omar Guelleh*, who had been in power since 1999, retained his position as the country's authoritarian strongman, and the ruling RPP stayed in power. Parliamentary elections were held on 24 February but only one opposition party, the *Union pour la démocratie et la justice* (UDJ), took part, while the other opposition parties – namely the *Rassemblement pour l'Action, la Démocratie et le Développement Ecologique* (RADDE) and the *Alliance Républicaine pour la Démocratie* (ARD) – boycotted the elections. Guelleh's RPP won 94% of the vote, a result that corresponded to 58 of 65 seats in parliament, while the UDJ received seven seats. The parliament was elected for a five-year term, and women received a 25% quota of the seats. However, voter turnout was low because the elections were not perceived as free and fair and the outcome had been foreseeable. *Abdoulkader Kamil Mohamed* continued to serve as Djibouti's prime minister, having held this position for a decade. The small country and its economy remained under the iron grip of the president and his extended family, but in light of the age of the president, who was born in 1947, power squabbles continued within the dominant Somali-Issa clan and between members of the Issa and ethnic Afar groups. *First lady Kadra Mohammed Haïd* was highly influential; reportedly, she was pulling the strings in the background. Hailing from the Somali-Issa clan, she placed members of the clan in various important positions, including the governor of the central bank, the head of the Constitutional Court, and the deputy speaker of the national parliament. The political system was highly personalised and based on patronage networks. Djibouti ranked 130th out of 180 countries in the 2023 Transparency International Corruption Perceptions Index, based on data from 2022.

This resulted in a repressive political climate, and *civil liberties* were almost non-existent. There was no freedom of the press, and the government was in control of Djibouti's few radio and television stations. 'La Voix de Djibouti', the only internet opposition radio station, was forced to continue broadcasting from France. As in previous years, the Freedom House Index of 2023 ranked the country as 'not free', and Djibouti held rank 126 out of 180 countries in RSF's press freedom ranking, based on data from 2022. Human rights activists remained under scrutiny, and in mid-March, the vice-president of the French organisation International Federation for Human Rights (FIDH), Alexis Deswaef, was expelled from the country during a fact-finding mission. He was arrested at his hotel and forced onto a plane to Ethiopia, while a programme officer of the organisation was turned away by the authorities upon her arrival; both human rights observers had been in the possession of a valid entry visa. Before his expulsion, Deswaef had met human rights activist Zakaria Abdillahi, the former president of the Ligue Djiboutienne des droit humains, who had been a victim of arbitrary persecution and surveillance for many years. He also held talks with several civil society representatives and opposition leaders. The political situation in the country remained stable during the year, and the Afar-dominated rebel movement *Front pour la Restauration de l'Unité et de la Démocratie* (FRUD armée) was largely inactive, unlike in the previous year.

Foreign Affairs

Djibouti continued to serve as landlocked Ethiopia's only sea outlet and retained its strategic importance as a host to several *international military bases* operating to protect the sea passage through the Bab al-Mandeb Strait through the Red Sea towards the Suez Canal. In the ongoing conflict between President Guelleh and the UAE-based port company DP World, related to the Doraleh Container Terminal, the government suffered a new set-back when a US court enforced awards from the London Court of International Arbitration worth $486 m against Djibouti in mid-February.

The government maintained its historically close relations to *Saudi Arabia*, and in early April, President Guelleh sent a letter to Crown Prince Mohammed bin Salman through Ambassador Day-Eddine Said in which he pledged to strengthen mutual cooperation in all fields. Saudi foreign minister Prince Faisal bin Fahan received the letter and discussed bilateral relations with the ambassador. In mid-May, President Guelleh attended the annual *Arab League* summit in Jeddah and discussed the conflicts in Sudan and Yemen, which he characterised as the main challenges for the Arab world. He also welcomed Syria's return to the League. However, on 29 September, Saudi Arabia's arch-foe *Iran* announced the re-establishment of diplomatic relations with Djibouti, which had been stalled for seven years. The foreign ministers of the two countries met on the sidelines of the 78th session of the UNGA in New York, and Djibouti's minister of foreign affairs, Mahamoud Ali Youssouf, confirmed that his government welcomed the re-establishment of relations. Relations with *Egypt* also remained warm, although no high-level visits took place during the year. In February, medical aid was delivered from Egypt to Djibouti as a sign of friendship and to strengthen cooperation in the medical field.

The close cooperation between Djibouti and its much larger neighbour *Ethiopia* continued; the two countries' economies remained strongly intertwined due to Ethiopia's dependence on Djiboutian ports to handle its foreign trade activities. However, disagreements related to port fees charged by Djibouti strained relations to a certain extent. On 5 April, a high-level delegation led by the vice-president of Prime Minister Abiy Ahmed's Prosperity Party, Adem Farah, arrived from Addis Ababa to discuss bilateral cooperation and issues such as drought, migration, and regional security. However, after Abiy claimed in autumn that his country had a historical right to access to the sea and to control a Red Sea port, Djibouti rejected the claim on 19 October, as Eritrea and Somalia had done before.

Kenya's president William Ruto visited Djibouti on 11 June, met with President Guelleh and both leaders agreed to introduce a visa-free travelling scheme to strengthen cooperation and to pursue their strategic partnership. In December the two countries agreed to establish a parliamentary friendship group. Foreign minister Mahamoud Ali Youssouf visited *Rwanda* and, along with his Rwandan counterpart Vincent Biruta, signed three bilateral agreements regarding mutual visa exemptions, the improvement of air services and the promotion and protection of investments.

Relations with *Somalia* were close, and on 30 January, Djibouti's defence minister Hassan Omar Mohamed met with his Somali counterpart Abulqadir Mohamed to discuss ongoing military operations against the al-Shabaab militia. On the next day, a joint meeting of the defence ministers of Somalia, Kenya, Djibouti, and Ethiopia took place in Mogadishu with the purpose of discussing joint anti-terrorism measures, including cooperation between the Somali National Army and members of the AU peacekeeping operation African Transition Mission in Somalia (*ATMIS*). This was the first meeting of this kind since 2007. Djibouti was an active member of ATMIS and had a military presence in Somalia's Hiran region. President Guelleh also tried to mediate in the ongoing conflict between Somalia and the internationally unrecognised government of *Somaliland*. In early April, he reached out to Somali president Hassan Sheikh Mohamud and Somaliland's leader Muse Bihi Abdi to resume stalled talks to settle their dispute, and a dialogue conference took place at the end of December under Guelleh's mediation.

Djibouti took over the *IGAD* chairship from Sudan and hosted the organisation's first summit since 2019 in the presence of leaders and officials from Kenya, Ethiopia, Somalia, South Sudan, Sudan, and, after a long time, Eritrea, which had severed its IGAD membership 16 years ago in protest at Ethiopia's military activities in Somalia during that period. On the agenda were discussions about the ongoing conflict in Sudan and the peace process in South Sudan.

Djibouti retained its close relations with former colonial power *France*. On 14 December, French foreign minister Caterine Colonna and minister of the armed forces Sébastien Lecornu visited Djibouti. They held talks with government officials, including the president, in a constructive atmosphere and discussed the future and the financial demands of the French military base in the country. The *US government* played close attention to regional developments in the Horn of Africa and reinforced its military presence at its base in Camp Lemonnier. After the beginning of the civil war in Sudan in April, the US sent additional troops to Djibouti to facilitate evacuation measures. In late May, the US special envoy for the Horn of Africa, Mike Hammer, met government officials during a visit to Djibouti and Ethiopia to discuss bilateral cooperation and regional conflicts in the Horn. He also met IGAD executive secretary Workneh Gebeyehu. In mid-August, the US acting assistant secretary of defence Mara Karlin travelled to Djibouti, where she discussed regional security issues with officials from the US Africa Command (AFRICOM) and met with President Guelleh in the company of AFRICOM commander General Michael Langley to reaffirm her country's commitment to the mutual defence relationship. US secretary of defence Lloyd Austin met with Djibouti's president and defence minister on 23 September during his first trip to Africa to discuss regional security issues, including Djibouti's engagement for ATMIS. However, in late December, Djibouti's foreign minister stated that his country was reluctant to participate in the US-led naval coalition against the *Houthis in Yemen* to contain attacks against international sea travel in protest at Israel's military engagement in the Gaza Strip, despite potential harms to its economy.

China maintained close relations with Djibouti, its military base which opened in 2017 remaining operational and hosting approximately 2,000 troops. On 6 August, members of the RPP met members of the Chinese Communist Party to discuss future cooperation. The US base Camp Lemonnier was staffed with some 4,000 military personnel and additional third-country civilian employees. It was used to reload US warships involved in the anti-Houthi operations that started in October. *Japan* and *Italy* retained a small military presence as well, and the *EU military Operation Atalanta* was extended in January until the end of 2024 with the aim of controlling piracy and protecting vulnerable shipping, countering drugs trafficking and participating in the weapons embargo on al-Shabaab in the Red Sea and Indian Ocean.

Socioeconomic Developments

Djibouti's *development strategy* continued to rely on FDI and the development of its ports and infrastructure. The implementation of renewable energy projects, which had been a focus of the government for several years, advanced gradually. Due to the country's strategic location at the Bab el-Mandeb Strait, international military bases continued to contribute substantially to the state's budget; the same held true for Djibouti's role as sea outlet for landlocked Ethiopia. As in previous years, China was an important foreign investor, and the Chinese-constructed Doraleh Multi-Purpose Port was of crucial importance for the handling of imports and exports. In addition, a variety of Chinese enterprises were active in the Djibouti International Free Trade Zone. This was operated as a joint venture with the Djibouti Ports and Free Zone Authority and provided services such as commerce, logistics, and processing. The Djibouti *railway*, which had also been established with Chinese financial support, became fully operational again after the end of the Covid-19 crisis. In July, the World Bank granted $730 m via the International Development Association to upgrade the Addis–Djibouti corridor, which was seen as a vital trade route and a lifeline for Ethiopia's population of 120 m.

Djibouti retained its commitment to sustainable development and to its development plan 'Vision Djiboutie 2035', which expressed the aim that the country should become the leading commercial and logistics hub in East Africa and that it would achieve 100% *energy self-sufficiency* through *renewable energy* resources by

2030. An important step in this direction was achieved when Amea, a UAE-based independent power producer, signed an agreement with Electricité de Djibouti (EDD) to install a 25 MW solar farm in Grand Bara which was supposed to produce 55 GWh per year for some 66,500 people and support the country's strategy to reduce CO_2 emissions. In addition, Djibouti launched a 60 MW wind farm in early September located near Lake Ghoubbet that was supposed to increase power production by almost 50%, thereby reducing the country's dependence on imported energy. In previous years, 60% to 80% of consumed power had to be imported from Ethiopia. The project was financed by a consortium of investors including the Africa Finance Corporation and the Dutch Entrepreneurial Development Bank and was worth $122 m. In late May, IGAD held a workshop with the purpose of validating and endorsing Djibouti's National Blue Economy Strategy related to the sustainable economic exploitation of marine and aquatic resources.

Over the year, Djibouti signed various grant *agreements with foreign donors* and investors to foster development in different fields. On 5 April, Djibouti and the AfDB signed three agreements worth €22 m in grants with the purpose of strengthening the health sector, improving energy efficiency, and supporting the reform of the financial sector. More specifically, the agreements aimed at improving access to maternal and neo-natal healthcare for vulnerable population groups, improving energy efficiency of public buildings, and strengthening the national banking and financial system to accelerate the development of the productive sector. On 12 May, the Islamic Development Bank signed an agreement with Djibouti valued $600 m over three years to boost development in the fields of energy, agriculture, health, and private sector development. The EIB lent €79 m to the country for the improvement of water desalination and sanitation including wastewater treatment. The grant was repayable over a period of 25 years.

In mid-June, the *IMF* concluded its periodic staff visit to Djibouti and stated that economic growth had slowed down in 2022 due to international trade disruptions and the conflict in Ethiopia. However, port activities improved in 2023 after the 2022 Pretoria Peace Agreement had put an end to the war in Ethiopia. The organisation recommended to the government that revenue collection should be improved, expenditure efficiency should be enhanced, and governance should be strengthened to invest more in human capital development and in inclusive growth. Similarly, the *World Bank* expected a recovery of Djibouti's economy and a GDP increase of 4.7%. It also stated that the inflation rate had fallen from 11% in July 2022 to only 1.2% one year later. However, the bank complained that tax revenues were diminishing due to tax exemptions and mounting public debt servicing costs, while Djibouti's banking sector had remained stable. The World Bank expected a positive development and rising growth rates of over 5% for the near future but warned that regional tensions, the worsening Middle East conflict, and the accumulation of public debt might put this forecast at risk. However, negotiations with creditors about debt restructuring reportedly took a positive turn during the year.

Djibouti's population remained exposed to *endemic poverty* despite fulfilling the criteria for belonging to the low-middle-income country category. Chronic unemployment remained high; it was projected at 28% by the ILO. The last available WFP annual report, from 2022, estimated that 35% of the population lived in poverty, with 21% being exposed to extreme poverty. According to report, Djibouti ranked 93rf out of 125 countries, which meant the population was affected by a serious level of hunger. The UN's *Integrated Food Security Phase Classification* (IPC) stated that about 250,000 people, corresponding to 21% of the population, would experience acute food insecurity, especially in the remote rural areas of the country, where 40% of the population was affected. Migrants and refugees were also highly vulnerable; in December, the IOM indicated in its migration trends for the country that migration from Ethiopia had increased by 21% due to reduced border controls and rumours that boat departures from Obock to the Arab Peninsula had resumed. According to the UNHCR, Djibouti hosted some 30,000 refugees, mainly from Somalia, Ethiopia, and Yemen.

Despite the prevailing poverty among the population, the government remained focused on its *space programme*, launched in 2021. In mid-January, it signed a $1 bn MoU with the Chinese Hongkong Aero Space Technology Group to build an international commercial space port including a rocket and satellite launch site in Northern Obock. On 14 November, the country launched its first satellite, called Djibouti-1A, on a SpaceX transporter with the purpose of tracking environmental change across the country and pursuing the SDGs related to climate change at national and regional levels. The programme was run in cooperation with the French Centre Spatial Universitaire de Montpellier. For the future, Djibouti intended to build its own astronautical and space academy according to minister of higher education and research Aboubaker Hassan.

Eritrea

Nicole Hirt

No political changes took place in Eritrea, and the country remained an autocracy under its long-term president Isaias Afewerki, who has been in power for more than three decades. The ruling People's Front for Democracy and Justice (PFDJ) was the only party allowed and there was no implemented constitution, no functioning parliament and judiciary. The human rights situation remained extremely worrying. Eritrean troops continued to occupy parts of Ethiopia's Tigrayan territory, and adult citizens were obliged to participate in the open-ended national service. The country's economy was under the firm grip of the military and the PFDJ's ruling elite, while the majority of the population depended on diaspora remittances for subsistence. The diaspora was polarised between government supporters and opponents, and in summer violent clashes between the groups occurred in various European countries, in Israel, and in North America. The president established close relations with Moscow during the year, and relations with China, which controlled Eritrea's mining sector, remained close.

Domestic Politics

The political situation in Eritrea remained unchanged and the autocratic system under the long-term rule of President Isaias Afewerki continued. No implemented constitution has been in place since independence in 1993, and no elections were held. The president ruled the country with an iron fist and relied on a few personal advisors, including Yemane Gebreab, the head of the political affairs department of the ruling *People's Front for Democracy and Justice* (PFDJ), and the financial head of the PFDJ Hagos Gebrehiwot 'Kisha'. Afewerki also relied on high-ranking military personnel, specifically on General Filipos Woldeyohannes, the leader of Eritrea's defence forces in the absence of an appointed defence minister, and Abraha Kassa, the head of the National Security Office. Eritrea has not had a legislative body since the National Assembly convened for the last time in 2002, and the *judiciary* was in an extremely poor state, with almost no regular court proceedings taking place. The criminal justice system was characterised by arbitrary arrests of suspects and a complete lack of due process. Civil law remained in the hands of *customary institutions* and there was a severe lack of qualified jurists. The last regular meeting of the cabinet of ministers was held in 2018, and the health of some of the elderly ministers had reportedly already deteriorated by then. The PFDJ remained the only legal political party, but it was largely inactive as a political body. The president had no intention to reform the political system, and the open-ended national service which had been introduced in 2002 and had since triggered a continuous mass exodus of the younger generation. On 22 February, the president gave an interview on EriTV in which he blamed the US for its long-term hostility towards his country and claimed that the Tigray People's Liberation Front (TPLF) had planned the war in Tigray (see below) with support from Washington. He claimed that the Pretoria peace agreement had also been worked out by the US government to prevent the TPLF's total military defeat.

The *human rights situation* in the country remained extremely worrying, and Eritrean citizens did not enjoy any kind of civil liberties. All citizens remained under obligation to perform national service, which consisted of several months of military training, followed by unspecified periods of forced labour for the military or the PFDJ's economic enterprises. In February, a HRW report stated that in previous months, house-to-house searches for alleged draft evaders had been carried out and family members had been arbitrarily detained and expelled from their houses to put pressure on those who had gone into hiding to avoid being sent to Tigray as soldiers. On 6 March, the UN's deputy human rights chief Nada Al-Nashif addressed the UNHRC and reported that the situation in Eritrea remained dire, with government authorities that continued to commit atrocities enjoying complete impunity. She also confirmed that all political prisoners had remained in detention. On 9 May, the special rapporteur for human rights in Eritrea, Mohamed Abdulsalam Babiker, presented his report regarding the human rights situation and came to similar conclusions. He wrote that the indefinite national service had a negative impact on the economic, social, and cultural rights of Eritreans and that the rule of law continued to be non-existent. Civic space remained completely closed, and Eritreans had no access to independent information, while arbitrary detention remained common.

Access to the internet remained extremely limited, only available in urban areas through internet cafés controlled by the government; the connection speed stayed extremely low. The population continued to feel reluctant to talk openly on the phone due to the fear of being supervised by the state's security agents, and exchange of news and opinions with Eritreans living outside the country was severely restricted. Eritrea ranked 174th out of 180 countries in Reporters Without Borders' 2023 *press freedom* ranking based on 2022 data. The improvement from rank 179 in the previous year was a result not of any kind of progress towards freedom of information but rather of the deteriorating situations in other countries. As usual, the limited number of press outlets and radio stations were under the control of the Ministry of Information and its head Yemane Ghebremeskel. Radio Erena, EriSat, and other online news outlets produced news in the diaspora, but it was hard to receive such news in Eritrea due to the risk of being detected and labelled an opposition sympathiser. After civil war broke out in Sudan in April, the Eritrean government reportedly deported more than 3,500 refugees from that country by capturing evacuation buses on their way from Khartoum to safer areas. Some of these refugees were later detained.

Religious freedom continued to be heavily restricted, including through close government surveillance of the legal religious denominations, namely the Orthodox, Catholic, and Lutheran churches and Sunni Islam. In January, Release International reported that some four hundred Evangelical Christians were languishing in Eritrean jails, exposed to torture and inhumane prison conditions. On 25 April, International Christian Concern reported that 103 college students had been detected while worshipping and arrested in a crackdown. They were transported to the overcrowded Mai Sirwa prison near Asmara. Generally, all kinds of Pentecostal churches and the Jehova Witnesses remained banned.

Eritrea held rank 161 out of 180 in Transparency International's 2023 *Corruption Perceptions Index* based on data from 2022, while a lack of reliable data persisted. Corruption among army officials continued with impunity. For instance, national service recruits had to pay bribes for benefits such as holiday extensions.

In the *diaspora*, violent clashes between government supporters and opponents took place in several European countries, the US, Canada, Israel, and Australia. These clashes happened in response to the annual festivals organised by the government with the support of its diplomatic missions and transnational organisations, including the Young PFDJ and several so-called cultural associations. A new *opposition movement*, which labelled itself 'Blue Revolution' (a reference to Eritrea's flag from the time of its federation with Ethiopia, which had been chosen as the symbol of the movement), became prominent among Eritreans during the year. Members of this movement's militant wing, named Brigade N'Hamedu, attacked police officers who were attempting to protect festival visitors in different cities: for instance, on 9 July, 26 police officers were hurt in the German city of Giessen, where the opposition movement held a violent protest in an attempt to interrupt the annual Eritrea Festival; and in September, 39 members of the police force were injured in a similar event in Stuttgart, some of them seriously. In Stockholm similar riots occurred relating to the annual Eritrea Festival, and dozens of people were injured. Similar clashes took place during the Edmonton Festival in Canada on 21 August, and in Tel Aviv more than a hundred people were injured on 3 September, when government supporters had organised an 'Eritrea Day'. The protesters claimed that the festivals served as tools to collect money for the regime in Eritrea and to spread hate speech and propaganda, while government supporters referred to their democratic right to celebrate their government during such meetings in countries where the right to assembly was granted.

Foreign Affairs

Eritrea's military presence in Tigray continued after the entry into force of the Pretoria Declaration of Permanent Cessation of Hostilities by the federal government of Ethiopia and the TPLF in November 2022. Eritrea had not been an official party in the Tigray war and did not take part in the Pretoria negotiations. Accordingly, the country was not a signatory of the peace agreement. In January, international media outlets such as 'The Economist' and the Canadian 'Globe & Mail' reported that Eritrean troops kept looting and attacking civilians, especially in the area around the town of Adigrat. Eritrea also maintained close links to militant Amhara militias that had a presence in parts of the Tigrayan territory, and President Isaias retained a network of informants all over Ethiopia. Reportedly, Eritrea was also involved in the military training of the Amhara Fano militias. On 30 January, US ambassador to the UN Linda Thomas-Greenfeld confirmed the continuous presence of Eritrean troops in Tigray.

On 2 February, President Isaias travelled to Kenya to discuss peace efforts in Ethiopia with his Kenyan counterpart William Ruto. During a joint press conference by the two leaders, Isais appeared visibly annoyed when journalists asked him questions regarding the presence of his troops in Tigray, and he declined to answer. According to analysts, Isaias was not pleased with the Pretoria agreement and saw it as a plot engineered by the West to secure the survival of the TPLF, while he regarded that organisation as his personal arch-enemy. On 20 March, the Biden administration stated that all parties involved, among them Eritrea, had committed *war crimes* during the Tigray war, including crimes against humanity, yet without announcing any particular political consequences. On 22 April, the newly installed Tigray interim administration deplored the fact that Eritrean troops still occupied several administrative areas in northern and parts of north-western Tigray. On 27 May, CNN reported that it had evidence that Eritrean troops had stopped a UN-led humanitarian mission from entering the village of Gemhalo in northern Tigray and that the Eritrean military regularly prevented the population from accessing humanitarian aid. Similarly, the AU observer mission was reportedly denied access to the town of Humera on 11 May. Deutsche Welle reported that there was evidence of a massacre carried out by Eritrean troops in the Tigrayan city of Adwa in late October 2022, which took the lives of some three hundred people. Eritrea's foreign ministry called all accusations 'unsubstantiated and defamatory' and linked them to alleged US hostility towards Eritrea.

Despite simmering *tensions between Eritrea* and the federal government of *Ethiopia*, members of Eritrea's top military leadership, including General Abraha, travelled to Ethiopia at the invitation of the Ethiopian National Defense Force to visit intelligence and security facilities. However, *relations between Isaias* and *Ethiopian prime minister Abiy Ahmed* deteriorated further when the latter claimed in October in front of members of his government that Ethiopia had a historical right of access to the sea and that the landlocked country should be in control of a Red Sea port. These claims raised the alarm among the neighbouring countries along the Red Sea coast, namely Eritrea, Djibouti, and Somalia. Eritrea had been part of Ethiopia from the time of its federation with the Ethiopian empire in 1952 until the military victory of the Eritrean Liberation Front in 1991, which rendered Ethiopia landlocked. There were still revisionist tendencies among many Ethiopian nationalists, some of whom regard Eritrea's independence as a historical mistake. In December, Ethiopian media reported waves of arrests among Eritrean communities residing in Addis Ababa and other parts of the country, perhaps in an attempt to weaken the surveillance system established by the Eritrean authorities in the aftermath of the 2018 peace agreement.

Eritrea's relations with *Somalia* remained positive, and thousands of Somali troops were sent to Eritrea to receive military training upon the request of Somalia's government. On 13 March and once more on 8 October, President Hassan Sheikh Mohamud travelled to Asmara to discuss bilateral ties and regional matters. On 11 April, Eritrea's foreign minister Osman Saleh and presidential advisor Yemane Gebreab went on a working visit to *Kenya*, where they met President Ruto. During President Isaias' February visit to Nairobi, the two countries had agreed to abolish entry visa requirements to enhance bilateral relations, and Ruto encouraged

Eritrea's return to IGAD as an active member. In fact, Eritrea rejoined the Horn of Africa's regional organisation in June, 16 years after Isaias had suspended the country's membership in 2007 in protest at Ethiopia's military intervention in Somalia in 2006. Eritrea's Ministry of Information pledged that the country would henceforth be ready to work for peace, stability, and regional integration.

After the outbreak of civil war in *Sudan* between the Sudanese Armed Forces (SAF) led by Abdel Fattah al-Burhan and the Rapid Support Forces (RSF) under the control of Mohamad Hamdan Dagalo, better known as Hemedti, in April, President Isais did not clearly side with one of the opponents. Hemedti had visited Eritrea on 13 March, weeks before the outbreak of hostilities, to discuss bilateral relations and reportedly to attempt to weave an alliance between the RSF and Eritrea. However, on 11 September, SAF chief and head of Sudan's Sovereign Council Abdel Fattah al-Burhan visited Asmara to discuss strengthening bilateral relations as well, and members of his delegation were assured that Isaias supported the safeguarding of Sudan's territorial integrity and a diplomatic solution to the conflict. Eritrea's relations with the government of *South Sudan* remained friendly, and on 4 April, minister of foreign affairs Osman Saleh and his constant companion Yemane Gebreab paid a visit to President Salva Kiir to deliver a message from President Isaias regarding bilateral cooperation and regional developments.

Eritrean relations with the *UAE*, which had considerably strengthened its ties with Ethiopia, remained poor. On 16 November, the pro-government website Tesfanews accused the UAE on X (formally Twitter) of being behind Prime Minister Abiy's demands to obtain Red Sea access due to its own rivalry with *Saudi Arabia*. This could also be seen as an attempt by Isaias to further strengthen his ties to the Saudi kingdom. The president visited Saudi Arabia several times during the year. On 28 February, he travelled to Riyadh to meet government officials. In mid-November, he attended the Saudi Arabia–Africa summit and met with Saudi prime minister Crown Prince Mohammed bin Salman. He was accompanied by several government officials, including Hagos Gebrehiwet 'Kisha', the PFDJ's head of economic affairs, who rarely went on official state visits abroad. Relations with *Egypt* remained stable. Isaias visited Cairo on 12 July, met with President Abdel Fatteh al-Sisi, and attended the summit of leaders of the countries neighbouring Sudan. On 12 October, Osman Saleh and Yemane Gebreab met with Egypt's foreign minister Sameh Shoukri to discuss efforts to stop the war in Sudan.

President Isaias was keen to maintain his close ties with *Russia*, which had been strengthened by his decisive support for the Kremlin's invasion of Ukraine in 2022. On 27 January, Russia's foreign minister Sergey Lavrov met with the Eritrean president in Asmara during his second tour of Africa to discuss the enhancement of bilateral ties in mining, information technology, education, and health. Reportedly, Russia was interested in establishing a military base on Eritrean territory, but no official news pointing in that direction was released. Eritrea's ambassador to Moscow, Petros Tseggai, claimed in a January interview with the Russian media outlet Sputnik that his president had no interest in the establishment of any foreign military bases. On 30 May, Isaias travelled to Russia for a four-day working visit and discussed bilateral relations with President Putin and other government officials. During the meeting, the Eritrean president criticised the 'unipolar world order' under US dominance and demanded a move towards a 'new, civilised order', in which Russia was supposed to play an important role. He also participated in the Russia–Africa summit in St Petersburg at the end of July. According to a note on the Kremlin's website dated 28 July, Isaias issued a message in which he declared that there was no war and not even a conflict between Russia and Ukraine, but that in fact a war had been 'declared by NATO on Russia'.

Eritrea also had close and stable ties with *China*. The two countries had established a strategic partnership in 2022. President Isaias was invited to visit China in mid-May and met with President Xi Jinping on 15 May, who lauded Eritrea's independent foreign policy and the country's safeguarding of its own sovereignty, security, and development path. Xi also hosted a welcome banquet for Eritrea's president at the Great Hall of the People.

Eritrea's relations with the *US* and the *EU* remained poor due to the president's harsh criticism of the democratic West and the 'unipolar world order' under US dominance, and his assertion of alleged long-term Western conspiracies against Eritrea, including continued support for the TPLF. The targeted sanctions imposed by the EU and the US in 2021 against the PFDJ, its National Security Office, the Hdri Trust Fund, and the Red Sea Trading Corporation were not lifted, and Yemane Gebreab complained in an interview he gave to Black Agenda Report on 12 April that the sanctions violated international law. However, he visited *Italy* in the company of Osman Saleh to discuss strengthening bilateral ties with government officials. No details of the conversations were published, but the possible curbing of the entry of refugees from Eritrea to Italy was among the main Italian motives to meet the Eritrean officials.

Socioeconomic Developments

Eritrea's *economic system* remained a highly controlled command economy characterised by extreme constraints on the private sector based on a militarised society. The open-ended national service remained in place for all adult Eritreans, and recruits had to serve as forced labourers for enterprises run by the military and the PFDJ. The government received significant additional income through the 2% diaspora tax levied on all incomes earned by millions of Eritreans nationals and people of Eritrean origin living permanently outside the country. The population depended ever more on private remittances sent by their relatives from abroad because forced recruitment into the national service, which often lasted for decades, deprived them of the opportunity to make a living through their own income.

Basic consumer goods remained scarce, and access to potable water and a reliable electricity supply was restricted. The FAO warned that erratic rainfall might cause a poor harvest. UNICEF's 2023 *Humanitarian Action for Children report* stated that the country was highly vulnerable to economic, climatic, and external shocks; 1.1 m people were in urgent need of humanitarian assistance, among them 745,600 children. According to the report, around 98,000 children were orphans and 30,000 were disabled. In addition, 44% of all households were female-headed because their husbands had been detained, had been forced into labour in other parts of the country, had fled the country, or had been killed in armed conflicts. These numbers disclosed the negative impact of Eritrea's high levels of societal militarisation and its military involvement in the armed conflict in Tigray (2020–22) on children as the most vulnerable group among the population. UNICEF also stated that only one in five children in the country was receiving the necessary minimum diet and that malnutrition was common.

The *education sector* had been in a process of disarray for years due to the mass exodus of the younger generation caused by the open-ended national service, resulting in turn in a massive lack of qualified teachers. It was common practice for graduates of Eritrea's colleges to be forced to serve as teachers in the framework of the national service without being able to choose their place of assignment or the subjects they must teach to the overcrowded classes. In addition, students who wanted to finalise their secondary education still had to pass the 12th school year at the Sawa military camp, where they suffered from physical and psychological mistreatment. According to UNICEF, primary school attendance improved slightly and the retention rate to class five increased to 85.7%. The drop-out rate for secondary schools was 45.6%. The quality of education was poor, with the rate of those reaching the minimum mastery level for literacy and numeracy at grade five standing at 37.6% – meaning that almost two-thirds of students left school without having acquired the ability to read and write and mastered the basic rules of arithmetic.

The WHO did not publish any news about the progress of Eritrea's *Health Sector Strategic Development Plan* for the years 2022–26 or about possible achievements related to the SDG 3 health targets. Similarly to the education sector, the health sector suffered from a severe lack of qualified personnel due to the national service policy, which led to a high outflux of trained health personnel and low motivation among those who remained due to a lack of payment or freedom of choice for the national service recruits who were assigned to work in the sector.

The 2023 outlook of the AfDB projected that Eritrea's GDP would grow by 2.6% in 2023, a very similar rate to the two preceding years. It stated that Eritrea could profit from rising metal prices but would remain in debt distress, with a public debt-to-GDP ratio of 164.7%. Inflation rose to 7.5% in 2022 due to higher energy and food prices. In April, the AfDB approved a grant of $50 m for the construction of a 30 MW *photovoltaic power plant* in the city of Decamhare in Southern Region with the aim of approving electricity supply.

As always, the government refrained from publishing a state budget, and potential financial flows from foreign countries allied with Eritrea's government, such as Saudi Arabia, China, and increasingly Russia, could not be determined. It was also unclear what proportion of state revenue was derived from the diaspora tax, and the amount of informal remittances sent from Eritreans abroad to support their relatives at home was unknown. There was a complete lack of transparency regarding the allocation of state revenues to different sectors and to military spending. The *banking system* remained in a rudimentary and outdated state and did not provide basic services such as ATMs or digital banking. As in previous years, the withdrawal of cash and private investments was heavily restricted, severely hampering the functioning of the private sector.

Eritrea did not receive *EU* development funding and did not profit from the *World Bank*'s lending programme due to payment arrears. President Isaias's increasingly critical rhetoric against the US and Western countries in general and his praising of Russia's leadership and China's policies could be seen as an indicator that he sought support from authoritarian countries rather than accepting Western aid and its related conditionalities.

China's involvement in the country's *mining sector* became even stronger than in previous years when the Australian company Danakali sold its 50% share of the *Colluli potash project* to Chinese company Sichuan Road and Bridge in March after having developed the project for 13 years. The mine, situated in the Dankalia desert in Eritrea's Southern Red Sea Region, is considered to be the world's most significant source of sulphate and potash and could be operational for up to two hundred years after production is begun. Eritrea's National Mining Corporation (ENAMCO) held the second-largest share in the project. The Bisha Copper-Zinc Mine, established by a Canadian company, continued to be run by Chinese Zijin Mining Company in cooperation with ENAMCO; no information about its profitability was available. Eritrea remained the only African country not to have become a member of the AfCFTA.

Ethiopia

Hallelujah Lulie and Jonah Wedekind

Following the November 2022 Pretoria Cessation of Hostilities Agreement (CoHA) signed between Ethiopia's government led by the Prosperity Party (PP) and the Tigray People's Liberation Front (TPLF), Ethiopia's 2023 political landscape was largely defined by contestation over implementing the peace deal. A schism in the Ethiopian Orthodox and Tewahedo Church (EOTC), led by bishops from Oromia region dioceses staging a breakaway from the central Holy Synod, resulted in protests. Public grievances reflected growing perceptions – particularly among Amhara constituents – of Oromo elite dominance over the multinational federation. An escalation of the Fano insurgency in Amhara and sporadic attacks by the Oromia Liberation Army (OLA) in western and southern Oromia compromised security and local government authority. The Southern Nations, Nationalities and Peoples Region (SNNPR) was dissolved with the creation of the South Ethiopia and the Central Ethiopia regions, bringing the count to 12 regional and 2 city states in the federation. Foreign relations with the West continued to normalise despite the government's rejection of independent investigations into human rights abuses during the war and increasing curtailment of the press and political space. Ethiopia was admitted to the BRICS group and sought loans and debt relief from bilateral creditors to alleviate fiscal constraints posed by external debts and inflation. Negotiations with the IMF for debt restructuring stalled, resulting in the country defaulting on its Eurobond credit. Conflict and drought, exacerbated by inflation, left 20 m people in need of food aid across southern, south-eastern, and northern Ethiopia. Government socioeconomic priorities were questioned, given Prime Minister (PM) Abiy Ahmed's penchant for urban beautification and palace projects for which funding sources are opaque. Commodity export earnings reduced slightly while electricity exports gained in importance. Ethiopia and Egypt could not find a technical compromise on the operation of the Grand Ethiopian Renaissance Dam (GERD) following its fourth filling. Declaring construction over 90% complete, landlocked Ethiopia turned from the Nile to the Red Sea and Gulf of Aden. Somalia was angered by Ethiopia's signing of an MoU with Somaliland, granting access to the latter's coastline in return for Ethiopia recognising its statehood.

Domestic Politics

In January, three Oromo archbishops unilaterally announced the establishment of an *independent Oromia Orthodox synod seeking to break away from the EOTC, shaping the political, security, and social developments of the year*. The declaration was strongly rejected by the EOTC's central Holy Synod, which excommunicated the three archbishops. The resulting schism in one of the oldest institutions in Ethiopia was characterised by claims of demographic shifts and simmering ethnic, political, and ideological divisions in the Church, as well as between Church and state. Differences in the understanding of Ethiopia's history and disagreements on the EOTC's preferences in language – using Amharic and Ge'ez over other languages including Afaan Oromo in liturgy and sermons – and symbols – using a unitary Ethiopian flag instead of a federal one – were raised by the breakaway group as reasons necessitating the split. The three archbishops, led by Abuna Sawiros, also complained that despite having the second-largest Orthodox population in Ethiopia, Oromo priests, bishops, and believers were not adequately represented in the Church. The EOTC rejected this, labelling the rebellion a 'political project'. Leading figures including the EOTC secretary, Archbishop Petros, accused the PM and government of supporting the split, widening tensions between the EOTC and the government. *A mass-mobilisation by EOTC followers in early February protesting the breakaway* quickly turned political. A federal-government-negotiated settlement in mid-February resulted in the breakaway bishops dropping their demands. Despite his portraying himself as the peacemaker, Abiy's perceived tacit support for the split worsened elite fragmentation within the PP leadership and constituency and accelerated the diminishing of Abiy's support base among EOTC followers and in Amhara. In July, appointments of archbishops in Tigray emboldened autocephaly in the Tigray Synod, which had accused the EOTC of 'supporting genocide' during the 2020–22 Tigray war, rejecting the EOTC's apology earlier in the month for not speaking out against the war. The crisis worsened state – Church relations and dented the historic position and role of the Church in the Ethiopian public and political space.

A statement by the Oromia regional government in May announcing *the construction in Addis Ababa of a palace for the Oromia region was met with criticism.* The regional government was accused of violating the city's constitutional status as the seat of the federal government and the self-rule rights of Addis Ababans. In March, mass demolitions of houses and buildings deemed 'illegal' in 'Shaggar' city of Oromia, which effectively surrounds Addis Ababa, reignited debates over the identity and ownership of the capital and its environs. The regional government maintained that Oromia was a sovereign regional state and Addis Ababa its capital. The Amhara opposition accused the demolition campaign of seeking to change the demography of the capital through the Shaggar project in the interests of the Oromo. The demolitions included churches and mosques, raising outrage and anger among the faithful and their representatives. In March, the Ethiopian Human Rights Commission (EHRC) labelled the demolitions illegal and against international and human rights laws.

Opposition members challenged the PM and finance minister Ahmed Shide in parliament about the funding sources for and necessity of prominent urban beautification projects in Addis Ababa. Of concern was Abiy's 'Chaka' (forest) project, costs for which were estimated to exceed $10 bn while construction (including a palace) is expected to expand over 500 ha and displace city dwellers in the Yeka sub-city district.

The unresolved issue of 'contested areas' between Tigray and Amhara, differences on the magnitude and pace of the DDR (Disarmament, Demobilization, and Reintegration) programme, and frustration with reconstruction and recovery processes continued to frustrate the progress of the peace process. On 3 February, PM Abiy met with senior TPLF figures and former leaders of the Tigray Defense Forces (TDF) for the first time since the war began in November 2020. The meeting reviewed the implementation of the Pretoria agreement and post-war recovery and reconstruction efforts. A month later, the Council of Ministers approved a guideline to establish an 'Inclusive Interim Regional Administration of Tigray', and on 23 March Abiy appointed Getachew Reda, TPLF member and former minister of information (2012–16) during the government of the Ethiopian People's Revolutionary Democratic Front (EPRDF), as head of the TIRA (Interim Regional Administration of Tigray). Among other things, the TIRA was mandated to oversee the DDR of an estimated 270,000 former combatants, the return and settlement of IDPs, and the normalisation of relations with Addis Ababa and regional states of the federation, all of which proved complex to implement in practice due to range of factors including continued contestation over Amhara forces' control of the West and South Tigray zones and the de facto administrations in Welkait-T(s)egede, Setit-Humera, Tselemti, and Raya, established during the war. The need for accountability for atrocities committed during the war was emphasised by the Tigray authorities and international partners. A domestic transitional justice framework was adopted to address atrocities and human rights violations and abuses committed by all parties. However, the government rejected the findings and recommendations of an independent investigation by the UN's International Commission of Human Rights Experts on Ethiopia. The government's transitional justice bill has passed many stages since then and was presented for consultation by the Ministry of Justice in October. Numerous stakeholders expressed concern that the framework fell short of its initial objectives.

While it succeeded in stopping the war in Tigray, *the Pretoria agreement resulted in the gradual unravelling of the political and security coalition against the TPLF*. Discontent among the Amhara polity on the spirit, content, and implementation of the agreement spiked in 2023. The establishment of Shaggar and alleged role of the federal and Oromia regional governments in the EOTC crisis added to the rapid fragmentation of the political and security alliance between the federal government and Amhara political and armed groups. Fears of a possible ideological and security realignment between the federal government and the TPLF also fuelled anxiety and speculation. The sense of betrayal and uncertainty shaped relations between the federal government and Amhara political forces in Ethiopia and the diaspora. In early 2023, the diaspora-supported Eskinder Nega, a former journalist and chair of the Balderas for True Democracy Party, declared the formation of the Amhara Popular Front (APF), an armed movement akin to the Fano aiming to unseat the government through force.

In April, *the federal government's move to demobilise and reintegrate regional special forces into the ENDF was met with mass defection from the Amhara special forces and mobilisation of the Fano armed movement* against the regional and federal governments. According to minister of peace Binalf Andualem more than half of the Amhara regional special forces had defected in April and May, rejecting the government's call for demobilisation of the regional special force and resulting in a stand-off with the ENDF. Ensuing demonstrations in most cities in the Amhara region, including Gondar, Bahir Dar, Kobo, and Debre Birhan, were met with government curfews. The federal decision to centralise the monopoly of violence and pursue nationwide DDR, overseen by the National Rehabilitation Commission, was introduced in April against the backdrop of CoHA and ensuing political differences and growing power competition between the leadership of the Amhara and Oromia PP factions. Citing the number of Oromo figures in the top leadership and command structure of the military, the Amhara opposition and diaspora labelled the ENDF an institution working for Oromo interests ('Oromummaa army'). Special forces and

Fanos alike rejected demobilisation as a purported scheme to weaken the Amhara military capabilities and consolidate Oromo's control over the national security sector. The Amhara opposition and nationalists referred to the threat from the not fully disarmed TDF and uncertainties over what CoHA calls 'contested areas' between Tigray and Amhara – in West Tigray (Welkait-T(s)egede) and South Tigray (Raya) – to justify the need for the regional special force. The impasse on the resolution of the territorial dispute continued to undermine trust and reconciliation between the former warring parties. The leaders of the Fano, the informal and locally fractured Amhara militia which took part in the Tigray war alongside government forces, held that the existence of the Amhara special forces was an insurance policy for the region in case of an attack by the TPLF's TDF or the federal government's ENDF. A government attempt to deal with the escalation by releasing prominent Fano leader Zemene Kassie on 4 June gave impetus to the expanding armed movement. Zemene Kassie declared that the Amhara nation faced an unprecedented existential threat and called for the total mobilisation of the Amhara people. Prominent figures of the diaspora, former leaders of opposition parties and protest movements, and artists who had supported Abiy and his government joined in expressing their support for the armed resistance to oust Abiy. These included Andargachew Tsege and Neamin Zeleke, two figures critical in mobilising support for the government during the Tigray war.

The following months witnessed a significant escalation of violence between the Fano and Amhara and federal security forces across the region. The vice-president of the Amhara regional state and head of Amhara PP, Girma Yeshitila, was assassinated in April. *In July and August, Fano forces over-ran and briefly controlled major cities in the region, including the regional capital Bahir Dar and Gonder. The regional government requested federal intervention. On 4 August, the federal government declared a state of emergency* (SoE). Significantly, this SoE had a nationwide application. Subsequently, the federal government arrested Yohannes Buayalew, former vice-president of the Amhara regional state and member of the Amhara Regional Council, accusing him of supporting the armed movement. Christian Tadele, a member of opposition party the National Movement of Amhara (NAMA) in the House of People's Representatives and Kassa Teshager, an opposition member of Addis Ababa City Council were also arrested, as were hundreds accused of supporting Fano. The former regional president, Gedu Andargachew, opposed the SoE in parliament. Gedu, also a former foreign minister and national security advisor to Abiy during the Tigray war, was allegedly put under house arrest. The crisis resulted in regional state president Yilkal Kefale and his team resigning. On 25 August, the Amhara regional council appointed Arega Kebede, a former head of the regional militia, as sixth president of the regional state under Abiy's tenure – demonstrating the government's leadership crisis in and attempt at securitising the region.

While Amhara was witnessing unprecedented political instability and insecurity, *Oromia, which had experienced a protracted insurgency since 2019, attempted to end a devastating conflict affecting civilians, security, and governance across the state.* The OLA had over-run towns, successfully launched prison breaks, and disrupted major transport corridors in 2022, but was pushed to the fringes by a government counter-offensive early in 2023. *Shifting ideological and political alliances in Ethiopia and growing recognition of the political and power stalemate in Oromia laid the ground for peace talks.* A February statement to the regional council by Oromia regional state president Shimelis Abdisa pleaded for a peaceful resolution and asserted a commitment to ending the conflict. The following months saw progress: the first round of talks took place in May in Zanzibar, Tanzania. The talks, observed by the US, EU, and IGAD, articulated the problem, agreed on a code of conduct, and ended on a good note despite failure to reach a deal. Statements by both parties acknowledged the progress made and expressed readiness to continue the process. The second round took place in November, with the participation of the three most senior political and military leaders of the movement, including the head of the insurgency, Kumsa Diriba, known by his nom de guerre Jaal Marroo – a testament to the high hopes that facilitators and the parties had of reaching a deal and the depth of the preparations ahead of the talks. The two parties reached consensus on wide-ranging issues including power-sharing in the Oromia regional state government. However, *an agreement was not reached due to differences on reform and restructuring of federal institutions and processes*, with the parties blaming each other for the breakdown of the talks. There was no ceasefire during the talks, and sporadic clashes and military campaigns by the government and OLA continued throughout the year.

Continued demands from numerous ethnic and cultural groups for regional statehood or an elevation of administrative status, recognition, and autonomy continued to shape politics and governance. *The disintegration of the former SNNPR, which started with the formation of the Sidama and South West Ethiopia regions in 2019 and 2021, continued.* The rest of the region was divided into two following a controversial, contested referendum held in February for South Ethiopia Region (SER). The creation of SER as the 11th regional state resulted in the remaining SNNPR zones falling into Central Ethiopia Region (CER) as the 12th state, ending the existence of the SNNPR on 19 August. Political and social movements demanding regional statehood in Wolayta Zone (SER) and Gurage Zone (CER) were suppressed by political and security crackdowns targeting members of the zonal administration, scholars, activists, and journalists. The results of the referendum in SER and the lack of a referendum for CER, as well as the government's so-called 'cluster' approach of distributing administrative centres and departments in different zones of the newly established states, resulted in further protests and interethnic violence. Analysts saw the federal government as testing out a 'geographic' federalism in the south, which the PP initially implicitly favoured over 'multinational' federalism, though it was constrained constitutionally in implementing this model elsewhere as public opinion remained sharply divided. In May, a study by the government-funded Policy Studies Institute on possible amendments to the constitution met with public condemnation.

Inter-regional boundary clashes continued to claim lives and disrupt governance in areas bordering the Afar and Somali regional states. Regional militia and armed groups from the two regions clashed repeatedly, resulting in the death and displacement of civilians. Repeated attempts to resolve the so-called Affar–Issa conflict did not result in durable peace. Sporadic clashes over checkpoints and administrative boundaries in the Oromia–Somali borderlands, particularly around Babille along the trade route from Harar to Jigjiga, also raised tensions between the two regions. The area, which saw over 1 m people displaced during the political transition (2017–19), remains vulnerable to conflicts between the Oromia and Somali regions as it hosts the Qoloji IDP camp, the largest displacement settlement in the country, on contested territory.

Reporting on or in insurgency areas in Amhara and Oromia was risky for domestic and foreign journalists, with access severely restricted. The government warned reporters not to promote the agendas of groups it labels 'terrorist' and routinely arrested those reporting critically on the government's handling of the insurgencies. The Ethiopian Human Rights Defenders Centre counted up to 30 detention incidents in 2023. In May, the Ethiopian Mass Media Professionals Association called on the government to reverse the imprisonment of journalists (dozens, according to RSF) and to uphold the Media Law, passed in 2021 but since curtailed by the PP government. Stricter legislation on hate speech, designed to counter increasingly ethnicised online hate speech, has also been abused by the government for arbitrary arrests. RSF noted that most press freedom gains under Abiy's government have been reversed since the outbreak of the civil war. Ethiopia's press freedom score was 41.3, ranking it 141st out of 180 countries (based on 2022 data), down from 99th before the Tigray war started in 2020. According to Freedom House, Ethiopia scored 10/40 and 10/60 for political rights and civil liberties respectively; with a total score of 20/100, the country was designated 'not free', dropping three points since the 2022 country report.

Foreign Policy

Efforts to rebuild relations and repair damage caused to the image and reputation of the government and the country by the Tigray war were the foreign policy priority. With political instability and civil war in Sudan, Ethiopia aspired to rebrand itself a responsible actor ready to retake its regional political and security role and project itself as an anchor state of the Horn. This failed to convince diplomats, particularly in the West, so soon after the signing of CoHA. Abiy visited Khartoum in January to address rising tensions between the military and the Rapid Support Force. Ethiopia's attempt to mediate conflict in Sudan did not succeed. One month later, Abiy attended the Somalia-Frontline States Summit in Mogadishu, aimed at enhancing regional security cooperation, and he visited South Sudan in March to seek to strengthen bilateral ties. *Declining relations with Eritrea and a new president in Somalia ended the Addis–Asmara–Mogadishu axis that had shaped Horn politics and security between 2018 and 2021.* Ethiopia–Eritrea relations cooled and uncertainty and mistrust widened between Addis Ababa and Asmara as Abiy's relations with the TIRA improved. Abiy's surprise visit to Cairo on 12 July to meet with President Abdel Fattah al-Sisi was part of attempts to signal Ethiopia's return to regional diplomacy and normalise its foreign affairs post-CoHA. The talks focused on the GERD and the Sudan conflict. A joint statement by the two leaders committed to finalising the agreement in four months. However, the latest round of talks held in December failed. Cairo accused Ethiopia of deliberately hindering progress to create a fait accompli, while Ethiopia accused Egypt of 'colonial era mentality'.

Ethiopia was admitted to the BRICS group in August, joining officially on 1 January 2024. Addis Ababa presented this as a diplomatic victory, despite uncertainty over its actual diplomatic and economic dividends. The decision, taken at a BRICS summit in South Africa, to accept Ethiopia served the government's attempt to reassert the country's relevance in the global space, in the face of changing geopolitical dynamics and falling out of favour with the West after the civil war. Abiy attended, holding a series of sideline meetings with President Xi Jinping of China, PM Narendra Modi of India, and South African president Cyril Ramaphosa. Ethiopia also used the platform to gain more concessions from Beijing on the payments on debt maturing in 2023/24 as part of the common framework agreement. As part of a growing focus on the Asia Pacific region, Abiy received Hayashi Yoshimasa and Park Jin, foreign ministers of Japan and South Korea respectively, in August.

Addis made coordinated efforts to consolidate rapprochement with the West following the decline in relations during the Tigray war. A joint visit to Addis Ababa by French foreign minister Catherine Colonna and her German counterpart Annalena Baerbock in January was a signal of improving relations with major European powers. The two ministers met Abiy and discussed a wide range of issues including DDR, transitional justice, and progress on implementing the CoHA. Two months later, US secretary of state Antony Blinken visited Addis, focusing on progress on the Pretoria peace agreement, the security and human rights situation, and post-conflict economic recovery efforts. The April visit by the Italian PM Georgia Meloni was another major diplomatic victory for Addis Ababa, heralding progress in normalising relations with EU member states, followed by the May visit of German chancellor Olaf Scholz, further consolidating normalisation despite remaining points of contention. In February, PM Abiy visited Germany, France, Austria, Italy, and the

Czech Republic to participate in major multilateral forums and bilateral meetings to strengthen development cooperation. In November, the Czech PM Petr Fiala made an official visit to Ethiopia, meeting with Abiy and visiting the Ethiopian Air Force base and headquarters in Bishoftu, where Czech technicians are stationed. An agreement on military aviation including refurbishment of L-39 aircraft was the first security and military agreement between Ethiopia and EU member states since the Tigray war.

The numerous partnership platforms and international forums organised by emerging and middle powers and regional players continued to provide space for Ethiopian diplomacy. In July, Ethiopia attended the Russia–Africa Summit and Economic Forum in St Petersburg. Abiy and his delegation met with President Vladimir Putin to discuss economic and military cooperation. In October, Abiy met Xi Jinping in Beijing while on a state visit and attending the Third Belt and Road Forum for International Cooperation, during which the two countries announced the elevation of their partnership from Comprehensive and Enduring Strategic Cooperative Partnership Level to All-Weather Strategic Cooperation Partnership Level. Abiy also participated in the COP28 in the UAE in December, where he tried to highlight his tree-planting campaign as a pillar of Ethiopia's green diplomacy. He met Sheikh Mohammed Bin Zayed Al Nahyan and other world leaders on the sidelines of the forum. The Saudi–Africa Summit in November was another platform where the PM actively sought economic support.

Chronic foreign-exchange shortage, decline in FDI, slowed growth, and rising unemployment put negotiations with international financial institutions at the heart of foreign policy objectives. Efforts to be included in the IMF programme and secure World Bank support guided relations with the US and socioeconomic decisions including lifting subsidies, introducing new taxes, and monetary measures. In his August visit to Addis Ababa, World Bank president Ajay Banga asserted the need for more radical reforms, including devaluation of the Ethiopian birr (ETB), national bank independence, and government expenditure for an agreement on a bailout package.

The bold claim by Abiy on Ethiopia's natural right to access the sea was one of the most consequential foreign policy developments. In parliament, Abiy made the issue of maritime access, which he asserted as an 'inalienable right', an existential issue for the survival and prosperity of the Ethiopian state and its people. The quest for landlocked Ethiopia's direct and sovereign access to the sea should 'no longer be considered as taboo', Abiy said in an address broadcast on state television on 13 October. Abiy further stated that Ethiopia's existence as a state was linked to the two strategic waters of the Red Sea and the Blue Nile. He asserted that Ethiopia needed to own a port and that peace in the region depended on 'balanced mutual sharing' between landlocked Ethiopia and its neighbours. The statement created nervousness in Eritrea, Djibouti, and Somalia.

Socioeconomic Developments

Following one of the lowest GDP growth rates in the last decade for 2022 (IMF: 3.8%; UNDP: 3.0%), the *IMF and UNDP projected an economic rebound in 2023* (6.1% and 5.0% respectively). This factored in expectations of post-war reconstruction in northern Ethiopia and adjustments to supply chain shocks incurred from the Covid-19 pandemic and the Russia–Ukraine war. With the country dogged by currency and consumer goods inflation, mounting domestic and foreign debt, and reduced investor confidence due to an insecure business environment, the IMF projected a conservative 0.3% increase to 6.4% for 2024. The government's statistics were more optimistic, declaring that a growth rate of 7.5% had been achieved in 2022/23 and projecting 7.9% for 2023/24, according to the Ethiopian Statistical Service (ESS).

Hyperinflation was a major drain on growth. Particularly, the inflation of consumer and intermediate goods (food, fuel, fodder, fertiliser) remained stubbornly high during the year. Headline inflation peaked at around 35% in late 2022 but finally eased in 2023 from 34.2% in March to under 30% in December (UNDP). Food inflation stood at around 33.9% in early 2023 but gradually decreased over the year (ESS). However, disaggregated data suggests that some consumer goods, such as eggs and the staple injera, doubled in the first half of the year, while the government sought to stabilise the prices of other goods – such as sugar and edible oil, which had increased by around 50% in 2022 – through additional imports financed by loans from the central bank. Irregular, short-term fluctuations in the price of teff grain, the key ingredient for injera, from ETB 5,000 to ETB 10,000 between February and March, raised suspicion of artificial shortages. This aggravated rows between Amhara and Oromia regional leaders, who accused each other of transport blockades, and also raised fears that if inflationary economic trends were to worsen, they could fuel contentious issues.

Senior Ethiopian economic analysts and Cepheus, a local market consultancy, publicly questioned the growth and inflation figures published by the ESS, which superseded the Central Statistics Agency as part of the Ethiopian Statistical Development Programme launched by the Ministry of Planning and Development to improve economic data accuracy. Mamo Mihretu, a former World Bank employee and macroeconomic advisor to Abiy, was appointed as the new governor of the National Bank of Ethiopia (NBE) in January. By July, he had publicly acknowledged that inflation posed a 'cost-of-living crisis' for citizens. To curb inflation, in August the NBE issued policies to limit domestic credit growth (at 14%), increase interest rates on central bank loans (from 16% to 18%), and incentivise exports by increasing the retention rate of foreign-exchange export earnings. Mamo ambitiously declared that the plan was to reduce headline inflation to 24% by mid-2024.

The gradual devaluation of the national currency by a combined 25% between 2018 and 2022 put the spotlight on the gaping discrepancy between the average official exchange rate and the black market rate (circa ETB 55 for $1 versus ETB 110–115 for

$1 respectively). Following IMF/World Bank expert visits to Ethiopia in April, World Bank president David Malpass expressed concern over the 'parallel' exchange rate and suggested the need for a 'unified' one. Since then, it was reported that a devaluation and the floating of the birr was imminent, although the Ministry of Finance repeatedly called such reports 'false rumours' to calm local business and investor fears that a depreciated Birr would in the short-term increase inflation further, propel the parallel market, and thus hamper diminishing profits. Controversially, a draft plan for Ethiopia's second Homegrown Economic Reform agenda (HGER 2.0) suggested correcting 'the exchange rate misalignment'.

The ambition of HGER 2.0 was to 'unlock new growth potentials' by improving productivity in all economic sectors, expanding privatisation, and enhancing export promotion, import substitution, and diaspora remittances. A government-linked review of HGER 1.0 acknowledged that external shocks (esp. Covid-19, the Ukraine war), civil war in Ethiopia, and macroeconomic imbalances (rising inflation and debt pressure, unemployment, exchange deficit) had restrained if not reversed key liberalisation reforms. HGER 2.0 formed the basis of negotiations between the government and the IMF for debt restructuring and reanimating the sluggish economic liberalisation process which PM Abiy had promoted at the start of his tenure. The PM announced in June that Ethiopia would continue moving away from the EPRDF's dogmatic 'developmental state' to an 'entrepreneurial state' model favouring public–private partnerships. Yet the state remained interventionist. Regional conglomerates (e.g. Tumsa, Tiret) constituted crucial state levers for facilitating and regulating the transfer of strategic assets, properties, and resources to party-loyal ethnic elites. Ethiopian Investment Holding (EIH), established in 2022, took charge of the portfolios of over half of all state-owned enterprises (SOEs) (26 in total), including Ethio Telecom, Commercial Bank of Ethiopia, and Ethiopian Airlines – though its role is to oversee the partial privatisation of SOEs in the medium term.

External debt threatened the stability and sustainability of Ethiopia's inflationary post-war economy. The debt-to-GDP ratio was 46.37%, while total debt was $63.2 bn (internal $35.5 bn, external $27.8 bn). Ethiopian officials faced crucial discussions with IMF staff on a potential $2 bn lending programme and debt restructuring (with repayment suspension until 2025) subject to structural reforms, including those outlined in HGER 2.0. These did not result in an agreement. By year's end, Ethiopia had defaulted on interest payments on its $1 bn Eurobond, to the tune of a $33 m coupon. Abiy downplayed this, saying: 'this is not too much for us to pay, it is just two days revenue of Ethiopian Airlines'. This elicited suggestions that Ethiopia had voluntarily defaulted on debts owed to multilateral Paris Club creditors, in an effort to seek further repayment suspensions. Rating agencies labelled the move a 'selective default', with Fitch downgrading Ethiopia's long-term rating to CC (from CCC in 2022), signifying an increased risk of defaulting on its local currency-denominated debt in 2024 – a potential 'sovereign default'.

At the June Summit for a New Global Financing Pact in Paris, Abiy lamented that Western creditors continuously forced Ethiopia to focus on debt rather than development. Seeking alternative external fiscal support, Ethiopia secured a two-year debt repayment suspension for its bilateral loans from China ($14 bn, amassed since 2006 under the EPRDF). Abiy lauded Ethiopia's inclusion in BRICS, which will potentially provide future access to alternative, albeit less significant, loan frameworks such as BRICS's New Development Bank and Contingency Reserve Arrangement. In 2022, the Ministry of Finance had acknowledged that it embraced 'off-balance sheet' financing to spread out Ethiopia's accumulated debt burden. Economists assume that this resulted in off-sheet domestic loans from the NBE (money-printing) and unaccounted-for bilateral loans from non-Paris-Club creditors, such as the UAE, at higher interest rates than multilateral ones. The scramble to seek alternative loans and debt relief, according to UNDP, revealed Ethiopia's diminishing capability to service debt, constrained by its foreign-exchange deficit, foreign-exchange reserves which fell to $1 bn in June, covering less than one month of imports, and a current account deficit narrowing to 2.9% of GDP from 3.8% in 2022.

In its struggle to drive down the foreign-exchange deficit, the government sought to clamp down on illicit trade of key export products, including artisanal gold, the stimulant cash crop *khat*, tobacco, and livestock among others, which the government's Ministry of Trade and Regional Integration (MoTRI) estimates to contribute to about 55% of Ethiopia's capital flight. Porous border trade customs and customs tax evasion also resulted in ineffective import-export taxation and constitute a drain on available government revenues. Tax non-compliance among urban small business owners has become the norm under the PP government, according to several studies. Insecurities in areas of insurgencies (e.g. West Oromia) and where government legitimacy partially broke down (e.g. in Fano-controlled areas of Amhara) made it difficult for regional governments to raise taxes effectively everywhere. With regional states instructed by the federal government to raise 50% of their budgets, this resulted in a race between regions to raise revenues for export commodities such as khat, culminating in a September clash over the location of a customs checkpoint in the contested Oromia–Somali borderlands. *Total export earnings decreased by 12% from $4.1 bn in 2021/22 to $3.6 bn in 2022/23. Coffee continued to be Ethiopia's most exported commodity, earning $1.6 bn, around one-third of overall export earnings* (MoTRI). Despite surging global coffee prices, Ethiopia shipped 20% less coffee than in the previous year. Record-breaking revenues in 2022 declined by 23% in 2022/23, according to the Ethiopian Coffee and Tea Authority. In 2022, gold rivalled coffee as the second most exported product, but extraction rates relied largely on Saudi investment group MIDROC's controversial Laga-Dambi gold mine, while insecurities and start-up problems of large firms in western Oromia (e.g. Tulu Kapi), and burgeoning artisanal mining and smuggling (e.g. in Tigray and Benishangul-Gumuz), resulted in capital flight and export fluctuations. As a result gold exports dropped by 60% in early 2023, but they had recovered by the end of the year. Monopolisation and inter-regional struggles over strategic resources, notably salt in Afar and edible oil crops in 'contested' Amhara/Tigray areas, which could easily cover national demand, resulted in Ethiopia having to import these goods – an unnecessary drain on foreign exchange. In January, the prominent minister of mines and petroleum (MoMP), Takele Uma, was dismissed from his position, in which he had revamped the MoMP and sought to put mining on an equal footing with agriculture. The latter still constitutes the bedrock of the economy, with 79% of total export earnings while industrial sector accounts for 11.8% (MoTRI). Manufacturing accounted for one-fifth of total exports, representing 4.6% of GDP (compared with 5.9% in 2022; UNDP statistics). Local manufacturing satisfied 38% of domestic demand, with costly imports covering the rest. Despite a domestic energy deficit, earnings from electricity exports to Sudan, Kenya, and Djibouti continued to expand, from $93.5 m in 2022 to $96.4 m in 2023.

Struggling with year-on-year export fluctuation, the NBE maintained a ban on up to 40 luxury items, instituted late in 2022 to cut spending and promote the local manufacturing industry. Further austerity measures included the successive slashing of fuel subsidies – which increased fuel prices by over 90% compared with mid-2022, taking the price of benzene and diesel to ETB 77.65 and ETB 79.75 by August. Government subsidy cuts were outsourced to consumers, with further knock-on effects for transport and food costs. *Citizens bore the brunt of high inflation and the government's cost-cutting measures.* Underemployed people resorted to desperate income-generating measures, resulting in increased petty corruption and brokerage of everyday economic transactions. Ethiopia scored 37 on a scale of 0 (highly corrupt) to 100 (very clean), in Transparency International's Corruption Perceptions Index (2022 data), ranking 98th out 180 countries. There was an uptick in unregulated 'housemaid' brokerage from Ethiopia to Gulf states, while the Ethiopian government announced a plan in April to 'export' 500,000 female domestic wage labourers to Saudi Arabia. A kidnapping economy has reportedly also emerged in rural areas and the outskirts of major cities, as organised groups – often accused of being OLA members – seek incomes through ransom. In February, the Ministry of Education reported that only 3.3% of 896,642 students, many of them conflict affected, had passed their high school leaving exams. Cohorts of failed students thus risk swelling the ranks of unemployed, disenfranchised youths potentially seeking a cause or insurgency to rally behind. Despite the CoHA, insurgencies in Amhara and Oromia, disputes over occupied territories in Tigray, and sporadic clashes over administrative boundaries elsewhere continued to disrupt social services, aid deliveries, and economic activities.

The national fiscal crisis resulted in a tightening of federal budget allocations for 2023/24, reaching the lowest share in a decade. Capital expenditures declined from 39% to 35.5%, while recurrent spending stayed relatively constant at 61%. The total approved federal budget for 2023/24 was ETB 801.6 bn, according to government figures. While this was presented as a 1.9% increase from 2022/23, when inflation rates (circa 30–35%) are factored in the budget likely declined by around $1 bn and total capital expenditures by 7%. According to UNICEF, 71.5% of the approved budget was allocated to federal government expenditures, 26.7% to regional governments, and 1.7% to the SDGs. Regional budgets failed to cover outstanding salaries of public servants towards the end of the year. Multiple regional governments, including in Amhara– where government legitimacy was already low, with numerous local cadres defecting to the Fano insurgency factions – announced their inability to cover salaries. The National Rehabilitation Commission reportedly required $850 m to implement the CoHA-related DDR programme to demobilise over 370,000 ex-combatants. The federal government could cover only 15% of the costs and sought to secure international donor funds, suggesting that it lacked the funds to pay and ensure the loyalty and service of disgruntled officials or to pacify regional and rogue militants (e.g. Amhara regional forces and Fanos).

Western nations made the lifting of restrictions on aid, development, and lending programmes conditional on progress on implementing the CoHA, including unfettered humanitarian access to conflict-affected areas. *The US announced the easing of economic support restrictions in June, though USAID and WFP temporarily halted food aid from June to November following the discovery of a 'scheme' of systematic syphoning of foreign food aid deliveries*, the distribution of which the Ethiopian government had insisted on controlling itself. The government agreed to ease its grip on UN/WFP aid deliveries thereafter. Early-year droughts in south and southeastern Oromia resulted in similar feuds between regional government and CSOs and activists demanding more food aid deliveries to the Borana zone. The 2023 UN Humanitarian Response Plan estimated that 20 m were dependent on food aid. By August, the overall $2.2 bn food aid appeal for Ethiopia was only 25% secured, according to the UN; by December, FEWS NET reported that food assistance had been at 'record-breaking levels' in 2023, particularly in war-affected Tigray, northern Amhara, and the drought- and flood-affected southern and south-eastern Oromia and Somali regions. With the onset of war in Sudan, over 100,000 people crossed into Ethiopia, with 47,000 registered as refugees or asylum seekers, according to UNHCR, compounding the fact that Ethiopia hosted over 1 m refugees. The IDP crisis, amounting to 3.4 m displaced and 2.5 m returned/relocated in 2023 (UNHCR), also continued as a result of the OLA and Fano insurgencies in Amhara and Oromia.

A decision over reinstituting the preferential trade scheme with the US (the AGOA) remained outstanding, awaiting review in July 2024. Industrial Parks (IPs) – which were central to Ethiopia's state-led development strategy over the last two decades under the EPRDF and accounted for 40% of manufacturing exports by 2020 and 90,000 jobs in 2021 – suffered the consequences of Ethiopia's war economy and post-war insecurities. Some of the 13 IPs were operating at lower capacity (e.g. Hawassa IP) or were dormant (e.g. Bahir Dar IP) due to AGOA shortfalls, while others in Amhara and Tigray (e.g. Kobolcha IP, Mekelle IP) were affected by conflict. The government financed the post-war reconstruction of IPs in Tigray but ordered the Industrial Parks Development Corporation (IPDC) to halt the construction of three additional IPs (Aysha, Asosa, and Bishoftu). Plans announced in 2022 by the IPDC to privatise IPs and thereby finance outstanding loan repayments of other parks to ease the government budget deficit (ETB 281 bn, circa 2.48% of GDP), saw no serious bidders. In May, the Ethiopian Investment Commission revealed that over 50 foreign investors had vacated their spots in IPs as a result of theft, bureaucracy and supply bottlenecks, foreign-exchange shortages, and restricted profit repatriation. The sluggish privatisation of SOEs was similar in the sugar sector under the stewardship of the government's Ethiopian Sugar Industry Group: eight sugar estates went up for sale in 2022 and while the government declared in March 2023 that over 20 private bidders had shown an interest in the tender, the deadline for bids was extended until October. By year's end, no sugar estate was sold, with investors perturbed by high start-up and reparation costs and risks of rural resistance.

Despite the signing of the CoHA and hopes for a more secure investment environment, FDI flows to Ethiopia marked a 14% decline since 2021, reaching $3.7 bn, though Ethiopia remained the second-largest FDI recipient in Africa, according to UNCTAD. The UN estimated that around 450 of a total 5,000 manufacturing firms have ceased production nationwide given external shocks since 2020. Domestic firms were not able to fill the FDI gap, lacking capital endowments and export capacities. To counter the FDI flight, in September the NBE approved the opening of foreign-exchange offshore accounts for a selection of strategic foreign investors, to enable profit repatriation and currency conversion. Earlier in the year, the government had announced that it would open the banking sector to five foreign banks in the next five years (alongside the 29 local banks), though this would be limited to foreign banks opening local subsidiaries or joint venture acquisitions restricted to 60% local bank ownership. The government began the groundwork for establishing its first ever Ethiopian Securities Exchange, set to launch in 2024. Despite this, investors grew impatient with reforms. Ethio Lease, the only foreign-owned financial services company in Ethiopia, with a licence to procure critical equipment in US dollars and lease them to firms operating in Ethiopia in ETB, announced in November that it would close its operation. Like many foreign investors, Ethio Lease, owned by US-based Africa Asset Finance Co., cited the government's inability to ease foreign-exchange restrictions and local currency inflation for its decision.

Kenya

Njoki Wamai

Kenya's domestic politics were defined by contestation between the ruling Kenya Kwanza coalition and citizens due to the high cost of living, along with disagreements on the integrity of the electoral commissioners and the August 2022 election process. Disgruntled citizens protested over the failure of the 'Hustlers' government led by President William Ruto to fulfil its promises, especially on reducing the cost of living. The opposition coalition Azimio La Umoja, led by Raila Odinga, organised the frustrated masses for regular anti-government protests on Mondays, accusing President Ruto of failing to address alleged electoral malpractice in the previous election and the introduction of economic policies that raised the cost of living for ordinary people exponentially. The police responded brutally, leading to the deaths of protesters before the bipartisan National Dialogue Committee (NADCO), with the involvement of both Kenya Kwanza and Azimio la Umoja, was formed to end the protests and address the issue of inflation. Insecurity was widespread due to activities of pastoralist militia and al-Shabaab in the northern part of the former province of Rift Valley and the North Eastern region, which spilled over from the election year. President Ruto offered to intervene militarily in Haiti, and Nairobi continued to lead African multilateral efforts to obtain climate debt justice for the continent. Socioeconomic developments included economic recovery from the Covid-19 pandemic and an increased economic growth rate, driven by favourable weather conditions that boosted agricultural production. Unstable financial markets and a depreciating Kenyan shilling increased inflationary pressure and drew widespread criticism, making Kenya Kwanza increasingly unpopular by year's end.

Domestic Politics

Domestic Kenyan politics were defined by optimism and disappointment in equal measure for both supporters and critics of the Kenya Kwanza coalition led by President William Ruto. President Ruto's first year in office was marked by a spike in the cost of living, prompting nationwide demonstrations and resulting in a growing number of extrajudicial killings by the police. The first quarter of the year was defined by *anti-government protests over inflation* and by alleged electoral malpractice committed in the August 2022 election by the Independent Elections and Boundaries Committee (IEBC), as well as the IEBC's alleged failure to address the issue. The new government reacted violently to protests, leading to deaths and injuring of journalists, politicians, and protesters. Raila Odinga, the opposition coalition leader, called on the international community to hold Ruto and his government to account for police brutality and reversal of democratic gains. Attempts by Tanzanian president Samia Suluhu Hassan and former Nigerian president Olesegun Obasanjo to reconcile the Kenya Kwanza and Odinga-led Azimio La Umoja coalitions finally led to bipartisan talks among elites known as the *NADCO*. The talks were co-chaired by Wiper leader Kalonzo Musyoka from the Azimio coalition and majority leader Kimani Ichung'wah from Kenya Kwanza. The committee presented a report to Ruto and Odinga which addressed the electoral disputes but failed to address the most pressing issue of cost of living, drawing criticism from Martha Karua, an Azimio La Umoja co-principal. Democratic gains made by the opposition were undone as many Azimio La Umoja members of parliament joined the ruling coalition, leading to a weaking of the parliamentary opposition. These members were subjected to disciplinary measures at party level and cases at the political party's tribunal, which surprisingly ruled in support of the 'political party-hopping' which is common among party elites in Kenya.

President Ruto *reshuffled his cabinet* in October for the first time, one year after making initial appointments, drawing both support and criticism from supporters of those ministers demoted to less powerful portfolios. Musalia Mudavadi, a trusted coalition partner from the populous Abaluhya ethnic group who previously served as prime cabinet minister, was appointed foreign affairs cabinet secretary, an extra role created following Ruto's appetite for advancing Kenya's foreign affairs and given to Mudavadi in light of his calm diplomatic demeanour, unlike that of the previous cabinet secretary Alfred Mutua, who was moved to tourism. The previous holder of that position, Peninah Malonza, was moved to the less glamorous docket as cabinet secretary for the EAC as well as receiving responsibility for arid and semi-arid land (ASAL). Another woman minister, Aisha Jumwa, was handed ministerial responsibility for gender, and Rebecca Miano became the trade secretary, leading a powerful ministry. Politicians who saw a reduction in their executive role included Moses Kuria, the former trade minister, who was moved to the less powerful public service docket. President Ruto's appointments of women remained largely tokenistic, in roles such as gender affairs and ASAL, as he reserved the powerful positions for male cabinet secretaries. This stands in sharp contrast to his predecessor Uhuru Kenyatta, who had appointed women to those ministries. In July, the High Court of Kenya dismissed the appointment of 50 chief administrative secretaries (CASs) by President Ruto in March. The court termed the appointments unconstitutional following a petition by the Law Society of Kenya challenging the appointment process. The judges ruled that it was not the intention of the framers of the constitution to create 50 positions of deputy cabinet secretaries or to deputise 22 cabinet secretaries. This court ruling was welcomed by a majority of Kenyans, who considered the appointments unfair to the taxpayers given the rising wage bill.

On *devolution*, the culture of impeaching governors continued with Kawira Mwangaza, who was the first governor to be impeached since the election in December 2022. In the first impeachment by the members of Meru County Assembly, a special senate committee probed her impeachment charges and termed them unsubstantiated. In November, Mwangaza was impeached again; she survived a second time when the senate found seven charges laid against her by the assembly unsubstantiated and false. Mwangaza had been the governor of Meru County since August 2022. She was among seven women governors widely known as the 'G7' elected in 2022, increasing the number of women governors from three in the 2017 elections to seven after the 2022 elections. Mwangaza was charged with abuse of office, nepotism, and gross misconduct, charges to which she pleaded not guilty, arguing that she was a victim of patriarchy and rivalry from male candidates in the gubernatorial race who supported protracted wrangling advanced by members of county assemblies to oust her.

On *human rights*, the 2023 Amnesty International country report raised concerns over the failure of the Kenyan government to protect the right to life enshrined in the constitution. Security forces committed extrajudicial killings and enforced disappearances with impunity in attempts to suppress protesters. Kenyan security forces killed at least 57 protesters during the year, but police officers were yet to be held to account for these unlawful killings by year's end. Member of parliament George Peter Kaluma led a campaign and tabled a homophobic bill in April intended to criminalise same-sex unions and any lobbying for LGBTQ+ rights. This was after Uganda had adopted the Anti-Homosexuality Act 2023, which threatens the right to freedom of speech of LGBTQ+ individuals while introducing harsher penalties for same-sex unions and homosexuality, on 21 March.

Kenya was ranked 'partly free' with a score of 52 out 100 on 'freedom of speech' and 'right to assembly', according to the 2024 Freedom House report (based on 2023 data). The country scored average on political rights and civil liberties, with 22/40 and 30/60 respectively, similarly to the 2022 ranking.

On *political and civil rights*, the year was marred by widespread police brutality towards citizens, the media, and opposition politicians. This was despite Ruto's proclamations in his election campaign and inaugural presidential speech that he would bring an end to police brutality and human rights violations. Ruto did not openly condemn police brutality against protesters, and this only emboldened the Kenyan police, leading to 57 deaths, 300 arrests, and scores being injured, including protesters, bystanders, journalists, and opposition politicians, according to Amnesty International. Ruto continued in the footsteps of his predecessor President Kenyatta in violating fundamental freedoms in the guise of national security. Despite the backsliding on fundamental rights by the executive, in February the Kenyan Supreme Court delivered a precedent-setting ruling in protection of marginalised groups when it upheld a lower court ruling that allowed for the registration of an LGBTQ+ organisation.

The country scored 66 out of 100 in the 2024 Freedom House Internet Freedom Index (based on 2023 data), a decrease from the previous year's score of 68 (0 being least free and 100 most free). Internet networks and social media sites were freely available without widespread government restriction. However, in February, the streaming company Netflix was forced to sign an agreement with the Kenyan Film Classification Board (KFCB) to restrict LGBTQ+ content. The Supreme Court allowed the communications authority to install a device management system (DMS) in May, granting the regulator access to personal customer data from service providers without consulting the general population. In May, at least eight Kenyan government ministries were reported to have been hacked by a hacking group affiliated with the Chinese government to access data related to the country's debts to China. On the right to privacy, a scandal emerged in July when cryptocurrency company Worldcoin launched in about 35 countries, including Kenya, offering cryptocurrency tokens of up to 7,000 Kenyan shillings (KSh) after scanning individuals' eyeballs. Thousands of Kenyans, especially unemployed youth, thronged several malls across the country to have their eyeballs scanned for biometrics for the reward. The Office of Data Protection Commission later banned the company after Kenyans online criticised the regulatory officials for failing to protect Kenyans' right to privacy.

The online social media space in Kenya continued to be manipulated for political and economic interests by politicians, companies, and individuals. The 'bloggers for hire' phenomenon of anonymous social media personalities using their collective social media to chase clout to shape public opinion and manipulate online information continued without any disciplinary measures. Women politicians and activists with significant online presence bore the brunt of this, with cyber-violence directed towards women including online sexual violence through a network of accounts paid to discredit them. These bloggers for hire are paid by companies and sometimes individuals working for government to position content in the top trending topics in Kenya, according to Freedom House. President Ruto's chief administrator secretary, Denis Itumbi, who has also referred to himself as the 'Hustlers Bureau intelligence chief' for the Kenya Kwanza coalition, has often been accused of creating this culture of bloggers for hire, including the '36 bloggers' during the Jubilee elections in 2013 and 2017 who were alleged to be working with him in spreading fake news in Uhuru Kenyatta's campaigns. During the year under review, these bloggers continued to inundate social media spaces with propaganda and fake news on political elites using sponsored hashtags, targeted advertising, and disinformation. Violence catalysed by these bloggers increased against women politicians, opinionated women in the online space, and non-binary individuals who were publicly humiliated using gendered hate speech. Despite the increasing violence against women in the cyber-space in Kenya, the National Cohesion and Integration Commission (NCIC) did not act to curb the spread of this new type of violence.

On *corruption*, Kenya scored 31 and was ranked 126th out of 180 in 2023 (based on 2022 data) in the Transparency International Corruption Perceptions Index, indicating that corruption was still a significant challenge. This was a decline from a score of 32 and from rank 123 in 2022. In the longer term, Kenya had averaged 24.23 points on the index from 1996 until 2023, reaching an all-time high of 32 points in 2022, from a record low of 19 points in 2002 during the authoritarian Daniel Moi regime. The average global score was 43, with over two-thirds of countries scoring below 50. The 2023 report highlighted a global trend of weakening justice systems which had reduced accountability and allowed corruption to thrive. The Transparency International Kenya report attributed the decline in Kenya's ranking to the few graft cases that had been successfully prosecuted in 2023. Many graft cases dragged on excessively, and others resulted in acquittals after the new regime made no effort to review cases or appeal. The collapse of the Arror-Kimwarer dam graft case involving KSh 63 bn was one such example that eroded public confidence in the Office of the Director of Public Prosecutions (ODPP), led by Nurdin Haji. During the year, some members of parliament also attempted to water down anti-corruption laws by repealing certain provisions of the legislation which governs the investigation, prosecution, and punishment of corruption, including the Anti-Corruption and Economic Crimes Act (ACECA), 2003. The auditor-general's report for 2023/24 exposed rampant corruption in the devolved counties, especially in Vihiga, Migori, and Nairobi.

On *security*, according to the 'Terror Attacks and Arrests Observatory' published by the Nairobi-based Centre for Human Rights and Policy Studies (CHRIPS), terrorist attacks decreased by 6.5% from 77 in 2022 to 72 reported incidents in 2023. This was attributed to numerous terror attacks being foiled by security officials. CHRIPS further reported that during the year, 178 people were killed, compared with 116 in 2022. The affected counties included 25 attacks in Mandera, 21 in Lamu, 23 in Garissa, and three in Wajir; June saw the highest number of attacks, at 19, with at least 58 fatalities and 58 injured people. Fatalities in the year included 75 security officials, 68 al-Shabaab militants, 30 civilians, and two government officials. Among the 151 people injured in the year were security officials at 93, civilians at 45, and al-Shabaab militants at ten. Three people were kidnapped: two in Lamu and one in Garissa. Fifty-nine people were arrested for terror-related offences, of whom 16 were Kenyans, ten Tanzanian, three Somali citizens, one Ugandan, and 29 of undisclosed origin, according to CHRIPS data.

Pastoralist militia groups were involved in *banditry, cattle theft, and conflicts* with large-scale landowners in northern Kenya and the northern Rift Valley despite increased government operations to subdue them. In February, security forces implemented a three-day amnesty period for members of militias to hand in illegal weapons. According to Armed Conflict Location and Event Data Project (ACLED), Kenya recorded nearly 250 political violence events and 240 reported fatalities between 1 January and 24 March 2023. Pastoralist militias were involved in almost 30% of violent activity in the country. Garissa County saw the highest number of reported fatalities, with 37 resulting from violent extremism, and Turkana County followed, with 27 reported fatalities from pastoralist militia activities.

The rainy seasons reduced the incidence of violence, but existing tensions and disruptions to schooling continued due to the prevalence of small arms and light weapons (SALWs) in northern part of the former province of Rift Valley, brought in to the country via porous borders with neighbouring countries. The government conducted military-led operations against the militia and also invested in infrastructure development such as roads and schools, redressing decades of state neglect in the region, in an attempt to encourage militias to change their livelihoods. Kenya has a history of violence against security officials, and the disappearance and alleged assassination of government officials. Corruption by government officials, intra-party competition during elections, and organised crime were among the drivers of violence. Political youth wings and vigilante groups were reported to have assaulted party rivals and local officials in early 2023, according to ACLED.

Foreign Affairs

Nairobi continued to invest in *bilateral and multilateral relations* across the region and beyond, determined to strengthen its geostrategic and geoeconomic position. President Ruto's first year in office was marked by numerous international trips amid the rising cost of living and his support for Kenya's controversial police intervention in Haiti. Between January and September, Ruto made a total of 35 visits to 23 countries, including 11 bilateral trips for state visits and 24 visits for multilateral summits and meetings, making him the most well-travelled president in the first year of his term compared with all of his predecessors. Regionally, Uganda, Tanzania, and Ethiopia played host to the Kenyan president five, six, and four times respectively. Internationally, he made most the visits to the US (four) and France (three), signalling his continued focus on the East Africa region and the West, unlike his predecessors Uhuru Kenyatta and Mwai Kibaki. The *bilateral state visits* made by President Ruto included France (24 January), Belgium (29–30 March), Rwanda (4–5 April), the UK for the Coronation of King Charles III (6–7 May), Israel (9–10 May), Djibouti S (12 June), Comoros (6 July), Congo-Brazzaville (7–8 July), Mozambique (10–12 August), Uganda (13 August), and India (4–6 December).

President Ruto attended 24 *multilateral* summits and meetings, including in East Africa and the Horn on issues related to climate change and green energy as well as summits in Europe, China, and the Middle East. These included the Feed Africa Summit, Senegal (25–26 January); the 20th and 21st Extraordinary Summits of the EAC Heads of State, Burundi (4 February and 31 May); the 36th Ordinary Session of the AU Assembly, Ethiopia (17–19 February); the Energy Transition Dialogue in Germany (27–28 March); the AU Heads of State Summit, Uganda (26 April); a bilateral meeting in the Netherlands (7–8 May); the Pan-African Parliamentarians Summit, South Africa (17 May); the 22nd COMESA Heads of State and Government Summit, Zambia (7–8 June); the IGAD Summit in Djibouti (11–12 June); the 111th Annual ILO Conference in Switzerland (15–16 June); the Global Pact Finance Summit, France (22–23 June); the IGAD summit in Ethiopia (10 July); the World Bank Africa Meeting (25–26 July) and the Africa Food Systems Forum (7 September), Tanzania; the US for the 78th UNGA and a business visit (15–25 September); the 3rd Belt and Road Initiative Summit, China (15–18 October); the Future Investment Initiative, Saudi Arabia (24–25 October); the Three Basins Summit, Congo (28 October); the Saudi Arabia–Africa Summit, Saudi Arabia (10–11 November); the 5th G20 Compact with Africa, Germany (20–21 November); F the EU Parliament, France (21 November); the EAC High Level Forum on Climate and Food Security (23–24 November), Tanzania; and the UN Climate Change Conference in UAE (1–4 December). The gains made from the numerous trips are yet to be recorded, and criticism continued from Kenyan taxpayers and the opposition on excessive government spending for international meetings.

President *Ruto equally hosted several prominent leaders to promote bilateral agreements and multilateral summits* during year. These bilateral visits centred on regional security, economic, and green energy agreements. The visiting leaders included Eritrea's president Isaias Afwerki, who visited Kenya for the first time in 11 years in February; US first lady Jill Biden (February); Japan's prime minister Kishida Fumio (May); German chancellor Olaf Scholz (May); Singapore's prime minister Lee Hsien Loong (May); the late Iranian president Ebrahim Raisi (July); South Sudan's Salva Kiir (August); Indonesian president Joko Widodo (August); US secretary of defence Lloyd Austin (September); Angolan president João Lourenço (October); King Charles III and Queen Consort Camilla for a state visit (October); Czech Republic's prime minister Petr Fiala (November); and Romanian president Klaus Iohannis (November). Nairobi hosted South Sudan's president, Salva Kiir, Libya's Mohamed al-Menfi, and Congo's Denis Sassou Nguesso for more than two visits each in 2023 for private and summit meetings. The numerous and expensive diplomatic visits hosting various dignitaries came at a high cost to the Kenyan taxpayer. By December, State House had exceeded the six-month budget by KSh 447 m, leading the public to question President Ruto's commitment to the budgetary discipline and fiscal responsibility promised in his manifesto.

On *international peace and security*, Ruto actively built Nairobi's geostrategic position as a peace and security player in the world. The president offered the UNSC and the US government 1,000 police officers to assist the Haitian National Police to tackle widespread gang violence in July. This led to a court petition on 9 October by Kenyan civil society and opposition political party the Third Way Alliance blocking this deployment. Different groups and citizens opposed to the deployment cited Kenya's unresolved security issues at home, and Kenyan police's unwarranted use of force and corruption record. Despite these concerns, the cabinet passed a resolution to deploy officers to Haiti, and on 24 October the High Court extended the block. The Kenyan parliament, with majority government-supporting members, approved the deployment in November, but it had not been implemented by the end of year.

On *regional peace and security*, Kenya's diplomatic credentials in the region were put to the test by Sudan's General Abdel Fattah al-Burhan when he rejected President Ruto to lead Sudan peace talks in April. Ruto had been appointed as the chair of the IGAD-led mediation process. The IGAD quartet group comprising Kenya, Djibouti, South Sudan, and Ethiopia was created to support a structured, unified, and inclusive IGAD-led peace process. In November, Khartoum agreed to Ruto-led IGAD mediations known as the Jeddah Peace Talks, though tensions remained due to mistrust between the warring parties in Sudan.

On *EAC neighbours*, Nairobi's diplomatic and trade relations with Dar es Salaam, Kampala, and Mogadishu improved as the president made six trips to Tanzania and five to Uganda, making Tanzania the country visited most often by the president in his first year. Differing Covid-19 containment measures during the tenure of President John Magufuli had soured relations between Nairobi and Dar es Salaam, but President Kenyatta had attempted to ease relations after the death of Magufuli in March 2021. Ruto and Tanzania's President Suluhu amended 23 trade barriers hindering their commercial relationship, further enhancing their trade relations.

Bilateral relations with Mogadishu continued to improve despite ongoing tensions between the two countries resulting from the previous sea border dispute and the threat of al-Shabab militants. In May, Kenya agreed to open its three border points with Somalia after 12 years. The opening of the Mandera, Lamu, and Garissa border points was expected to improve regional security by easing trade and the movement of people. The mission mandate of the EAC *Regional Forces* (EACRF) ended in the DRC in December. The EACRF was a joint force with EAC forces deployed in 2022 whose mandate was mainly to buffer the frontlines against M23 rebels to encourage peaceful dialogue for peace and stability in Eastern DRC. Kenya sent 900 Kenya Defence Forces (KDF) soldiers to the EACRF mission, which was considered ineffective by Kinshasha. EACRF was replaced by SADC troops with a mandate to use armed force in December. During the government of Kenyatta (2013–22), Kenya had played a central role in facilitating peace talks between the Ethiopian government forces and Tigray region forces in November 2022. President Ruto opted for economic cooperation with Ethiopia, aware of the tensions in Kenya–Ethiopia relations based on geostrategic and economic rivalry between the two countries.

At a multilateral level, Ruto continued to champion climate justice for Africa and investment in green energy. Nairobi hosted the African Climate Action Summit (ACS) from 4 to 6 September. The ACS was co-hosted by the Government of Kenya and the African Union Commission (AUC) pursuant to an AU Assembly decision adopted during its 36th Ordinary Session on 19 February. The summit positioned Africa in solidarity with the rest of the world for global climate action, under the theme 'Driving Green Growth and Climate Finance Solutions for Africa and the World'. Deliberations focused on the nexus between climate change and Africa's development, with special emphasis on addressing climate justice by increasing investment in Africa.

Socioeconomic Developments

Emerging markets and developing economies such as Kenya recorded considerably higher growth rates than the global average in the year under review, according to the Kenya National Bureau of Statistics 2024 Economic Survey. Kenya's *economy recovered* from the previous year's drought and the slow global economic environment caused by the Covid-19 pandemic. The economy grew in accordance with

AfDB's projections of 5.6% in 2023, driven by a rebound in agricultural production due to increased rainfall, a growing service industry, and increased household consumption. The service sector contributed the most to GDP at 55.4%, followed by agriculture 21.8%, industry 16.8%, and other sectors 6.0%. Significantly, the performance of the agriculture sector improved also due to government intervention, including a fertiliser subsidy programme; the real growth of the agricultural sector was 7.0 % with increased outputs of maize (+38.8%), wheat (+16.1%), rice (+19.1%), and tea (+6.6%).

According to the Kenya UN Drought Response Dashboard, despite increased rainfall in the last quarter of 2023, the number of people who experience hunger remained high. According to the Famine Early Warning System Network (FEWSNET), in the pastoral areas, forage and water resources significantly improved following the October to December short rains. This improved productivity and increased food and incomes for households, but despite this more than 1.5 m people in pastoral areas remained at crisis levels of food insecurity as of December, according to FEWSNET. Pastoral families found coping strategies to minimise food and grass consumption. Recharged water levels across northern Kenya kept livestock in grazing areas.

Despite the increased economic growth, *energy and food inflation* increased. According to the KNBS (Kenya National Bureau of Statistics), the inflation rate by December was 6.6%. The high rate was caused by high commodities prices in transport, housing, water, electricity, fuel, and food. In particular, a spike in fuel costs, an increase in VAT, and the removal of subsidies on petroleum products by the Ruto government increased energy costs, which influenced food prices. The increased fuel prices also increased production and transportation costs, further driving up the costs of food and non-food commodities. The low market availability of staple foods following successive low-production seasons ensured that staple food prices were high.

The KNBS 2024 Economic Survey (capturing data from 2023) also reported that *national government revenue* – largely drawn from taxes, including 41.7% income tax, 23.2% VAT, 11.8% excise taxes, 5.7% custom taxes, and 6.1% other taxes, alongside 9.8% non-tax sources – increased considerably compared with the previous year. The *taxation regime* received a lot of open criticism from citizens, as high taxes and increased taxation were not matched with adequate service delivery by the state. Kenya's *unemployment rate* was 5.6%, according to ILO assessments. An increase in unemployment was linked to increased inflation, the skills gap, and the effects of Covid-19, climate change, increased population growth, and urbanisation.

On *international trade and balance of payments*, Kenya's exports grew by 15.4% due to increased agricultural revenues. Kenya's top exports were tea (KSh 188.7 bn), horticulture (KSh 187.47 bn), clothing (KSh 45.5 bn), coffee (KSh 34.6 bn), and iron and steel (KSh 32.3 bn). Kenya's leading export destinations were Uganda, Pakistan,

Netherlands, Tanzania, the UK, and the US. KNBS data shows that Kenya's imports originated mainly from China, the UAE, India, Malaysia, and Japan. The highest import volumes during the year were for petroleum (KSh 606.0 bn), machinery (KSh 289.9 bn), vegetable fats (KSh 139.1 bn), iron and steel (KSh 120.8 bn), and non-milled wheat (KSh 93.8 bn). The trade balance narrowed from a deficit of KSh 1,617.6 bn in 2022 to KSh 1,604.1 bn in 2023. The prolonged Russia–Ukraine war continued to have a knock-on effect on commodity prices, especially the price of wheat, which was among the main import goods.

Kenya's *growing public debt* remained a serious concern. As of December, the country's total debt stock was approximately 69.1% of GDP, equivalent to $71.20 bn and composed of 31.3% domestic debt and 37.8% external debt, according to the National Treasury and Economic Planning Monthly Bulletin. Following the 2021 debt crisis, Kenya embarked on a 38-month IMF programme in April 2021, running to mid-2024, supported by a $2.34 bn funding plan, aimed at strengthening fiscal and debt management. Kenya's debt remained above the IMF's recommended minimum import cover, leading to a mismatch between demand and supply of US dollars, which resulted in the temporary depreciation of the Kenya shilling and a slump in exchange rates. The *Kenyan shilling weakened by 22% against the US dollar* between July and September, according to a Kenyan Treasury quarterly report, and by December, the shilling was trading at KSh 156 to the US dollar compared with KSh 101 in November 2019. This also had an impact on inflation, as Kenya is dependent on petroleum imports for fuel, and existing debt servicing costs. A reduction in bilateral debt obligations to China from $7 bn in 2021 to $6.6 bn at the end of 2022 was registered and an increase in multilateral borrowing through the Eurobond was recorded, with President Ruto indicating a possible foreign policy shift away from China.

Kenya's tourism sector recovered after declining arrival figures during the pandemic years. The 2023 'Annual Tourism Sector Performance Report' by the Kenya Tourism Research Institute reported an increase in tourism revenue of 34.0% compared with 2022. This revenue was generated by holiday tourists and conference tourism, which increased by 11.0% in 2023.

The education sector continued with the implementation of the new Competence Based Curricula (CBC) amid challenges. Some of the challenges encountered included inadequate infrastructure in learning institutions, inadequate human capital (teachers, trainers for special needs education and STEM), natural calamities and human conflict, disrupted provision of education, and the high cost of training and administration of examinations. In August, the Presidential Working Party on Education Reform (PWPER), established in September 2022 to examine challenges affecting education sector in Kenya, presented its report to the president. The working party addressed, among other things, access, relevance, equity, quality, governance, and financing of education as well as experiences in implementing

Competency Based Education (CBE). The working party recommended the development of a sessional paper on education based on the 2023 report which would guide policy for basic education, tertiary education, training, and research.

On *migration*, according to UN data, 774,370 refugees and asylum seekers were registered in Kenya in 2023. They were hosted mainly in two camps in Dadaab (49%) and Kakuma (37%) while others were living in urban areas (14%). The refugee countries of origin were neighbouring countries due to conflict and authoritarian governments, including Somalia (56%), South Sudan (23%), DRC (7.8%), Ethiopia (5.1%), Burundi (4.2%), Sudan (1.5%), Uganda (0.5%), Eritrea (0.4%), and Rwanda (0.4%). Around 650,000 refugees received support, including 500,000 children who accessed Early Childhood Development (ECD) schools, according to UNHCR. The 2023 'Global Report on Internal Displacement' (GRID) by the Internal Displacement Monitoring Centre reported that by December, 40,000 people were displaced because of conflict and violence and 649,000 people were displaced largely by floods. The International Displacement Monitoring Centre recorded this as the highest number of displaced people from Kenya since data first became available for the country in 2008.

With regard to *health*, the government intensified efforts to speed up universal health coverage (UHC) through the promised Social Health Insurance Fund (SHIF). The SHIF is President Ruto's flagship project seeking to provide affordable healthcare to all Kenyans, set to replace the 57-year-old National Health Insurance Fund (NHIF). The SHIF was enacted by passing enabling legislation such as the Social Health Insurance Act 2023, the Digital Health Act 2023, and the Facility Improvement Fund Act 2023 despite criticism. The proposed bills created a national health tax at 2.75% of gross salary for salaried employees and for every household. Critics argued that a proposed increase in individual health insurance contributions undermined the right to health for those who could not afford the premiums. The proposals were also criticised due to the ineffectiveness and corruption of the NHIF. Despite promises of universal healthcare, the infant mortality rate was still high at 30.629 deaths per 1,000 live births, according to the UNICEF/World Bank 'Levels and Trends: Child Mortality' report for 2023.

The national rollout of the SHIF by the Social Health Authority (SHA) is set for implementation in 2024 and expectations are high in a country where universal healthcare has remained a dream.

Rwanda

Erik Plänitz

In 2023, Rwanda underwent significant domestic and foreign policy shifts under President Paul Kagame's leadership. Military restructuring further solidified Kagame's authority, addressing concerns over Rwanda's involvement in conflicts such as the M23 insurgency in the DRC. Political opposition faced constraints amid allegations of interference, though there were instances of hope, such as the acquittal of an opposition figure. Tensions with the DRC escalated over accusations of Rwandan support for rebel groups, leading to diplomatic strains. However, efforts to ease tensions were initiated by the US, reflecting Rwanda's diplomatic engagements beyond its immediate region. Relations with neighbouring countries saw both improvements and set-backs, with Rwanda strengthening ties with Uganda while facing border closures with Burundi. Economically, Rwanda experienced robust growth. Efforts to stabilise inflation and address unemployment were underway, aided by IMF agreements and fiscal consolidation plans. Despite challenges such as climate change and migration policy controversies, Rwanda maintained its regional leadership in governance and economic development.

Domestic Politics

Rwandan president Paul Kagame announced a *cabinet reshuffle* affecting several ministries. The changes, revealed on 22 August, include the appointment of Albert Murasira as the minister of emergency management, replacing Solange Kayisire. Murasira, formerly the minister of Defence, was replaced in that position by Juvenal Marizamunda two months prior. Other new ministers include Marie-Solange Kayisire for local government, Gaspard Twagirayezu for education, Jeannette Bayisenge for service and labour, and Dr Valentine Uwamariya for gender and family promotion. The reshuffle was part of a broader series of changes initiated by Kagame.

The zero-tolerance strategy towards *corruption* cases was felt by the former minister of state for culture, Edouard Bamporiki, on 9 January. The High Court found him guilty of corruption and sentenced him to five years in prison. He was dismissed by Kagame in May 2022 over corruption allegations, having allegedly accepted bribes. After a slight downward trend in recent years, Rwanda ranked 49th in Transparency International's Corruption Perceptions Index based on data from 2023, with a score of 53 out of a maximum possible 100 points. This put Rwanda in fourth place in sub-Saharan Africa and first place in East Africa.

In addition to the cabinet, Kagame fundamentally *restructured the army leadership* and that of the security agencies. On 7 June, he appointed Juvenal Marizamunda as the new defence minister, Mubarak Muganga as the new chief of defence staff, and Vincent Nyakarundi as the new army chief of staff. Marizamunda had previously served as chief of correctional services and deputy inspector-general of police. Jean Bosco Ntibitura became the new director-general of the National Intelligence and Security Service. Felix Namuhoranye assumed the position of inspector-general of the Rwanda National Police on 20 February. The former police chief, Dan Munyuza, was appointed ambassador to Cairo on 2 August, amid allegations of human rights abuses by human rights organisations.

Kagame's *military reshuffle* was seen as part of a long-term strategy to consolidate power rather than a response to the recent military coups on the continent. The shake-up involved the retirement of 83 senior officers, including 12 generals, and 86 non-commissioned officers, on 30 August. One notable retirement was that of James Kabarebe, Kagame's former army chief of staff, minister of defence, and closest ally. This was seen as a move to address concerns among Western governments and the UN regarding Rwanda's involvement in the humanitarian crisis in eastern DRC. Kabarebe was implicated in a UN report on Rwanda's role in the insurgency of the *Mouvement du 23 Mars (M23)* in the DRC. He was appointed minister for regional cooperation on 27 September, retaining a special position within Kagame's power apparatus.

The reshuffles within the armed forces and security agencies' headquarters were viewed as a carefully planned strategy to prevent any military commander from building a faction that could challenge Kagame's hold on power. Additionally, the reshuffle involved personnel transfers between Mozambique's Cabo Delgado province and Rwanda. It was speculated that Kagame might be creating space to gradually promote his children to top command positions, with his eldest son Ivan and another son, Ian, being mentioned. Ian Kagame, a graduate of the Royal Military Academy at Sandhurst, currently serves in the Presidential Guard.

The restructuring of the leadership further strengthened Kagame's position regarding the *presidential elections* scheduled for 15 July 2024. Kagame declared his candidacy on 20 September in an interview with 'Jeune Afrique'. At the time of writing, Frank Habinza was the only opposition candidate to have declared his candidacy, officially nominated at the party congress of the Democratic Green Party on 13 May.

As the 2024 general elections in Rwanda approached, political opposition faced constraints both within and beyond the ruling party. Senior Rwandan Patriotic Front (RPF) officials criticised a traditional clan meeting on 9 July arranged by influential leaders, characterising it as interference in Rwandan unity. According to media reports, officials present at the gathering were briefly detained and interrogated.

On 22 February, the Nyarugenge High Court acquitted university professor and *opposition* figure Christopher Kayumba. He was acquitted of rape allegations after spending 17 months in detention. The accusation surfaced after he founded a regime-critical online newspaper and a political organisation. Following an appeal by the prosecution against the ruling, the High Court sentenced Kayumba to a two-year suspended sentence for his involvement in a rape case on 2 November. The court found him guilty of committing the crime against his former maid.

On 20 April, the High Court sentenced six former members of the Democratic Forces for the Liberation of Rwanda (FDLR) to five years in prison. The prosecution had sought 25 years, including for conspiring against the government, but the court found only the establishment of an armed group to have been proven.

HRW reported on 10 October that Rwanda's government had engaged in a campaign of 'extraterritorial repression' involving the murder, attacking, and disappearance of critics beyond its borders. According to HRW, over a dozen cases of such incidents, including killings, kidnappings, enforced disappearances, and physical attacks against Rwandans in the diaspora, were documented. The Rwandan government rejected HRW's findings, calling them a distorted picture and emphasising the progress made in advancing the rights of Rwandans. The situation was reflected in international rankings. In the Freedom of the World Index 2024, based on data from 2023, Rwanda was again classified as not free, its score remaining at 23 out of 100. The tense situation of the media was reflected in the Freedom of the Press Index.

According to data from 2023, Rwanda improved slightly from position 136 to 131. Reporters Without Borders ranked Rwanda last in East Africa in its annual report, 144th out of 180 for the year 2023, compared to 131st in the previous year.

Rwandan *journalist* John Williams Ntwali, known for producing critical content about the government, was killed in a road crash on 18 January. The 44-year-old editor of the newspaper 'The Chronicles' died when a speeding vehicle collided with the motorcycle he was riding as a passenger. Ntwali, who had faced multiple arrests in his two-decade journalism career, also owned the YouTube channel Pax TV, recognised for providing a rare outlet for critical reporting in Rwanda. The driver involved in the accident was fined $920 for involuntary manslaughter on 7 February. Human rights organisations suggested that Ntwali was a target, stating that he was on a hitlist of Rwandan reporters critical of the government. HRW called for a prompt and effective investigation into Ntwali's death, emphasising that he had joined a list of individuals who challenged the government and died in suspicious circumstances.

Rwandan government critic *Paul Rusesabagina* was released from prison after over 900 days. Released on 24 March, he was set to fly to Qatar, which played a role in facilitating his release, and then to the US. Rusesabagina was convicted in September 2021 for supporting an armed rebel group. His sentence was commuted by a presidential order, according to justice minister Emmanuel Ugirashebuja, who cautioned that under Rwandan law, commutation does not erase the underlying conviction. US president Joe Biden and secretary of state Antony Blinken welcomed Rusesabagina's release, expressing gratitude to Rwanda, with Belgium also supporting the move. Rwanda credited both the US and Qatar for resolving the case, emphasising the importance of resetting the US–Rwanda relationship. Rusesabagina faced allegations of having backed the National Liberation Front (FLN), a rebel group associated with attacks in Rwanda in 2018 and 2019. Despite denying any connection to the incidents, he was the founder of the opposition organisation Rwandan Movement for Democratic Change (MRCD), perceived as having ties to the FLN's militant activities.

The *security forces* in Rwanda operated mainly on the border with the DRC. On 24 January, Rwandan military forces fired artillery at a DRC fighter jet allegedly violating Rwandan airspace. The DRC claimed that the incident had occurred on its soil, with the jet returning safely to Goma airport. On 15 February, Rwandan military forces reportedly clashed with about 12 suspected members of DRC military forces near Rusizi. Rwanda claimed that the DRC forces had entered no man's land and fired at a border post, while the DRC argued that they had been pursuing criminals near the border. On 3 March, Rwandan Defence Force (RDF) soldiers and the Armed Forces of the DRC (FARDC) engaged in a brief exchange of fire at the border in Rubavu. The clash occurred after an alleged crossing from DRC to Rwanda by a

FARDC soldier, resulting in the soldier's death. In July, RDF soldiers were reportedly deployed to the border with DRC in Rubavu, Rutsiro, and Nyabihu. The deployment was in response to alleged communication from the FDLR about planned attacks and grenade throwing in the area.

Foreign Politics

The year's foreign policy was defined by the further deterioration of relations with the *DRC*. Rwanda was accused by the DRC of supporting the rebel group the *M23* in the conflict in North Kivu. While Rwanda denied this, a report presented to the UNSC by the UN Group of Experts on 13 June implicated the Rwandan government. According to the report, Rwanda had supported the M23 through troop reinforcements, equipment, and assistance in command structures. Specifically, the report named five commanders of the RDF as supporters. In response to the report, a spokesperson for the US State Department called on Rwanda to withdraw its troops from the DRC. Rwanda rejected the report and, in turn, demanded a halt to Congolese support for what it called the *genocidal FDLR militia*. According to Rwanda, the militia was fighting alongside the FARDC and had repeatedly advanced into Rwandan territory in recent years. Peace negotiations were expected to make further progress in January. However, a spiral of accusations and the boycotting of negotiations brought the talks to a standstill. On 19 January, Rwanda accused the DRC of abandoning the peace deal agreed in Luanda, Angola, in November 2022. The intended peace meeting between the presidents was postponed, and accusations and threats continued. Qatari diplomats had scheduled a meeting in Doha on 23 January with Kagame and the president of the DRC, Félix Tshisekedi. However, the gathering was unexpectedly cancelled when Kinshasa withdrew its participation at the last moment. This decision caught Qatar off guard, especially considering that it was Tshisekedi who had initially sought mediation for the conflict in eastern DRC.

On 17 February, the AU Peace and Security Council in Addis Ababa endorsed the EAC's decisions for adequate deployment in the east of the DRC but avoided blaming any member state. The council called for de-escalation and a resumption of dialogue between Rwanda and the DRC. The Kenyan-led East African Regional Force that was deployed in December 2022 initiated its withdrawal from North Kivu in December 2023 after its mandate renewal was refused by the DRC due to perceived ineffectiveness in combating rebel groups in the region, including the M23.

On 13 March, Congolese foreign minister Christophe Lutundula confirmed that the DRC had cut diplomatic contact with Rwanda, accusing it of backing the M23. Rwanda, in turn, alleged the recruitment of foreign mercenaries by the DRC, indicating preparation for war. President Kagame dismissed the allegations, justifying Rwandan forces' entry into Congolese territory as a response to FDLR rebels, alleging DRC's support for them. Kagame revealed having reached out to M23 rebels under the Nairobi and Luanda peace processes, urging them to withdraw from occupied areas.

Heightened tensions alarmed the UN, leading the secretary-general's special envoy for the Great Lakes region, Huang Xia, to call for maximum restraint and dialogue between the two countries on 17 October. Speaking before the UNSC, Xia expressed deep concern over the deteriorating security situation, highlighting the potential for a direct conflict between the DRC and Rwanda, each accusing the other of supporting armed groups within their territories.

President Tshisekedi accused Rwanda of violating a regional peace agreement in May and reiterated these allegations during a summit in Bujumbura, Burundi, in June. The accusations included aggression and repeated violations of DRC's territorial integrity and international agreements related to peace efforts in eastern DRC.

In August, US secretary of state Antony Blinken announced that the presidents of Rwanda and the DRC had agreed to initiate talks to ease tensions in eastern DRC. The talks between Blinken and Kagame continued at the World Economic Forum in Davos on 16 January 2024.

In November, the US urged DRC and Rwanda to de-escalate the situation along their common border. Director of national intelligence Avril Haines visited the two countries on 19 and 20 November, with both presidents offering commitments to de-escalating tensions. The specifics of their promises drew on previous African-led negotiations in Nairobi and Luanda.

As tensions persisted, President Tshisekedi compared President Kagame to Adolf Hitler on 9 December, alleging expansionist aims and threatening a similar fate. This sharp rhetoric further strained the already tense relationship between the two leaders.

Despite mediation efforts, military tensions escalated in January 2023 when Rwandan forces reportedly fired at a Congolese fighter jet, leading to accusations of deliberate aggression and acts of war by both parties. On 28 January, the FARDC warned that Rwandan troops had crossed into Congolese territory. FARDC claimed that RDF special forces had entered Masisi Territory, North Kivu, planning false flag attacks against Congolese ethnic Tutsis. The tension escalated on 29 January when DRC police clashed with Rwanda soldiers on an island in Lake Kivu.

On 3 March, a cross-border security incident occurred at the Petite Barriere border post between Goma city and Gisenyi. A soldier of the Republican Guard of the FARDC was killed by a Rwandan soldier, leading to an exchange of fire. Congolese reinforcements reportedly killed two Rwandan soldiers. A similar incident had occurred at the same border post in November 2022.

Recent developments indicate a positive shift in relations between Rwanda and *Uganda*. The 11th Joint Permanent Commission (JPC) held at the Kigali Convention Centre between 22 and 24 March marked a significant milestone in revitalising bilateral ties. MoUs were signed in key areas such as political consultation, immigration, mutual legal assistance, and judicial cooperation. Despite past strains, both nations expressed a commitment to resolving their differences, emphasising their historical bond.

The meeting highlighted a thaw in relations that began when General Muhoozi Kainerugaba, special advisor to president of Uganda Yoweri Museveni, visited Rwanda in 2022. The focus shifted towards implementing decisions to *address conflict causes* comprehensively. This included removing trade barriers and harmonising cross-border cooperation. The improved relations were evident in the opening of a new border post at Rwempasha–Kizinga on 5 July. Uganda also signed a deal with Turkish firm Yapi Merkezi to revive construction of the *standard gauge railway* line connecting the port of Mombasa to Kampala and Kigali in May. Yapi Merkezi, the same company contracted for the Tanzania standard gauge railway, was to undertake the project's construction on the eastern and western sides of Malaba–Kampala–Kigali. Rwanda completed preliminary engineering designs for the line from Kampala to Kigali.

Economic cooperation between Uganda and Rwanda increased during the year, with power trading between Rwanda and Uganda poised to begin. Completed projects such as the Shango Substation and the Mirama–Shango 220kV Transmission Line facilitated regional power exchange. The positive trajectory in relations suggested a new dawn for cooperation between the two countries, with various projects and initiatives aimed at fostering economic and social development in the Great Lakes region.

Relations between Rwanda and *Burundi* significantly deteriorated, marked by the closure of the border on 11 January 2024 by Burundi. President of Burundi Évariste Ndayishimiye accused Rwanda of hosting and training RED-Tabara, which claimed responsibility for an attack near Burundi's border with the DRC in December 2023. Rwanda consistently denied these allegations.

The closure was expected to negatively impact cross-border trade and the movement of people between the two nations. After the previous year's rapprochement efforts, the renewed allegations were a major set-back in relations and diplomatic progress.

Rwanda also strengthened its relations with countries in *West Africa* and the Sahel region. In mid-April, Kagame visited *Benin, Guinea, and Guinea-Bissau*.

During a meeting with president of Benin Patrice Talon on 14 April, the two leaders signed cooperation agreements. Kagame pledged *military support to help Benin* address the spillover from the jihadist conflict at its northern border with

Burkina Faso. Talks between Benin and Rwanda on military and logistical cooperation began in 2022. Kagame expressed readiness to work with Benin to secure its borders, and details of the cooperation, including supervision, coaching, training, and joint deployment, were discussed. The meeting addressed the terrorist threat and ways to strengthen cooperation in dealing with it.

During a visit by Kagame to Guinea, interim president of *Guinea* Mamady Doumbouya expressed admiration for Rwanda's developmental model. Kagame arrived in Conakry, Guinea, on 17 April. The two presidents aimed to strengthen bilateral relations and create a bridge between Conakry and Kigali. Kagame expressed willingness to collaborate with Guinea and extended an invitation to Doumbouya to visit Rwanda soon. Agreements were reportedly signed during the visit on the opening of diplomatic representations and direct flights between Conakry and Kigali, and an MoU on post, telecommunications, information technology, communication, and state digitisation. Kagame also visited Guinea-Bissau, where visa-free travel agreements were signed along with cooperation deals in tourism, trade, and education sectors.

Military relations were expanded with *Burkina Faso*. Burkina Faso's chief of staff of the armed forces, Céléstin Simporé, visited Kigali on 10 November for military cooperation talks. The meeting involved discussions on ways to enhance *defence cooperation between Burkina Faso and Rwanda*. Simporé was received by his Rwandan counterpart Mubarak Muganga and defence minister Juvenal Marizamunda.

In Southern Africa, Rwanda maintained its military presence in Mozambique and was involved in combat operations in the Cabo Delgado province. Among other actions, the RDF repelled a militant attack in Chinda village, Mocimboa da Praia district, northern Mozambique, on 20 October. Earlier in the year, on 15 April, the RDF had conducted an operation in support of Mozambique's army, neutralising 17 militants and detaining at least 40 suspected militants.

This military presence *increasingly strengthened Rwanda's role in Mozambique's political and economic system*. Mozambique's council of ministers approved a bill on 1 March for the ratification of an extradition agreement with Rwanda, signed in 2022. The agreement allowed for the extradition from one country to the other of individuals, including political refugees, accused of crimes. The move raised concerns, as many Rwandans fleeing political persecution have sought refuge in Mozambique amid a wave of killings and kidnappings. The approval was criticised in the media, with the 'Zambezi' newspaper stating that Mozambique's president, Filipe Jacinto Nyusi, was giving Rwanda a free hand to persecute opponents in Mozambique.

In the CAR, Rwanda retained its strong role and even expanded it, according to a report by the ICG dated 7 July. A report by French public broadcaster RFI on 20 February detailed the growing influence and operations of the Wagner Group in CAR. The report, based on an independent investigation and leaked documents, highlighted Russia's sponsorship of anti-UN demonstrations in Bangui and the establishment of troll factories in several countries for disinformation campaigns targeting the US. Despite pressure from the US on CAR's allies, including Rwanda, to reduce Russia's influence, the president of CAR, Faustin-Archange Touadéra was reportedly determined to deepen relations with Moscow. Rwanda may not have been able to push back against Wagner, but it had to intervene at least once to rescue the mercenaries. Rebel attacks on Wagner Group camps were reported on 30 March in Nième near Bouar, resulting in casualties. A subsequent ambush on 29 March left two soldiers dead and three Wagner mercenaries injured. Rwandan troops from the UN Mission in CAR (MINUSCA) intervened to assist the mercenaries during an attack in Bossemptele on 4 April, resulting in casualties on both sides.

Relations with states in the Global North did not significantly cool off in the face of the conflict in the DRC. President of France *Emmanuel Macron*'s visit to the DRC on 3 March was noteworthy for its avoidance of overt criticism of Rwanda, despite pressure from Congolese authorities. Macron refrained from announcing sanctions and instead called on all parties involved, including Rwanda, to 'take responsibility' for the situation in the region. This diplomatic approach suggested a cautious stance by France, perhaps aiming to maintain a delicate balance amid regional tensions. The lack of explicit condemnation implied that France was navigating its relations with Rwanda with strategic prudence, acknowledging the complexity of the geopolitical landscape in the Great Lakes region and Rwanda's role in Mozambique.

Relations with the USA benefited from the release of Paul Rusesabagina. Following the UN report on Rwanda's role in the M23 insurgency, *sanctions were imposed on six individuals*. Among them, for the first time, was Andrew Nyamvumba of the RDF, a heavyweight in politics. According to the US Treasury, Nyamvumba had been responsible for directing operations for the RDF's 3rd Division, which had engaged in attacks on Congolese army positions and camps alongside M23 fighters in 2022. The UN Group of Experts on Congo reported in June that Nyamvumba played a coordinating role in RDF operations. However, the US limited itself to this individual punitive action.

Regarding relations with the *EU*, there was a notable development involving the imposition of sanctions on a senior Rwandan army officer, Jean Pierre Niragire. He had led Rwandan special forces deployed in the DRC's eastern province of North Kivu since May 2022. The *EU sanctions* were imposed due to Niragire's direct involvement, along with his unit, in Rwanda's alleged aggression against the DRC. The EU's justification for including Niragire on the sanctions list revolved around the accusation that the RDF aimed to strengthen the M23 in eastern DRC. The EU claimed that the RDF was supporting M23 by providing troops and equipment. M23 was accused of being a subsidiary of the Rwandan army, contributing to insecurity in the region and committing serious human rights violations. Rwanda consistently denied these allegations, particularly those linking it to the M23 insurgency in North Kivu.

Socioeconomic Developments

Rwanda experienced *robust economic growth* in 2023. The World Bank reported growth of 7.6% in the initial three quarters of the year. The strong output in manufacturing and services sectors offset weaker-than-expected agricultural production and a slowdown in construction. Despite this, the economic situation slightly improved compared with previous years. *Inflation decreased* significantly over the year. While it was at 21.7% in November 2022, it dropped to 11.2% in November 2023. Although the government missed its target, it was able to stabilise the situation. According to the National Institute of Statistics, GDP increased by 8.2% in 2023.

In August, labour market data from the National Institute of Statistics revealed that the overall *unemployment rate* remained at 18.0%, nearly unchanged from August 2022. Gender disparities persisted, with women experiencing a higher unemployment rate of 21.9% compared with men at 14.8%. Young people aged 16 to 30 years faced a relatively higher unemployment rate of 21.0%.

In the *budget* presented on 15 June for the fiscal year 2023/24, finance minister Uzziel Ndagijimana announced an increase in expenditures by 5.6% to approximately $4 bn. Ndagijimana stated that 63% of the budget was covered by domestic revenues, with external loans making up 24% and external grants contributing 13%.

In response to the economic challenges, the government of Rwanda outlined a credible fiscal consolidation plan to ensure macroeconomic stability. The World Bank's Economic Update report emphasised the importance of mobilising additional resources beyond the government budget. The government aimed to address challenges by implementing a tighter monetary policy stance while allowing for greater exchange rate flexibility.

Rwanda engaged with the IMF under the *Policy Coordination Instrument* (PCI) and Resilience and Sustainability Facility (RSF). The first reviews of these arrangements were discussed in meetings with the IMF mission on 4 April, resulting in a staff-level agreement on economic and financial policies. The IMF mission praised Rwanda's strong economic growth but highlighted inflationary pressures and external vulnerabilities. The team recommended building policy buffers, implementing tax laws for domestic revenue, and advancing monetary policy reforms. The mission also commended Rwanda's efforts in pandemic response, socioeconomic resilience, climate change reforms, and institutional capacity strengthening. On 24 May, the executive board of the IMF finally approved the disbursement of

$74.6 m under the RSF. On 14 December, the board approved a new 14-month credit facility for Rwanda, totalling $268.05 m. Of this amount, Rwanda could immediately access $138.84 m. This agreement was part of the IMF's stand-by credit facility (SCF) and RSF. According to the IMF, the board's decisions permitted an immediate disbursement of approximately $49.49 m under the RSF and around $89.35 m under the SCF.

Rwanda's *mineral export earnings* witnessed significant growth, reaching $609 m in the first six months of 2023, as reported by the Rwanda Mining, Petroleum, and Gas Board. The mining sector, the second-largest export revenue earner after tourism, saw increased revenues due to investments in mineral processing, value addition, and mineral diversification. Gold, cassiterite, wolfram, coltan, and new minerals such as amblygonite, lithium, and beryllium contributed to the rise in export earnings. The government aimed to achieve $1.5 bn in annual mineral export revenues by 2024.

A joint venture agreement involving Aterian PLC, Rio Tinto Mining and Exploration Ltd, and Kinunga Mining Ltd, signed on 1 August, highlighted Rwanda's foray into lithium exploration. The project encompassed 2,750 hectares in Southern Province and included the identification of 19 pegmatite zones for lithium, caesium, and tantalum.

The establishment of a $100 m cement manufacturing plant, as part of a joint venture with West China Cement, aimed to address the supply deficit in the construction industry. The plant, located 50 km south-west of Kigali, targeted annual production of 1 m metric tonnes, making it the largest in the country. This venture promised to contribute to the construction industry and offer cheaper cement options.

To support the struggling *agricultural sector*, the EIB pledged investments of €100 m during COP28. The programme provided financial support for enterprises owned and managed by women. This funding initiative aimed to bolster investments in enhancing agricultural productivity, facilitating better financial access within the agricultural sector, and fostering the economic empowerment of women. A minimum of 30% of the overall funding in this fresh initiative was to be specifically allocated to female entrepreneurs or businesses with a predominantly female workforce.

Again, Rwanda faced challenges related to *climate change*, with heavy rain leading to *floods and landslides* in several parts of the country. From 19 March onwards, floods hit the areas of Rusizi and Rubavu. On 6 May, the government allocated nearly $100 m to repair damaged infrastructure and assist affected families. The floods left around 9,000 people homeless and destroyed 50 schools. In a collaborative effort with international partners, including the Agence Française de Développement (AFD), EIB, Cassa Depositi e Prestiti (CDP), and the IFC, Rwanda announced a cooperative approach to mobilising an additional €300 m for climate resilience.

This initiative complemented existing financing arrangements, such as the RSF with the IMF. The partnership focused on policy reforms, capacity development, and financing arrangements to accelerate climate investment and build resilience.

Rwanda remained in the spotlight of *international migration policy* this year. After the British High Court of Justice had deemed the proposal to deport asylum seekers to Rwanda legal on 19 December 2022, the Court of Appeal overturned the verdict on 29 June, confirming Rwanda as an unsafe destination. The case was reheard before the Supreme Court on 9 October. The Court of Appeal's decision was upheld. In response, the UK government presented the Safety of Rwanda (Asylum and Immigration) Bill on 7 December 2023. The bill asserted Rwanda as a secure haven for asylum seekers, irrespective of its actual safety conditions. Notably, the bill would limit individuals' ability to challenge their transfer to Rwanda within UK courts.

Rwanda continued its work with the UNHCR. As of November, according to UNHCR, there were over 135,000 *refugees and asylum seekers* in the country. UNHCR flights from Libya to Rwanda also continued during the year. On 9 March, 150 asylum seekers from Libya reached Kigali.

Rwanda's *international marketing campaign* also continued. On 27 August, the five-year partnership between the football club FC Bayern Munich and Visit Rwanda began. The sponsorship amount was undisclosed. FC Bayern was the third club to be sponsored by Visit Rwanda, following Arsenal (UK) and PSG (France). Furthermore, the country took steps to host global sports competitions, including the 2025 World Road Cycling Championships, and in March, it served as the venue for the 73rd Congress of the International Football Federation (FIFA).

Seychelles

Anthoni van Nieuwkerk and Benedikt Kamski

Seychelles has seen an increase in political pluralism in recent years. In anticipation of elections in 2025, two new political parties made their appearance: the Seychelles United Movement (SUM) and the Seychelles National Alliance Party (SNAP). Despite the country's strong standing in the Transparency International Corruption Perceptions Index, several members of the political establishment were arrested for alleged misappropriation of funds during the year. Seychelles maintained friendly relations with its close neighbours in the Indian Ocean and prioritised strategic relations with long-standing allies India, China, and the EU. President Wavel Ramkalawan used global platforms to call for more cooperation in addressing climate change, ocean conservation, sustainable development, and maritime security. By the end of the year, Seychelles featured a solid economic recovery yet significantly lower growth rates compared with the previous year. Tourism and fisheries remained key growth drivers, with significant potential in digital finance and other knowledge-intensive services. Seychelles continued to be among the leading voices in the 'blue economy' movement, using oceans for sustainable growth and jobs while preserving ecosystems.

Domestic Politics

In the 2020 general election, the opposition party Linyon Demokratik Seselwa (LDS) defeated the long-standing United Seychelles Party (USP), leading to a peaceful power transition. LDS currently holds a majority in the National Assembly, while the former ruling USP obtained 10 of 35 seats. President Wavel Ramkalawan and the LDS will remain in power until the next general election scheduled for September 2025. Seychelles has seen an *increase in political pluralism* in recent years. In the year under review, two new political parties made their appearance. The SUM was registered in August, followed by the SNAP in November as the eighth political party. Both announced that they would participate in the coming legislative and presidential polls. The Electoral Commission of Seychelles (ECS) signed an MoU with the Election Commission of India on 26 September. The agreement, finalised during the visit to Seychelles of India's chief election commissioner, Shri Rajiv Kumar, focused on sharing experiences and expertise and exploring the digitalisation of the electoral process.

In October, in an unexpected development, the Magistrates' Court charged eight individuals, including Patrick Herminie, the leader of the USP, of witchcraft. Herminie, who had announced that he would stand in the presidential elections, said that his arrest was a politically motivated attempt to destroy his image and that of his party. Charges included *possession of items for witchcraft, conspiracy to perform witchcraft, and procuring related services*.

Former minister Maurice Loustau-Lalanne and finance official Lekha Nair were arrested on 23 November on charges of money laundering and corruption, followed by former first lady Sarah Zarqhani Rene on 27 November. In December, Seychelles police raided Alpha Consulting, linked to the Pandora Papers leak of 2021 that exposed the financial offshore dealings of public officials and wealthy individuals around the globe. The raid was part of an investigation into concealed ownership of British shell companies. Among Alpha's clients was Yevgeny Prigozhin, whose company Wagner Group was sanctioned in 2019.

In the 2023 *Corruption Perceptions Index*, Seychelles achieved a ranking of 20th out of 180 countries (based on 2022 data), a rank it shared with France and the UK and that made it again the top-ranked nation in SSA. President Ramkalawan expressed pride in this accomplishment.

The *Freedom in the World 2024 report* (based on 2023 data) gave Seychelles a score of 79 out of 100 ('free'), unchanged from the previous year. However, the country dropped 21 places on the World Press Freedom Index – from 13th place in 2022 (the highest ranking in SSA) to 34th in 2023. Controversially, Seychelles lost the greatest number of points in the legislative and social indicators. The government and the ruling LDS openly expressed disappointment with the score, while the chair of the

Association of Media Practitioners of Seychelles noted that it was due partly to a change in the methodology used for the index.

In August, the Seychelles National Assembly commenced debates on the recommendations made by the *Truth, Reconciliation, and National Unity Commission* (TRNUC) in its final report. The National Assembly will consider proposed reparations and how they will be carried out. The TRNUC was established in 2018 to work on settling past political divisions and grievances that were a result of the coup d'état in Seychelles in 1977. The final report of the commission was submitted to President Ramkalawan in March.

Foreign Affairs

In February, the minister of foreign affairs and tourism stated that 'a more equitable and sustainable world order should be based on cooperation, dialogue, solidarity, respect for the sovereignty of nations and the rights of individual nations and individuals'. Minister Sylvestre Radegonde emphasised the principles that guided Seychelles' foreign policy, which he said reflected the values, culture, aspirations, and principles of the Seychellois people.

Seychelles maintained friendly relations with its close neighbours in the *Indian Ocean* and prioritised strategic relations with long-standing allies India and China, as well as the EU. After a 27-year hiatus, the US embassy reopened in June. The office is headed by a *chargé d'affaires* while the ambassador to Seychelles and Mauritius is based in Port Louis, Mauritius: the two nations have cooperated in various areas in recent years, such as in signing a bilateral agreement on countering illicit transnational maritime activity operations in July 2021, and have worked together regarding the climate crisis and drug trafficking, among other issues. The US views Seychelles as an important partner in providing security in the Western Indian Ocean. In October, the US embassy announced a collaboration with the Ministry of Education focusing on English language teaching and STEM (science, technology, engineering, and mathematics) education.

Relations with *India* deepened. In July, an agreement was reached to undertake training through joint military exercises, sharing of knowledge from military experts seconded to the Seychelles Coast Guard, maritime surveillance, assistance on community projects, and capacity building in various fields. In November, Seychelles announced that it would receive a grant amounting to 35 m Seychellois rupees (SCR; $5.7 m) from India to finance high-impact community development projects through a newly signed MoU, as well as further cooperation on youth, sport, and tourism.

The government attended the 3rd Belt and Road Initiative Forum for International Cooperation in October in *Beijing*. Over the years, China has assisted Seychelles through the building of several infrastructural projects. An ongoing project is the new headquarters for Seychelles Broadcasting Corporation, funded by the Chinese government. In July, a Confucius Institute opened at the University of Seychelles, focusing on language training.

In October, Seychelles and the *EU* held their 10th Political Dialogue in Victoria, led by Sylvestre Radegonde and EU ambassador Oskar Benedikt, with representatives from ten EU member states. It was agreed to enhance cooperation in maritime security, ocean management, fisheries, trade, investment, climate change, and environmental protection, acknowledging the positive impact of the Sustainable Fisheries Partnership Agreement (SFPA) on Seychelles' fishing industry. The EU welcomed the Maritime Environment Fund to help clean up Seychelles' waters. The parties reviewed the EPA support programme for economic diversification and SME support, with the EU committing to assist in improving Seychelles' tax governance rating.

In April, Seychelles and Mauritius met to discuss common interests and concerns, focusing on the interests of Small Island Developing States (SIDS) and advancing collective economic development. Due to the Covid-19 pandemic, the parties had last met in Port Louis in 2017, and had had to postpone their subsequent meeting until 2023.

President Ramkalawan visited the Maldives in June and announced that bilateral relations would be elevated to a higher level. The two countries pursued common issues including maritime security, climate change, economic development, tourism, and the establishment of the Multidimensional Vulnerability Index (MVI) and the Loss and Damage Fund.

In May, members of parliament from countries of the *Indian Ocean Commission* met in Seychelles. Agence Française de Développement (AFD) announced funding for a project on governance, peace, and stability (GPS) over the course of two and a half years to support action against IUU (illegal, unreported, and unregulated) fishing and drug trafficking and to enhance peace and stability in the region.

In his address to the UNGA in September, Ramkalawan called for *global cooperation in addressing climate change, ocean conservation, sustainable development, and maritime security*. At COP28 in Dubai, the Seychellois delegation emphasised the health impacts of climate change and President Ramkalawan called for more equitable access to the Loss and Damage Fund and urged for simpler financial mechanisms for high-income SIDS such as Seychelles. Recent surveys suggest that $22 m is needed for infrastructure and coastal erosion alone, and $600 m for climate adaptation and mitigation over the next decade.

In September, Seychelles became the 18th member of the *Ocean Panel*. The Ocean Panel is a high-level global initiative that allows world leaders to build momentum and work towards a sustainable ocean economy in which effective protection, sustainable production, and equitable prosperity go together. President Ramkalawan was also elected as the new president of the SIDS DOCK, an initiative of the Alliance of Small Island States (AOSIS), meant to transform the energy sectors of AOSIS members and address adaptation to climate change.

Socioeconomic Developments

By the end of the year, Seychelles showed solid *economic recovery*, though at a much slower pace than in 2022. GDP growth declined considerably compared with the previous year, in line with World Bank estimates that foresaw a moderation in growth from approximately 8.9% down to 3.3%. In August, the Ministry of Finance, National Planning and Trade had already revised its growth projections downward by 1.2% to 4.2% due to lower-than-expected numbers of tourism arrivals. Overall, the contraction in growth illustrated Seychelles' high degree of vulnerability, as a tourism-dependent economy, to external factors, including supply chain disruptions. Despite these challenges, tourism and fisheries remain *key growth drivers*, alongside significant untapped potential in digital finance and other knowledge-intensive services. Tourist arrivals increased, nearly reaching pre-pandemic levels. Germany and Russia led tourist numbers in early 2024, with European tourists making up more than 70% of the total arrivals of approximately 342,000. Overall, the services sector continued to dominate Seychelles' economy, contributing approximately 66% of GDP. The information and communication sector grew by 16% year-on-year in Q2 2023, partly due to increased demands by visitors for broadband. Financial and insurance activities increased by 33%.

According to AfDB data, the *fiscal deficit* saw a slight increase, rising from 1.5% of GDP in 2022 to 1.9% in 2023. Nevertheless, the debt-to-GDP ratio showed improvement, decreasing by 2.2% to 56.7% in 2023, indicating growing efficiency in public debt management and ongoing economic recovery. Conversely, the current account deficit increased to 8% of GDP due to higher import costs. External reserves also improved, with import cover increasing from 3.2 months in 2022 to 3.7 months in 2023. The financial sector remained well capitalised yet highly concentrated, with the top three banks holding 80% of total assets, deposits, and loans. The proportion of non-performing loans rose slightly, from 6% in 2022 to around 7% in 2023, primarily due to borrowing during the Covid-19 pandemic.

Seychelles has established itself as a prominent *offshore financial centre*, offering services in banking, insurance, and investment management. Trade and transport are other vital sub-sectors, with the country's strategic Indian Ocean location making it a key transit point for goods moving between Africa, Asia, and the Middle East. More than 200,000 companies have been registered since the Seychelles International Business Companies Act was introduced in 1994, with steadily growing numbers of new incorporations, according to government figures.

On 2 November, finance minister Naadir Hassan presented the 2024 *budget* of SCR 10.64 bn to the National Assembly. The budget focused on key areas such as health, education, housing, sports, community development, public safety, transportation, and national development. To encourage workers, the government planned to reform taxes on bonuses and performance-based salaries. A new tax system would provide exemptions on voluntary pension contributions by employers and offer a five-year tax holiday for new businesses in priority sectors. Additionally, the VAT Act was to be revised to prevent booking platforms from charging VAT commission, and taxes on certain battery-operated vehicles were to be lowered to support environmental protection efforts.

On 18 October, Seychelles launched the GEF-7 project to enhance biodiversity conservation and promote nature-based solutions within the blue economy. The launch was attended by minister for agriculture, climate change and environment Flavien Joubert and various stakeholders. The initiative will focus on managing Marine Protected Areas (MPAs) through Marine Spatial Planning (MSP) to protect ecosystems and foster sustainable economic growth. Funded with $4.95 m from the Global Environment Facility (GEF), the project aims to improve institutional and financial mechanisms, as well as monitoring and enforcement capacities, for effective MPA management. It will run until September 2029.

The World Bank reported that Seychelles achieved or surpassed all targets under the $56 m ECF approved by the IMF in May 2023. Seychelles also integrated climate financing needs into its investment plan, as required by the $46 m Resilience and Sustainability Facility loan, resulting in a combined disbursement of $20.4 m (1% of GDP) in 2023. Although Seychelles will require nearly 5% of GDP annually for climate change mitigation, it currently spends only 0.9% of GDP per year. Global rating agency Fitch anticipated ongoing multilateral support for Seychelles' climate adaptation, leading to increased budgetary spending on climate issues in the medium term.

Seychelles leads the *blue economy movement*, using oceans for sustainable growth and jobs while preserving ecosystems. Facing an annual financing gap of $14.4 m for climate change mitigation, the country raised $15 m through a blue bond backed by the World Bank and introduced debt refinancing for ocean conservation. The government allocated over 4% of its budget to environmental efforts and started a sustainable environment levy for visitors in April 2023. Relying mainly on concessionary financing, Seychelles is also encouraging private sector investment in green energy and eco-friendly transport through a public–private partnership law and a strong financial sector.

At the end of 2023, Mahé Island's northern region experienced severe weather, including heavy rainfall, landslides, and floods, as well as a major explosion in a crucial industrial zone. These events caused extensive damage to commercial buildings, homes, and public infrastructure. On 7 December, Bloomberg reported that

Seychelles had declared a *state of emergency* due to a blast at an explosives depot owned by a local construction company and flooding resulting from heavy rains. Building resilience, economic diversification, and climate change adaptation is crucial for Seychelles' future stability and growth.

Somalia

Faduma Abukar Mursal

Somalia faced internal power struggles and dealt with widespread military offensives and humanitarian challenges during the year under review. The increased military offensives throughout the country and a hardening social climate intensified tensions. Several armed clashes over the voting system between regional security forces and armed opposition groups sometimes led to the latter declaring themselves autonomous. President Hassan Sheikh Mohamud made efforts to integrate Somalia into regional organisations, where the country was described increasingly as a business- and investor-friendly environment. By contrast, the humanitarian situation remained dire, especially following heavy floods that affected over 1 m people.

Domestic Politics

Following his second-term election in 2022, the president of the Somali federal government (SFG), Hassan Sheikh Mohamud, set the tone of his second presidency with increased military offensives throughout the country, the mobilisation of civilians as militias, financial sanctions, and an intensive hold on the media. The SFG together with traditional regional leaders announced on 28 May that they had agreed on a series of reforms to the country's political system, such as the introduction of universal suffrage and direct elections for the office of the president, national representatives, and local and regional councils. Local elections to be held under the new system are scheduled for June 2024. However, these reforms faced opposition, including clashes between security forces of the regional polities and armed opposition groups, leading at times to the latter declaring themselves autonomous.

The SFG, together with US forces and regional allies, was focused on the *military offensive to defeat jihadist fundamentalist group al-Shabaab*. Shortly after re-election in 2022, President Hassan Sheikh Mohamud announced an '*all-out war*' against the group. In February 2023, leaders of Somalia, Kenya, Ethiopia, and Djibouti issued a plan calling to 'search and destroy' al-Shabaab by stepping up military operations. There were two phases of large-scale military operations, with a short pause during the heavy floods at the end of the year. In November, the government and its partners conducted clearing operations around the town of Xuddur, the Bakool and Bay regions, in small villages in Galmudug such as Barag Mohamud Daaud, and on both banks of the Shabelle river in Hirshabelle State.

During the year, the number of airstrikes significantly increased. They were conducted by Kenya, Ethiopia, the US, and, in June, the first official airstrikes by the UAE. The second phase of the 'total war' started in August, with intensified airstrikes, especially those operated by the US Africa Command, justified as 'collective self-defence' airstrikes. Amnesty International, newspaper outlets such as 'Goobjoog' and 'The New York Times', HRW, and al-Shabaab spokespeople reported the killing of civilians in these campaigns, and the disruption of telecommunications services. Furthermore, the government called on clerics, regional administrations, and civilians to mobilise themselves as militias that would support government military efforts. The government also engaged in what was labelled a 'financial war', which consisted of the blocking of the bank accounts and mobile money accounts of merchants accused of having facilitated the flow of money to al-Shabaab.

The year was marked by an *electoral crisis in the wake of the municipal elections*. In May, the National Consultation Council (NCC), which comprises all of the federal member state (FMS) presidents (apart from Puntland) and the federal president and prime minister announced the decision to hold the first direct local elections in June 2024, ahead of the parliamentary and presidential elections scheduled for November 2024. Significantly, the political leaders also announced the introduction of a presidential system replacing the current parliamentary one.

In Puntland, voters went to the polls on 25 May to elect district councils. Until then, the region of Puntland had used an indirect, clan-based electoral system to select its political representatives. The opposition accused the incumbent president Said Abdullahi Deni of seeking to manipulate the electoral process and extend his mandate. Aside from the postponement of polling in three districts, the media reported that voting had taken place peacefully. The ruling Kaah Political Association was the main winner. Seven parties were competing for 774 seats, and the Kaah won a total of 286 seats. In Hirshabelle State, the political row within the administration escalated in June when the current leader of the administration Ali Abudllahi Hussein, also known as Gudlawe, sacked former governor Ali Jeyte Osman. The disagreement was reported to be about the tax reforms, and the fact that taxes from the Hiran region had not been deposited in the Bank of Hirshabelle. Osman rejected his dismissal and declared himself president of a self-declared autonomous region of Hiran, one of the two regions that make up the Hirshabelle polity (the other being Middle Shabelle). By year's end, the consequences of this self-declaration were yet to be seen.

In February, the situation in Las Anod worsened dramatically, with clashes between forces of Somaliland and local militias called the Sool, Sanaag, and Cayn-Khatumo forces (SSC-Khatumo, also known as Dhulbahante militias) throughout the rest of the year. Las Anod is the administrative capital of the Sool region, and located between Somaliland and Puntland. Somaliland claims the regions of Sool, Sanaag, and Cayn (SSC) as part its territory on the basis of colonial-era boundaries. Inhabitants of the region, often considered to be Dhulbahante, accused Somaliland of operating an 'economic embargo' on the region and deplored the presence of Somaliland forces.

On 5 February, the conference of Dhulbahante clan representatives took place in Las Anod. After the conference, participants said that they did not recognise Somaliland's administration and wanted to be part of Somalia, and demanded the withdrawal of Somaliland forces from Sool. The president of the self-declared independent Somaliland, Muse Bihi Abdi, rejected this decision in the name of the defence of the territorial integrity of Somaliland. On the same day, clashes broke out between Somaliland armed forces and the SSC-Khatumo forces. From February until the end of the year, there were continuous *on-and-off clashes around Las Anod*. After deadly clashes, Somaliland withdrew forces from an important military base in the village of Tukaraq, east of Las Anod, by the end of February. Several efforts at mediation, including by the SFG and Ethiopia, were unsuccessful, as were international calls for de-escalation of the fighting. The Khatumo forces insisted on the withdrawal of Somaliland forces. After a military pushback on 25 June, Somaliland's President Bihi reiterated his commitment to defending territorial integrity but expressed willingness to engage in negotiations with Dhulbahante elders. According to human rights observers, dozens of civilians were killed and injured amid the fighting. Significantly, Somaliland forces were accused of indiscriminately shelling the town, damaged hospitals, schools, and mosques and displacing tens of thousands of people. The use of mortar shelling and the heavy artillery exchange killed many civilians, damaged key social infrastructure such as the hospital of Las Anod on 8 July, and resulted in the withdrawal of the NGO MSF, announced on 24 July. During July, the frontline shifted away from Las Anod to neighbouring areas such as the villages of Oog and Guumays. In August, the Khatumo forces achieved a major victory by capturing the Goojacade army base and several smaller outposts on the outskirts of Las Anod from the Somaliland forces. This meant that there was no presence of Somaliland troops in the region.

On 5 August, Abdulkadir Ahmed (known as Firdhiye), was elected chair of the self-declared SSC-Khatumo state's 45-member executive council and started a campaign for the recognition of the new administration as a region. The leader of SSC-Khatumo, the newly self-declared administration of the Dhulbahante community, began negotiations with the SFG on its admission as an FMS. In October, Firdhiye visited Mogadishu and reiterated the desire to create a new administrative region, and the SFG recognised SSC-Khatumo as interim administration on 19 October.

The Las Anos crisis also directly affected the *electoral process in Hargeisa, the capital city of Somaliland*. When the conflict arose, several politicians in the opposition condemned Bihi's approach in Las Anod, and a few senior officials resigned or switched sides. For example, in March, two Dhulbahante clan members, Abdirisaq Ibrahim Mohamed 'Attash', who founded the Waberi political association, and Saleban Essa Ahmed 'Xaglatoosiye', announced their withdrawal from Somaliland politics and called for Somaliland forces to leave Las Anod. The deputy commander of army, Lieutenant General Suleiman Barre Gesood, defected in early June, and the speaker of the House of Representatives, Abdirisaq Khalif, resigned. Another opposition party, Waddani, accused Bihi of using the Las Anod conflict to delay elections originally scheduled for November 2022. Amid the electoral dispute, the electoral commission set election dates in July and announced that political party elections were scheduled for December and the presidential vote for November 2023. This decision contradicted the demands of the opposition because the elections would take place with a delay of two years and the presidential election would take place before those of the parliament. In August, the ruling Kulmiye party elected Bihi as its candidate for the presidential election, and interior minister Mohamed Kahin as new party chair. In order to reduce the tensions, elders from the Haber Jeclo clan proposed in August to combine the political party and presidential elections so that they would take place at the same time in November 2024. *After the withdrawal Somaliland's forces from Sool, the electoral disputes in Somaliland deescalated visibly. In August*, Bihi accepted the compromises proposed by the elders of the Haber Jeclo and announced simultaneous political party and presidential elections for 13 November 2024.

The hijacking of several vessels along the Somali coast sparked worries about the return of piracy in the area. For about a decade, armed Somali pirates had scoured the waters off the Somali coasts, forcefully boarding vessels and demanding ransoms of millions of dollars. The hijacking of ships had considerably reduced with the introduction of extensive maritime security measures along East Africa's coast by the EU-led naval mission, Atalanta. The attacks resurged in November when an Iranian fishing vessel, 'Almeraj 1', was hijacked, as well as a tanker, 'Central Park', off the Yemeni coast. Several other Iranian fishing vessels believed to be engaging in illegal fishing, which threatens the livelihoods of local fishing communities, were also hijacked. The Somali government called for greater international support.

The state of human rights and the protection of civilians remained dire. The increase in fighting in several parts of the country resulted in greater numbers of conflict-related deaths and injuries in several sections of the population, including unarmed civilians. In continuity with previous years, human rights abuses by state, non-state, and foreign actors occurred regularly. According to several organisations, including HRW, the International Committee of the Red Cross (ICRC), and Amnesty International, the actors involved in these violations included both government bodies and al-Shabaab. The total war that the government announced had a great death toll. Aside from the airstrikes that resulted in several civilian casualties, the Somali government and its various authorities carrying out military offensives did not hand over al-Shabaab cases to civilian courts, instead carrying out executions, sometimes as a result of military court proceedings. Moreover, the government intervened in an expanding range of aspects of social life. In this regard, on 22 February, HRW deplored the fact that the Senate had passed a law granting the National Intelligence and Security Agency (NISA) broader powers of detention and surveillance.

Both targeted and indiscriminate attacks by al-Shabaab in the form of IEDs, suicide bombings, shelling, and targeted killings occasioned a high number of civilian deaths. Al-Shabaab was responsible for several attacks in urban settlements and on military bases where the president of the SFG was staying, notably the siege of Pearl Beach Hotel in June, and in Dhusamareb and Mahas in September.

The *Freedom in the World* report for 2024, based on data from 2023, ranked Somalia as 'not free', with a score of 8/100, as in the previous year. On political rights the country scored 2/40, and on civil liberties 6/60. Restrictions on the media were important components of the government's total war campaign. The federal government banned social media platform TikTok, messaging service Telegram, and gambling app 1XBET in August. Similar reports on the obstruction of freedom of the press were reported in Somaliland, in particular a ban on BBC services. The secretary-general of the Somali Journalists Syndicate (SJS), Abdalle Ahmed Mumin, was sentenced by a court in February for two months and arrested a third time for voicing concerns about a government directive restricting reporting on national security issues. In August, security forces arrested Mohamed Ibrahim Osman Bulbul, a journalist working for Kaab TV in the capital, for reporting on cases of corruption in the police forces. He was finally released under the order of a high court judge. On 15 May, Somaliland police arrested journalist Bushaaro Ali Mohamed near the border with Ethiopia and sentenced him to one year in prison for 'tarnishing the image of state institutions'.

Somalia had a score of 11/100 and ranked in the last place out of the 180 countries ranked in Transparency International's Corruption Perceptions Index 2024 (based on 2023 data). In March, President Hassan Sheikh Mohamud endorsed bills to fight corruption. In July, a highly publicised series of trials of government officials accused of corruption by the Banadir Regional Court was televised. The government sued several government officials, including four high-profile statesmen, on charges of corruption, embezzlement, and abuse of power. The dozens of officials under scrutiny included the former director of the Immigration and Citizenship Agency, Mohamed Aden Koofi, who was accused of embezzlement; Abdulkadir Ilmi Ali, for corruption; and Osman Hassan Osoble, Abdikafi Hassan Mohamed, and Muhiyedin Hassan Juru in the Ministry of Finance, charged with misappropriating public funds.

Foreign Affairs

President Hassan Sheikh Mohamud made visible diplomatic efforts to integrate Somalia into regional organisations and to secure military and financial support from international partners. For instance, Somalia made important steps towards becoming the eighth member of the EAC. It was admitted into the EAC bloc at the Summit of EAC Heads of State on 24 November and was set to become a full member in March 2024.

By contrast, the *relationship with the UN was marked by reports of aid diversion, and the withdrawal of AU Transition Mission (ATMIS) troops*. In September, the UN published a report on 'widespread and systematic' diversion of food aid that was intended to avert famine in the country, this was given by the EU as its justification for temporarily suspending its funding to the WFP. The UNSG appointed George Conway as the new deputy special representative for Somalia.

The *withdrawal and replacement of ATMIS in Somalia* with the Somali army was a major concern throughout the year. In March, the EU approved an additional €110 m to support Somalia's armed forces and ATMIS in Somalia. By the end of June, the first phase of troop withdrawal had begun, and 2,000 soldiers were replaced by Somali security forces, composed of various units trained by regional forces and foreign armies, such as those of the US and Türkiye. In September, the Somali government requested a delay to the withdrawal of an additional 3,000 troops. In November, the UNSG suspended the withdrawal of ATMIS troops scheduled for the end of the year.

The so-called Somalia Quint met for a fourth time in October in Ankara. This group, composed of Qatar, Türkiye, the UAE, the UK, and the US, met under the theme 'Security and Stabilisation in Somalia' and expressed support for the SFG and the intensified military offensive. Each of these countries also maintained close bilateral cooperation with Mogadishu. For instance, President Mohamud met with Turkish president Recep Tayyip Erdogan, who committed to continuing the training of the soldiers of the so-called Gorgor Brigades in Türkiye, to training the Somali National Army to use Turkish drones, to covering the salaries of government officials and civil servants, and to the guarding of the Somali coastline. In February, the UAE and Somalia signed a security agreement strengthening military and security collaboration.

Bilateral relations with the US continued to be close, mostly in the form of military support. The Biden administration had redeployed troops to Somalia starting in 2022, reversing a decision by former president Donald Trump to remove US troops from the country. In January, the US pledged $9 m in new military aid to Somali forces, the first direct military support since US forces, including Special Forces, returned to Somalia in 2022. The US acknowledged having conducted over a dozen airstrikes, primarily in central Somalia – in the form of reactive strikes but also preventive ones as so-called 'collective self-defence'.

Bilateral relation with Eritrea continued to grow closer. In May 2022, Asmara and Mogadishu had improved bilateral cooperation with the signature of an agreement covering defence, security, diplomatic, and political cooperation between the two countries. After decades of tensions between the two, their rapprochement was often reported to be a result of the fact that both the Eritrean president Isaias Afwerki and Hassan Sheikh Mohamud were worried about the Ethiopian government's open claims to secure access to the Red Sea, which grew louder during 2023. The Somali president travelled at least four times to Asmara, and Somalia dispatched its first ambassador to the Eritrean capital.

Relations between the SFG and the Ethiopian government were marked by growing tensions, especially by the end of the year, with a controversial MoU with Somaliland that became public on 1 January 2024. Ethiopian prime minister Abiy Ahmed and Somaliland president Muse Bihi Abdi met on 31 December and signed the MoU, which would allow Addis Ababa to gain access to a commercial port and a leased military base on the Red Sea coast in exchange for the official recognition of Somaliland's sovereignty. The SFG considered this MoU as compromising the territorial integrity of Somalia, and sought international partners such as the EU to condemn it.

Socioeconomic Developments

The socioeconomic landscape was marked by a dire humanitarian situation, resulting in part from heavy flooding. The country remained highly dependent on the importation of food as well as donor support to meet humanitarian needs. By November, the federal government had declared an emergency after torrential rains triggered floods that affected over 700,000 people and displaced over a million across the country.

The SFG budget was based largely on donor contributions. The federal government's official budget for the year amounted to $977 m. Around 70% of the budget ($667 m) came from donors, with domestic revenue making up a little less than 30%.

Reliable data on GDP growth figures and inflation rates was scarce and based largely on estimates. The AfDB estimated Somalia's GDP growth at 2.8% in 2023, up from 2.4% in 2022. The growing services sector, the recovery of agriculture from drought, and household consumption and investment were the main drivers of this growth. Inflation in Somalia was estimated at 6.1%. The government started implementing a currency exchange programme to introduce a new Somali shilling by 2026, which should gradually replace US dollars and counterfeit Somali shillings.

In terms of fiscal deficit, Somalia remained in high debt distress, but its recognition in the debt relief programme reduced the risk of debt distress to moderate, according to the AfDB. In July, Somalia received a $75 m grant from the World Bank – the second of two grants for building institutions – and support to qualify for full and irrevocable debt relief under the HIPC initiative. In November, Somalia and the IMF reached an initial agreement that would allow the release of $100 m, which would help Somalia to qualify as a HIPC and entitle it to debt relief. In December, the IMF and the World Bank approved the HIPC initiative to provide debt service savings for Somalia of $4.5 bn. After this HIPC completion point, the external debt of Somalia fell, from 64% of GDP in 2018 to about 6% in 2023.

Humanitarian conditions were extremely precarious throughout the year. After Somalia had faced five consecutive below-average rainfalls, the Gu rains from March to June were better than forecasted, helping to reduce some of the immense constraints, including food price hikes. However, the rains also resulted in flash floods throughout the country, especially in the states of SouthWest, Hirshabelle, Jubaland, and Galmudug. The floods forced tens of thousands of people to flee in parts of the country, destroyed farmland and infrastructure, and resulted in an estimated one hundred or more deaths. The government and also al-Shabaab created emergency relief committees.

According to UN data, almost 3 m people were internally displaced in 2023, and 70% of them required food assistance and emergency aid. Armed confrontations, floods, and droughts were the main causes, and affected populations across the country, especially in the regions of Bay, Mudug, and the Middle and Lower Jubbas. As of August, Somalia was host to over 30,000 registered refugees and asylum seekers, mainly from Ethiopia and Yemen, some 700,000 Somali refugees and asylum seekers were displaced in neighbouring countries, and a further 1.5 m people were internally displaced. Between October and December, the UN estimated that nearly

4.3 m people were acutely food insecure. Based on trends since August 2023, it was predicted that over 1.5 m children would be acutely malnourished by July 2024.

Humanitarian agencies operated in difficult conditions, their workers facing challenges such as armed confrontation, targeted attacks, and the difficult weather conditions. There were also restrictions imposed by parties to the conflict. For example, in July, al-Shabaab blocked routes into Baidoa town. Also in July, MSF announced its withdrawal from Las Anod because of increased armed confrontation, recurrent attacks on medical facilities, and injuries to medical staff.

The *overall public health situation in the Somali areas remained precarious*, with limited health services and uneven coverage, and a significant cholera outbreak. Reliable data about vaccination rates, including Covid-19, was not available.

The Mogadishu Lighthouse, built on the edge of the old port in the early 1900s during the Italian colonial period, partially collapsed in May because of a lack of maintenance.

South Sudan

Daniel Large

The elections scheduled for December 2024 were a salient feature throughout the year. In July, current president Salva Kiir announced that he would stand in the ballot. Efforts to prepare the legislative and institutional framework for the elections were contested and behind schedule. The weakening of Riak Machar's SPLM-IO (Sudan People's Liberation Movement in Opposition) continued, and opposition groups outside the 2018 peace agreement remained fragmented, with sporadic clashes with government forces. The major event impacting South Sudan's domestic and foreign affairs was the outbreak of armed conflict in Khartoum on 15 April, which caused new insecurity, refugee flows, and uncertainty over oil exports through Sudan. Salva Kiir took a leading role in IGAD-sponsored regional efforts to mediate the conflict, working with both the Sudanese Armed Forces (SAF) and the Rapid Support Forces (RSF) in a year that saw him travel widely, from Riyadh to New York and Moscow. A decade after the irruption of conflict in December 2013, South Sudan faced new levels of displacement, humanitarian need, and suffering, including food insecurity, and was confronted with the continuing effects of conflict and climate change.

Domestic Politics

According to the original political timetable agreed in the September 2018 Revitalised Agreement on the Resolution of Conflict in South Sudan (R-ARCSS), before this was extended by two years in August 2022, South Sudan's transitional period was supposed to end with elections this year. Not only was the transitional period not supposed to last so long: it was also supposed to involve reforms geared towards enhancing security, economic development, transitional justice, and political change. Such an agenda for change was not unfamiliar in historical terms; the subdued 40th anniversary of the Bor mutiny on 16 May 1983, now associated with the founding of the Sudan's People's Liberation Army (SPLA), was a reminder of past grand visions of a better, reformed 'new Sudan', the protracted armed struggle and suffering that accompanied its pursuit, and questions about what had been gained by independence in 2011.

At a political rally on 5 July in Wau, Western Bahr el Ghazal, President Salva Kiir pledged that the *delayed elections* scheduled for December 2024 would proceed and that he would stand for president. As the year progressed, a series of developments indicated formal advances in the electoral timetable but were contested and mostly involved shallow steps in the creation of the legal and institutional framework for elections. In early September, President Kiir ruled out another extension of the transitional period and cautioned against violence by his political opponents if they lost the elections. First Vice-President Riak Machar confirmed his support for the elections at various points but expressed concern that the conditions for a credible ballot were not in place.

Parliament hurriedly passed the National Election Act, 2012 (Amendment) Act 2023 on 18 September. There were complaints that speaker Jemma Nunu Kumba had failed to allow opposition MPs sufficient time to debate the bill, which was signed into law by Kiir not long afterwards. The SPLA-IO, asserting that the bill ran counter to the peace agreement and would result in an undemocratic election, boycotted the vote and walked out over a late amendment giving the president elect the right to appoint an extra 5% of legislators. The Act contained new provisions to add elections for the administrative areas of Abyei, Ruweng, and Pibor, to increase the number of elected MPs from 250 to 332 and the number of Council of States members from 40 to 56.

In November, Kiir reconstituted the National Election Commission, a key body for the elections, together with the Political Parties Council and the National Constitution Review Commission (NCRC). These were examples of official measures formally important to the holding of the elections, albeit accompanied by questions about their likely effectiveness and resourcing; the 2023/24 national budget, for instance, failed to provide sufficient funds for these reconstituted bodies to operate effectively. A rare rally by some 12 opposition parties in Juba on 18 November demanded access to participation in the elections.

Kiir swore in members of the NCRC in December, but multiple concerns persisted over the elections among opposition politicians and in civil society quarters. SPLM-IO parliamentarians cited restrictions on Riak Machar's freedom of movement. The tenth anniversary of the irruption of violence in Juba on 15 December 2013 provided a sobering milestone. A statement by Remembering the Ones We Lost, a public memorial project, called on the government and all armed groups to end violence, and again asked for 15 December to be made National Memorial Day.

There were new political appointments and reshuffles across the year, some more controversial and important than others. In January, Peter Lam Both became SPLM secretary-general. In March, *Kiir sacked defence minister Angelina Teny*, the wife of Riek Machar, and was accused by the SPLM-IO of unilaterally violating the terms of the peace agreement. Teny was replaced by former Upper Nile state governor Chol Thom Balok. The stand-off ended only in September, when Kiir appointed Teny as the new interior minister. A November reshuffle saw Dak Duop Bichiok replace Kuol Athian Diing as the new minister of public service and William Anyun Kuol appointed minister of trade and industry. After violence in the state of Warrap, Kuol Mur Mur replaced Manhiem Bol Malek as its governor. Presidential affairs minister Barnaba Marial Benjamin was replaced by Bangasi Joseph Bakosoro, a move that appeared connected with the latter's political influence in the state of Western Equatoria and how this might help Kiir's electoral prospects there.

In terms of civil liberties, the targeting of civil society activists, journalists, and media, human rights defenders, lawyers, and protesters continued within South Sudan, starting in January when the National Security Service (NSS) arrested six media staff of the South Sudan Broadcasting Corporation over a leaked video showing Kiir appearing to urinate on himself during a public event. Such targeting also extended beyond South Sudan; in February, for example, NSS agents and Kenyan police abducted Morris Mabior Awikjok, former civil servant turned activist, and rendered him to Juba. One trend observed by civil society groups was an increase in cyber-attacks. The *National Security Service Act* 2014 (Amendment) Bill 2023 was revised over the year and was presented to parliament for its third reading in September. Freedom House graded South Sudan 'not free' in its Freedom in the World 2024 report, with a score of 1 out of 100, ranking it as one of 15 'Worst in the World' countries out of 67 countries designated 'not free' based on data from 2023. The World Press Freedom Index 2023 ranked South Sudan 118th out of 180 countries (for 2022). In June, South Sudan ratified the AU Protocol to the African Charter on Human and People's Rights on the Rights of Women in Africa, and the country acceded to the Convention on Cluster Munitions in August. In October, the UN Commission on Human Rights in South Sudan reported 'entrenched systematic repression' of the media, human rights defenders, and civil society. Just after this, the government postponed the visit of the UN special rapporteur on the human rights of internally displaced persons, Paula Gaviria Betancur.

As Riak Machar's *SPLA-IO became politically and militarily weaker*, the government became stronger through opposition defections. A series of SPLA-IO members from Machar's former strongholds in Jonglei and Unity defected over the year to join Kiir's government. In October, the defection of two important commanders from Unity and Jonglei, Lieutenant General Simon Maguek Gai and Lieutenant General Michael Wal Nyak, reduced its military capacity in both states. In December, tensions between Machar's forces and those of Simon Maguek Gai triggered sporadic fighting in Unity state. After arriving in Juba in May, Shilluk Agwalek militia leader General Johnson Olony met Kiir in June and agreed to integrate his forces into South Sudan's national armed forces, the South Sudan People's Defence Force. Others who switched sides to join the government included members of Simon Gatwech's SPLA-IO Kitgwang faction, deputy chief of staff of the South Sudan United Front/Army Dickson Gatluak, and National Salvation Front commander Kenyi Warrior.

New negotiations between the government and armed groups and opposition entities outside the 2018 peace agreement were held amid shifting opposition alignments. In Rome, talks facilitated by the Community Sant'Egidio between the Transitional Government of National Unity and opposition groups under a new banner, the Non-Signatories South Sudanese Opposition Group, resumed in March but were adjourned without success. On 3 April, invoking the 'need for united opposition' to 'change the regime in Juba', a new South Sudan Federal Democratic Alliance was declared in Khartoum. Signatories included the SPLM/A Kitgwang, the National Salvation Front, and various new groups but excluded former SPLA chief of staff Paul Malong, former SPLA commander Stephen Buay, and former SPLM general secretary Pagan Amum.

In terms of violent conflicts, the ceasefire mostly held, despite sporadic fighting between government forces and those outside the R-ARCSS and intercommunal conflict in many parts, but the *outbreak of fighting in Sudan* on 15 April was a serious development. As well as triggering refugee flows and economic ripple effects, this had security implications. The risks of conflict spilling over into South Sudan were evident when a group of RSF fighters entered Renk county, Upper Nile, on 19 April, prompting the army to issue an ultimatum for the group to disarm or leave. The new civil war in Sudan meant more international attention on Khartoum, on top of attention directed towards Ukraine and Ethiopia, and less external pressure on Kiir's regime in Juba to meaningfully advance on creating and resourcing the institutional framework for the delayed elections.

By the metrics of the 2018 R-ARCSS, the UN Mission in South Sudan (UNMISS), and the Reconstituted Joint Monitoring and Evaluation Commission, the timetable was behind schedule and South Sudan was, as frequently stated, 'not ready' for elections. Concern was by no means confined to international quarters but emanated first and foremost from within the country. In December, for instance, over 70 local civil society organisations issued a statement warning that South Sudan was 'not ready for inclusive, free, fair, credible and peaceful' elections following a conference in Juba. Another reading, based more on the actions of Salva Kiir's leadership, however, suggested that the official implementation process around the R-ARCSS and its elections component was not so much behind schedule as proceeding according to a different timetable and logic predicated upon the Kiir's intent to guarantee that the elections would further strengthen his power, or at the least officially confirm the political-military status quo, while adding the veneer of renewed legitimacy in international eyes. As such, by balancing international pressure around the election timetable with the pursuit of an agenda based on strengthening his power, the tactical manoeuvring of Kiir's leadership was instrumentalising the December 2024 elections process. The prospect of elections increasingly looked to entail official choice but a predetermined outcome.

Foreign Affairs

The UNSC renewed UNMISS's mandate for another year in March, keeping the ceiling of 17,000 military personnel and 2,101 police personnel and further emphasising civilian protection. In April, the UNHRC renewed the Commission on Human Rights in South Sudan's mandate for another year. The UNSC's renewal of sanctions and the arms embargo until 31 May 2024 was denounced by South Sudan's foreign ministry as 'deplorable'; in June, the AU Peace and Security Council called for the lifting of the arms embargo on grounds relating to the implementation of the peace deal. The UNSC renewed the mandate of the Panel of Experts until 1 July 2024, with China, Russia, Ghana, Mozambique, and Gabon abstaining. In November, the UNSC extended the mandate of the UN Interim Security Force for Abyei for a year.

UNMISS became more involved in election-related activities over the year and expressed fairly regular public concerns about the process. In March, the head of UNMISS, Nicholas Haysom, warned that South Sudan faced a 'make or break' year in 2023, and that its leaders should hold 'inclusive and credible' elections in 2024 to implement the peace agreement. In May, the UNSC decided that actions impeding 'the conduct or legitimacy of free and fair elections in South Sudan, including by impeding or distorting pre-election preparatory activities', could be used to justify sanctions. In December, Haysom again warned the UNSC that 'South Sudan is not yet in a position to hold credible elections'.

Pope Francis finally visited South Sudan on a three-day 'pilgrimage for peace' in February, accompanied by the archbishop of Canterbury, and the moderator of the General Assembly of the Church of Scotland. Presiding over an open-air mass with some 100,000 attendees at the John Garang Mausoleum in Juba, he denounced tribalism, financial wrong-doing, and corruption, called for end to violence, and proclaimed 'May hope and peace dwell in South Sudan'. During the pope's visit, President Kiir reiterated his commitment to the Rome talks process, but their subsequent resumption led nowhere. In December, on behalf of President Kiir, minister of presidential affairs Bangasi Joseph Bakasoro asked Kenya's president William Ruto to mediate between the government and the non-signatories to the 2018 peace agreement.

There were developments in South Sudan's relations with neighbouring and other important states. In March, Ethiopian prime minister Abiy Ahmed visited Juba for talks with Kiir. In April, South Sudan deployed some 345 additional soldiers to the DRC as part of the EAC Regional Force's fight against the M23 rebel group, but this force withdrew in December with the rest of the troops. The acting minister of foreign affairs, Deng Dau, met his counterpart, Sheikh Abdullah bin Zayed Al Nahyan in Abu Dhabi on 11 April, signalling ongoing relations between Juba and the UAE. In August, South Africa's deputy president Paul Mashatile, appointed special envoy on South Sudan in March, visited Juba, where he offered to assist with resolving 'challenges that may hinder free and fair elections'.

By far the most significant factor in South Sudan's regional relations was the outbreak of conflict in Sudan in mid-April. This followed signs of progress between South Sudan and Sudan earlier in the year, notably over the disputed region of Abyei. In January, General Abdel Fattah al-Burhan, chair of the Sovereign Council of Sudan, held talks about Abyei with President Kiir in Juba. On 9–10 April, follow-up talks in Khartoum chaired by the deputy chair of the Sovereign Council of the Sudan and head of the RSF, General Mohamad Hamdan Dagalo (known as 'Hemedti'), and South Sudan's presidential advisor on national security, Tut Gatluak, produced agreement on peacefully resolving the Abyei dispute. Shortly afterwards, however, on 15 April, fighting began in Khartoum, after which IGAD appointed Kiir as leader of its Mediation Support Unit dealing with Sudan, along with his Kenyan and Djiboutian counterparts. Kiir's leadership of IGAD's mediation between the Sudanese warring parties involved failed efforts to agree a ceasefire. In May, he hosted representatives of the SAF and the RSF in Juba for separate talks, to the consternation of Burhan's leadership. One notable characteristic of Kiir's Sudan conflict diplomacy was his efforts to engage both Burhan and Hemedti and not take sides. Indeed, his efforts to engage with these leaders took precedence over other active relations with a disparate range of other Sudan movements, including the SPLM-North.

Important strands of Juba's diplomatic engagement with conflict in Sudan involved relations with other involved powers, notably Egypt and Saudia Arabia, that overlapped with its official IGAD mediation role. Sudan featured prominently in Juba's relations with Cairo. In July, Kiir attended the Sudan's Neighbouring States

Summit in Cairo, where he called for a national Sudanese-led mediation process to end the conflict. He returned to Cairo in November to meet Egyptian president Abdel Fattah al-Sisi, after which South Sudan and Egypt agreed to waive an age requirement and registration fees for South Sudanese students enrolling at Egyptian universities. Following efforts to enhance relations that pre-dated the outbreak of violence in Sudan, Saudi Arabia's Royal Court advisor and the kingdom's former minister of state for African affairs, Prince Ahmed Kattan, visited Juba in August for talks with Kiir. In November, Kiir travelled to Riyadh for the inaugural Saudi Arabia–Africa leaders' summit.

The EU and US remained major donors and continued to engage, despite tensions over sanctions and election-related issues. The EU sanctioned Gatluak Nyang Hoth, commissioner for the county of Mayendid, and Gordon Koang Biel of Koch county, under its human rights sanctions regime, for 'widespread and systematic use of sexual violence as a war tactic'. In July, the EU added James Mark Nando on the same basis. In June, the US Treasury Department announced sanctions on Major General James Nando and Governor Alfred Futuyo for their involvement in sexual violence. In August, the US Department of State, Department of Labor, and Department of Commerce issued a 'South Sudan Business Advisory' that highlighted the risks for US businesses and individuals of doing business in the country, especially with 'enterprises with ties to the South Sudanese government'. In November, the Troika group of the US, UK, and Norway expressed concern at the 'persistent lack of political will' over peace agreement implementation and election preparedness.

A familiar pattern continued of discord between South Sudan and its US and European partners counterposed with closer ties with Russia and China. Juba's relations with Moscow saw notable developments: a delegation attended the International Parliamentary Conference 'Russia–Africa in a Multipolar World' in March, and Vice-President Taban Deng Gai led South Sudan's participation in the Russia–Africa summit in St Petersburg in July. The headline event came in September, when Kiir visited Moscow and met President Putin at the Kremlin. Relations between Juba and Beijing progressed further in terms of interconnected political and economic strands. These featured regular contact, including an April visit by an SPLM delegation led by Peter Lam Both to China where he signed an MoU with Liu Jianchao, head of the Chinese Communist Party's International Department. In August, the Chinese embassy handed over a new China-aided TV studio production and broadcasting complex in Juba and, in a historic first, South Sudan's basketball team defeated China at the FIBA Basketball World Cup.

The prominence of President Kiir's role in attempting to respond to conflict in Sudan, its most important neighbour and a guarantor of South Sudan's 2018 peace agreement, was striking in view of South Sudan's history of conflict with Khartoum before 2005 and independence in 2011. It was accompanied by further changes in his ministers dealing with foreign affairs. In March, Kiir sacked foreign minister Mayiik Ayii Deng and replaced him with his deputy Deng Dau Deng, before sacking Deng and appointing James Morgan, previously South Sudan's ambassador to Ethiopia. Kiir's foreign trips over the year suggested confidence in his domestic political position. In September, for instance, as well as visiting the Kremlin, he visited Ugandan president Yoweri Museveni in Kampala, met UNSG António Guterres, and addressed the UNGA in New York. In November, however, the enhanced presence of security forces in Juba during Kiir's trip to Saudi Arabia prompted rumours of a coup attempt – a reminder of how difficult circumstances remained within South Sudan.

Socioeconomic Developments

Claims that South Sudan's first National Economic Conference, held in Juba in September, would offer 'a roadmap for South Sudan's economic prosperity', contrasted with the entrenched reality of dire economic circumstances. In August, President Kiir sacked finance minister Dier Tong Ngor and replaced him with Bak Barnaba Chol, who hails from Kiir's home state, an appointment that seemed to indicate an intent to tighten Kiir's control of public resources. In October, a presidential decree sacked Bank of South Sudan governor Johnny Ohisa Damian and appointed James Alic Garang, a former IMF official, to the post. In December, the World Bank estimated that South Sudan's economy had stagnated in 2022/23, contracting by 0.4% in 2023. Inflation averaged 3.3% in the first nine months. The country's annual CPI increased from 5.8% in December 2022 to December 2023, with a 23.9% increase in Juba. South Sudan again ranked 171st of 180 countries in the 2023 Transparency International Corruption Perceptions Index (scoring 13 out of 100 for 2022). The depreciation of the South Sudanese pound (SSP) against the US dollar continued, despite various attempts by the central bank, which attributed the devaluation to rising commodity prices and difficult domestic and global conditions, to respond. By December, the SSP–dollar exchange rate represented a 40% depreciation against the dollar compared with a year previously, with the SSP officially trading at SSP 1,068 (and 1,100 informally).

The IMF approved a $114.8 m disbursement in March to help address South Sudan's urgent balance of payment needs. In May, an IMF staff team visited for talks on its February 2023 Staff Monitored Program (SMP). In December, after a further visit to Juba, the IMF finalised its consultations and review of the SMP in South Sudan and enumerated multiple challenges faced by the authorities, including financing the December 2024 elections.

The minister for finance and economic planning presented the 2023/24 budget to the National Assembly on 20 June, setting out an estimated SSP 2.11 trillion

($2.06 bn) in expenditures, SSP 1.84 trillion ($1.80 bn) in revenue, and a deficit of SSP 267 bn ($261 m). On 17 July, a public hearing on the proposed budget gave air to criticism and dissatisfaction from different quarters. On 22 July, the SPLM-IO parliamentary caucus cautioned that the insufficient allocation of funds to critical tasks outlined in the R-ARCSS would put both the August 2022 road-map and the 2024 elections at risk. Despite SPLM-IO opposition, the budget was passed on 11 August.

In December, the World Bank reported that while it was difficult to estimate the total debt situation, South Sudan remained at a high risk of debt distress for external and domestic debt. An IMF/World Bank Debt Sustainability Analysis update indicated external public debt worth $2.76 bn (some 54% of GDP) as of 1 March. Over half of this (some $1.3 bn) was owed to commercial creditors via high-cost, short-maturity debt. External debt service amounted to an estimated 7.5% of GDP in 2022/23.

The oil sector faced uncertainty and challenges on multiple fronts as Nilepet, the national oil company, prioritised *increasing production*. In January, President Kiir appointed Bernard Amour Makeny as Nilepet's new managing director. Makeny visited China in October, where, backtracking from the previous plan to take over China National Petroleum Corporation (CNPC) oilfields when contracts expire in 2027, he asked CNPC to boost oil production. Long-standing under-investment, investor concerns, and uncertainty over 2027 and flooding had contributed to reduced production. Oil output ran at about 130,000–140,000 barrels per day (bpd), with the 2023/24 budget projecting oil production at 132,000 bpd. Attempts to boost the industry included multiple exploration-related MoUs being signed and the sixth annual South Sudan Oil and Power conference in Juba in June. The impact of conflict in Sudan became a major issue. Reported threats by the RSF in June to blow up the main oil export pipeline if South Sudan did not stop paying transit fees to the SAF, for instance, underscored the renewed vulnerability of South Sudan's oil exports through Sudan's evolving conflict landscape, the potential risks to South Sudan ruling political-military elites revenue, and need to find new export routes. In June, a new Emergency Response Team, working with its Sudanese counterparts to minimise disruption to oil exports via Sudan, announced that all essential supplies for the oil sector would be imported via Mombasa, with Port of Djibouti also being considered. Talks were held with Kenya over oil export routes and trucking oil. An MoU signed in August with Ethiopia and Djibouti featured the option of building an export pipeline.

Flooding remained a widespread problem, mostly affecting the Nile and Lol rivers and the Sudd marshlands. Drought affected Aweil and Rumbek, according to the IGAD Climate Prediction and Applications Centre drought watch. The ongoing effects of such 'climate shocks', including the lingering effects of previous flooding, contributed to climate-driven forms of conflict in parts of the country, such as Tonj East county. These also disrupted food production, contributing to worsening food security. In November, areas in Jonglei and Unity were classified as in IPC Phase 5 (Catastrophe), and 11 counties in Jonglei, Unity, Upper Nile, Northern Bahr el Ghazal, and Eastern Equatoria as in Phase 4 (Emergency). According to the 2023 INFORM Risk Index, South Sudan ranked as the country second most vulnerable to natural hazards globally and among the top five countries most vulnerable to the impact of climate change.

The impact of conflict in Sudan on refugee flows into South Sudan represented a major development as the country struggled to respond to and cope with this influx. The macro figures were stark in December, when OCHA reported a total of 9.4 m people in need, including refugees; 2 m IDPs, of whom some 40,000 were in POC sites, 2.5 m South Sudanese refugees (including 924,000 in Uganda, 683,00 in Sudan, and 419,000 in Ethiopia); 361,000 refugees in South Sudan; and 476,000 registered people crossing from Sudan. Food insecurity was at its highest levels since 2011, with 5.78 m acutely food insecure and 1.7 m malnourished children. For the vast majority, particularly those outside the capital, the transitional period had not brought clear benefits. On top of the government's budgetary relegation of services in favour of security and other priorities, the international relief effort substituting services for the state faced a tough combination of increasing needs and declining resources. The 2023 Humanitarian Response Plan requested $1.7 bn to target 6.8 m people, for instance, but was funded only at 46% as of 5 September. In December, an independent evaluation of UNMISS's protection of civilians, requested by the UNSC, credited UNMISS with remaining a 'highly relevant peacekeeping mission' but, pointing to scale of challenges, noted that 'finding a last solution to the country's political problems' was key. The prospects that the scheduled elections would do so were bleak.

Sudan

Antoine Galindo and Augustine Passilly

The horizon rapidly darkened after the signing of a framework agreement at the end of 2022 supposed to enable the democratic transition interrupted by the coup of 25 October 2021 to resume. The head of the Sudanese Armed Forces (SAF), Abdel Fattah al-Burhan, and the head of the very powerful paramilitary Rapid Support Forces (RSF), Mohamed Hamdan Dagalo, also known as Hemedti, were unable to agree on a central point of the treaty, the integration of the RSF into the national ranks. The tensions, latent for several months, led to the outbreak of a war in April. The army headquarters, the airport in the heart of the capital, and the presidential palace quickly became scenes of violent clashes. Eventually, the RSF took over most of Khartoum and Jazeera states and the west of the country, confining the SAF to the east and north. From the first days of the conflict, many civilians and eminent personalities asserted their neutrality and their opposition to the war. This led to the creation of a broad coalition, Taqaddum, by the end of October. However, this momentum did not prevent the ethnicisation of the clashes. Efforts by the international community to bring the conflict to an end also failed. The US and Saudi Arabia did manage to extract a declaration of principle from the two belligerents on 11 May, but this was quickly violated. The so-called 'Jeddah process' remained at a standstill at the end of the year, as did the potential meeting between the two generals, which IGAD had announced on 9 December would never take place. Faced with the failure of mediation attempts, the US and the UK imposed sanctions on individuals and companies supporting the war effort.

Time was running out for a country whose economy was in tatters. Only the gold sector made any progress, as it was used to supply both sides with weapons, fuel, and other basic necessities. Civilians paid a heavy price for the tug of war between al-Burhan and Hemedti. By the end of the year, the hostilities displaced 6.7 m people, while 17.7 m Sudanese were food insecure. Famine was threatening, a cholera epidemic was raging and more than 70% of hospitals were out of action in towns affected by the fighting.

Domestic Politics

The year began in Khartoum with widespread excitement: on 5 December 2022, a framework agreement had been signed, laying the foundations for a new collaboration between the military and part of the political class. The document provided for the organisation, from January onwards, of several roundtables intended to enable progress to be made in five areas: transitional justice, reform of the security services, revision of the 'Juba Peace Agreement' (JPA) of October 2020, dismantling the regime of former president Omar al-Bashir, and resolving the political crisis in the eastern states of the country. Although far from being unanimously approved, this document was supposed to enable the country to get out of the rut it had been in for over a year of political instability.

In October 2021, the president of the Transitional Sovereignty Council (TSC), Abdel Fattah al-Burhan, and his deputy, Mohamed Hamdan Dagalo, known as Hemedti, took power from the transitional civilian government of Prime Minister Abdallah Hamdok, plunging the country into uncertainty. For a full year, Sudan found itself hostage to a growing rivalry between the two TSC generals and a political class incapable of organising itself to confront them. Until the 2021 coup, the political class was mainly grouped within the Forces of Freedom and Change (FFC), the coalition on which Hamdok relied to govern. The FFC was initially made up of political parties and civil society groups that had taken part in the transitional government between 2019 and 2021, as well as the parties that signed the 2020 JPA. Following the coup of 2021, the coalition broke up and two groups emerged. On the one hand, FFC – Central Council (FFC-CC or FFC-1), the largest group, was made up mainly of the historic members of the coalition, including the National Umma Party (NUP), the Sudanese Congress Party (SCP), the Unionist Alliance, the Arab Socialist Ba'ath Party, the Civil Society Initiative, professional unions, and a few JPA signatories grouped under the banner of the Sudanese Revolutionary Front (SRF).

On the other hand, the FFC Democratic Bloc (FFC-DB or FFC-2), was driven mainly by two former rebel groups, Minni Minawi's Sudan Liberation Movement (SLM-MM) and Gibril Ibrahim's Justice and Equality Movement (JEM), together with smaller parties such as the Democratic Alliance for Social Justice and other groups mainly from the periphery.

The 5 December framework agreement failed to resolve the crisis and led to the crystallising of tensions between January and March 2023. Some of the agreement's opponents feared that it would completely undermine the 2020 JPA, which since the fall of Omar al-Bashir's (1989–2019) regime had represented the main matrix of Sudan's political transition. Following the JPA, several rebel groups negotiated key portfolios and positions in the transitional government. This was the case, for example, with the SLM-MM, which won the governorship of the Darfur region (which includes five states) in April 2021 and key positions in the Ministry of Mines in February 2021. The JEM bargained a position at the head of the Ministry of Finance and Economic Planning. Other groups obtained seats in the TSC. Clinging to these positions, which they feared losing, SLM-MM and JEM threw their full weight behind slowing down the process triggered by the 5 December framework agreement. Former cadres of al-Bashir's regime, who were still very influential within the army and the state apparatus and who controlled large sections of the economy, also worked hard to thwart the agreement. They refused to let a new democratic transition harm their interests and dismantle their economic empire. The 5 December process, initially intended to last only a few weeks, was also delayed by growing divisions between the political parties in the FFC, particularly over the names of those who should make up any hypothetical future government that might have emerged.

The main stumbling block was the reform of the security sector. This point, which had already caused considerable turbulence during the 2019–21 transition period, crystallised the tensions between Hemedti and al-Burhan at the beginning of the year. The JPA, like the framework agreement, provided for the integration of the RSF, the paramilitary force controlled by Hemedti, into the command of the SAF, the regular army led by al-Burhan. Al-Burhan and his camp wanted to impose a rapid integration timetable of two years while Hemedti wanted a period of ten years or more. The RSF was created in 2013 and its independence was enshrined in law in 2017, ratified by parliament. This officially incorporated the militias into the government's military apparatus under the direct command of the president, while the defence minister remained responsible for overseeing the SAF. The RSF soldiers were initially former Janjaweed fighters, Arab fighters from Darfur active during the Darfur war from the early 2000s. After the fall of al-Bashir's regime in 2019, to which it contributed, the RSF was given free rein to develop, recruit, and establish itself as a key player in the transition, backed by a powerful gold trade and an economic empire controlled by the Dagalo family.

During the first four months of the year, while Khartoum was negotiating the reform of the security services, the RSF carried out major troop movements from North Darfur, its historic stronghold, throughout the country.

At the same time, the resistance committees – grass-roots organisations very active during the revolution and present throughout the country – and a whole section of civil society continued to demonstrate against the military. Most of them were against the framework agreement and called for the SAF and RSF to be removed from power. Before this document was signed, some pro-democracy parties such as the Ba'ath dissociated themselves from the FFC-1. The SCP had already left the coalition in November 2020, refusing in particular to continue working with the military.

Tensions rose a notch on 12 April, when RSF movements around the airport of Merowe, a town in the north of the country, triggered the ire of the SAF as well as a verbal escalation between Hemedti and al-Burhan. Sensing that the situation was spiralling, the Quad for Sudan, comprising the US, UK, UAE, and Saudi Arabia, tried a last-ditch mediation led by the Saudi ambassador to Khartoum, Ali Bin Hassan Jaffar. Unfortunately, the mediators were unable to get the two men to meet, and on the morning of 15 April, the first shots were fired around Merowe airport and at the Soba military base in the south of Khartoum. At the same time, clashes broke out in several parts of the capital, plunging Sudan into chaos and sending millions of refugees onto the roads.

During the first weeks of the conflict, the capital Khartoum was the scene of violent clashes. While the SAF indiscriminately bombed civilian residential areas, the RSF, which has no air force, carried out guerrilla offensives, using civilian homes as camouflage. The fighting was concentrated around a few key sectors and buildings: army headquarters, where the SAF command was based; tank headquarters in the south of the capital; Khartoum International Airport in the heart of the city; and the presidential palace. By the end of the year, the RSF had taken control of most of the capital, confining the SAF to the suburbs of Omdurman, Khartoum's twin city, and to the Jazeera region in the south, where the two Nile rivers meet. The SAF also retained control of the north and east of the country.

Numerous political and community groupings, and even armed groups, refused to immediately align themselves with one or other of the belligerents. At the end of April, the Civilian Front for Ending War and Restoring Democracy was set up, a first attempt at a common front signed by political parties, professional unions, representatives of civil society, and resistance committees, as well as 131 eminent personalities. In the months that followed, political and civil movements, many of them exiled in Cairo, Addis Ababa, Nairobi, or Kampala, tried to speak with one voice. But political divisions and the polarisation of the war made this dialogue difficult and delayed the formation of a coalition. Two poles emerged, in Cairo and Addis Ababa, where competing conferences were organised during the summer.

Although involved behind the scenes from the start of the conflict, former prime minister Abdallah Hamdok did not agree to take on a leadership role until October, when the Taqaddum coalition was formed in Addis Ababa. Made up mainly of the political core of FFC-1, Taqaddum also brought together civil society players, members of resistance committees, and professional organisations. From its inception, Taqaddum was traversed by a wide range of currents and plagued by dissension. Although it aimed to provide a third, non-aligned voice in the conflict, the proximity of some of its members or sympathisers to the RSF cast doubt on the neutrality of the group, which also struggled to broaden its base.

Initially courted by Taqaddum, the formations of the FFC-DB and certain rebel groups that had signed the JPA remained non-aligned until November, before siding with the SAF. The decision was precipitated by the extreme violence and ethnicisation of the conflict in Darfur, from where the two main FFC-DB groups, JEM and SLM-MM, originate.

In Darfur, dozens of tribal chiefs from Arab and non-Arab communities signed a pledge of neutrality in May amid fears that the region would once again descend into ethnic clashes. The conflict in the 2000s pitted Arab fighters, supported and financed by Khartoum, against the non-Arab black peoples of Darfur, including the Fur, Massalit, and Zaghawa. But the tribal leaders' call for neutrality did not prevent the conflict from spreading and becoming ethnicised.

From the outset, the ethnic shift was most marked in El Geneina, the capital of West Darfur. Its governor, Khamis Abdallah Abakar, a Massalit, was assassinated by the RSF on the night of 14–15 April, after denouncing an ongoing 'genocide' a few hours earlier on the Saudi channel Al Hadath. On 24 April, the town was the scene of violent clashes, with the SAF abandoning local residents to their fate. Arab militias allied with the RSF systematically attacked non-Arab populations, particularly the Massalit. Tens of thousands of them tried to flee the violence to the northern suburb of the town, Ardamata, where there was an SAF base. Many continued on to Chad. After taking control of the town, the RSF replaced the murdered governor with his deputy, Al Tijani Karshoum, a Rizeigat Arab, the community to which Hemedti belongs.

The town of Nyala, in South Darfur, was also the scene of violent clashes between the SAF and RSF – first, in the early days of the conflict, on 16 April, over control of the airport. Then in July, six Arab herding community leaders (Habaniya, Beni Halba, Tarjam, Taaisha, Rizeigat, and Fallata – the latter of Fulani descent) from South Darfur rallied behind the RSF, which finally succeeded in capturing the town on 26 October, after three days of intense fighting led by the brother of Hemedti, Abdelrahim Dagalo, the RSF's number 2. As a result of the fighting, the SAF lost the headquarters of 16th Infantry Division, considered to be the headquarters of the SAF command in Darfur. Following this, the RSF seized the base of 21st Division of the SAF in Zalingei, the capital of Central Darfur, and then the base of 20th Infantry Division in Ed Daein, the capital of East Darfur.

It was this offensive that convinced JEM and SLM-MM, the two Darfurian rebel groups whose base was essentially made up of Zaghawa, to join forces with the SAF, raising fears of a major battle around the army's last stronghold: at the end of December, only the capital of North Darfur, al-Fasher, was not yet administered by the RSF.

In the states of Kordofan and Blue Nile, in the south and south-west of the country, a political dimension was added to the ethnic conflict. The Nuba Mountains, the stronghold of Abdelaziz al-Hilu's Sudan People's Liberation Movement North (SPLM-N), straddle these two regions. Their inhabitants, the Nuba, although belonging to non-Arab communities, have refused to choose sides. Al-Hilu, a longstanding campaigner for a secular Sudan, had always refused to ally himself with the Sudanese army, which he considered to be under the orders of the former cadres of al-Bashir's theocratic regime. While it concentrated most of its energies on fighting the SAF, the SPLM-N also had to contend with assaults by the RSF, notably in the Tukma and Dilling areas of South Kordofan, where, allied with local Arab tribes, they sought to dislodge the Nuba. In North Kordofan, the conflict crystallised around El Obeid, the regional capital, controlled by the SAF and besieged from May onwards by the RSF.

Although 2023 had begun on a hopeful note with the framework agreement that was supposed to pave the way for a return to democratic transition, it ended in chaos. On 18 December, the RSF seized Wad Madani, the Jazeera capital where almost half a million of the capital's inhabitants had taken refuge, increasing the city's population fourfold. Its capture once again put 300,000 people on the road and jeopardised commercial operations, the delivery of humanitarian aid, and health centres.

Only the north and east of the country, controlled by the SAF, remained relatively untouched by the fighting, though the military intelligence services carried out numerous arrests and abuses against activists, politicians, journalists, and anyone associated with the pro-democracy movement, perceived as a threat by the SAF general staff and their advisors, whose new capital was now established in Port Sudan, on the shores of the Red Sea.

Corruption worsened, with Sudan dropping two places on Transparency International's Corruption Perceptions Index for 2023 (based on 2022 data) compared with the previous year. Against this backdrop, a quarter (24%) of users of public services had paid a bribe in the past year.

Almost completely closed to the international media since the outbreak of the conflict, the country has become very hostile to national journalists. On 10 October, Halima Idris Salim became the fourth reporter to be shot dead while covering the war, and cases of harassment were frequent. Reporters Without Borders ranked the country 149th out of 180 for 2023 (based on 2022 data), making it one of the nations globally where press freedom is most restricted.

Foreign Policy

Aware that a conflict was inevitable in the short to medium term, al-Burhan and Hemedti engaged in diplomatic competition throughout 2022 and continued during the first quarter of 2023. The two men had travelled extensively in the sub-region, in search of future allies.

Sudan is a junction point between the Sahel, Central Africa, the Horn of Africa, and the Arabian Peninsula, so its stability is a major issue for many countries in the region. Oil extracted from the oilfields of neighbouring South Sudan transits through Sudan. The Gulf states see it as a granary. Egypt sees it as a potential ally in its rivalry with Ethiopia over the waters of the Nile. Chad shares a very porous border with Darfur, where a conflict could have major consequences for stability in N'Djamena.

As soon as the first shots were fired in April, international observers began to worry about the possible involvement of regional players in the conflict – particularly Egypt, whose close ties with al-Burhan led to fears that the SAF might be aligned, and UAE, where Hemedti maintains a tentacular influence and where the Dagalo empire sells its gold, which it uses to finance the conflict.

To prevent a regional conflagration, international and regional organisations tried to tackle the issue, albeit in an uncoordinated fashion. Initially led by the US and Saudi Arabia, a limited mediation between representatives of the two belligerents was set up in Jeddah, on the other side of the Red Sea. This resulted in a handful of ceasefires; these were never really respected but did allow thousands of foreign nationals trapped in Khartoum to be evacuated between 22 and 23 April. The mediation also led, on 11 May, to a declaration of principle by the two belligerents on respect for humanitarian law, which was soon trampled underfoot.

The repeated failures and lack of inclusiveness of the Jeddah mediation earned the US State Department a great deal of criticism, but it never changed its approach to the mediation and kept a tight rein on the talks. Despite numerous attempts, the regional organisations did not immediately succeed in obtaining a seat at the negotiating table, forcing them to set up their own platforms. On 16 April, IGAD charged four of the region's heads of state (Djibouti's Ismaïl Omar Guelleh, Ethiopia's Abiy Ahmed, South Sudan's Salva Kiir and Kenya's William Ruto) with the task, but they were never able to get to Khartoum, and their proximity to the belligerents rendered their attempt futile. Ruto was suspected of having close links with Hemedti, while Kiir's regime had historical ties with the SAF.

Amid this cacophony, the AU, largely sidelined, also tried to make its presence known – first by seeking to support civil initiatives, and second by making repeated appeals to the international community to respect the principle of subsidiarity, by virtue of which responsibility and leadership for public action lie with the competent entity closest to those directly affected by that action. It was on the basis of this principle that the three African countries (Gabon, Ghana, and Mozambique) that are members of the UNSC blocked any attempt at a resolution at the UNSC headquarters in New York during the first weeks of the conflict, and that the IGAD and the AU fought over the leadership of the mediation. For its part, Cairo organised a summit of Sudan's neighbouring countries on 13 July, attended by Chad's transitional president Mahamat Idriss Déby; Salva Kiir; Eritrean president Isaias Afwerki; Faustin-Archange Touadéra of CAR; Mohamed al-Menfi, president of Libya's Presidential Council; Abiy Ahmed; Ahmed Aboul Gheit, secretary-general of the Arab League; and Moussa Faki, president of the AU Commission.

Despite numerous attempts at mediation, the belligerents remained deaf to calls for a return to calm. Faced with the escalation of the conflict and the increasingly obvious impasse in the mediation in Jeddah, on 1 June, the US Treasury Department enacted a first set of sanctions, initially targeting 'affiliated companies fueling both sides of the conflict'. In Washington's sights were Al Junaid and Tradive General Trading, two companies at the heart of the Dagalo family empire, which finances the RSF. The US also targeted a galaxy of companies that gravitate around the military-industrial complex, such as Defense Industries System, whose close links with the SAF and former executives of al-Bashir's regime have been brought to light by numerous investigations.

From September onwards, the US Treasury also imposed sanctions on individuals. On 6 September, the assets of Abdelrahim Dagalo were targeted. Then, on 28 September, influential advisors of the SAF, such as Ali Karti, were targeted for their activities against peace, security, and stability in Sudan. Ali Karti, a former foreign minister under al-Bashir, was considered to be one of the main architects of the war. Behind the scenes, he spent the four years following the fall of al-Bashir activating politico-religious support networks, notably in Türkiye, drawing on a vast business network inherited from the three decades of dictatorship. At the same time, the US Treasury sanctioned GSK Advance Company Ltd, a company specialising in information and security technologies run by influential members of the SAF, and Aviatrade, a military supplies company based in Russia that supplies the RSF.

Finally, on 4 December, the Treasury announced a new round of sanctions against Taha Osman Ahmed al-Hussein, the former head of al-Bashir's presidential office, who played a central role in 'advancing the war efforts of the RSF'; Salah Abdallah Mohamed Salah (Salah Gosh), former head of Sudanese intelligence, who 'in the past publicly advocated that the SAF overthrow the civilian government of Sudan'; and Mohamed Etta Elmoula Abbas, who led the efforts of the Sudanese Islamist Movement (SIM) in Türkiye. The UK sanctioned six companies on 12 July: Al Junaid, GSK Advance Company Ltd, and Tradive General Trading (RSF), and Defensive Industries Systems, Sudan Master Technology, and Zadna International Company for Investment (SAF). On 9 October, the European Council subsequently adopted Common Foreign and Security Policy (CFSP) Decision 2023/2135 concerning restrictive measures due to activities undermining stability and political transition in Sudan, which was to serve as a framework for the sanctions announced at the beginning of 2024.

Despite calls from some civil society players and the international community, the UAE, widely singled out as a hub for the trade in illegal Sudanese gold mined and exported reportedly by all warring parties, was not concerned by sanctions and continued to support the RSF behind the scenes. On 9 July, the UAE government inaugurated a field hospital in the Chadian town of Amdjarass to help Sudanese refugees. In early November, the authorities claimed to have treated 12,367 patients, in response to accusations by the 'New York Times' that the facility was actually being used to treat wounded RSF fighters but also as a cover for delivering weapons and drones to these paramilitaries. Suspicions were aroused after more than a hundred flights linking Abu Dhabi to Amdjarass were identified between June and September. It was in fact in mid-June that the use of drones by the RSF was first spotted.

While the RSF benefited greatly from military, logistical, and financial aid from the UAE, which Abu Dhabi has denied, the SAF was reportedly also able to rely on discreet help from Egypt and on the financial networks of Islamist movements close to the former regime in Qatar and Türkiye.

After being exfiltrated from the SAF headquarters in Khartoum to Port Sudan on 26 August, al-Burhan embarked on a two-week international tour in preparation for the UNGA in New York. After an initial stop-over in Cairo on 29 August, the general visited South Sudan on 4 September, Qatar on 7 September, Eritrea on 11 September, and Türkiye on 13 September. He then flew to New York to polish his statesmanlike stature at the UNGA podium. On the sidelines of the event, he held talks with the chief prosecutor of the ICC, Karim Kahn, and the Saudi foreign minister, Faisal bin Farhan al-Saud. He was photographed with the US under-secretary of state for African affairs, Mary Catherine Phee, aka Molly Phee. More importantly, while in transit at Shannon Airport in Ireland on his way back to Port Sudan, al-Burhan was pictured with Ukrainian president Volodymyr Zelensky. The two men exchanged views on the presence in Khartoum of Russian fighters from the Wagner militia, whose proximity to the RSF had been the subject of numerous investigations. The links between the SAF and Kiev go back well before the start of the war. In particular, Ukraine had benefited from arms deliveries via Khartoum at least since March 2022. While the presence of Russian fighters alongside the RSF could not be proven by the end of the year, there was much less doubt about the presence of Ukrainian fighters.

Hemedti did not leave Sudan after the start of the war, preferring to delegate his international policy to a handful of trusted advisors, in particular Youssef Ezat al-Mahri, a close associate of the Dagalo clan, who made numerous more or less formal trips to East Africa, the Gulf states, and Europe. On 9 December, at the end of an extraordinary IGAD summit on Sudan, the member countries announced that Hemedti and al-Burhan had agreed to meet before the end of the year. However, the meeting never took place, as the SAF had dismissed IGAD's declarations out of hand and had made such a meeting conditional on the withdrawal of the RSF from all public infrastructures and civilian dwellings. It was not until 27 December that Hemedti left Sudan for the first time since the start of the war, embarking on a regional tour taking him to Ethiopia, Kenya, Djibouti, Rwanda, and South Africa.

Socioeconomic Developments

The outbreak of war had a devastating impact on Sudan's already ailing economy. The AfDB forecasted GDP growth of 2% for 2023. Ultimately, the year ended with a fall in GDP of 18.3%, according to the IMF's provisional calculation. These estimates should be treated with caution, as few data are available, particularly in areas controlled by the RSF.

In the SAF-dominated north and east of the country, the value of the Sudanese pound (SDG) collapsed. In April, the US dollar was trading at SDG 580; by the end of the year, it was almost SDG 2,000. The de facto government's revenues plummeted by around 80%. The capital, where a third of the country's economy was concentrated before the war, fell into the hands of the RSF at the start of the conflict, leaving most businesses out of action. The bulk of the country's taxes now came from the port of Port Sudan and, to a lesser extent, from the towns under the rump of the SAF in the east and north. Consequently, the budget balance was expected to continue to fall in 2024 to –2.8%, according to projections by the African Economic Outlook team. The fiscal deficit widened to 9.1% of GDP in 2023 as tax revenue declined from 5.6% of GDP in 2021 to 2.0% in 2023, according to AfDB figures. The current account deficit widened to 7.3% of GDP due to weak export performance. The coup of 2021 halted progress towards the completion point of the HIPC debt reduction initiative which could have improved the debt situation of the country.

To compensate, the de facto government in Port Sudan printed banknotes, with the result that annual inflation rose to 171.5%. It should be noted that inflation was already very high in 2022, when it reached 138.8%, and in 2021, when it climbed to 359.1%. Once again, the lack of data can distort the figures, while in areas affected by conflict, considerable price rises are reported. Commodities such as sugar and rice have risen almost 20 times. Most banks in the capital, where they are concentrated, were looted following the outbreak of the war in April. Banking applications such as Bankak came back into service in May, enabling Sudanese people to receive support, particularly from the diaspora. But these applications were often interrupted because of power cuts and localised telecommunications suspensions. From July, some foreign banks managed to relocate outside Khartoum, but access to cash remained a real challenge.

The only sector that thrived despite the fighting was gold exploration – which the de facto government bought with newly printed currency in order to stock up on arms, fuel, and other essentials. Around 7 to 8 tonnes of gold were produced each month in the north and east of the country before the outbreak of hostilities. By the end of the year, the monthly figure had risen to 10 tonnes. The number of gold miners doubled, encouraged by a reduction in state-imposed regulations. In the west, in the hands of the RSF, at least 5 tonnes of gold were exported illegally to Chad every month. This was clear proof that gold was fuelling both sides of the conflict. Most of the private sector collapsed, and the giants that remained, such as DAL Group and CTC Group, had to accommodate the military, for example by paying exorbitant fees at checkpoints or even supplying battalions.

Sudan remained the world leader in the production of gum arabic, although the sector was also cut back. Exports are generally between 100,000 and 120,000 metric tonnes; in 2023, they did not exceed 60,000 metric tonnes. In addition to the logistical difficulties caused by the conflicts, the weather was not favourable to the crop. The same applied to other crops, while farmers received barely any support from the government regarding seeds or fertilisers. As a result, famine threatened.

By the end of the year, several districts of Khartoum state and large areas of the three Kordofan states (North, West, and South) and the five Darfur states had reached the final stage before falling into a state of famine, according to the Famine Early Warning Systems Network. In all, 17.7 m Sudanese were acutely food insecure, more than a third of the country's population of some 46 m. The major markets in towns governed by the RSF, notably El Geneina (capital of Western Darfur) and Nyala (capital of Southern Darfur), or besieged by the RSF, such as El Obeid (capital of North Kordofan), virtually ground to a halt. At the same time, civil servants were regularly deprived of their salaries for several months at a time and rarely receive them in full.

The displaced populations were the most vulnerable. In total, the war threw more than 6.7 m men, women, and children onto the roads between April and December. Of these, 1.3 m took refuge in neighbouring countries, mainly Chad, South Sudan, Egypt, Ethiopia, and CAR, where they survived in extremely precarious conditions. Sudan was already hosting nearly 1 m refugees before the outbreak of hostilities in April. Many returned home, adding to the burden on the new host countries. If the fighting continues, the IOM estimates that more than 3.2 m refugees and migrants affected by the crisis in Sudan could need vital aid in Sudan's neighbouring countries throughout 2024. To make matters worse, both sides of the conflict obstructed the delivery of humanitarian aid. Only local initiatives, notably the Emergency

Response Rooms (ERRs) run by young volunteers, were able to intervene in areas controlled by the RSF.

In addition to food security, the health situation deteriorated. A cholera epidemic was declared in Gedaref state on 26 September. Three months later, the Federal Ministry of Health and the WHO recorded 224 cholera-related deaths in nine states. In the areas affected by the conflict, particularly in Khartoum, more than 70% of hospitals were out of action. Most schools did not reopen following 15 April, depriving 19 m children of an education. Tens of thousands of people died in the fighting, but there were no reliable estimates so far. In El Geneina alone, a UN group of experts estimated that between 10,000 and 15,000 local residents were killed in 2023 during an ethnic cleansing. In October, OCHA chief Martin Griffiths spoke of 'one of the worst humanitarian nightmares in recent history' since the conflict broke out in Sudan.

Lastly, 89,000 people were affected by the annual floods between July and the end of October, which claimed at least ten lives.

Tanzania

Kurt Hirschler and Rolf Hofmeier

Developments towards further liberalisation of the political space were again contradictory. Some presidential decisions early in the year raised hopes of continued liberalisations, but these were increasingly disappointed as the year progressed. President Samia Suluhu Hassan lifted the ban on political rallies that had been in place since 2016, set up a commission to review the criminal justice bodies, and initially continued an open and constructive dialogue with the political opposition. However, the authorities responded with repression to strong criticism from the opposition and parts of civil society of an agreement on port management with a state institution from Dubai. In addition, the government postponed the promised review of the constitution until after the 2025 elections, and the reform of election-related laws fell far short of expectations. At the end of the year, the two main opposition parties announced that they would abandon or review their reconciliation approach towards the government. Within the long-ruling CCM (Chama cha Mapinduzi/Party of the Revolution), attempts to heal controversies between opposing factions were noticeable. Relations with the international community and neighbouring countries remained good and unproblematic, and Hassan's renewed intensive international travel was accompanied by efforts to promote trade relations and attract investments. The economy again proved to be largely resilient to multiple internal and external shocks. Tanzania recorded a satisfactory GDP growth rate of above 5%, but due to persistent high population growth this had little effect on poverty reduction.

Domestic Politics

At a meeting with the 19 registered political parties on 3 January, Hassan announced that she would *lift the ban on political rallies* imposed by her late predecessor, John Magufuli, more than six years earlier. She stated that this move was part of her so-called 4Rs strategy: Reconciliation, Resilience, Reform, and Rebuild. The decision was widely welcomed as an important, albeit delayed, step towards rebuilding democracy in the country. The ban had been imposed as an extrajudicial presidential order, as the constitution guarantees the right to assembly. It was used selectively against opposition parties and resulted in frequent arrests of opposition members and clashes between their supporters and security forces. Particularly for opposition parties, rallies are crucial as they are the most important tools for communicating with voters. Upon the lifting of the ban, opposition parties started to conduct series of rallies throughout the country, particularly the front-runner CHADEMA (Chama cha Demokrasia na Maendeleo/Party for Democracy and Progress) and the second-strongest ACT-Wazalendo (Alliance for Change and Transparency – Patriots), which was the junior partner in the constitutionally required Government of National Unity (GNU) with the ruling CCM in Zanzibar. These rallies were attended by thousands of people and remained peaceful and without incident. The rallies also served to revitalise the parties' organisations, which had largely collapsed during the restrictive years under former president John Magufuli (2015–21). The demonstrations were characterised by a generally conciliatory tone, particularly towards President Hassan, but also by calls for more far-reaching reforms ahead of the next civic elections in 2024 and the general election in 2025, such as a repeal of several restrictive laws dating from the Magufuli era, the establishment of independent electoral commissions, and the overdue revision Tanzania's constitution.

In response to this gradual political opening since President Hassan had taken office, two prominent *CHADEMA leaders returned from exile*. CHADEMA's presidential candidate for the 2020 elections, Tundu Lissu, returned on 25 January from Belgium, where he had been living since an assassination attempt in 2017. On 1 March, the former Arusha MP Godbless Lema returned from his exile in Canada, having fled after the disputed 2020 elections upon receiving death threats. Both politicians were welcomed by thousands of celebrating supporters on their return.

On 8 March, *Hassan attended a meeting of CHADEMA's women's wing* as guest of honour to celebrate International Women's Day. She explained this unprecedented step of attending a meeting of the main political competitor with reference to her desire to build a new unified nation with political competition without violence. She described CHADEMA as an ally, acknowledging that there was also resistance from conservatives in both parties. She also renewed her commitment to reviving the constitutional revision process. Numerous CCM officials and members of the CCM Women's Association also took part in the public procession preceding the meeting.

As another step towards enhancing democracy and the rule of law, on 31 January the president inaugurated a *commission tasked with reviewing the country's criminal justice bodies*. According to Hassan, the criminal justice system was in total chaos, since ethical guidelines were not observed. She pointed out that people without power or money rarely got justice, due to the immense extent of corruption. Further to allegations of corruption, criminal justice bodies were often accused of human rights violations, abuse of power, arbitrariness, lack of transparency, inefficiency, and incidences of political interference. Hassan tasked the commission with reviewing the work of the police force, the Prevention and Combating of Corruption Bureau, the Drug Control and Enforcement Authority, the National Prosecutions Services, and the Prisons Service within six months. She pointed out that 70% of the population saw the police force as the most problematic institution in terms of access to justice. The 11-member commission was chaired by the widely respected former chief justice Mohamed Chande Othman and the retired chief secretary Ombeni Sefue and consisted of current and former senior state officials, some of whom were perceived as responsible for human rights violations committed by state institutions during their active years. No independent experts or representatives of CSOs were appointed to the commission. On 15 July, the commission presented its report to President Hassan, in which it proposed several technical and structural reforms to the criminal justice architecture. Among other things, it proposed removing the arrest authority from regional and district commissioners and other administrative leaders, with the intention of avoiding arbitrary, politically motivated arrests. Other authorities with arrest powers should collaborate with the police force and use only police detention facilities to hold suspects, in order to allow citizens to determine which institution had arrested their relatives and where they were being held. The commission also recommended reversing the trend towards the militarisation of public institutions such as the Fire and Rescue Force, the Immigration Department, the Wildlife Management Authority, and Tanzania Forest Services, which had led to complaints of harassment and torture being carried out by these institutions.

The continuing debate about long-overdue constitutional reforms highlighted the *contradictions of Hassan's reconciliation agenda*, leading to a weakening of the confidence of the opposition parties in the seriousness of the government's reform promises and ultimately to the *withdrawal of the two major opposition parties from the dialogue process*. In October 2022, a task force on political reforms set up by Hassan had recommended the resumption of the constitutional revision process, as vehemently demanded by the opposition. After Hassan publicly reaffirmed her commitment to a new constitution, the minister for justice and constitutional affairs explained on 25 March in the parliamentary budget debate that TSh 9 bn ($3.88 m) had been added for the constitutional and electoral laws review processes.

At a meeting organised by the Tanzania Centre for Democracy on 22 and 23 August, which brought together representatives from the government, political parties, CSOs, and development partners, participants agreed that the time available to *overhaul the constitution* before the 2025 elections was too short. Instead, some minimum constitutional reforms should be implemented before the elections, such as the introduction of independent electoral commissions and of independent candidates and the right to challenge the presidential election results in court. In view of the lengthy dialogue between the government and CHADEMA, as well as Hassan's statements, this result was somewhat surprising. The postponement of the constitutional reform was a disappointment and defeat, particularly for CHADEMA and its chair Freeman Mbowe, who had been a driving force behind the reconciliation approach towards the CCM despite internal scepticism. The other major opposition party, ACT-Wazalendo, on the other hand, had long favoured immediate electoral reforms before the elections and comprehensive constitutional reform after 2025. In mid-September, at a three-day meeting of political party leaders, Hassan finally *ended the debate on constitutional reform* before the upcoming elections. A lot of time would be needed to draft the bills and to provide information and education to the population, she explained.

But already in June, the surprisingly harsh *clampdown on critics of a government agreement* with a foreign investor had increased doubts about the government's commitment to moving away from the undemocratic practices common under Magufuli. On 10 June, the National Assembly approved the upscaling to the implementation stage of an *intergovernmental agreement* that had been concluded with the Emirate of Dubai in October 2022 on *port management and investment cooperation* between the Tanzania Port Authority (TPA) and the Emirati company DP World. A few weeks before this vote, alleged details of the agreement had circulated on social media along with accusations that the government was selling out the country to foreign interests. The government was accused of having already signed the contracts and granted DP World extensive rights over the port for 100 years. However, key government officials, including Hassan, transport minister Makame Mbarawa, and the director-general of the TPA, dismissed all allegations as untrue. They stated that the contract procedures complied with generally prescribed standards and that the management of port terminals by private companies was common practice worldwide. This would strongly improve productivity in the notoriously inefficient port. The government expected a reduction in processing times at the port and an increase in revenue of at least 200%. Despite these assurances, the public debate about the deal widened, with civil society activists, lawyers, and even religious leaders mobilising against the agreement. It also took on a populist and economic nationalist tone. CHADEMA quickly recognised the potential impact of the dispute and launched a campaign in July under the slogan 'Save Our Ports'. The CCM also recognised the explosive nature of the issue: from mid-July, secretary-general Daniel Chongolo and vice-chair Abdulrahman Kinana responded with their own campaign, defending the port deal at rallies. However, the government responded to the criticism not only with explanations but also with *bans on rallies and arrests*, thus resorting to the repressive methods of the Magufuli era. Several people were arrested, summoned, or threatened, at least briefly, for opposing the port deal. On 19 June, the police arrested 18 participants in a banned protest in Dar es Salaam; they were released unconditionally after a few days in custody. In mid-July, prominent lawyer and activist Rugemeleza Nshala was arrested and summoned after criticising the port deal in a social media discussion. Lawyer Boniface Mwabukusi and CHADEMA politician Mdude Nyagali were arrested some days after holding a press conference. All reported having received death threats. Mwabukusi had represented four citizens in a lawsuit against the port deal before the High Court in July. The court, however, dismissed the case in mid-August. After Mwakubusi called on the population to hold mass demonstrations in mid-August, police inspector Camilius Wambura declared that the police would find and arrest all instigators and that people who had made 'seditious and treasonous' statements would be 'dealt with' according to the law. Former parliamentarian and opposition leader Willibrod Slaa was arrested in mid-August. Slaa, Mwabukusi, and Nyagali were released on 18 August under strict reporting conditions, facing treason charges. On 11 September, police arrested Tundu Lissu along with several aides and security guards at a hotel in Arusha for allegedly holding an unlawful assembly and 'preventing police from doing their work'. They were released on bail later that evening. While national and international human rights organisations condemned the authorities' crackdown on peaceful demonstrations and expressions of opinion, information minister Nape Nnauye justified the police actions with alleged calls for the violent overthrow of the government. President Hassan accused opposition politicians of using their new freedoms not to rebuild their parties but rather to insult others.

As a result of these developments, but also in order to position themselves strategically for the upcoming elections, *both major opposition parties declared an end to the dialogue with the CCM* and that they would prepare for a competitive election campaign. For CHADEMA, Mbowe, the strongest supporter of reconciliation talks with the CCM, stated in November that these talks had stalled since June and that five issues on the original agenda had remained untouched. Lissu also accused the CCM of having no interest in real reconciliation and declared the talks dead.

In *Zanzibar*, President Hussein Mwinyi launched a *reconciliation committee* at the end of May, consisting of five members each from CCM and ACT-Wazalendo, tasked with developing proposals for a proper structure for the GNU, the introduction of an independent Zanzibar Electoral Commission (ZEC), and a legal challenge to the presidential election results. By year's end, however, *ACT expressed dissatisfaction* and even questioned its continued participation in the GNU. Senior party members complained about allegedly unfulfilled promises made to it upon its joining the GNU, in particular the reform of the ZEC and the repeal of the Zanzibar Election Act to ensure fairer elections in 2025. The party was also outraged by Mwinyi's reappointment of the former ZEC director, whom the ACT accused of being responsible for rigging the 2020 elections. ACT's demand for the establishment of a juridical commission of inquiry to investigate human rights violations during the 2020 elections was not addressed, and nor was the demand for compensation and medical care for ACT members arrested during those elections. The party complained about alleged disrespect and only limited power in government. Party leader Zitto Kabwe alleged that a 31 October by-election in Mtambwe, Pemba, won by the ACT candidate, was marred by massive irregularities and attempts at vote-rigging by the authorities. According to Kabwe, the same methods had been used in the highly controversial 2020 elections. He even accused Mwinyi of orchestrating chaos and the killing of innocent civilians. On 24 August, Mwinyi appointed seven members of the ZEC, including two members from the opposition and two women, to prepare for upcoming elections.

Following the postponement of the constitutional debate and the unexpectedly repressive reaction to critics of the port deal, the promised *review of electoral laws* was an important indicator of the government's genuine willingness over substantial democratic reforms and the implementation of Hassan's proclaimed 4Rs policy. The East African Court of Justice (26 May) and the African Court on Human and Peoples' Rights (13 June) criticised some existing laws against which representatives of opposition parties and civil society had filed lawsuits. However, three election-related bills that the government tabled in parliament on 10 November fell far short of expectations. These were the National Electoral Commission Bill 2023, the Political Parties Affairs Laws (Amendment) Bill 2023, and the Presidential, Parliamentary, and Local Government Elections Bill 2023. The disappointment of the opposition parties and other stakeholders related mainly to the fact that the bills did not provide for an independent National Electoral Commission (NEC). The bills also ignored other demands, such as the registration of independent candidates, judicial challenge to the presidential election results, and the introduction of a 50 + 1 threshold for the presidential election. Given the massive irregularities in the 2019 civic and 2020 general elections, the independence of electoral staff would have been an important measure to build trust in the democratic process. The proposed National Electoral Commission Bill provided that NEC members would no longer be appointed directly by the president but would be nominated by a 'special recruitment committee'. The committee would then forward at least nine proposals to the president, from which she would select a maximum of five NEC members. According to the draft law, the selection of the NEC chair and vice-chair would remain the sole responsibility of the president. The use of civil servants as returning officers had been widely criticised as restricting the impartiality and independence of election staff. The demand that the NEC should hire their own staff was, however, not complied with. Parliamentary debate on the bills was postponed until February 2024, pending scrutiny by a special House committee that would also involve public participation. Opposition parties, activists, and religious leaders, however, demanded the withdrawal of the bills from parliament.

Through the year, the president *replaced several senior government members and administration officials*. In January, she appointed 37 new district commissioners and transferred 48 others. One month later, she replaced several ministers, deputy ministers and permanent secretaries, three regional commissioners, and the top executives of three government institutions. While swearing in the new staff, Hassan hinted that inefficiency and conflicts within the agencies were the cause for the reshuffle. Hassan made further changes to the cabinet in early July and late August, including expanding the cabinet, creating two new ministries by splitting up existing ones. Several ministers swapped their dockets. Particularly notable was the appointment of energy minister January Makamba, a key Hassan supporter and experienced campaign strategist, to the prestigious post of foreign minister. The appointment of minerals minister Doto Biteko to the newly created position of deputy prime minister (with simultaneous transfer to run the energy ministry) may also have been a strategic move to strengthen Hassan's position. Biteko was one of the few remaining Magufuli loyalists in the cabinet. Although Hassan had successfully secured her own power base in the CCM and largely sidelined inner-party opponents, there were still Magufuli loyalists in the CCM who rejected her departure from Magufuli's policies and opposed her candidacy for the 2025 election. Biteko's promotion was viewed by some observers as a move to secure the support of members of Magufuli's former inner circle – also in view of the bad mood among the population due to the high cost of living and allegations that Hassan was selling the country to foreigners in connection with the port deal, and in recognition of Magufuli's continued popularity among the population.

The somewhat surprising appointment of the controversial former Dar es Salaam regional commissioner *Paul Makonda* to the sensitive post of ideology and publicity secretary by the CCM's National Executive Committee on 22 October also indicated that Hassan wanted to secure the support of the party wing still close to Magufuli. During his time in office, Makonda had been considered among Magufuli's closest associates and a devout follower. As a populist and a hardliner, he was known primarily for involvement in gross human rights violations, partly illegal actions, suppression of the political opposition, crackdown on freedom of expression, and open incitement against LGBTQ+ people. This had earned him the rare citation as *persona non grata* in the USA. Makonda had, however, worked closely with the current president in the 2014 Constituent Assembly and was considered to be an absolutely loyal confidant – probably another reason to bring him on board to support Hassan in the underlying trench warfare between different CCM party factions before the next elections.

On 27 November, *CCM secretary-general Daniel Chongolo unexpectedly submitted his resignation*, having been confirmed only in mid-January. His resignation was triggered by leaked WhatsApp messages containing sexual content, which, as he explained, had tarnished his image. Political commentators speculated that Chongolo had fallen victim to internal power struggles between various CCM factions. The June protests against the port deal may have made it clear to Hassan and the CCM that their re-election in 2025 was not securely assured and prompted them to *abandon the 4Rs reconciliation course*. With a view to containing political opposition, reforms were no longer pursued and within the CCM, Hassan sought to strengthen party unity while at the same time ensuring the loyalty of potential rivals.

The *Personal Data Protection Act 2022* (which came into effect on 1 May 2023) was based on international data protection standards and intended to enable participation in the global digital economy. It provided for matters relating to the protection of personal data and established guiding principles and conditions for collection and processing of personal data. The Act also established the Personal Data Protection Commission, which would be responsible, among other things, for the registration of data processors and data collectors. On 13 June, the National Assembly passed the *Media Services Act 2016 amendments*. The amendments removed some restrictive provisions of the 2016 Act, but fell short of the expectations of media stakeholders, who criticised the fact that the government's control over the media sector was not sufficiently limited and that unclear regulations allowed the arbitrary withdrawal of media licences. Other laws, such as the Cybercrimes Act 2015, the Statistics Act 2015, and the Access to Information Act 2015, also continued to *restrict press freedom*. In its 2024 *World Press Freedom Index*, based on 2023 data, RWB ranked Tanzania 97th of 180 countries (with a score of 54.8), a significant improvement compared with the previous year (rank 143rd, score 44.02). *Freedom House* characterised Tanzania as 'partly free', with a score of 36/100, as in the previous year.

After years of preparatory work, extensive consultations with various stakeholders, and multiple delays, the National Assembly passed the *Universal Health Insurance Bill* for Tanzania Mainland on 1 November, signed into law by Hassan on 6 December. The bill introduced compulsory health insurance for the entire population and merged the formal public health insurance and the Community Health Fund. The new health insurance will cover a standard benefit package; additional benefits are to be covered by private health insurance. The insurance will be financed partly by individual contributions and partly by increased government support and subsidies to enable the inclusion of approximately 26% of the population who live below the national poverty line and cannot afford contributions. Taxes on carbonated and alcoholic drinks, cosmetics, gambling, and certain electronic transactions, as well as a fee on motor vehicle insurance, will be used for this purpose.

On 5 September, in a milestone judgment, the African Court on Human and People's Rights ordered the *abrogation of all laws authorising the use of corporal punishment*. In late November, the deputy minister for constitutional and legal affairs, Pauline Gekul, was removed from her position within hours of being linked to grave allegations of violating human rights by assisting in the torture and maltreatment of one of her employees.

The *conflict between the government and Maasai communities* over the expansion of a hunting area and the associated relocation of Maasai groups from Ngorongoro District, which had escalated in 2022, continued, albeit at a lower intensity. On 15 August, security forces arrested 39 Maasai in the Ngorongoro Conservation Area after a community meeting, accusing them of attacking journalists. Police later arrested Ngorongoro MP Emmanuel Shangai on allegations that he had organised these attacks. Maasai representatives successfully sought international support for their concerns. In late January, the African Commission on Human and People's Rights visited the area and expressed concern about claims of inadequate consultation and information regarding the relocation and resettlement programmes, as well as allegations of reduction of vital social services in the areas demarcated for the envisaged hunting blocs. In late May, a delegation of Maasai representatives travelled to Europe to seek support for their cause to stop the ongoing evictions and human rights violations. European governments, EU institutions, and NGOs were directly or indirectly involved in tourism and conservation projects, including in the district of Ngorongoro. A three-member-delegation from the European Parliament was to travel to Tanzania on 4 September for an independent observation mission but was denied entry by the authorities. The government had earlier already stopped observation missions by the UN special rapporteur on the rights of indigenous peoples and UNESCO World Heritage. In a 14 December resolution, the European Parliament urged the Tanzanian government to immediately halt the forcible evictions of Maasai communities and to avoid any measures that negatively impact the lives, livelihoods, and cultures of these communities.

In a related case, on 20 July, the World Bank confirmed the registration of a request for inspection from two *residents of the Ruaha National Park* (RUNAPA), supported by the Oakland Institute, a US-based CSO. The request related to alleged government violations of the World Bank's safeguarding policies and procedures in a project funded by the World Bank to improve the management of natural resources and tourism assets in RUNAPA. According to the request, communities in five villages with an approximate population of 21,000 people were threatened with eviction. The request alleged that the affected communities had not received meaningful consultation, and that community members had been subjected to violence by rangers, including seizure of cattle.

The human and civil *rights of LGBTQ+ people were increasingly restricted*. Several such people were arrested and at least four were each sentenced to 30 years in prison. On 17 April, information minister Nape Nnauye told the National Assembly that the government had shut down over 3,360 social media accounts and websites allegedly involved in 'promoting homosexuality'. The registrar of NGOs deregistered at least three LGBTQ+ advocacy organisations for alleged failure to comply with laws regulating NGOs. On 2 April, the National Council of NGOs executive committee began investigating 29 CSOs for allegedly 'promoting homosexuality'. In February, education minister Adolf Mkenda banned several children's books from schools, claiming that they violated local cultural norms.

Foreign Relations

Tanzania once again maintained *good relations with the international community*. This was underlined by Hassan's presence at many important global and regional meetings, as well as numerous trips abroad. These foreign trips also served to promote economic cooperation and to attract investments.

Tanzania continued to avoid clear condemnation of the *Russian war in Ukraine*, citing the country's multilateral orientation. Tanzania remained absent in the vote on a UNGA resolution on 23 February which called for the immediate and unconditional withdrawal of Russian forces from Ukraine, and the country had mostly abstained from previous resolutions condemning Russian aggression. It supported UN resolutions in October and December that related to the *Israel–Hamas war*, calling for an immediate and sustained humanitarian truce and cessation of hostilities, as well as an immediate ceasefire and the unconditional release of the hostages.

Following Hassan's visit to the US in 2022, *US vice-president Kamala Harris* visited Tanzania between 29 and 31 March as part of her three-country African trip.

Harris pledged $560 m of bilateral American assistance and also promised further US economic engagement. The US remained among the most important donors to various programmes in the areas of democracy and good governance, health, biodiversity and food security, education, and women's empowerment.

Indonesia's President Joko Widodo visited Tanzania between 21 and 22 August. It was agreed to establish a Joint Permanent Commission to facilitate communication and cooperation between the two governments, as well as cooperation in the areas of health, energy, agriculture, defence, minerals, and the blue economy. In 2021, according to the Ministry of Finance, Indonesia had been Tanzania's fourth-largest trading partner, with a significant trade surplus in Indonesia's favour.

From 9 to 11 October, Hassan was on a *state visit to India* at the invitation of India's President Droupadi Murmu. In addition to meetings with her and Prime Minister Narendra Modi, the programme included participation in a business and investment forum in New Delhi. Foreign minister January Makamba held talks on a comprehensive strategic partnership based on four pillars: development cooperation, maritime security, defence cooperation, and joint investments in trade.

The long-standing relations with *China*, Tanzania's most important trading partner and foreign investor, remained stable and close. Over 100 Chinese investors took part in the China–Tanzania Investment Forum in Dar es Salaam on 25 September.

German president Frank-Walter Steinmeier met Hassan for political talks during his official visit from 30 October to 1 November. He also met German and Tanzanian business leaders as well as CSO representatives. On his second day, Steinmeier travelled to Songea (Ruvuma Region) to visit graves of the victims of the colonial Maji Maji war and to speak with descendants of the victims. Steinmeier stated that he bowed to the victims of German colonial rule and asked for forgiveness for the actions of the German state.

From 16 to 19 November, *Romanian president Klaus Iohannis* performed an official visit and signed two agreements, on economic, scientific, and technical cooperation in the agricultural and environmental sectors and on collaboration in response to disasters and international humanitarian aid.

On 16 and 17 March, Hassan, accompanied by several ministers, made her first state visit to *South Africa* to discuss security cooperation and trade opportunities between the two countries.

From 23 to 25 October, Hassan visited *Zambia* as guest of honour for celebrations of the 59th anniversary of independence. Among eight cooperation agreements that she signed with President Hakainde Hichilema were for the construction of a natural gas pipeline and for the provision of 20 ha of land for a dry port facility near Dar es Salaam, specifically for consignments destined for Zambia.

Despite a dormant border conflict between the two countries that had been dragging on for several years, relations with *Malawi* remained friendly. From 5 to 7 July, Hassan visited the neighbouring country and attended the celebrations for the 59th anniversary of independence as guest of honour. In late March, the government donated $1.0 m to Malawi and provided 1,000 tonnes of food and medical aid to support victims of a devastating cyclone.

The government also donated $1.0 m to *Türkiye* as humanitarian aid for the victims of a devastating earthquake in February. Türkiye had become an increasingly important trading partner and investor in recent years.

Relations with the *neighbouring EAC member states* remained predominantly cordial, characterised by cooperation in the economic and infrastructural fields. *Rwanda*'s President Paul Kagame was in Dar es Salaam for a working visit on 27 and 28 April, during which he discussed with Hassan, among other things, possibilities for facilitating more trade between their countries. On 25 May, Hassan and *Uganda*'s president Yoweri Museveni commissioned a jointly used hydroelectric power station on the Kagera River, the border between the two countries. In addition, the construction of the controversial East African Crude Oil Pipeline (EACOP) oil pipeline was further discussed and the project of a natural gas pipeline was agreed (see 'Socioeconomic Developments'). Similarly to previous years, the generally good relations with *Kenya* were marred only slightly by *trade disputes*. In early June, at least 200 trucks were stuck at Kenya–Tanzania border towns Namanga and Holili. The trucks, hired to export maize to Kenya, were denied exit since the Tanzanian authorities had stopped issuing export permits to Kenyan traders. In 2022, the government had issued new regulations requiring all foreign traders to register their companies in Tanzania as condition for obtaining an export licence. In mid-May, the government banned foreign traders from buying products directly from farmers, requiring them to buy only through companies registered in Tanzania. On 10 June, representatives of both governments agreed to stop the border blockade and to allow the trucks to proceed.

Resumed fighting in the *Congolese province of North Kivu* led to a new influx of about 14,500 *refugees*. At the end of the year, Tanzania was hosting about 250,000 refugees, mainly from Burundi and the DRC. Towards the end of 2023, government officials threatened to expel the remaining Burundian refugees, as their country of origin was considered peaceful.

Socioeconomic Developments

Tanzania's economy once again proved *largely resilient* to multiple internal and external shocks. Slow but steady improvements in the business and investment climate, structural reforms, constructive cooperation with the international community, and lessened political risks resulted in a renewed 'B2 Positive' rating by Moody's Investors Service in April, and a rating of 'B Positive' with stable outlook by Fitch in June. According to the World Bank, *GDP growth increased to 5.2%* from

4.6% in 2022, with the service sector accounting for about half of the growth, led by the strong performance of the financial and insurance, tourism, and transportation sub-sectors. The industrial sector also recorded growth, with particular contributions from mining, manufacturing, and construction. The important agricultural sector (accounting for around 70% of the population) saw only limited growth, as repeated floods and prolonged droughts destroyed livestock and farmland. With a strong monetary policy and temporary subsidies for fuel, fertiliser, and staple foods, the government successfully curbed *inflation* to 3.8%, well below the 5% target. Food inflation was also reduced from around 10% to 2.3%, although prices for important staple foods continued to rise at an already high level.

Despite continued respectable GDP growth rates, progress towards substantial *poverty reduction* remained limited. Although the percentage of people living below the national poverty line was marginally reduced, to 26.5%, the absolute number of people below the poverty line continued to rise, to 15 m, due to high population growth of 3%.

The government took out further substantial *loans*, especially to finance large infrastructure projects. However, according to a joint IMF–World Bank debt sustainability analysis in April, the risk of *debt distress remained moderate*. Due to a reduced trade deficit and an increased service trade surplus, the *current account deficit* was reduced from $5.3 bn (7.7% of GDP) to $2.8 bn (3.9%). However, this improvement did not have a positive impact on the central bank's *foreign exchange reserves*. Gross reserves fell from $5.2 bn (end 2022) to $4.5 bn – equivalent to four months of imports.

On 15 June, finance minister Mwigulu Nchemba submitted the *2023/24 budget* to parliament. Total *expenditure* was budgeted at TSh 44,388 bn (about $18.6 bn), an increase of only 7.0% over the previous year. The budget proposal envisaged a lower share for development expenditure (31.7%) than in previous fiscal years (36%), and increased current expenditure (68.3%). The *revenue forecast* encompassed increased domestic tax and non-tax revenue projections, decreased domestic and external non-concessional borrowing (17.0%), and slightly increased grants and concessional loans from development partners (12.3%).

At the end of March, the *controller and auditor-general* presented his report for the 2021/22 financial year. It revealed that losses of non-commercial state organisations had increased dramatically to TSh 303.8 bn. Two-thirds of this deficit was incurred by the insurance fund NHIF, which spent TSh 204 bn more than it earned. But commercial parastatals such as the Railway Corporation and the electricity supplier TANESCO were also heavily indebted. Fourteen organisations, such as Air Tanzania, made considerable losses. As in previous years, the report also revealed substantial misuse of public resources. The annual report of the *anti-corruption agency the Prevention and Combating of Corruption Bureau (PCCB)*, submitted at the same time, showed that it had filed charges for TSh 8.4 bn in evaded taxes and

TSh 2.6 bn in stolen public funds. Transparency International's 2023 *Corruption Perceptions Index* ranked Tanzania 87th of 180 countries (score 40), a slight improvement compared with the 2022 ranking (94th) and score (38).

The government further pursued the realisation of the controversial $3.5 bn EACOP from Hoima in western Uganda to Tanga. On 21 February, it issued a construction licence for what will be the world's longest heated oil pipeline (1,443 km). Human rights and environmental concerns raised by international NGOs and some political parties led to the withdrawal from the project of several international banks and insurers. According to the government, 99% of the people who would be displaced by the project had accepted and already received compensation payments. However, the NGO Global Witness reported that some people affected by the relocation had been intimidated by security forces and forced to agree; many had also allegedly been underpaid for their land. Unlike in Uganda, no public protests against the project were observed. On 10 November, the respective energy ministers signed a bilateral agreement to build a *natural gas pipeline* from gas fields in southern *Tanzania to Uganda*, where the gas will be used for power generation and industrial purposes.

After the government had, in June 2022, signed an Initial Host Government Agreement with energy companies Shell and Equinor to build a $42 bn *LNG export terminal* in Lindi Region, further negotiations were successfully concluded in May. Subsequently, a Final Host Government Agreement was to be signed but newly appointed energy minister Biteko proposed extensive changes to the negotiated agreements, as some aspects were allegedly disadvantageous for Tanzania. Renegotiations had not been concluded by the year's end. The signing of the final investment decision was targeted for 2025 and the start of production planned for 2030.

The government continued to pursue the goal of ending the chronic undersupply of *electricity* by 2025. While the commissioning of the controversial 2,115 MW *Julius Nyerere Hydropower Plant* mega-project on the Rufiji River was announced for early 2024, the government was working on the realisation of further projects. On 14 March, finance minister Nchemba signed concessional loan agreements with the AfDB and the French Development Agency (AFD) to finance the *Kakono Hydroelectricity Project* on the Kagera River in north-western Tanzania. In addition to $161.47 m from the AfDB and $120.52 m from the AFD, the project obtained a $39.44 m grant from the EU. The run-of-river project was scheduled to be operational by the end of 2028 and to add 88 MW to the power grid. At end-December, energy minister Biteko announced that the *Regional Rusumo Falls Hydroelectric Project* was 99% complete and had started production. The power plant was jointly operated by Tanzania, Rwanda, and Burundi on the Kagera River and was expected to generate 80 MW on completion (to be shared between the three countries). On 29 May, the electricity company TANESCO signed a contract with China's Sinohydro

Corporation to build Tanzania's first ever *solar power plant*. The first phase was scheduled for completion in mid-2024 with a capacity of 50 MW.

Large *solar projects* were also initiated on *Zanzibar*'s main island Unguja (currently supplied with electricity from the national power grid through a submarine cable with 100 MW capacity). At end-March, the US company Astra Energy announced having received a site from the Zanzibari government for the construction of a 'Clean and Renewable Energy Park'. The project was to comprise 42.5 MW of solar generation. In mid-May, the government signed a power purchase agreement with two companies to build Zanzibar's first utility-scale photovoltaic solar plant, with a capacity of 180 MW. This $140 m project was to be implemented by a Mauritian-based company owned by Tanzanian billionaire Rostam Aziz.

At the end of January, work began on the fourth phase of the *Standard Gauge Railway (SGR)*, on the 165 km Tabora–Isaka section. In July 2022, the government had awarded the $900 m contract to Turkish company Yapi Merkezi, which – in partnership with a Portuguese firm – had already been contracted to build three of the six other sections. According to the government, sections one and two (Dar–Morogoro–Makutupora), under the responsibility of Yapi Merkezi, were about 95% completed, and section three (Makutupora–Tabora) was 67% completed. In early August, a 13-day strike by some 2,000 mostly Turkish workers exposed the company's financial distress. The workers complained that they had not received a salary for seven months. Upon compelling the company to pay five months' salary, the workers ended the strike. To solve the financial bottleneck and raise additional funds for the $10.4 bn SGR project, finance minister Nchemba travelled to Europe in late September and obtained pledges from Spain and Sweden.

The national airline *Air Tanzania (ATCL)* continued to make negative headlines. In a dispute with Airbus over non-delivery of spare parts for defective engines, ATCL turned to the African Airlines Association in March to increase pressure on Airbus. Two aircraft had been grounded since October 2022 causing high losses. Airbus had not yet paid the contractually agreed compensation. In February, the government set aside TSh 10 bn to cover the losses. Focus areas of the bailout included addressing employee grievances, long-standing debts, and unauthorised borrowings. In its financial report, the CAG pointed to the airline's continued high loss of TSh 35.2 bn (approx. $15 m) in 2021/22. On 3 June, ATCL took delivery of its first ever cargo aircraft, a Boeing 767-300F, capable of carrying up to 54 tonnes of cargo. The plane was expected to reduce the costs of Tanzanian agricultural, fishing, and livestock exports. However, the joy over the delivery was marred by the CAG report revealing 'anomalies' in the purchase of the freighter. Apparently ATCL had submitted an invoice for $86 m to pay the final instalment (instead of $37 m actually due). Hassan dismissed the director-general of the Tanzania Government Flight Agency, to pave the way for an investigation.

In late February, the first ever *Tanzania–EU Business Forum* took place in Dar es Salaam. It assembled over 600 business leaders from the EU and representatives of the Tanzanian government and the business community. The meeting was part of the EU's Global Gateway initiative and, according to the EU, raised about €1 bn for investments in Tanzania.

After the country had been plagued by prolonged droughts, the *El Niño weather phenomenon* caused heavy rains and floods towards the end of the year, especially in the north and north west and some coastal regions. Numerous people lost their lives, livestock was killed, and agricultural land, as well as private and public infrastructure, was damaged or destroyed. A torrent of mud, rocks, and logs devastated the northern town of Katesh and a neighbouring village on 3 December. The *mudslide disaster* claimed 87 lives, injured many people, and left an estimated 5,600 people homeless. Hassan cut short her attendance at the COP28 climate change conference in Dubai to visit the area and promised that the government would build new houses for all who had lost their homes.

Uganda

Moses Khisa and Sabastiano Rwengabo

Uganda progressively recovered from the disruptive effects of the Covid-19 pandemic and the reverberations of the war in Ukraine. It also maintained its regional and international diplomatic engagements. The political outlook was generally calm and uneventful except for isolated attacks by Allied Democratic Forces (ADF) rebels in western Uganda and a deadly al-Shabaab attack on Ugandan forces in Somalia. Domestic institutions were stable and relatively functional but also dysfunctional, with huge corruption scandals in the Office of the Prime Minister and militarism continuing its creep into civilian institutions. The economy grew at an average GDP of 5.3% but major human development indicators changed only slightly, and the national debt shot past the threshold of 50% of GDP. Uganda played a prominent role in regional affairs, joined the EAC Regional Force deployed in DRC, and remained active in the AU, Non-Aligned Movement (NAM), G77+, and UN activities. The country continued as Africa's leading refugee-hosting country and contributor to troops to the AU Mission in Somalia.

Domestic Politics

Government and policy stability remained a key priority for the ruling National Resistance Movement (NRM) government under President Yoweri Museveni in the post-2020/21 general elections, post-Covid-19 pandemic, and post-Ebola epidemic landscape. The state maintained a substantial monopoly on the use, or threat of use, of force through the different armed forces – the Uganda People's Defence Forces (UPDF); the Special Forces Command (SFC); the Chieftaincy of Military Intelligence (CMI); the Uganda Police Force (UPF) and its Criminal Intelligence and Investigations Directorate and Counter-Terrorism Directorate; the Uganda Prisons Services; and paramilitary groups. Private security companies, local and foreign, remained under police oversight and provided commercialised security services especially to urban elites and the middle class, as well as private businesses.

While no armed group significantly threatened to overthrow the central government, there were acts of terrorism linked to the ADF rebel group operating in the Rwenzori Mountains and the forested eastern DRC. The ADF has evolved into an Islamic fundamentalist group, initially linked to al-Qaida and currently a Central Africa affiliate of Islamic State (ISIS/ISIL). On 16 January, an ADF bomb attack reportedly killed 17 people and injured 20 in a church at Kasindi, in the DRC province of North Kivu, a few kilometres from the border with Uganda. On 16 June, the ADF moved into Uganda and attacked Lhubiriha Secondary School, near the border town of Mpondwe, Kasese District, killing 42 people: 37 students, 4 community members, a security guard, and 6 students were abducted. It was reported that 20 of the students were hacked with machetes, and the attackers threw a grenade into the dormitory, killing 17 other students. In October, the ADF killed one person and burned a truck at the Mpondwe–Lhubiriha border with the DRC. As the UPDF carried out air raids against the ADF in the DRC, on 17 October, the same ADF cell attacked tourists in Queen Elizabeth National Park, killing two foreign tourists and a local driver and burning their vehicle. On 15 October, the BBC reported that the police had foiled an ADF plot to bomb churches in the central district of Butambala. On 31 October, several of these attackers were reportedly killed in a joint security operation around Lake Edward in Queen Elizabeth National Park, near the Kayanja Landing site, Kasese District. The forces again killed two and injured one on 12 December in Kibaale Forest National Park.

The ADF cells remained active across a large swath of western Uganda. For example, on 5 December, they attacked the village of Nkoko in the sub-county of Kitswamba, Kasese district, hacking one Betty Biira to death and seriously injuring her son, Harrison Masereka. They also abducted a man, one Aston Agaba, whom they took away. On 18 December, security forces hunting for these attackers found Agaba dead in Kibaale Forest National Park in Kamwenge district, nearly

100 kilometres away from Nkoko. On 18 December, the same ADF group reportedly killed ten people at Kitehurizi Trading Centre, Kamwenge District. On Christmas Day, the ADF attacked another village, Nyabitusi, in Kamwenge, killing a 75-year-old woman and her two grandchildren and burning their bodies. However, the ADF was the only insurgent group that engaged in acts that threatened Uganda's national security, and government responded to this threat using its armed forces and security apparatus, in cooperation with neighbouring DRC.

Overall, the UPDF and UPF possessed minimum capabilities to maintain order and security, and they suffered from notable shortcomings and lapses, such as inadequate professionalism, the slow pace of intelligence processing and action, corruption and abuse of authority, impunity, and politicisation. The military and intelligence services were especially influenced by political elites – the president; his son, who throughout the year was involved in political mobilisation under a group called MK (Muhoozi Kainerugaba) Movement; close associates of the first family; and 'Bush War historicals'. This created incentives to manipulate the security forces, leading to compromises in their ability to provide impartial and professional security to all citizens. Incidents of violent crime, such as armed robberies, also at times raised doubts about the government's control over the use of force.

In addition to criminals, police and military personnel and private security guards were involved in a number of shootings, some motivated by crime and others by rage and anger. In May, state minister for labour and MP for Oyam North Constituency Colonel (Rtd) Charles Engola was shot dead by his bodyguard, Private Wilson Sabiti, at his residence in Kyanja, a Kampala suburb. On 6 May, an unknown gunman shot dead controversial social media influencer Ibrahim Tusubira (alias Isma Olaxes) in Kyanja Central Zone, Nakawa Division, Kampala. On 12 May, police constable Ivan Wabwire shot dead a Ugandan-Indian money lender, Uttam Bhandari, on Parliamentary Avenue, Kampala, over a loan payment. There were also low-profile criminal murders, even though the police reported a 1.5% decrease in the number of registered crimes.

In addition to pursing a military response to ADF cells in both the DRC and Uganda, the military retained its presence in domestic socioeconomic and political spaces. For example, the deputy inspector-general of police remained an army general, Major General Tumusiime-Katsigazi, as did the police chief of staff, Major General Abel Kandiho. The agricultural programme Operation Wealth Creation (OWC) remained in the hands of military personnel: the chief coordinator was the president's half-brother, General Salim Saleh. The UPDF retained representation in parliament, which it had had since 1996. The Ministry of Internal Affairs was headed by generals: minister General Kahinda-Otafiire, junior minister General David Muhoozi, permanent secretary Lieutenant General Joseph Musanyufu, director of citizenship and immigration control Major General Apollo Gowa, commissioner of passport control Brigadier General Johnson Namanya-Abaho, and commissioner of immigration control Colonel Geoffrey Kambere. Brigadier General Henry Isoke headed the State House Anti-Corruption Unit, which its former head, Colonel Edith Nakalema, was appointed to head the Investors Protection Unit in State House on 5 May. In other words, militarisation continued to extend beyond the security sector, into public service institutions, duplicating or supplanting pre-existing civilian institutions and personnel.

Government–opposition relations retained a contentious character as minimum consensus remained elusive on key political issues, such as national dialogue, presidential succession, the role of the military, and respect for civil liberties. Governance indices for 2023 showed continued underperformance in key areas. Freedom House scored Uganda 35 out of 100 overall, with 10 out of 40 in political rights and 24 out of 60 in civil liberties in the 2024 Freedom in the World report (based on 2023 data), and described the country as 'not free'.

The NRM retained power through patronage and other forms of political corruption, intimidation, and politicised prosecution of opposition leaders. The civil society and media sectors faced legal and extra-legal harassment, state violence, and intimidation. For several days in September, police claimed 'disturbances to public order' to halt mobilisation activities by the leading opposition party, the National Unity Platform (NUP) of Robert Kyagulanyi, alias Bobi Wine. A police statement on 19 September offered justification for this, saying that 'While the NUP insist that their mobilisation tours were peaceful, we had credible intelligence on how they were determined to confront police and attract ugly scenes. Their unregulated processions caused significant risk to the public, motorists, pedestrians, bystanders and participants.' In October, Bobi Wine claimed he had been placed under house arrest after he returned from South Africa, but authorities claimed they were escorting him from the airport.

There were judicial moves against basic civil liberties. On 26 July, a magistrate issued an arrest warrant against opposition politicians Kizza Besigye and Samuel Lubega Mukaku, demanding that police produce them in court on 25 August. The two had been detained the previous year for allegedly inciting violence after participating in protests in Kampala. In June 2023, the same court, presided over by another magistrate, dismissed charges for want of prosecution, but the charges were reinstated in July. By the end of 2023, the charges remained and the case was unresolved.

Police used the infamous Public Order Management Act (POMA) 2013 to constrain the opposition. But on 26 March, the Constitutional Court nullified parts of Sections 5 and 10 of it. The Computer Misuse (Amendment) Act, passed in 2022, was subjected to Constitutional Court review, and in January the court ruled that Section 25 of the Act, prohibiting electronic communication that would 'disturb the peace', was unconstitutional. Provisions against the 'misuse of social media', however, remained in effect. On 27 April, police arrested 11 female opposition MPs for protesting police brutality as they tried to enter the premises of the Ministry of Internal Affairs. Throughout the year, opposition politicians and supporters faced state suppression whenever they tried to assemble. A group of young Ugandans claiming to be NUP supporters were arrested in and around Kampala in March, arraigned in a magistrate's court on 19 May, and charged with possession of IEDs. On 6 June, their charge sheet was amended to terrorism and committed to the High Court. Their case had not been heard by year's end. Terrorism is a capital offence in Uganda.

Uganda's unicameral legislature remained dominated by the ruling NRM. Of the 556 seats, 353 directly elected members represent single-member constituencies; 146 are reserved for women; 30 members represent special interest groups (youth, older people, workers, the military, and disabled people); and ex-officio members, primarily presidential ministerial appointees, hold 27 seats. The NRM had 336 out of 499 directly elected seats while also occupying the presidency. The NUP maintained its 57 seats; Forum for Democratic Change (FDC) 32; and four other opposition parties had fewer than 30 seats combined.

Parliament debated and passed more than 25 bills, including the Alcoholic Drinks Control Bill 2023. Arguably, the most controversial was the Anti-Homosexuality Act (AHA), which explicitly criminalised same-sex acts and prescribed very harsh penalties, with provisions targeting LGBTQ+ people including 'Aggravated homosexuality', which carries the death penalty. The president assented to the bill on 26 May. The law garnered international news headlines and condemnation from the USA, UK, and the UN, among others. The Constitutional Court began hearing a legal challenge to the law in mid-December. While several states and organisations criticised the law, others supported it – especially in the region, which might suggest that some countries on the continent seek to follow Uganda's example.

Several special/by-elections were held during the year. The NRM's Uthman Mubarak Mugisha won a by-election to become the chair of Hoima District in western Uganda, replacing his father, Kadiri Kirungi, who died in a motor accident on 17 March. An NRM-leaning independent candidate, Emmanuel Omoding, won the 23 February parliamentary by-election for Serere County, Eastern Region. Mary Akol of the NRM won the 16 June by-election for district chair, Bukedea District, Eastern Region. In Oyam County North, Oyam District, Northern Region, a parliamentary by-election held on 6 July was won by Eunice Otuko Apio of the opposition Uganda People's Congress (UPC).

Corruption – scandals and responses to them – remained a big problem. While Uganda has elaborate laws and institutions for combating official corruption, such as the Anti-Corruption Act 2009, the Inspectorate of Government, the Office of the Auditor General, the police's Criminal Investigations and Intelligence Department, and parliament's Public Accounts Committee, corruption was endemic mainly due to impunity, collusion, and their relationship with imperatives of regime survival.

An Inspectorate of Government report noted that 'Ugandan citizens often only access essential public services if they pay a bribe to the public servants who function as gatekeepers of these services'. The report revealed, among other disturbing findings, that: (a) 'The total cost of corruption in Uganda is estimated to be [Ugandan shillings, USh] 9.144 tn per year (about $2.4 bn) equivalent to 44% of total government revenue in 2019; (b) The highest total cost of corruption was estimated for the environmental protection sector – at about USh 2.8 tn per year; and (c) the cost of corruption in healthcare amounts to nearly USh 191 bn per year and in the education sector to about USh 278 bn per year'. The report revealed that the police and the Ministry of Finance, Planning and Economic Development were particularly affected by corruption. Procurement is a major channel for corruption.

In March, President Museveni ordered government advertising to be routed through the Uganda Broadcasting Corporation (UBC) and government-print advertising through the New Vision Printing and Publishing Company, both state owned. Private media entities opposed the shift, and the president rescinded the directive in August. Relatedly, in February, a rift developed between the managing director for the National Society Security Fund (NSSF), Richard Byarugaba, and the minister of gender, labour and youth development, Betty Amongi, over Byarugaba's alleged refusal to release funds to the minister's office to implement a new law providing for expansion of NSSF coverage and ensuring compliance. In turn, the minister reportedly declined to renew Byarugaba's contract and mobilised more than 100 workers to sign a petition to the president and herself requesting an investigation into Byarugaba's management of NSSF projects, illegalities, and award of contracts and procurement deals. On 18 August, the minister appointed Byarugaba's deputy, Patrick Ayota, as substantive NSSF managing director and refused to reappoint the former, against the NSSF board's recommendation. In September, Byarugaba petitioned court, and on 4 December, High Court judge Musa Ssekaana set 7 March 2024 as the date of the court ruling on the case.

In April, a huge corruption scandal erupted in the Office of the Prime Minister. Vice-president Jessica Alupo, prime minister Robina Nabanja, parliament speaker Anita Among, and finance minister Matia Kasaija were implicated in the diversion of house-roofing iron sheets meant for distribution among former Karimojong warriors. Others cabinet officials implicated were the minister for Karamoja affairs and her deputy, Mary Goretti Kitutu and Agnes Nandutu; Rebecca Kadaga, deputy prime minister and minister for East African community affairs; Amos Lugoloobi, deputy minister for finance and planning; and technical officials. Overall, 26 ministers faced criminal prosecution for corruption along with 30 MPs. Government spokesperson Ofwono Opondo said the scandal was 'unprecedented in the history of the NRM administration'. Kitutu, Nandutu, and Lugoloobi were arrested and temporarily imprisoned. But in June, the director of public prosecution (DPP), Jane Frances Abodo, closed 17 files related to the scandal; by end of the year, none of the political and technical leaders had been dropped from their positions or prosecuted. Transparency International's 2023 Corruption Perceptions Index (based on 2022 data) ranked Uganda 141st out of 180 countries (26 out of 100 index points).

Foreign Affairs

Uganda retained a key role in regional integration, peacekeeping missions, and peace and security measures. The *deployment of the UPDF* in DRC (in place since 2022) remained and Ugandan was part of the AU Transition Mission in Somalia (ATMIS). In September, the DRC government allowed joint operations between the UPDF and the Congolese *Forces armées de la république démocratique du Congo* (FARDC), to expand anti-ADF military operations to new areas – up to the territory of Mambasa in Ituri Province.

The UPDF was also part of the EAC Regional Force (EACRF), a multinational force deployed in eastern DRC in November 2022 to restore peace and stability. The EACRF drew from EAC partner states Burundi, Kenya, South Sudan, and Uganda. Following the near expiry (on 8 September) of the mandated period, an EAC summit on 5 September extended the duration of the mandate of the EACRF and the Status of Forces Agreement for a further three months, from 9 September to 8 December. On 21 December, the EACRF completed its withdrawal from eastern DRC amid a mixture of successes and set-backs. On 15 December, it was replaced by the SADC Mission in the DRC (SAMIDRC), comprising troops from Malawi, South Africa, and Tanzania.

Uganda also continued regional and international anti-terrorism operations through ATMIS, formerly the AU Mission to Somalia (AMISOM). Under S/RES/2687 (2023), the UNSC authorised AU member states to deploy up to 17,626 uniformed personnel to ATMIS until 30 September 2023, and 14,626 personnel from 1 October to 31 December, inclusive of 1,040 police personnel from 1 January 2024 until 30 June 2024 and to complete the Phase 3 drawdown of 4,000 ATMIS personnel by the latter date. It affirmed readiness to review these figures in light of the proposal requested in paragraph 41 to the Resolution. The Resolution also *encouraged* the traditional donors to ATMIS to continue supporting it until its planned exit by 31 December 2024, and asked the AU and Somali authorities to evaluate the process and update the UNSC in April 2024 about Phase 3 of the ATMIS drawdown.

On 25 May, fighters from al-Shabaab attacked an AMISOM forward operating base housing Ugandan forces in Bulo Marer, Lower Shabelle Region, Somalia, 130 km south west of Mogadishu, killing 54 UPDF soldiers (al-Shabaab claimed to have killed 137), including their commander, Lieutenant Colonel Edward Nyororo. While President Museveni tweeted that 'Our soldiers demonstrated remarkable resilience and reorganised themselves, resulting in the recapture of the base by Tuesday', a temporary court martial in Mogadishu on 1–2 November, chaired by Brigadier General Robert Mugabe, indicted two senior UPDF officers accused of 'cowardice' following the devastating attack. Majors Steven Oluka and Zadock Obor had commanded two military bases in south-west Somalia and had reportedly failed or refused to encourage soldiers under their command to fight courageously when al-Shabaab attacked on 26 May. Instead, they reportedly fled to Golweyn Forward Operating Base after coming under attack, leaving behind their junior commanders and men, resulting in the highest casualty numbers for the AU force, and the Ugandan contingent in particular, since deploying to Somalia in 2007.

Uganda retained its role as one of the world's largest refugee-hosting countries and the leading one in Africa. By year's end, it hosted 1,577,502 refugees and 37,660 asylum seekers, 57% (920,642) of them under 18. The majority were from South Sudan (923,658) and DRC (505,738), with the remainder from Somalia, Rwanda, Eritrea, Ethiopia, Burundi, and Sudan.

Uganda also continued to play an important role in *regional and international diplomatic engagements, negotiations, and high-level exchanges*. President Museveni attended the second Russia–Africa summit in St Petersburg in July. Uganda sent former prime minister Ruhakana Rugunda as a peace envoy to Ukraine and Russia together with AU chair President Azali Assoumani of the Comoros, Senegal's President Macky Sall, Zambia's Hakainde Hichilema, South Africa's Cyril Ramaphosa, Egyptian prime minister Mostafa Mabdouli, and Florent Ntsiba, minister of state and director of cabinet of the president of the Congo. This was a peace mission by the AU, the first of its kind by African leaders. They visited Ukraine on 16 June, to try to help end the then nearly 16-month-old Russia–Ukraine war. *Al Jazeera* reported that President Zelensky of Ukraine told the delegation 'to ask his Russian counterpart Vladimir Putin to free political prisoners from Crimea and beyond'. The team then met President Putin, Russian foreign minister Sergey Lavrov, and presidential aide Yury Ushakov, in St Peterburg, on 17 July.

By end of the year, Uganda was preparing to host the 27th Conference of Speakers and Presiding Officers of the national parliaments of the independent sovereign states of the Commonwealth (CSPOC); the 19th Summit of the Heads of States and Governments of the 120-member NAM; and the 3rd Summit of the 134-member Group of G77+China under the UN Conference on Trade and Development (UNCTAD). Uganda was set to assume leadership of these institutions in early 2024.

Military/defence and security cooperation agreements with the DRC, and under the EAC, remained operational. Uganda retained defence attaches at the EAC secretariat in Arusha and in other diplomatic missions, and participated in EAC meetings at technical, council, and summit levels. In September, Sudan's Abdel Fattah al-Burhan held talks with President Museveni in Entebbe while the leader of the

Rapid Support Forces (RSF), General Mohamed Hamdan Dagalo, met Museveni in December. These meetings were part of the preparations for the forthcoming IGAD summit in 2024 to resolve the Sudanese political crisis and devastating civil war.

On 6 February, Uganda's foreign affairs ministry informed the UN Office of the High Commissioner for Human Rights in Uganda that it would not renew its agreement beyond the three-year term ending that same month; the office closed on 5 August. Relatedly, the National Bureau for NGOs produced a report, reported in the media on 12 February, identifying 22 NGOs accused of 'promoting homosexuality' and 'forced recruitment' of schoolchildren into homosexuality. It recommended banning groups involved in 'promoting LGBTIQ activities', suggested individual activists should be publicly profiled to prevent them from civil society engagement, and pointed to foreign funders of such NGOs.

Socioeconomic Developments

In the 2022/23 fiscal year, the Ministry of Finance, Planning and Economic Development (MOFPED) revealed that Uganda's GDP growth averaged 5.3% (higher than the 4.7% of the previous year) amid recovery from the Covid-19 pandemic and despite the projected global slowdown in economic growth from 3.4% in 2022 to 2.9% in 2023. The effects of the war in Ukraine were beginning to be felt in terms of imported inflation and high fuel prices. The Half Year Macroeconomic & Fiscal Performance Report for Financial Year 2022/23, released in February, indicated that Uganda's economy remained resilient in the first half of 2022/23 amid global turbulence, with GDP growth of 7.5% during the first quarter (an improvement from 2.7% growth during the first quarter of 2021/22). General improvement in the level of economic activity, and in sentiments about economic and business conditions in the country, were evident in the high-frequency indicators of economic activity especially in the second half of the year. In March, MOFPED reported improvement in economic activity since the start of 2022/23 and in the high-frequency indicators of economic activity.

Annual headline inflation declined to 2.7% for the year ending September 2023 compared with 3.5% recorded for the year ending August 2022. The Ugandan shilling depreciated by 1.2% in September (as did all EAC partner states' currencies, as the US dollar continued to strengthen), having traded at an average mid-rate of USh 3,738.02 compared with USh 3,689.12 in August. Lending rates for foreign-currency-denominated credit declined from a weighted average of 9.18% in July to 8.57% in August.

Government operations in September resulted in a fiscal deficit of USh 231.89 bn, against a programmed deficit of USh 216.83 bn. There was a domestic revenue shortfall of USh 158.89 bn due to both tax and non-tax revenues performing below their respective targets for August, traded at a deficit of $64.41 m with EAC partner states compared with the $23.98 m in July 2023, mainly due to deficits registered with Tanzania and Kenya, which more than offset the surpluses registered with the DRC, South Sudan, Rwanda, and Burundi.

According to a 13 October update from the International Trade Administration (ITA) of the US Department of Commerce, the health sector had received 6% of the 2023/24 national budget with donor funding comprising nearly 80% of these resources. Out of Uganda's 23 sites licensed to manufacture medicines and health supplies, only 13 were involved in commercial production of pharmaceuticals. Despite opportunities such as growing demand for medical supplies and equipment and manufacturing of generic pharmaceuticals (in a country importing 80% of essential medicines and medical supplies), there are pressing challenges including dependence on foreign-sourced technology, machinery, and associated high-skilled expertise, as well as dependence on imported active pharmaceutical ingredients.

The AfDB projected that despite higher commodity prices, tighter financial conditions, and continued global supply chain disruptions, Uganda's economy would remain resilient to external shocks. The Bank of Uganda (BoU) had raised the policy rate from 6.5% in 2022 to 10%, and it retained this in 2023. But the AfDB further showed that Uganda's estimated climate finance needs were $17–$28 bn during 2020–30, with an average financing gap of $1.3–$2.2 bn a year, underscoring the need to mobilise private investment to close this gap.

On 15 June, the government announced the national budget, under the theme *'Full Monetisation of Uganda's Economy through Commercial Agriculture, Industrialisation, Expanding and Broadening Services, Digital Transformation and Market Access'*. It projected GDP growth of 6% in 2023/24 and estimated the size of the economy at USh 184.3 trillion ($49.4 bn) compared with USh 162.9 tn ($45.6 bn) the previous year. Government showed that the agriculture sector had grown by 5% (despite the dry spell in the first quarter), with food crops, livestock, and fishing performing well. Industry, driven by manufacturing and construction in the oil and gas sector, grew at 3.9%. Total private sector credit increased from USh 19.5 trillion in May 2022 to 20.5 trillion in April 2023, representing annual growth of 4.8%, while commercial bank interest rates increased from 18.8% in April 2022 to 19.3% in April 2023 due to increase in the Central Bank Rate (CBR) to 10% from October 2022.

Government provided long-term, affordable capital, totalling USh 2.77 trillion, through the Uganda Development Bank, Emyooga (Presidential Initiative on Wealth and Job Creation), the Agricultural Credit Facility (ACF) under the BoU, and the Small Business Recovery Fund. While these funds were accessible to large, medium-sized, small, and micro-enterprises, they were not enough to cover the investment needs of the private sector, forcing many private sector actors to borrow at hefty commercial bank rates of between 18 and 20% and informal money lenders' rates that were even higher. The 2023/24 budget allocated USh 1.1 trillion to the Parish Development Model (PDM) as part of Parish Revolving Fund (PRF), to be lent to agribusiness investors at community level. The high cost of borrowing complicated private sector profitability in an economy afflicted by infrastructure deficits, bureaucratic slowdowns, and corruption.

The BoU reported two treasury bill auctions and one treasury bond auction in December 2023, which raised USh 1,020.16 bn, of which USh 549.55 bn was from treasury bills and USh 470.62 bn from treasury bonds. Out of this, USh 761.73 bn was used for refinancing, USh 258.44 finance other budget items. The BoU reported that export earnings grew by 83.2% from $335.77 m in December 2022 to $615.05 m in December 2023, driven mainly by increased earnings from gold, which grew from $0.63 m in November 2022 to $258.79 m in November 2023. FDI inflows into Uganda grew from US$1.36 bn in April 2022 to US$1.5 bn for the year ending April 2023 (over 4% of Uganda's GDP). FDI was influenced by oil and gas sector investments. Pre-oil investment will average $2 bn annually until first oil is achieved in 2025.

Uganda's debt for 2023 reached unprecedented levels. According to the IMF, quoting the auditor-general's report, public debt rose to USh 96.1 trillion ($25.3 bn, 52% of GDP) as of June 2023. Of this, USh 44.6 trillion was domestic while USh 52.8 trillion was from foreign sources. This implied that interest payments on loans took a hefty portion of the national budget and domestic revenues, leaving little for public expenditure on development and service delivery. According to the BoU's December report, escalating debt servicing costs were straining tax revenue collection, with USh 32 out of every 100 collected going towards debt servicing. The BoU projected that external debt servicing would account for 35% of GDP in 2024/25. According to the IMF, before Covid-19, Uganda's public debt was 34.6% of GDP in 2018/19; this increased to 50.6% in 2021/22, and was projected to reach 53% in 2023/24, which 'surpasses the IMF's recommended threshold of 50% for low-income countries'.

The 2023/24 UNDP HDI (based on 2022 data) was 0.54, with Uganda ranked 158th out of 193 countries and territories (an improvement from 166th position in 2022). Nearly one-third of the population (28.4%) were below the global poverty line. There was 37.4% volatility in agricultural productivity, 29.9% in supply chain infrastructure, and zero food security and access policy commitments.

Uganda's human security indices during 2023 were poor. According to the Integrated Food Security Phase Classification (IPC), the first 2023 harvest together with the second 2023 planting and harvesting seasons (August 2023 – January 2024) revealed disturbing findings about food insecurity especially in 12 refugee host districts. An estimated 846,000 people (20% of the population analysed) faced high levels of *acute food insecurity*, classified in IPC Phase 3 or above (Crisis or worse). Another 58,000 people were classed in IPC Phase 4 (Emergency). The six districts classified in IPC Phase 3 or above were Adjumani, Kiryandongo, Kyegegwa, Lamwo, Obongi, and Yumbe. Food and nutritional insecurity here was especially acute because Uganda hosted more than 1.4 m refugees in 13 districts. During April–August, there was below-average food and livestock production in Karamoja (north-eastern Uganda). All nine districts of the sub-region of Karamoja were classified in IPC Phase 3 (Crisis). A significant portion of Karamoja's population (45% of 582,000 people) faced high levels of acute food insecurity. An estimated 102,000 people (8%) were classified in IPC Phase 4 (Emergency), while 480,000 people (37% of the population analysed) were classified in IPC Phase 3 (Crisis). Both Karamoja and refugee host areas face negative impacts of climate change (poor rainfall performance, waterlogging, flash floods); endemic pests and diseases; persistent land conflict between refugees and host communities; and increasing food prices, dependence on humanitarian food aid for refugees, and a weak food security governance infrastructure.

The WHO reported that as of December, Uganda had had a total of 171,888 confirmed Covid-19 cases and 3,632 confirmed deaths. The July–September WHO Country newsletter reported a 51% decline in smoking between 2014 and 2022, dedication to eliminating hepatitis B, and a week-long scoping mission to tailor Uganda's capacity to implement initiatives on epidemic preparedness and response. The October–December newsletter reported reductions in HIV infections among newborns (by 77%, from 20,000 cases in 2010 to 5,900 in 2022), evolving strategic multisectoral partnerships to transform the health system and workforce, and the country's strong immunisation and health surveillance systems. Overall, however, access to healthcare services especially in rural areas and for the urban poor remained seriously inadequate due to health sector inefficiencies, corruption, and non-prioritisation of equal access to quality healthcare.

On 1 May, specialist doctors went on strike over allowances. They were followed by medical officers special grade (associate consultants) on 10 May. There was also a demonstration by pre-medical interns on 15 May. The medical personnel, through the Uganda Medical Association (UMA), had held several meetings with officials from the Ministry of Health and Parliament, but their grievances had not been attended to. In response to these strikes, in the budget speech the government stated that it would, 'in the next few weeks, resolve the plight of medical interns and doctors designated as senior house officers, in view of their important role in supporting the healthcare system', and in the meantime it 'provided USh 22.6 bn to clear outstanding arrears for medical interns and senior house officers for the financial year ending June 2023'.

PART 6

Southern Africa

David Sebudubudu

The state of democracy remained diminished across the region, and this was affirmed by democracy indices. The quality of elections held during the review period was suspect, and human rights violations were a concern in many countries. Meanwhile, a trend of low economic growth rates was sustained across regional countries, including in the regions' largest economy, South Africa. Regional economies also grappled with climate-associated natural disasters, diseases, and food insecurity, among other challenges. The sub-regional organisations maintained their integration and cooperation agenda, with no major shift recorded.

Elections, Democracy, and Human Rights

In *Zimbabwe*, domestic politics was defined by preparations for the country's harmonised elections, which were held on 23 August, with a fractured opposition. The election outcome was deemed unacceptable by the opposition Citizens Coalition for Chance (CCC), which cited fraud. Election observers including the SADC election observer team declared that the election did not meet standards that define democratic elections – much to the chagrin of President Emmerson Mnangagwa and his government. The opposition Movement for Democratic Change – Tsvangirai (MDC-T) was rocked by instability and dramatic collapse. The ruling Zimbabwe African National Union – Patriotic Front (ZANU-PF) confronted internal divisions. The state sustained its repressive character amid reports of violence, human rights violations, and harassment of political opponents. Reports of corruption also continued as the country struggled with its economic distress.

Equally, *Eswatini* held its dubious and questionable elections on 29 September. Political parties are not allowed in the country, making its elections a sham, yet SADC as usual deployed election observers – making its commitment to democracy doubtful. The killing of a pro-democracy activist, Thulani Maseko, sparked violent protests that led to two protesters losing their lives. The country attracted wide disapproval over its human rights violations.

In *Madagascar*, the first round of presidential elections was held on 16 November. The elections were dented by opposition protests, violence, and accusations of irregularities in the lead-up to the polls. Ten opposition candidates called on voters to boycott the elections, citing an 'institutional coup' by President Andry Rajoelina. Rajoelina emerged as the winner with 59% of the votes, with voter turnout put at 46.4%, 'the lowest in the entire history of Madagascar'. The opposition condemned the results. Human rights violations were a major issue as the state displayed its repressive character to quell opposition protests.

Mozambique conducted municipal elections on 11 October amid accusations of fraud and violence being made in certain quarters. Portuguese Resistência Nacional Moçambicana (Renamo) leader Ossufo Momade objected to the outcome of the municipal elections, saying that its credibility was in doubt. In light of irregularities associated with the elections, calls for reform were made. The country's democratic space diminished, and police repression was evident as the force tried to contain protests. Human rights violations were evident during the year under review. A draft non-profit organisations law meant to curb money laundering and the financing of terrorism met disapproval as it was felt that it stood to hinder freedom of assembly and association. The insurgency in the province of Cabo Delgado continued despite efforts to contain it. As part of its effort to enhance its military capability, the country introduced compulsory military service, a decision that was disapproved of by the opposition Renamo. Meanwhile, the country declared that the $500 m secret debt with Swiss Bank UBS, associated with the $2 bn corruption scandal, had been scrapped, thus easing the country's debt obligation.

In *Botswana*, there were no major changes recorded in domestic politics. President Mokgweetsi Masisi and former president Ian Khama sustained their public ruction, which shaped domestic politics, with the Directorate of Intelligence and Security Services (DISS) at the centre of this conflict – attracting criticism. Efforts to bring their disagreement to an end were not successful. Opposition cooperation was disrupted by internal cleavages, while corruption remained a major issue despite President Masisi's posture against it. However, a major development that stands to shape the country's economy was a new ten-year sales agreement concluded between the government and De Beers, and 25 years' extension of mining licences for Debswana (a company jointly owned by the government of Botswana and De Beers).

In *Angola*, the opposition National Union for the Total Independence of Angola (União Nacional para a Independência Total de Angola, UNITA) tried to impeach President João Manuel Gonçalves Lourenço for destabilising the democratic process, without success. Hélder Pitta Gróz stepped down as attorney-general after differing with President Lourenço over matters of appointment to the position of vice attorney-general, but the president reappointed him to the position for five years after four months. President Lourenço declared his commitment to fighting corruption, yet reports of corruption persisted. For instance, eight judges proposed to the Superior Council of Judicial Magistrates that it put the presiding judge, Joel Leonardo, on suspension while a corruption probe against him was in motion. Human rights violations were sustained.

Lesotho's domestic politics remained fractured. Prime Minister Samuel Matekane's ruling coalition found itself in a precarious position despite the promise that Matekane held for the country. The opposition tried to topple his government through a motion of no confidence, but it was unsuccessful, nipped in the bud by security chiefs who came to Matekane's aid, declaring that they would not sanction a change of government. Matekane was criticised for giving preference to his business cronies.

In *Malawi*, President Lazarus Chakwera and the ruling Tonse Alliance attracted criticism, with the opposition Democratic Progressive Party (DPP) calling on Chakwera to relinquish his position in light of his failure to manage the economic crisis that was besieging the country. The country recorded a rise in grain prices and insufficient fuel and foreign exchange while the Malawi kwacha was devalued. As in the previous year, intra- and inter-party wrangling involving both the ruling party and opposition parties continued.

In *Mauritius*, democracy diminished. As the democratic space shrank, a culture of censorship intensified. Interestingly, election petitions that emerged following the 2019 general elections either were set aside by the Supreme Court or applicants decided to pull them back.

The domestic scene was not active in *Namibia*. Following the re-election of Netumbo Nandi-Ndaitwah (NNN) in 2022 as the ruling South West African People's Organization (SWAPO), the party's vice-president, President Hage Geingob, initially appeared hesitant to endorse her as the party's presidential candidate in the elections scheduled for November 2024. As NNN put in motion efforts to cement her position in the party's gatherings, the president eventually declared her his successor. Even then, there was pressure from some party members for a party congress to select a presidential candidate – suggesting that not all were embracing NNN as the party's presidential candidate. On issues affecting minorities, the Supreme Court decided that same-sex marriages between Namibian citizens and foreigners were permissible and legitimate, thus allowing their foreign spouses to enjoy the same rights as those involved in opposite-sex marriages. The decision met with disapproval in certain quarters, including among some members of parliament, in turn giving rise to a private member Marriage Amendment Bill that was approved but was yet to be validated by the president.

In *South Africa*, the political landscape was dominated by preparations for the 2024 elections. This landscape fragmented during the year under review. President Cyril Ramaphosa enacted the Electoral Amendment Act, permitting independent candidates to compete for provincial and national elections, which put into effect a 2020 decision of the Constitutional Court. While the ruling African National Congress (ANC) considered the formation of the Multi Party Charter (MPC) by various opposition parties under the tutelage of the Democratic Alliance (DA) inconsequential, the formation of the uMkhonto weSizwe (MK) Party, associated with former president Jacob Zuma, sent vibrations across the political spectrum regarding the possible damage it could cause to ANC support especially in the province of KwaZulu Natal. Meanwhile, investigations by three institutions into President Ramaphosa's 2020 *Phala Phala* game farm scandal cleared him. Following her removal as the public protector, Busisiwe Mkhwebane immediately joined the opposition Economic Freedom Fighters (EFF) as a member of parliament.

In *Zambia*, President Hakainde Hichilema's government grappled with the country's debt situation as efforts to contain it were in motion. Meanwhile, the Public Order Act, which was used to curtail public gatherings, continued to be a public issue that caused divisions as efforts to have it repealed were underway. President Hichilema carried out a cabinet reshuffle in line with his anti-corruption posture. This stance seemed to be paying dividends as the country's ranking improved on *Transparency International's Corruption Perceptions Index*. The opposition Patriotic Front (PF) was afflicted by internal divisions. Some opposition members of parliament tried to impeach the Speaker of the National Assembly, Nelly Mutti, for 'abrogating the constitution', without success. Minority rights remained a public issue.

Corruption continued to present a major challenge across regional countries despite the anti-corruption stances declared by several leaders – suggesting a deficit in accountability. This attests to the fact that good governance has eluded most regional countries. According to the 2023 Corruption Perceptions Index, which ranks 180 countries around in the world, most regional countries fared badly based on the positions they assumed in the index – suggesting a serious challenge of corruption. Out of 180 countries, Botswana was 39th, Mauritius 55th, Namibia 59th, South Africa 83rd, Lesotho 93rd, Zambia 98th, Malawi 115th, Angola 121st, Eswatini 130th, Madagascar and Mozambique joint 145th, and Zimbabwe, the region's worst performer, at 149th position. On Transparency International's scale ranging from 0 to 100 where 0 is highly corrupt and 100 very clean, Botswana, regarded as the region's least corrupt country obtained a score of 59, and Zimbabwe, the region's most corrupt, a score of 24. Transparency International's scores and rankings suggest that corruption remains a major barrier to development that diverts a lot of resources.

Democracy and governance indices presented a state of democracy that was also diminished across regional countries. The *EIU Democracy Index*, an authoritative and widely used source of reference especially for investors and governments, offers comprehensive ratings of countries globally for the state of democracy. The 2023 Democracy Index considered 167 countries, scoring them on a range of 0–10 and categorising them as full democracy, flawed democracy, hybrid regime, or authoritarian regime. Out of the 12 regional countries under consideration, the Democracy Index presented Mauritius as the only full democracy in the region with a score of 8.14; Botswana (7.73), Lesotho (6.06), Namibia (6.52), and South Africa (7.05) as flawed democracies; Malawi (5.85), Zambia (5.80), Madagascar (5.26), and Angola (4.18) as hybrid regimes; while Mozambique (3.51), Zimbabwe (3.04), and Eswatini (2.78) were deemed authoritarian regimes. This suggests that the culture of democracy is yet to be established in the region.

Socioeconomic Developments

Owing to several factors confronting Southern African economies, including the region's largest economy, South Africa, the AfDB estimated that economic growth for the region would decline to 1.6%, down from around 2.5% in 2022. Depressed economic activity in South Africa, whose economy was projected to have grown at around 0.8%, and climate-associated disasters that adversely affected several countries in part contributed to this diminished economic growth in the region. Economic growth in the SACU was put at 1.2%. The debt burden remained a challenge for several counties in the region. For instance, in Zambia it was a major preoccupation for the government. Due to sustained low growth rates, regional economies were confronted by under-development challenges.

As in the previous year, climate-associated disasters and disease outbreaks afflicted several regional economies, thus retarding economic growth. Cyclone Freddy and associated rains caused a lot of destruction in a number of countries and led to flooding and loss of lives especially in Madagascar, Malawi, and Mozambique. Madagascar was first battered by Tropical Cyclone Cheneso in January, which caused destruction and loss of lives and displaced several thousands of people. In February, Cyclone Freddy killed at least 17 people in Madagascar. Overall, it was estimated that around 299,000 people were affected while 41,000 houses were damaged by Cyclone Freddy. The cyclone affected areas that had not yet recovered from cyclones Batsirai and Emnati in 2022. The impact of Cyclone Freddy was more felt more heavily in Mozambique, where several provinces were ravaged, with around 1.1 m people affected. It was further reported that around 198 people died, at least 184,000 people were unsettled, more than 199,000 houses damaged, and around 390,000 hectares of land devastated. Associated with the cyclone was a flare-up of cholera cases, thus aggravating the wreckage it caused. Malawi was also affected by Cyclone Freddy: 1,216 people were reported to have died. Cyclone Freddy dislodged more than 659,000 people while more than 204,800 hectares of crops were destroyed. Zimbabwe received a lot of rain associated with the cyclone, with a few homes and schools damaged and at least two deaths reported. In Mauritius, one death was recorded while at least 500 people were displaced by the cyclone. Some parts of Eswatini, South Africa, and Zambia also received a lot of rain associated with the cyclone. Zambia also had to deal with the challenge of anthrax and cholera outbreaks, and Zimbabwe also experienced an outbreak of cholera. Malaria was a challenge in several countries, while food insecurity was also an issue of concern across several regional countries.

Socioeconomic barriers remained a challenge across regional economies. The 2024 Heritage Foundation *Index of Economic Freedom*, which appraised the state of economic activities in 184 countries for 1 July 2022 to 30 June 2023, concluded that the entire global economy was 'mostly unfree'. The Index classifies countries according to whether they are 'free', 'mostly free', 'moderately free', 'mostly unfree', or 'repressed'. Mauritius was rated 'mostly free', securing a global rank of 19th/184 and a score of 71.5; Botswana 'moderately free' with a score of 68.0 and world rank of 36th/184. Namibia (96th with a score of 57.5), Madagascar (97th and a score of 57.3), Eswatini (107th and a score of 55.6), South Africa (111st and a score of 55.3), Angola (118th with a score of 54.3), Malawi (129th and a score of 52.1), Lesotho (133rd and a score of 51.9), and Mozambique (141st and a score of 50.7) were judged 'mostly unfree'. Zambia (152/184) and Zimbabwe (172/184) were rated 'repressed' with scores of 48.4 and 38.2, respectively. The ratings suggest that regional countries in the main did not offer a conducive environment for economic activities.

Sub-regional Organisations

The sub-regional organisations maintained their integration and cooperation agenda. On 20 February, SACU completed its tariff offer to the AfCFTA following its approval by Botswana, thus demonstrating SACU's commitment to the AfCFTA as all its members had sanctioned the agreement that established the AfCFTA. On 5 April, a virtual second SACUM/UK EPA Trade and Development Committee meeting was held. On 1–2 June, the SACU secretariat, in cooperation with the AfCFTA secretariat and the UNDP, held 'an information-sharing workshop on the AfCFTA and a regional dialogue on emerging market opportunities for the SACU region', in Johannesburg, South Africa. The 8th SACU summit was held on 29 June in Ezulwini, Eswatini. Lesotho took over, from Eswatini, the rotational positions of SACU structures of the SACU Summit chair, Council of Ministers chair, and Commission chair – from 15 July 2023 to 14 July 2024.

The SADC also sustained its regional integration agenda. On 11 July, a virtual Extraordinary SADC Organ Troika Summit was held to consider the state of security situation in the region. The 43rd Ordinary SADC Summit of Heads of State and Government took place in Luanda, Angola, on 17 August. At the end of the summit, Angolan president João Lourenço replaced DRC president Félix Tshisekedi in the revolving position of SADC chair. In the same vein, Zambian president Hakainde Hichilema succeeded Namibian president Hage Geingob to the position of chair of the Organ on Politics, Defence and Security Cooperation.

Angola

Jon Schubert

Following last year's hotly contested election, and the rather narrow re-election of President João Lourenço, this year was by contrast politically relatively uneventful, though it saw the first ever opposition motion to dismiss a sitting president – a process still open by the end of the year. The country's foreign politics saw a more proactive role in regional peace efforts and, notably, a rapprochement with the United States. The economic situation was dire, especially after the government phased out fuel subsidies, which triggered widespread but swiftly repressed citizen protests. Generally, the human rights situation and press freedom deteriorated, while a book featuring the alleged 'confessions' of the late ex-president José Eduardo dos Santos made minor waves.

Domestic Politics

In July, following President João Lourenço's speech to parliament, opposition parties called the head of state a dictator and announced that for the first time in Angolan history, they would submit a *request to dismiss the president from his functions*.

In their address to the National Assembly, the largest opposition party, the National Union for the Total Liberation of Angola (União Nacional para a Libertação Total de Angola, UNITA), said that Lourenço's government was acting against democracy, social peace, and national independence, alleging that the president had 'subverted the democratic process in the country and consolidated an authoritarian regime that undermines peace'. Predictably, the leadership of the ruling Popular Movement for the Liberation of Angola (Movimento Popular de Libertação de Angola, MPLA) called the move 'irresponsible'. Yet despite its majority in parliament the party's politburo felt it necessary to give clear orientations to its parliamentarians, with politburo secretary for information Rui Falcão saying that it had 'instruct[ed] its parliamentary group to take all measures to ensure that the Angolan parliament is not instrumentalised in the realisation of designs based on a clearly subversive, immature and politically totally irresponsible agenda'.

Still, on 12 October, UNITA formally submitted its *impeachment request* to parliament, signed by 90 MPs. The 100-page document included 200 pieces of documentary evidence and 40 witness testimonies. UNITA's parliamentary leader, Liberty Chikaya, said that the courts now had to decide on the validity of the form, but that it was parliament's prerogative to decide on the motion. While some independent deputies voiced scepticism about the usefulness of the process, others said that it was an important impulse, as it would force Angolans to read their constitution in detail. The plenary session to discuss the motion on 14 October was held behind closed doors, and MPLA deputies voted against it, without any debate. Opposition deputies later circulated video recordings via social media that revealed a tense climate in the hall, with the opposition shouting 'shame!' and 'dictatorship!'. On 20 December, UNITA submitted the motion to the Constitutional Court, together with a complaint about the MPLA's 'illegal votation' in parliament, in view of forcing MPLA deputies to 'respect the constitution'. In its filing, UNITA identified and denounced more than 170 violations of the Public Procurement Law, as well as a 'frightening increase' in violations of budget execution rules. Chikaya said the impeachment process had been sabotaged and delayed, but that this was only the beginning. While the process remained without any actual consequences until year's end – perhaps unsurprisingly given how partisan the courts still were – it certainly showcased a more assertive opposition, a year after the contested re-election of Lourenço in August 2023.

Barring such parliamentary high drama, the year in politics did not offer many substantial surprises: in January, the *attorney-general*, Hélder Pitta Gróz, resigned from his position after he had, in a ministerial meeting in December 2023, voiced his disagreement with President Lourenço's imposition of a personnel change in the vice-attorney-general position. Reports said that President Lourenço had deemed Pitta Gróz's attitude 'unacceptable', not least because it revealed how directly the presidency was interfering in judicial affairs. Yet four months later, in April, Pitta

Gróz was reconfirmed in his position for another five-year mandate by the president, with Inocência Pinto appointed as his deputy. In other personnel changes in public administration, former Constitutional Court judge Guilhermina Prata was in January named ambassador to France. Commentators quipped that Lourenço was thus reviving Angola's diplomatic representations as the 'valley of the fallen', where disgraced and/or former MPLA comrades could find a sinecure and appropriate geriatric medical treatments unavailable in-country, regardless of any political or managerial competence required for the position.

Another controversy in the *judiciary* marked the whole year: in March, eight judges of the Supreme Court submitted a motion to the Superior Council of Judicial Magistrature (Conselho Superior da Magistratura Judicial, CSMJ) to suspend their presiding judge, Joel Leonardo, while the corruption investigation into his person recently opened by the attorney-general's office was underway. The CSMJ, conveniently also headed by Leonardo, said that it would assess the legality of the motion. Yet only hours before being confronted by his colleagues, Leonardo installed various of his family members in positions across the court's administration. In April, investigative journalist Rafael Marques said that Leonardo had also ordered the unfreezing of General Higino Carneiro's accounts while the latter was being investigated for corruption and money laundering. In May, the Order of Lawyers motioned to call on President Lourenço to 'invite' Leonardo to resign from his functions 'without prejudice to the presumption of innocence' while the investigation was ongoing, especially as Lourenço had only in March publicly expressed concern about an investigation into the president of the Audit Court, Exalgina Gambôa, who promptly resigned from her functions. In June, however, Leonardo, still in post, was made part of the president's protocollary reception committee and opened a tender for 'food procurement cards', akin to a credit card for purchases at a specific supermarket chain, for the court's judges. The newspaper 'Novo Jornal' calculated that judges would be able to spend the equivalent of $1,200 per month, on top of their already very generous salaries and in-kind subsidies.

In January, the Ministry of Territorial Administration (MAT) announced that it had concluded public consultations about the government's planned *territorial administrative reordering*. The division of the two largest provinces, Moxico and Cuando Cubango, to create two additional new provinces, as well the increase in the number of municipalities from 146 to 518, had been met with the 'broad approval of the population', according to the MAT. Various civil society organisations, however, including rural development NGO ADRA (Acção para o Desenvolvimento Rural e Ambiente) and the Angolan Industrial Association (AIA), said that they had not been consulted and were not in favour. In addition to widespread suspicions that the new division would help the MPLA to consolidate its grip on the rural vote by adding two provincial electoral circuits, salary and representation costs for municipal administrations were also predicted to treble, to 5.5 bn kwanza ($6.5 m).

In March, UNITA's youth wing, the United Revolutionary Youth of Angola (Joventude Unida Revolucionária de Angola, JURA), elected Nelito Ekuikui, UNITA's provincial secretary for Luanda, as its new president. Speaking on the occasion of Ekuikui's election, UNITA president Adalberto Costa Júnior warned of the 'atmosphere of persecution of young people' the country was experiencing, saying that JURA had to be an 'estuary of hope'.

In December, speaking at the ordinary meeting of the MPLA's central committee, President Lourenço pointed to reforms and measures to strengthen and diversify the economy, hailed the party's 'courageous' fight against corruption and impunity, and denounced the 'forces' that were funding efforts to 'overthrow' the MPLA, the one 'political party truly committed to the fight against corruption'.

Yet despite such public proclamations about intensifying the fight against it, *corruption* remained a central issue. In January, the newspaper 'Expresso' published details of offshore trusts linked to a former manager of state oil company Sonangol, Orlando José Afonso; the same month, the vice-governor of Bengo province admitted that public servants had colluded in the illegal granting of land concessions. In March, a Transparency International report revealed that the former national customs director, Silvio Franco Burity, was the beneficiary of two BVI-registered companies that owned property assets in and around London. In April, Africa Intelligence reported that since Lourenço ascended to the presidency in 2017, construction company Omatapalo had netted the equivalent of $3 bn in state contracts, 90% of which came from simplified contracts awarded by presidential decree without public tender. In June, the Amsterdam Appeals Court found Isabel dos Santos, the former president's daughter, guilty of having embezzled €52.6 m from Sonangol via her Netherlands-based Esperaza Holding, ordering the restitution of the funds and the payment of €181,000 in legal fees to Sonangol. Dos Santos, for whom an international arrest warrant had been issued by Angola, stated from her exile in Dubai that the court's decision clearly showed a 'lack of understanding of normal business operations'. In December, the UK High Court froze £580 m of Isabel dos Santos's assets, following a suit by Angolan mobile operator Unitel, a company she founded and directed during her father's time in power. Also in December, the Swiss Office of the Federal Prosecutor opened a case against Swiss-based commodity trader Trafigura for having bribed an unnamed Angolan official with €4.3 m between 2009 and 2011, which would have benefited the company by up to $143.7 m in gains from illicitly obtained supply and freight contracts.

On World Press Freedom Day in May, the Angolan Union of Journalists deplored set-backs to *press freedom*, with reporters complaining about the tightly circumscribed professional environment they were facing. In March, the government had suspended the independent YouTube news outlet Camunda News. On the Reporters Without Borders Press Freedom Index, the country dropped by 25 positions from the previous year, to 125th out of 180 countries, making it the only Portuguese-speaking African country experiencing such a drop and to be classed as 'unfree'.

The *human rights* situation remained dire: in the northern exclave province of *Cabinda*, any civic activism expressing a desire for greater autonomy was severely repressed. Activists meeting privately in March to share experiences of peaceful activism saw their meeting interrupted by the police, who detained over 40 people, seven of whom were still in detention by April. A delegation of civic activists travelled to Luanda in December to report to foreign embassies and advocacy organisations that 'Cabinda was a living hell', with poverty and widespread destitution on the rise, all fundamental rights violated, and all civic expression of discontent met with repression and arbitrary detentions. Activists described degrading detention conditions in locales improper even for animals to live in.

Rights and justice were an issue beyond Cabinda too. In March, the Justice and Peace Commission of the Catholic Bishop's Conference of Angola and São Tomé (Conferência Episcopal de Angola e São Tomé, CEAST) did not mince its words when it said, at its yearly National Peace and Reconciliation Day, that Angola needed a new constitution because, in practice, institutions were 'hostage' to the party in power: 'institutions are losing credibility at national and international level because of corruption and impunity, although the state media endeavours to show a different image of Angola', the bishops' note stated. In June, Friends of Angola, an advocacy group based in Washington, DC, wrote an open letter to the UN rapporteurs on human rights, freedom of expression, and freedom to peaceful assembly and association to express concern about a draft law on NGOs that the Angolan parliament had approved in May. The law was ostensibly designed to comply with international regulations against terrorism and money laundering, but CSOs had not been consulted; moreover, the letter stated, the current law 'fails to address these risks and instead imposes arbitrarily harsh regulatory, supervisory, and disciplinary measures that will greatly restrict the independence and autonomy of Angolan civil society organisations'.

Even rallies that were less openly oppositional were banned: in March, when citizens of Luanda sought to hold a vigil for the recently deceased popular Mozambican rapper Azagaia, they were dispersed by the police. The national director of human rights, Yanick Bernardo, later said that the authorities had not been properly notified of the planned vigil. Protests against rising fuel prices were also met with force: in May, the police in Huambo opened fire on demonstrators, killing five, and a similar protest in Cabinda was impeded from even forming when the police violently detained protest organisers. In October, 200 citizens were arrested in Saurimo, Lunda Sul, for 'creating disorder'; by November, most were still being detained without charge. In June, the police used 'excessive force' to disperse a protest by ambulant women vendors in Luanda. And in the remote eastern provinces of Moxico and Cuando Cubango, CSOs also reported that up to 300 members of the *Lunda-Chokwe Protectorate Movement*, an autonomist movement for the diamond-rich east, had been detained under degrading conditions and without formal accusation in prisons in Moxico's provincial capital, Luena.

The government also resumed *forced demolitions* of people's houses, which according to the government were built in unauthorised areas, such as around the new Luanda International Airport in Bom Jesus and in Zango, Viana, both in Luanda province. In May, 14 citizens were detained in Bengo province as they protested against housing demolitions there; upon their release three days later, they complained of physical mistreatment and the denial of medical attention.

In a slightly more positive development, the leader of the Lunda-Chokwe Protectorate Movement, José Mateus Zecamutchima, who had been arrested in 2021 after a violently repressed popular demonstration in Cafunfo, Lunda Norte, was released in March as part of a larger *amnesty* law. At a press conference following his liberation, Zecamutchima said he had been a political prisoner, as it was ludicrous to think that he had been organising a rebellion in the Lundas from his Luanda home. Rather, it had been a spontaneous protest of the population there against the misery and violence they were experiencing daily. The president of the opposition *Bloco Democrático* party, José Filomeno Vieira Lopes, interviewed at the margins of the press conference, confirmed that it was 'natural for groups to organise, and to advance political demands for administrative autonomy and financial autonomy. And the state, because it is not democratic, does not know how to engage in dialogue, it only knows how to repress.' In June, the rapper and activist Gilson da Silva Moreira, better known as 'Tanaice Neutro', was also released after two years in jail, following appeals by Amnesty International and Angolan civil society. Tanaice Neutro had been arrested in January 2022 after calling the authorities incompetent and the president a clown on social media, and sentenced to 15 months' imprisonment in October 2022. Earlier release on medical grounds in May had been denied by the minister of interior, Eugénio Laborinho.

The amnesty law was signed, in part, to address chronic *overcrowding in prisons*; when prison services celebrated their 44th anniversary in March, this was recognised by authorities and civil society as an ongoing concern. The 'inhuman' conditions in jails were aggravated, as lawyer Ezequiel Candeeiro noted, by the Angolan principle of jailing first, investigating second: on average, he said, 10 to 20 individuals were remitted to prison per day, yet while their process is supposed to be instructed within four months, in many cases a person can wait for six months for an accusation to be made, languishing in jail for a year or even two without formal accusation.

Foreign Affairs

In June, Angola hosted a quadripartite peace conference to analyse and coordinate peacebuilding efforts, especially in the conflict between DRC and *Rwanda*. The mini-summit was attended by heads of state from countries across SADC,

EAC, CEMAC, and CIRGL (International Conference on the Great Lakes Region). In August, Angola took up the rotating SADC presidency; a second, extraordinary SADC summit in Luanda in November decided on the strategic orientation of the SADC peacekeeping mission in the DRC (SAMIDRC) that would take over after the expiry of the mandate of the EAC's military mission and during the gradual withdrawal of UN peacekeeping mission MONUSCO. Angola itself would provide 450 troops.

In July, President Lourenço visited *Botswana* for a two-day state visit with a view to reinforcing bilateral cooperation – the first ever such state visit by an Angolan head of state. Both countries expressed 'concern' over the security situation in northern Mozambique. Ties with *Zambia* were also strengthened via a January agreement to develop an oil and gas pipeline and electricity transmission, and the attribution of the Lobito Corridor concession in July (see socioeconomic developments, below). Across the rest of the sub-region, no notable developments were recorded.

In June, the president of *Egypt*, General Abdel Fattah el-Sisi arrived for a 48-hour working visit to deepen bilateral collaboration in areas from defence and intelligence to healthcare, education, and energy. In August, the king of *Saudi Arabia* sent a message of cooperation and support to President Lourenço, receiving in return reassurances about support for Riyadh's bid to host the Expo 2030. The opening of direct flights from Doha in November was also a signal of Angola's desire to increase investments from *Qatar*.

Further abroad, *China* remained the country's biggest bilateral lender, signing a €231 m loan agreement with Angola in January. The Angolan treasury lauded the loan as 'very advantageous', with a repayment schedule of 20 years and below-market interest rates, which were still to be negotiated but, for the first time, were not directly backed by oil production as a collateral. Chinese foreign minister Qin Gang, in Luanda for the celebration of the 40th anniversary of bilateral relations, emphasised China's willingness to support Angola in 'opposing external interference, independently choosing its development path, and safeguarding national sovereignty, security and development interests'. And in December, concluding 12 years of arduous negotiations, Angolan foreign minister António Tete, flew to Beijing to sign a Reciprocal Investment Protection Agreement to improve legal security for investors. The bilateral trade volume reached $23.7 m, making Angola China's second-largest commercial partner in Africa.

Angola sought to counterbalance China's weight by more actively courting the *US*, and years of paid lobbying efforts paid off when, in late November, President Lourenço met with *US* president Joe Biden in Washington for a working meeting – not as solemn as an official state visit, but with concrete economic objectives for both sides: for the US, seeking to secure access to strategic minerals for e-mobility via the Lobito Corridor that links the mining regions of DRC and Zambia to the Atlantic Coast; for Angola, the ongoing need to diversify its economy. Both presidents stated that the partnership was 'more important than ever', with the US announcing investments to the tune of $950 m in the Lobito Corridor and another $250 m for solar energy development. Earlier in November, secretary of defence Lloyd Austin had visited Luanda to build up 'stronger defence relations and exploring avenues for greater military-to-military cooperation between the US and Angola'. Following his US trip, Lourenço travelled to Dubai to attend COP28.

Angola was also courted by *Russia*: in January, foreign minister Sergey Lavrov visited Luanda with a view to reinforcing ties between the two countries – this after Angola had abandoned its neutral position and, in October 2023, joined the majority of countries that had condemned Russia's war of aggression in Ukraine, a move interpreted in Russia as a shift towards the US (similarly, Lourenço's absence at the BRICS summit in August was seen as clear distancing from Russia). While President Lourenço, at the concluding press conference, reiterated Angola's encouragement for a ceasefire, Lavrov reminded Angolan audiences that 'the West could betray its allies' from one moment to the next and that the good relations between Russia and Angola were 'not subject to the vagaries of geopolitics, but based on a spirit of solidarity and mutual support'.

Beyond the superpowers, Portugal and Brazil remained among the most important economic and political partners, owing to historic ties and linguistic proximity. *Portugal* has registered a marked increase in immigration from Angola over the past five years, Portuguese migration services reported in January. In June, Portuguese prime minister António Costa visited Luanda to sign a new cooperation agreement for 2024–27 and bolster the existing credit line by half a billion euros to €2 bn. The visit also saw the signing of a memorandum between the Ports of Sines and Algarve company and the Barra do Dande development corporation. Two technical cooperation agreements signed in September were expected to help align Angola with EU debt and financing regulations and allow for further €500 m to be disbursed.

In August, Brazilian president Luiz Inácio Lula da Silva visited Luanda, with a view to restarting bilateral ties which had cooled off under his predecessor Jair Bolsonaro. Lula underscored the importance of South–South cooperation and *Brazil*'s commitment to debt cancellation for African countries, as well as continued interest in infrastructural development. He also quipped to Lourenço at the public press conference that he had 'rarely seen such well-behaved press', which the Angolan Union of Journalists interpreted as a subtle but clear criticism of a 'passive' media landscape that was 'hostage to political power'. The two countries also signed an agreement to combat leprosy, including an investment of 9 m Brazilian reais ($1.8 m).

In February, King Felipe IV and Queen Letizia of *Spain* arrived in Luanda for a two-day visit to reinforce bilateral ties and open a business forum for entrepreneurs of the two countries. This was a clear signal that the relationship was strong and important after last year's brief legal wrangles over the repatriation of former president dos Santos's body after he passed away in Barcelona in July 2022.

In March, *French* president Emmanuel Macron visited Luanda to renew economic ties beyond the dominant oil production; an agreement to rehabilitate the agricultural sector included a €200 m aid package. In May, President Lourenço visited the UK to attend the coronation of King Charles III. In October, *North Korea* closed its embassy in Luanda, likely because of international sanctions and a concomitant drop in foreign revenues.

In November, Angola introduced *visa-free travel* for visitors from 98 countries, including another 14 African countries beyond the SADC, all of the EU plus Norway and Türkiye, Russia, the US, Canada, Mexico, Brazil, Australia and New Zealand, as well as 16 smaller island countries in the Caribbean and Oceania. In the first quarter after this was introduced, 18,719 foreign travellers benefited from visa-free entry, the migration services reported – though only 3% of these travellers came purely for tourism. Finally, in December, Angola left *OPEC* after it sought to cut outputs to prop up prices; the organisation 'no longer served Angolan interests', said oil minister Diamantino Azevedo.

Socioeconomic Developments

Angola's economy remained almost completely dependent on petroleum revenues, which dropped by 23% compared with the previous year owing to lower prices and declining production. Angolan economists, however, commented that in addition to the dependency on a single commodity, it was government spending priorities that were causing the persistent crisis. The editor of economy newspaper 'Expansão', João Armando, in a July editorial, lamented the inexplicable expenses, 'from the fleets of cars we compulsively buy, the huge subsidies we increase every year for public office holders, the pharaonic salaries paid to some companies and public institutions, to the thousands of consultants we import without knowing exactly what for, to the recurrent purchase of new equipment and services with overpriced contracts, the hundreds of business or first class trips we pay for family and friends of public office holders, to the lack of rigour and transparency in many contracts, it is the desire to buy, buy, buy, always more and more expensive'. Among such expenses were the rehabilitation of protocolar installations in the Futungo de Belas palace complex in Luanda, budgeted at $60 m, as well as the water heating and cooling system of the presidential palace, for $1.3 m.

In May, the National Oil and Gas Regulatory Agency, ANPG, bought the former seat of Banco Económico (formerly known as Banco Espírito Santo Angola, BESA) to serve as its new headquarters, at a reported price of $100 m. The same month, ANGP signed an exploration agreement with TotalEnergies Angola and Sonangol for blocks 20 and 21 in the Kwanza Basin, for a forecast investment of $5 bn.

Despite such new investments, in June, the national currency, the kwanza (Kz), suffered a further, record devalorisation, when its value dropped by 37% over the previous month, to Kz 804 to $1; in the informal market, a $100 bill fetched Kz 100,000, leading to further rises in costs of living. This was because the basic foodstuffs used in the CPI, such as frozen chicken, rice, and cooking oil, continued to be largely imported from abroad. Accordingly, with 40% of the population already living in *poverty*, many more Angolans were facing destitution.

The state budget allocated 7.7% of government expenditure to the education sector and 6.7% to health, representing an increase of 25% and 45% over the previous year, respectively. An analysis of budget execution in the first semester published in October, however, revealed that initial budget revenues had been too optimistic, and that, in order to avoid a forecast deficit of Kz 7.4 bn ($8.7 m) the government had been making cuts: only 31% of the budget for social spending had been executed, while 56% of the defence and security budget had been spent. This was indicative of the government's real spending priorities but also of the state of government revenues, which still depended overwhelmingly on oil production and were conditioned by debt repayment, largely to China.

In response to budget problems, in June the government withdrew *fuel subsidies* completely, so that the price of a litre of gasoline was hiked overnight from Kz 160 to 300 ($0.20 to 0.35). A vague plan to supply the drivers of collective taxis, upon which most Angolans rely for their everyday transport, with refuelling cards worth Kz 7,000 per day, was rolled out haphazardly and too late. Protests across the country erupted, resulting in several deaths and injuries, and a week later, the president dismissed *Manuel Nunes Júnior* as minister of economic coordination, replacing him with *José de Lima Massano*, the then governor of the National Bank, with vice-governor Manuel Dias taking the helm at the bank. In October, minister of finance Vera Daves said that the government was re-evaluating the subsidy cuts and that all options were on the table. Yet at year's end, budget discussions revealed plans for further price increases for fuel and electricity.

While still in post, Nunes Júnior had announced 'concrete measures' against unemployment, albeit without specifying what these measures might be. By the end of the year, the official *unemployment* rate had risen to 31.9%, with 80% of the workforce active in the informal sector.

In June, the increasingly decapitalised Sovereign Wealth Fund (Fundo Soberano de Angola, FSDEA) reported losses of $195.6 m for the previous year, following profits of $62.9 m in 2021. The fund, initially created with a reserve of $5 bn, had been led from 2013 to 2018 by former president dos Santos' son, José Filomeno 'Zénú' dos Santos (who was after that imprisoned for corruption and money laundering) but had been further decapitalised by the expense of fighting the Covid-19 pandemic and assisting in municipal development. Its current head, former finance minister Carlos Alberto Lopes, blamed the war in Ukraine and high interest rates on capital markets for the fund's poor performance. In August, at the opening of the Municipalities and Cities Fair in Lubango, President Lourenço also said that the economic crisis was a global phenomenon, not limited to Angola, and that this was 'not the time to point fingers at anyone' but rather one in which to 'roll up the sleeves and work more'.

In November, after almost 20 years of construction and budget overruns and at an estimated total cost of $7.5 bn, Africa's 'largest white elephant', the new Luanda International Airport, was inaugurated. Although it was still unclear who would operate the airport, and where trained and certified personnel from air and border control to runway maintenance would be found, transport minister Ricardo d'Abreu was confident that within the planned concession period of 30 years, the airport would reach its full planned capacity of 15 m passengers per year, attracting transit passengers currently travelling via South Africa. Economic analysts pointed out, in increasingly exasperated tones, that Luanda's current '4 de Fevereiro' international airport saw a yearly volume of about 1.3 m passengers, while Johannesburg's O.R. Tambo Airport had seen 17.4 m passengers in 2023. Based on 3.4% annual passenger volume growth previsions for Africa by IATA, the new airport would reach its full capacity by 2093, especially as it was, at the moment, only provisionally certified. In March, national air carrier TAAG had admitted that a joint venture signed with Cabo Verdean TACV in the previous year had not 'left the paper' because both companies were facing problems and restructuring. In an in-depth interview, the retired former vice-minister of transports, Hélder Preza, said that the new airport would be a drain on revenues for decades to come and questioned the necessity of building a new airport in Mbanza Congo, Zaire province, which had been designated a World Heritage Site in 2017. That new airport, Preza said, would 'have the capacity to receive Boeing 777 aircraft. The question is: how likely is it that, in the next 20 years, that airport will receive 300 passengers from Paris, Frankfurt or wherever?' As such, airport development was an apt metonym for the government's overall economic vision for the country.

A slightly more concrete development was the signing, in July, of a 30-year concession agreement for the operation of the *Lobito Corridor* with the Lobito Atlantic Railway consortium, composed of commodity trader Trafigura, construction company Mota-Engil, and rail operator Vecturis, in the presence of the presidents of Zambia and DRC. The consortium, which had won last year's public tender, planned to invest $455 m in Angola and another $100 m in the DRC to manage and run cargo operations and the maintenance of the rail lines. Also, in the province of Benguela, Carrinho Group concluded the construction of its complex of 17 food processing plants. And in July, newspapers reported that funding for the first phase of construction of the new petroleum refinery in Cabinda, a loan of $355 m, had been secured. In October, the government also announced that a contract had been signed to resume construction of the much-delayed Lobito refinery, with China National Chemical Engineering (CNCEC), at a value of $6 bn, to be concluded within 40 months. Planning and earthworks had started between 2012 and 2016 but had to be suspended after Sonangol was unable to continue paying the constructor, then the Brazilian company Odebrecht.

While the fascination with big infrastructure continued, including yet another promise to finally start building the long-promised Lunda surface metro, most other sectors of public life were marked by *severe deficiencies*, from health, education, water, and sanitation to public transport, road maintenance, courts, public attendance services of the administration, and basic food security.

In June, doctors threatened a strike over salary arrears while the national union of teachers denounced unpaid salaries since May. A strike of *higher education* professors started in February; it was suspended temporarily in May to allow for the academic year to end well, but the union continued to deplore working conditions, low salaries, and the lack of any government response. In September, the minister of higher education affirmed that apart from salaries, 'all problems' had been resolved, and that the next strike, announced for November, would not paralyse the sector, a view not necessarily shared by university teachers. The WHO 2023 tuberculosis report named Angola as the lusophone country with the highest incident and fatality rates, 119,000 and 19,000, respectively, for the previous year. In the first trimester, Luanda hospitals registered a rise in *malaria* deaths; medical professionals pointed to widespread precarity and a lack of basic sanitation, including rubbish disposal, as main causes. Covid-19 vaccination ceased to be a requirement for entry in July.

Road fatalities were still among the world's highest: in October, the media reported an average of 50 traffic-related deaths per day. A planned measure to improve road safety, to allow the application of tinted window screens only by companies selected and licensed by the national police was, however, halted in April after the Ministry of Interior alleged some 'irregularities' in the process. Indeed, newspaper 'Novo Jornal' had revealed that several high-ranking police officers were active in the tinted window business. In September, the Luanda provincial government also banned moto-taxis from 50 main roads with a view to 'regularising' the sector; drivers complained about the lack of dialogue in the process and that the measure was effectively pushing them out into the periphery of the city.

In June, German engineering company Gauff revealed plans to produce 'green hydrogen' for export to the EU at the Laúca dam. The director of the hydroelectric plant, Moisés Jaime, expressed optimism, saying that the project would allow turbines to operate at full capacity and that this would constitute a new source of revenues; meanwhile, the Social and Political Observatory of Angola noted that only 42% of Angolans had access to *electricity*, saying the country should rather invest in distribution networks.

In June, a prominent lawyer, Benja Satula, and his wife, psychologist Solange Faria, launched a book titled 'Confessions of a Statesman', based on 'psychographic messages' transcribed from conversations between the spirit of the late president dos Santos and Faria, who, as Angolans were intrigued to discover, was also a spirit medium. In the book, dos Santos's spirit opened up about murky episodes of his leadership and the MPLA's history, stating that he felt betrayed and humiliated by the party after Lourenço's ascendancy to power. While many, especially MPLA luminaries, dismissed the book as pure fiction, others noted that Satula had been dos Santos's lawyer from 2017 to 2022, and that the 'psychographic messages' were potentially a way to circulate information that would otherwise have been protected by attorney–client privilege.

Botswana

David Sebudubudu

The tension between President Mokgweetsi Masisi and the former president, Ian Khama, intensified, with reports of possible mediation without success. Meanwhile, the Directorate of Intelligence and Security Services (DISS) continued to attract disapproval for its deceitful character. The independence of the judiciary and other critical public institutions such as the Directorate on Corruption and Economic Crime (DCEC) and the Independent Electoral Commission (IEC) remained public issues, and reports of corruption and maladministration continued. Opposition cooperation talks were in motion, yet divisions and internal wrangling were apparent. Despite Khama's efforts to disparage Masisi's regime, the country sustained positive foreign relations. Socioeconomic developments were dominated by a new ten-year sales agreement between the government and De Beers, and mining licences for Debswana (a partnership between the Botswana government and De Beers) were extended for 25 years from 2029 to 2054, following intense negotiations – a critical development considering the role of diamonds in the country's economy. However, the economy remained vulnerable to external shocks, and the country continued to be afflicted by socioeconomic challenges.

Domestic Politics

On 8 February, the 2022 Delimitation Commission responsible for defining the boundaries of the country's 61 constituencies submitted its report to President Mokgweetsi Masisi, as prescribed in the constitution. The *Botswana Patriotic Front (BPF)* sustained *internal divisions and ructions for the control of the party*, with some senior members quitting the party. On 13 January, there were suggestions that former president Ian Khama was considering standing for the presidency of the BPF. Meanwhile, on 13 January, Khama was not successful at the High Court in his effort to challenge the warrant of arrest issued against him in December 2022. On 1 February, the vice-president of the BPF, Caroline Lesang, resigned from the party, noting that it was 'being used in personal reconciliation negotiations'. It was believed in certain quarters that she was referring to the party patron, Khama, as there were emerging reports at the time of him reconciling with President Masisi in the personal feud that had been raging since 2018, immediately after Khama stepped down from the presidency at the end of his term. A number of BPF members also resigned around the same time as Lesang. In February, newspaper 'The Monitor' reported that BPF leader Biggie Butale had pledged to work closely with Khama to ensure that the party was stable. In the same month, media reports also suggested that Khama was likely to go back to the ruling Botswana Democratic Party (BDP) after President Masisi had indicated at a BDP meeting in Shoshong that he was looking forwarding to the day when he could settle his differences with Khama and even discouraged party members from fuelling their feud. Immediately, Khama declared that he had asked his brother Tshekedi Khama, the BFP secretary-general, to go back to Botswana to start the mediation process with Masisi, or a person nominated by Masisi. The *Botswana Federation of Public, Private and Parastatal Sector Unions (BOFEPUSU)* and the *Botswana Federation of Trade Unions (BTFU)* were among those that embraced suggestions of mediation between the two leaders. Contrary to these suggestions, however, no mediation talks were begun.

On 21 March, a BPF National Executive Committee (NEC) member, Guma Moyo, declared that he had left the party, although he would remain in the Umbrella for Democratic Change (UDC), following 'a very tense' meeting of the NEC at which Khama, blamed Butale and Moyo for 'having been sent to destabilise' the party. Moyo had declared his intention to contest the position of party president against Khama. On 27 March, Tshekedi Khama wrote to Butale asking him to stop engaging in party activities as party president, in light of his declaration at the BPF NEC meeting on 20 March that he was quitting the party; Butale denied having made such a declaration and continued his involvement in party activities. On 5 April, Butale announced that the party's NEC HAD approved the suspension of Tshekedi Khama, deputy secretary-general Vuyo Notha, deputy treasurer Robert Mariba, and secretary for political education Prince Bosilong. On 6 April, Notha asked the party's members of parliament and councillors to a meeting on 15 April in Phikwe, in defiance of the party leader and purported suspension, suggesting divisions within the party. On 26 April, the High Court validated that Butale was the lawful leader of the BPF. On 29–30 April, the BPF held its National Conference and Extraordinary Congress in Gaborone, at which it decided, among other things, to join the UDC and to allow the party president and the NEC to lead the party to the 2024 general elections. In May, media reports suggested that Khama was considering forming a splinter party, but he ultimately decided not to quit the BPF.

On 5 June, the BPF NEC put Butale on a 90-day suspension for, among other things, deciding on the dates for a by-election in the constituency of Serowe West and approving the names of the candidates competing in party primary elections to represent the party in the by-election. Mephato Reatile was made acting president of the party. The party also announced suspensions of Moiseraele Master Goya and Reitumetse Aphiri. Butale and Aphiri immediately contested their suspensions in court, with success: on 24 July, the High Court set aside the 5 June suspensions and found that Ian Khama, Tshekedi Khama, Lazarus Lekgoanyana, Ford Moiteela, Prince Bosilong, Motswasele Kganetso, Kolaatamo Malefho, Lawrence Ookeditse, and Amogelang Mokwena had been disrespectful of an April High Court decision. On 7 August, the High Court decided on a 30-day incarceration suspended for 12 months for all of them save for Ian Khama, who was awarded a warning.

In a separate matter, on 4 July the secretary of the BPF Disciplinary Committee, Barulaganye Letang, put Butale on suspension for 90 days while awaiting a disciplinary hearing for, among other things, allowing 'BPF members to campaign against the party and its decisions at Mmaphula East ward by-election, having failed or neglected to declare and or account for finances received ... on behalf of the party and working with the BDP to destabilize' the party. On 9 July, despite supposedly being suspended himself, Butale put Mephato Reatile, Kolaatamo Malefho, and Lawrence Ookeditse on suspension. On 10 July, publicity secretary Ookeditse announced the suspension of Butale, Moiseraele Master Goya, and Phagenyana Phage. On 13 July, the BPF expelled Biggie Butale and Moiseraele Master Goya from the party. The same day, Butale wrote to the Tshekedi Khama contesting his expulsion, noting that the Disciplinary Committee and the NEC 'does not have capacity to suspend or expel' him on the basis of the reasons advanced in his letter. On 14 July, Butale challenged the decision in court; on 2 August, High Court judge Zein Kebonang ruled against him. On 3 August, the BPF announced the member of parliament for Jwaneng Mabutsane, Mephato Reatile, as its president until the party held its congress. On the same day Butale appealed Judge Kebonang's decision, but he decided to withdraw the appeal on 23 August. He tried to delay the implementation of Kebonang's decision before High Court judge Itumeleng Segopolo, without success, as the decision was made by a judge of equal standing. On 23 August, he also made an urgent attempt on urgency before High Court judge Boipuso Makhwe to have his suspension and expulsion by the party delayed while the decision was still being reviewed by the court – without success, as the court decided the matter was not urgent because the decision had been made on 13 July. Butale made another urgent attempt before High Court judge Michael Motlhabi to obtain the delay. While this review was pending, on 17 September the BPF elected a new NEC. Mephato Reatile was elected party president, Thoko Muzila vice-president, Carter Morupisi national chair, Lawrence Ookeditse secretary-general, Neo Oagile deputy secretary-general, Lararus Lekgoanyane treasurer, and Fox Segwai deputy treasurer. Ford Moiteela was elected national organising secretary, Amogelang Mokwena information and publicity secretary, Shadrack Baaitse secretary for international affairs, Kesego Lesaso secretary for public education, Elijah Masedi secretary for public health, Patrick Mathe secretary for sport, Molatedi Bareki secretary for economic affairs, Victor Jimmy Mphee secretary for political education, Prince Moitoi secretary for labour, and Thatayaone Tauyakgale secretary of constitution and legal affairs. Owing to divisions within the BPF, on 14 November Biggie Butale and his associates formed the Botswana Republican Party (BRP), and media reports indicated that some of his supporters were expected to quit the BFP for the new party.

In July, the 'Weekend Post' newspaper reported that save for Mozambican president Filipe Nyusi and Zimbabwe president Emmerson Mnangagwa, the SADC heads of state had decided not to attend the US–Africa Business Summit in Gaborone, Botswana, and instead held a meeting with Ian Khama in Maputo, Mozambique, to discuss a report produced by Khama in June entitled 'Chronicles of Persecution 2018–2023'. The report was shared with the Commonwealth leaders, SADC leaders, the EU, and embassies based in Botswana. In it, Khama alleged 'serious disregard for human rights and the rule of law' by President Masisi. The report was anticipated to be discussed at the 43rd SADC Summit in Angola in August. As expected, the report met with disapproval from government and in turn triggered an intense media campaign, including in international media, prompted by the government to contain the damage caused to President Masisi, his government, and the country.

The *Directorate of Intelligence and Security Services (DISS)* retained its deceitful character. In February, the 'Weekend Post' reported that the DISS had claimed there was a secret plan to kill President Masisi, conceived in South Africa. As with previous reports, this was not substantiated. On 5 April, the 'Botswana Gazette' reported that DISS director-general, Peter Magosi, had been accorded a two-year contract extension. On 24 February, the newspaper 'Mmegi' reported that the DISS HAD sacked its deputy director-general of operations, Kenamile Badubi, who had been on suspension. Surprisingly, on 1 March, the 'Botswana Gazette' reported that the DISS had 'reinstated' Wilheminah 'Butterfly' Maswabi, who was in 2019 charged with possession of unexplained property, false declaration of a passport, and financing of terrorism in relation to 100 bn pula supposedly stolen from Bank of Botswana, in association with Ian Khama former DISS director-general Isaac Kgosi, and South African businesswoman Bridgette Motsepe, and put into offshore bank accounts and South African banks. In 2021, Maswabi had been cleared of all charges as the High Court decided that the case was based on 'fabricated evidence'. In 2022, the Court of Appeal affirmed that it had been proper to clear Maswabi of possession of unexplained property and false declaration of a passport but unfitting for the High Court to clear her on a charge of financing of terrorism as this had been withdrawn by the state. Subsequent to the Court of Appeal decision, the chief justice, Terence *Rannowane*, who was part of the panel that decided on the appeal, wrote to President Masisi declaring again that the case was based on 'fabricated evidence'. In March, the 'Weekend Post' reported that the DCEC had 'discreetly' obtained a warrant of arrest against Tshekedi and Anthony Khama, who were in exile in South Africa. On 4 August, the Court of Appeal invalidated a 2022 High Court decision in which it had decided that the state should return ten guns belonging to Isaac Kgosi, and sent the case back to the High Court again for trial.

On 20 July, the DISS detained 'Mmegi' editor Ryder Gabathuse and senior reporter Innocent Selatlhwa, attracting immediate condemnation from various quarters, including the Botswana Editors Forum and the Botswana Chapter of the Media Institute of Southern Africa (MISA Botswana). During the arrest, one of the DISS agents was reported to have made a remark to the effect that 'I am a warrant myself', when they were asked about an arrest warrant – which was telling about the operations of the DISS. On 27 September, the 'Botswana Gazette' reported that the DISS director of research and analysis, Botho Seboko, had resigned after falling out with the DISS director-general Peter Magosi 'over undisclosed matters'. Seboko had been revealed by Unity Dow in 2022 as the person using the pseudonym 'France Museveni' on social media, to the chagrin of Seboko, who in turn decided to sue Dow for defamation. In July, it was reported that the DISS was delaying the return of Khama's official residence, State House Number 4, to his private security despite a decision by the High Court in June requiring this.

On 2 March, the president of BOFEPUSU, Johannes Tshukudu, criticised President Masisi for disregarding 'abuse of power and state resources' by the DISS, stating that 'we should be worried as a country when our president and leader does not see all of these things or when he seemingly ignores all these facts before him. They [DISS] are supposed to be providing intelligence, the investigating powers are not with them. Now we find ourselves in situations where the DISS does everything from investigations to prosecution and even court judgements delivery', and as a result, the 'judiciary is in disarray'. Later in the year, on 16–17 September, BOFEPUSU held an elective congress in Francistown and elected Gotlamang Oitsile as president. Oitsile pledged that BOFEPUSU would play a key role in ensuring that the *Public Service Bargaining Council (PSBC)* was revived.

Reports of *corruption* and *maladministration* were sustained. On 3 February, the 'Botswana Guardian' reported that a major Chinese company, Unik Construction Engineering, which had been assigned a government Moshupa Sanitation tender under doubtful conditions in 2020, was simultaneously 'also constructing a state-of-the-art mansion' for President Masisi's mother in Moshupa, Masisi's home village. It was reported that completion of the house was anticipated to coincide with that of the Moshupa Sanitation project in April 2023. The newspaper reported that the house was 'part of kickbacks' from the company for securing government projects. The company rejected these reports. In February, the 'Botswana Gazette' reported that the DISS, the DCEC, and the Botswana Unified Revenue Service (BURS) had raided some law firms and the Gaborone City Council (GCC), seized documents, and put ten employees of the GCC in detention in relation to 'property fraud involving collusion with a cartel of Nigerians and Zimbabweans, as well as tax evasion in the city'.

Meanwhile, the legal tussle over shares in the 550 m pula (P) Water Utilities Cooperation project in Goodhope involving President Masisi's sister and nephew continued to play out in public throughout the year. The project had been won by G. & M. Building Services Property Limited, a company in which Masisi's sister Boitumelo Phadi Mmutle was a shareholder. Masisi's nephew Olebile Joseph Pilane was contesting a 40% shareholding in the company, alleging according to court records that 'his company shares were illegally transferred to Kelebogile Monnawatshipi and Tswelakhumo Ventures, each getting 20% after he refused to donate 5% of the Goodhope water supply tender contract sum to Botswana Democratic Party as instructed by Huashi Li, the managing director of Precon Construction, a company in joint venture for the project'. Media reports suggested that the BDP treasurer Star Dada was expected to give evidence in court in relation to 'the circumstances under which the Botswana Democratic Party received the P 200,000 cheque from a Chinese citizen, money alleged to be 5% of the total tender profits'. Media reports also suggested that Peter Magosi was expected to offer evidence in court in relation to the conditions under which he requested Pilane to recover a copy of the P 200,000 cheque paid to the BDP. The case attracted public attention. In November, the 'Botswana Guardian' reported that Masisi had conceded that his 'government is corrupt' and reasserted his anti-corruption posture.

The independence of the DCEC remained a political issue. On 24 May, President Masisi decided to terminate the contract of the director-general of the DCEC, Tymon Katlholo, three months before it officially lapsed on 31 August. Katlholo had been on suspension since 2 June 2022, 'a day after he appeared before Parliamentary Public Accounts Committee'. Tshepo Pilane was immediately made acting director-general of the DCEC. On 20 July, Pilane was replaced by Festus Matshameko. Pilane's replacement was made a day following his appearance at the Public Accounts Committee, suggesting lack of independence, and interference in the work of the anti-corruption agency. On 8 September, Botlhale Makgekgenene was appointed director-general of the DCEC. Makgekgenene had previously worked as a DCEC deputy director-general.

Issues concerning the independence of the *judiciary* were sustained. On 14 February, Maun High Court judge Bugalo Maripe decided against Chief Justice Rannowane's decision to relocate a case that involved another High Court judge, Gabriel Komboni, and Rannowane from Maun to Gaborone to be presided over by a panel of judges chosen by Rannowane. The case involved the transfer of High Court judge Komboni from Gaborone to Francistown by Rannowane. In December, the Court of Appeal affirmed that there was 'no valid appeal', dismissed Rannowane's urgent appeal against Maripe's judgment, and called for the execution of his judgment to be stayed, registered on 6 April. Interestingly, on 18 December, High Court judge Gabriel Komboni registered his resignation.

In March, the 'Weekend Post' reported that Rannowane and High Court judge, Gaolapelwe Ketlogetswe were attempting 'to reconcile' regarding a complaint by Ketlogetswe in August 2022 to President Masisi in which he accused Rannowane and the minister for state president Kabo Morwaeng of 'interference' in a case involving the former minister of finance and member of parliament for Lobatse constituency Thapelo Matsheka's contentious detention in relation to the alleged ritual murder of Tlotso Karema. The case reinforced concerns over judicial independence, which has become a public issue. On 16 April, the 'Sunday Standard' newspaper reported that in the words of the 2022 US State Department's 'Country Report on Human Rights Practices' for Botswana, the country's judiciary 'has lately faced questions over its independence from the executive'.

On 7 March, the Court of Appeal affirmed a 2022 High Court decision that the Forest Hill 9KO farm was owned by Bamalete Tribal Territory. The case had attracted controversy in 2022 after Kgosi (Chief) Mosadi Seboko of the Balete tribe announced that President Masisi had informed 'her that he has the power to meddle with the judiciary', a suggestion that was rejected by the Office of the President. Interestingly, on 14 March, 'Mmegi' reported that parliament had decided to replace Kgosi Seboko from the Pan-African Parliament (PAP) with a specially elected member of parliament and former minister, Unity Dow, a decision that Dow immediately condemned and declined to accept. It immediately emerged that Kgosi Seboko had not resigned from the PAP. During the vote to substitute Kgosi Seboko, Dow was not the only BDP member of parliament to go against the party caucus decision. In its attempt to clarify this, on 15 March, the BDP stated that Kgosi Seboko had 'ceased' to be a member of the PAP in line with the 2022 parliament decision that 'sought to dissolve the then existing parliamentary committees and to reconstitute them into committees that will reflect the composition of parties in parliament and therefore, the wishes of the voters in the past elections'. Following Dow's decision to decline to be voted into the PAP committee, the BDP caucus decided on replacing Kgosi Seboko with specially elected member of parliament and assistant minister of trade and investment, Beauty Manake, while Mephato Reatile, who had defected to the BPF in 2020, was replaced with another BDP member of parliament, Christian Greef. Subsequently, the BDP parliamentary whip, Liakat Kablay, registered a complaint regarding Dow's conduct, and she was accorded 14 days by the party's Disciplinary Committee to offer her defence. On 16 May, Dow addressed a press conference at which she criticised the BDP and its government for being intolerant and failing to ensure that the DISS operated under the law, noting that there was 'trust deficit' and that 'our democracy and economy are under threat'. She announced her resignation from the BDP. Later in the year, on 2–3 September, the BDP held its 59th National Council and Extraordinary National Congress in Palapye. On 7 November, Dow joined the Botswana Congress Party (BCP).

On 20 February, the Botswana National Front (BNF) secretary for health and social welfare, Andrew Motsamai, resigned from the party's NEC. On 19 April, it was reported that the BNF had removed Moeti Mohwasa, a close ally of the BNF and UDC leader Duma Boko, from the UDC NEC. It was further reported that Boko, secretary-general Ketlhalefile Motshegwa, party chair Patrick Molutsi, and its Women's League president Bonang Nkoane would represent the BNF at the UDC NEC. Media reports suggested that the BNF leader had called for a meeting of the BNF executive committee in relation to the ousting of Moeti Mohwasa from the UDC NEC. However, on 21 April the BNF restored Mohwasa to the UDC NEC, with some suggesting it was at the insistence of Boko – suggesting divisions within the party. On 15 June, the BNF announced the resignation of its secretary for information and publicity Justin Hunyepa. Still in June, the BNF Youth League president resigned. On 16–18 July, the BNF held its annual conference under the heading 'Nurturing a political vanguard for socioeconomic transformation and prosperity for all' in Shoshong. On 13 October, BNF Women's League president Bonang Nkoane left the party, citing the need to focus on her personal life and professional career, among other factors. On 9 November, media reports suggested that she had joined the ruling BDP.

On 17 April, the Alliance for Progressives (AP) withdrew from *AP–BCP–BLP cooperation talks*, in line with a decision of the party's executive committee of 15 April, citing 'issues of concern'. The decision followed media reports that suggested parallel talks had taken place between the AP and the UDC and that the AP leader Ndaba Gaolathe and UDC leader Duma Boko had held a meeting in South Africa to discuss ways they could cooperate in the 2024 elections. It was further reported that 'majority of AP leaders prefer to work with UDC for 2024 elections'.

The BCP held its conference in Tutume on 15–17 July, and decided to compete in the 2024 general elections not under the UDC. On 3 August, the BCP decided to withdraw from court a case in which it was contesting the suspension of its leader Dumelang Saleshando and its secretary-general Goretetse Kekgonegile from the

UDC, following its decision to participate in the 2024 general elections outside the UDC. The BCP held its party primary elections on 7 October. Meanwhile, the Botswana Movement for Democracy (BMD) elected Thuso Tiego as party president on 9 September.

There were a few by-elections held. On 25 March, two council by-elections were held in Bosele ward, Gaborone Bonnington North, and Grootlaagte, Ghanzi North; they were won by UDC and BDP candidates, respectively. On 29 April, the UDC won another council by-election in Mapoka/Nlapkhwane ward, Tati West constituency. On 24 June, it won a further by-election in Mmaphula East ward, Palapye constituency. On 21 April, it was declared that Tshekedi Khama had ceased to be the BPF member of parliament for Serowe West constituency in line with Section 68 (1) (b) of the constitution and Standing Order 16.2 of the National Assembly, which render a parliamentary seat vacant if a member fails to attend two successive meetings of parliament. On 8 July, the Serowe West constituency by-election was held and the seat retained by the BPF. On 9 December, the BCP won a council by-election in Lepokole/Borotsi ward, Bobonong constituency.

On 20 July, President Masisi set in motion the national *Mindset Change Campaign*, which seeks to rally citizens around the country's vision and propel its development and transformative agenda, founded on 'pillars of high-performance culture', as it strives to become a high-income country by 2036. The campaign was received with mixed reactions.

Issues concerning *minorities* continued to attract controversy. On 22 July, the Evangelical Fellowship Botswana (EFB) and churches staged a walk in protest against the Penal Code Amendment Bill No. 29 of 2022, which sought to give legal validity to homosexuality, urging members of parliament not to approve the Bill. The Bill was in line with the 2019 High Court decision that legalised homosexuality, affirmed by the Court of Appeal in 2021. Meanwhile, it was reported that *the Lesbians, Gays and Bisexuals of Botswana (LEGABIBO)* had reminded President Masisi of the pledges he made when they were at his office in January 2022. On 1 August, the government decided to defer the Bill 'to allow for a rigorous examination of the constitutional issues raised'. The decision to defer the Bill met with approval from LEGABIBO, which was against it being discussed in parliament and urged the government to 'uphold the Court of Appeal decision and pass the Bill'. Some reports suggested that the decision to defer the Bill was a result of pressure from religious groups.

On 4 October, the UDC communicated with the IEC that it was uneasy over a number of processes, methods, and practices that it felt had 'the effect of undermining the core functions and constitutional obligations of the Commission' in relation to the 2024 general elections. On 27 October, the IEC responded to the UDC without acceding to its demands but assured the UDC that it was operating within its mandate as defined by the law. On 31 October, the UDC secured a temporary court order that allowed it to observe and monitor the national registration exercise scheduled from 1 to 30 November, while awaiting a final decision on the application on or before 7 November. Subsequently, on 31 October, the IEC decided to change the registration exercise dates to 13 November–8 December. On 10 November, the High Court affirmed the 31 October decision. This allowed the UDC to observe and monitor the national election registration exercise. Subsequent to this court decision, the IEC immediately decided to defer the national election registration exercise indefinitely. Interestingly, on the same day, Chief Justice Rannowane notified the UDC that he had decided to enlist three judges, namely Gaolapelwe Ketlogetswe, Bengbame Sechele, and Taboka Slave, for the main application in the case between the UDC and the IEC, citing considerable public interest in the case. At the time that Rannowane made this decision, the case was before Judge Ketlogetswe. On 14 November, the UDC successfully secured a temporary order that restricted and proscribed Rannowane from enlisting the three judges, thus deferring the main application until a decision has been made on the empanelment of judges. Subsequent to this, the IEC wrote to Ketlogetswe requesting him to recuse himself from the empanelment case, citing conflict of interest. Ketlogetswe did not accede to the IEC request, and in turn the IEC made an application to court calling for his recusal. On 6 December, Judge Tebogo Tau decided to allow the IEC to appeal Ketlogetswe's order of 10 November on an urgent basis, thus staying Ketlogetswe's decision while the appeal was being heard. Judge Tau stated that allowing the UDC to record voters' names and identity numbers seemed 'intrusive'. On 19 December, the Court of Appeal reversed Ketlogetswe's decision of 10 November.

On 3 November, Ignatius Moswaane, the UDC member of parliament for Francistown West, and 20 others were put in detention for taking part in a demonstration without a permit. The demonstration was in opposition to 'Zimbabweans who they allege are taking away their economic chances'. They were released on bail on 5 November. On 6 November, Baratiwa Mathoothe, the BPF member of parliament for Serowe North constituency, was put in custody, allegedly for sharing the State of the Nation (SONA) speech 'before being released or before it was read by President Mokgweetsi Masisi'; he was set free the following day.

On 28 December, the 'Sunday Standard' reported on a planned 'secret meeting' in Angola to reconcile Ian Khama and President Masisi, to be moderated by former Nigerian president Olusegun Obasanjo and the president of Angola, João Manuel Gonçalves Lourenço. On 29 December, government instead announced that President Masisi had travelled to Angola to meet Lourenço, who also served as chair of the SADC. It was reported that President Masisi's visit was meant among other things to inform President Lourenço on the Botswana government's stance on Ian Khama's 'self-imposed exile' and that of some of his family members. It was also reported that 'President Lorenzo informed President Masisi that he had been approached by former Presidents of Nigeria and South Africa on behalf of Former President Lt. Gen Khama, to help pave the way to address issues around the self-imposed exile of Former President Khama and to help resolve his differences with President Masisi', suggesting that no meeting took place between Khama and Masisi in Angola on 28 December.

Foreign Affairs

The country sustained its *foreign relations*, marked by several international trips and a handful of in-bound visits. The vice-president of the European Commission, Josep Borrell Fontelles, visited on 27–28 January; the president of the Swiss Confederation Alain Berset on 6–8 February; Flanders Region minister for finance, budget, housing and immovable heritage Matthias Diependaele on 26–28 March; and Angola's President Lourenço on 20–22 July.

President Masisi took part in the second Dakar Summit on Agriculture and Agribusiness, Dakar, Senegal, on 25–27 January; visited Namibia on 8 January; travelled to Dallas, Texas, on 25 February–6 March; attended the 36th AU Ordinary Session, 18–19 February; took part in the 2023 United Nations Water Conference in New York on 22–24 March; travelled to Switzerland on 29 April–3 May; attended the coronation of King Charles III in the UK on 6 May; attended the inauguration of Nigerian president Bola Ahmed Adekunle Tinubu on 29 May; travelled to the DRC on 9–12 May; visited Namibia on 26 June; attended the closing session of the Disarmament, Demobilisation and Reintegration (DDR) process in Mozambique on 23 June; took part in the virtual Extraordinary SADC Organ Troika meeting on 11 July; attended the 60th birthday celebration of King Letsie II on 17 July in Maseru, Lesotho; attended the 43rd SADC Ordinary Summit in Luanda, Angola, on 17 August; travelled to Bahamas on 12–15 September; took part in the Group of 77 and China meeting in Havana, Cuba, on 15–16 September; attended the 78th session of the UNGA in New York on 19–23 September; joined the Bits and Pretzels conference in Munich, Germany, on 24–26 September; attended the Annual Africa Down Under (ADU) conference in Perth, Australia, on 6–8 September; joined the World Children's Day Sub-Regional Celebrations in Walvis Bay, Namibia, on 19 November; took part in the United Nations COP28 in Dubai, UAE, on 1–2 December; travelled to the USA on 11–18 December; and visited Angola on 28 December and Pemba, Mozambique, on 30 December.

Vice-president Slumber Tsogwane attended the second session of the UN Habitat Assembly on 5–9 June and the inauguration of Zimbabwean president Emmerson Mnangagwa on 3 September. The minister of foreign affairs Lemogang Kwape took part in the meeting of the Non-Aligned Movement contact group in response to

Covid-19 on post-pandemic global recovery in Baku, Azerbaijan, on 2 March; the 22nd Commonwealth Foreign Affairs Ministers Meeting (CFAMM) in London, UK, on 15 March; the SADC Ministerial Committee of the Organ (MCO) on Politics, Defence and Security meeting in Windhoek, Namibia, on 20–21 July; and the 4th Singapore–Sub-Saharan Africa High-Level Ministerial Exchange visit in Singapore on 29–31 August. Kwape also travelled to Seoul, South Korea, on 15–20 October and attended the 173rd General Assembly of the International Exhibitions Bureau in Paris, France, on 28 November. The acting minister of foreign affairs and minister of defence and security Kagiso Mmusi undertook a fact-finding visit to Malawi on 19 March following destruction brought about by Cyclone Freddy. On 29 July, Botswana decried the coup in Niger, and on 9 October, it denounced Israel–Palestine hostilities.

Socioeconomic Developments

A major socioeconomic development for the year was that in September the government and De Beers entered into a new sales agreement for another ten years, and mining licences for Debswana (the partnership between the Botswana government and De Beers) were extended for 25 years from 2029 to 2054, following intense negotiations. In the terms of this sales agreement, the share of Debswana's rough diamonds allowed and assigned to the Botswana government, through its Okavango Diamond Company, to process will gradually rise from 25% to 50% over the ten-year agreement period, thus allowing Botswana to play a significant role in the diamond value chain.

The economy remained susceptible to external shocks, and its performance reflected global trends. *Economic growth* was estimated at 3.2% (down from 6.7% in 2022). The 2023/24 revised budget-projected revenues stood at P 81.67 bn and expenditure at P 88.79 bn, resulting in a deficit of P 7.13 bn, compared with an initial P 7.59 bn. According to the 2023/24 budget, customs and excise exceeded minerals as the main contributor of revenue, at P 24.93 bn (31.2% of total revenue). Minerals followed at P 23.34 bn (29.3% of revenues). The country's foreign reserves rose to P 64.90 bn, up from P 60.80 bn. In January, the government obtained $100 m from the OPEC Fund.

Compared with 2022, *inflation* eased during the year and was kept within the Bank of Botswana target of 3–6%, registering at 3.5% in December (down from 12.4% in December 2022). As part of its efforts to control inflation within its medium target of 3–6%, at its meetings in February, April, June, August, and October, the Bank of Botswana decided to sustain the *Monetary Policy Rate (MoPR)* (interest rate) at 2.65%. However, on 7 December, it decreased the MoPR from 2.65% to 2.4%.

Meanwhile, *fuel prices* remained unstable. On 13 January, they were decreased. On 1 March, an increase was made. On 21 June, another decrease was introduced, followed by another rise on 13 September. A further increase was made on 25 October, and a decrease was introduced on 15 November.

The country continued to grapple with socioeconomic challenges, and these have not registered any notable shift – thus presenting a menace to the country's development trajectory. Consequently, the government was under pressure to sustain its social protection and welfare programmes to support vulnerable groups. Unemployment was put at 25.9% during the third quarter of 2023, and the poverty prevalence rate was registered as 20.8% by the *2021 Pilot National Multidimensional Poverty Index*. Poverty was more intense in rural than in urban areas. HIV continued to present a challenge, with a prevalence rate of 20.8%, according to the 2021 Fifth Botswana AIDS Impact Survey (BAIS V). However, on 6 November the government reported that it had exceeded all of the 95–95–95 UNAIDS targets, which seek to detect 95% of those with HIV, offer antiretroviral medication to 95% of those detected, and realise 95% suppression of the viral load of those under treatment by 2030. The rate of perinatal transmission of HIV was sustained at under 2%.

Eswatini

Marisha Ramdeen

Eswatini, classified as a lower-middle-income country with an approximate population of 1.2 m people, continued to experience political and socioeconomic challenges in the year under review, with 70% of the population living below the poverty line. The 2023 national elections and the National Dialogue Process dominated the political landscape. A failed health system remained a concern, as did food and water insecurities.

Domestic Politics

The year commenced on a tragic note when pro-democracy activist and human rights lawyer Thulani Maseko was *assassinated*. This drew widespread condemnation by various human rights organisations, including the National Union of Metalworkers of South Africa, the South African Federation of Trade Unions, the Law Society of South Africa, and the United Nations, among others. The assassination, together with other political and social grievances, incited further civil and political protests. On 27 January, a petition delivery march was held, attended by various political parties and civil society groups, including the People's United Democratic Movement (PUDEMO), the Swaziland Youth Congress (SWAYOCO), the Economic Freedom Fighters (EFF) Swaziland, SWALIMO (the Swaziland Liberation Movement), the Communist Party of Swaziland (CPS), the Trade Union Congress of Swaziland (TUCOSWA), and the Swaziland Rural Women's Assembly. According to the 'Times of Eswatini', the march turned violent when two marchers were shot. TUCOSWA organised a May Workers Day march where thousands of workers convened and were urged to take action against the closure of the University of Eswatini. The university closed indefinitely on 16 March due to ongoing strikes by employees. It thereafter reopened on 8 May following an agreement signed by the Association of Lecturers, Academic and Administrative Personnel (ALAAP) and the National Workers Union of Swaziland Higher Institutions (NAWUSHI) which led to the suspension of the strike.

Voter registration began in May, and by June 583,428 people were registered to vote. Campaigns for the primary elections took place on 23 August, and the national *elections* were held on 29 September 2023. As political parties remained banned, only individuals were able to stand for the primaries. As a result of this system, opposition parties were divided on whether to boycott the elections. According to the 'Daily Maverick', 'only about a dozen of those nominated during primaries last month are known to have ties to the opposition'. The newspaper further indicated that AU and SADC observers were pleased with the electoral process and that the elections were held peacefully and in an orderly manner. As a result of the vote, 51 male and 8 female MPs were elected to the lower house of parliament by King Mswati.

Following the elections, King Mswati convened the *Sibaya*, or National Dialogue Process, on 23 October to address the political dissent that had erupted since June 2021, when violent civil unrest took place. The Sibaya was intended to enable the public to voice their opinions and engage with the king. An amount of 30 m emalangeni (E, equivalent to 30 m South African rand, ZAR) was allocated for the dialogue. As part of this process, the public submitted their statements to King Mswati through a council of governors assigned by him to process the submissions made. On 28 October, King Mswati officially closed the process. The Eswatini Ministry of Information, Communication and Technology shared King Mswati's remarks on the Sibaya, in which he stated that 'Cabinet Ministers had an opportunity to educate the nation about the different charters that needed ratification … and noted the submissions by the nation'. Following the conclusion of the Sibaya, King Mswati appointed Russell Mmemo Dlamini as the new prime minister, as well as 20 senators. While the government was satisfied with the National Dialogue Process, activists and political groups refused to accept the Sibaya as a legitimate process of deliberation on political matters. The Multi-Stakeholder Forum (MSF), which comprised civil society and political formations, did not participate in this process, and nor did PUDEMO.

While some democratic norms were demonstrated in the form of the elections and the National Dialogue Process, *human rights violations*, exhibited in several situations, remained a concern. On 1 June 2023, former MPs Mthandeni Dube and Mduduzi Bacede Mabuza, who had called for political reforms and had been arbitrarily detained for nearly two years, were found guilty of terrorism, sedition, and murder. They faced up to 20 years in prison. According to HRW in its 2023 report, 'Political dissent and civic and labour activism are subject to harsh punishment under the Terrorism Act of 2008 and the Sedition and Subversive Activities Act of 1938'.

Findings by the Afrobarometer survey released in 2023 suggested that the level of gender-based violence had increased by 14% over the previous year. In order to counter ongoing terror attacks and violence, the government allocated E 1.17 bn to fight against terrorism, crime, and gender-based violence (GBV). In addition, King Mswati warned the nation against ritual murders committed by those who hoped to be elected to parliament.

Foreign Affairs

Eswatini remained a member of the UN, the AU, the SADC, and the Commonwealth of Nations. Eswatini was also a member of the SACU and COMESA. The 8th Summit of the SACU Heads of State and Government took place on 29 June, in Eswatini.

On 3 February, the EU, via its humanitarian assistance agency, European Civil Protection and Humanitarian Aid Operations (ECHO), and the Finnish Red Cross *donated an ambulance* to the Baphalali Eswatini Red Cross Society.

In February, Eswatini and Bangladesh *signed an MoU* on the 'Establishment of a Comprehensive Consultation Mechanism' and another on 'Contract Farming and Agricultural Cooperation'. Bangladesh further committed to contribute $25 m over the next three years; current trade was at $3 m. However, it was made clear by the Bangladeshi delegation that this agreement would exclude any trade in arms or any other form of military equipment.

The ICC received formal complaints in March over crimes against humanity, filed by EmaSwati for Change (EFC), a human rights and advocacy organisation formed by EmaSwati based in the US.

King Mswati officially opened the *Zimbabwe International Trade Fair* on 28 April, the theme of which was 'Transformative Innovation and Global Competitiveness'. Taiwanese president Tsai Ing-wen attended Eswatini's independence day celebrations in September, where agreements were signed between the two countries regarding their trading partnership.

In October, at the commemoration of Germany National Day, King Mswati, represented by MP Prince Chief Mshengu, reiterated the need to strengthen the diplomatic relations between the two countries.

In light of the civil unrest in Eswatini, several countries presented statements in *condemnation of human rights violations*. In February, the European Parliament passed a resolution that urged the EU to consider suspending donor funding to Eswatini amid the allegations of human rights violations. Meanwhile, a demonstration took place outside the offices of the consulate of Eswatini in Johannesburg where picketers demanded that the government of Eswatini leave South Africa in the absence of democratic reforms. The demonstrators included the South African National Education, Health and Allied Workers Union (NEHAWU) and the South Africa Communist Party (SACP). In April, the Organisation of Africa Trade Union Unity (OATUU) condemned the violation of workers' rights in Eswatini. In May, several US senators introduced a resolution that condemned the human rights record of the government of Eswatini and the killing of Thulani Maseko. In June, the African Commission on Human and People's Rights (ACHPR) adopted Resolution 554, pertaining to the political climate in Eswatini and ongoing extrajudicial killings by King Mswati's security forces and mercenaries. The ACHPR expressed concern about the violent killing of Maseko and other human rights defenders. The resolution also raised other concerns regarding allegations of the violation of the right to life, dignity, and freedom of movement, assembly, and expression, enshrined in the African Charter in Human and People's Rights and international instruments.

Socioeconomic Developments

According to the AfDB's Eswatini Economic Outlook, the country's *GDP growth* was maintained at 3.5%, at an amount of approximately $11 bn at the end of 2023. The mining industry contributed 2% of GDP, largely through coal and quarry mining. Inflation rose from 5.3% in January to 6.0% in May. The most recent exports included scented mixtures, raw sugar, industrial fatty acids, oils, and alcohols, sawn wood, and non-knit women's suits. Export destination countries included South Africa, Kenya, Nigeria, DRC, and Mozambique. In addition to the country's produce, there were positive infrastructural developments, particularly in the telecommunications industry. The Eswatini Post and Telecommunications Corporation (EPTC) launched the fastest, most reliable and affordable fibre internet service in June. MTN Eswatini, which remained the biggest tax contributor, presented a report to stakeholders in August detailing a commitment to boosting economic growth and social progress. The ZAR 250 m Matsapha Lusushwana Lifestyle Mall was operational in July and created around 1,500 jobs.

Maize remained a staple in the country; the harvest was completed in June, with an estimated 85,000 tonnes produced, a decline of 15% compared with previous years. According to the FAO, the reduction in the harvest was due to fluctuations in seasonal rainfall, particularly dry spells in January and March, which are crucial months for maize development. The decline in maize production led to increased costs for EmaSwati, and *food inflation* increased to 15.7%. The Integrated Food Security Phase Classification (IPC) report published in August 2023 indicated that 'approximately 238,500 people (20%) of the population were estimated to be facing acute food insecurity and requiring urgent humanitarian assistance in September 2023'. In response to the food and nutrition crises, international NGOs, including Salesian Missions and Feed My Starving Children, sent a shipment of food that increased nutrition for approximately 2,300 people.

Water insecurity also posed a threat, given that 40% of rural communities lacked access to clean and safe water and 25% of the infrastructure that existed, such as taps and toilets, was not functional. Government efforts were underway to address the water crisis. On 20 June, the acting minister of natural resources and energy officially opened the ZAR 2.5 m Lozitha Water Scheme. This project was one of the ministry's interventions to ensure that every liSwati could access safe drinking water. The scheme received its water from a mountain stream. Part of the water scheme included the availability of sanitation facilities, expected to further reduce waterborne diseases; the community of Lozitha achieved 100% sanitation coverage through guidance from the Ministry of Health.

HIV/AIDS remained prevalent. Current life expectancy in 2023 was 61.05 years, and statistics revealed by Business Insiders Africa suggested that the average liSwati will not live beyond the age of 57 years in coming years, with Eswatini ranked seventh among the ten African countries expected to have the lowest life expectancy. The health situation was further compounded by a crippled health system. Health facilities faced several challenges that included shortages of ARVs, reduced levels of immunisation against measles for children, limited support for patients with kidney disease, an outbreak of cholera, limited medical supplies such as bandages and medicines, and a breakdown of laboratory equipment for chemotherapy treatments. In July, patients protested at the Mbabane Government Hospital due to the lack of drugs and poor services. In November, the minister of health stated that those who had played a role in the collapse of the health system would face consequences, and in December, eight civil servants were interviewed by the police as part of investigations into the shortage of medical drugs in public health facilities.

However, the government undertook some health initiatives, including vaccinations. During the country's first ever Human Papillomavirus (HPV) vaccination campaign, launched in June by Her Royal Highness Inkhosikati laMatsebula, a total of 46,674 schoolgirls were vaccinated across the country. The incidence of HPV was fuelled by high HIV rates, which also increased the incidence of cases of cervical cancer. In December, the minister of finance launched the End Malaria Fund Border Resource Mobilisation campaign to help raise funds to eradicate the disease.

Eswatini launched its 2022 Eswatini Violence Against Children and Youth Survey (VACS) report in September, in which it indicated that from 2007 to 2022, 'there were notable reductions in all forms of violence against girls and young women in Eswatini'. In spite of this, GBV remained increasingly high. A report by the Ministry of Health titled 'Situation Analysis of SRH including HIV and GBV Services for Adolescents and the Youth in Eswatini' noted that a study had suggested that 47.5% of adolescents (15–19 years) and 37.5% of young adults (20–24) believed that it was justifiable for a husband to beat his wife in certain circumstances. The government was called upon by politicians, civil society, and the public to declare GBV a national crisis. According to the 'Swaziland News', in November, the king spoke against GBV at the End of Year Service at Lozitha Palace, where he encouraged men and women to live together in peace without violence. King Mswati appointed Lydia Sijabulile Dlamini as the first woman to serve as acting national commissioner of the Royal Eswatini Police Service (REPS).

The king also commissioned thousands of girls to cut reeds as part of the ongoing *annual Umhlanga Reed Dance ceremony*. The young women participated in the double celebration of the king's 55th birthday and the country's 55 years of independence.

Lesotho

Roger Southall

Wealthy businessman Samuel Matekane had led his newly formed Revolution for Prosperity party (RFP) to victory in Lesotho's October 2022 general election, taking power at the head of a three-party coalition. As a newcomer to politics, he had promised the country a new start and committed to using his business skills to overcome the political strife which had destabilised the nation and delayed the national reform process. However, predictions that he would find it difficult to surmount the established patterns of politics were confirmed when in October 2023, opposition parties announced that they had the necessary support in parliament to oust him – only for their move to be frustrated by Lesotho's security chiefs stating that they would not allow this to happen. Matekane subsequently strengthened his position by bringing four more parties into his coalition, yet the future of Lesotho's politics remained uncertain.

Domestic Politics

The 2022 election brought about far-reaching changes in the composition of Lesotho's parliament. The RFP, formed by Matekane in March 2022, had come from nowhere to win 57 of the 80 single-member constituency seats in the country's mixed-member proportional representation electoral system. Because this gave it more seats than was justified by its proportion of the total votes cast (38.9%), it was not entitled to any further allocation of the seats awarded to parties to reflect their share of the national vote. Consequently, it searched for partners to form a coalition government and found them in the Alliance of Democrats, which had won five seats, and the Movement for Economic Change, which had won four. This gave the coalition 66 seats in the 120-seat parliament.

As long as the coalition remained intact, it would enjoy a comfortable working majority. However, many Basotho were understandably wary. Lesotho had been governed by successive coalitions since 2012, all of which had proved unstable. Why should this one be any different? After all, an Afrobarometer survey published after the election reported that a substantial majority (57%) of respondents thought that all or most MPs were corrupt, and that this encouraged parties to split and politicians to switch parties during any one parliament. Furthermore, although there were high hopes that Matekane's background would translate into his running an effective and corruption-free government, these hopes were accompanied by fears that he might use his position to further his business interests, with critics alleging that he had made his millions by winning lucrative government road construction contracts through his close relationship with Pakalitha Mosisili when the latter was prime minister.

All of this reflected a widespread lack of trust in Lesotho's politics. This was underlined by Amnesty International calling on the new government to address a pervasive culture of impunity within the security forces. It alleged that the police and the Lesotho Defence Force had been responsible for repeated violations of human rights. Afrobarometer cited this as a major concern, with 81% of respondents agreeing that individuals found guilty of political crimes or human rights violations should be held accountable. Only 18% favoured granting them amnesty to allow the country to move forward.

The public's disillusionment with Lesotho's politics-as-usual was why, on 5 April, Matekane came out swinging at the Manthabiseng Convention Centre in Maseru with an upbeat report to the nation on his government's first 100 days in office. Here was the nation's new housekeeper announcing a far-reaching spring clean! He had drawn up performance-based contracts for himself as prime minister, for his ministers, and for all public servants. He claimed early successes in the fight against crime and corruption. Outstanding debts to contractors owed to government had largely been paid, and the Ministry of Finance had discovered the whereabouts of 3.5 bn maloti (M) out of M 6.1 bn which had been reported missing by the auditor-general. Fourteen schools had been built since the government had taken office. All this may have sounded impressive, yet Matekane was fully aware that in the longer term he would be judged by his ability to proceed with the much-delayed national reform process. He was soon to find that the road to reform was strewn with obstacles.

Lesotho's Westminster-style constitution had allowed for a concentration of power in the hands of the prime minister. This had become increasingly evident from 2012 as successive prime ministers had sought to cope with the uncertainties of coalition politics. As a result, flaws in the constitution had become increasingly apparent. These included insufficient checks on the powers of the prime minister, erosion of the independence of the judiciary, a blurring of civil–military relations (which had encouraged recurrent military interventions in the political arena), a lack of professionalism in the civil service, and the inability of parliament to hold the executive accountable. Political analyst Hoolo 'Nyane, observing from the University of Limpopo, viewed the climax of these deficiencies as having been reached in 2014–15 under then prime minister Thomas Thabane, who capriciously changed the leadership of the judiciary and security forces to suit his ends, arbitrarily prorogued parliament, and shuffled the entire senior cadre of the civil service. The resulting political turmoil (Thabane's government collapsed in 2015) had led to increasing pressure for constitutional reform, notably from the SADC.

All recent governments had formally committed to reform. A key moment was reached when enactment of the National Reforms Dialogue Act of 2018 led to the establishment of the National Leaders' Forum (NLF) and the National Dialogue Planning Committee (NDPC). The latter was convened in 2019, resulting in the creation of the National Reforms Authority (NRA), a 35-member multi-stakeholder body including representation of political parties and civil society organisations. However, although it drafted important constitutional amendments, it was controversially closed down by Prime Minister Moeketsi Majoro when it came to the end of its officially stipulated time span in mid-2022.

Faced by SADC impatience with his move, Majoro sought to revive the process by pulling together the NRA's incomplete drafts into a Tenth Amendment to the Constitution Bill, colloquially known as the 'Omnibus Bill'. Under pressure of time before the forthcoming election, he attempted to rush this through parliament, along with a related National Assembly Electoral (Amendment) Bill, without regard for constitutional voting thresholds for altering different clauses of the constitution. Neither law had been passed by the time parliament came to the end of its five-year term on 13 July 2022.

Under pressure from the SADC, Majoro declared his bills' failure to pass a 'state of emergency' and recalled parliament, which now hurriedly passed them into law. However, parliament's action was successfully challenged in the High Court on the grounds that its failure to pass the two bills was not an emergency, resulting in this latest chapter in the reform process being aborted.

This was the complicated and messy situation which Matekane faced when he took office. The dilemma he faced was whether the government should lead the reform process itself or reconvene a multi-stakeholder body like the NRA. One option Matekane now contemplated was dividing the reforms into three categories – ordinary, special, and referendum-bound amendments – in an attempt to comply with the amendment clause in the existing constitution. However, the danger in this was that amendment to the constitution would end up proceeding piecemeal, whereas the National Dialogue had concluded that changing the constitution's basic structure was possible only through the formulation of an entirely new constitution, which could pass only following approval in a referendum.

Matekane met with opposition leaders in February to discuss the way forward, but despite talk of collaboration, no agreement was reached. This confirmed the government in its determination to press ahead unilaterally, and it proceeded to pass the National Assembly Electoral Amendment Bill, as it had been formulated in 2022, through parliament. This prohibited any attempt to remove a prime minister within three years of an election; likewise, MPs would be banned from switching parties for the first three years of a new parliament. Predictably, this move was bitterly denounced by Mathibeli Mokhothu, the leader of the opposition, who accused the prime minister of 'cherry-picking' pieces of legislation that suited him rather than seeking opposition support for a revived Omnibus Constitutional Bill, which would require a two-thirds majority in parliament for approval. Matekane, he stated, was not serious about reform.

There were simultaneous rumours that opposition parties were stirring dissent within the RFP among those of its MPs who felt that Matekane had ignored their claims to preferment, allegations being made that the prime minister had been appointing former business cronies to senior positions in government. Events culminated in the submission of a motion of no confidence in parliament on 16 October. This was put by Mokhuthu's Democratic Congress with the backing of smaller parties and, supposedly, RFP rebels. However, although the opposition had claimed the support of 64 MPs, Matekane survived.

He was saved on the day by the speaker of parliament announcing that he was deferring the no-confidence motion until the outcome of a Constitutional Court challenge made to it by an RFP MP, who had asked it to put any no-confidence motion on hold until after the completion of the national reforms process. Although this was unlikely to succeed, as the motion was perfectly constitutional under the Westminster-style system, the speaker's ruling deferred the matter. However, the saga was brought to an abrupt halt that same evening, by the intervention of the security forces.

Matekane had met with police commissioner Homolo Molibeli, Defence Force commander Lieutenant General Mojalefa Letsoela, and National Security Service director General Pheello Ralenkoane, ahead of the parliamentary session, and had made a bid for their support. They responded by issuing a joint declaration, on the evening of 16 October, that they would not allow a change of government to happen. Stating that it was their duty to uphold the constitution and maintain national security, they denounced those bent on removing the government as motivated by selfish interests. The Basotho people had ordered that the constitution be amended and a change of government would therefore not happen. What would take place was a continuation of the national reforms process.

The security chiefs' statement was backed by the LDF mounting a roadblock outside parliament, and according to Mokhutu, illegally searching MPs, looking for firearms. On a wider canvas, critics criticised the opposition for provoking an unnecessary crisis, Matekane for misusing the army to fight his battles, and the security chiefs for threatening a coup in a replay of Lesotho's recurrent political crisis. Nonetheless, the SADC's silence suggested that Matekane had its support.

In the wake of this drama, Matekane strengthened his position by coaxing the Basotho Action Party (BAP; six MPs), the Lesotho Congress of Democrats (three), and two smaller parties into joining his coalition. Meanwhile, the reforms process had stalled. Although the government pledged to reintroduce the Omnibus Bill in the National Assembly in the new year, opposition leaders vowed not to participate in the reform process until the government fired the heads of the security services.

Foreign Affairs

Matekane had gone out of his way at his inauguration as prime minister to impress upon South African president Cyril Ramaphosa his commitment to implementing the national reform process. The postponement of the latter by the judgment of the High Court that the Omnibus and the National Assembly Electoral (Amendment) Act were unconstitutional had tried the patience of both South Africa and the SADC, and if Matekane, as an unknown quantity to both, was going to receive their support, he needed to convince them that his commitment to the reform process was genuine.

Matekane's government conveyed the same message when the Panel of Elders of the SADC, led by former president of Tanzania Jakaya Kikwete, made a four-day visit to Lesotho on 7–11 February 2023, following the decision by the SADC Summit of Heads of State and Governments to establish an Oversight Committee and Mediation Reference Group to oversee the implementation of reforms. Although the official communiqué issued at the end of the visit was as bland as most such communications, it is clear that the political and security situation in Lesotho was central to its discussions.

The progress being made towards the implementation of the national reforms process was also taken up strongly at the inaugural meeting of the Bi-National Commission (BNC) established to strengthen relations between South Africa and Lesotho in September. An agreement to elevate the existing Joint Bilateral Commission of Cooperation, an inter-ministerial body, between the two countries to the BNC, a summit of the two heads of government, had been made in November 2021. Its purview covered the entire span of relations between the two countries, of which defence and security, migration, and water stood out as clear priorities.

In the wake of statement issued by the security chiefs following the postponement of the no-confidence debate, opposition parties addressed a warning to Ramaphosa, as the SADC's facilitator of the security situation in Lesotho, and Zambian president Hakainde Hichilema, as chair of the bloc's Organ on Politics, Defence and Security, that Lesotho was at risk of a coup. There was no officially communicated response, although Hichilema doubtless pressed Matekane on the matter when he made a one-day visit to Lesotho on 2 November.

The only other development of note was Lesotho's signing of the Free Trade Area Agreement between COMESA, the EAC, and the SADC on October 27.

Socioeconomic Developments

The AfDB reported that Lesotho's economy had grown by 2.5% in 2022, driven by growth in services (2.6%), construction (8.1%), fiscal stimulus, and Covid-19-related spending. This was an improvement on the 1.6% growth in 2021. Inflation rose to 8.3% in 2022, from 6.1% in 2021, owing to higher inflation in South Africa, the country's main trading partner. In 2022, the fiscal deficit narrowed to 4.3% of GDP, from 4.8% in 2021, due to a rebound in SACU revenue. It was financed with government savings and borrowing. The current account deficit increased to 6.8% of GDP in 2022, from 4.2% in 2021, owing to higher imports, financed through South African capital transfers.

GDP was projected to grow 2.1% in 2023 and 2.6% in 2024, driven by the huge infrastructure construction works of the Highlands Water Project, involving tunnels and dams and higher government capital spending. However, the fiscal deficit was projected to increase to 5.5% in 2023 and 5.1% in 2024, owing to a projected decrease in government revenue arising from a drop in SACU revenue. The current account deficit was projected to narrow to 5.8% of GDP in 2023 and 5.1% in 2024, due to projected recovery in remittances. The Bank predicted that the main risk to the macroeconomic outlook remained the fragile fiscal situation globally, a resultant weakening demand for Lesotho's exports, and reducing investor confidence.

Real GDP per capita grew by 1.5% in 2022, up from 0.3% in 2021, and was projected to grow by 1.0% in 2023 and 1.5% in 2024. However, poverty remained endemic, with half the population living below the national poverty line in 2017. According to 2021 data, youth unemployment stood at 33.2%, compared with overall unemployment of 24%, while 500,000 people were food insecure.

Madagascar

Richard R. Marcus

Madagascar's economic growth continued to be solid in 2023, with 3.8% growth in GDP. Inflation remained high at 9.9%, but this was an improvement on the 11.2% of 2022. Agricultural production and manufacturing continue to be faulted. While 2023 saw improved rains and diminished drought conditions, the south of the country continued to face long-term acute food insecurity due to climate change-induced famine, with 1.5 m people facing IPC (Integrated Food Security Phase Classification) 3 (Crisis) or higher-level food insecurity. Multilateral and bilateral donors continued to recognise the urgency and the need to increase both humanitarian relief and long-term portfolio investments. The consequential 2023 presidential elections dominated Malagasy political space, urban social conditions, and decision-making throughout the year. Originally scheduled for 9 November, they were postponed to 16 November by the High Constitutional Court (HCC) due to political unrest. Incumbent president Andry Rajoelina won 58.95% of the vote in the first round, thereby obviating the need for a run-off poll and securing a second five-year term. International observers approved the elections, but they exposed both the centralising and illiberal tendencies of the president and the weakness of the opposition.

Domestic Politics

January saw a surge in *pre-electoral* activity. Potential presidential candidates, including former president Marc Ravalomanana, began touring the country. Malagasy politics has been dominated by the competition between Rajoelina and Ravalomanana since military forces close to Rajoelina overthrew Ravalomanana in 2009. Rajoelina and Ravalomanana, both from the historically privileged Merina ethnic group of the central highlands, competed directly in the second round of the 2018 presidential elections. Entering a new election year, there was considerable public exhaustion at the dominance of these two candidates. Vocal southern MP Siteny Randrianasoloniaiko saw his star rising and began touring on 26 January with a focus on the growing poverty in the country under Rajoelina's leadership. He worked on building a populist base and positioning himself as a voice of the people against an alliance of Merina and what he characterised as internationally driven economic extraction. Significant parts of the international community raised geopolitical concerns about his ties with Russia at the expense of Europe and the US and his antipathy towards mining and other global industries.

Former president Hery Rajaonarimampianina announced that he would return to Madagascar from France in order to compete. Civil society was collectively raising concerns about what it described as the authoritarian tendencies of the Rajoelina government and seized on delays in electoral list reforms as an example of political manipulation. There was significant criticism of the performance of individual cabinet members, and a high level of expectation that there would be a cabinet reshuffle. This materialised on 20 February, with eight ministries – National Defense; Foreign Affairs; Justice; Labor and Civil Service; Public Works; Transport and Meteorology; Energy and Hydrocarbons; and Youth and Sports – seeing new leadership. While the reshuffle was well received, the timing and selections brought accusations from the opposition that Rajoelina was moving to surround himself with loyalists and protect against military intervention.

President Rajoelina took a sharp turn in his political framing in February, releasing a new campaign message, 'Here and Now'. Moving away from his focus on long-term needs in his list of *velirano* development goals, he turned his focus to underscoring the meeting of the immediate needs of the population. The immediate needs to address – such as rice subsidies, educational expansion, and an emergency social action plan – were significant, defensible, and clear, but the geographic locations were clearly strategic, with a focus on areas where Rajoelina sought to boost his re-election prospects. This pattern continued throughout the year. For their part, the UN, EU, and other international partners relayed concerns over progress in electoral preparation but rebuffed entreaties by Prime Minister Christian Ntsay to provide funds to help to finance the elections.

On 31 March, the minister of interior and decentralisation, Justin Tokely, announced that for 'All political parties, whether they are with the regime or from the opposition ... Public meetings in the open air, or on public roads, will be formally prohibited. They must take place indoors.' He added: 'All events must have the approval of the competent local authorities'. This declaration, carrying the force of a decree, was viewed by the opposition and many observers as a significant restriction intended to limit the organisation of political competition. While the decree applied equally to all parties, President Rajoelina could continue to make political speeches as president unfettered by location restrictions. A 4 April joint declaration by the EU, Germany, US, France, Japan, UK, Switzerland, and Norway denounced the move as an acceleration of the decline in the political climate and a challenge to human rights standards. The relative quiet of the Independent National Electoral Commission (CENI) let to opposition accusations that it had lost its neutrality.

By June, President Rajoelina had secured his electoral momentum. He travelled not as a candidate but as president to Vakinankaratra, Ikongo, Ambanihy, Haute Matsiatra, Anosy, Androy, Atsimo-Andrefana, and Amoroni'i Mania, where his re-election prospects were in question, in order to provide immediate, short-term relief in food security, education support, vocational rehabilitation, public infrastructure, and other livelihood areas. At the same time, opposition candidates had little to offer, and public disquiet over the president did not translate into support for Ravalomanana. Siteny Randrianasoloniaiko's incoherent messaging, particularly in the Sava region, led to an unsuccessful tour and diminished prospects. Other candidates, including Hajo Andrianainarivelo and Tahina Razafinjoelina, failed to launch. The electoral terrain was clearly uneven as the Rajoelina government further limited campaigning by stationing security forces at opposition rallies, but also as there was no viable competitor. It became clear that Rajoelina would win a plurality of votes in November; the question was whether he would secure the 50% necessary to win a victory in the first round of voting or whether there would be a run-off second round.

On 15 June, a press report revealed that Rajoelina had taken French citizenship. According to Article 42 of Madagascar's constitution, 'A Malagasy adult who voluntarily acquires a foreign nationality loses his Malagasy nationality'. Opposition leaders filed a grievance on 12 July that President Rajoelina was no longer Malagasy and was thus ineligible to run for president. The HCC found in Judgement No. 04-HCC/AR of 22 August 2023 that it 'was not competent to say and judge that Rajoelina Andry Nirina has lost Malagasy nationality', thereby rejecting the request for a public hearing and the invalidation of Rajoelina's candidacy. This led to claims that the HCC had joined the CENI in lacking independence.

In August, election preparations were still far behind and the international community had done little to realise the election funding basket. The US and Japan contributed, raising the basket to just over half of the $8.8 m requested by the CENI. Rajoelina continued to use security forces to clamp down on public rallies, international donors raised concerns about government transparency, and the president's chief of staff, Romy Andrianarisoa, was arrested on corruption charges in the UK, but the implosion of the opposition would have been enough to leave him in pole position.

Under *Article 52 of the Malagasy constitution*, a president seeking re-election must step down in advance of the election. Presidential powers are to be exercised in trust by the president of the Senate, but Senate president Herimanana Razafimahefa declined to serve on 8 September. If there is an impediment to the Senate president serving, power is transferred to a collegial government with limited authority led by the prime minister. The HCC affirmed the collegial government on 9 September, but President Rajoelina was accused by the opposition of again manipulating the control of power and access behind the scenes. Opposition rallies became more fervent. While they antagonised security forces with intent, forces responded with limited restraint leading to conscribed violence. The opposition began a quixotic demand for reform to institutions, the dissolution of the HCC and the CENI, and a transitional government.

As rallies turned to *protests*, on 2 October, police began deploying tear gas. Marc Ravalomanana sustained minor injuries at a protest on 7 October, leading protesters to became more violent, rallying around renewed calls for Rajoelina to be disqualified due to his citizenship and for the dissolution of the HCC and CENI. On 12 October, the HCC moved the election from 9 to 16 November to allow for a cooling-down period. The elections went off smoothly, and on 25 November, the CENI announced that Rajoelina had won 59%, securing victory in the first round. Randrianasoloniaiko came in second with 14%, followed by Ravalomanana with 12%. Safidy, a Malagasy CSO providing election observers, found irregularities including instances of money changing hands for votes and insufficient ballot security. International observers, including SADC and Liberal International, observed inconsistencies in electoral materials and in the timely opening and closing of polling stations, and limited training of poll workers. However, observers and the international community concluded that the margin of victory was greater enough to exceed any impact on the outcome from electoral irregularities. The HCC confirmed the results on 30 November and President Andry Rajoelina was inaugurated on 16 December. The opposition rapidly turned its attention towards the 2024 legislative elections.

While the worst concerns about *instability* did not materialise, 2023 marked significant democratic backsliding. Varieties of Democracy lowered the Madagascar Accountability Index score from 0.61 in 2022 to 0.42 in 2023. It noted falls in the Electoral, Liberal, Egalitarian, and Deliberative Democracy Indices. At year's end,

Rajoelina found himself under pressure to respond to popular frustrations in his second mandate, address short-term stability, and to engage with international donors concerned with transparency, accountability, and freedom of expression.

Foreign Affairs

President Rajoelina began the year under greater pressure from the international community but with few signs of a change in the status quo. Madagascar has remained close to France since independence, and France remains Madagascar's most critical trading partner. Relations with the EU, other European countries, and the US have gone through challenges under Rajoelina, but Madagascar has persisted in maintaining its Western alignment, and Western powers have provided significant reprieve to Rajoelina's political centralisation to allow this to happen. At the same time, Rajoelina has improved Madagascar's relationship with China, leading to an increase in the value of Chinese imports from $7.9 m in May 2022 to $19.2 m in May 2023, but President Rajoelina has consistently limited political influence from countries that might disrupt strong relations with France, the US, and the EU.

Madagascar has sought to maintain a path of non-alignment in order to court new investment, but this has been challenging. Early in the year, the EU and the US made it clear that they viewed the neutrality of Madagascar in voting on the Russia–Ukraine war in the UN as support for Russia. Indeed, Madagascar had fired its minister of foreign affairs for voting in favour of a UN resolution condemning the Russian invasion. Concerned about these relationships, Madagascar voted on 23 February with the Western international community on a UN resolution calling for a peaceful resolution to the conflict. For many in Madagascar, this was read as a capitulation to Western demands. It invoked concerns raised about Covid-19 restrictions that Madagascar falls to more neocolonial influence.

The international community took note early in the year that the lack of preparedness for the elections was itself destabilising for the country. The US ambassador to Madagascar, Claire Pierangelo, met in March with HCC president Florent Rakotoarisoa to help bolster the strength of the court and insist on its neutrality. She continued throughout the month to meet with Landy Mbolatiana Randriamanantenasoa, minister of justice, and Christine Razanamahasoa, president of the National Assembly, to push for free, credible, and transparent elections. Graham Maitland and Simon Pierre Nanitelamia of the UN Department of Political and Peacebuilding Affairs met with foreign minister Yvette Sylla in March to stress the need for dialogue, openness, and transparency. The OIF began an audit process to identify flaws in voter registration and future execution. EU ambassador Isabelle Delattre Burger was a forceful interlocutor with President Rajoelina throughout

2023, including at a meeting on 21 March in which she expressed concern about the need to improve the legal framework of elections.

Relations between Madagascar and SADC remained strong in 2023. The executive secretary of SADC, Elias Mpedi Magosi, met with Sylla on 23 March and President Rajoelina on 24 March, committing to support for the agricultural sector, investment in agri-business, the creation of employment opportunities.

The great challenge throughout the year was that international donors, including the World Bank, IMF, and bilateral donors, continued to fund development projects at high levels, but the diplomatic community was slow to provide requested funds in support of the elections. In April, Isabelle Delattre Burger made it clear that the EU contribution would be marginal compared with 2018 support. President Rajoelina gathered ambassadors from Japan, the EU, UK, France, and Germany, as well as the US deputy chief of mission, to discuss how the reluctance to fund elections due to concerns over election preparations was perpetuating the challenge. A meeting on 9–10 June between President Rajoelina and French president Emmanuel Macron began to break the impasse. The UNDP agreed to provide some of the requested funding to the CENI to increase transparency and inclusion. France, the US, and Japan followed suit, and the $8.8 m request was ultimately met.

While funding helped to ensure that the *electoral process* could be executed without significant flaws, the concerns of the international community mounted with the March decree limiting outdoor rallies, the emergence of security forces at opposition events in August, and the continued narrow political space created by the president. In September EU ambassador Burger urged the government to finalise a law on the protection of human rights defenders that had languished since 2018. As security continued to deteriorate in October, the international community was vocal but took little action. UNHCR called on the Malagasy government to 'ensure respect for human rights and the rule of law throughout the electoral period'. Notably, ambassadors from the US, EU, and France were all at the beginning of their four-year terms of service in 2023, holding significant initiatives to be developed under the auspices of their governments. The higher priority was to maintain the relationships necessary to undertake core initiatives rather than press on government transparency or the expansiveness of electoral participation.

In December, following his inauguration, President Rajoelina announced new partnerships. A 19 December partnership with China became the first agreement of Rajoelina's second term. The AfDB announced $268 m in funding shortly thereafter. There were stern warnings from the EU and the US about the need to engage in dialogue and protect freedom of expression, but key initiatives, including inclusion in the US AGOA, remained in place. President Macron's 15 December letter summed up the position of most of the international community well. He congratulated President Rajoelina on his electoral victory, but also highlighted 'divisions that emerged' during the election campaign, particularly over Rajoelina's French nationality. Macron stated: 'I hope that the divisions that appeared during the recent election campaign will be overcome'. He called for consolidation of trust and dialogue in Malagasy society and said that 'France will be sensitive to this'. With attention already on the 2024 legislative elections, it did not appear that consolidation, reconciliation, or listening were priorities of the newly inaugurated president.

Socioeconomic Developments

The majority of Madagascar's population remained in subsistence agriculture, with 64% living in rural areas, even though agriculture, forestry, and fishing accounted for only 21.1% of GDP in 2023. This is part of a pattern of continued decline in the sector, from 35% in 1995, contributing negatively to growth. The drop in agriculture without a complementary rise in employment in other sectors has led to improved macroeconomic stability and global economic engagement marked by steadily increasing unemployment and poverty. According to the World Bank, the only sector that has seen marked growth relative to GDP between 2013 and 2023 is construction. Madagascar's Gini coefficient of 42.6 (comparable to those of DRC and Peru) was an indicator of how poorly the economic gains over the past decade have been distributed.

Madagascar's economic growth continued to be solid in 2023, with 3.8% growth in GDP by IMF figures, but this was insufficient to demonstrate a reversal in the long-term decline in real GDP per capita tied to population growth. Inflation remained high at 9.9%, but this was an improvement on the 11.2% of 2022. Public frustration continued as the price of rice, the food staple, remained stubbornly high. Energy prices also remained high, with a particular impact on electricity in urban areas. Since 2017, the average electricity price in Madagascar has fluctuated between $117.34 and $194.91/MWh. While the general trend has been downward, season spiking and insufficient supply marked by grey-outs have added to public frustration. According to the Bloomberg Climatescope, Madagascar's power score of 1.82 ranks it at number 48 among emerging markets and number 75 in the global power ranking. This is a drop of 26 places from 2021 to 2022 (the most recent scores available). The blame has been placed largely on the inefficiencies of Jirama, the long-embattled national water and electricity corporation. Specifically, investment is low, inefficiency is high, wholesale power markets do not exist, purchase power agreements (PPAs) are few and far between, and government intervention in targeted taxes or carbon prices has been a challenge.

Poverty in Madagascar has been steadily worsening. The 2023 UNDP Multidimensional Poverty Index ranked Madagascar as the fifth country from the bottom of its list, after Niger, Chad, CAR, and Burundi, with 68.4% of the population living in multidimensional poverty and 45.8% in severe multidimensional poverty. Taking into account PPP, 80.7% of the population lived in poverty. The intensity of deprivation worsened and access to health, education, drinking water, sanitation, and financial resources remained weak. A recent World Bank analysis found that the trends of the last decade are explained by market and governance failures, climatic shocks, and the Covid-19 pandemic. Natural disasters have cost the economy 1% of GDP. Overall consumption growth has been positive but low for the bottom 60% and negative or close to zero for the top 40% at the national level. A change in direction will require a radical reshaping of the economy. Subsistence agriculture has been highly impacted by climate change. The private sector has seen stagnant productivity. There has been an inadequate supply of infrastructure and essential services including education. A comprehensive reform agenda focused on the necessary conditions for rapid industrial and service employment growth in urban areas and renewed productivity gains in the agricultural sector is critical.

Madagascar accounts for over 70% of the world's vanilla, which represents $600 m in Malagasy export earnings. The market was volatile in 2023. In January, US ambassador Claire Pierangelo first raised concerns over monopolistic business practices with President Rajoelina. The high price of $250 per kilo was a burden on international companies. A delegation of US and Canadian importers boycotted a January meeting when they learned that Mamy Ravatomanga would be in attendance. Ravatomanga is a highly influential advisor to President Rajoelina but is seen in the international community as distorting market activities for personal benefit, if not outright corruption.

Despite the political upheavals, the international donor community has remained committed to Madagascar. In January, World Bank country representative Marie-Chantal Uwanyiligira continued to express strong concerns about transparency and accountability but increased the World Bank's Madagascar portfolio by $250 m with the Madagascar Resilience and Safety Net Project the same month. While the total portfolio neared $3 bn in 2023, fiscal commitments rose to $1.05 bn. In March, the World Bank released its new 2023–27 Country Partnership Framework focusing on raising living standards, improving job opportunities, political economic analysis for intervention in key sectors (particularly energy), and the financial and livestock sectors. It noted, and committed to working with, existing constraints including a lack of structural transformation, insufficient government investment in human capital, political instability, economic shocks, and climate-change-induced shocks. This is a departure from previous years, in which it sought to either address primary constraints or condition aid on their change.

On 29 June, the IMF released its fourth review under the ECF. It found programme performance mixed, raising concern over the energy sector and finding reform of Jirama to be insufficient and growth to be decelerating, in part because of high inflation. Structural factors were largely blamed, but the IMF strongly noted the poor government performance in tax administration reforms, public debt management, and other key areas. Improvement in budget execution, transparency, and governance were viewed as critically needed, an extension of previous IMF findings. Despite these concerns with government performance and political stability, the IMF committed to its ECF fund dispersal.

On 12 May, a new mining code was adopted by the National Assembly after years of contestation. It quickly passed the Senate and moved into law. The World Bank, a leading actor in the writing of the code, returned to the table in February in advance of the parliamentary session. Engagement with the government and Rio Tinto, the lead in the QMM consortium in Tolagnaro and one of the most influential companies in the sector, was significant. Among the major changes in this new mining code were the upward revision of the royalty rate from 2% to 5%, the reduction of the validity period of an exploitation permit from 40 to 25 years, and the reduction by half of the surface area authorised for any type of exploitation. The code remains controversial because only 2% of the royalty goes to local government while 3% remains with the central state, in contrast to the government's decentralisation rhetoric.

On 19 January, Tropical Cyclone Cheneso made landfall between Antalaha and Sambava in north-eastern Madagascar. Thirty-three people were killed, 20 were left unaccounted for, tens of thousands were displaced, and more than 20,000 homes, schools, and medical facilities were severely damaged. Tropical Cyclone Freddy followed, making landfall on 21 February in Mananjara about 1500 km south, causing five deaths and significant damage to rice production. The damage was magnified because the region had still not recovered from Cyclone Batsirai, which landed a year earlier.

Rains improved in the south of the country, lessening drought, but the long-term impacts of climate-change-induced changes in rain patterns left soils fragile and famine an ongoing concern. The regions of Anosy, Androy, and Atsimo-Andrefana saw, according to IPC data, 1.5 m people facing Phase 3 (Crisis) or higher-level food insecurity. The UN and other organisations referred to the situation in southern Madagascar as one of the first climate-change-created changes to livelihoods. The long-term impacts of climate change, including the sale of cattle and other reserves, a higher percentage of the population slipping into extreme poverty, high levels of regional migration, an increase in insecurity in some areas, and a rise in cattle theft, will impact the region long into the future. An area of approximately 200,000 square kilometres without road infrastructure has helped to create a near-stateless zone, fuelling the diminution of governance throughout the region. The World Bank, AfDB, UNDP, USAID, and other donors have recognised the growing urban–rural divide and the need for structural change.

Malawi

George Dzimbiri and Lewis Dzimbiri

The Tonse Alliance administration continued to face criticism from various quarters of society for, among other things failing to tame the country's looming economic crisis and inability to manage and administer the Affordable Inputs Programme (AIP) in time. The AIP programme was marred by many hindrances such as a reduction in the number of beneficiaries, the failure of beneficiaries to access the fertilisers and seeds, and corruption. Consequently, most Malawians are likely to experience hunger in the following year because most poor Malawian farmers rely absolutely on the programme. The year also saw intra- and inter-party conflicts in both the ruling and opposition political parties. Malawi enjoyed good relations with other countries and international agencies, thereby receiving monetary and material support. The year witnessed a substantial devaluation of the national currency, the kwacha, by 44%. As a result, commodity prices skyrocketed amid declining revenues from tobacco sales. The devaluation of the kwacha triggered industrial actions in various organisations and sectors of the economy. The year was also marked by acute shortage of foreign-exchange currency, forcing some firms in both the public and the private sector to suspend manufacturing and packaging activities. The shortage left the government struggling to pay for fuel imports, and thus led to an acute shortage of fuel for three consecutive months.

Domestic Politics

Intra- and inter-party conflicts ensued during the year. Intra-party conflicts were noticeable both in the opposition parties and in the ruling Tonse Alliance. On 12 August, the High Court granted the leader of the opposition in parliament, Kondwani Nankhumwa, an injunction that restrained the DPP Disciplinary Committee from summoning him to a hearing. The Disciplinary Committee had summoned Nankhumwa, also the DPP Southern Region vice-president, to a hearing on 3 August, alleging that between 15 and 25 July, he had conducted rallies in the Southern Region without seeking permission from the erstwhile governing party.

On 14 September, around 44 DPP members of parliament (MPs) vowed to oppose any aspirant who would dare challenge party leader Peter Mutharika at the party's elective convention set for July 2024. The development came barely four days after DPP legislator Mark Botomani accused fellow legislator Chipiliro Mpinganjira of organising a meeting of Mutharika's sympathisers on 10 September. Towards the end of September, the DPP expelled its publicity secretary, Nicholas Dausi, with immediate effect, also sacked him as its MP. A public notice of the decision indicated that the expulsion followed a recommendation by the Disciplinary Committee and a decision by the central executive committee. It was alleged that Dausi, a former publicity secretary of the party, was being sacked for misconduct. However, when contacted, Dausi maintained that he was yet to receive communication from the party on his expulsion.

In a related development, Peter Mutharika criticised 'some individuals' in the party who considered themselves more important than anyone else. While Mutharika did not name the individuals, he was referring to wrangles in the party orchestrated by Nankhumwa, who was challenging decisions made by a faction sympathetic to Mutharika. In December, DPP director of legal affairs Charles Mhango had written to embattled secretary-general Grezelder Jeffrey asking her to repay 107 m kwanza (MK) that she had allegedly received to pay election monitors in the 2020 presidential elections but had never paid. While this was unfolding, Nankhumwa was launching his campaign for the DPP presidency at Golden Peacock Hotel in Blantyre. On 12 December, the High Court judge Simeon Mdeza rejected a plea by some DPP members who wanted to stop other party members from holding the National Governing Council (NGC) meeting that had been called by Jeffrey. The members, including Shadric Namalomba, Chipiliro Mpinganjira, Jean Mathanga, and others, wanted the court to stop the meeting, slated for 12 December, and were challenging their absence from the NGC members' list. Towards the end of October, disagreements had ensued in the DPP as the party's spokesperson Shadric Namalomba maintained that its leader, Mutharika, was eligible to contest the September 2025 presidential election. However, Nankhumwa's camp claimed that Mutharika was not eligible to contest, citing provisions in the party's constitution that bar him after having served for two terms. This was happening days after Simeon Mdeza had ordered the party to hold a convention within 90 days.

Inter-party conflicts also took place. On 28 September, the DPP, Malawi's main opposition party, pushed for the resignation of President Lazarus Chakwera over a looming economic crisis resulting in fuel shortages, scarcity of foreign exchange, and increased grain prices. A government spokesperson said that pushing Chakwera to resign was unrealistic. Dalitso Kabambe, a presidential aspirant for the DPP and former governor of the Reserve Bank, told reporters that the country's economy was heading into a crisis. He said the problem was that the Chakwera administration had no expertise in managing the economy. In June, the attorney-general, Thabo Chakaka Nyirenda, gave a four-day ultimatum to the DPP to pay MK 59.9 m in costs initially ordered by the High Court. This related to a case that the DPP lost when it sought constitutional interpretation after the High Court ruled that four DPP electoral commissioners had been appointed illegally. The four, appointed by Mutharika on 7 June ahead of the June 2020 elections, were Arthur Nanthulu, Steve Duwa, Linda Kunje, and Jean Mathanga.

The government was also at loggerheads with *civil society* (CSOS). On 12 November, opposition parties and human rights organisations in Malawi voiced strong criticism of President Chakwera and his administration for dispatching 221 young Malawians to engage in agricultural work in Israel. That decision was implemented in the wake of Israel's recent aid contribution of $60 m (£47 m) aimed at supporting Malawi's economic recovery. The labour export deal was criticised amid concerns over the secrecy with which it was done and the potential risks to citizens at a time when Israel was in a conflict with the Palestinian group Hamas. In a related development, civil rights groups in Malawi condemned government for choosing to abstain from a vote calling for a ceasefire in Gaza. The vote on the protection of civilians, especially women and children, and upholding legal and humanitarian obligations in Gaza took place at the UN on 17 August. The Human Rights Defenders Coalition (HRDC) and another grouping, Youth and Society (YAS), described Malawi's abstention as 'not only irresponsible, hypocritical, but a disgrace'. YAS executive director Charles Kajoloweka that said Malawi's action was an immoral abdication of its international human rights obligations as a UN member. On 12 August, some MPs rebuked the government for failing to discipline controlling officers who had mismanaged public resources in ministries, departments, and agencies (MDAS). According to the auditor-general's report for the period under review, payment vouchers worth MK 5.5 bn had been submitted to auditors without the necessary supporting documents attached.

The major culprits were State Residences, the Parliament of Malawi, the Malawi Defence Force, the Ministry of Youth and Sports, and the Ministry of Foreign Affairs and International Cooperation. There were also accounting queries regarding Malawian embassies in Egypt and Berlin in Germany. The other main culprits were the Southern Africa Tuberculosis and Health System Support Project, the Ministry of Transport and Public Works, the Department of Immigration and Citizenship Services, and the Legal Aid Bureau.

Foreign Affairs

Malawi continued to enjoy *good relations with other countries and international agencies, and received financial and material support.* On 20 January, the US government, through USAID, signed an administrative agreement with the World Bank to contribute $4.4 m (MK 4.5 bn) to kickstart a new social protection multi-donor trust fund and support the government of Malawi to scale up and strengthen existing shock-responsive safety nets and their delivery systems. The trust fund allowed the government to provide unconditional cash transfers to the most vulnerable Malawians and deliver cash for work to households at risk of extreme hunger. According to the US ambassador to Malawi, David Young, the trust fund was expected to significantly expand a cash-for-work programme that provided temporary jobs. The project would enhance Malawi's climate resilience through forest and soil restoration, watershed recovery, and other climate-smart enhanced public works.

On 26 April, Russia's ambassador to Malawi handed over 20,000 tonnes of fertiliser to the country. The donation amounted to 3% of Malawi's annual national fertiliser requirement of 600,000 tonnes. During the handover ceremony, Malawi's minister of agriculture, Sam Kawale, said that the fertiliser was a major boost for the country amid shortages in the government-sponsored Affordable Inputs Programme (AIP), which sells seeds and fertiliser to poor farmers at cheaper prices. Similarly, on 6 July, the minister of health, Khumbize Kandodo Chiponda, received a donation of 165 tonnes of medicines and medical supplies from the Republic of India worth over MK 2 bn. Speaking at the donation ceremony, the Chiponda expressed gratitude to the government of India for the timely donation.

President Chakwera made *several trips within the year.* On 28 July, he left for China amid concerns that his frequent travels were draining the public purse as well as exerting pressure on low forex reserves. But the government justified the trips, saying that the benefits accrued far outweighed the costs. Prior to his departure from Kamuzu International Airport in Lilongwe, the president said that he would utilise the visit to China, where he was attending the China–Africa Economic and Trade Expo (CAETE) from 29 June to 2 July, to negotiate for debt relief from the bilateral agreements made in the past.

In a related development, on 12 November, Chakwera went to Saudi Arabia and Egypt. He backed these trips by saying they were key to the country's goal of becoming self-reliant and that they would help Malawi boost its economy through the agriculture, tourism, and mining sectors. While in Saudi Arabia, the president was expected to witness the signing of a $20 m (MK 22 bn) loan agreement between Malawi and the Saudi Fund for Development for the construction of the Mangochi–Makanjira road. From Saudi Arabia, he proceeded to Cairo, Egypt, for the Intra-African Trade Fair on 13 November.

On 6 November, President Chakwera suspended all foreign trips by government officials, including himself. The announcement was made in a nationally televised address as part of what he called tough measures to heal the Southern African nation's economy. He also directed all ministers who were outside the country to return and said that the suspension would be in place until March 2024. He said that any travel deemed absolutely necessary during that period had to be submitted to his office for his personal authorisation. The president unveiled a range of austerity measures, including cutting by 50% fuel entitlements for cabinet ministers and senior government officials. These measures came in the midst of severe criticism that Chakwera was making frequent foreign trips, thereby depleting meagre forex. His announcement was meant to lead by example by curtailing his travel plans. As part of the measures, he also directed the minister of finance to include provisions for a reasonable wage increase for all civil servants in the mid-year budget review.

Socioeconomic Developments

On 29 January, Malawi *dropped on the HDI* despite having improved its position by five places in the 2020 Mo Ibrahim Index of African Governance. According to the report, Malawi faced challenges on human development especially in access to health and education, moving from position 23 in 2020 to 18 in 2022 due to higher scores in the areas of security and rule of law. Malawi underperformed on poverty reduction and social protection.

On 8 March, minister of finance and economic affairs Sosten Gwengwe *presented the 2023/24 national budget to the National Assembly*. It was pegged at MK 3.87 trillion, 35.7% higher than the previous year's MK 2.85 trillion budget, which had increased to MK 3.04 trillion by the end of the financial year on 31 March. The allocation of the Malawi Human Rights Commission (MHRC) was maintained at MK 1.375 bn and that of the Office of Ombudsmen at MK 1.254 bn. The allocation to the health sector was MK 283.5 bn, representing 10% of the national budget. Gwengwe sounded optimistic that Malawi Revenue Authority would achieve the MK 1.6 trillion target it had been tasked to collect.

Various *acts of legislation* kept parliament busy. On 12 April, parliament approved the long-awaited Disaster Risk Management Bill, which replaced the Disaster Relief Preparedness Act of 1991. The bill provided some ray of hope in terms of systematic response to disasters. On 14 June, President Chakwera assented to bills that were approved by parliament in April. The seven bills were Bill No. 1 of 2023: Malawi University of Science and Technology (Amendment), Bill No. 8 of 2023: Supplementary Appropriation (2022/2023), Bill No. 9 of 2023: Disaster Risk Management, Bill No. 10 of 2023: Financial Crimes (Amendment), Bill No. 12 of 2023: Defense Force, Bill No. 13 of 2023: Mines and Minerals, and Bill No. 41 of 2022: Press Trust Reconstruction (Amendment). Among other things, the Disaster Risk Management Bill sought to align the law with developments in the area of disaster preparedness, risk reduction, and response and recovery.

On 7 December, parliament passed the Ombudsman (Amendment) Bill 2023 after close to one and half hours of scrutiny. This bill sought to amend the Ombudsman Act (Cap. 3:07) in order to clarify and strengthen the legal framework of the jurisdiction and mandate of the Ombudsman. Minister of justice Titus Mvalo said that the bill would clarify the functions and powers of the Ombudsman by, among other things, aligning them with the broad jurisdiction and mandate conferred by Section 123 of the Constitution and enhancing them generally to ensure the effective discharge of the Ombudsman's mandate, conferred under Section 123. On 17 December, parliament introduced Bill No. 22 for the Data Protection Act, 2023. In particular, the bill sought to provide a comprehensive legal framework for the regulation of personal data in compliance with internationally accepted principles of data protection. Notably, the bill would require the registration of data controllers and processors of significant importance.

On 23 December, parliament also approved Bill No. 23 of 2023: Persons with Disabilities. The bill repealed the Disability Act of 2012 and the Handicapped Persons Act of 1971. The new legislation would regulate all matters regarding disabled people in Malawi. Presenting the bill to the House, the minister of gender, Jean Sendeza, said the Handicapped Persons Act was outdated, having been enacted in 1971, before the current constitution was adopted.

The year witnessed *high inflation*. The year-on-year inflation rate for January 2023 stood at 25.9%, up from 24.5% in December 2022. Food and non-food inflation rates were at 30.5% and 20.40%, respectively. The national month-to-month inflation rate for January stood at 4%, the food inflation rate was at 4.7%, and the non-food inflation rate was at 12.4%. Headline inflation for the first half of 2023 averaged 27.48%, an increase from an average of 16.25% recorded in the corresponding period in 2022. Average food inflation for the first half of 2023 was 34.75%, up from an average of 20.47% recorded in the corresponding period in 2022. Non-food inflation increased to an average of 19% in the first half of 2023, from an average of 12.03% in the corresponding period in 2022.

Total treasury bill applications in October stood at MK 25.72 bn, and MK 25.79 bn was allotted, representing a 0.27% rejection rate. In October, the government conducted several treasury note auctions, including two-year, three-year, five-year, seven-year and ten-year treasury notes. The auctions raised a total of MK 156.34 bn from MK 156.34 bn in applications, resulting in a nil rejection rate. The weighted average yields were 26.75%, 28.00%, 30.00%, 32.00%, and 33.00% respectively. Total maturities (for October) stood at MK 116.44 bn, resulting in a net withdrawal of MK 84.78 bn.

Tobacco sales went up during the year: Malawi recorded a 55% increase in 2023 season. Figures from the market regulator, the Tobacco Commission (TC), indicated that the country had realised a total of $282.618 m, up from $182 m previous year. With Malawi needing $250 m every month for imports, the $282 m realised in 2023 was enough to keep the wheels of the economy running for 34 days. Tobacco leaf fetched an average price of $2.35/kg, compared with $2.14/kg in 2022. However, the 2023 tobacco selling season was a little shorter than last year's, with a total of 17 weeks compared with last year's 20 weeks.

The policy rate was hiked during the year. On 5 May, the monetary policy committee of Reserve Bank of Malawi raised the policy rate to 24% from 23%. The central bank kept its benchmark lending rate unchanged at 24.0% up to 27 October, citing a recent moderation in inflationary pressures and weak domestic economic growth.

The year also witnessed *the devaluation of the Malawian kwacha*. The Reserve Bank of Malawi devalued the national currency by 44% in November 2023; as of 24 November, it was trading at MK 1,685/$1, compared with MK 1,116 in late October. The bank stated that the devaluation of the kwacha followed an assessment conducted that, among other factors, indicated that 'supply–demand imbalances remained in the market despite adjustments of the exchange rate through the auction system'.

Fuel and gas prices were also increased during the year. On 10 November, the Malawi Energy Regulatory Authority (MERA) announced an increase in fuel prices from MK 1,746 to MK 2,530 per litre for petrol and from MK 1,920 to MK 2,734 per litre for diesel. MERA made the announcement after the Reserve Bank of Malawi had announced the 44% devaluation of the kwacha. MERA considered recent trends in world petroleum products prices as well as exchange rate movements and their impact on energy prices. MERA also increased average electricity tariffs from MK 123.26/kilowatt-hour (kWh) to MK 173.70/kWh, effective 10 November. The electricity tariff was also hiked more than 44% following the fall of the Malawi kwacha against the US dollar. The price of paraffin was increased from MK 1,261 to MK 1,910 per litre.

Prices of farm produce also went up during the year. Retail maize prices experienced a 5% increase in October, rising from MK 692 in the final week of September to MK 732 in the final week of October. The increase occurred at the onset of the lean season, represented a notably smaller change compared with the same period in the previous season (when prices increased by 23%, but from a much higher base). Consistent with the typical trend, Southern Region recorded the highest monthly average maize retail price of MK 775/kg, with the peak weekly retail price (MK 883/kg) noted in Luchenza in Thyolo. Central region maintained relatively stable prices, with the monthly average settling at MK 710/kg. Two markets in Central region even recorded a modest price decline: Mitundu in Lilongwe (4%) and Mchinji (1%). This could be attributed to local availability of maize as farmers were releasing previously withheld stock to use in purchasing farm inputs, and to pay for labour as they prepared for the upcoming farming season.

Labour disputes intensified during the year. The Civil Servants Trade Union (CSTU) and Teachers Union of Malawi (TUM) cancelled their nationwide strikes planned for 9 January following negotiations with government. The government agreed to salary increments effective April. The unions had originally announced their intention to strike following the collapse of negotiations on 16 December 2022. On 16 October, the Professional Drivers Union of Malawi and Truck Drivers Union of Malawi called for a nationwide strike over salary and welfare grievances. It was expected that transport and freight disruptions would be likely during the work stoppage. On 14 December, over a thousand workers marched and staged a sit-in at Electricity Supply Corporation of Malawi (ESCOM) operations in the cities of Blantyre, Lilongwe, and Mzuzu to protest a pittance wage offer. ESCOM offered a 10% increase but workers said that they wanted a 44% rise to protect the value of their wages against the increasing cost of living after the devaluation of the kwacha by the Reserve Bank.

Mauritius

Roukaya Kasenally

This was an important political year, with a number of populist measures passed by the current regime despite a fragile economy exacerbated by the Russia–Ukraine war, monetary policy tightening, and elevated inflation. According to the official estimates, the Mauritian economy achieved recover to its pre-pandemic level in 2023, with GDP forecasted to grow at 7.1% (Statistics Mauritius), driven mainly by the tourism sector.

Domestic Politics

All political party leaders had their sights set on the electoral agenda as the country prepared itself for the scheduled election in 2024. Three of the mainstream political parties – the Mauritius Labour Party (MLP), the Mouvement Militant Mauricien (MMM), and the Parti Mauricien Social Démocrate (PMSD) – launched their alliance for the forthcoming election. This was the first time in post-independence Mauritian politics that these three political parties had rallied together to fight a general election. Two of the leaders – Navin Ramgoolam (MLP) and Paul Berenger

(MMM) – were in their late seventies, and it was widely speculated that the 2024 general election would be the last one they would contest. However, neither party initiated the process of identifying or nominating a new leader. In fact, the process of succession planning within Mauritian political parties was practically non-existent.

An important win for the prime minister and his ruling party was that all electoral petitions that were filed following the 2019 general election were either rejected by the Supreme Court or ultimately withdrawn by the applicants.

The island's democratic credentials continued to plummet. The Varieties of Democracy (V-Dem) 2023 report classified Mauritius as 'a democracy in steep decline' while the International Institute for Democracy and Electoral Assistance's (IDEA's) Global State of Democracy 2023 categorised Mauritius as one of the six countries in Africa that had experienced 'the greatest number of declines over the last five years'. Institutions had been completely taken over by a rapidly expanding executive, in the process eroding the checks on the exercise of executive power. This was quite evident in parliament, where the speaker of the house – a political nominee of the current prime minister – systematically silenced opposition members: during the 30 parliamentary sittings held between 28 March to 20 December 2023, there were 35 expulsions of opposition MPs by the speaker. Parliamentary mechanisms such as the Private Notice Question (PNQ) and Prime Minister's Question Time (PMQT) were systematically distorted to the advantage of government MPs. The long-overdue municipal elections (last held in 2015) were once again postponed, with the amendment of the Local Government Act to extend the term of the current councillors by two years. This meant that the councillors had been in office for ten years without going through an election.

Two key constitutional positions, the Director of Public Prosecutions (DPP) and the Commissioner of Police (CP), were at loggerheads, with potentially grave implications for law and order in Mauritius. The original bone of contention was the decision of the DPP not to contest a magistrate's decision to allow the conditional release of a well-known anti-government political activist, Bruneau Laurette. In a public declaration, the CP accused the DPP of creating an 'evil precedent' and subsequently filed a constitutional complaint in the Mauritian Supreme Court against the DPP. This was the first time that such an open and hostile confrontation had occurred between these two offices, and it had not been resolved at the time of writing. The DPP is considered one of the most important guardrails of judicial independence, as the office is vested with a series of powers when it comes to criminal proceedings under the Constitution of Mauritius (Section 72, 3). However, there have been numerous attempts to bring the Office of the DPP under executive control – namely in 2017 with the proposed (but aborted) Prosecution Commission and more recently with the enacted Financial Crimes Commission (2023).

The economy deteriorated because of the introduction of a number of *populist* measures that depleted the treasury and the Bank of Mauritius reserves.

The 2023/24 budget introduced for the first time an 'independence allowance' of 20,000 Mauritian rupees (MUR), which was made available to all those turning 18 between 1 January and 31 December 2023, amounting to some 15,000 beneficiaries. It was not clear whether this was a one-off or a recurrent feature. The measure attracted a fair amount of criticism and was seen as a means of enticing first-time voters in a pre-election year. Another promised *populist* measure since the current government took office has been the staggered increase in universal pension – automatically given to any Mauritian citizen of 60 years and above. The latest statistics suggest that some 250,000 beneficiaries are entitled to the pension, representing just under a quarter of the population. A number of key parastatal institutions, such as the Central Electricity Board and the State Trading Corporation, accumulated combined deficits amounting to MUR 10 bn in 2023, thereby putting at risk the functioning of core industries.

A culture of censorship, control, and surveillance deepened in the country, with a number of institutions such as public universities, segments of the media, and certain civil society organisations practising self-censorship. Reporters Without Borders (2023) emphasised what it considered 'a media landscape that is highly polarised' and an increase in 'online attacks against journalists'. A measure that has cast a chilling effect on civil liberties and political rights is the mandatory re-registration for all SIM card holders, with failure to do so resulting in automatic deactivation. It is estimated that there are some 2.5 m active SIM cards for a population of 1.3 m in the country. The new Mauritius National Identity Card (MNIC) 3.0 is being tested and finalised, making the island one of the most digitalised within the African continent. The MNIC will cost the public purse MUR 378 m.

Foreign Affairs

Mauritius is in the middle of the Indian Ocean – courted because of its position in a region at the centre of a highly contested game among key global players. The outbreak of war between Israel and Palestine and an increased number of attacks by the Yemen-based Houthi rebels in the Red Sea have further emphasised the need for maritime security and the management of territorial waters and trade routes in the Indian Ocean region. The changing geopolitical and geo-security situation weighed significantly on islands in the Indian Ocean to act strategically – Mauritius included.

Relations between Mauritius and India continued to strengthen. Mauritius was invited as a 'guest country' to the G20 Summit hosted by India. The conspiracy of silence around one of Mauritius's outer islands – Agalega – continued regarding what exactly the infrastructure being built there will be used for. Satellite imagery showed a three-kilometre airstrip and a deep-water jetty. Construction on the island started in 2019, and the inauguration of the infrastructure was expected to take place in early 2024. The development was fully funded by the government of India. The governments of both India and Mauritius insisted that Agalega would not become a military base but rather that the development was meant to facilitate security and safety manoeuvres in the waters of the Indian Ocean and to help Mauritius manage its extensive Exclusive Economic Zone of some 2.3 m square kilometres.

Following the signing of the Comprehensive Economic Cooperation and Partnership Agreement in 2021, Mauritian exports to India increased from $1 m in 2022 to $3.7 m in 2023. Despite this seeming to indicate a win–win situation for Mauritius and India, there are growing concerns that Mauritius is *aligning itself too closely with India*.

Discussions with the UK government on the return of the Chagos Archipelago continued. HRW launched a scathing report in which it referred to the forced displacement of the Chagos people and ongoing abuses as 'crimes against humanity committed by a colonial power against an indigenous people'. A number of rounds of negotiation were conducted between Mauritius and the UK. In a statement made in the UK parliament, the minister for overseas territories, commonwealth, energy, climate and environment had the following to say on the Chagos progress: 'These discussions have built understanding between the two sides, and covered issues relating to ensuring the continued effective operation of the joint UK/US military base on Diego Garcia; resettlement of the former inhabitants of the Chagos Archipelago; strengthening our cooperation on a range of issues such as environmental and marine protection, improving security and tackling illegal activities in the region'. Unfortunately, there was hardly any progress on these fronts. In fact, there has been a growing reluctance to commit from the UK, in light of certain opinions formulated by the former prime minister of the UK, Boris Johnson, that 'Mauritius is a close ally of China'.

Following the signature of the first continental Free Trade Agreement (FTA) between China and Mauritius in 2021, the inaugural Mauritius–China FTA Cooperation Forum was held in Mauritius, allowing the FTA to be further fine-tuned. The Chinese shipping company Huanghai Shipbuilding Company delivered a 8,200 deadweight tonnage multi-purpose vessel to Mauritius. The vessel, costing approximately $20 m, was fully financed by the Mauritius Shipping Corporation and will be used for transportation within the islands of Mauritius.

Mauritius hosted a number of key conferences, such as the third Africa Partnership Conference (APC) and third Ministerial Conference on Maritime Security and Safety. Relations with other traditional diplomatic and economic partners such as the EU, France, and Japan remained cordial.

Socioeconomic Developments

GDP growth in 2023 was sustained by the 31% annual growth in tourism, the 28.6% growth in construction, the 10.4% growth in agriculture, and the 4.8% growth in the financial services sector. The number of tourist arrivals for 2023 surpassed expectations, and was estimated to have reached 1.3 m. This seems to be a commendable feat, although the footprint that such an increase in tourism will entail in terms of the island's environmental and ecological conditions is worrying.

The investment rate increased slightly in 2023, reaching 21.7% of GDP, with private sector investment growing significantly by 16.2% in 2023 compared with 9.6% in 2022, reaching MUR 109 bn. On the other hand, public sector investment stood at MUR 32.8 bn in 2023. The 'building and construction work' segment consumed MUR 94 bn, out of which MUR 39.9 bn went to residential buildings – including social housing projects initiated during the year.

On 21 July, Standard & Poor's (S&P) reaffirmed the 'investment grade' status of Mauritius, underscoring the importance of the country as a safe and an attractive jurisdiction for attracting global business inflows. Meanwhile on 25 July, Moody's upgraded the scorecard-indicated outcome of Mauritius to Baa1–Baa3 (it was previously Baa3–Ba2) based on the economic growth achieved by the country in 2022 as well as improved fiscal consolidation.

Final consumption expenditure of households and government, the major component of expenditure on GDP, increased by 8.6% to MUR 534.3 bn in 2023. The final consumption expenditure of households grew by 2.6% compared with 3.3% in 2022, while that of government declined by 1.5% after growth of 6.4% in 2022. The headline inflation rate was put at 7.0% in 2023, compared with 10.8% in 2022 (Statistics Mauritius), largely reflecting the still-elevated costs of energy and commodity imports. From 2022 onwards, the Bank of Mauritius embarked on tightening its monetary policy stance by increasing the key repo rate to 4.5%. This rate was maintained throughout 2023 and contributed to balancing the macroeconomic fundamentals of inflation and GDP growth.

Total export proceeds for 2023 stood at MUR 104 bn (a decrease of 1.4% from 2022) while total imports amounted to MUR 284 bn (a decrease of 2.7% from 2022). The trade deficit for 2023 was put at MUR 180 bn, around 3.4% lower than the deficit of MUR 186.6 bn in 2022. On the fiscal front, government debt stood at 69.6% of GDP at the end of September compared with 70.6% in June. Public sector gross debt improved to 79.6% of GDP in September compared with 81.2% in June. According to the IMF, further fiscal consolidation promoting economic growth was needed, alongside strengthening monetary policy effectiveness.

As economic activity picked up in 2023, the unemployment rate continued to drop, standing at 6.3% at the end of the third quarter. The youth unemployment rate decreased in the third quarter to 17.8%, from 24.8% in the corresponding quarter of 2022. In July, the monthly minimum wage of MUR 11,575 was boosted by a monthly allowance of MUR 3,425 (MUR 2,000 + MUR 1,425 as top-up) financed from the Contribution Sociale Généralisée, introduced in 2020 for the pooling of pension contributions from employer and employee. In December, the government announced that the National Minimum Wage payable to full-time employees would increase to MUR 16,500 monthly from January 2024.

Gender inclusion remains one of the Achilles' heels of the Mauritian socio-economic system, despite some important gains. The national budget 2023/24 announced that all listed companies must have a minimum of 25% women on their boards. Mauritius moved up seven places in the Global Gender Gap Index 2023, ranked at 98th. The LGBTQ+ community witnessed a major victory following a decision by the Supreme Court to decriminalise consensual sodomy. Prior to that, it was an offence under Section 250 of the Mauritian Criminal Code which goes back to 1838.

The Mauritian education system finally realigned itself to its pre-Covid-19 structure. The University of Mauritius – one of the most established public universities – made its way, for the first time, into the Times Higher Education World Ranking 2023. It ranked between 1001st and 1200th out of 2,325 universities on a range of measures. The quality of education, especially higher education, remains satisfactory, as evidenced by the number of both public and private universities on the island. The country maintained its third place in Africa on the World Education Forum.

Mauritius was ranked 106th out of 193 countries most vulnerable to climate disaster risk by the World Risk Report 2023. In view of the ongoing vulnerability of the country as a member of the group known as small island developing states (SIDS), MUR 1.6 bn was earmarked in the 2023/24 national budget for the setting up of a National Environment and Climate Change Fund (NECCF). A delegation led by the minister of environment attended COP28. Mauritius has a particular stake in the Loss and Damage Fund as one of the SIDS.

Mozambique

Lorraine Dongo

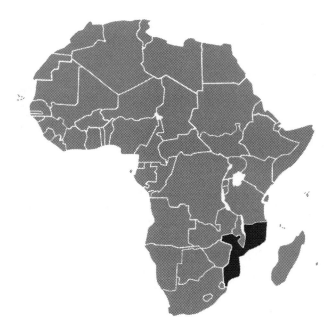

Mozambique navigated a year marked by critical municipal elections amid fraud allegations, challenging its democratic integrity. Efforts towards economic stabilisation saw the resolution of the 'hidden debt' scandal and the initiation of a sovereign wealth fund, reflecting a stride towards financial transparency. The devastation wrought by Tropical Cyclone Freddy highlighted vulnerabilities and deficiencies in disaster response mechanisms. Internationally, Mozambique balanced historical alliances and complex geopolitical interests, particularly in its active role within the UNSC. The year underscored Mozambique's journey towards reform and governance improvement, and the ongoing struggle with security concerns in Cabo Delgado against a backdrop of socioeconomic challenges.

Domestic Politics

In October, Mozambique held its sixth *municipal elections*, critical for its democratic progress, despite facing allegations of *electoral fraud, violence, and misconduct*. These claims, raised by the Mais Integridade consortium and echoed by civil society and opposition parties, particularly Renamo, raised serious doubts regarding the elections' integrity. Renamo's leader, Ossufo Momade, contested the official results, citing discrepancies, and urged peaceful protests and legal action instead of resorting to armed conflict. Former National Elections Commission president Brazão Mazula also criticised the electoral process, highlighting disorganisation and potential irregularities.

The controversies triggered *protests* and calls for *electoral reform*, particularly after Frelimo claimed victory in 56 municipalities, a figure reduced from 64 due to court-ordered *recounts and reruns*, with Renamo victorious in four. These disputes also involved Paulo Vahanle, Nampula's mayor and a Renamo member, who was suspended over allegations of misconduct, including organising a protest that had been deemed risky, accentuating tensions between Renamo and the Frelimo-led government. Amid these events, a disagreement emerged over Frelimo's proposal to postpone *district elections*, opposed by Renamo, which emphasised constitutional adherence and governance concerns. This debate shed light on Mozambique's *political complexities* as the country moves towards further decentralisation.

The 2024 *general elections* were slated for 9 October, with anticipation surrounding Frelimo's candidate selection given President Nyusi's ineligibility for re-election due to *term limits*. The recent *electoral controversies* have shaped the political climate, posing challenges to Mozambique's democratic evolution and future election integrity. The situation highlighted the imperative for *reforms, transparency, and accountability* to ensure the electoral process reflects the will of the Mozambican people, as the country stands at a critical juncture in its political journey.

Mozambique's *civic space* deteriorated from 'obstructed' to 'repressive' according to CIVICUS, while Freedom House categorised the country as 'partially free' in relation to *freedom of expression*. This decline was linked to incidents of *police violence* following the 11 October municipal elections, including the tragic killing of a 16-year-old in Chiúre, condemned by Amnesty International as a breach of international human rights standards.

The aggressive *police response* to *peaceful protests*, utilising tear gas and live ammunition, exemplified issues of *excessive force*, prompting calls from Amnesty International for investigations and the release of detained opposition supporters. Concerns were raised regarding a *proposed draft law on non-profit organisations*, criticised for potential government interference, which threatens freedom of assembly and association under the pretext of countering money laundering and the financing of terrorism. Notable incidents of police using lethal force and arbitrary detentions were reported during various public gatherings, such as the funeral procession of Mozambican rap star Edson da Luz and a health fair held by medical doctors, alongside ongoing kidnappings with alleged police involvement. Despite criticism by the attorney-general regarding police and judicial complicity in these kidnappings, resolutions to the cases remained elusive. In a specific instance of public dissent, residents of *Ressano Garcia* protested on 8 July against the police's inadequate crime control efforts, accusing them of complicity in rampant murders and kidnappings. The police's violent dispersal of the protest, using weapons of war, highlighted broader dissatisfaction with police conduct in Mozambique.

Further scrutiny came from the *Centre for Public Integrity*'s (CIP's) critical review on 19 April of annual report of the *Mozambique attorney-general* (AG) to parliament. The CIP highlighted shortcomings in the AG's report, particularly the inadequate coverage of human rights abuses, gender-based violence in Cabo Delgado, environmental crimes, and corruption, indicating leniency towards serious crimes, including financing of terrorism and corruption in the extractive industry.

Moreover, on 10 June, the *Center for Democracy and Human Rights* (CDD) initiated legal action against the *president of the Matola Municipal Council, Calisto Cossa*, for a contentious public tender awarded on 31 May for an Integrated Municipal Management System (SIGEM), valued at 518,503,427.42 meticais (MZN). The tender, awarded to the MCNet (Mozambique Community Network)/Axis Solutions consortium and reported by 'Jornal Notícias', was challenged by the CDD for its lack of transparency and alleged legal violations, raising concerns about the misuse of public funds. These developments painted a grim picture of Mozambique's civic environment, where government and police actions severely limited freedoms. The fight against corruption, human rights abuses, and mismanagement of public funds called for more effective and transparent governance.

In June, Mozambique marked a historic step towards lasting peace with the closure of *Renamo*'s final *military base in Gorongosa, Sofala Province*, as part of the *Disarmament, Demobilization, and Reintegration* (DDR) process. This significant event, attended by Mozambique's President Filipe Nyusi, Renamo leader Ossufo Momade, and international figures, symbolised a commitment to peace and sustainable development. The closure event on 15 June in Gorongosa's Nota neighbourhood brought together notable figures, highlighting a shared resolve towards reconciliation and national healing. This progress, while marking the end of a long-standing armed struggle, did not address the ongoing conflict in Cabo Delgado, where Islamist terrorists continued their assaults. However, it opened new avenues for addressing such security challenges, promising a new era of peace and prosperity for Mozambique.

On 29 September, President Nyusi commemorated the *90th birthday of Mozambique's first president, Samora Machel*, with a message of resilience against terrorism. Drawing parallels between Machel's anti-colonial leadership and the current fight against terrorism in Cabo Delgado, Nyusi reaffirmed the nation's commitment to unity, peace, democracy, and wellbeing, echoing Machel's ideals. This came amid ongoing efforts, supported by Rwanda and the SADC, to counter the insurgency in Cabo Delgado, highlighting Mozambique's enduring spirit in confronting contemporary security challenges.

Mozambique saw *security improvements*, notably in the *north*, despite ongoing conflict with the *ISIS-linked group al-Shabaab*. Joint efforts by *Mozambican, Rwandan, and SADC forces* facilitated the return of displaced persons, though challenges such as access to basic needs and infrastructure damage persisted. The killing of an alleged al-Shabaab leader failed to halt the group's activities, signalling a persistent threat.

Human rights concerns arose over the conduct of *the Southern African Development Community Mission in Mozambique* (SAMIM) forces and national security practices, even as Mozambique's global standing improved with its UNSC non-permanent membership. Military interventions in the *Cabo Delgado insurgency* achieved some mitigation, hinting at possible investment resurgences, despite corruption scandals and the mishandling of corpses by forces attracting criticism. Future tasks for Mozambique include managing the terrorist threat, improving governance and transparency, and leveraging natural resources. The potential restart of *TotalEnergies' LNG projects* depends on improved security and humanitarian conditions, offering economic recovery hope amid ongoing insurgency risks, highlighting the need for sustainable development and adherence to human rights and law.

A major legislative amendment extended *compulsory military service*, from two years to a mandatory five for general troops and up to six for special forces, to enhance the armed forces' capability in responding to threats such as al-Shabaab. Defence minister Cristóvão Chume highlighted the necessity of the amendment on 15 November, aiming to reduce foreign military dependence. However, this extension sparked debate over the *impact on youth employment* and the *absence of reintegration strategies*. HRW emphasised the risk of rights violations, urging Mozambique to ensure respectful implementation of the reform. The law, supported by Frelimo and the Movimento Democrático de Moçambique (MDM) but opposed by Renamo, signified a shift towards national defence self-reliance, with effects on the *al-Shabaab conflict* and wider societal implications.

Concurrently, Mozambique pursued peace through a dialogue workshop on 29–30 November, emphasising *interreligious dialogue* (IRD) in conflict resolution in *northern Mozambique*. Organised by the King Abdullah bin Abdulaziz International Centre for Interreligious and Intercultural Dialogue (KAICIID) and partners, the workshop brought together religious, youth, and women's leaders.

On 2 October, Mozambique's economy and finance minister Max Tonela, alongside deputy attorney-general Angelo Matusse, announced the cancellation of *over $500 m in secret debt* with Swiss Bank UBS, which had absorbed Credit Suisse. These loans were linked to a corruption scandal involving state-owned companies borrowing around $2 bn for security services, in dubious circumstances. Finalised on 30 September, the deal significantly reduced *Mozambique's debt burden*, stemming from loans in 2013 and 2014 intended for national security but embroiled in bribery and mismanagement allegations. Despite the cancellation of Credit Suisse's remaining $450 m debt, Mozambique retained the right to pursue legal action against Privinvest, VTB, and Portuguese bank BCP for their roles in the scandal. Legal proceedings, particularly against *Privinvest*, are ongoing.

In May, Mozambique's parliament unanimously approved the *Cashew Law*, shifting from the *World Bank*'s late-1990s deregulation policies. The law raises the surtax on raw cashew exports from 18% to 22% to boost domestic processing and support over 1.4 m smallholder farmers. Furthermore, on 13 December, Mozambique's law-makers approved the creation of a *sovereign wealth fund* to manage LNG *export revenues*, projected to surpass $6 bn annually by the 2040s. Tonela announced the fund as a key step towards economic recovery from the 2016 hidden debt scandal, aiming for transparency and sustainable development. With an expected accumulation of about $91.7 bn from LNG exports, the fund will allocate 60% of revenues to the state budget and save the remaining 40% for long-term security. The governing party Frelimo supported the law, while opposition parties called for greater transparency and inclusivity in the fund's management to ensure equitable benefit distribution. These measures, from resolving the hidden debt scandal to enhancing the cashew industry and establishing a sovereign wealth fund, accentuate Mozambique's strategic efforts to secure financial recovery, transparency, and sustainable economic development.

Foreign Affairs

In January, Mozambique began its term as a non-permanent member of the UNSC, underlining its global influence. By March, it had made history by assuming the *council's presidency*. Led by Pedro Comissário, Mozambique's UN representative, along with foreign minister Verónica Macamo and President Nyusi, discussions focused on women in peace and security, and the global terrorism threat. They spotlighted global challenges in Afghanistan, DRC, South Sudan, Syria, and Sudan, proposing further discussions on Ukraine. This was significant, as Mozambique has grappled with Islamic militancy since 2017, aiming to prioritise 'the Africanization of terrorism'. Reflecting the intricate balancing act that smaller nations must perform in the geopolitical arena, Mozambique abstained from condemning *Russia's actions in Ukraine. Mozambique's historical ties with Russia*, dating back to the liberation struggle against colonialism, further illuminate the complex interplay of past alliances and present foreign policy.

On 17 February, during her New York visit, Verónica Macamo emphasised the critical role of the *Northern Integrated Development Agency* (ADIN) in combating terrorism in Cabo Delgado. She stressed the importance of integrating *armed interventions* with *reconstruction and development* efforts that prioritise young people, women, and the displaced. Macamo noted a decrease in terrorist activities but highlighted the ongoing challenges faced by approximately *1.4 m displaced individuals*. This discussion took place following her meeting with Amina Mohammed, the UN deputy secretary-general.

Simultaneously, in a move intended to bolster regional stability, the EU Council committed *€20 m to support the Rwanda Defence Force's operations in Cabo Delgado*, which have been ongoing since July 2021. This funding, aimed at sustaining Rwanda's deployment, will cover essential equipment and strategic airlift expenses, reinforcing collective efforts to combat terrorism in the region. Further reinforcing international military support, the *43rd SADC Summit in Luanda* on 17 August resolved to extend the regional military mission in Mozambique for another year to continue addressing the Cabo Delgado insurgency, highlighting the sustained *regional commitment to peace and stability* since the mission's inception in 2021 with approximately 2,000 troops.

On 13 July, the EU Training Mission in Mozambique (EUTM MOZ) hosted the UK Foreign Affairs Select Committee at the *Katembe Training Camp*. Commodore de Brito briefed British MP Alicia Kearns and her committee on the mission's initiatives, which are focused on strengthening *Mozambique's armed forces* and securing the region of Cabo Delgado. The visit was part of the UK's counter-terrorism inquiry, enhancing its understanding of Mozambique's defence and financial strategies against *terrorism* and efforts to address *conflict-related sexual violence*. Subsequently, on 15–16 August, General Michael Langley from the US visited Mozambique to discuss strengthening *US–Mozambique security ties* through an integrated approach aimed at stabilising *northern Mozambique* and resolving the ongoing conflict in Cabo Delgado. This visit aligned with the *US Strategy to Prevent Conflict and Promote Stability*, which includes a comprehensive ten-year regional plan.

The 2023 *Africa Amnesty Month*, marked by events on 11–12 September in Maputo, aimed to promote peace and disarmament across Africa, facilitated by collaborations between UNREC (the UN Regional Economic Communities), the AU, and the Mozambican government, with notable attendees including ambassador Ewumbue-Monomo and AU high representative Mohamed Ibn Chambas. Later in the year, during *transnational crimes debates* at the UN headquarters in New York in December, Macamo addressed Mozambique's humanitarian situation and resilience efforts. Moreover, from 11 to 13 December, French minister Chrysoula Zacharopoulou visited Mozambique, announcing an additional *€10 m in support for Cabo Delgado*, further reinforcing France's *humanitarian commitment* to the region.

On 1 March, in Rome, Mozambique's agriculture minister, Celso Correia, met with FAO director-general Qu Dongyu, emphasising Mozambique's commitment to *sustainable agriculture*. He outlined Mozambique's progress towards agricultural self-sufficiency, stressing the need for technology transfer and improved seed access post-floods. Correia reported a significant reduction in hunger, stating that less than 10% of the population was food insecure, with 90% having stable diets. He emphasised the importance of these achievements and advocated for long-term agricultural support. On 29 May, in Maputo, Vietnam's deputy minister of agriculture, Nguyen Quoc Tri, and Mozambique's Olegário dos Anjos Banze discussed expanding *agricultural cooperation* at the fourth Vietnam–Mozambique Intergovernmental Committee meeting. They focused on enhancing cashew processing, irrigation, and animal feed production, reflecting Mozambique's proactive approach to strengthening its agricultural sector and international partnerships.

On 4–6 April, in Maputo, President Nyusi and Zambian president Hakainde Hichilema discussed strengthening *bilateral ties*. A notable achievement was the revival of the *Mozambique–Zambia Permanent Mixed Commission*, which reached consensus on defence, security, and economic sectors. The talks resulted in agreements in the social communications sector, plans for direct flights between Maputo and Lusaka, and potential oil transport and railway projects. On 10 August, *Kenyan president William Ruto's visit to Mozambique* strengthened the diplomatic and economic relationship between the two countries. The visit resulted in the signing of *eight MoUs* spanning legal assistance, training, investment, the blue economy, and driving licence recognition, emphasising the countries' commitment to bilateral cooperation.

In May, during a New York visit, President Nyusi pledged to enhance *health cooperation* with Brazil, focusing on vaccine production in Africa. Nyusi discussed post-pandemic immunisation efforts with UN News and Brazil's foreign minister Mauro Vieira. He emphasised *Mozambique's Covid-19 strategy*, including the *'One district, one hospital' project* to improve health service access. Nyusi praised the partnership with *Brazil's Fiocruz* for setting up a pharmaceutical factory and training health professionals in Mozambique. Health minister Armindo Daniel Tiago's visit to Brazil in November aimed to advance Mozambique's healthcare sector, with a goal of establishing a hospital in every district by 2030. The visit resulted in agreements to enhance Mozambique's health services through Brazilian expertise in medical training, pharmaceuticals, and biotechnology. This collaboration aligned with the WHO's support for *Mozambique's health investment strategy*, focusing on developing modern healthcare facilities.

At the third *International Labour Conference* in Geneva on 12 June, Mozambique's labour minister, Margarida Talapa, highlighted the country's commitment to decent work, displaying a *revised Labour Law* submitted to parliament. Since 2017, Mozambique has launched employment policies, established support bodies for youth and technical education, and made strides in combating child labour with ILO support.

On 20 June, Belgium announced a €25 m *climate cooperation* programme with Mozambique, aiming to enhance the country's climate resilience, especially after *cyclones Idai, Kenneth, and Freddy*. This programme, *Belgium's first bilateral climate initiative*, allocates €2.5 m for *'loss and damage'* and implements a *'debt-for-climate swap'* cancelling €2.4 m of Mozambique's debt for climate investments. Mozambique, along with Belgium and the *Africa Carbon Markets Initiative*, is developing a carbon credit regulatory framework, aiming for 95 m annual carbon credits by 2030 from forestry and renewable sources. Announced on 15 March by Mozambique's Environment Ministry, this plan aimed to boost investments and community benefits, highlighting Mozambique's active role in global carbon markets and commitment to sustainable development through innovative financing.

During his African tour in August, *Indonesian president Joko Widodo* made his first visit to Mozambique, joining President Nyusi at the Mozambique National Festival of Culture. This event celebrated *cultural diversity and diplomacy*, featuring traditional ceremonies and performances by 1,500 Mozambican artists, and underscored the strong cultural and diplomatic ties between Indonesia and Mozambique, setting the stage for future collaborations. On 28 September, President Nyusi inaugurated the *Mozambique–China Cultural Center* at Eduardo Mondlane University, a significant development in Mozambique–China cultural relations. The $50 m centre, financed by the Chinese government and built by the Yanjian Group, includes a 1,500-seat auditorium among other facilities, coinciding with the tenth anniversary of the Belt and Road Initiative, symbolising deepening ties and mutual commitment to cultural exchange. Later in the year, on 27 November, *Japan's foreign minister Kamikawa Yoko* met with Mozambique's Verónica Macamo to further enhance relations within the *Free and Open Indo-Pacific Partnership*. Their discussions focused on economic, security, and cultural exchanges, notably Mozambique's engagement in the Osaka Expo and the promotion of 'Sake Yasuke', a cultural symbol made from rice grown in Cabo Delgado, further highlighting the dynamic and growing cultural diplomacy between Mozambique and its *Asian partners*.

President Nyusi addressed the *UN Climate Ambition Summit* in New York on 21 September, highlighting Mozambique's meteorological improvements, including *weather stations* in over half of its 154 districts. Nyusi discussed ongoing updates to *early warning systems*, including new radars supported by the AfDB, and emphasised regional collaboration and Mozambique's transition to *hydro and solar energy*. Later in the year, the first *Mozambique–EU Investment Forum* took place on 22–23 November, focusing on diversifying trade and investments with a particular emphasis on *clean energy*. *EU commissioner Kadri Simson*'s visit highlighted cooperation and energy initiatives, emphasising the EU's commitment to supporting Mozambique's energy infrastructure development.

In October, Italian prime minister Giorgia Meloni's visit to Mozambique, alongside President Nyusi and Eni's head Claudio Descalzi, focused on exploring the potential of Mozambique's *offshore gas fields*, especially the Coral field in the *Rovuma basin*. The discussions emphasised *Italy's investment* in Africa's *energy sector*, focusing on Mozambique's burgeoning LNG production through the Coral South floating LNG project, operated by Eni and its partners. Meloni emphasised Italy's commitment to allocating 70% of its climate fund to Africa, urging Italian businesses to explore broader investment opportunities in Mozambique. Aligned with these energy discussions, on 1 November, President Nyusi met India's minister of petroleum and natural gas, Hardeep Puri, in Maputo to discuss expanding *Indian investment in Mozambique*. They discussed sectors beyond energy, including agriculture, transport, and communications. Puri praised Nyusi's forward-looking approach and the mutual benefits of investment, including job creation. They explored opportunities in railway rolling stock and agriculture for both local consumption and export markets. Puri invited Mozambique to join the *Global Biofuel Alliance*, underscoring India's $11 bn investment in Mozambique's energy sector.

Caminhos de Ferro de Moçambique (CFM) announced the resumption, on 11 December, of the *Machipanda line* passenger service, enhancing *Zimbabwe–Mozambique* connectivity and reinforcing social ties between the two countries. This followed the rehabilitation and modernisation of the line inaugurated by presidents Nyusi and Emmerson Mnangagwa on 23 November.

On 13 November, *Mozambique's Frelimo and Angola's People's Movement for the Liberation of Angola* (MPLA) celebrated their strong political cooperation in Maputo, underscoring their historical ties and mutual development interests. The meeting emphasised organisational training and financial sustainability, honouring the unity forged during their independence struggles.

At *COP28* in Dubai (30 November to 13 December), President Nyusi emphasised the importance of meeting *Paris Agreement* goals. He urged for increased research funding and innovation to aid communities in adapting to climate change, and promoted the collaborative management of miombo forests, innovative finance models, and Mozambique's contribution to the *African carbon market*. Transport and communication minister Mateus Magala stressed the importance of sustainable practices in Mozambique's *transport sector*. He highlighted investments in resilient infrastructure and early warning systems and advocated for climate-compatible mobility and partnerships for green industrialisation, including Maputo's Bus Rapid Transport (BRT) and biofuel projects. One side event organised by Mozambique focused on *climate finance* challenges for *PALOP countries* (Países Africanos de Língua Oficial Portuguesa, the Portuguese-speaking African countries, namely Mozambique, Angola, Cabo Verde, Guinea-Bissau, and São Tomé and Príncipe) in addressing transparency, coordination, and capacity issues. Dr Albano Manjate, deputy director of monitoring and evaluation at the Ministry of Economy and Finance Mozambique and Focal Point for the Green Climate Fund (GCF), highlighted bureaucratic obstacles and the need for clear funding, displaying PALOP's commitment to improving climate finance through cooperation and innovation.

Socioeconomic Developments

In February, Mozambique was struck by *Tropical Cyclone Freddy*. Cyclone Freddy made landfall in *Inhambane* on 24 February and in Zambezia on 11 March, causing unprecedented rainfall and widespread destruction across multiple provinces, displacing thousands. On 15 March, the National Institute of Disaster Management (INGD) reported severe damage caused by Freddy's winds and rains, worsening existing floods since early February, especially in *Zambezia Province*.

Various stakeholders made substantial efforts in *response to the disaster*. President Nyusi allocated MZN 250 m for *Zambezia's recovery*, emphasising a broad rehabilitation strategy, and establishing a Technical-Scientific Commission for climate change. International support, including $150 m from the World Bank, a $5.75 m USAID grant, and $1.85 m in emergency aid from the EU, was crucial. UNICEF provided over $1.2 m in health and WASH (water, sanitation, and hygiene) supplies, supporting cholera vaccination campaigns, and ensuring educational continuity for affected students.

Cyclone Freddy worsened a *cholera outbreak*, spreading to *11 provinces* by May, with over 30,000 confirmed cases. The Ministry of Health's *mass vaccination campaigns*, supported by the WHO and UNICEF, were critical in mitigating the outbreak's impact. Various responses from the EU, UNICEF, and other partners provided crucial aid in water, sanitation, shelter, and education, highlighting the significance of coordinated action in crisis response.

In December, OCHA released 'Humanitarian Needs and Response Plan Mozambique', shedding light on the country's *humanitarian situation*. In 2023, Mozambique saw over 570,000 IDPs return to their places of origin, driven by improved security and the desire to rebuild livelihoods. However, around 670,000 IDPs in north-eastern Cabo Delgado and south-western Pemba, Metuge, and Mueda continued to face challenges, requiring ongoing humanitarian assistance. *The Legal Identity programme*, evaluated by minister Helena Mateus Kida in February, aimed to issue legal documents to 90,000 people in conflict-affected areas by September.

According to *official figures on the economy* accessed by Lusa News, Mozambique's state revenue surged by 12.7% to MZN 321,921 bn (€4,675 bn), driven primarily by increased corporate income tax. The Ministry of Economy and Finance reported that the state budget execution from January to December reached 92.2% of projected collection, nearly meeting the government's annual revenue projection of around MZN 349,114 m (€5,000 m). Taxes accounted for 90% of the total revenue collected in 2023, amounting to MZN 293,589 m (€4,263 m), reflecting a 11.6% increase but with an execution rate of only 93% of predictions. VAT generated almost MZN 63,455 m (€921.5 m), covering 69% of the yearly budget. The gross amount of VAT charged was MZN 75,994 m (€1,103 m), with MZN 12,539 m (€221.3 m) deducted in tax refunds. Corporate income tax increased by 74% to MZN 90,117 m (€1,308 m), exceeding the government's expectations by 115%. GDP expanded by 5.01%, up from 4.16% in 2022, with average annual inflation decreasing to 7.13%, a 3.17 percentage point decline from the previous year.

In March, Mozambique introduced a *visa exemption programme* for citizens of 29 countries under Decree No. 10/2023. Official government figures showed that between 1 May and 30 June, 12,325 foreigners entered Mozambique under this initiative. Notable beneficiaries during the initial 60-day period included visitors from the US (3,020), Portugal (1,509), China (1,332), the UK (1,327), Germany (739), and France (831).

On 17 January, the CIP criticised the *Single Salary Table* (TSU) for illogical salary setting and lack of study of financial sustainability, amid government financial struggles. Adjustments were made, but the CIP called for a complete overhaul. Journalist Fernando Lima suggested salvaging the TSU with substantial actions. Deputy minister of state administration and public service Inocêncio Impissa acknowledged the issues and promised reforms. An IMF report in November 2023 revealed that the TSU's projected cost had soared from MZN 19.2 bn to MZN 28.5 bn over 2022/23 due to rollout complexities. Errors in realigning public servants and underestimating costs led to reliance on expensive domestic financing. The government pledged reforms, including audits and fiscal adjustments, aiming to reduce the *wage bill* to 13% of GDP by 2024.

Despite some positive signs, Mozambique continued to grapple with *high poverty rates*, with per capita GDP growth at 1.3%. Poverty remained a pressing challenge, with 62% of Mozambicans living on less than $0.63 per day and 80.6% of children classified as poor. To address these issues, the World Bank supported Mozambique with 35 projects worth $6.2 bn, focusing on poverty reduction and sustainable development.

President Nyusi was honoured with Mozambique's national award for Disaster Risk Management, Environment, and Climate Change on 30 January, as reported by 'Banca e Seguros' magazine. This recognition, announced during the *International Conference on Sovereign Insurance against Disasters, Environment and Climate Change* in November, acknowledged Nyusi's 'selfless efforts in the fight against the harmful impacts of natural disasters' across Africa and Mozambique, and his success in 'institutional reforms' enhancing the country's resilience against extreme events.

The Netherlands Development Cooperation (SNV) convened a significant meeting in Maputo on 19 April, as part of the *BRILHO Energy Africa Programme*. The focus was on the *Gender Equality and Social Inclusion Seal* (GESIS) for Mozambique's off-grid energy sector, aimed at ensuring equitable energy access. Funded by the University of Sheffield's Economic and Social Research Council (ESRC) Impact Accelerator Accounts and supported by the UK and Sweden, GESIS, led by BRILHO alongside partners such as the Ministry of Mineral Resources and Energy (MIREME) and CESET (Community Energy Systems and Sustainable Energy Transitions), reflects a collective effort towards inclusive and just energy access, aligning with Mozambique's goal of achieving universal electricity access by 2030.

Transport and communications minister Mateus Magala highlighted Mozambique's plans to establish a *battery manufacturing facility* using its graphite resources for the *electric vehicle (EV) battery sector*. This initiative aligned with Mozambique's green mobility objectives and was aimed at reducing import reliance. During the *Mozambique–European Union Investment Forum* on 21–23 November, Max Tonela emphasised the importance of minerals such as graphite and lithium for electric motors and batteries. This reflected Mozambique's strategic focus on processing essential minerals to meet the rising demand for electric vehicles in the EU.

In November, minister for mineral resources and energy Carlos Zacarias reported considerable progress in the construction of Mozambique's largest gas-fired power plant, the *Temane Thermal Power Plant*. With completion rates at 60–65%, the project aimed to enhance Mozambique's energy autonomy and reduce cooking gas imports by around 70%.

The US, through the *Millennium Challenge Corporation* (MCC), pledged over $500 m to Mozambique in 2023 to stimulate economic growth and combat climate change impacts, primarily in Zambezia Province. This investment focused on critical infrastructure projects, including a new bridge over the Licungo River and improvements to rural transport networks. It was also intended to promote sustainable fishing practices and ecosystem management to support commercial agriculture and coastal livelihoods. Senior officials from both nations underscored the compact's significance for Mozambique's socioeconomic advancement and environmental resilience.

In September, the China Road and Bridge Corporation (CRBC) unveiled plans to construct a *light rail system* in Greater Maputo, slated to be operational in 2024. The project aimed to address transportation challenges in the capital by connecting the former Maputo International Fair site with the suburb of Zimpeto. The CRBC, with a track record of infrastructure projects in Mozambique, had conducted feasibility studies and public consultations for the initiative. Additionally, CRBC expressed interest in rehabilitating National Highway Number 1, with the first phase scheduled for May 2024.

Beginning in mid-2023, Mozambique's *healthcare system* faced significant disruptions due to *strikes* by doctors, nurses, and pharmacists demanding better salaries and working conditions linked to government pay reforms under an IMF-backed programme. These strikes nearly paralysed medical services in Maputo, leaving only maternity services operational. On 31 July, health minister Armindo Tiago announced a vaccination campaign targeting children aged 9 to 59 months in response to a *measles crisis*. This campaign focused on regions with the highest incidence rates, such as Niassa and Zambezia, as well as addressing vaccination gaps widened by Covid-19 and other public health emergencies. The campaign in light of concerns expressed during a high-level mission on 11 December by Gavi, the Vaccine Alliance, about Mozambique's limited access to *childhood vaccinations*, deeming the country highly vulnerable. In a meeting held in Maputo with President Nyusi, Gavi head David Marlow stressed the need for comprehensive immunisation efforts, considering challenges such as cyclone disruptions to health systems.

On 25 July, Saíde Júnior, the financial administrator of Aeroportos de Moçambique, announced the planned reopening of the *Mocímboa da Praia airfield* in Cabo Delgado, closed due to terrorist activities, by the first quarter of the following year. The reopening, after a three-year hiatus, was intended to drive socioeconomic development by restoring a vital transportation link within the province and to other regions. This development, expected to require two months of rehabilitation work, followed improved security conditions in an area significantly affected by conflict and displacement since 2017.

During a visit on 23–28 July, an EU delegation assessed the impact of EU financial assistance, emphasising the importance of the *EU–Mozambique partnership*, budget support, and the monitoring of human rights and political freedoms. The EU has allocated €428 m for 2021–24 through various budgetary instruments to support Mozambique in areas such as green growth, youth development, and governance. The delegation also highlighted Mozambique's *youth potential* and encouraged investment attraction through the European Fund for Sustainable Development Plus (EFSD+).

In September, Thai Mozambique Logística (TML) announced a $500 m investment to begin constructing the *Macuse port and rail link project* in mid-2024. The unveiling occurred on 11 November in Quelimane, during the launch ceremony for the Macuse–Chitima railway-port complex project, with a budget exceeding MZN 2.7 bn. Shareholders of TML had already secured MZN 500 m for the port's construction. The initial phase was to cover 2.4 kilometres on the Macuse side and 2.9 kilometres on the Supinho side. It will have the capacity to export 2 m tons of Portucel wood, handle ships of up to 60,000 tons, employ 8,000 Mozambicans, and include facilities such as a logistics service park and a fuel supply terminal. Manuel Latifo, representing the shareholders, mentioned that the resettlement of 70 affected families would be completed by February 2024. Chawal Naparia, president of the Zambezia Business Council, stressed the importance of local companies as primary suppliers to the harbour operators.

In October, Mateus Magala announced a $290 m investment for the *Beira Port* during the Beira Corridor Business Forum. This investment was slated to triple the port's container handling capacity and enhance cargo facilities over the next

15 years, contingent on market trends. The plan included vital enhancements such as dredging the port's access channel and rehabilitating the Machipanda railway line, improving connections with Zimbabwe.

Furthering its commitment to port development, the government revealed plans, as reported by 360 Mozambique on 22 November, for a substantial investment exceeding $2 bn in the *Port of Maputo*. This investment, currently under negotiation with the Maputo Port Development Company (MPDC), was projected to significantly expand the port's handling capacity, contributing over $8 bn to the state over 25 years. The expansion aligned with a broader vision to upgrade infrastructure, promote industrialisation, and stimulate economic activity along transport corridors. Additionally, August 2023 marked the 120th anniversary of the Port of Maputo, celebrated under President Nyusi's leadership, accentuating the port's remarkable growth from managing 5 m tons of cargo in 2003 to 27 m tons in 2022.

During the November and December *anti-domestic violence campaign*, the project "Community Leaders Are Allies in a Solidarity Movement for Gender Equality and Women's Rights to End Early Unions in Mozambique" launched on 8 November in Xai-Xai, Gaza Province. Led by UN Women Mozambique and funded by the Catalan Agency for Development and Cooperation, the project aimed to empower community leaders in five districts of Gaza to combat violence against women and girls, along with harmful traditional practices. On 4 December, Mozambique's parliament speaker, Esperança Bias, called for stringent punishment for domestic violence perpetrators, highlighting the need for increased vigilance and reporting. Government data revealed alarming statistics, with 3,923 cases of physical violence and 1,504 cases of psychological violence recorded between January and September. The minister of gender, children, and social action, Nyeleti Mondlane, advocated for *gender equality* and conducted various awareness-raising activities during the campaign, with support from UN Women Mozambique.

On 13 December, Mozambique's Ministry of Mineral Resources and Energy finalised a $5 bn agreement with a consortium led by EDF, the French power giant, for the *Mphanda Nkuwa Hydropower Project* in Tete Province. Besides EDF, this consortium, selected through a competitive process initiated in June 2022, includes TotalEnergies and Sumitomo Corporation, in partnership with Mozambique's Electricidade de Moçambique (EDM) and Hidroeléctrica de Cahora Bassa (HCB). The project aims to generate 1,500 megawatts in its first phase, significantly boosting Mozambique's electricity production capacity and potentially benefiting over 3 m households in Southern Africa. Projected to cost $4.5 bn, it is slated for completion by 2031 and encompasses a dam, a power station with four turbine-generator units, and a 1,300 km high-voltage transmission line from Tete to Maputo. Additionally, in November, the Mphanda Nkuwa Hydropower Project Implementation Office (GMNK) launched a *Professional Internship Programme* for Mozambican graduates, to equip them with practical skills in managing large projects.

On 5 May, *Mozambique's National Hydrocarbon Company* (ENH) secured a historic 40% stake in the *Angoche block*, marking a significant increase from its typical 10–15% participation in *mineral resource exploration*. This move, announced by ENH administrator Rudêncio Morais, led to negotiations with the National Petroleum Institute and the Ministry of Mineral Resources and Energy for improved participation terms. Contracts were expected to be finalised between June and July, reflecting efforts to enhance ENH's role in resource exploration and increase the national stake in the sector without bearing research costs.

In May, Mozambique expanded *mining and oil exploration* benefits to districts and provinces in alignment with President Nyusi's Economic Acceleration Package. This initiative granted administrative divisions the revenue from a 7.25% tax on exploration activities, supplementing the existing 2.75% revenue share to communities. Furthermore, the government introduced reforms in customs clearance, excise taxes, and rail-port concession contracts to improve governance and stimulate economic growth.

On 13 September, the African Development Fund allocated $6.73 m to Mozambique for the *Institutional Support Project for the Business Environment and Governance*, part of the Economic Acceleration Package. This initiative aimed to refine the business landscape and governance by simplifying administrative procedures for businesses, fostering investment-conducive policies, and evaluating tax incentives for eco-friendly investments. It also targeted enhancing public spending efficiency and transparency, benefiting various government ministries and the private sector.

In November, President Nyusi launched a *water supply system in Dombe*, Manica, benefiting over 6,000 residents, with an expected reach of 8,000. Funded with MZN 35 m, partly from the UK, the initiative addresses water scarcity caused by *Cyclone Idai in 2019*. Additionally, health brigades were deployed across four provinces – Tete, Zambezia, Nampula, and Cabo Delgado – to monitor *diarrhoeal diseases amid cholera concerns*, highlighting a proactive approach to public health alongside infrastructure development.

Rio Tinto settled with the SEC (Securities and Exchange Commission) for $28 m over allegations linked to its *2011 Mozambique coal assets acquisition*, resolving a pending lawsuit before Judge Analisa Torres in November. The company addressed claims of having overvalued the assets, bought for $3.7 bn and sold at $50 m. Former chief executive officer Tom Albanese accepted a $50,000 penalty, while former chief financial officer Guy Elliott disputed the charges.

On 11 December, Mozambique initiated an *air quality monitoring project*, unveiling its first station in Boane District, inaugurated by the deputy minister of transport and communications, Amilton Alissone. The station was to monitor pollutants and noise pollution in real time, aiding environmental management. Plans included expanding to ten stations across municipalities and provinces.

During the second Ordinary Session of the National Trade Facilitation Committee in December, Mozambique introduced *a new phytosanitary certificate* to strengthen the quality evaluation of exports and imports. Minister of industry and trade Silvino Moreno announced the certificate's role in detailing methodologies for cleaning, treating, and enhancing product quality, particularly for plants and animals, to prevent disease transmission across borders.

Namibia

Henning Melber

In a relatively quiet year of domestic politics, a gradual economic recovery from the downturn since 2015 was registered. An increase in tourism and significant foreign direct investments, mainly in the mining sector and the exploration of oil and gas, and the prospects of grand-scale green hydropower projects were a welcome boost. But unemployment and poverty remained major challenges, as did the degree of public debt and the continued need for fiscal prudence. In foreign relations, the 'Go East' and pro-Russia policy continued.

Domestic Politics

The congress of the South West African People's Organisation (SWAPO), the former liberation movement and since independence the party in government, had in late November 2022 re-elected *Netumbo Nandi-Ndaitwah* (often referred to as NNN) as the party's vice-president. Following previously established practice, this was understood to be a confirmation that she will be the successor to President Hage Geingob as the official party candidate for the country's presidential elections, expected to take place in November 2024. However, President Geingob seemed reluctant to openly support her. This was a matter of much speculation during the first months of the year. While Team NNN began actively campaigning, with party meetings and public events in different regions to consolidate support, President Geingob on various occasions finally gave his confirmation of Nandi-Ndaitwah as the elected and recognised successor. But influential members of the party continued to demand another party congress to officially elect the presidential candidate for the next elections. This signalled that not all seemed to be at ease with having, for the first time, a female candidate likely to occupy the highest state office. During the year, a significant number of aspirants from different parties as well as independent individuals announced their ambition to join the competition for votes.

In his *State of the Nation Address* on 16 March, President Geingob diagnosed economic resilience and offered a positive prognosis for recovery but considered the high unemployment rate, especially among young people, as a potential threat to stability. He stressed that more than 30% of the population received some form of social grant. He snubbed the opposition parties when abruptly leaving the National Assembly before answering the second round of questions posed to him in the subsequent debate.

On 16 May, the Supreme Court ruled (by four to one) that *same-sex marriages* entered into by Namibian citizens with foreign partners in other countries must be recognised in Namibia as legally valid. This will entitle the foreign spouse to the same residence rights accorded to spouses in opposite-sex marriages, even though same-sex marriages cannot be entered into locally. This caused a public outcry, including *homophobic hate campaigns*. These led to the cancellation of several public events of the gay community, which so far has been able to organise such events freely and publicly.

The majority of members of parliament, from different parties, actively opposed the court's judgment. To bypass the ruling, a SWAPO MP introduced in the National Assembly for the first time a 'private member's bill', which allowed for direct tabling. This *Marriage Amendment Bill* would narrow the definition of 'spouse' of the Marriage Act of 1961. Adopted by most law-makers regardless of party affiliation on 11 July, the bill was subsequently modified to prohibit same-sex marriages and marital unions between transgender individuals. After endorsement by the National Council, it was finally passed in record time on 23 September. Since then, it has been with the president's office waiting for the signature of the head of state. Reportedly, it is being scrutinised for compliance with the country's constitutional principles. Both the Supreme Court ruling and the homophobic outbursts it triggered also received considerable attention internationally. The matter furthermore caused concerns about whether the independence of the judiciary and the rule of law have been fully respected by the response of law-makers in not abiding by the ruling and thereby possibly being in contempt of court.

In another contested matter, the domestic discord over the bilaterally negotiated *German–Namibian Joint Declaration* continued. On 19 January an application was filed at the Namibian High Court by Bernadus Swartbooi, leader of the second-largest opposition party the Landless People's Movement, the Ovaherero Traditional Authority, and nine communities as members of the Nama Traditional Leaders Association. The lawsuit demanded a judicial review to set aside the decision of the speaker of the National Assembly to note the Joint Declaration and to instead declare it unlawful in terms of Namibia's constitution as well as in breach of a motion adopted by the National Assembly in 2006. In addition, on 23 February, seven special rapporteurs of the OHCHR submitted largely identical letters to the German and Namibian governments. They expressed grave concern at the alleged failure to ensure the right of the Ovaherero and Nama to meaningful participation, through self-elected representatives. As they argued, 'international law requires the States to obtain the free, prior, and informed consent of the Indigenous Peoples concerned through their own representatives before adopting and implementing legislative or administrative measures that may affect them'. Both governments dismissed the criticism in their replies by mid-year.

A public outcry over state expenditure for *Namibia's participation in COP28* was motivated by the sheer size of the delegation, which included the president's wife and their children. In a statement, the president's office offered reassurance that 'not a single cent of public funds has been spent on the children of the first couple', but demands to present the evidence of the private purchase of their flights and receipts for other expenses as proof of this were ignored. However, it was admitted that for administrative purposes the children had been registered as delegates to the conference. The matter again brought to the fore public concern over the abuse of taxpayers' money to finance the privileges of those in office.

A growing tendency of *interethnic animosities* reanimated previous debates about whether members of the Oshiwambo-speaking population (the main political base of SWAPO) are benefiting from preferential employment in the public service. During the year, President Geingob attended several ethnic-regional cultural festivals in different parts of the country as a guest of honour to celebrate local traditions. This caused a debate over whether such recognition would foster tribalist tendencies, or if it was not rather a recognition of the country's *leitmotif* of 'unity in diversity'.

International rankings presented a mixed picture, with the country again scoring high for *media freedom*. In the Freedom of the Press Worldwide Index by Reporters Without Borders, Namibia regained the top score in Africa at rank 22, one position below Germany, several above the UK, and even further ahead of the USA. But in a hitherto unique act of interference, the editor-in-chief of the state-owned daily newspaper 'New Era' was suspended in October for critical comments he had published on the legal system and the risk of the undermining of the rule of law. He had not been reinstated by year's end. Journalists organised in the Namibia Media Professionals Union continued to campaign, without success, to be officially recognised as a trade union.

As in 2022, Namibia scored was 8th out of 146 countries in the Global Gender Gap Index, the highest rank of all African countries. In contrast, levels of gender-based violence remained high. According to the UN Population Fund (UNFPA), at least a third of women in the country experience physical violence from an intimate partner at some point in their lives. In the Global Peace Index the country advanced by six places to 56th, making it the seventh of seven African countries with 'high peace'. In contrast, according to the WHO, Namibia's suicide rate stood at 9.7 per 100,000 people, the highest rate recorded in Africa.

Foreign Affairs

President Geingob undertook nine *international trips*, down from 19 the year before, reducing his travel days from 74 to 41. These foreign visits were the AU Summit in Addis Ababa (18/19 February), a state visit to Pretoria (20 April), the SADC Summit in Luanda (16/17 August), the BRICS Africa Summit in Johannesburg (22–24 August), an 11-day stay in New York during the opening sessions of the UNGA (17–24 September) with a stop-over in France, the African Energy Week conference in Cape Town (16–18 October), the European Commission's Global Gateway Forum in Brussels (25/26 October), the funeral of former Finnish president Martti Ahtisaari in Helsinki (13 November), and a 14-day stay in Dubai to participate in COP28 (30 November to 13 December). Accompanied for COP28 by a large delegation and the first lady and their children, the expenses were a matter of public discussion upon the president's return (see above).

High-ranking *foreign visitors* to Namibia from 11 countries were recorded during the year. They included US first lady Jill Biden, who stayed from 22 to 24 February. She was reassured by Namibia's first lady of the firm friendship between their respective countries. Finland's president Sauli Niinistö undertook a state visit on 27/28 April in the company of a business delegation. Following a BRICS meeting in South Africa, India's foreign minister Subrahmanyam Jaishankar visited from 4 to 6 June, flagging a strong interest in closer cooperation in the energy sector. Sharing India's interest, not least in the local potential of green hydrogen production, on 19 June the Danish and Dutch prime ministers Mette Frederiksen and Mark Rutte, respectively, made a joint working visit to discuss with President Geingob a partnership with Rotterdam as the European harbour hub for a large hydropower collaboration project. Cuban president Miguel Díaz-Canel y Bermúdez was the guest of honour at the annual Heroes' Day celebrations (26 August).

Close relations with *Botswana* were consolidated. Presidents Geingob and Masisi met on 24 February at the Trans-Kalahari/Mamuno Border Post to launch the use of identity documents for travel between the two countries. On 26 June, Masisi met Geingob again for a one-day working visit. Relations with *South Africa* played a prominent role; President Geingob's state visit was the first since 2012. The special relationship between the respective governing parties the ANC (African National Congress) and SWAPO were underlined by the fact that, as part of the programme, President Geingob addressed the National Executive Committee of the ANC. On 13 October, Geingob welcomed South African president Cyril Ramaphosa for the third session of the Bi-National Commission (BNC). Co-chaired by the two presidents, the meeting of the BNC, founded in 2022, followed an agreement reached during Geingob's state visit to South Africa on 20 April. On 27 November, Geingob criticised South Africa's handling of SACU to its own advantage, preventing the industrialisation of other members of the customs union. He also called on South Africa to respect international law regarding the Orange River as a natural border between the two countries, over which Namibia wanted partial jurisdiction. South Africa maintains that the entire river is part of its territory.

Friendly relations with *Russia* were further cultivated. Namibia abstained from all resolutions in the UNGA to condemn the Russian invasion of Ukraine. During his state visit to South Africa, Geingob declared that he did not support the ICC decision to arrest Putin and questioned the court's jurisdiction. On 19 July, in a unusual gesture beyond the ordinary diplomatic protocol of the letter of credence, Geingob received the new Russian ambassador Dmitry Lobach for a one-to-one conversation at State House. On Twitter/X, Geingob posted the same day: 'I reassured him of Namibia's continued commitment to strengthen bilateral cooperation with Russia for the prosperity of our two countries'. Meeting Russia's deputy prime minister Yury Trutnev in Windhoek on 8 December, the minister of international relations and cooperation, Netumbo Nandi-Ndaitwah, also deputy prime minister and the anticipated SWAPO candidate for the presidential elections in November 2024, declared that Trutnev's visit would demonstrate the commitment to strengthening bilateral relations and cooperation. She urged her technical teams to ensure implementation of signed legal frameworks.

At the end of December, the minister publicly announced a turnaround regarding the *EU–OACPS (Organisation of African, Caribbean and Pacific States) partnership agreement*. In early November, she had said that she was declining the signing of the so-called Samoa Agreement, argued that the obligations it created would violate Namibia's constitutional principles, harm local industries, and hinder development. Following further negotiations and clarifications with the EU, after an intervention by President Geingob, the cabinet reversed the decision. The agreement was signed on 19 December in Brussels.

With over 2,000 Namibians having filed applications for asylum in the UK, of which fewer than 10% were regarded as justified, the British government announced on 19 July the *withdrawal of visa-free entry to the UK*. Namibians would now be required to apply for a visa to travel to or transit through the UK.

Relations with Germany continued to focus on the bilateral negotiations over the Joint Declaration on how to terms with the genocide committed between 1904 and 1908 in the colony of South West Africa. Addressing German-speaking Namibians in late October, foreign minister Nandi-Ndaitwah revealed that another round of negotiations had taken place in Windhoek from 4 to 6 October. According to her, the focus had been on three unresolved issues, namely 'the amount offered, the 30 year payment period and whether the final joint declaration would bring finality to Germany's obligations towards Namibia in the context of genocide'. At another meeting in early December in Berlin, the delegations seemed to establish further common ground. On 9 December, Christoph Retzlaff, director for sub-Saharan Africa and the Sahel at Germany's Federal Foreign Office, confirmed on X that he had held 'constructive and trustful talks with Technical Committee of Government of Namibia'.

During the General Assembly debate on the Israeli *incursion into Gaza* on 26 October, Namibia's permanent representative to the UN delivered a strongly worded statement in support of the right to self-determination of Palestine and demanded the unreserved withdrawal of Israel and the cessation of all hostilities. In light of Namibia's abstentions on Russia's invasion of Ukraine, this indicated a lack of coherence in terms of principled normative values on the right to self-determination and the protection of national sovereignty. As an analysis by the local Institute for Public Policy Research concluded in November, 'human rights cannot be described as a determinative guide in Namibian foreign policymaking'.

Socioeconomic Developments

On 22 February, finance minister Ipumbu Shiimi presented the *annual budget* for 2023/24. He was once again confronted with a precarious balancing act, which he sold as an effort to reconcile fiscal prudence with economic stimulation and social transfer provisions. The total budget of 84.6 bn Namibian dollars (ND) (with an operational budget of ND 66.1 bn) was a new record. Public debt crossed the ND 150 bn mark, amounting to over 70% of GDP. Public service costs of ND 32.9 bn (38.9% of the budget) remained unsustainably high. The declared priority of social spending was only in part supported by the allocations. The ranking illustrated the mismatch: while education received a record ND 20.6 bn, or 28.4% of the budget, health and social services trailed with ND 9.7 bn, only the fourth-largest allocation. Public safety, with ND 14.1 bn or 19.4% of the budget, came second, and interest payments as debt servicing ranked third, with ND 10.2 bn or almost 12% of the budget. The anticipated increase of over 71% in SACU revenue, from ND 14.2 bn in the previous financial year to ND 24.3 bn or 32.5% of total revenue income of ND 74.7 bn, offered some leeway for modestly higher social transfers. An increase of ND 100 for old-age pensions was basically an inflation-related adjustment, not an improvement in real purchasing value. Not surprisingly, therefore, the comments by pensioners included as an appendix to the budget speech were generally a confirmation that they cannot afford anything beyond attempting to satisfy basic needs. In contrast, the extension of the disability grant for the under-18 age group to those over 18 was a welcome elimination of age-related discrimination. The increase in 'sin taxes' (alcohol and tobacco) was an obvious way to raise revenue income, but it remained unexplained why the increase in tax on sparkling wine was markedly smaller than that on other alcohol and tobacco, when those who drink such wine tend to be those who can afford a higher price for the status symbol. This seemed not so much a pro-poor but more a pro-rich adjustment. In contrast, the announcement of the doubling of the tax-free allowance on annual income from ND 50,000 to 100,000 was welcomed, though not immediately effective. It seemed to have been put on the reserve list for next year's budget, when the country will be in an election year.

The *mid-year budget review* was tabled by finance minister Shiimi on 31 October and increased the budget from ND 86.4 bn to 89 bn. Debt servicing (statutory expenditure) increased to ND 11.8 bn and the debt reached ND 153.8 bn. Tax income was estimated to be ND 3.8 bn higher than expected. The overall budget deficit remained at 4.2% of GDP. The economic growth rate was predicted to be 3.5% for the year and 2.9% for 2024. Close to a hundred *state-owned enterprises* remained a fiscal burden. Following a cabinet decision, they were to have been incorporated under a parent company with a total capital of ND 119 bn, following the model of Malaysia. In his speech, Shiimi criticised the so-far missing implementation of the decision and the inefficiency and lack of rentability of most of these parastatals. Their continued subsidisation remained a fiscal risk and required resources which otherwise would have benefited social sectors.

Social expenditure remained a means of survival for *people in dire need*. In September, a total of 625,398 people (of some 2.5 m) were receiving the monthly old-age pension or disability and vulnerable children grants. The number of people expected to experience food insecurity from October 2023 to March 2024 was estimated at 695,000. In October, the annual inflation rate was assumed to be 6%, but price increases in basic food commodities remained much higher. According to a release of the local WFP in April, unemployment was at 34% overall, with youth unemployment at 48%. Almost 60% of all people in *employment* worked in the informal sector. Local companies in the construction sector continued to ail, with a decrease in activity, and agriculture faced continued adversity due mainly to weather conditions, which limited crop and livestock productivity. The Neckartal Dam project, which had promised up to 15,000 job opportunities in the southern Kharas Region, remained stagnant because of lack of funds for investment in the second phase of infrastructural implementation. In contrast, tourism recovered from the disastrous effects of the Covid-19 pandemic. Diamond mining and the fishing industry remained other important employment sectors. But overall, employment rates did not match the increase in numbers of people reaching working age, and huge numbers competed for the few advertised jobs.

Big hopes were linked to the boost in the search for *fossil fuel*. Since 2021, the Canadian company ReconAfrica has drilled for oil and gas in an ecologically highly sensitive area of the Okavango Delta. Despite massive local and international protest and a dubious legal situation, the explorations have continued. Offshore licences in the Orange Basin have been issued to other major international oil companies such as Quatar Energy, Shell, and Total Energies. Shell announced that it would spend a quarter of its budget for deep-sea exploration in 2023/24 on its search along the Namibian coast, since results so far had been promising. But uncertainty remained in terms of how fields could be developed with a water depth greater than 2,000 metres and reservoir depth of 6,000 metres in what is a high-risk/high-return frontier area. Commenting on the hype over a possible oil bonanza, the World Bank warned, with reference to the case of Nigeria, against equating with discoveries with the promise of economic development.

With the signing of several MoUs for the development of *green energy*, in combination with the expected discovery of large amounts of oil and gas, there were expectations of the country becoming the continent's future energy hub. However, various legally binding obligations in relation to these projects remained undisclosed. During COP28, President Geingob revealed that Namibia was advancing nine hydrogen projects and had its eye on longer-term financial commitment exceeding (US) $20 bn to establish a thriving green fuels industry. But the necessary supply of water remained a concern for the implementation of some of the projects. The main attention was on the mega hydropower project with the German Hyphen Hydrogen Energy company in the Tsau ǁKhaeb National Park, much to the concern of environmental groups. Despite the best natural conditions to produce ammoniac, local experts articulated concerns over the implementation and the advantages or benefits for the local population. A legally fixed and binding normative framework for such operations remained absent. The secrecy which surrounded the negotiated agreement created suspicions over the lack of transparency and accountability and fuelled mistrust that loopholes could benefit grand-scale corruption. At the end of May, President Geingob categorically dismissed any public interference. In a statement, the Legal Assistance Centre bemoaned the fact that this came at a time of serious questions about the project's environmental impact and economic viability, 'to push through a controversial project that will have a massive impact on the citizens'. At the end of the year, the government announced that it had entered a partnership with Hyphen, with government's 24% ownership share estimated at over ND 14 bn. While the World Bank welcomed the window of opportunity offered by green energy, it warned against losing sight of other potential opportunities for development.

Uranium production, almost exclusively under the ownership of Chinese companies, regained momentum through higher world market prices. The annual primary production of uranium oxide amounted to about one-tenth of the world's volume. Plans to open a fifth mine in Erongo Region were announced by Bannerman Energy. In a commercial farming region near the Kalahari, Russia's state-owned Rosatom faced vehement opposition from local farmers and the Ministry of Agriculture to its going ahead with plans for a massive uranium project because of fear of irreversible damage to the existing ground water reserves.

Huge deposits of *strategic minerals and rare earth elements*, much-sought essentials in demand as part of a global energy transition, added to the attraction of Namibia as an investment opportunity. In June, the government announced a ban on exporting unprocessed critical minerals such as crushed lithium ore, cobalt, manganese, graphite, and rare earth metals and elements, with the aim of strengthening the sustainability of the extractive industry through local processing, refining, and recycling capacity. This caused conflict with the Chinese mining company Xinfeng, which continued to export lithium unrefined, claiming to have a valid licence to do so, while constructing a lithium processing plant. At COP28, Geingob announced that Namibia would join the EU Critical Raw Materials Club. In November, the pilot stage was inaugurated of the first carbon-neutral iron ore mine worldwide.

The Ecological Threat Report 2023 included Namibia under high-risk countries, but because of its relative peace it was not classified as a 'hot spot'. The Africa Wealth Report 2023 recorded an increase since 2012 of 20% in the number of US dollar millionaires, to 2,100. It devoted an entire chapter to Namibia, titled 'Africa's new frontier'.

South Africa

Sanusha Naidu

The year under review was occupied with preparations for the impending seventh national and provincial elections scheduled for 2024. The body politic of the state became increasingly fractious, with political parties holding leadership conferences and preparing for their aggressive electoral campaigns. On the international front, the country had to contend with increasing criticism of the lack of consistency between its foreign policy ideals and actions, while at the domestic level, the government faced acute push-back from CSOs and communities regarding the lack of economic growth, inadequate service delivery, and a deepening socioeconomic crisis.

Domestic Affairs

The year began with the ruling party, the African National Congress (ANC), resuming the unfinished business of its *55th Elective Conference*. With the party convening a hybrid platform, delegates were convened to vote for 80 members to make up the National Executive Committee (NEC) and adopt policy recommendations. In closing the conference, *President Cyril Ramaphosa* noted that the renewal of the party was a critical foundation for consolidating internal unity. The conference resolved to address critical challenges affecting the country, including important reforms to build the economy, the chronic unemployment crisis, the energy disaster, and the urgent need to transform the economy and deepen social protection for the majority of South Africans in terms of access to affordable basic services and a living wage. Some analysts saw the conclusion of the conference as a victory for President Ramaphosa in consolidating his position for a second term as head of state after the 2024 elections.

Several other political parties also held their elective conferences. The official opposition, the Democratic Alliance (DA), saw the re-election of *John Steenhuisen*, who received a landslide 83% of the votes while *Helen Zille* remained as chair of the *Federal Executive*. Steenhuisen noted in his victory speech that the overwhelming victory had given him the confidence and a mandate to take the opposition party to a bigger electoral victory in the 2024 elections. But the DA conference also faced some internal challenges. One of the issues was whether the party should have a deputy leader. The proposal was rejected by delegates, albeit by a small margin, and this was viewed by critics as the party resisting to the potential for two centres of power that a deputy leader position could create. While some delegates felt that the position of a deputy leader would be adopted at the *DA's 2028 congress*, others bemoaned the fact that the rejection of the position was more about mitigating the possibility of former Johannesburg mayor Dr Mpho Phalatse contesting the leadership of the party, after being elected as deputy leader.

Despite the DA holding a successful elective conference, the bigger challenge for the party was that its executive leadership was criticised for not being racially inclusive. The party had been plagued by an exodus of black leaders, which was seen as disruptive to the DA's identity as a multicultural organisation. In fact, the issue of race in the party placed it in an invidious position in terms of attracting black voters in the 2024 national and provincial elections and growing its electoral footprint. Party leaders in Gauteng such as *Solly Msimang* downplayed the issue of race and argued that an obsession over race in the DA needed to be reconsidered beyond parochial narratives. For Msimang, the party represented a broader contextual proposition of building a prosperous country for all. But some analysts were quick to refute such claims, noting that race is still very much part of the socioeconomic fabric of the state given that the majority of the black population are confronted by high levels of poverty, inequality, and unemployment while the wealth of the country remains in the control of the white minority. Therefore, the electoral landscape of the country remained defined by race and class divisions.

The 2020 *Phala Phala* saga continued to make headlines, with the investigation by the *South African Reserve Bank (SARB)* releasing its findings, noting that it 'could not conclude' that President Ramaphosa violated any exchange control regulations or was in breach of foreign currency rules. In its media statement, the SARB stated that based on the documents it had reviewed, it was unable to establish whether a 'perfected transaction' had taken place and therefore could not conclusively determine whether there had been a contravention of the relevant exchange control regulations. In addition it highlighted that since the legal prerequisites underpinning the 'perfected transaction' seemed not to have been fulfilled, it would appear that the transaction was incomplete (that is, the buffalo that was the primary entity in the transaction had not been delivered), and thus 'there was no legal obligation under exchange control regulations of 1961 to declare the foreign currency'. At the same time, the DA brought a *Promotion of Access to Information* (PAIA) application to the *South African Revenue Services* (SARS) requesting that the records pertaining to the sale be made public. In its response, the tax agency found that there was no record of declaration relating to the transaction. This was confirmed in an affidavit by the legal specialist overseeing the matter. While opposition parties took this finding to mean that President Ramaphosa had engaged in an illicit transaction that contravened the *Prevention and Combatting of Corrupt Activities Act* (PRECCA), SARS confirmed that in auditing the president's companies that owned the *Phala Phala* farm, it had found Ramaphosa to be tax compliant.

In June, the final agency to absolve the president from any wrong-doing in the Phala Phala affair was the Public Protector's Office. Following more than a year investigating the matter, the acting head of the institution, *Advocate Kholeka Gcaleka*, found Ramaphosa's head of VIP protection services, Wally Rhoode, to have abused state resources while dismissing all allegations against the president. According to the findings, Rhoode had unlawfully pursued an investigation against the alleged perpetrators using state resources. In addition, Advocate Gcaleka found that was there no conflict of interest between the president's involvement in the farm and his position as head of the state. The Public Protector went further, noting that there was no evidence to suggest that the president had benefited from 'paid work' based on the daily operations of the farm.

Opposition parties and civil society actors disparaged the findings of all three institutions, accusing them of bias and collusion aimed at protecting the ANC president and head of state. Towards the end of the year, three suspects allegedly involved in the Phala Phala farm theft were arrested by the police agency, the Hawks. Despite Gcalek facing legal challenges regarding the Phala Phala findings, the ad hoc committee in parliament overseeing the appointment of the next *public protector* had recommended the nomination and appointment of Gcaleka as head of the office. In September, the former public protector, Advocate Mkhwebane, was *impeached* by the National Assembly in a historic decision taken since the democratic dispensation in 1994. Mkhebane became the first head of a Chapter Nine institution to be removed from office. In November, President Ramaphosa accepted the committee's recommendation and officially appointed Gcaleka as the country's *public protector*.

Following her impeachment, Mkhebane joined the Economic Freedom Fighters as a member of parliament.

As the year progressed, the 2024 election loomed large in the body politic of the state. In August, a group of several opposition parties led by the DA convened a two-day conference to explore the possibility of a grand political coalition. Initially referred to as the *Moonshot Pact* by the DA leader at the party's April federal congress, the parties attending the conference (ActionSA, Inkatha Freedom Party, Freedom Front Plus, United Independent Movement, Spectrum National Party, and the Independent South African National Civic Organisation) agreed that the group agreement should be identified as the *Multi-Party Charter* (MPC). The MPC was viewed as a mechanism thaElectot could potentially unseat the ANC from power. Motivated by the ANC possibly losing its dominance at the polls and getting less than 50% in the 2024 elections, the stakeholders in the MPC saw an opportunity to increase their election footprint, reaping higher benefits at the expense of the ANC. While each of the political parties in the MPC will contest the elections independently, the MPC was conceptualised as deepening a common vision towards a coalition engagement.

Despite the formation of the MPC highlighting that South Africa's democratic landscape was shifting towards coalition politics, there were mixed views on the viability of the Charter. The immediate question confronting the MPC was who would lead the Charter. From the start there was ambivalence about using the term 'Moonshot Pact'. This was because members of the other parties felt that this would imply that the DA was both the face of and the dominant actor in shaping the principles of the Charter. The other issue that analysts raised was whether the MPC was cohesive, in spite of the declaration highlighting that it demonstrated an intention to engage politically in the long term. Given the contested nature of political party relations in the country, this posed a risk around how post-election engagements would evolve around forming a *coalition manifesto*. New parties such as *Rise Mzansi* and *Build One South Africa* were more cautious in joining the MPC, feeling that their electoral debut would be more successful if they participated of their own accord. Finally, the ruling party dismissed the MPC, with President Ramaphosa calling it a 'sideshow'.

Even though the ANC did not see any threat from the MPC, the formal launch of the uMkhonto weSizwe (MK) party in December became more of a thorn in the side of the ruling party. Registered in September, MK's arrival on the electoral scene illustrated not only the fragmented nature of the country's political system but also the fractious internal conditions within the ruling party. Speaking at the MK's launch, former president *Jacob Zuma* dropped a bombshell when he said that he could no longer vote or campaign for Cyril Ramphosa's ANC. In what some analysts and media agencies interpreted as an incendiary statement, Zuma went on to belligerently claim that voting for the current leadership of the ANC would be a betrayal of 'one of the great liberations movements of our time ... that ... today is not the once great movement that we loved and were prepared to lay down our lives for'. Zuma's inflammatory statement noted with some level of political vengeance that 'the new people's war starts today. The only crucial difference is instead of the bullet this time we will use the ballot.'

Political pundits, in assessing the impact of the new party on the ANC, noted with concern that *KwaZulu Natal*, the major electoral support base for the MK among Zulu voters, was becoming increasingly volatile, with tensions rising between the two political parties. Speculation was rife that the ANC could lose control of the province, with MK posing a serious threat to the ruling party's largest provincial branch structure. The formation of MK – was the name of the ANC's military wing during the liberation struggle – created tensions for the ruling party, including the question of who owned the trademark of the military wing, disbanded in 1993. This posed an identity crisis for the ruling party regarding its credibility and legitimacy in claiming liberation credentials. The ANC was also confronted with an institutional dilemma regarding former president Zuma's assertion that despite not voting for the ANC, he would remain a lifelong member of the party. This contradicted the *ANC's constitution*, which states that any member showing support for or becoming a member of another party must be brought before a disciplinary commission hearing and/or has to resign from the party as a member. In response, the ANC remained muted on the matter.

The period under review saw President Ramaphosa sign the *Electoral Amendment Act* of 2023 in April. The amendment allowed for independent candidates to be included and nominated to contest the national and provincial elections. The amendment, which gave effect to the Constitutional Court's decision in 2020 noting that it was unconstitutional to prevent independent candidates from participating in the general elections, required that the minister of home affairs establish an electoral reform panel to deliberate over how the electoral system would accommodate the change in the Act. Unfortunately, the Electoral Amendment Act faced difficulties. The immediate challenge was that the minister of home affairs had missed the deadline as stipulated in law that the *Electoral Amendment Panel* should have begun within four months of the Electoral Amendment Act taking effect. Civil society group OUTA (the Organisation Undoing Tax Abuse) raised concerns that the panel should have been technically convened by 19 October. This was despite the home affairs minister issuing a government gazette in June/July inviting members of the public to nominate suitably qualified people to serve on the panel. OUTA argued that the delay in the process would severely hamper the preparations for the *2024 elections*, especially the electoral reforms that needed to be undertaken according to the Constitutional Court's 2020 decision. By mid-December, the home affairs minister had issued a second public call for nominees, following a decision by the Joint Sitting of the Portfolio Committee on Home Affairs and the Select Committee on Security and Justice and Correctional Services, arguing that the nominations received lacked democratic representation.

The second issue raised as a result of the Electoral Amendment Act was the question of what would be the criteria for *independent candidates* to become eligible and contest the elections. The matter in contention was the number of signatures independent candidates had to obtain to qualify as what the *Independent Electoral Commission (IEC)* identified as a 'contestant' in the 2024 elections. In December, the Constitutional Court decided that 1,000 signatures was a sufficient requirement for independent candidates to be able to contest the election, rather than the original threshold of 15,000.

At the same time, in August, the Constitutional Court ruled against the application brought by the *Independent Candidate Association of South Africa* requesting 'that the 200/200 split in seats allocated in the National Assembly' should be considered on the basis 'that an independent candidate must get many more votes than political party candidates in order to gain a seat in the National Assembly, because independents were allowed to compete only for 200 regional seats and not the 200 'compensatory seats allocated only to political parties in the national elections'. In the application, the association 'suggested that the playing fields would be levelled if the split were 350/50 seats'.

In the judgment, Justice Nonkosi Mhlantla highlighted that 'the 200/200 split passed constitutional muster, because it was grounded in proportional representation and would have little risk of "overhang" (where there were more elected officials than seats in the national assembly)'. The judgement also upheld the rationality of the Electoral Amendment Act reform, with Justice Mhlantla reiterating the explanation provided by the IEC that 'there was no mechanism under the current Act to correct the problem should overhang occur, and the association had not presented any viable solution to "combat the risk" that the IEC would not be able to declare the election'. This decision was welcomed by both parliament and the IEC.

The period under review saw the passing of important political figures. In September, the founder and leader of the Inkatha Freedom Party (IFP) and long-serving traditional Zulu prime minister to the *Amazulu king, Dr Mangosuthu Buthelezi*, passed away at the age of 95 two weeks after being admitted into hospital. The long-standing leader of the IFP was hailed by President Ramaphosa 'as an outstanding leader in the political and cultural life of our nation'. The ANC also lost senior struggle icons including the former secretary-general, *Jessie Duartes*, and the *Pahad brothers (Essop and Aziz)*, who had served in the Mbeki administration.

In June, the ANC expelled its controversial former secretary-general *Ace Magashule*, following a disciplinary committee hearing over 'accusations of misconduct and other breaches of party rules, while also facing charges of corruption in a criminal case'. The committee found that Magashule had been in contravention of several of the party's rules.

Within the DA, there were tensions between MP *Ghaleb Cachalia* and the leadership of the party. The fallout centred around Cachalia's comments regarding the Israel–Palestine conflict. Cachalia publicly criticised Israel's response to the 7 October Hamas attacks and called it a *'genocide'* on social media platform X (formerly Twitter). Cachalia was warned about making any published statements regarding the situation in *Gaza*, as this was seen as contradicting the DA's official policy (which was unclear) without having the authority to do so and contravening a caucus directive that empowers the shadow minister for international relations only with the right to make commentary or statements on the issue. Defiant, Cachalia did not adhere to the party's rules, was removed from his position as shadow minister for public enterprises in parliament by Steenhuisen, and became a backbencher. Tensions between Cachalia and Steenhuisen deepened.

As 2023 drew to a close and despite the many political talking points, no one could forget the *Economic Freedom Fighters* (EFF) storming the stage during President Ramaphosa's *State of the Nation address in February*. The leader of the EFF, Julius Malema, dismissed it as nothing more than a 'peaceful protest' and noted in the group's court argument that MPs have the right to protest. The court, however, had a different interpretation of the situation. The *Red Berets* were found 'guilty of gross disorderly misconduct', Malema and five others were banned from attending the 2024 State of the Nation, and were ordered to pay a fine. In December, the National Assembly approved the suspension of Malema and five senior members for a month without pay. The report, which allowed for sanctions to be imposed against the implicated MPs, was seen as a serious breach of the *Powers and Privileges Act*, which governs the behaviour of MPs. Other political highlights included the DA instituting court proceedings against the ANC demanding the abolishing of its *cadre deployment policy*, which the opposition party argued perpetuated corruption and was unconstitutional and unlawful. Linked to the issue of cadre deployment, the DA was successful when the Supreme High Court dismissed the ANC's two earlier appeals to release its cadre deployment records to the DA under the Promotion of Access to Information Act (PAIA). Despite the ruling, the matter was still pending as it was taken to the Constitutional Court for review.

Foreign Affairs

It was a mixed year for the country regarding international engagements. Following condemnation of the government's stance regarding the *Russian* conflict with *Ukraine* and what some saw as an ambiguous foreign policy, the state once again came under the spotlight in February for its *joint military exercises* with Russia and China. Mainstream media both domestically and internationally, including sections of academia and policy think tanks, objected to South Africa participating in the exercise. The overarching criticism was that by engaging in the naval drills, South Africa was ignoring the foundation of its foreign policy principles and respect for human rights in favour of *'non-alignment'* or neutrality in the face of Russia violating the sovereignty of Ukraine.

In March, the pretrial chamber of the ICC issued an arrest warrant for Russian president *Vladimir Putin*. This added to South Africa's 'Russia dilemma'. With South Africa hosting the *15th BRICS Heads of State Summit* in August, the predicament for the government was that being a signatory to the Rome Statute and member of the ICC, it was obligated to arrest President Putin if he landed on South African soil or intended to participate in the summit. Speculation on how South Africa would address the situation revolved around whether the Ramaphosa government would defy the ICC's mandate and invite Putin to the Summit, or seek to sway the ICC towards the view that its jurisdiction could be applied because *Russia* is not a member of the ICC. Wanting to avoid an embarrassing debacle such as the one that the government had faced after not complying with the ICC arrest warrant against former Sudanese president *Omar al-Bashir*, who attended the AU summit in 2015, the Ramaphosa Presidency was acutely aware of the global and domestic pressure that the situation posed for South Africa's international credibility.

Fake news and speculation began to emerge that South Africa's close relationship with Moscow would see the country withdrawing from the ICC. Despite the misinformation fuelling popular opinion, in July the South African Presidency confirmed that President Putin would not be attending the BRICS Summit. The months of speculation put to rest the ongoing saga of 'Will he or wont he'? In its statement, the Presidency noted that the decision was made following discussions between the two sides and highlighted that it was a mutual agreement. The Russian foreign minister represented Putin at the summit.

In May, another storm brewed regarding the docking of a Russian vessel called the *Lady R*, towards the end of December 2022, at the *naval base in Simonstown*, Cape Town. Allegations were made by US ambassador *Reuben Brigety* that weapons had been loaded onto the vessel. Ambassador Brigety's intransigence over his claim that South Africa had violated international sanctions caused a stir domestically and internationally. Of course, in typical South Africa fashion, the government at first dithered in response to the allegations and then replied that there was no credibility to the claims. The minister of defence, in her comment on the situation, emphasised that the equipment in question was a sales order dating back to 2018 for the *South African National Defence Force* (SANDF).

President Ramaphosa instituted a commission of inquiry to investigate the allegations. The commission found no evidence to support Ambassador Brigety's claims, but there were still unanswered questions around why the vessel had turned off its automatic navigational system before entering the naval base, and why it was 'conducting its operation under the cover of darkness'. There were muted mentions of the involvement of the UAE. Nevertheless, the findings vindicated the South African government and raised the ire of the ANC and the *South African Communist Party* (SACP), which called for Ambassador Brigety to be recalled by the US for making spurious statements and not producing the evidence he claimed he had. Even some editorials in mainstream media pages were unrelenting and accused the ambassador of lying, saying that he therefore 'must go'.

While President Ramaphosa recognised that the allegations had impacted negatively on the country's economy due to currency shocks and the reputational risks for the state, he was more cautious in his response, focusing on resolving the issue amicably with *Washington*, which he considered more important since diplomatic relations had become strained. This was against the backdrop of the US being incensed about Pretoria's relationship with Russia, China, and *Iran*, which were seen as rogue states. The view from the US was that SA appeared to be abandoning its engagement with Washington in favour of Russia and China. Relations became fragile, as some congressional representatives called for South Africa to be removed from the *AGOA* as well as for a review of bilateral relations between the two sides. Despite the underlying stresses, the 20th AGOA Forum was hosted in Johannesburg. In his opening address, President Ramaphosa noted that the US was a significant trade partner for the continent while also inviting 'US retailers, importers, and large corporates to see Africa as a key industrial procurement source, a place that is integral to a more resilient supply chain'.

In August, the government hosted the 15th BRICS Summit. The major discussion centred on the expansion of the grouping that was decided on by the heads of state at the 14th Summit in China. The focus of the discussions was the criteria, principles, and norms that would be applied in admitting new members. There was also speculation that a single BRICS currency would be launched. The summit outcomes proved to be pivotal for the bloc, signalling, as one analyst commented, 'a new era of cooperation'. Six new members were invited to join the group as of 1 January 2024. Initially, Indonesia was seen as one of the six but it declined due to domestic considerations with its pending presidential elections. Four of the six members (*Egypt*, Iran, *Saudi Arabia*, and the UAE) were from the *Middle East and Africa* (*MENA*) region. Some commentators saw this as BRICS deepening its Middle East policy. The other two countries making up the final six were *Ethiopia* and *Argentina*. There was uncertainty (at the time) about whether Argentina would accept the invitation. As it turned out, the populist presidential candidate, Javier Milei, who was elected the country's leader in December, had noted that the South American nation's alignment was with the US and formally declined the invitation.

Though the BRICS Summit was hailed as a success, there remained uncertainty over what criteria were used to identify and invite the six countries to join the group. This became a contentious issue, casting doubt on what accession rules informed the decision. In the final analysis, it was decided that foreign ministers would present a cohesive framework on the admission criteria to 16th BRICS Summit, to be hosted by Russia in Kazan. Another important outcome of the summit was the agreement to further develop the *BRICS Pay system* of using local currencies as a form of payment. In the final communique, the *New Development Bank* was tasked with overseeing this process. BRICS Pay should not to be confused with the creation of a single BRICS currency; in fact, the deliberations of the summit had made it clear that launching a BRICS currency was not feasible. South Africa was praised for hosting a successful summit and playing a significant role in smoothing tensions in the group over expansion.

In December, South Africa lodged an application of genocide against the State of *Israel* with the ICJ. The case was officially known as the *Application of the Convention on the Prevention and Punishment of the Crime in the Gaza Strip (South Africa v. Israel)*. South Africa argued that Israel had committed and was committing acts of genocide against Palestinian people living in Gaza that contravened the *Genocide Convention*. In the application, South Africa asked the ICJ to consider provisional measures including the immediate suspensions of Israel's military operations in and around Gaza. South Africa was both lauded and criticised for instituting the application. The application followed the South African government recalling its ambassador in early November, together with other diplomatic officials. In response later in November, Israel recalled its ambassador from Pretoria after the *Department of International Affairs and Cooperation* (DIRCO) démarched the Israeli ambassador regarding public comments made by the diplomat over the country's stance on Israel's response to Hamas' 7 October attacks and the situation in Gaza. The DIRCO minister, Dr Naledi Pandor, 'speaking during the debate in the National Assembly [on] the Israel–Palestine conflict [noted] that [Ambassador] Belotsercovsky has been making a number of comments without having had any discussion with senior members of the government of South Africa'. According to the DIRCO statement, the ambassador was 'called upon to conduct himself in line with the Vienna Conventions, which accord heads of diplomatic missions certain privileges and responsibilities, key among which is to recognise the sovereign decisions of the host nation'.

The escalating tensions in the Middle East also saw increasing pressures domestically, with public opinion divided between lobby groups on both sides either supporting or dismissing the ICJ application and South Africa's positioning on the matter. Despite the intense backlash at times against the South African government and criticism levelled against state authorities for being duplicitous in their foreign policy engagements and raising the spotlight only on Israel's aggression, the Ramaphosa presidency was resolute and noted that no country should be seen as above international law, which must be applied in a fair, equitable, and just manner. In short, for the South Africa government the application was about applying *international humanitarian law*, whereby the rights of all people should be upheld with impartiality, as well as ensuring that where inconceivable acts of aggression are committed against vulnerable people, especially children, the world must act to uphold international law and not become muted as in the case of the *Rwandan genocide*.

Socioeconomic Developments

At the end of 2023, the political and socioeconomic landscape of the country was bleak. The picture was one of a country going into the 2024 elections with an embedded set of structural problems exacerbated by high levels of unemployment, lack of access to service delivery, deepening acts of criminality, and a fractured body politic.

Economic growth continued to decline in 2023. The *South African Statistical Agency* noted in its 2023 annual growth report that overall growth rate was 0.6%. This showed signs of an economy becoming structurally weaker. Economic activity remained anaemic, with lacklustre performance in major sectors such as mining, agriculture, manufacturing, and industry. The main sectors driving growth in the economy were finance, real estate, and business services, at 1.8%.

Unemployment remained a primary factor, with weak labour productivity. In the last quarter of 2023, unemployment edged up to 32.1% from 31.9% in the third quarter. This instability in the job market was also due to the construction and agriculture sectors shedding 108,000 and 35,000 jobs respectively. Even though the mining sector, which has been the mainstay of the economy, saw the creation of 37,000 jobs in the fourth quarter, industry experienced poor growth and threatened job cuts.

The major concern with the state of unemployment was that out of a working-age population (aged 15–64) of about 41 million people, based on the expanded definition of unemployment and including those not actively seeking work, only around 16.7 m people were in some form of employment. This must be contextualised in terms of the actual labour force, which stood at 24.6 m, with 16.4 m people considered 'not economically active'.

Youth employment, measured between the ages of 18 and 24, increased to 59.7% in the fourth quarter from the 59.4% recorded in the third quarter. Overall youth unemployment was at 50.4% by year's end. The stark picture represented a peak in youth unemployment in 2023 driven by factors such as low levels of skill and education, an economy still recovering from the impact of *Covid-19*, intergenerational inequality, and socioeconomic disadvantages. The unemployment data also revealed that women were more affected than men. Meanwhile, the South African Reconciliation Barometer survey released by the Institute for Justice and Reconciliation noted that 'deep poverty and economic inequality [persisted] in South Africa and are among the country's most significant obstacles to reconciliation'.

Ordinary South Africans faced a record-breaking 332 days of electricity blackouts. The public electricity entity, *ESKOM*, struggled with frequent breakdowns of power units, executive leadership, and management crisis, with the resignation of chief executive officer *Andre de Ruyter* at the end of 2022. Before stepping down in March, de Ruyter revealed in an explosive media interview that there had been an attempt on his life through poisoning with cyanide a day after he had announced his resignation. De Ruyter believed that the poisoning attempt was linked to his accusations of ruling-party corruption and alleged that mafia-like crime syndicates were operating in the electricity utility.

The electricity outages created a debilitating effect for small business entrepreneurs, who struggled to absorb the financial costs. There was little relief from government to address the concerns of small to medium-sized businesses. For ordinary citizens, the rise in electricity tariffs increased the cost of living. The economy continued to stutter with fuel hikes, transport costs, and high inflation costs.

At the end of May, the SARB increased the repo rate from 7.75% to 8.25%, which saw the country's official interest rate increasing to 9.25% from 1 June. The SARB governor noted that the increase was due to escalations in electricity costs, higher oil prices, and currency volatility. The governor was clear that maintaining the inflation in the 3–6% range was as critical as ensuring that the budget deficit was under 3% of government spending. The latter was further compounded by increases in fuel prices that saw consumer inflation set at 5.5%, with food becoming more expensive. Food insecurity became a real socioeconomic concern in the country.

In November, the finance minister delivered the *Medium-Term Budget Policy Statement*, in which he highlighted that the country's 'economic and fiscal outlook over the medium term remains weak, reflecting the cumulative power cuts, the poor performance of the logistics sector, high inflation, rising borrowing and a weaker global context'. The country also became more vulnerable to *climate change*, creating added pressure on people's lives and material conditions and on state resources.

Zambia

Edalina Rodrigues Sanches

President Hakainde Hichilema's economic diplomacy efforts to find a swift resolution to the debt situation produced mixed results. Discussions around the revision of the Public Order Act, which restrict public gatherings, remained polarised. The United Party for National Development (UPND) won most by-elections. The main opposition party, the Patriotic Front (PF), faced strong internal disputes, with procedures for electing the new party leadership being highly contested. Opposition MPs filed an impeachment motion against the speaker of parliament, who was accused of having committed gross misconduct and violations of the constitution. There were significant improvements in the fight against corruption. Zambia strengthened ties with Western countries, the SADC, and Israel, but China continued to be an important trade and investment partner. Switzerland, China, DRC, South Africa, and Zimbabwe were the country's major commodity export destinations. However, the trade surplus dropped significantly, mainly due to lower copper production. The IMF had several meetings with the country to monitor macroeconomic developments. IMF reviews of the country's development under the ECF arrangement allowed Zambia direct access to financing. The failed deal on debt relief under the

G20 Common Framework raised further uncertainty over the country's capacity to tackle the debt crisis. The economy grew slightly, but rising inflation and costs of living led to a deterioration in citizens' standards of living.

Domestic Politics

The *revision of the Public Order Act* (POA) remained a polarising issue. On 16 January, the Zambia Development Law Commission (ZDLC) submitted a proposal to repeal and replace the POA, alongside a draft of the Public Gatherings Act, to the Ministry of Justice and the Ministry of Home Affairs for consideration. The POA had been the subject of much scrutiny in 2022 for granting excessive powers to the police, which some argued could suppress the exercise of fundamental rights such as freedom of association and assembly. Throughout the year, the ZDLC publicly condemned several episodes in which the POA was used against civilians and members of political parties to limits rights of assembly. Information minister Cornelius Mweetwa offered reassurance of the government's commitment to engaging in further consultations with stakeholders in order to refine the Act and ensure its swift progress through parliamentary processes.

There were *reshuffles in cabinet* aiming at signalling the government's commitment to political integrity and administrative efficiency. On 6 July, President Hakainde Hichilema of the UPND fired Luapula provincial minister Derricky Chilundika, following the appearance of incriminating audio recordings suggesting Chilundika's involvement in illegal mining activities related to the rare gemstone, sugilite. On 26 September, a *cabinet mini-reshuffle* led to the dismissal of Chushi Kasanda as minister of information and media, with Mweetwa assuming this portfolio. Princess Kasune was nominated Central Province minister after the transfer of Credo Nanjuwa to Southern Province. The president took steps to enhance administrative efficiency, transferring and replacing permanent secretaries in the Ministry of Livestock and Fisheries and the Ministry of Information and Media. Towards the end of year (26 December), another scandal led to the resignation of foreign minister Stanley Kakubo, after he was involved in a social media frenzy over alleged dealings with a Chinese businessman.

In October, a directive of the Registrar of Societies instructing political parties to hold *intra-party elections* for vacant positions within 60 days elicited mixed reactions among political leaders and their respective parties. In the major opposition party, the Patriotic Front (PF), Miles Sampa, MP for the constituency of Matero, unexpectedly took the lead and organised a convention at Lusaka's Mulungushi International Conference Centre (a government complex) on 24 October to elect new office bearers. The next day, a list of new office bearers, with Sampa as PF president, was sent to the Registrar of Societies for approval. However, the procedure was considered unlawful as it had excluded other candidates who had expressed interest in standing for the PF presidency. The party leadership subsequently accused Sampa of indiscipline, expelled him from the party, and asked the speaker of the National Assembly, Nelly Mutti, to declare his seat vacant. The speaker's later validation of Miles Sampa as the PF new president sparked protests from several PF MPs who, alongside several independent law-makers, notified the clerk of the National Assembly on 3 November of their intention to impeach the speaker for, among other charges, abrogating the constitution. On 7 November, Mutti issued 30-day suspensions to 19 of these MPs, in a move seen as a response to the *motion of impeachment*. On 10 November, Mutti was reported by a PF parliamentarian to the Anti-Corruption Commission (ACC) for actions that disregarded the constitution and the rule of law.

Internal wrangling within the PF continued, and on 6 December, the party's secretary-general Morgan Ng'ona wrote to Mutti informing her of the party decision to immediately expel nine of its MPs due to gross misconduct and indiscipline, namely failure to report activities to the party.

The ruling UPND won most councillor *by-elections held during the year*. On 20 January, four by-elections were held in the wards of Itala (Luapula Province), Kapanda (Northern Province), Kashikishi (Northern Province) and Nyatanda (North-Western Province). Candidates of the opposition – the PF and the Socialist Party (SP) – received the most votes in the first two, while the UPND candidate won by a narrow margin in the two wards. On 20 April l, three by-elections were held, in Muchinda (Central Province), Chitimukulu (Copperbelt Province), and Katilye (Northern Province), all won comfortably by the UPND.

Zambia's classification in the EIU Democracy Index 2023 remained the same as in 2022, with an aggregate score of 5.80/10 and an overall ranking of 78. The categories in which the country had the best ranking were *electoral process and pluralism* (7.92/10) and *political culture* (6.88/10). The country performed worst in the three categories of *functioning of government* (3.64/10), *political participation* (5.0/10), and *civil liberties* (5.59/10).

During the year, there were several episodes where *rights of assembly were restricted*. In March, the police arrested four members of a feminist group for allegedly planning a demonstration aimed at promoting homosexuality. Same-sex sexual activity is prohibited under the Penal Code. In October, protesters were prevented from demonstrating against the high cost of living amid soaring inflation and a severe economic crisis (as reported by Voice of America). These and other episodes continued to raise contestation against the POA alleging its use as a political tool by the government.

For the first time in a decade, Zambia's Transparency International (TI-Z) *Corruption Perceptions Index score improved*, from 33 to 37 points on a 100-point scale, 0 being highly corrupt and 100 very clean. The country was ranked 98th in the world in the index (up from 116th in 2022). This improvement followed important initiatives such as 'the establishment of the Economics and Financial Crimes Court as well as integrity mechanisms such as Integrity Committees, gift policies, and service charters which proliferated across many public institutions; reduced political corruption due to the elevation of the fight against corruption under the UPND administration; and a general improvement in the bribery situation within the public sector, partly due to the rollout of the Electronic Government Procedures in many institutions' (TI-Z). Towards the end of the year, it was announced that the ACC was formulating a law to compel all government employees to declare their assets.

On 22 December, parliament passed the Marriage (Amendment) Act, which set the marriageable age at 18, without exception, for all marriages, including customary marriages. This represented remarkable progress towards safeguarding children's rights, and the nation's commitment to eradicating child marriage: Zambia's previous dual system of statutory and customary laws permitted marriage between 16 and 21 years of age with parental consent, but marriage under 16 years could be allowed with the consent of a High Court judge.

Foreign Affairs

President Hichilema's foreign policy approach continued to prioritise economic diplomacy, aiming to restore the country's credibility with creditors and multilateral organisations and tackle the debt crisis. *China* remained an important partner; ties with *Western countries*, the SADC, and *Israel* were strengthened.

During the UNGA resolution (A/ES-10/L.25) calling for an immediate ceasefire between Israel and Hamas and demanding aid access to Gaza, and unlike most African countries, Zambia joined the 45 countries that abstained (the US and Israel voted against the resolution).

On 8 April, Zambia withdrew its support concerning the request made for an advisory opinion of the ICJ on the legal consequences arising from the policies and *practices of Israel in the Occupied Palestinian Territory*, including East Jerusalem. The country's statement defended the position that the peaceful resolution of the Israeli–Palestinian conflict could 'only be achieved through direct bilateral negotiation' and that both sides should comply 'with the Israeli–Palestinian agreements entered into within the context of the Middle East peace process and Security Council resolutions 242 (1967) and 338 (1973)'.

President Hichilema visited more than 20 countries and states in 2023 in the context of official or state visits or to attend summits and important political events. In January, he visited *Angola* (11–12), UAE (16–18), *Senegal* (25–26), and *Namibia* (31). In Angola, Hichilema and President João Lourenço discussed the need to consolidate peace and security in the Great Lakes region, particularly CAR and the eastern part of the DRC. They also recognised the need for further collaboration. Six new legal instruments were signed in the areas of energy, infrastructure, education, trade, and justice. In the UAE, Hichilema attended the Abu Dhabi Sustainability Week and sought cooperation opportunities in the areas of energy, mining, finance, and hospitality. In Namibia, he attended the Emergency Extraordinary SADC Troika Summit to discuss ways of addressing the political and security situation in the SADC region. In February, Hichilema attended the 36th Ordinary Session of the assembly of the AU in Ethiopia (17–19) and in March (5–9), the 5th UN Conference on the Least Developed Countries. In April, Hichilema visited *Mozambique* (4–6), where he held bilateral talks with President Filipe Nyusi on trade, investment, and infrastructure development, discussed issues related to peace and security in the SADC region, and signed MoU in the field of media and information. On 26 April, he attended the 6th Transform Africa Summit. In May, he was present in the *Coronation of Charles III and Camilla* in the UK (5–9) and travelled to *Paris* to hold bilateral discussions with French president Emmanuel Macron to expedite *Zambia's debt restructuring process* (10).

In June, Hichilema visited Poland (15), and he travelled to *Ukraine and Russia* as part of the African Peace Initiative to promote dialogue and peaceful negotiations between the two nations. He also attended the Summit for a New Global Financing Pact in Paris (22–23). During this summit, Zambia negotiated a deal to restructure $6.3 bn in debt owed to governments abroad, including China (Reuters).

In July, Hichilema attended the official handover ceremony of the Lobito Corridor operations in *Angola*, at the invitation of President Lourenço (4). In *Ghana* (7–9), Hichilema and President Nana Akufo-Addo held bilateral talks on trade and investment and signed a range of MoUs in crucial sectors, including trade and export promotion, tourism and culture, skills promotion, youth and sports, science and technology, and collaborative efforts to combat illicit drug trafficking. Between 31 July and 2 August, Hichilema was in *Israel* at the invitation of Israeli president Isaac Herzog. The two countries signed a *General Framework of Agreement* on further cooperation in the areas of education and culture, agriculture, water, green economy and environment, ICT, and economy.

On 26 August, Hichilema travelled to South Africa to attend the 15th BRICS summit. In September, he made a state visit to *China* (10–16) at the invitation of President Xi Jinping. The two heads of state jointly witnessed the signing of *multiple bilateral cooperation documents* in such fields as Belt and Road Initiative cooperation, green development, digital economy, and investment cooperation. Hichilema also visited *Mozambique* for the inauguration of the renovated Nacala Port (7). In November, he attended SADC summits in *Lesotho* (2) and *Angola* (4), the Saudi Arabia–Africa summit (9–10), and the 5th G20 Compact with Africa Summit in *Germany* (19–21) and made a state visit to *Italy* (21–23). On the sidelines of the

28th COP28 in Dubai (30 November–12 December), Hichilema held bilateral discussions with Emmanuel Macron and with China's executive vice-premier Ding Xuexiang.

Several regional and Western leaders visited Zambia. The country hosted the 2023 *Summit for Democracy* (S4D2) on 29–30 March, which gathered delegates from the US and 21 African countries; and Kamala Harris visited on 30 March, reassuring the country of the US's continued support for a 'speedy completion of Zambia's debt treatment and restructuring'. On 1–3 November, Hichilema received the German president Frank-Walter Steinmeier. The subject matter of bilateral talks between the two leaders included cooperation in water and sanitation, agriculture, small and medium-sized enterprise (SME) development, and energy, trade, and investment, among other significant sectors.

On 18 December, President Hichilema held a bilateral meeting with the French minister of state for development Chrysoula Zacharopoulou at State House in Lusaka. The visiting minister reaffirmed France's commitment to collaborating with Zambia as well as supporting the finalisation of the debt restructuring. The two sides signed a *Joint Declaration of Intent* to develop the partnership for enhanced collaboration in areas such as food security, water and sanitation, and forestry sustainable management.

Socioeconomic Developments

The *economy grew* by between 4% and 8% between the first and fourth quarters of the year, slightly improving the year's average by 0.8% compared with 2022 (Zambia Statistics Agency/ZAMSTATS). The growth was attributed mainly to the positive performance of the industries of information and communication and construction. Inflation levels went up from 9.4% in January to 13.1% in December (ZAMSTATS). This was mainly attributed to an increase in the cost of food items (including food and non-alcoholic beverages) but also non-food items (housing, water, electricity, gas and other fuels, transport, clothing and footwear). At the province level, inflation was higher in Lusaka and Western provinces, with lower values in Eastern and Luapula. The cost of living, as measured by the *Jesuit Centre for Theological Reflection* (JCTR), increased for Lusaka from 9,047.31 kwacha (K; $364) in January to K 9,157.41 ($370) in December.

The stock of external debt amounted to $15.6 bn by the end of September (IMF). This included $14.2 bn attributed to the central government and $1.4 bn in guaranteed external obligations. The domestic debt stock increased, while external financing remained constrained (IMF).

There were *several interactions between the Zambian government and the IMF*. Following her visit to Zambia on 22–24 January, Kristalina Georgieva, managing director of the IMF, issued a statement highlighting 'Zambia's efforts to improve the use of public resources', commending the 'government's efforts to improve transparency and tackle corruption', and stressing the need for a swift resolution of the debt situation. Between 22 March and 5 April, IMF staff held meetings with Zambian authorities to reach an agreement on the conditions for initiating the first review of the 38-month ECF arrangement (approved on 31 August 2022).

On 22 June, Georgieva commended the *agreement reached between Zambia and its official creditors for a debt treatment under the G20 Common Framework*. In a press release, she stated: 'I warmly welcome Minister of Finance Situmbeko Musokotwane's announcement that the Zambian authorities have reached an agreement with their official creditors on a debt treatment, consistent with the objectives of the IMF-supported program'. On 13 July, the executive board of the IMF completed the first review of the 38-month ECF arrangement providing the country with access to Special Drawing Rights (SDR) of 139.88 m (about $189), bringing Zambia's total disbursements under the arrangement to around $374 m.

An IMF mission visited Zambia between 25 October and 8 November to discuss progress on economic and financial policies and prepare the second review under the ECF arrangement. The second review was concluded on 20 December, allowing for an immediate disbursement of SDR 139.88 m (around $187 m), bringing Zambia's total disbursement under the ECF to SDR 419.64 m (around $561 m).

On 24 November, Zambia announced *the failure of debt negotiations under the G20 Common Framework*. The government stated that there were objections from bilateral creditors, 'who say the terms of the deal are not comparable to relief offered by a group of countries including France, China and India' (Reuters).

According to the FAO's 'Crop Prospects and Food Situation' report, *cereal production increased by 22.9%* for the 2023/24 consumption period: from 2,653,805 megatons (mt) in the previous season to 3,261,686 mt. The report signalled Zambia's *record high prices of maize*, and their effect on food access and security. The Integrated Food Security Phase Classification (IPC) for September estimated that more than 3 m people were facing *acute food insecurity* and attributed this mainly to 'shocks and hazards experienced in the country such as prolonged dry spells, pests, diseases, high input and food prices'.

The annual *copper production* was estimated at 682,000 tons (from over 700,000 tons in 2022). As result, the total volume of refined copper exported in 2023 was around 779,400 mt while that of 2022 hovered at around 898,400 mt, representing a 13.2% decrease (ZAMSTATS). This had an impact on *export earnings, which dropped significantly*.

Zambia trade surplus decreased to K 6.2 bn compared with K 44.5 bn in 2022 (ZAMSTATS). Switzerland was the major export destination, accounting for 45% of total export earnings (up from 38.5% in 2022). The other top four commodity export destinations (as a percentage of total export earnings) were China (21.4%); DRC

(10.7%, up from 8.1%); South Africa (4.8%) which was not in the top 5 in 2022; and finally Zimbabwe (3.4%, down from 3.6%). These five countries collectively accounted for 86% of Zambia's total export earnings in December. The main export products were copper anodes for electrolytic refining (Switzerland, China), sulphur of all kinds (DRC), cobalt oxides and hydroxides and commercial cobalt (South Africa), and Portland cement (Zimbabwe). The novelty this year was the emergence of South Africa, replacing Singapore as the fourth major destination (ZAMSTATS).

In November, the government announced a *salary increment* of K 550 across the board for civil servants, to become effective on 1 January 2024. This followed ten days of negotiations involving representatives from 19 workers' unions in Chilanga District. The parties also agreed on an increase in the rate of transport allowance (from 15% to 20% of the monthly basic salary) and the rate of meal allowance (from K 100 to K 130).

Health minister Slyvia Masebo announced the promotion of 2,424 health workers, out of whom 311 were in medical roles. The promotions resulted in net entry-level positions totalling 1,452 across the health sector. The country *recorded an outbreak of cholera* in October 2023, mainly in Lusaka and Ndola, the country's two largest cities.

Zimbabwe

Amin Y. Kamete

The year was dominated by another controversial election. Alleged intra-party struggles in the ruling party ZANU-PF and the waning Movement for Democratic Change-Tsvangirai (MDC-T) persisted. The Citizens Coalition for Change (CCC), led by Nelson Chamisa, became the main opposition party as the MDC-T imploded. Another highlight of the year was the CCC's post-election woes, allegedly engineered by ZANU-PF. Accusations persisted of repression, human rights violations, and harassment. On the international scene, 're-engaging' with the West was a recurrent theme. There was no let-up in economic adversity. There was no discernible recovery from humanitarian and socioeconomic challenges, which were compounded by a cholera outbreak.

Domestic Politics

Having won some crucial by-elections the previous year, the CCC became the *main opposition political party*, pushing the MDC-T into obscurity. Through reported acts of repression directed at the CCC, the government seemed to confirm that it regarded the CCC as ZANU-PF's main rival. On 1 January, in what was interpreted as ZANU-PF colluding with the MDC-T, the justice, legal, and parliamentary affairs minister, Ziyambi Ziyambi, announced that ZANU-PF and the MDC-T – still the official parliamentary opposition – would share more than 1.4 bn Zimbabwean dollars (ZWL) under the Political Parties Finance Act. With 70.03% of the 2018 vote, ZANU-PF would receive ZWL 985.9 m; the MDC-T, which had 29.97% of the vote, would get ZWL 422.5 m. Some small political parties complained that the arrangement was unfair, as it favoured 'big' parties.

Through the government gazette on 31 May, President Emmerson Mnangagwa announced that *harmonised elections would take place on 23 August*. The announcement set 2 October as the date for a presidential run-off should it be required. The harmonised elections would comprise presidential, parliamentary, and local council elections. The proclamation was made at a time when there were raging parliamentary debates over electoral reforms. The election ended up being contested by 18 political parties and 11 presidential candidates.

There was *turmoil in the MDC-T* which led to the party's implosion. In February, Elias Mudzuri, the MDC-T vice-president, 'fired' party president Douglas Mwonzora for breaching the party's constitution. Mudzuri claimed that Mwonzora had not followed the constitutional procedure for holding the party congress. In response, on 6 February, Mwonzora expelled Mudzuri and six senior members from the party. He recalled Mudzuri from Senate, alleging that he had ceased to be a member of the MDC-T on 1 February. Mudzuri and the other suspended members hinted that they would form a splinter group challenging Mwonzora's leadership. In March, Mwonzora lost the High Court case in which the expelled members challenged the expulsions.

On 21 June, *the MDC-T suffered a major set-back* when the nomination court rejected the application of the party's 87 aspiring MPs to register as election candidates due to unpaid nomination fees. This effectively meant that the Zimbabwe Electoral Commission (ZEC) had barred the 87 from contesting the elections. On 27 June, the MDC-T lost a High Court case in which it had asked the court to order the ZEC to register these 87 candidates. On 8 August, Mwonzora *announced that the MDC-T had withdrawn from the presidential election*. He claimed that it was impossible for the country to conduct free, fair, and credible elections, describing the forthcoming presidential election as a 'farce' and a 'sham' which was 'far from free and unfair'.

Despite the suspension of by-elections and with just a few months to go before the 2023 general elections, Mwonzora's MDC-T *continued to recall people elected on the MDC-T ticket* whom Mwonzora claimed had been expelled from the party. They were being punished for backing the CCC. On 27 February, the MDC-T recalled three councillors from Norton Town Council. In the same month, the party recalled the mayor of Kadoma and three Kadoma councillors. Six other councillors were recalled from Kwekwe and Mutare.

Alleged ZANU-PF factionalism intensified after the proclamation of election dates which triggered primary elections to decide ZANU-PF candidates. In March, ZANU-PF postponed its primary elections. There were speculations that this was a reaction to suspicions that the party had been infiltrated by the pro-Mugabe 'Generation 40' (G40) faction. However, ZANU-PF spokesperson Mike Bimha explained that ZANU-PF had postponed the elections because it was overwhelmed by the number of candidates. On the weekend of 27 May, several ZANU-PF heavyweights, including ministers, lost in the primary elections. This fuelled reports of the existence of factions linked to Mnangagwa and his deputy Constantino Chiwenga. The reports of factionalism intensified following revelations of the existence of a ZANU-PF elections monitoring wing calling itself Forever Associates of Zimbabwe (FAZ). Ntokozo Msipha, the spokesperson for Tyson Wabantu, a political formation linked to Savior Kasukuwere, the self-exiled, pro-Mugabe former ZANU-PF political commissar and cabinet minister, confirmed the alleged 'infiltration', claiming that the faction had 'overwhelmed the system by fielding our own candidates throughout the country'.

In a move that had implications for ZANU-PF, on 19 June, *Kasukuwere announced his candidacy for the presidency*. This had the potential to split the ZANU-PF vote, with Mugabe loyalists voting for Kasukuwere. ZANU-PF reacted by branding Kasukuwere a 'criminal' with no ability to win over the public. This was widely interpreted as an indication that ZANU-PF was worried about his candidature, a view seemingly confirmed when the police stated that they had two outstanding warrants of arrest for Kasukuwere and would arrest him if he came to Zimbabwe. Kasukuwere filed an application seeking the cancellation of his warrant of arrest to allow him to contest. On 12 July, the High Court nullified Kasukuwere's nomination as a presidential candidate. The ruling followed an urgent court application by an unknown ZANU-PF activist, Lovedale Mangwana, who sought Kasukuwere's disqualification on the basis that he had been living outside Zimbabwe for more than 18 months. It was widely believed that ZANU-PF was behind the application. The court barred Kasukuwere from telling anyone that he was a presidential candidate. Kasukuwere filed an appeal at the Supreme Court, which he lost on 28 July. He took his case to the Constitutional Court. On 8 August, he lost this case too, with the Constitutional Court declining to grant him direct access to argue against the Supreme Court ruling.

Allegations of *state-sponsored political violence and human rights abuses* resurfaced during the year, as did reports of repression of CSOs and activists. There were reports of attacks on CCC members, particularly in rural areas. In early January, some villagers in Murehwa were injured when suspected ZANU-PF members reportedly attacked CCC supporters in the district. According the CCC, the villagers, mostly elderly, had been meeting at the homestead of a party member. On 14 January, police arrested 25 CCC members while they were attending a private meeting in Budiriro,

Harare. Among those arrested were MPs Amos Chibaya and Costa Machingauta. They were allegedly also physically assaulted. The arrested CCC members were charged under Section 37 of the Criminal Code for 'participating in gathering with intent to promote public violence, breaches of the peace or bigotry'. They appeared in court on 16 January and were granted bail on 27 January. *Job Sikhala*, CCC's deputy chairperson, who had been arrested in 2022, remained in prison for the rest of the year. In the period leading up to the elections, the authorities were accused of what Human Rights Watch described as failure 'to take necessary steps to ensure that the general election ... meets international standards for free and fair elections'.

In what was seen as the government's *'weaponising' of the law* to target opposition activists, critics, and people speaking against corruption, on 28 April the opposition Transform Zimbabwe leader, Jacob Ngarivhume, was sentenced to four years in prison for incitement to protest against corruption and the government's mishandling of the economy. On 11 December, the High Court quashed the conviction and sentence. In May, journalist Hopewell Chin'ono was acquitted on charges brought against him for obstructing the course of justice after he had posted opinions of an ongoing case on social media. On 15 August, police arrested 42 members of the CCC. They appeared in court on 17 August, facing charges of blocking traffic and disrupting order during a campaign event.

After the elections, *allegations of abuse and repression* continued. The CCC accused the state for a spate of kidnappings of its party members and pro-democracy activists. On 2 September, newly elected CCC councillor Womberaishe Nhende and activist Sonele Mukuhlani were allegedly abducted, tortured, and drugged by suspected state agents. On 4 September, when their lawyers Doug Coltart and Tapiwa Muchineripi visited Nhende and Mukuhlani in hospital, they were arrested on charges of obstructing justice after they told police that they could not interview the two because of their mental and physical condition. On 23 October, James Chidakwa, a former MP, was allegedly abducted, assaulted, and injected with an unknown substance. On 16 November, the Zimbabwe Human Rights Commission (ZHRC) released a statement expressing concern over political violence and human rights violations.

The *harmonised election elections* to elect the president, legislators, and councillors were held on 23 August. In some areas, the voting was extended to 24 August. Before the elections, there were the usual accusations of violence and bias on the part of the security forces and public media in favour of ZANU-PF. The ZHRC noted that 'the public media (electronic and print) by and large, reported more in favour of the ruling party while the private media reported more favourably on opposition political party activities'. Despite some reports of pre-election civil rights violations, characterised by alleged threats, intimidation, and coercion, all observer missions generally agreed that the elections were held in a peaceful environment.

In some constituencies, there were *logistical and technical problems*. These included the late delivery of voting materials to polling stations, late opening of polling stations, and polling stations running out of ballot papers. Most of the affected constituencies were urban areas, which are regarded as opposition strongholds. This generated accusations that the ZEC was deliberately trying to favour ZANU-PF. Polling stations affected by the issues were allowed to compensate for lost time by extending voting hours. Consequently, voting was extended to 24 August. The elections saw the heavy involvement of affiliate groups, the most prominent being FAZ, a pro-ZANU-PF outfit which had significant influence in the electoral process.

As in previous elections, the ZEC announced the parliamentary results as they were received. It announced the presidential results on 26 August. When all *election results* were announced, ZANU-PF won both the parliamentary and the presidential elections. Although ZANU-PF won the majority of council seats, as expected, the CCC dominated in the urban areas. Significantly, *ZANU-PF failed to secure the two-thirds parliamentary majority* necessary to change the constitution. It secured 177 seats; the CCC had 103. This meant ZANU-PF had 56.18% of the vote while the CCC had 41.46%. In the presidential election, Mnangagwa got 2,350,711 votes (52.6%) while Chamisa had 1,967,343 votes (44.03%). Mnangagwa was inaugurated on 4 September.

While the smaller contesting parties readily conceded, the *CCC rejected the election results*, condemning both the process and the outcome. Chamisa alleged 'blatant and gigantic fraud' and indicated that the CCC had not ratified the results, which he claimed had been 'hastily assembled without proper verification'. Mnangagwa dismissed the allegations and challenged the CCC to act. On 25 August, election observers from the EU, the Commonwealth, and the SADC said the elections had failed to conform to regional and international standards. Among the concerns they raised were issues with the voters' roll, the banning of opposition rallies, biased state media coverage, and voter intimidation. The condemnation by the SADC team riled ZANU-PF and the government. Singled out for attack was Nevers Mumba, Zambia's former vice-president, chairperson of the SADC observer mission. Signalling their refusal to recognise the legitimacy of Mnangagwa's presidency, on 3 October CCC legislators boycotted Mnangagwa's State of the Nation address.

After the elections, *the CCC suffered major set-backs*. In October, Sengezo Tshabangu, hitherto virtually unknown, claiming to be the CCC's interim secretary-general, wrote to Jacob Mudenda, the speaker of parliament, and to the local government minister, stating that he was recalling some CCC legislators and councillors. He recalled 15 MPs, 9 senators, and 17 councillors. The CCC promptly disowned him, saying that they did not know him. Chamisa wrote to Mudenda advising him to ignore Tshabangu's letter. In November, Tshabangu asserted that he was recalling 13 more legislators, including senior CCC members Fadzayi Mahere, Amos Chibaya, and Gift Siziba. There were strong suspicions that Tshabangu was sponsored by ZANU-PF: the speculation was that the party wanted to force by-elections in order to grab parliamentary seats from the CCC to get the two-thirds majority it needed to change the constitution to secure Mnangagwa a third term as president.

This seemed to be confirmed when despite the matter still being before the courts, on 20 October, Mnangagwa announced 9 December as the date for by-elections to replace the recalled CCC legislators. On 14 November, after CCC took the case to court, the High Court temporarily stopped the recall. Mudenda ignored the ruling and effected the recall order on the same day. On 1 December, Mnangagwa set 3 February 2024 as the date for additional by-elections following the recalling of more CCC MPs by Tshabangu. On 1 December, the Supreme Court rejected an appeal filed by the first 15 recalled legislators. The court ruled that the group had failed to prove that they were still CCC members and had not cited the CCC in their appeal.

In a further set-back for the CCC, on 7 December, the High Court barred its candidates from running in the 9 December by-elections. Tshabangu had declared that they could not stand as CCC candidates without his approval. The apparent ease with which Tshabangu got his legal victories led to an intensification of accusations that the judiciary was 'captured', with CCC spokesperson Promise Mkwananzi stating that 'the courts have ceased to be a just and neutral arbiter of disputes'. In the controversial 9 December by-elections, ZANU-PF won seven seats; the CCC won two seats in Bulawayo.

In March and April, Al Jazeera broadcast a three-part documentary entitled 'Gold Mafia' exposing a long-running gold-smuggling and money-laundering cartel that implicated senior figures in the government and ZANU-PF. Opponents were quick to use the documentary for political purposes, arguing that it confirmed endemic corruption within the party and the government. Due to the ensuing outcry, the government was forced to respond. On 6 April, the Reserve Bank of Zimbabwe (RBZ) froze assets of some of the people implicated. Monica Mutsvangwa, the information minister, announced that the government had instructed the responsible departments to act.

ZANU-PF held its 20th Annual National People's Conference in Gweru from 27 to 28 October. The theme was 'Towards Vision 2030 through Industrialisation and Modernization'. One of the notable conference outcomes was the amendment of ZANU-PF's constitution to reorganise its departments. Mnangagwa stated that the revised constitution had 'given more impetus and clarity in defining the functions and responsibilities of the party's departments and the general structures of the party'.

On 11 September, *Mnangagwa announced his new cabinet*. Chiwenga, who remained vice-president, was replaced as health minister by Douglas Mombeshora. Soda Zhemu, previously the energy minister, became the mines minister, with his replacement being Edgar Moyo, the former deputy primary and secondary education minister. Winston Chitando, former mines minister, was named local government minister, as July Moyo moved to the public service, labour, and social welfare portfolio. Monica Mutsvangwa was moved from information to women's affairs and SMEs. The information portfolio was given to former ICT minister Jenfan Muswere. Tatenda Mavetera became the ICT minister. Sithembiso Nyoni became the industry and commerce minister, replacing Sekai Nzenza, who had failed to secure a parliamentary seat. Mnangagwa's son, David Mnangagwa, was appointed deputy finance minister while his nephew, Tongai Mnangagwa, was named deputy minister of tourism and hospitality. Critics accused Mnangagwa of rewarding loyalists and relatives.

Foreign Affairs

Zimbabwe's relations with countries and organisations in the Global South remained strong. There was no discernible shift in relations with OECD countries and multilateral lenders. The government and its supporters continued to attribute Zimbabwe's economic woes to 'illegal' Western sanctions and to accuse the opposition, private media, activists, and critics of being used by the West.

Mnangagwa's inauguration on 4 September was marred by low international turnout. This was interpreted as signalling Zimbabwe's further isolation. Only three African presidents were among the few notable dignitaries: Cyril Ramaphosa (South Africa), Félix Tshisekedi (DRC), and Filipe Nyusi (Mozambique). The other SADC and AU leaders who were invited did not show up. Mnangagwa had reportedly sent 69 invitations to sitting presidents and former heads of state.

Zimbabwe remained active in, and maintained good relations with, regional organisations *the SADC, COMESA,* and *the AU*. However, relations were tainted when the regional bodies did not rubber-stamp the elections. On 26 August, the SADC and the joint AU and COMESA observer missions publicly questioned the legitimacy of Zimbabwe's elections for the first time in history. On 27 August, in his first post-election comments, Mnangagwa dismissed his African critics. He called on 'all our guests to respect our national institutions', insisting that Zimbabwe was a sovereign state. The regional bodies, however, continued to ignore the CCC's refusal to recognise the legitimacy of Mnangagwa's presidency.

On 27 September, Zambia, which held the *SADC Troika* chair, convened a virtual meeting where among other issues discussed was the SADC Electoral Observation Mission (EOM) report on Zimbabwe's disputed harmonised elections. The Troika members accepted EOM's preliminary statement, making it an official SADC report. It also criticised the behaviour of Zimbabwean authorities. On 4 November, Mnangagwa attended the Extraordinary Summit of the Heads of State and Government of the SADC in Luanda. Contrary to popular expectations, Zimbabwe was not discussed. According to the communiqué, the summit merely 'noted' the EOM report. Some analysts interpreted this as an endorsement of the report and a vindication of the mission. Notably, on 26 September, the Ministerial Committee of the Organ Troika had 'noted with concern, the personal attacks and threats ... on the media' directed at the head of EOM, Nevers Mumba, and Zambian president Hakainde Hichilema 'by individuals in both ... ZANU-PF ... and some in high level positions in the Government of Zimbabwe'. On 25 October, the SADC Anti-Sanctions Day – the annual symbol of solidarity with Zimbabwe and a call for the lifting of sanctions imposed by some Western nations – was observed.

In *other visits*, Mnangagwa attended the 36th Ordinary Session of the Assembly of Heads of State and Government of the AU on 18 and 19 February in Addis Ababa. He held bilateral meetings with other leaders. Zimbabwe participated at the Twenty-Second Summit of the Authority of Heads of State and Government of COMESA, in Lusaka on 8 June. Foreign affairs minister Fredrick Shava represented the country. On 31 May, Mnangagwa arrived in Malawi for a three-day state visit. On 22 May, he left for Egypt for a state visit that coincided with the 58th annual assembly of the AfDB Group and the 49th meeting of the African Development Fund. He was expected to engage representatives of creditor nations as Zimbabwe sought to clear arrears and resolve its national debt. On 21 September, Mnangagwa addressed the 78th session of the UNGA. Among the issues he spoke about were sustainable development goals and 'illegal, unilateral economic sanctions' on Zimbabwe.

On 30 January, *Belarusian president* Alexander Lukashenko arrived in Zimbabwe for a two-day state visit. He held talks with Mnangagwa aimed at strengthening cooperation between the two countries. On 9 October, Mnangagwa hosted the Saudi minister of state for foreign affairs, Adel bin Ahmed Al-Jubeir, who was on an official visit to Zimbabwe. Among the issues discussed were bilateral relations and 'opportunities for their further development across various fields'. On 10 November, Mnangagwa attended the inaugural Saudi Arabia–Africa summit in Riyadh. On 1 December, he arrived in Dubai for the UN Climate Change Conference (COP28).

Zimbabwe had generally good relations with *South Africa*. On 5 October, Mnangagwa joined President Ramaphosa on a tour of Zimbabwe's new customs office at the Beitbridge border. The two met during the launch of South Africa's Border Management Authority in Musina. Among other issues, the two leaders discussed border management challenges. On 4 September, Ramaphosa was one of the three African heads of state who attended Mnangagwa's inauguration. ANC secretary-general Fikile Mbalula openly backed ZANU-PF and the Zimbabwean government. Immediately after the election, Mbalula congratulated Mnangagwa for his victory. In September, Mbalula accused Chamisa of perpetuating 'the entrenchment of neocolonialism and imperialism'. He reaffirmed the ANC's ties with ZANU-PF despite its 'committing blunders'. On 5 September, Mnangagwa met Mbalula at State House. When criticised, Mbalula defended celebrating ZANU-PF's triumph, saying that he supported democracy. On 5 September, he declared that there would not be fresh elections in Zimbabwe, as demanded by the CCC. He went on to block a public lecture at Wits University to discuss the controversial elections. The lecture was to be addressed by Zimbabwean academic Ibbo Mandaza.

A great deal happened regarding the *Zimbabwe Exemption Permit (ZEP)*. On 4 June, the Pretoria High Court ordered South Africa's Department of Home Affairs (DHA) not to arrest or deport ZEP holders. On 7 June, DHA extended the deadline for ZEP holders to change to another immigration status to 31 December 2023, and on 28 June, the High Court ordered the DHA to further extend the deadline to 30 June 2024. On 9 November, the High Court confirmed that ZEPs would be valid until June 2024. On 1 December, Zimbabweans who had been granted ZEPs in 2009 were granted automatically extended permits valid until 29 November 2025.

Zimbabwe maintained good *relations with China*. On 27 May, foreign affairs and international trade minister Frederick Shava visited China. During the visit, China's foreign minister, Qin Gang, pledged to help Zimbabwe oppose 'external interference and sanctions' while building its own path to development. On 28 August, foreign ministry spokesperson Wang Wenbin stated that the Chinese observer mission to the Zimbabwean elections believed that the elections had been held 'in a peaceful and orderly fashion with active participation by the people'. On 30 August, President Xi Jinping congratulated Mnangagwa on his re-election and promised to promote bilateral ties. On 4 September, Xi's special envoy, Zhou Qiang, the vice-chair of the National Committee of the Chinese People's Political Consultative Conference, attended Mnangagwa's inauguration. Mnangagwa met with Zhou at State House.

Relations with Russia remained strong. Mnangagwa attended the Russia–Africa summit in St Petersburg on 27 and 28 July. He held a meeting with President Putin on the sidelines of the summit. Putin offered a helicopter to Mnangagwa. Russia endorsed Mnangagwa's election victory, saying that the results showed 'popular expression of will' and demonstrated 'wide support' for Mnangagwa. On 27 July, Russia and Zimbabwe signed a cooperation agreement on the use of atomic energy for peaceful purposes. The Russian news agency, TASS, signed a cooperation agreement with Zimbabwe's news agency, New Ziana. The agreement centred on bilateral cooperation in information exchange, staff training, and mutual visits. On 28 August, the Russian foreign ministry declared that Russia would continue 'developing comprehensive partnership and mutually beneficial cooperation with Zimbabwe'. On 20 November, Russian ambassador to Zimbabwe Nikolai Krasilnikov paid a courtesy call on Mnangagwa. He stated that Russia would enhance its partnership and cooperation with Zimbabwe and was confident that, led by Mnangagwa, Zimbabwe would achieve its Vision 2030 of becoming an upper-middle-class economy.

There was no change in *relations with the EU*. On 28 February, the EU extended the two remaining restrictive measures against Zimbabwe, comprising the arms embargo and the targeted assets freeze against the Zimbabwe Defence Industries (ZDI). Despite this, at the start of the year, it appeared that Zimbabwe–EU relations were improving. The EU celebrated Europe Day on 12 May where it hosted Zimbabwean government officials. It deployed one of the largest observer missions to monitor the 2023 elections. On 25 August, the EU Election Observation Mission (EU EOM) concluded that 'curtailed rights and lack of level playing field led to an environment that was not always conducive to voters making a free and informed choice'. In its final report on 17 October, the EU EOM reiterated its initial observations that the elections were flawed, highlighting the 'largely calm' but 'disorderly' environment on election day and the climate of retribution in the post-electoral period. On 25 October, Chiwenga, Zimbabwe's vice-president, claimed that Zimbabwe had lost more than \$150 bn since 2001, due to sanctions imposed by the EU and other Western countries. On 19 September, the EU announced that it was withdrawing \$5 m in financial support from the ZEC because of its lack of independence and transparency in the disputed August elections.

There was little change in *Zimbabwe–UK relations*. On 5 May, Mnangagwa arrived in London for King Charles' coronation. There were protests by parliamentarians and Zimbabweans disgruntled with Mnangagwa's invitation. Zimbabwe touted Mnangagwa's attendance as an indication of the success of its 're-engagement'. According to the UK sanctions list, five individuals and one entity (ZDI) were still subject to an asset freeze. The individuals were Kudakwashe Tagwirei (businessman), Owen Ncube (former security minister), Anselem Sanyatwe (former Presidential Guard commander), Isaac Moyo (Central Intelligence Organisation director-general), and Godwin Matanga (police commissioner-general). They were targeted for alleged 'human rights violations and corruption'. Responding to a question in the House of Lords, on 6 July the UK foreign secretary, James Cleverly, said that the UK was concerned by the ongoing detention of government critics in Zimbabwe, including Job Sikhala. He reported that the minister of state for development and Africa, Andrew Mitchell, had raised these concerns, and the case of Job Sikhala specifically, with Mnangagwa, when they met in the margins of the King's coronation.

The UK's policy paper on UK–Zimbabwe development partnership, published on 17 July, indicated that Zimbabwe remained a UK government priority country on human rights. It noted that Zimbabwe's key human development indicators were some of the lowest in the region. According to the paper, the UK was 'committed to supporting Zimbabwe on its path to long-term, inclusive, and resilient development, democracy, and prosperity'. In the financial year 2023 to 2024, the UK allocated Zimbabwe an ODA budget of £29.5 m. On 31 August, the minister for development and Africa released a statement stressing that the UK shared 'the view of the Election Observation Missions' preliminary statements that the pre-election environment and election day fell short of regional and international standards'. In November, UK ambassador to Zimbabwe Peter Vowles said that the UK was keen to see Zimbabwe readmitted to the Commonwealth.

Relations with the US did not improve. On 1 March, the US extended sanctions against Zimbabwe, citing ongoing repression which presented 'a continuing threat to peace and security in the region'. In a message to the US Congress, President Biden said that Zimbabwe had not made any reforms to warrant the lifting of the sanctions. On 26 August, the US embassy expressed concerns about Zimbabwe's general election, claiming that it fell short of the requirements of the country's constitution and regional guidelines. Zimbabwe rejected the claims. On 4 December, US foreign secretary Antony Blinken announced more sanctions on Zimbabwe in light of electoral malpractice and human rights abuses. Some targeted individuals would now be restricted from getting travel visas. The US embassy indicated it would not reveal the names of those affected by the visa restrictions but stated that they were known. According to the embassy, Zimbabwe had 59 individuals and 39 entities on the sanctions list.

There was no change in relations with *multilateral organisations*. According to an AfDB report of 11 July, Zimbabwe's total consolidated debt amounted to $17.5 bn. Debt owed to international creditors stood at $14.04 bn, debt to multilateral creditors at $2.5 bn. Zimbabwe was in arrears. Most of the arrears were to multilateral development banks, including the AfDB, the World Bank, and the EIB.

Socioeconomic Developments

Economic indicators did not change significantly. According to the RBZ, the CPI for all items at the end of December was 113.22. The annual inflation rate was 26.5%. Monthly inflation was highest in June at 12.1% and lowest in February at −3.7%. In a bid to stabilise the currency, on 24 July, the RBZ announced the launch of gold coins to be sold to the public. In October, the IMF estimated that real GDP was projected to grow by around 4.8%, supported by strong activity in mining, agriculture, and energy. Growth was expected to drop to 3.5% in 2024. In May, the Confederation of Zimbabwe Industries (CZI) projected that *manufacturing sector capacity utilisation* had fallen to 56.1% in 2022. It forecast a capacity utilisation level of 70.9% in 2023.

Figures from the budget statement showed that nominal GDP at market prices was ZWL 119,017 bn. The current account surplus was projected to close the year at $244.4 m, down from $305 m in 2022. The World Bank put Zimbabwe's total reserves (including gold) at $598.6 m for 2022. According to the finance ministry, the total public and publicly guaranteed debt (PPG) stock at the end of September, amounted to ZWL 96.71 trillion, which translated to 81.3% of GDP. The debt comprised an external debt of ZWL 69.36 trillion and a domestic debt of ZWL 27.4 trillion. In US dollar terms, total PPG debt amounted to $17.7 bn, with external debt amounting to $12.7 bn and domestic debt standing at $5 bn. The bilateral and multilateral debt stood at $9.1 bn, with 76% being principal arrears, interest arrears, and penalties. According to the RBZ, for the period January to June, total foreign currency receipts were $5.6 bn, up from $5.4 bn in 2022. Diaspora remittances were $919 m compared with $797 m in 2022. According to claims by the Zimbabwe Investment and Development Agency (ZIDA), Zimbabwe attracted $8 bn in FDI, which was double ZIDA's intended target. The RBZ reported that in December, the trade deficit grew by 84% to $268.8 m. Compared with December 2022, the deficit widened by 94% from $138.4 m. According to the 2023 Global Multidimensional Poverty Index (MPI), Zimbabwe had a value of 0.110 with 6.8% of the population in severe poverty.

Zimbabwe experienced several *humanitarian challenges*. According to UNICEF, 3 m people were in urgent need of humanitarian assistance and protection in the country; 2.2 m of these were children. In addition to the economic crisis, there was a cholera outbreak and food insecurity. The Vulnerability Assessment Committee (ZimVAC) estimated that 2,715,717 people (26% of rural households) would be 'food insecure' during the peak hunger period. UNICEF estimated that 1.5 m people (972,000 women and 528,000 men) would need 'life-saving health, HIV and nutrition services'. Among them were 1.1 m children, comprising 572,000 girls and 528,000 boys. In February, the first *cholera* case was reported. By the beginning of December, 10,263 suspected cases, 1,409 confirmed cases, and 230 deaths had been recorded. Responding to the outbreak, on 17 November, the authorities declared a state of emergency in Harare.

According to the most recent UNAIDS estimates, the prevalence of *HIV/AIDS* among adults was 11%, translating to about 1.2 m adults living with HIV/AIDS. HIV prevalence was higher among women (13.7%) than men (8.2%). The number of children aged 0 to 14 living with HIV was 75,000. The number of deaths due to AIDS was estimated at 20,000. The proportion of adults and children living with HIV/AIDS receiving ARV therapy was 96% and 69%, respectively.

On *demographic indicators*, according to estimates, the crude death rate stood at 7.6 per 1,000 people. Average life expectancy was 62.6 years. The infant mortality rate was 34.96 deaths per 1,000 live births. There were no official estimates for net migration. Macrotrends put the figure at −3.96 per thousand. The most recent estimate for adult literacy was 89.7%, in 2021.

The challenges persisted in *education and health* delivery systems. Most of them related to staffing, equipment, and funding. Strikes and threats of strikes continued.

Even before schools reopened in January, the militant Amalgamated Rural Teachers Union of Zimbabwe (ARTUZ) announced that members would embark on an indefinite nationwide strike when schools reopened. They were demanding a 110% wage hike. Before schools reopened for the second term in May, ARTUZ said that teachers were 'incapacitated' and would be reporting for duty only twice a week. In October, the Zimbabwe Teachers' Association reported that around 300 teachers were leaving the country each month. On 10 January, Mnangagwa signed the Health Services Bill, outlawing organised protests by healthcare workers. They face a fine or imprisonment of up to six months. Official statistics revealed that more than 4,000 health workers, including some 2,600 nurses, had left Zimbabwe in 2021 and 2022.

On 30 November, finance and economic development minister Mthuli Ncube presented the *2024 national budget* with the theme 'Consolidating Economic Transformation'. The budget had a projected expenditure of ZWL $53.9 trillion, translating to 18.3% of GDP. It proposed ZWL 51.2 trillion in tax revenue and ZWL 2.7 trillion in non-tax revenue. Mthuli introduced new taxes and hiked several tariffs. Among the most controversial was a 'wealth tax' on homes and rises in tollgate and passport fees. When amended proposals were passed in parliament on 15 December, many of the hikes had been slashed due to a public outcry.

Printed in the United States
by Baker & Taylor Publisher Services